HISTORY OF THE
WAR IN SOUTH AFRICA
1899-1902

HISTORY

OF THE

WAR IN SOUTH AFRICA

1899–1902

COMPILED BY DIRECTION OF
HIS MAJESTY'S GOVERNMENT

BY

MAJOR-GENERAL SIR FREDERICK MAURICE, K.C.B.

WITH A STAFF OF OFFICERS

VOLUME II

The Naval & Military Press Ltd

Published by
The Naval & Military Press Ltd
5 Riverside, Brambleside, Bellbrook
Industrial Estate, Uckfield, East Sussex,
TN22 1QQ England
Tel: +44 (0) 1825 749494
Fax: +44 (0) 1825 765701
www.naval-military-press.com

In reprinting in facsimile from the original, any imperfections are inevitably reproduced and the quality may fall short of modern type and cartographic standards.

NOTE TO THE READER.

The following circular letter was sent out during the composition of the present volume, and is now published to explain the conditions under which the history has been compiled :—

"In sending round these proofs for comment, I am anxious to appeal to all who can throw light upon any points within their knowledge to do so. Now that the first volume has been published, it must, I think, be clear to all that our only object has been to state the true facts as far as we are able to get at them. This seems to have been generally recognised; but our success entirely depends on our obtaining all the criticism and evidence we can. The first drafts of the first volume were very different from the text as published; but, though this was due to the evidence we subsequently obtained from those to whom they were sent, yet in many instances the corrections were furnished with expressions of great indignation that the account was not in accordance with facts known to the writer, but not previously supplied to us. We cannot make bricks without straw; and though the mass of material to be dealt with is very great, it often fails us at important points. It is to fill in these deficiencies that we submit the story as we have it, to those who can give us better evidence. On one point a fiction has gone abroad which may much interfere with this. It has been freely stated that the volume was much 'sub-edited' in the interest of Departments concerned. There is not one word of truth in this. We have held no brief for anyone and no Department or Office has asked us to modify one word in their own interest. The only subject on which any Office asked for change was that mentioned on page 1, Volume I., viz., any phrase that might affect our relations with our Boer fellow-subjects. Otherwise the narrative has been written exactly as we should have written it if we had been publishing a volume on our own account, except that under no other circumstances whatever could we have had complete evidence as to the truth."

F. MAURICE.

CONTENTS.

VOLUME II.

CHAP.		PAGE
I.	Relief of Kimberley. Situation before starting.	1
II.	Relief of Kimberley. Passage of the Riet and Modder	15
III.	Relief of Kimberley. French enters Kimberley	28
IV.	How Kimberley was prepared for siege.	39
V.	The Siege of Kimberley	54
VI.	Pursuit of Cronje	73
VII.	Pursuit of Cronje (*continued*)	87
VIII.	The Battle of Paardeberg	106
IX.	The Investment of Cronje's Laager	145
X.	The Surrender of Cronje	162
XI.	From Paardeberg to Poplar Grove	180
XII.	Poplar Grove	194
XIII.	Driefontein	208
XIV.	The Occupation of Bloemfontein	230
XV.	Gatacre and Clements from Cape Colony join hands with the main army	241
XVI.	Lord Roberts seizes the Waterworks, despatches French to Thabanchu, and by an action at Karee Siding is enabled to restore the railway bridge northwards over the Modder.	259
XVII.	Operations in the Orange Free State during the halt at Bloemfontein. Sannah's Post.	274
XVIII.	Operations in the Orange Free State during the halt at Bloemfontein (*continued*). Reddersburg	300

CHAP.		PAGE
XIX.—Defence of Wepener		314
XX.—The Spion Kop Campaign. The First Stage		334
XXI.—The Spion Kop Campaign. The Flank March to Trickhardt's Drift		350
XXII.—The Spion Kop Campaign. The Capture and Evacuation of Spion Kop		379
XXIII.—Vaal Krantz		403
XXIV.—Relief of Ladysmith. The Capture of Cingolo		423
XXV.—Relief of Ladysmith. The Capture of Monte Cristo; the right bank secured		447
XXVI.—Relief of Ladysmith. Crossing of the River; attack on Wynne's Hill		463
XXVII.—Relief of Ladysmith. Hart's Hill		481
XXVIII.—Relief of Ladysmith. Pieters Hill		501
XXIX.—Relief of Ladysmith. Pieters Hill (*continued*)		515
XXX.—The Defence of Ladysmith. From the action of Lombards Kop to the attack of January 6th, 1900		531
XXXI.—The Defence of Ladysmith. Wagon Hill		555
XXXII.—The Defence of Ladysmith. Last phase of Siege, 7th January to 3rd March, 1900		571

APPENDICES.

NO.		PAGE
1.	Letter from Lieut.-General Kelly-Kenny to Lord Roberts, 17th February, 1900	589
2.	Casualties, etc., in the principal Engagements described in Volume II.	590
3.	Detail of Entrenching carried out by the Royal Engineers and 14th brigade during the investment of Cronje's Laager	602
4.	Prisoners taken at Paardeberg	603
5.	Redistribution of the Mounted Infantry into Four brigades on the 6th March, 1900	605
6.	Return of Troops marching into Bloemfontein on its surrender, 13th March, 1900	606
7.	Reasons for the removal of Lieut.-General Gatacre.	614
8 (A).	General Sir R. Buller's orders, 8th January, 1900	616
8 (B).	General Sir R. Buller's orders, 9th January, 1900	619
8 (C).	Natal army organisation, 8th January, 1900	620
8 (D).	Orders issued to Colonel the Earl of Dundonald, 10th January, 1900	622
8 (E).	The Concentration of Supplies at Springfield, January, 1900	622
8 (F).	General Sir R. Buller's special order to the Troops, 12th January, 1900	623
8 (G).	Telegram from Sir R. Buller to the Secretary of State for War, 13th January, 1900	624
8 (H).	Secret orders issued by General Sir R. Buller to Lieut.-General Sir C. Warren, 15th January, 1900	625
8 (I).	Force under the command of Sir Charles Warren on leaving Springfield for Trickhardt's Drift, 16th January, 1900	626

NO.		PAGE
8 (J).	Force under the command of Major-General the Hon. N. G. Lyttelton at Potgieters Drift and Springfield	627
9 (A).	Lieut.-General Sir Charles Warren's orders for the march to Trickhardt's Drift, 16th January, 1900	629
9 (B).	Letter from Sir R. Buller to Lieut.-General Sir C. Warren, 17th January, 1900	631
9 (C).	Messages exchanged between Sir C. Warren and the Earl of Dundonald, 18th January, 1900	631
9 (D).	Sir C. Warren to Sir C. F. Clery, 19th January, 1900	633
9 (E).	Sir C. Warren to the Earl of Dundonald, 20th January, 1900	633
9 (F).	Sir C. Warren to Sir R. Buller, 19th January, 1900	633
9 (G).	Orders issued by Sir C. Warren to Sir C. F. Clery, 19th January, 1900	633
9 (H).	Sir C. Warren to Sir C. F. Clery, 20th January, 1900	634
9 (I).	Sir C. Warren to Chief of Staff, 21st January, 1900	634
9 (J).	Sir C. Warren to Sir R. Buller, 21st January, 1900	634
9 (K).	Sir R. Buller to Sir C. Warren, 22nd January, 1900	635
9 (L).	Force orders by Sir C. Warren, 22nd January, 1900	635
9 (M).	Orders by Sir C. Warren for the occupation of Spion Kop, 23rd January, 1900	636
9 (N).	Attack orders issued by Major-General Coke, commanding Right Attack, January 23rd, 1900.	637
9 (O).	Brigade orders by Major-General Woodgate, 23rd January, 1900	637
9 (P).	Force orders by Sir Charles Warren relative to the occupation of Spion Kop.	638
10 (A).	Colonel Crofton's Message	639
10 (B).	Lieut.-General Warren to Major-General Lyttelton, 24th January, 1900	639
10 (C).	Heliogram from someone unknown on Spion Kop to Major-General Lyttelton, 24th January, 1900 .	639
10 (D).	Major-General Talbot Coke to Lieut.-General Warren, 24th January, 1900	640
10 (E).	From Colonel Thorneycroft to Chief Staff Officer to Sir C. Warren, 24th January, 1900.	640
10 (F).	From Colonel Thorneycroft to Sir C. Warren, 25th January, 1900	640

APPENDICES.

NO.		PAGE
10 (G).	MAJOR-GENERAL LYTTELTON TO LIEUT.-GENERAL WARREN, 24TH JANUARY, 1900	641
10 (H).	LIEUT.-GENERAL WARREN TO MAJOR-GENERAL LYTTELTON, 24TH JANUARY, 1900	641
10 (I).	FORCE ORDERS ISSUED BY LIEUT.-GENERAL WARREN ON THE EVENING OF THE 24TH JANUARY, 1900	641
10 (J).	LETTER FROM LIEUT.-GENERAL WARREN TO COLONEL THORNEYCROFT, 24TH JANUARY, 1900	642
11 (A).	ORDERS FOR THE OPERATIONS AT VAAL KRANTZ, 3RD FEBRUARY, 1900	643
11 (B).	2ND BRIGADE ORDERS, 7TH FEBRUARY, 1900	645
11 (C).	ORDERS FOR THE RETIREMENT FROM VAAL KRANTZ	645
12.	EXPENDITURE OF AMMUNITION BY THE ROYAL ARTILLERY DURING THE RELIEF OF LADYSMITH, 14TH-28TH FEBRUARY, 1900	647
	EXPENDITURE OF AMMUNITION BY THE NAVAL GUNS DURING THE SAME PERIOD	648
	EXPENDITURE OF AMMUNITION BY THE NAVAL GUNS DURING THE PRINCIPAL ACTIONS ON THE TUGELA	649
13.	SIR REDVERS BULLER'S REASONS FOR NOT PURSUING THE BOERS ON THE 28TH FEBRUARY, 1900	651
14.	DEFENCE OF LADYSMITH.—DECISION OF BOER COUNCIL OF WAR VETOED BY SUBORDINATES	654
15.	DEFENCE OF LADYSMITH.—EXPENDITURE OF AMMUNITION DURING THE SIEGE. HOSPITAL STATISTICS	655

LIST OF MAPS AND FREEHAND SKETCHES.
VOL. II.

MAPS.

No. 18.	OPERATIONS ON THE UPPER TUGELA.	January 10th to February 10th, 1900.	
No. 19.	SPION KOP.	January 17th to 26th, 1900.	*Area of Operations.*
No. 19 (A).	SPION KOP.	January 17th, 1900.	*Position of Troops at Sunset.*
No. 19 (B).	SPION KOP.	January 18th, 1900.	*Position of Troops at Sunset.*
No. 19 (C).	SPION KOP.	January 19th, 1900.	*Position of Troops at Sunset.*
No. 19 (D).	SPION KOP.	January 20th, 1900.	*Position of Troops at Sunset.*
No. 19 (E).	SPION KOP.	January 21st, 1900.	*Position of Troops at Sunset.*
No. 19 (F).	SPION KOP.	January 22nd, 1900.	*Position of Troops at Sunset.*
No. 19 (G).	SPION KOP.	January 23rd, 1900.	*Position of Troops at Sunset.*
No. 19 (H).	SPION KOP.	January 24th, 1900.	*Position of Troops at Sunset.*
No. 19 (I).	SPION KOP.	January 25th, 1900.	*Position of Troops at Sunset.*
No. 19 (J).	SPION KOP.	January 26th, 1900.	*Position of Troops at Sunset.*
No. 20.	SPION KOP.	January 24th, 1900.	*The Situation at about 9 a.m.*
No. 20 (A).	SPION KOP.	January 24th, 1900.	*The Situation at about 3 p.m.*
No. 20 (B.)	SPION KOP.	January 24th, 1900.	*The Situation at Sunset.*
No. 21.	VAAL KRANTZ.	February 5th, 1900.	*Position of Troops at 11 a.m.*
No. 21 (A).	VAAL KRANTZ.	February 5th, 1900.	*Position of Troops at Sunset.*
No. 21 (B).	VAAL KRANTZ.	February 6th, 1900.	*Position of Troops at Midnight.*
No. 21 (C).	VAAL KRANTZ.	February 7th, 1900.	*Position of Troops at Sunset.*
No. 22.	RELIEF OF KIMBERLEY.	February 10th—14th, 1900.	*Movements of Troops.*
No. 22 (A).	RELIEF OF KIMBERLEY.	February 15th, 1900.	*Movements of Troops.*
No. 22 (B).	RELIEF OF KIMBERLEY.	February 16th and 17th, 1900.	*Movements of Troops.*
No. 23.	PAARDEBERG.	February 18th, 1900.	*Situation about 8 a.m.*
No. 23 (A.)	PAARDEBERG.	February 18th—19th, 1900.	*Situation at Night.*
No. 24.	PROTECTED BIVOUAC AND WORKS NEAR PAARDEBERG.	February 21st to 27th, 1900.	
No. 25.	PAARDEBERG TO BLOEMFONTEIN.	February—March, 1900.	
No. 26.	POPLAR GROVE.	March 7th, 1900.	*Situation at 11.30 a.m.*
No. 27.	DRIEFONTEIN.	March 10th, 1900.	*Situation at 3.30 p.m.*
No. 28.	ENVIRONS OF KIMBERLEY.	*Situation early in February,* 1900.	
No. 29.	KIMBERLEY.	*British Works and Positions at the End of the Siege.*	
No. 30.	RELIEF OF LADYSMITH.	February 14th to 27th, 1900.	*Area of Operations.*
No. 30 (A).	RELIEF OF LADYSMITH.	February 18th, 1900.	*Dispositions after capture of Green Hill and Monte Cristo.*
No. 30 (B).	RELIEF OF LADYSMITH.	February 22nd, 1900.	*Dispositions at dusk.*
No. 30 (C).	RELIEF OF LADYSMITH.	February 23rd, 1900.	*Dispositions at night.*
No. 30 (D).	RELIEF OF LADYSMITH.	February 27th, 1900.	*Dispositions at evening.*
No. 31.	DEFENCE OF LADYSMITH.		
No. 32.	LADYSMITH.	January 6th, 1900.	*Action at Wagon Hill and Cæsar's Camp. Situation at* 2.30 *a.m.*
No. 32 (A).	LADYSMITH.	January 6th, 1900.	*Action at Wagon Hill and Cæsar's Camp. Situation at* 5 *p.m.*
No. 33.	SANNAH'S POST.	March 31st, 1900.	
No. 34.	WEPENER.	April 9th to 24th, 1900.	
No. 35.	NORTH CAPE COLONY AND PART OF THE ORANGE FREE STATE.		
No. 36.	SOUTH AFRICA.	Map showing the approximate situation on the 1st April, 1900.	
No. 37.	INDEX MAP TO VOLUME II.		

FREEHAND SKETCHES.

UPPER TUGELA.
POTGIETERS DRIFT.
COLESBERG.

RELIEF OF LADYSMITH. *View from Clump Hill.*
RELIEF OF LADYSMITH. *View from Hart's Hill.*
LADYSMITH.

MAPS TO VOLUME II.

THE note on the Maps of Volume I. begins with some remarks on the general mapping of South Africa at the time of the war. As regards the special maps in this volume, the following remarks give the material upon which each is based, and from these an idea can be formed as to the degree of accuracy of each. The maps are numbered consecutively on from those of Volume I., in which there were seventeen. As regards Nos. 18, 19, 20, 21; the first (No. 18) is made up of reductions of those surveys of Spion Kop and Vaal Krantz and of Major S. C. N. Grant's, R.E., survey round Colenso made at the same time. Over these areas the map (No. 18) is reliable, but the rest of the map, made up from the four-miles-to-an-inch Natal maps, based on compilations of the farm surveys, is deficient in detail. The three last are based almost entirely on special surveys made after the relief of Ladysmith by Lieutenants J. W. Skipwith and R. Ommanney, R.E. In No. 20 has been incorporated some detail from a sketch made by the Staff of the 10th brigade. Nos. 22, 25 and 28 are based upon small scale maps compiled from the farm surveys; as in the case of all the maps based on like material, they must not be accepted as very accurate. All reliable sketches of localities, such as those of Modder River (Map 12), Magersfontein (Map 13), Paardeberg (Map 23), Poplar Grove (Map 26), Kimberley (Map 29), have been incorporated. Maps 23 and 24 are reproductions of sketches made by Major H. M. Jackson, R.E., and Captain C. De W. Crookshank, R.E., respectively, shortly after the operations illustrated. Maps 26 and 27 are reductions of some large scale sketches received from the office of the D.A.Q.M.G. for Intelligence, Pretoria. Map 29 is a reduction of a large scale survey made during the war by Mr. C. D. Lucas, of Kimberley, under the direction of Captain W. A. J. O'Meara, R.E. Map 30 is made up of the sketch made by Major S. C. N. Grant, R.E., in 1890, and the area on the north and south completed from the farm surveys. Maps 31 and 32 are reproductions from a map compiled under the direction of the D.A.Q.M.G. for Intelligence, Pretoria, in 1905, from various sources. Maps 33 and 34 are from special sketches made by Captain C. W. Gordon, Northumberland Fusiliers, and Lieut. P. O. G. Usborne, R.E. Map 35 is a reprint of No. 9 (Vol. I.), with a few additions and corrections incorporated from sketches of localities which have become available since Map No. 9 was prepared.

The panoramic sketches issued with this volume are facsimile reproductions of a selection made from a number executed by the late Captain W. C. C. Erskine, Bethune's Mounted Infantry.

THE WAR IN SOUTH AFRICA.

CHAPTER I.

RELIEF OF KIMBERLEY.*

SITUATION BEFORE STARTING.

IN the last chapter (XXVI.) of Volume I. it was shown that the elaborate measures taken by Lord Roberts to impose upon the Boers proved entirely successful. No one was so completely deceived as Cronje himself. In vain had his subordinates warned him that his position at Magersfontein, however strong, had been prepared against a frontal attack only, and that his lines could be rolled up by a turning movement. His obstinate conviction that there would be no change in the British strategy made him reply: "The English do not make turning movements; they never leave the railway, because they cannot march." † His force had lost much of its mobility. The veld had been eaten down; many of the Boer horses had become unfit for service, others had been sent away to graze at a distance; thus the number of men without horses now formed a considerable proportion, probably as much as one third, of the strength of the Boer commandos. The burghers, accustomed from old habit and tradition to the continuance of family life, had, in not a few cases, been joined in camp by their wives and children, and a great quantity of baggage had accumulated. Cronje's force was, in fact, suffering from that inevitable deterioration

Cronje, outwitted by Lord Roberts, clings to Magersfontein.

---
* See map No. 22.

† "My Experiences of the Boer War," by Count Sternberg (page 114); see also "War Notes," by Colonel de Villebois Mareuil (page 232).

and loss of energy which inaction causes among irregular troops. Nevertheless, the burghers were yet to show that, when roused, their stubbornness in battle was still unimpaired.

Ground to be traversed on march.

The reasons which determined Lord Roberts' choice of the route for his army have been set forth in the first volume; but the favourable nature of the country to the eastward (or left) of Cronje's position must now be more particularly detailed. Compared to the other parts of the theatre of war in which the British and the Boers had as yet met in arms, the rolling downs of the centre of the Orange Free State were almost void of features. The deep beds of the rivers were formidable obstacles when defended by resolute men, as the battle of the Modder had shown, and as the defence of Cronje's laager at Paardeberg was to prove. Otherwise the ground was open, for the scattered kopjes offered few points that could not be turned by superior numbers. Yet the task in hand was beset with difficulties. To relieve Kimberley, and cut off Cronje from his sources of supply, celerity of movement was essential. It was in order to ensure such celerity that Lord Roberts and his Staff, ever since they landed at Cape Town, had been engaged in reorganising the transport.* Much as had been done in this respect, especially for the cavalry, it would be impossible to rely on the cavalry alone. The infantry and artillery must be available in close support, and the main burden of the fighting must be borne by them. Now, the problem of rapidly moving forward these two arms, difficult always, was doubly so in the war in South Africa, most of all at the time of year when the march must begin.

Heat, dust, dearth of water.

February is the hottest month of the year in the sub-continent. Though the part of the Orange Free State which the troops were about to invade is some four thousand feet above sea level, the sun's rays were very powerful; the soil was loose, sandy, and extraordinarily dusty. Water was alarmingly scarce. Except in the beds of the rivers and streams, which at this season are usually reduced to a series of small pools connected by a trickle of current mainly running in underground channels, there was but little surface water in the Orange Free

* Volume I., Chapter XXVI.

RELIEF OF KIMBERLEY.

State. Such farms as are not fortunate enough to have a frontage to a permanent stream, rely on dams and reservoirs; but the supply in these was very low, and likely to prove inadequate for the needs of a large number of animals and men. No rain had fallen for many weeks; and the plains offered but little food for the hardy country-bred oxen, still less for the English horses, on which most of the cavalry regiments were mounted. The veld formed a fairly good surface for the movement of wheeled transport on a broad front; but two streams, the Modder and the Riet, barred the way between Kimberley and the Orange river. Owing to the steepness of their banks, they could only be crossed at drifts, in some cases ten to twelve miles apart. Again, Lord Roberts was about to execute a flank march around a mobile enemy knowing every inch of the ground, in a country that had not been surveyed for military purposes. He might be attacked either from the north and east by the commandos which were investing Kimberley and by Cronje's troops, or from the south-east by part of the burghers who faced Clements at Colesberg, and by reinforcements of Free Staters drawn from Natal.

To meet the water difficulty the army was to move in great detachments, at such relative intervals of time and space that, while each covered its own line of communications, it was within supporting distance of its neighbour. Ramdam, a well-watered farm nearly due east of Graspan, and about four miles across the frontier, was chosen as the starting point of the invasion. From Ramdam General French's cavalry division was to march to the Riet, some twelve miles eastward, seize the fords known as Waterval and De Kiel's Drifts, and then, moving rapidly northwards, attempt to make good the crossings of the Modder, some fifteen or twenty miles east of the Magersfontein position. The infantry divisions, following in successive échelons, were to support General French's mounted troops. After the Modder had been crossed, much must depend on the movements of the enemy, but it was expected that the infantry divisions, as well as the cavalry, would be needed for the relief of Kimberley, and that that town would become the base of the

Mode of march to meet difficulties.

subsequent advance on Bloemfontein. Until the direct road to Kimberley was freed from the presence of the enemy, a line of supply was to be opened from the Modder River camp to the army, *viâ* Jacobsdal, as soon as the upper drifts of the Modder had been secured.

<small>Positions of the troops, 8th Feb., 1900.</small>

The assembly between the Orange river and the Riet had placed the troops by February 8th, 1900, as follows: One brigade of mounted infantry (Hannay's), still lay at Orange River station; the rest of the cavalry division and the whole of the VIth division (Kelly-Kenny) were at Modder River camp, while the VIIth division (Tucker) encamped at Graspan and Enslin. The IXth division (Colvile) was as yet incompletely organised. One of its brigades—the 3rd (Highland)—was still under Lord Methuen's orders at the Modder camp; the other, the new 19th, was in process of formation at Graspan. In the cavalry division not one of the three cavalry brigadiers—Broadwood, Porter, or Gordon—had yet arrived to take over their newly-organised commands. Some days were therefore needed to consolidate the component parts of the hastily-formed army corps into a homogeneous whole. But circumstances suddenly arose which appeared to render delay dangerous, and, indeed, impossible.

<small>Situation at Kimberley.</small>

The siege of Kimberley* had been rather a passive investment than an active attack. The Boer officer commanding the investing force, General Ferreira, trusted mainly to the effects of a mild bombardment and of starvation. He justly reckoned the large civil population a weakness on which he could count. From a military point of view, Colonel Kekewich had found no difficulty in holding his own against the enemy, and, through Lord Methuen, on the 19th of January had reported to the Commander-in-Chief that he had sufficient supplies to maintain the defence until the 28th of February. But there was anxiety as to the effect which prolonged hardship and danger was producing upon the enormous mass of besieged non-combatants. Suddenly their nerves were exposed to an unexpected strain. The 94-pr. (Creusot), disabled on the 7th of December by Sir A. Hunter's sortie from Ladysmith,† had been sent to Pretoria,

---

* See Chapter V. † See Chapter XXX.

RELIEF OF KIMBERLEY.

and been repaired there in the workshops of the Netherlands Railway. The Pretoria authorities decided to try its effect on Kimberley. Cronje wished to secure the gun for Scholtz Nek, but this proposal was successfully resisted by General Ferreira, and on the 7th of February "Long Tom" began to burst its large shells over the town. This seriously alarmed the inhabitants, and made them so anxious for the end of the siege that, on the 9th of February, Colonel Kekewich felt obliged to signal a special report to Lord Roberts. The Field-Marshal understood from this that the danger of surrender had become imminent, and he ordered an advance for next morning. This was found to be impossible, as the army was not yet sufficiently equipped with transport to march. The Commander-in-Chief, therefore, on the 10th of February, signalled to Kekewich to deliver to the inhabitants of Kimberley a strongly-worded message from himself, of which the following is an extract: *Arrival of "Long Tom."* *The C.-in-C. promises speedy relief.*

> "Many days cannot possibly pass before Kimberley will be relieved, as we commence active operations to-morrow. Our future military operations depend in a large degree on your maintaining your position a very short time longer, and our prestige would suffer severely if Kimberley were to fall into the hands of the enemy."

To the Commander of the garrison the Field-Marshal promised, in another cipher message, the fullest support in all measures which he might find necessary to take to ensure the continuance of resistance to the enemy, and added: "You can assure all who are now apprehensive that we shall strain every nerve to relieve you, which will, I hope, be in a few days' time."

Nor was this the only disquieting intelligence which reached Lord Roberts at this critical moment. On the 26th January he had telegraphed to Sir Redvers Buller:— *Anxiety because of Spion Kop failure.*

> "I am much concerned to hear that Spion Kop position has been abandoned. . . . . Unless you feel fairly confident of being able to relieve Ladysmith from Potgieter's Drift, would it not be better to postpone the attempt until I am in the Orange Free State? Strenuous efforts are being made to collect transport, and I am hopeful of having sufficient to enable me to move on or about the 5th February. If White can hold out, and your position is secure, the presence of my force on the north of the Orange river should cause the enemy

to lessen their hold on Natal and thus make your task easier. Reports from Boer camp point to their being fagged and unable to cope with our artillery fire. It seems, therefore, most desirable to maintain as bold a front as possible for the next ten days."

Correspondence thereon.

Next day two telegrams, both dated the 26th, arrived from the War Office. These were sent when news of the failure at Spion Kop was received in London. One was despatched in duplicate by Lord Wolseley to Sir Redvers Buller and Lord Roberts, the other from Lord Lansdowne to the latter officer. The first ran as follows :—

"In the event of your thinking it possible that your next endeavour to relieve Ladysmith may be unsuccessful, would it not be feasible for White to break out at night with all his mounted men, and as many others as he could carry in carts, and all or part of his guns, and get across the Tugela river? It would seem that the most likely moment for this endeavour might be perhaps when you are engaged on Tugela river, or immediately afterwards if you did not have decisive success. S. of S. authorises me to say that if you adopt this suggestion, Government is quite prepared to give you every support, but please understand that you are left entirely unfettered."

This message was explained and cancelled by a further telegram from Lord Wolseley on the 27th :—

"It has been pointed out to me that my telegram of yesterday is capable of misinterpretation. Please understand that it is not intended to suggest that the best course for White to pursue is to cut his way out; on the contrary, this plan, if practicable at all, should only be adopted when all the expedients for extricating him have failed. In view of Lord Roberts's subsequent communication to you, you had better regard the telegram as cancelled."

The second, that from Lord Lansdowne, was thus worded :—

"Please tell me what you think of the situation in both colonies as affected by the check to Buller on the Tugela, and what should be done if he fails to relieve Ladysmith. Is there in Natal any place which might be made impregnable, to all intents and purposes, and would enable General Officer Commanding with, say, 10,000 men, to contain a considerable number of the enemy, by which means the rest of Buller's force could be freed to join you?"

On receipt of these despatches Lord Roberts, on the 27th, again telegraphed to Sir Redvers Buller :—

"Give me the earliest information of the reply you propose to send the Commander-in-Chief. White's action seems to me to depend entirely upon the time he can hold out; the longer he can do so, the more chance I have of affording help from this side. White named the 15th February as the latest date, but if he could possibly hold out until the end of the month, I should hope to be able to give him and you material assistance. By the latter date I ought to be near Bloemfontein, having meanwhile relieved Kimberley. The fact of my threatening Bloemfontein will probably relieve the hostile pressure in Natal, and thus enable Ladysmith to be relieved even before the end of February.

"For White to break out would be a desperate venture, and the abandonment of the position he has so long defended, and of the sick and wounded, would be a severe blow to our prestige throughout South Africa, and would in no small degree embarrass future operations."

On the 27th Lord Roberts telegraphed, through Sir Redvers Buller, to the Commander of the Ladysmith garrison:

"I beg you will yourself accept and offer to all those serving under you my warmest congratulations on the heroic and splendid defence you have made. It is a matter of the deepest regret to me that the relief of Ladysmith should be delayed, but I trust that you will be able to hold out later than the date named in your recent message to Buller. I fear that your sick and wounded must suffer, but you will realise how important it is that Ladysmith should not fall into the enemy's hands. I am doing all that is possible to hurry on my movements, and shall be greatly disappointed if by the end of February I have not been able to carry out such operations as will compel the enemy to materially reduce his strength in Natal."

Previous to the receipt of this message, but on the same day as its despatch, Sir George had heliographed to Sir Redvers Buller, offering spontaneously to break out of Ladysmith with 7,000 men and 36 guns, but not concealing the physical weakness of his troops.* On the 28th, in reply to the Field Marshal's message, General White stated that by sacrificing (*i.e.*, using as food) the rest of his horses, he could hold out for another six weeks.

On the 29th January Sir Redvers reported to Headquarters:—

"My plan for next try to relieve Ladysmith is to turn the Spion Kop position by the east, crossing the Tugela three times and using a new drift, just discovered, which makes all the difference, as it enables me to reach a position I had hitherto considered inaccessible. I am only waiting for the battery of Horse Artillery from India, and, if it arrives, I hope to attack on Wednesday at 4 p.m.

* See Chapter XXXII.

Vaal Krantz correspondence.

"The death-rate in Ladysmith is now eight to ten a day, and their hospital stores have run out, so delay is objectionable. I feel fairly confident of success this time, as I believe the enemy had a severe lesson last week and are very disheartened, while we are all right. One can never safely attempt to prophesy, but so far as my exertions can, humanly speaking, conduce to the required end, I think I can promise you that I shall in no case compromise my force."

As regards the War Office's suggestion, that if it became necessary to abandon Ladysmith, Natal might be held by 10,000 men, Sir Redvers Buller reported that 30,000 would in his opinion be needed. The Field Marshal therefore decided to give General Buller a free hand in his design of pushing for Ladysmith *via* Vaal Krantz, and on the 29th January he telegraphed to the War Office:—

"Buller's plan for another attempt to relieve Ladysmith appears feasible; he seems confident of success and is evidently more cheerful."

On the 6th of February Sir R. Buller informed Lord Roberts that he had pierced the enemy's lines at Vaal Krantz, but that, owing to the difficulty of carrying flanking positions still occupied by the enemy, any further advance could only be effected at a loss of from 2,000 to 3,000 men. He added:—

"I am not confident, though hopeful, that I can do it. The question is how would such a loss affect your plans, and do you think the chance of the relief of Ladysmith worth the risk? It is the only possible way to relieve White; if I give up this chance, I know no other."

Lord Roberts replied immediately:—

"Ladysmith must be relieved even at the loss you anticipate. . . . . . Let your troops know that the honour of the Empire is in their hands and that I have no possible doubt as to their being successful."

But on the following day Sir Redvers Buller reported that he had decided that it would be useless waste of life to try to force a passage, which, when forced, would not "leave me a free road to Ladysmith." He proposed, therefore, to try another route east of Colenso, but added: "My view is that I have a forlorn (hope) chance at both places; but if I get through

RELIEF OF KIMBERLEY.

here, I am not at Ladysmith by a long way, while if I get through there, I relieve the place." And on the 9th he again telegraphed to Lord Roberts :—

"The operations of the past three weeks have borne in upon me the fact that I had seriously miscalculated the retentive power of the Ladysmith garrison. I now find the enemy can practically neglect that, and turn their whole force upon me. I am not, consequently, strong enough to relieve Ladysmith. If you could send me reinforcements, and if White can hold out till they arrive, I think it might be done; but with a single column I believe it to be almost an impossibility. I shall continue attacking as it keeps the enemy off Ladysmith, but think the prospects of success are very small."

Buller asks for reinforcements for relief of Ladysmith, 9th Feb., 1900,

In a later telegram of the same date he further stated that :

"It is right that you should know that in my opinion the fate of Ladysmith is only a question of days, unless I am very considerably reinforced. Wherever I go, the enemy can anticipate me in superior force. I turned yesterday from Vaal Krantz and am moving towards Colenso; the enemy have left Vaal Krantz and are now at Colenso; they do in six hours and seven miles, what takes me three days and twenty-six miles."

This unexpected demand for the despatch of immediate reinforcements to Natal reached the Commander-in-Chief at the Modder camp at a moment when, although it added to his anxieties, the doubt whether Kimberley would stand firm for many more days rendered it impossible for him to grant it.

On the 10th February, Lord Roberts, after reviewing the previous communications which had passed between himself and General Buller, pointed out to him that, "to send you large reinforcements now would entail the abandonment of a plan of operations the object of which was explained to you on 26th January, and in the prosecution of which, I am convinced, lies our best chance of success both in Natal and on the north of Cape Colony.' Such a course would involve endless confusion and protracted delay, and, as Cape Colony is weakly held, might not improbably lead to a general rising of the disaffected Dutch population. I must therefore request that, while maintaining a bold front, you will act strictly on the defensive until I have time to see whether the operations I am undertaking will produce the effect I hope for. The repeated loss of men on the Tugela line

which cannot be granted.

without satisfactory results is what our small army cannot afford."

General Buller's reply to these instructions was dated two days later, and ran as follows :—

"Your resumé of telegrams is quite correct, except that you have omitted your answer of 16th January to mine of the 15th, which you quote. In it you said: Begins: 'I am concerned to hear you can expect very little help from White, as that is the sole chance of Ladysmith being relieved.'—Ends. I took the words 'sole chance' as a direct intimation that I was not to ask for reinforcements, and I should not have done so now had it not been represented to me that I ought to tell you I did not think I was strong enough to save Ladysmith unless reinforced. Pray do not think that I wish to lay my troubles on you. I quite admit that I miscalculated the retentive power of Sir George White's force. I thought he would hold at least 10,000 men off me—I doubt if he keeps 2,000, and I underrated the difficulties of the country. I don't know your plans or where your troops are, and the last thing I wish to do is to involve your plans in confusion. I merely state the fact that I think Ladysmith is in danger, and that I find myself too weak to relieve it. But as you value the safety of Ladysmith, do not tell me to remain on the defensive. To do that means to leave the whole Boer force free to attack Ladysmith. Sir George White has repeatedly telegraphed, 'I trust to your preventing them throwing their strength on me'; and again, 'the closer to Ladysmith you can establish yourself the better chance we shall have.' I feel sure this is right policy, and I hope you will not say that I am to rest supine and leave Ladysmith alone. . . . As I have before said, I will do all I can, and you may rely that I will not compromise my force."

It is of interest to compare General Buller's appeal with the latest intelligence possessed at this moment by the Boers as to the condition of affairs in Ladysmith. On the 8th of February, the State Secretary at Bloemfontein received the following report from the Free Staters' Headquarters before Ladysmith :

"A deserter from Ladysmith, who seems trustworthy, states 'that the place is on its last legs, and that the troops have for the last two days been fed on half a pound of horseflesh and one biscuit a day; they are in a state of starvation and disheartened. The cattle are sick, and their meat has been condemned by the doctors. The troops at the outset of the siege numbered 12,500; of the 7,500 now remaining about 2,000 are down with fever and dysentery and 2,200 are wounded. They expect to be relieved by the 18th instant; if this does not happen they will make an attempt to force their way through. White has been ill with fever since the 4th, and Hamilton has taken command. He does not know where Hunter is. . . . .'"

RELIEF OF KIMBERLEY.

This telegram, although not accurate in its details, suggests the probability of another general attack on Ladysmith, if Sir R. Buller had assumed a passive attitude. The last Boer telegrams which reached Jacobsdal, prior to its capture by the British troops on 15th of February, announced that "Ladysmith was on its last legs."

On receipt of this appeal Lord Roberts telegraphed on the 13th that he had no desire that Sir Redvers should adhere to a passive attitude, and left it to him to do whatever he thought best, relying on his assurance that he would not compromise his force.

The critical situation in Natal made the need of vigorous action in the western theatre of war more than ever urgent. On the afternoon of the 10th the Chief of the Staff communicated to the Lieut.-General of the cavalry division the Commander-in-Chief's anxiety as to the position at Kimberley, and informed him that the cavalry must relieve the town "at all costs." Lord Kitchener added that the hope of directly relieving Ladysmith had gone. The same evening the Field-Marshal visited the cavalry lines and explained to the officers of the division the nature of the task which had been assigned to them. On the morning of the 11th the movement began. The cavalry division was ordered to march to Ramdam, where it would probably be joined by Hannay's mounted infantry brigade, which had left Orange River station on the previous evening. The VIIth division was also to move to Ramdam, its camps at Enslin and Graspan being taken over by the VIth division from Modder River camp. The IXth division, whose brigades (3rd and 19th) had still to be brought together from the Modder, Belmont, and Graspan, was directed to complete its organisation and equipment as rapidly as possible. In order to deceive the enemy all tents were to be left standing.

Prompt action essential.

Cavalry to relieve Kimberley "at all costs."

Advance begins, 11th Feb., 1900.

For the cavalry division six days' rations for the men, and five days' forage for animals, were carried with the troops, as follows:

(a) Three full days' of both in the supply columns.

(b) Two days' food and one day's forage in regimental reserves.

(c) The remainder on the men and horses.

Five per cent. of led horses also accompanied the division. In the infantry divisions the men carried two days' rations and the brigade mule transport two more; for subsequent supplies they were dependent on the convoy system described in Volume I., Chapter XXV.

Orders for the 1st division. Before leaving Modder River camp the Field-Marshal instructed Lord Methuen, with the Guards', the 9th brigade, and his divisional troops, to continue to hold the ridge to the north of his camp beyond the right bank of the Modder and Riet rivers, and to cover the railway bridge and its approaches. He was to watch the enemy with the utmost vigilance, but to act entirely on the defensive until he received information of the occupation of Jacobsdal by British troops; he was then to establish a fresh line of communications with Lord Roberts through that place. He was warned that, pending the arrival of further reinforcements from England, his line of communications to the south was weakly guarded.

Movements of Hannay's column, 9th Feb. In the execution of the orders for the movements of the 11th only one column, that of Colonel Hannay, came into contact with the enemy. His troops consisted of the Carabiniers and one squadron of the 14th Hussars * (belonging to the 1st cavalry brigade), the 2nd, 4th, 5th, 6th and 7th regiments of mounted infantry, two companies of New Zealanders, two squadrons of Kitchener's Horse, and one company of Rimington's Guides. At 3 p.m. on the 9th, while encamped on the south of the Orange river, he had received written orders from Army Headquarters to march to Ramah Spring on the right bank of the river, half-way between Orange River bridge and the British post at Zoutpans Drift.† The crossing of the bridge was much delayed by the number of trains running. The railway bridge is over a quarter of a mile long, and, as originally constructed

---

* The Headquarters and the other two squadrons of this regiment were in Natal.

† See map No. 35.

RELIEF OF KIMBERLEY.

with an open floor, was only suitable for the passage of trains. The R.E. had planked over the floor so as to make it passable even for ox-wagons, but constant work day and night, and the greatest exertions on the part of the Sappers, were required to keep this narrow defile in repair during the strain to which it was subjected throughout the concentration. Owing to contradictory instructions from Army Headquarters, the column did not finally move off until 7.30 p.m., an unfortunate hour for the march of the newly-raised battalions of regular mounted infantry. Many of the rank and file crossed a horse that day for the first time in their lives. In the darkness of the night the horses often stumbled, and their riders fell. The animals went on with the column, leaving their masters on the ground, and when Hannay reached Ramah at 7 a.m., on the 10th, many men were absent. To allow the stragglers, as well as the baggage and supply wagons, which had been seriously delayed by several difficult dongas, to rejoin the column it was found necessary to halt all day at Ramah. *Night march with raw mounted infantry.*

During the 10th, the brigade was ordered to march next day to Ramdam, but after sunset a report reached Colonel Hannay that a Boer commando, on a rocky range of hills ten miles to the north-east, threatened his line of advance. A detachment under Captain (local Lieut.-Colonel) H. de B. de Lisle, consisting of the 6th mounted infantry, New Zealand mounted infantry, and New South Wales Rifles—in all about 1,000 mounted men with two machine guns—was sent in that direction with instructions to bivouac four miles out, and next morning "to drive through the hills," an operation which the experiences at Colesberg had shown to be very difficult against Boers holding a defile with magazine rifles. At dawn on the 11th the scouts ascertained that the enemy was posted in force on the kopjes, and was evidently expecting to be attacked. De Lisle held the front of the hills with one regiment, and attempted to turn the flanks with the remainder of his men, but without success; nor did a reinforcement of the 5th and half the 7th regiments of mounted infantry and a squadron of Kitchener's Horse enable him to drive away the defenders. But though de Lisle failed to *Hannay in action on 11th Feb.*

dislodge the Boers, he occupied their attention, and the transport was able to pass on in safety. Colonel Hannay, who came up at noon, decided to make no further effort to carry the hills ; he ordered de Lisle to confine himself to a demonstration sufficient to hold the enemy to his ground. Two companies were already so warmly engaged, at a range of six hundred yards, that it was found impossible to extricate them till nightfall. The transport and the remainder of the column marched on to Roodepan, a farm twelve miles to the south of Ramdam. This they reached at 4.30 p.m., but they were not joined by de Lisle's troops until midnight. Though Hannay's skirmish had so greatly delayed his march that he was unable to join the cavalry division on the 11th, yet his flanking movement to the eastward answered the purpose of the Commander-in-Chief, by causing the enemy to believe that he was demonstrating towards Koffyfontein. Hannay's casualties were four killed, twenty-two wounded, and thirteen missing. The numbers of the enemy engaged are stated by the Boer accounts to have been 226 men, under Commandant Van der Post.

CHAPTER II.

RELIEF OF KIMBERLEY.

PASSAGE OF THE RIET AND MODDER.*

THE orders for the 12th directed the seizure of one or more crossings over the Riet river by the cavalry division, supported by the VIIth division from Ramdam, the concentration at Ramdam of the VIth division from Graspan and Enslin, and of Hannay's brigade from Roodepan. To complete the IXth division (Colvile), the Highland brigade (MacDonald) was to move that day from Modder River camp to Enslin, a few miles from the neighbouring station of Graspan, where Colvile's other brigade (19th, Smith-Dorrien) was now assembled. Headquarters were to be transferred from the Modder River camp to Ramdam. The Commander-in-Chief, on the 11th, wrote to Lieut.-General Tucker : Movements ordered for the 12th Feb.

"I have told French that as soon as he gets across the Riet river to-morrow, he must discover where there is water for your division between the Riet and the Modder rivers. It is very desirable that you should reach the Modder from the Riet in two marches—it is about 30 miles—so that French's mounted troops should be relieved of the care of the pontoon bridge by your infantry. If French sends you a satisfactory report of the state of the country, I think you might safely march by night, or very early (2 a.m.), so as to save your men from the heat. Please remember with regard to the water that another division with a large force of artillery is following your troops.

"We have no certain information of the enemy coming from the Colesberg (south-east) direction, but it is just possible there may be a party of 2,000 trying to reach Jacobsdal, and it is likely you may come across some of their wagons, as they pass frequently between Jacobsdal and Fauresmith. Leave your ac-

* See map No. 22.

knowledgment of the receipt of this letter at Ramdam, where I hope to be to-morrow about noon, and keep me informed of your movements and of any information you may obtain about the enemy. Save your men as much as possible, but I hope nothing will prevent them being on the Modder at the point to be indicated to you by French on Wednesday " (*i.e.*, 14th February).

<small>Motives determining the route adopted.</small>

That movements of such importance would escape the observation of the enemy was more than Lord Roberts could expect. His first two days' march, in a south-easterly direction towards Bloemfontein were, therefore, useful in keeping up the illusion he had endeavoured to foster that that town, and not Kimberley, was the point at which he was aiming. He thus even still hoped yet further to take advantage of the enemy's knowledge of Sir Redvers Buller's original design. That design—a direct movement on Bloemfontein—when published in London newspapers before the embarkation of the army corps had been telegraphed to Pretoria. These lamentable indiscretions, as well as the information obtained by the Boers from documents captured at Talana, had been turned to good account. False orders for a concentration at Colesberg had been industriously circulated by his intelligence staff, while the true orders were communicated to as few persons as possible, and only sent to the troops at the last moment.* Yet, surrounded as Lord Roberts' camps were by zealous friends of the enemy, it seemed impossible that his real plan should not become known before the moment for the advance arrived. By moving at first towards Bloemfontein, he left his real intentions still uncertain, and tended to awake alarm lest the capital was still his immediate object, though the mode of approaching it had been changed from that originally proposed. The march at the same time enabled him to keep out of Cronje's observation, whilst the cavalry, without alarming him, drew near to that General's line of connection with the besiegers of Kimberley.

<small>Boers' intelligence department fails.</small>

The Boers had great advantages for obtaining correct reports. In every village and town in the British colonies, and in many of the farmhouses scattered through the frontier districts, there were both men and women regularly in the habit of supplying

* See Volume I., Chapter XXVI.

them with information. Large sums of money had been devoted to intelligence purposes in the years immediately preceding the war, and this expenditure had up to the outbreak of war been fruitful. Moreover, for the actual work of scouting in the field, contests with natives and the pursuit of game had trained the individual burgher to an unrivalled standard of skill. But, when war broke out, failure in organisation and the lack of a trained staff so completely threw away these trump-cards in the game, that a Boer secret official telegram, dated 7th December, 1899, admits that " the English possess better scouts and a better intelligence department than we do." A small corps of picked scouts, called Despatch Riders, had been organised; but these specialists were disliked by their comrades, and had of late been confined to the Colesberg area. At Magersfontein the shortage of horses and the slackness of the burghers in carrying out reconnaissances, had reduced that service to a low ebb.

Thus, owing to his faulty intelligence, Cronje was not fully informed of the British movements on the 11th. Of the marches of the infantry he does not appear to have been aware; and, despite the previous warnings of his subordinates that the concentration south of the Modder presaged some attempt to envelop him, he insisted that the arrival of the cavalry division at Ramdam was merely the preliminary to a demonstration to the eastward, similar in nature to those lately made against his western flank. Under this belief, on the afternoon of the 11th he directed Christian de Wet to take two guns and about 450 burghers and " drive back the British cavalry." De Wet, in his " Three Years' War," says he bivouacked that night close to the British troops at Ramdam, but the events of the following day point to his having halted on the right bank of the Riet, probably just east of Waterval Drift.

Cronje still fails to divine Lord Roberts' intentions.

General French's staff at Ramdam failed to get exact knowledge of De Wet's arrival on the 11th. The Field Intelligence department did not hear of De Wet's presence until the morning of the 12th, but they believed that Jacobsdal was held in some strength, and that the drifts across the Riet were probably watched. They felt uncertain whether these crossings would be defended. General French, with one staff officer, Major D. Haig, and a guide, on the afternoon of the 11th had reconnoitred to within four miles of the river, the banks of which, as observed from this distance, appeared to be low, flat, and devoid of cover.

Cavalry move for Riet on 12th Feb. at 2 a.m.

At 2 a.m. on the 12th, in bright moonlight, the cavalry division moved off from Ramdam, marching east-north-east towards Waterval Drift in three columns, Gordon's brigade (3rd) on the left, Porter's brigade (1st) in the centre, and Broadwood's brigade (2nd) on the right. Colonels Broadwood and Gordon had joined the division and assumed command of their respective brigades—the 2nd and 3rd—on the 11th of February. Colonel Porter was still commanding the 6th Dragoon Guards with Hannay's column, and did not actually take over the command of the 1st brigade from the senior regimental officer until the 14th. An interval of about 80 to 100 yards was preserved between the brigades, which were formed in column of regimental masses. The Horse artillery batteries were in rear of their respective brigades; Alderson's mounted infantry, the Field Troop, R.E., and the Pontoon Troop, followed the centre brigade. In a second line, three miles behind the centre column, were the bearer companies, field hospitals, and ammunition columns, escorted by two companies of mounted infantry. The supply column and transport, guarded by two squadrons of Kitchener's Horse, remained at Ramdam, ready to advance as soon as the actual point of passage over the Riet was decided upon. At 3.30 a.m. the moon set and the division halted, covered by outposts, while Rimington's Guides reconnoitred to the front. At 4.30 a.m. the plains in front were reported clear of the enemy as far as the river; and the march, covered by Major Allenby's squadron of the Inniskilling Dragoons, with a squadron of the Scots Greys in support, was resumed. The advance guard continued to lead towards Waterval Drift, which lay some six or seven miles to the eastward. Five miles higher up the Riet, *i.e.*, to the southward, is De Kiel's Drift. As the light improved, various features of the ground, which had not been noticed in the reconnaissance of the 11th, became visible to the west of the river. The approaches to Waterval

Drift from the west were flanked by kopjes on Lanshoek farm, a little to the north-west of the ford. De Kiel's Drift was covered to the west and south-west by a ridge named Waterval Hill, which appeared suitable for defensive purposes. French decided to push on to Waterval Drift and to seize it, if possible; but, if seriously opposed there, he proposed to demonstrate against it with a detachment, and with the rest of the division make himself master of De Kiel's. After demonstrating against Waterval Drift,

About 6 a.m. the advance patrols of the leading squadron came under rifle fire from the kopjes on Lanshoek farm. The enemy, in order to reconnoitre towards Ramdam, had crossed the river at dawn, and, on perceiving the advance of the British cavalry, had occupied the farm. The brigade division (O. and R. batteries) of the 3rd brigade, supported by the 9th and 16th Lancers, came into action against the hills. On this the enemy disclosed a field gun, which gallantly entered into an unequal duel, and dropped some shells close to General French and his staff. Under cover of Gordon's brigade (3rd) the remainder of the division took ground to the right, and seized Waterval Hill, as a preliminary to an attack on De Kiel's Drift. Gordon was directed to feint at Waterval Drift, and Broadwood's brigade (2nd) to hold Waterval Hill, on which, as a pivot, the 1st brigade and the mounted infantry were wheeled to the eastward. To carry out this plan Gordon gradually drew away from Lanshoek farm, and manœuvred as though about to make a dash at the Waterval Drift. On this De Wet withdrew his advanced parties across the river, and fell back to a low ridge on the right bank which covers that ford. From this ridge both his guns now came into action. By 9 a.m. the 1st brigade and the mounted infantry had completed their wheel to the right, and, facing eastward, awaited the report of the scouts, who were reconnoitring De Kiel's Drift.

The VIIth division, under Lieut.-General Tucker, had left Ramdam with its transport train at 7 a.m., and by 10 a.m. its advance guard reached Waterval Hill. The cavalry scouts reported the river line up to De Kiel's clear of the enemy, and, leaving Broadwood's brigade at Waterval Hill, French, with the

20   THE WAR IN SOUTH AFRICA.

1st brigade and mounted infantry, galloped for the drift. As he approached it, he found conditions peculiarly favourable for the passage of the river, as the left bank had considerable command over the right. The drift itself, although shown in the British staff map,* was not marked in the map of the country in possession of the Boers, and, perhaps for this reason, it was but very slightly held by the enemy. Some kopjes on the left bank were at once seized by the Scots Greys, and shortly before noon a party of Roberts' Horse forced the passage of the river, a little above the drift, with a loss of one officer killed and two men wounded. De Wet appears to have detached a portion of his force before dawn to Blaauwbank Drift, further to the east, and it was probably this detachment which now arrived on the scene of action. In any case, further Boer reinforcements now came up at speed from the east, and menaced French's right flank from the south side of the Riet; but they were quickly driven back by heavy artillery and rifle fire to a farmhouse 1,500 yards to the south. From this a few squadrons and a battery subsequently ousted them. Gordon had meantime detained in front of Waterval Drift the main body of the enemy, and De Wet, realising that his flank was turned, gradually withdrew. The whole cavalry division was thus able to concentrate on the right bank of the Riet at De Kiel's Drift. No pursuit of the enemy was attempted, as the horses showed signs of exhaustion from the great heat of the day. Two squadrons of the 10th Hussars were sent out in the afternoon to search for water to the north, and, though unsuccessful in their quest, succeeded in cutting the telegraph line between Jacobsdal and Koffyfontein in six places.

marginal note: The whole of the cavalry crosses at De Kiel's Drift.

From the top of Magersfontein Commandant Andries Cronje, a brother of General Cronje, had observed signs of fighting on the Riet in the morning, and had obtained leave to take 325 burghers of the Potchefstroom and Bloemhof commandos, with a Maxim-Nordenfeldt gun, to De Wet's assistance. Leaving

marginal note: Andries Cronje with reinforcements for De Wet arrives, too late to stop the cavalry.

---

* Prepared at Cape Town during the previous month under Colonel G. F. R. Henderson's supervision. See Volume I., page 15.

Magersfontein at 10 a.m., this reinforcement reached Jacobsdal at noon, but the Boers' ponies were too much out of condition for rapid progress, and a halt had to be made for three hours, some forty men being dropped in the village. The remainder pushed on at 3 p.m. and must have passed not very far from the scouting parties of the 10th Hussars. Seeing that the fight was over, Andries Cronje made his way eastward to Blaauwbank Drift and, late in the evening, joined De Wet on the far side of the Riet at Winterhoek Farm.

General Tucker, after a brief halt at Waterval Hill, had pushed on with his brigades and train to De Kiel's Drift, his battalions, but lately disembarked from England, being much tried by the burning sun and the lack of water on the march. The drift was found to be impracticable for wagons, but another ford was discovered a mile and a half to the eastward, and the transport of the VIIth division began to cross to the right bank, the infantry meanwhile taking over the outposts from the cavalry. There was little water in the bed of the river, but the banks at this new drift were very steep, and confusion quickly arose, due to a large extent to the fact that no staff officer had been detailed to regulate the crossing of the transport of the various units. French, as early as 11.50 a.m., had reported to the Commander-in-Chief that he hoped " to remain at the drift but a few hours and then press on," but at 8 p.m. the Chief of the Staff, who had ridden up from Ramdam (where Headquarters had now arrived), telegraphed to Lord Roberts that delay was unavoidable, and that the cavalry patrols had failed to find any water to the north of the Riet. The cavalry supply column had not yet arrived from Ramdam. General French had sent orders by field cable for its advance at 10.45 a.m., but, owing to the non-delivery of the message, which was directed to the " Baggage-master " (an expression unfamiliar to the orderlies), it had not started until late in the afternoon, and, after a break-down on the road, the head of the column only reached De Kiel's Drift at one o'clock on the morning of the 13th.

VIIth division follows cavalry to De Kiel's Drift.

During the 12th the VIth division (Kelly-Kenny), with a com-

22   THE WAR IN SOUTH AFRICA.

<small>Concentration and movements of other infantry divisions.</small>
pany of mounted infantry and two 12-pr. Naval guns, had concentrated at Ramdam without incident. Colonel Hannay's mounted infantry brigade also arrived at Ramdam, and thus became attached to Lieut.-General Kelly-Kenny's command. The Carabiniers, a squadron of 14th Hussars, and the New Zealand mounted infantry under Colonel Porter, followed and caught up the cavalry division at 9 a.m. on the 13th at De Kiel's Drift. Colvile's division was now complete at Enslin and Graspan, and ready to move.

The issue of the operations on the 12th had been favourable. Except for the slight opposition on the Riet, there was no sign as yet that Cronje had taken alarm. It seemed probable that the rapid advance northward, which had been planned for the morrow, might place at least some troops in possession of the crossings of the Modder. Two difficulties had, however, to be faced. The block at De Kiel's Drift had prevented French's men from drawing their supplies on the night of the 12th, and had shown that it would take at least another twenty-four hours before the transport train of both the cavalry and VIIth divisions could be moved across the river by that ford. The

<small>Water difficulties and block at De Kiel's Drift decide Lord Roberts to send cavalry to Modder a day in advance of infantry.</small>
second difficulty was the failure to find water north of the Riet. Without the certainty of water it seemed unwise to commit Tucker's battalions to a march of twenty-four miles across the veld to the Modder. Lord Roberts decided, therefore, that the VIIth division should remain halted for the 13th at De Kiel's Drift, to cover the passage of the transport; that French should move his cavalry northward and endeavour to seize a drift over the Modder and establish his brigades on the far bank; while the VIth division with Hannay's brigade should march to Waterval Drift. Even if French should encounter opposition too strong to be overcome by his mounted troops, at least one, if not two, infantry divisions would be within a day's march to support him. The IXth division was to march to Ramdam and act as a reserve.

<small>Boers, still deceived by Lord Roberts' movements,</small>
Meanwhile the situation on the enemy's side remained unchanged. Deceived, probably, by Hannay's movements on the 11th, De Wet believed that Koffyfontein was Lord Roberts'

immediate object. He therefore instructed Andries Cronje to move in that direction early next morning and take up a strong position in the hills south-west of that village. He detached 200 men under Commandant Lubbe to keep in close touch with the British cavalry. With the remainder he determined to await events at Winterhoek. To General Piet Cronje he had already despatched a written report by G. J. Scheepers —the head of his signallers—of the movement eastward of a large British force, estimated to be not less than 40,000 to 50,000 men.* He hoped that this report would rouse his superior to action before the toils had closed around him. But the old Boer leader still held stubbornly to his belief that the English could not march. Neither De Wet's message, nor the warnings of others who had seen the British columns, moved him. He could not read a map well enough to appreciate the importance of what had taken place, and laughed at a suggestion that the drifts over the Modder needed protection. The British force on the Riet was, he declared, "only cavalry, whom we shoot and capture."† Thus the upper reaches of the Modder were left unguarded save for piquets of Free State burghers who had been found unsuitable for employment in the front line. The existence of these piquets had been ascertained by the British Intelligence Staff.

<small>believe the British object to be Koffyfontein.</small>

French's division was unable to make an early start from De Kiel's Drift on the morning of the 13th, for the approaches to the ford were so hopelessly blocked by the infantry wagons that the cavalry supply column could not cross the river. Led horses with sacks had been sent during the night by French's Staff to the left bank to draw two days' supplies, but the process was a tedious one. At 7 a.m. the Cavalry Commander issued the following orders:

<small>French, delayed at De Kiel's Drift by infantry wagons, cannot march till 10.30 a.m. on 13th Feb.</small>

---

* De Wet, in "Three Years' War," asserts that he warned Cronje that the British troops were making for the Modder. But this statement appears inconsistent with his own dispositions, with the orders he issued to Andries Cronje, and with other Boer accounts.

† "My Experiences of the Boer War," by Count Sternberg.

His orders.

CAVALRY DIVISION MARCH ORDERS.
Headquarters, De Kiel's Drift,
13th February, 1900. 7 a.m.

1. The enemy has retired from the Riet apparently in a north and north-westerly direction.*
2. The General Officer Commanding intends to march to the Modder to-day to seize a passage over it, and establish the Division beyond it.
3. The Division will march at 9 a.m. to-day in the following order:

   (a) Porter's Brigade† in the centre, Broadwood's Brigade on the right, Gordon's on the left.
   (b) The mounted infantry (under Colonel Alderson) will follow the cavalry as closely as possible, escorting the ammunition column and pontoons, and accompanied by the Bearer Companies and Field Hospitals.

4. The baggage and supply columns with the ammunition wagons which are not horsed will follow with the detachment which marched into De Kiel's this morning under Colonel Porter, at an hour to be named by the latter.
5. The General Officer Commanding will march with the centre Brigade.

By Order,
D. HAIG, Major, D.A.A.G.

Colonel Porter was confidentially informed that the cavalry division would march northward, its left on Rondeval Drift, and was instructed to get all the cavalry division baggage and supply column across the Riet as rapidly as possible, and then follow.

The 16th Lancers were detached in the early morning to visit Waterval Drift, but after driving a few Boers away from that ford rejoined Gordon's Brigade.

The actual issue of supplies was not completed until 10 a.m. Half an hour later, in the presence of Lord Roberts, who had ridden over from Ramdam in the early morning, the division moved off in line of brigade masses with wide intervals, the artillery being placed on the inner flanks of the brigades. Two days' supplies were carried on man and horse. In rear followed Alderson's brigade of mounted infantry, guarding such of the ammunition columns as were horsed.

The cavalry division starts for Modder, 13th Feb., 1900.

* The cavalry had lost touch with the enemy on the previous afternoon. De Wet had in reality fallen back to the south-east.

† This brigade remained for the day under the command of the senior Regimental Officer—Lieut.-Colonel the Hon. W. Alexander, 2nd Dragoons.

Soon after starting, the flankers of the left brigade were fired at from the direction of Jacobsdal by the party of Boers who, left in that village by Andries Cronje the day before, were now moving towards De Wet; but these few skirmishers were driven off by a squadron of the 16th Lancers, while, to avoid delay, the direction of the column was diverted slightly to the eastward, and Blaauwboschpan Farm, eight miles north-east of De Kiel's Drift, was reached at 12.30 p.m. Here was found a well, which, it was estimated, would afford water for an infantry brigade. A report was, therefore, sent back by cable to the Chief of the Staff, and a squadron of Kitchener's Horse placed in charge of the well, with instructions to remain there until relieved by the infantry of Tucker's division, expected to follow next day. After half an hour's rest, French resumed the march. The time and appliances available had been insufficient to water the horses, which were already beginning to feel the effects of the severe heat.

Lubbe's scouts had meanwhile been watching the right flank of the division, and during the halt the Boer commandant had pushed forward and seized some small kopjes near Rooidam. These kopjes in some measure command the tracks which lead to the drifts across the Modder, twelve or thirteen miles to the northwards. The most western of these fords is that of Rondeval. Three miles up stream is Klip Drift; next comes Drieputs Drift, which, from its position at the end of a re-entering bend of the river was useless to the British; eight miles almost due east of Klip Drift is the ford of Klip Kraal. A few shells from the guns of the Horse batteries dislodged these scouts, but Lubbe's commando continued to march out of range of, but parallel with, French's right or eastern flank. At the time Lubbe's strength was believed to be between 700 and 1,000 men, but, from information obtained from Boer sources, the estimate appears excessive. The reports received by French during the march pointed to a possible attack on his flank while he was engaged in crossing the Modder, so, to deceive the burghers and to shoulder them off the path of the cavalry division, the direction of the 1st and 2nd brigades was changed

After skirmishing, French approaches Modder,

about 2 p.m. to the north-east. The two brigade masses wheeled half right, as though making for Klip Kraal Drift, while the 3rd held on northward towards the Rondeval passage. For a time Lubbe conformed to the movements of the main body of the cavalry, but about 3.30 p.m., when French approached Middlebosch Farm and saw the course of the Modder marked by the green bushes which here break the monotonous colouring of the veld, he also saw the commando crowding in haste across the drift at Klip Kraal. The feint had been successful. The Boers, indeed, had outstripped their foes, and had occupied the most eastern of the crossings; but by doing so they had placed a deep bend of the river between themselves and the western drifts, across which the British general proposed to force his passage. Pivoting the 1st and 2nd brigades again, but this time on their left flank and to the north-west, French left Lubbe to his own devices, and ordered the 2nd brigade (Broadwood's), with the 1st in support, to make a dash on Klip Drift, and the 3rd (Gordon's) to continue its advance on Rondeval Drift, the movements to be carried out as rapidly as the now exhausted state of the horses permitted. The brigades arrived simultaneously at the drifts about 5 p.m. Of the artillery, however, G. battery, under Major R. Bannatine Allason, attached to Broadwood's brigade, was the only unit able to come into action; the horses of the remainder were so worn out that they could not keep up with the cavalry. The 12th Lancers, under Lieut.-Colonel Lord Airlie, covered by the fire of the Household cavalry, attacked the Klip ford, while the 9th Lancers, under Major Little, assailed the Rondeval Drift. After a slight resistance the parties of burghers who were guarding these fords gave way. Lubbe was too far off to help them; and they sought safety in flight. Thus on the north bank of the Modder a continuous line of kopjes, extending between the two crossings and covering both, was seized and occupied. Some prisoners and the wagons of the Boer piquets fell into the hands of the cavalry. Only one officer and two men were wounded during these operations, but the heat and lack of water had told in a disastrous manner on the horses. Forty had died of exhaustion, and many more were incapable of further service. During the march from the Riet the cable of the field telegraph had been destroyed by a veld fire; written reports were, therefore, now sent back in duplicate by mounted messengers to the Chief of the Staff. Half the ammunition column, escorted by Lieut.-Colonel Alderson, reached the division shortly after dusk; but it was not until 6 p.m. next day, the 14th, that Colonel Porter joined with the remainder of the ammunition column and part of the supply column.

CHAPTER III.

RELIEF OF KIMBERLEY.

FRENCH ENTERS KIMBERLEY.*

Movements of the infantry, 13th Feb., 1900.

THE march of the VIth division, with two Naval 12-prs. under Lieut. F. W. Dean, R.N. and Hannay's brigade, from Ramdam to Waterval Drift (nine miles) was carried out on the 13th without contact with the enemy. The VIIth division remained at De Kiel's; the passage of its wagons to the north bank was not completed until after 1 a.m. on the 14th, as these necessarily had to make way for the cavalry supply column. The IXth division, to which the C.I.V. mounted infantry, a mounted company of the Grahamstown Volunteers, a squadron of Kitchener's Horse, and two Naval 4.7-in. guns, under Commander W. L. Grant, R.N., had been attached as divisional troops, arrived at Ramdam about noon on the 13th, and there bivouacked for the night. Lord Roberts' Headquarters were at De Kiel's Drift, but the Chief of the Staff had been detached to Waterval. Although the cavalry had reported the discovery on their march to Klip Drift of the well at Blaauwboschpan, and of water "probably sufficient for a division at a farm about four miles to the south of Middlebosch Hill," the Commander-in-Chief gave up his original intention of moving Tucker's division (the VIIth) by a direct march to the Modder.

The Transvaal commandos investing Kimberley, and those under Cronje covering that investment from the south, were at

* See map No. 22.

first supplied from the railhead at Klerksdorp, and the Free Staters, from Fauresmith and Bloemfontein; but latterly the commandos around Kimberley appear to have absorbed all supplies from the northern base, leaving Cronje dependent upon Fauresmith and Bloemfontein. Cronje's lines of communication, both through Jacobsdal and Fauresmith and along the Modder towards Bloemfontein, were now in the hands of the British troops; but, to set free French's division for its advance on Kimberley, it was necessary to replace his cavalry on the Modder by an infantry division. For the moment it was open to Cronje, had he been enterprising, to combine with Ferreira and concentrate in superior strength for an attack on French. The position of De Wet on the south-east had become known to the Headquarters staff. The despatch of Boer reinforcements to De Wet from Colesberg, or his reinforcement by the detachment which had fought Hannay at Wolvekraal were possibilities against which provision must be made. The Field-Marshal determined to give French immediate support by moving the VIth division during the night of the 13th-14th to Wegdraai, whence one more march would carry it to the Modder. The VIIth division was to advance on the 14th up the right bank of the Riet to Wegdraai, in support; the IXth division was ordered to move to Waterval Drift. From Wegdraai part of Hannay's mounted infantry, in accordance with Lord Roberts' original plan, would open up a line of communication with Methuen through Jacobsdal. Army Headquarters were moved to Waterval Drift, but Lord Kitchener was ordered forward to the Modder with the VIth division, in order to superintend the arrangements for the final advance on Kimberley. The fact that Cronje had remained stationary whilst the army was passing round him had now made the immediate relief of the besieged town a matter of secondary importance as compared with the complete isolation of Cronje's commandos; but, to make the stroke decisive, the separation of the Boer force investing Kimberley from Cronje seemed necessary, and this separation could only be effected by a rapid movement northward of the cavalry. Cronje's passive attitude made this advance

Cronje's communications.

Orders for the 14th Feb.

Motives for these.

possible. Even the arrival in his camp, on the afternoon of the 13th, of fugitives from Rondeval and Klip Drifts, failed to rouse him to a sense of his insecurity. He merely directed Commandants C. C. Froneman and T. De Beer, with some eight hundred burghers and a couple of guns, to move eastward with vague orders to drive back the enemy. With the remainder, now reduced to less than six thousand men, he still held stubbornly to his *rôle* of blocking any advance on Kimberley along the railway.

<small>Movements on the 14th Feb.</small>

In pursuance of Lord Roberts' orders, Lieut.-General Kelly-Kenny left Waterval Drift at 1 a.m. on the 14th with the VIth division and the 4th and 5th regiments of mounted infantry, the remainder of Hannay's brigade being left at Waterval to guard the crossing. Though Kelly-Kenny was not aware of the fact until the day had broken, the Chief of the Staff had marched with the VIth division. Wegdraai was reached at 10 a.m., after a skirmish with a small party of some thirty or forty Boers. There the main body of the column halted. During the day Lieut.-Colonel St. G. C. Henry reconnoitred with two companies of the 4th mounted infantry down the Riet to Jacobsdal, which he found evacuated by the enemy, though it still contained a large number of women, children, and non-combatants. This near approach to his head laager was reported by telegraph to Cronje, who, although for the moment he attached but little importance to it, sent out a detachment of the Jacobsdal commando, under Commandant Smut, to recover the village. The mounted infantry had already begun to fall back on Wegdraai, but a skirmish ensued, in which Colonel Henry was wounded. His companies were slowly withdrawn, being supported by the 1st Yorkshire, 1st Essex, and a battery which moved out a short distance from Kelly-Kenny's bivouac. At noon the IXth division reached Waterval Drift, bringing from Ramdam the ammunition park of the army and the three sections of the first supply convoy. On its arrival Hannay marched to Wegdraai with the 2nd and 6th mounted infantry, leaving the 7th mounted infantry to act as escort to Army Headquarters. At Wegdraai he was directed to guard for the night the divisional artillery

RELIEF OF KIMBERLEY.

and the supply and baggage train of the VIth division, and to escort them forward to the Modder next morning.

Lord Kitchener during the day had sent a staff officer to report on General French's situation at Klip and Rondeval Drifts, and had ascertained that, although not seriously molested, the cavalry division was being watched from the north by Froneman's force which, placed athwart the line of advance from the Modder on Kimberley, showed signs of an intention to envelop the British flank. Though the infantry of the VIth division had already made a nine-hours' march, the Chief of the Staff feared that any delay would give the Boers time to strengthen, both by entrenchment and reinforcement, the ground they held, and render its capture a costly task. When he pointed out to General Kelly-Kenny that the execution of the Commander-in-Chief's plans required a special effort, that general once more started his infantry and Naval guns. All ranks responded admirably to the call on them for further exertions. They marched off again at 5 p.m., and, notwithstanding drenching rain storms during the night, reached the drifts on the Modder at 1 a.m. on the 15th. Including détours, the division covered twenty-seven miles in twenty-three hours, no inconsiderable feat for troops who, just released from the confinement of a long sea-voyage, made this march in very hot weather over a sandy, treeless and almost waterless plain. The incidents of this night march were those common to similar operations in other parts of the theatre of war. To enable the direction of the column and the formation of the troops to be maintained, halts were frequent. The attention of the officers and non-commissioned officers was strained to the uttermost to keep the men on their feet. If a soldier dropped to the ground, he at once fell into the heavy sleep of physical exhaustion and could with difficulty be roused to resume his place in the ranks. So dense was the darkness that if a man strayed for a few yards across the veld he lost sight of the column and became a straggler. There were many such, of whom the greater part succeeded next day in rejoining their battalions. The divisional artillery and the train arrived on the Modder six hours later under Colonel

VIth division makes double march to join French at Klip Drift.

It reaches Klip Drift at 1 a.m., Feb. 15th, 1900.

Movements of other troops.

Hannay's escort. The VIIth division, to avoid the heat of the day, did not march from Waterval until 6 p.m. on the 14th, and arrived at Wegdraai at 2 a.m. the following morning.

<small>Cronje is made uneasy by the infantry march, but will not act decisively.</small>

The news that the VIth division had quitted Wegdraai and was moving north towards the Modder, reached Cronje on the night of the 14th; this passage round his flank of a large body of infantry at length produced a feeling of uneasiness in his mind, but he still persisted in believing that it was only a feint, and that the chief attack was to be expected along the railway. His main body, therefore, continued to occupy the Magersfontein positions, but, as a precaution, and possibly because the number of burghers had diminished, the foremost posts between the Modder and the Riet were withdrawn. The old Boer leader, moreover, during the night shifted his own Hoofd laager from Brown's Drift to a hollow on Bosjespan Farm, some two and a half miles to the eastward. It is difficult to understand the exact purpose of this change of site; it may have been due solely to a desire better to conceal his camp. Yet it would seem to indicate some wavering in judgment. Thus the Boer Headquarters, although the British staff knew it not, now lay unprotected six miles to the west of Rondeval Drift.

<small>He places his own camp in danger.</small>

<small>Condition of mounted infantry and of cavalry horses prevents discovery of Cronje's exposed Headquarters.</small>

The mounted infantry were too raw and untrained, as well as too much fatigued by their trying march from the 11th to the 14th, to make any such discovery. The horses of the cavalry division sorely needed rest, and, save for such outposts as were essential to the immediate security of his bivouacs, no reconnaissance was carried out on the 14th, as General French decided to reserve all he could for the task assigned to him for the following day. Even with these precautions, the fighting strength of the division was already considerably diminished by the breakdown of its animals. Of the cavalry, in addition to those dead, three hundred and twenty-six horses had become unfit to march. The artillery had also suffered severely. The whole of the horses of the ammunition columns had to be taken to complete the batteries, so that two out of the three columns had to be left parked on the Modder. For the third column only mules were available, but, by putting light loads on buck

RELIEF OF KIMBERLEY.

wagons, it was hoped that it would be enabled to keep up with the division.

During the night of the 14th Porter, with his force from Waterval Drift, arrived at Klip Drift. At daybreak on the 15th three days' supplies were issued to the cavalry, one of these being that due for the previous day. Owing to a deficiency in corn sacks, no regiment could carry with them more than two days' oats, and the units from India could scarcely manage even that quantity. By 8 a.m. the whole of the VIth division, with its two Naval guns, had crossed to the right bank of the Modder, and occupied the hills commanding the drifts.

<small>Porter joins French at Klip Drift.</small>

Froneman's commando, which had been increased by the arrival of some of Lubbe's burghers to about 900 men and two guns, during part of the 14th had threatened the front and flanks of the cavalry, but finally occupied two ridges, one running north-east from the neighbourhood of Cronje's laager, the other north-west from the loop of the river between Drieputs and Klip Drifts. These ridges converge, and about three miles from the Modder meet at a Nek from twelve to fifteen hundred yards in width, from which the ground slopes gently down to the river. Froneman had posted his two guns on the western ridge, which had been entrenched, and occupied about two miles and a half of front with his riflemen, who were so placed on both flanks that they could bring effective fire upon the Nek and the approaches to it.

<small>Boers under Froneman occupy ridges near Klip Drift.</small>

At 9.30 a.m. the cavalry division moved off in column of brigade masses; the 3rd brigade (Gordon) was in front, followed in succession by the 1st (Porter), the 2nd (Broadwood), and Alderson's mounted infantry. The guns were in battery column on the left of their respective brigades. Flanking squadrons watched the enemy on the left, while the advance guard (9th Lancers) led the march, which was to the north-east and parallel to the bend of the Modder, immediately above Klip Drift. For half an hour the division, under cover of the low kopjes which flank the right bank of the Modder, worked up stream; then French ordered the direction to be changed north-west towards Abon's Dam, where he hoped to find water for his

<small>French, relieved at Klip Drift by VIth division, marches against Froneman, at 9.30 a.m., Feb. 15th.</small>

horses. As the head of the column emerged on the open plain, the leading squadron of the advance guard came under a heavy musketry fire from the ridge on the right, at a range of about 1,500 yards. At the same time the two Boer guns on the western ridge, about 3,000 yards off, opened with shrapnel. Gordon's two batteries, O. and R. under Lieut.-Colonel F. J. W. Eustace, came at once into action against the burghers on the eastern ridge, while the Lieut.-General ordered Porter's brigade division, consisting of Q., T., and U. batteries, under Colonel A. N. Rochfort, to engage the enemy's guns. The fire of the Boer artillery was rapid and accurate, and immediately caused casualties: an officer and three gunners were killed, and three officers and eighteen of the other ranks wounded, while thirty-six horses were hit. Rochfort and Eustace's guns were now quickly supported by G. and P. batteries of Broadwood's brigade, the two Naval 12-prs. of the VIth division, which, under Lieut. Dean, R.N., had been hauled up a steep kopje on the north bank of the river, and by Kelly-Kenny's divisional field artillery, the 76th and 81st batteries. These silenced for a time the Boer artillery, which did not reopen until the Horse batteries moved on. During this artillery duel a squadron of the 16th Lancers had been pushed up the river, to prevent the enemy working round the right flank through the thick bushes which covered the bank. Although the Boer guns had ceased to fire the situation was difficult.

French orders forward the cavalry against the Nek. The ground between the river and the ridges was bare and open. It sloped like a glacis up to the connecting Nek. It was a sort of amphitheatre, two sides of which were held by the enemy. To send cavalry across it seemed a desperate expedient, yet delay would enable the Boer leaders to strengthen their entrenchments and bring up reinforcements, thus forcing an attack by infantry, which would cause delay and probably be costly. But the keen eye of the Cavalry General saw that the Nek joining the ridges was lightly held, and, although men riding across the amphitheatre towards it must be inevitably exposed to a heavy cross fire, he deemed it absolutely necessary then and there to pierce the enemy's line, even at the possible cost of many lives. He therefore sent against the Nek Gordon's brigade " at a fast gallop " and in extended order. Broadwood's brigade, with its two batteries under Lieut.-Colonel W. L. Davidson, followed in support at a distance of eight hundred yards. Porter's was kept as a reserve, feinting meanwhile to the northwest. The five remaining batteries, moving under escort of the mounted infantry, were to cover the charge by a vigorous bombardment. At this moment Gordon had only four squadrons of his brigade under his hand. One of the 16th Lancers was still scouting on the right flank, while one of the 9th Lancers was engaged, dismounted, against a detachment of the enemy on the eastern ridge. These four squadrons he deployed in extended order, eight yards between files, with the 9th Lancers on the right under Major M. O. Little and the 16th Lancers on the left under Major S. Frewen. The rear ranks formed a second line, twenty yards behind. During the deployment a party of seven men was sent forward under Lieut. A. E. Hesketh, 16th Lancers, to act as ground scouts, and to cut any wire fences which might impede the advance.

Placing himself at the head of his brigade, Gordon led it forward at a pace of about fourteen miles an hour, which he judged to be the fastest that the horses, in their enfeebled condition, could keep up. Broadwood's brigade, with the Divisional General and his staff, conformed to Gordon's advance. The Nek was about two miles off; the ground was good, and fortunately free from wire. The squadrons of the leading brigade came at once under a shower of bullets both from front and flanks, yet few fell. The extended formation, the pace of the charge, and the thick clouds of dust puzzled the burghers, while the supporting fire of the batteries shook their aim. Though bullets knocked up jets of dust all round the extended files, the casualties of the main body of the leading brigade were slight. The ground scouts specially attracted the enemy's attention : Lieut. Hesketh and two of his men were killed, and two others wounded. As the lines of Lancers approached at a steadily-increasing pace the crest of the Nek, the burghers manning it became nervous, shot worse and worse, and then mounted their ponies and galloped

The Nek is captured.

off in headlong flight. The few staunch men who stayed to the end were struck down or made prisoners. Gordon now wheeled the 16th Lancers to the left, sending part to pursue the enemy, who was retreating to the left front, and the remainder to occupy a kopje where a gun was thought to have been in action. The gun was not discovered, and the British troopers, riding 17 stone and mounted on weak and blown horses, had no chance of catching an enemy riding 14 stone on fresh animals, with a quarter of a mile start. The 9th Lancers were sent on to the north for about a mile, and occupied a second ridge. The 2nd and 1st brigades, followed by the mounted infantry and the remaining guns, passed in succession over the Nek without further opposition, and the division was then reformed.

Exclusive of the casualties already mentioned in the batteries, but inclusive of those of the party of ground scouts, the total losses sustained by the division in the attack had been only one officer killed, and fourteen men wounded. It was the most brilliant stroke of the whole war, alike in the prompt decision with which it was ordered and in the consequences which followed from it. The infantry nevertheless deserve their share of the credit. Without the extreme exertions of the VIth division on the 14th, carried on up to 1 a.m. on the 15th, French could not have left Klip Drift when he did and, had the Boers been given more time to prepare their defence and receive reinforcements, his attack would probably have been impossible. Nor must the effect of the quick recognition of the nature of the situation by Lord Kitchener and his eager pressing forward of the weary infantry to relieve the cavalry be left out of account as one of the decisive factors in the achievement.

French pushed on to Abon's Dam, which he reached at 11.45 a.m. A field telegraph cart which he had with him enabled General French to report his success to the Chief of the Staff, who at once telegraphed it on from Klip Drift to Lord Roberts. French mentioned that there was enough water at Abon's Dam and at a farm two miles to the north for an infantry division, and that he was leaving a guard of 100 mounted

RELIEF OF KIMBERLEY.　　37

infantry and two guns at each place. "The enemy," the despatch concluded, "has retired eastward and westward. I push on northwards."

Open country now lay between the British cavalry and the outworks of the besieged town. Ferreira's burghers had been far more sensitive about the movements of Lord Roberts' army than General Piet Cronje had been. They were not disposed to run risks in enterprises to the south in order to save their comrades from their dangerous position. On the night of the 13th-14th they had abandoned to the Kimberley garrison Alexandersfontein, the southern section of the line of investment, and, although some attempt was made on the following day and on the morning of the 15th to recover this lost ground, the effort was unsuccessful, and on the approach of the cavalry division across the open high veld the whole of the investing force fell back rapidly to the north and north-east, hoping to retreat over the Vaal. French's brigades, therefore, met with little further opposition, and that evening he was able to send by telegram direct to Klip Drift, and by flashlight *viâ* Lord Methuen's camp, the following report to the Chief of the Staff :

French moves on Kimberley. Besiegers give way before him.

Kimberley is relieved, 6 p.m., Feb. 15th, 1900.

"Have completely cleared enemy from south side of Kimberley, from Alexandersfontein to Oliphantsfontein, and now occupy ground. Entered Kimberley at 6 p.m. Besides post at Abon's Dam I have established another about six miles north of it, where water is abundant, but pumps required. I left there 200 mounted infantry. I captured enemy's laager at Oliphantsfontein with depôt of supplies and ammunition. Enemy has removed gun on south side of Kimberley, but I shall cross his communications to the north of Kimberley at dawn. Road between here and your camp now quite open. Kimberley garrison cheerful and well. You may rely upon my close co-operation with you in any attack you may make upon the enemy's position."

The 1st and 3rd cavalry brigades were bivouacked for the night at a camp near Blankenburg's Vlei,* on the east side of the town; the 2nd brigade, to which the Carabiniers were temporarily attached, had been halted at Alexandersfontein to the south, and remained there. The horses of all three brigades had again

* See map No. 29.

suffered severely from intense heat during this hard day, and still more from lack of water.

It will be observed that, while the infantry divisions were astride of Cronje's eastern lines of communication, the cavalry had now cut his communication with the Transvaal. It was suggested in the last chapter of Volume I. that Cronje, as a Transvaaler, was especially sensitive as to his communications with his native land. This view is confirmed by the indifference he showed to Lord Roberts' envelopment of his left flank. It is even possible that he cared little about the fate of Bloemfontein. At any rate his apathy ceased the moment he became aware that his northern line of communication had been closed by French.

Thus, without fighting a battle, but by audacity and skilful manœuvring, French, in conformity with Lord Roberts' plan, had not only worked right across Cronje's line of communications and relieved Kimberley from its long investment, but had driven in a wedge between Ferreira and Cronje shortly to prove fatal to the man who had sat still in his trenches.

Lord Roberts was well aware that heavy fighting was inevitable later to reap the full fruits of the success, but the work of the cavalry had ensured that, when the battle came, it would be fought under conditions which, as far as the fate of his immediate opponent, Cronje, was concerned, would make the victory decisive. He hastened to convey to Lieut.-General French his acknowledgments in the following telegram:

"I heartily congratulate you and the magnificent force you command on the vigour and endurance displayed by all ranks in the operations resulting in the relief of Kimberley. It is very satisfactory that there were so few casualties."

CHAPTER IV.

HOW KIMBERLEY WAS PREPARED FOR SIEGE.*

THE isolated position of Kimberley, and the probability that in the event of war with the Boer Republics it would be attacked, had been a source of anxiety to the military authorities at Cape Town for several years. Major E. A. Altham, Royal Scots, was sent to Kimberley in 1896 by Lieut.-General Sir W. Goodenough (then G.O.C. in South Africa), and in August of that year wrote : " The Government of the South African Republic have a strong feeling against the De Beers Mining Company, and against Mr. Cecil Rhodes, who owes his wealth to that company. The Free State, on the discovery of the diamond mines, claimed Kimberley as within its borders, and received comparatively but a small sum for the relinquishment of that claim. Kimberley is by far the most important place on the line of communications with Mafeking and, through Mafeking, to the north. Even if it should be thought impracticable to maintain that line of communication, the strategic value of Kimberley as a point from which it can be re-opened later in the campaign is very considerable ; but, in addition to these considerations, which may have a direct strategic bearing on the conduct of the campaign, there are others connected with Kimberley which would have an indirect but far-reaching effect. Except perhaps Cape Town, Kimberley is the richest prize which the enemy could capture, and lies at a tempting distance from his grasp. Its loss and any damage which might ensue to the mines

Isolation and importance of Kimberley causes anxiety in 1896. Major E. A. Altham's report on situation then.

* See maps Nos. 28, 29.

would not only be a heavy blow to the Cape Colony, but would also be most injurious to Imperial prestige throughout South Africa, and, while disheartening the loyalists, would greatly influence the waverers to take active part against us."

<small>Kimberley local troops in 1896.</small>

The only troops in Kimberley at that time were two local Volunteer corps, the Diamond Fields Horse, with a strength of 367 men, including an artillery troop armed with four old 7-pr. M.L. guns, and the Kimberley Rifles, about 400 strong. In order to protect the town and the mines, it was essential to hold a circuit of ten miles. Major Altham proposed to increase the local Volunteer forces, to re-arm and form into a separate battery the artillery troops of the Diamond Fields Horse, and to furnish the white miners with rifles and train them to shoot " on the lines of a burgher force, or in rifle clubs." He suggested that a defence scheme, which had already been discussed at Kimberley, should be submitted to General Goodenough. But out of the very small garrison of British troops then in South Africa General Goodenough had none available to garrison Kimberley, nor had he any control over the Volunteer corps in Cape Colony, which were administered by Colonial Staff officers acting under the direct orders of the Colonial Government. He therefore passed on Major Altham's report to Sir J. Gordon Sprigg, at that time Prime Minister of the Colony, and to the members of a Commission which, at the request of the Cape Ministry, had been assembled by the Governor (Lord Rosmead) to enquire into the organisation and efficiency of the Colonial forces. With the exception of the suggestion that the white miners should be armed and trained, the recommendations of the report·were approved by the Commissioners ; but, owing to political difficulties, no action was taken, and for similar reasons the preparation of a defence scheme by the local authorities in Kimberley was stopped.

<small>Lt.-Col. Trotter sent in June, 1898, by Sir W. Goodenough to prepare scheme of defence.</small>

But the clouds continued to gather in South Africa, and two years later, in June, 1898, Sir W. Goodenough, at the request of Sir Gordon Sprigg, sent another officer—Lieut.-Colonel J. K. Trotter, R.A.—to Kimberley with confidential instructions to draw up a definite scheme of defence.

HOW KIMBERLEY WAS PREPARED. 41

The town of Kimberley lies between its two principal diamond mines, the "Kimberley" and the "De Beers." The original settlement, the smaller township of Beaconsfield, is a thousand yards south-east of the present town. A mile and a half further to the south-east the little Boer village of Wesselton stands upon the lake known as Du Toit's Pan (see map No. 29). There are two other diamond mines, "Du Toit's Pan" and "Bultfontein," between Wesselton and Beaconsfield. The Premier mine projects into the plain a mile due east of Du Toit's Pan. Northeast of Kimberley the monotony of the veld is broken by plantations of eucalyptus trees surrounding the village of Kenilworth, a suburb erected some years before by Mr. Rhodes for the use of the white employés of the mines. To the south-west of Kimberley lies the main reservoir, which in normal times draws its supply of water by pipes from the Vaal at Riverton, nearly eighteen miles away (see map No. 28). The *terrain* encircling the two towns, Kimberley and Beaconsfield (both of which for the purposes of this narrative are included under the title of Kimberley), is on the whole favourable to defence. To the eastward a plain, unbroken save by the heaps of débris from the mines, stretches to a dark range of low kopjes on the Free State side of the frontier line. To the north the ground slopes gradually towards the valley of the Vaal river, the fall being crossed, some six miles out, by the wooded ridge of Dronfield. To the west of the town, separated from it by a shallow valley, rises Carter's Ridge, a wave of ground from which, at a range of four thousand yards, artillery fire could be brought to bear on the town itself. Southward the country rises and falls in almost imperceptible undulations until the commanding position of Wimbledon is reached, some six miles distant.

Description of the town and neighbourhood.

The heaps of débris much aided the defence. Built up by the accumulations of the tailings of the mines, they formed a series of large mounds some sixty to seventy feet high, skirting the town on the north, east and south. In front of these mounds a network of barbed wire fences effectually obstructed all approach except by the roads, while the electric searchlights, installed by the De Beers company to illuminate the fields of "blue" soil which were exposed to disintegrate in the open air, were available for military use. A few, however, of the débris heaps, such as those of the Premier mine to the south-east, and those of the Kamfer's Dam mines three miles to the north-west, were of doubtful advantage to the defence, as their occupation would cause undue extension, while, if not held, they would be dangerous.

<small>Mr. Schreiner having succeeded Sir Gordon Sprigg, no help from Cape Town is forthcoming. Utter decay of local forces in 1899.</small>

Colonel Trotter's scheme for the defence of this area was sent by Sir W. Goodenough to the War Office, but as Sir Gordon Sprigg had ceased to be Premier, no local action was taken. The Volunteers gradually dwindled in numbers till the Kimberley Rifles were reduced to two companies and the Diamond Fields Horse almost ceased to exist. At an inspection of the field battery early in 1899 it was still armed only with the four obsolete 7-pr. R.M.L., there were no horses for the guns, and only twenty-two officers and men appeared on parade. The breakdown of the Bloemfontein Conference in June, 1899, awoke the citizens of Kimberley to a sense of their danger. The Prime Minister of the Colony was asked to supply protection, or, at least, arms to enable the town to defend itself. Both these petitions were rejected, the Civil Commissioner being instructed to reply that " there is no reason whatever for apprehending that Kimberley is, or in any contemplated event will be, in danger of attack, and Mr. Schreiner is of opinion that your fears are groundless and your anticipations without foundation."

<small>War Office orders return to Kimberley of Lt.-Col. Trotter, July, 1899.</small>

The optimistic feeling of the Cape Ministry was not shared by the Military Staff at the War Office, whose anxiety about the safety of Kimberley was increased by their knowledge that part of the Boer plan of campaign was directed against the town, which was to be attacked as soon as war began. It was clear that out of the garrison of South Africa, which in August, 1899, was less than 10,000 men,* an adequate force of regular troops could not be allotted to so distant a post as Kimberley, and that the burden of its defence must fall principally upon its inhabitants. Orders were therefore telegraphed on 4th July to Sir W. Butler, then in command at the Cape, to send Lieut.-Colonel J. K. Trotter again to Kimberley to make confidential enquiries as to

* Volume I., page 1.

HOW KIMBERLEY WAS PREPARED. 43

the organisation of the defences. Lieut. D. S. MacInnes, R.E., was selected to assist him in his mission. The situation was a delicate one, as the General Officer Commanding the Imperial troops still lacked authority over the local Volunteers, and the Cape Government continued to maintain that there was no cause for any special preparation. In these circumstances it was thought desirable to keep two staff officers permanently in Kimberley to watch events, and, confidentially, to concert measures for defence with the leading inhabitants. Lieut.-Colonel Trotter, who had recently been appointed Chief Staff Officer of the South African command, could not be spared for any length of time from Headquarters at Cape Town, and, after reporting on the condition of Kimberley, he returned to the coast, being replaced by Bt.-Major H. S. Turner, The Black Watch, an officer who had for some years been in special employment in Southern Rhodesia, and was well known to, and popular with, South African colonists. Major Turner immediately placed himself in touch with the principal inhabitants of the town, and with their assistance was able to carry out valuable work. Preliminary arrangements were made for the organisation of additional local forces, and much information was obtained as to the Boers' preparations for war, while Lieut. MacInnes worked out in detail Colonel Trotter's scheme of fortification. Towards the end of July, Captain W. A. J. O'Meara, R.E., one of the ten Special Service officers sent out at that time from England for Intelligence duty, joined Major Turner, then acting as Staff Officer to Commissioner M. B. Robinson of the Cape Police, who, with the local rank of lieut.-colonel, had been appointed by the Cape Government to the command of the colonial forces, including the police detachments, around Kimberley. Early in September, Sir Alfred Milner persuaded his Ministers to send two thousand Lee-Metford rifles and a small quantity of ammunition to Kimberley, and to detail detachments of Cape Police to guard the more important points to the north and south of the town. He further suggested that a senior officer of the regular forces should be sent to report confidentially on the situation. Lieut.-Colonel R. G. Kekewich, Loyal North Lan-

Marginalia: Eagerness of leading inhabitants to assist Trotter is hampered by Mr. Schreiner's unwillingness to act. Major Turner replaces Trotter, and with Lt. MacInnes works out in detail on paper Colonel Trotter's scheme for defence of town. Arrangements for raising additional local troops. Sir Alfred Milner obtains some rifles and ammunition for Kimberley.

cashire regiment, was selected by Lieut.-General Sir F. Forestier-Walker for this duty, and on 11th September received personal instructions from Sir A. Milner to enquire carefully into the arrangements planned for the protection of Kimberley and of the communications to Mafeking on the north and to Orange River station on the south. If in Colonel Kekewich's opinion these arrangements offered reasonable security against immediate danger, the High Commissioner wished no further action to be taken; but if Colonel Kekewich became aware of any serious risk, either to Kimberley or to the communications with Cape Town, he was to report it at once. Colonel Kekewich was not informed that there was reason to believe that an attack on Kimberley formed part of the Boer plan of campaign. On political grounds he was told to keep his mission as secret as possible.

Bt.-Colonel R. S. S. Baden-Powell[*] was already at Mafeking inspecting the regiment which Lieut.-Colonel C. O. Hore had just raised, and a consultation as to the defence of the Cape frontier from Mafeking to Orange River took place at Vryburg on the 11th September between him, Brevet-Major Turner, Captain O'Meara, and Major H. J. Goold-Adams, the Resident Commissioner of the Bechuanaland Protectorate. On Colonel Kekewich's arrival at Kimberley on September 13th Turner and O'Meara at once explained to him the general situation. It was startling in its simplicity. The movements of the Boers showed that mobilisation had begun across the frontier, and that Kimberley was seriously threatened. There were no regular troops in the place, which was not fortified in any way, for work upon its defences had not yet begun. The local Volunteers were much below their authorised strength; so weak, indeed, were they that when called out for active service on October 4th they mustered only 540 strong. They were armed with Lee-Metford rifles, and, thanks to the exertions of Major W. H. F. Taylor, R.A., at that time commanding the artillery of the Cape Colonial forces, the four 7-pr. R.M.L. guns of the Diamond Fields Horse had just been replaced by better weapons, six 2.5-in. R.M.L. To protect the three hundred miles of railway

[*] See Volume I., pages 39, 42, 51.

HOW KIMBERLEY WAS PREPARED. 45

between Mafeking and the Orange river there were only the Volunteers at Kimberley, some half-dozen small posts of Cape Police, and a single company of sixty-one Volunteers at Vryburg.

Kekewich at once telegraphed to Headquarters to represent the urgent need for reinforcements, and on the 20th September the following troops reached him from Cape Town :— Sept. 20th, Kekewich asks for and receives reinforcements.

	Officers.	Men.
23rd company R.G.A. (with six 2.5-in. R.M.L. guns on mountain carriages)	3	90
7th company R.E.	1	50
Headquarters and 4 companies 1st Loyal North Lancashire regiment	9	413
Detachment Army Service Corps	1	5
Detachment Royal Army Medical Corps	1	5
	15	563

To this small force of regular troops was added, on the 26th, a mounted section of the Loyal North Lancashire, consisting of one officer and twenty-one men. Lieut.-Colonel Kekewich succeeded Commissioner Robinson in command of all Colonial troops in Griqualand West and Bechuanaland, and on the 13th October the Cape Police (District No. 2) were placed under his orders. By the 1st October various reinforcements of police had raised the numbers of those outside Kimberley to 446 of all ranks, distributed among posts at Kraaipan, Vryburg, Taungs and Fourteen Streams,* where there were also two 7-pr. field guns. There was also, under Major A. Bates, at the distant post of Kuruman in the wilds of Bechuanaland, a handful of Cape Police, who, unable to fall back on Kimberley before the invasion of the enemy, maintained a gallant resistance for many weeks Kekewich succeeds to command, Sept. 20th.

* See General Map of South Africa in map case of Volume I.

against overwhelming odds, and only surrendered at the last extremity.*

On the morning of the 28th September Captain O'Meara, who had been sent on the previous day by Kekewich on a bicycle to obtain information as to the situation at Boshof, a village in the Free State some thirty-three miles from Kimberley, reported that he had observed throughout the previous night the concentration of a large commando there. On receipt of this news the construction of the defences, which, owing to political reasons, it had been impossible to begin before the 18th, was pushed on with the utmost energy, and by 7th October the town was considered to be safe from a *coup de main*. Work, however, continued throughout the siege, as it was found necessary to include fresh ground to meet the varying dispositions of the enemy.

<small>Defence works, previously planned, are begun, 18th Sept., 1899, and on Sept. 28th, because of threatening news, are vigorously pressed forward.</small>

Though about eighty recruits joined the Volunteers during the first week after they were called out, their numbers† were wholly inadequate for the defence of the town, even with the regular gunners and infantry who reached Kekewich as a reinforcement on the 20th September. The numerical weakness of the Volunteer corps arose from no want of spirit on the part of the inhabitants, as was proved by their conduct during the siege. It was due rather to the imperfect appreciation of the danger of the situation which was prevalent throughout the Colony, and from the reluctance of the Cape Government to make any preparations for war. It therefore became necessary to carry out the arrangements made by Major Turner for the organisation of a Town Guard. On the 30th Sir Alfred Milner gave the necessary permission, and, within a week, more than 1,100 men had been enrolled, officers appointed, and non-commissioned officers of the regular troops detailed to give instruction in the use of the rifle and in simple drill. From these numbers

<small>Town Guard organised, Sept. 30th to Oct. 7th, 1899.</small>

---

* See Volume I., page 382, note.

† When embodied--
The Diamond Fields Artillery consisted only of 3 officers and 90 other ranks.
The Diamond Fields Horse ,, ,, 6 ,, 142 ,,
The Kimberley regiment ,, 14 ,, 285 ,,

HOW KIMBERLEY WAS PREPARED.   47

the force slowly grew until by the end of the siege it reached a strength of 2,750 men. The patriotism thus displayed by the inhabitants alone made it possible to occupy the wide circle of works necessary for the defence of the town. On 5th October, owing to the report of an intended attack, the "hooters" of the mines sounded an alarm at midnight, and the defences were manned for the first time.

President Kruger's ultimatum to the British Government expired on the 11th October, and next day the Boers crossed the frontier and occupied the railway station at Kraaipan, from which the police detachment, with Kekewich's consent, had fallen back on Mafeking two days before. Within a few hours of their occupation of Kraaipan the Boers had destroyed the railway at that point, and had captured an armoured train which was conveying two 7-pr. guns with ammunition from Vryburg to Mafeking. Captain R. C. Nesbit, V.C., Mashonaland Mounted Police, and the twenty-six men he commanded, after a stout resistance were compelled to surrender to the overwhelming artillery and rifle fire which was poured upon them by the burghers. *Hostilities begin, 12th Oct., 1899. Railway between Kimberley and Mafeking attacked.*

The movement of the commandos against the railway from Orange River to Mafeking was general. The police detachments who watched the line from Vryburg to Kimberley gradually retired southward, and as the line of investment drawn round Kimberley was at first a thin one, they all succeeded in joining Kekewich by the 22nd October, and proved a valuable reinforcement to his garrison. Kekewich had early realised that mobile infantry was urgently required for the defence of the large area enclosed by his works, and that the police and mounted volunteers were numerically insufficient for this purpose. In a conversation over the telegraph line to Cape Town a few hours before the wire was cut, he obtained Sir Alfred Milner's permission to raise a corps of mounted irregulars, under the title of the Kimberley Light Horse. *Kimberley Light Horse raised, Oct. 14th, 1899.*

On the 14th the telegraph lines north and south of Kimberley were cut, and a reconnaissance on the 15th in an armoured train ascertained that Boers with three guns were in possession of *On that day, the telegraph line being cut, Kekewich proclaims martial law.*

the railway between Spytfontein and Magersfontein. Lieut.-Colonel Kekewich, thus effectually cut off from railway and telegraphic communication with Headquarters, immediately proclaimed martial law and assumed supreme control of the civil population.

<small>Difficulties of Kekewich's task.</small>

In the lives of many men occurs an opportunity for distinction, but the majority fail to grasp it. It was not so with Lieut.-Colonel Kekewich. Called suddenly from the command of a battalion, where the scope of his energies was limited to the training of his men for battle, the fortune of war placed him in supreme charge of an invested town of nearly 50,000 inhabitants, defended by a garrison composed for the greater part of improvised troops, who were inadequate in numbers to hold the great length of line imposed upon them by the nature of the ground.

<small>The *personnel* of his command.</small>

Only one-eighth of his command were professional soldiers; the remainder consisted of Cape Police, well disciplined and hardy men, but not highly trained for war; the Kimberley Volunteers, whose military knowledge, like that of every other volunteer organisation, was necessarily scanty; the newly-raised irregular corps of Kimberley Light Horse, and the Town Guard, neither of whom had received any previous training at all. It is a truism that the less instructed are the men the better their leaders should be. But including one officer of the Army Service Corps, one of the R.A.M.C., and one recently retired from the infantry, Kekewich had but twenty-two professional officers under his orders, of whom by the 28th November four had been killed or permanently incapacitated for the remainder of the siege. The others were either volunteers or civilians. A few of the volunteers had gained experience and well-deserved honours in campaigns against the Kaffirs, but the majority had but a limited knowledge of the rudiments of the art of war, and were chiefly equipped with stout hearts and a determination to do their duty. The civilians, whose patriotism brought them from the desk or the warehouse to command their fellow-citizens in the trenches, were as ignorant as their men. It was not only in professional officers that Kekewich was grievously short-handed. In every garrison, even when the ordinary routine work has

HOW KIMBERLEY WAS PREPARED. 49

been cut down to the lowest point, the officer commanding must necessarily maintain a large correspondence, with many returns to prepare, many papers to catalogue and preserve for reference. This work is always carried out by highly-trained military clerks. But of these Kekewich had but one or two, and thus the commandant of Kimberley and his staff officers had to take upon their already overburthened shoulders the drudgery which should have been performed by non-commissioned officers.

Nor were these deficiencies in the *personnel* of the garrison counterbalanced by the excellence of the *matériel* at his disposal. To meet the modern artillery of the enemy he had only fourteen light field guns, twelve of which ranged up to 4,000 yards, while two could throw but half that distance. He was short of rifles. Two thousand Lee-Metfords had been sent to Kimberley a short time before the siege began, and the De Beers Company produced from their stores about 450 more. But these were not enough to re-arm some five hundred of the Cape Police, who concentrated on Kimberley, and to equip the Kimberley Light Horse and the Town Guard with the service weapon. The discarded Martini-Henrys were served out to the Town Guard, but there were not enough even of these old rifles for the whole of its members, and the last few men enrolled were served out with the obsolete Snider rifle, in default of a better fire-arm. Ammunition, the complement of rifles, was also deficient in quantity. Including half a million of rounds brought up country by the North Lancashire, the supply sent by Sir A. Milner, and about 650,000 rounds (of which many proved defective) supplied by the De Beers, there were about 1,500,000 Lee-Metford cartridges in Kimberley when the siege began. For the Martini-Henrys there were about 60,000 rounds. Small as was this amount of rifle ammunition, it could not be kept solely for use in action, for it was necessary to train the newly-raised troops to shoot, and their instruction necessarily consumed a large number of cartridges. Thus to the other anxieties of Colonel Kekewich and his staff was added that of carefully husbanding ammunition—difficult even with well-trained troops, infinitely more so with a garrison largely composed of hastily

His guns and ammunition.

raised levies. For the guns there were only 2,600 rounds, or less than 200 rounds for each piece of artillery; but this deficiency was partially made good during the siege. When the attitude of the Boers showed that an attack upon Kimberley was certain, the directors of the De Beers Company placed all the resources of their great mining industry at the service of Colonel Kekewich. They supplied labour for building the redoubts, horses and mules for the guns, for the Kimberley Light Horse, and for the six Maxims which the company possessed. Many of the works required for observatories and electric search-lights were designed and built by their officials. In November Mr. G. Labram, their chief engineer, whose remarkable knowledge, resource and versatility proved of the greatest service to the garrison, began to cast shells for the 7-pr. guns, and to make powder for them by blending blasting and rifle powder. Early in December he conceived the idea of building a gun heavier than any yet brought into action against the town; and on the 19th January a 4.1-in. B.L. gun, throwing a 28-lb. shell at an effective range of 8,000 yards, was fired for the first time. This improvised gun, named "Long Cecil" in honour of Mr. Rhodes, was very successful, and was fired 255 times during the remainder of the siege, the end of which Mr. Labram did not live to see, as he was killed by a shell on 9th February.

Invaluable help of the De Beers Company, and of Mr. Labram.

Labram's "Long Cecil."

Nature of the population of Kimberley.

The community for which the British commandant became responsible was of an exceptional character, due to the mining industry which had created it, and upon which its very existence depended. The dominant factor was the De Beers Company with its great staff of officials, and its workmen, who included a large number of natives collected from various parts of South Africa. Professional men, merchants, and native servants made up the remainder of the inhabitants. The municipal affairs of Kimberley were presided over by a mayor. When the town was first invested, Mr. R. H. Henderson held office; he was afterwards succeeded by Mr. H. A. Oliver. Both these gentlemen rendered valuable services to the military authorities; but from a civil point of view the real power, material and moral, was vested in the De Beers Company, and (although two other

HOW KIMBERLEY WAS PREPARED.　51

directors of that company were present) it may be said to have been concentrated in the hands of Mr. Cecil Rhodes. Mr. Rhodes, with characteristic courage, had hurried up from Cape Town and thrown himself into Kimberley on October 11th, determined to share the fate of the community over whose fortunes he had so long presided. Though in South African politics his influence had declined, in Kimberley his position was unchallenged and supreme. The population regarded him, not without reason, as the greatest empire-maker the sub-continent had yet seen; a large proportion of the irregular troops were employed in the mines of which he was the moving spirit; their future advancement in civil life greatly depended on his good will. Thus both from the political and financial aspect he was virtually the dictator of Kimberley, and his presence in the town during the siege necessarily became a potent factor in the situation.

The number of people within the lines of investment was at first not accurately known, but from a census taken during the siege it appears to have been about 48,000, of whom 18,000 were whites, while the remainder were drawn from races of varying colour and origin. This total included 12,000 women and 10,000 children. Attempts were made from time to time during the siege to reduce these numbers by despatching batches of natives by night through the Boer lines to their homes; but in most cases the enemy frustrated these efforts, and as the Boers were short of labour for their farms, the expediency of repeating the attempts was open to doubt. Number of the inhabitants.

The Kimberley defences (map No. 29), as the scheme was finally worked out by Lieut. MacInnes and approved by Colonel Kekewich, consisted of a series of redoubts with open gorges, which completely encircled the whole town and included the Kimberley and De Beers mines. A part of the front of this *enceinte* was protected by barbed wire and abattis, and efforts were made to restrict egress or ingress to points on certain roads at which movable barriers had been erected. A series of advanced works to the south-east guarded Beaconsfield. Kenilworth formed a salient projecting northward; the Premier mine Nature of the defence works.

was held as a detached post. An isolated redoubt on the southern road near Van Druyten's Farm, and another to the westward of the town covering Otto's Kopje mine, completed the defences. The main *enceinte* had a perimeter of about ten miles, but by the Kenilworth and Beaconsfield salients, this (exclusive of the Premier mine and other outworks) was increased to fourteen miles. The length of this line of defence was even more disproportionate to the garrison available to hold it than was that of Ladysmith to its garrison, but the value of the property at stake and the nature of the ground made it necessary to take the risks. The permanent distribution of the guns was as follows :—

23rd company Western division Royal Garrison Artillery.	2 guns at the reservoir, 2 guns near the pulsator, south of Kenilworth Dam ; they were moved later in the siege to Otto's kopje. 2 guns at the Premier mine.
Cape Police	2 guns in No. 2 redoubt north of Kimberley mine.
Diamond Fields Artillery ..	6 guns as a reserve in the Public Gardens, and employed with the mobile force as needed, usually a section at a time.

To each redoubt was assigned a permanent garrison of fifty men. The Town Guard were at first only required, as a whole, to be at their posts during the night, and seventy-five per cent. were set free during the day to follow their ordinary vocations. But, later, as the Boers closed in, it was thought necessary to keep more men on duty, and even during the daytime leave of absence was sparingly granted to these citizen soldiers. A conning tower and telephonic communications enabled the commandant to exercise at all times direct control over his entire force, and to watch the movements of the Boers from the various gun-positions with which they had encircled the town.

HOW KIMBERLEY WAS PREPARED. 53

In all sieges food and water are of the first importance. It was obvious that the water supply from the Vaal river would be cut off as soon as the investment of Kimberley began ; but on his arrival in September Lieut.-Colonel Kekewich had ascertained that there were springs of pure water at the bottom of the Premier mine, and it was partly for the sake of these that he included this mine within the area of his defences. A plan for utilising these springs was then discussed with the De Beers officials. Mr. Rhodes, on his arrival, undertook to pump 300,000 gallons into the waterworks reservoir—a supply which, carefully husbanded under the regulations of the martial law enforced by Colonel Kekewich, sufficed for the military and civilian population of the city. The reservoir and filter-bed were very strongly fortified, and held by a permanent garrison of two hundred men with two guns. Shortly before the declaration of war, supplies had been collected at Vryburg and Modder River stations and brought into Kimberley, while consignments of foodstuffs for stations along the railway to the north were detained in Kimberley, and, at the outbreak of hostilities, taken over by the military authorities. A rough estimate of the stock of food in the town was made then, and carefully checked in the middle of October. It was found that the amount would suffice for the time of investment then expected. A proclamation was issued fixing the price of meat at a slightly higher figure than the normal rate, and limiting the price of all other supplies to that which ruled before the communications were cut. The quantity to be sold to each individual was regulated from time to time by proclamation. Subject to these limitations sales were left at first in the hands of the ordinary tradesmen. Subsequently, to enable the military authorities to exercise a stricter control, a supply committee, composed of the chief inhabitants, was appointed with Captain H. V. Gorle, A.S.C., as chairman. The stocks of local dealers were bought up, and six depôts formed in different parts of the town for distribution to civilians in accordance with the approved scale of issue.

Supply of water and food.

CHAPTER V.

THE SIEGE OF KIMBERLEY.*

_{Boers appear before Kimberley.} THE first commandos to appear before Kimberley were those of Boshof, Jacobsdal and Kroonstad. Under the command of Wessels, who, later, was succeeded by Ferreira, they held a line from Oliphantsfontein, through Benaudheidsfontein to Alexandersfontein. As soon as Mafeking was surrounded Cronje sent them as reinforcements the Lichtenburg, Wolmaranstad and Bloemhof commandos, under General De la Rey (afterwards succeeded by Du Toit), whose command extended from Dronfield ridge and the intermediate pumping station on the north, through Carter's ridge on the west, to Wimbledon ridge on the south. During the months of November and December detachments of these Transvaalers went southwards to face Lord Methuen; they returned to their Headquarters in January, 1900, when the Free Staters were also reinforced from Cronje's force at Magersfontein. During the course of the siege the Boers dug many emplacements for their artillery, chiefly at the places just mentioned, and, in accordance with their usual tactics, so frequently transferred the pieces from one position to another that it has not been found possible to show on the map the situations of the guns on any given day.

_{Kekewich's active defence.} The general principle which Colonel Kekewich had laid down for his scheme of defence was to keep the enemy in constant fear of attacks from unexpected quarters. As soon as his mounted men were fit to take the field, he began a series of

* See maps Nos. 28 and 29.

THE SIEGE OF KIMBERLEY.

reconnaissances in force, and of raids against the dams and wells in the possession of the Boers. These were almost the only features of military interest in the annals of the investment, for, as will be seen, the enemy's bombardment was fitful and singularly ineffective. On the 20th October Bt.-Major Turner, who had been placed in command of all the mounted troops with the local rank of Lieut.-Colonel, made a reconnaissance to the north in the hope of destroying the Riverton waterworks, from which it was known the Boers drew much of their supply. The attempt failed, but at 4 a.m. on the 24th he again sallied out, in the same direction and for the same purpose, with a detachment of the Cape Police, Diamond Fields Horse, and Kimberley Light Horse, in all about three hundred men, intending to go as far as Riverton pumping station. The armoured train, under 2nd Lieut. A. McC. Webster, Loyal North Lancashire, worked with this party. The mounted troops reached Macfarlane's Farm, near the railway siding, at 7.15 a.m. No enemy was in sight, and, after an hour's pause, Turner pushed on, leaving half his force in occupation of a knoll and of the farm buildings. The main body of the patrol had advanced barely a mile towards Riverton when the outpost on the knoll signalled that Boers had appeared in a bushy valley east of Macfarlane's. Turner therefore returned to the knoll, and posted a party of the Cape Police to observe their movements. The enemy gradually increased in numbers, and threatened to cut off the armoured train from Dronfield siding. The armoured train was, therefore, ordered to withdraw, and fire opened on the burghers, who at once took cover. At 10.15 a.m. Turner heliographed to Kimberley for reinforcements, and Colonel Kekewich ordered two companies of the Loyal North Lancashire, under command of Major (local Lieut.-Colonel) W. H. E. Murray, to entrain for Macfarlane siding. Two guns of the Diamond Fields Artillery, two Maxims, and seventy Cape Police were despatched by road to Mostert's, a farm two miles north of Kimberley station, whence, at 11.30 a.m., in compliance with a further message from Turner, they were ordered to advance to Dronfield, where some of Turner's men had been sent back to meet them.

Reconnaissance of 20th Oct.

and of 24th Oct.

Reconnaissance of Oct. 24th, ending successfully, encourages defenders.

Meanwhile the enemy had received constant reinforcements from the eastward, and, thus strengthened, pushed through the bush to Dronfield ridge. Murray's train left Kimberley at 11.50 a.m. and reached the siding unmolested. It was now ordered back to Dronfield. The guns were approaching the ridge from the south, their escort having already passed it without observing the enemy. But, as the battery drew near, a sharp fire was opened on it from the summit of the ridge. Captain (local Major) S. May, Diamond Fields Artillery, who was in command, immediately came into action at a range of 1,500 yards. The enemy continued to creep forward, and was within 1,000 yards of the battery when Murray's train came steaming back, and a short distance south of Dronfield, halted under the enemy's musketry. The infantry from the train quickly formed for attack under cover of the railway embankment, and advanced against the ridge. They were received with a hot fusilade, but forced the burghers back into the valley to the north-east. Turner had, meanwhile, left the Macfarlane knoll, and was moving across the railway in échelon of troops. Dismounting his men he completed the enemy's discomfiture. The Boer commando, whose strength was estimated at 800, fell back towards Boshof, leaving their leader, Petrus Botha, dead on the field. The British troops, reinforced at 2 p.m. by a company of the Kimberley regiment, then returned to camp with a loss of three men killed and three officers and eighteen men wounded. This little fight did good in giving self-confidence to the irregulars and raising the spirits of the townspeople.

Boers, though closing in on town, fail to capture cattle.

Next day the enemy tightened his hold upon the town by bringing his nearest post on the south to within 6,000 yards of the Premier mine. On the 3rd November he attempted to capture the cattle of the garrison which were grazing to the north of Kimberley, but the raiders were driven off by the mounted troops. On the 4th, Commandant C. J. Wessels, "Head Commandant, Western Division, Orange Free State Burgher Force," formally summoned the Officer Commanding the garrison to surrender. If this demand were not complied with he requested that "all women and children" should be

Kimberley summoned to surrender, Nov. 4th.

THE SIEGE OF KIMBERLEY.

allowed to leave Kimberley, offering to receive all "Africander families" and to give safe-conduct to those of other nationalities. An armistice for this purpose was proposed for forty-eight hours. The offer to receive all women and children was notified by Colonel Kekewich to the Africander families, but of these only one took advantage of it. As regards the offer of a safe-conduct to the families of nationalities other than Africander, Kekewich had no transport with which to convey them to a place of safety, and Mr. Rhodes, on being consulted, was strongly of opinion that the publication of that portion of Wessel's letter might cause unnecessary alarm in the town. The receipt of this offer was not, therefore, generally made known.

On the morning of the 7th November the enemy's three guns posted on the ridge near Wimbledon opened fire on the section of the defences between Kimberley reservoir and the Sanatorium. Two guns mounted south-west of the Premier mine also came into action, but the range was extreme and their shells did no harm. *(Enemy's guns open fire, Nov. 7th, 1899.)*

On the 11th the bombardment was renewed from other points: three guns fired from Carter's ridge, a fourth from the ridge north of Kenilworth, and a fifth from the rise south of the Premier mine. The British artillery replied slowly, but with little effect. The enemy expended in all nearly four hundred shells, many of which fell within the town; but, fortunately, with only one casualty—a Kaffir woman who was killed in the street. As regards the number of rounds fired, this was the heaviest day's bombardment during the siege, although both on the 24th and the 25th January at least 300 shells fell amongst the houses. The shelling, the only form of attack during four months' investment, was very intermittent; the actual number of days of bombardment were only twelve in November, three in December, twelve in January, and thirteen in February. From time to time the Boers constructed additional gun-emplacements to the north, west and south, directing their fire both on the defences and on the inhabited portion of the town. Towards the end of January the number of guns bearing on Kimberley was increased to nine: one was posted south-east *(Nov. 11th. Bombardment increased with little effect.)*

58   THE WAR IN SOUTH AFRICA.

of the intermediate pumping station; another at Kamfer's Dam; three on Carter's ridge, and two on Wimbledon ridge; one at Alexandersfontein, and one at Oliphantsfontein Kop. Of these guns, two on Carter's ridge and the gun at Alexandersfontein fired cordite, the rest black powder.

During the first three weeks of November the mounted troops were constantly engaged on patrol and reconnaissance duty, and in warding off the attempts of the Boers to capture the cattle of the garrison. On the 23rd, the following message from Major R. N. R. Reade, Shropshire Light Infantry, D.A.A.G. for Intelligence on the staff of the 1st division, was received by Captain (local Major) O'Meara, who was now filling the double post of intelligence officer and chief staff officer to Colonel Kekewich :—

Hearing of Methuen's advance,

" Reade, Orange River, to O'Meara, 18th November. General leaves here with strong force on 21st November, and will arrive at Kimberley on 26th, unless delayed at Modder River. Look for signals by searchlight from us. They will be in code."*

Kekewich demonstrates in force on 25th Nov.

On the receipt of this message Colonel Kekewich determined to make a demonstration in strength on the 25th against the enemy's main position to the west and south-west of Kimberley in order to assist Methuen in his progress. Two columns, of a total strength of 1,124 men or nearly a quarter of the whole garrison, were therefore ordered to move out at daybreak. The one on the left, under Major (local Lieut.-Colonel) G. D. Chamier, R.G.A., consisting of four guns Diamond Fields Artillery, two Maxims with an escort of Cape Police, two companies North Lancashire, and one company Kimberley regiment, was to advance to the south-west, its left flank protected by the armoured train and a detachment of the Town Guard. The right column, composed of parties of the Loyal North Lancashire mounted infantry, Kimberley Light Horse, and Cape Police, in all 352 mounted men, with a section of the 7th company, Royal Engineers, was commanded by Major Turner. The troops moved off from their rendezvous at 3 a.m. At 4.40 a.m. the Diamond Fields

* See Volume I., Chapter XII.

Artillery guns came into action against the Ironstone Kopje south-west of the reservoir. The right column was concealed from view under cover of Otto's Kopje mine. Taking advantage of the enemy's attention being diverted by the fire of the left column, Turner led his men forward rapidly, and, disregarding the heavy musketry fire with which his approach was greeted, rushed the Boer redoubts on Carter's ridge with dismounted detachments of Kimberley Light Horse and Cape Police, about 70 men in all, and captured twenty-four unwounded and nine wounded men. The remainder of his force now moved forward and occupied the whole ridge; but at 7 a.m. the enemy showed signs of developing a counter-attack in superior numbers from the direction of Kamfer's Dam, and both the British columns fell back into Kimberley. Valuable information was obtained from the prisoners, and transmitted to Lord Methuen, to the effect that the strength of the commandos south of Kimberley was about 6,000, and that Cronje, with reinforcements from Mafeking, was travelling southward as rapidly as possible by train *viâ* Johannesburg and Bloemfontein, to oppose the relieving column. In this affair the guns fired 112 rounds; the infantry expended 40,000 cartridges.

During the night of the 25th–26th November two despatch riders slipped into the town through the enemy's lines with the news of the successful engagement at Belmont.* Forty-eight hours later communications were established by flash signal with Lord Methuen, who, having fought the battle of Graspan† on the 25th, was now advancing to the Modder. Unfortunately, the messages were of a trivial character, except one, which said that an official despatch from Methuen would be shortly signalled. This despatch, however, was not received, and the only information of value obtained from these communications was their place of origin, a farm called Klokfontein, on the south bank of the Modder. A transfer southward of considerable numbers of the besiegers had already shown that the relief column was advancing, and Colonel Kekewich decided to demonstrate

News of Belmont received, night, Nov 25th–26th.

* See Volume I., Chapter XIII.
† See Volume I., Chapter XIV.

next day against the line of investment so as to detain as many Boers as possible and thus diminish the opposition to Lord Methuen.

<small>Sortie of the 28th Nov., 1899, to keep besiegers before Kimberley.</small>

On the morning of the 28th Kekewich issued orders for a sortie in force to the south-west, in which 1,820 men, or nearly two-fifths of his total strength, were to be employed. His intention was, if possible, to seize the ridge from Wright's Farm, near the railway line, to Ironstone Kopje, but mounted troops were also to be detached to Carter's Farm. Colonel Kekewich had no intention to make a costly attack on Carter's ridge. The redoubts taken by Turner on the 25th were known to have been re-occupied by the Boers, and it was believed that they had been strengthened. Kekewich therefore gave orders that no attempt should be made to re-capture them, unless it was found that they were very weakly held. The troops detailed for the sortie were divided into three columns. The right column, under Turner, who, though wounded on the 25th, was still at duty, was composed of the mounted section of the North Lancashire, a mounted detachment of the Cape Police, the Diamond Fields Horse, and the Kimberley Light Horse, 633 in all, and was to issue by the barrier on Schmidt's Drift road. The centre column, under Chamier, consisted of a hundred mounted men (Cape Police and Kimberley Light Horse) under Major (local Lieut.-Colonel) T. C. Peakman, the Diamond Fields battery, a section of the 7th company, Royal Engineers, 3 companies, North Lancashire, and 2 companies of the Kimberley regiment. This column was ordered to debouch by the Kimberley reservoir. The left column, commanded by Major J. R. Fraser, Beaconsfield Town Guard, late of the North Lancashire regiment, was made up of 303 men of the Town Guard. It was to move along the railway from Beaconsfield station and hold the line on the left flank. The armoured train, under 2nd Lieut. Webster, North Lancashire, after first making a demonstration to the northward, was to aid this column.

The three columns started at 2.50 p.m. Chamier seized the Ironstone Kopje, and by 4 p.m. had occupied without resistance

THE SIEGE OF KIMBERLEY.

the ground from that point to Wright's Farm. Reporting this by heliograph to Kekewich, he added: " Propose taking up position overlooking Wimbledon and shelling Spitz Kop and Wimbledon ridge. Colonel Turner advances to Carter's." To this message Kekewich replied :

" Do as you think best, but the enemy's four redoubts west of Lazaretto appear to be strongly held, and you will doubtless require artillery to shell them out. Inform Colonel Turner."

The enemy's guns on Carter's ridge, although engaged by the Royal Garrison artillery from the reservoir, concentrated their fire on Chamier's infantry, while the Diamond Fields battery was in action against other Boer guns near Spitz Kop. Chamier now sent a company of the Loyal North Lancashire and a detachment of the Royal Engineers to Carter's farm, which they reached about 4.45 p.m., to find the mounted troops already in possession of the Boer laager. Colonel Turner's men had dismounted and became closely engaged with the enemy on the ridge to the westward. Observing this, Chamier sent to his support Major Peakman's squadron and two guns of the Diamond Fields artillery. Meanwhile Turner, placing himself at the head of a group of men in which mounted infantry, Cape Police, and Kimberley Light Horse were mingled, dashed forward and, with a determined rush, carried the two southern works of the enemy's line of redoubts on the ridge. The section of the Diamond Fields artillery now came into action with shrapnel at a range of 1,000 yards against the main redoubt on Carter's ridge, within 60 yards of which was one of the flank works occupied by Colonel Turner and a handful of men. The enemy's musketry was very severe, and Turner, while raising his head above the parapet of the captured work to fire his revolver, was shot dead. Notwithstanding the fall of their gallant leader, a plucky attempt to push forward was made by the leading detachment of British troops under Capt. T. H. Rodger, Diamond Fields Horse, but the excellent head cover of the Boer redoubt made it impossible to take it. The action was continued till dark, but the impetus of the sortie was spent. It would have been useless to persist. By Colonel Kekewich's orders, the troops were therefore withdrawn within the line early next morning, with a loss of two officers and twenty-two men killed, three officers and twenty-nine men wounded.

<small>On Dec. 2nd Kekewich hears of the Modder battle.</small>

This sally was well timed, for it took place during the battle of the Modder;* but, although searchlight communication had been established, Kekewich was not informed of the results of that battle until the 2nd December. Two days later a despatch was received from Lord Methuen conveying, in the High Commissioner's name, the decision† that, on the relief of Kimberley, the number of the inhabitants must be reduced, since communications might again be interrupted. Colonel Kekewich was, therefore, directed to make all arrangements for removal on the day the relief force should reach Kimberley of the surplus population, leaving only the troops and such persons as might be absolutely needed for purposes of municipal administration and for the working of the mines. The civil authorities were desired by the Colonial Government to co-operate cordially with the officer commanding troops in giving effect to these orders. In a further message, dated the 5th December, Lord Methuen informed Kekewich that the garrison would be strengthened by the other half battalion of the Loyal North Lancashire regiment and four Naval guns.

<small>Decision received, Dec. 4th, from Cape Town that the civil population must evacuate the town.</small>

It was impossible to keep these orders entirely secret, as in order to ascertain the number of inhabitants who could be sent away it was necessary to consult the local authorities and principal residents in confidence. To Mr. Rhodes the arrangements proposed for the future defence of the town appeared quite inadequate, and on December 7th Kekewich forwarded to Lord Methuen a remonstrance, in which Mr. Rhodes asked to be allowed to raise 2,000 volunteers in the Colony at his own expense, as a reinforcement for the garrison. If this were not allowed, he said, that the mines must be shut down, the white employés dismissed, and the 13,000 native employés handed

<small>Dec. 7th. Rhodes remonstrates.</small>

---

* See Volume I., Chapter XV.

† The reasons for this decision were set forth in Volume I., Chapter XI., page 209. The instructions had been given by Sir Redvers Buller.

over to the military authorities for disposal. On the 8th, Lord Methuen replied to Kekewich :—

"Please understand that I can give you one and a half battalions and Naval brigade, and you must cut your coat according to your cloth. I am arranging military defence with you, and Rhodes must understand that he has no voice in the matter." Dec. 8th. Methuen makes Kekewich responsible for carrying out order.

On the 11th Kekewich received a written despatch from the G.O.C., 1st division, instructing him that not a civilian or native was to remain in Kimberley after the relief "unless he satisfies you and myself that his services are essential for the protection of Kimberley, or some other good purpose." He was informed that fifteen trains would be assigned for the conveyance of food supplies into the town, and thirty for the removal of civilians, that the railway would probably be opened by the 15th, and that all the relief arrangements should be carried out by the 22nd. Arrangement for removal of civil population.

The proposed removal of the civilian population caused much discontent,* and strongly worded remonstrances were addressed by the Mayor and Chamber of Commerce to the High Commissioner; but Colonel Kekewich duly complied with his orders, and made the necessary preliminary arrangements. Renewed remonstrances by civil authorities.

Though between the 4th and the 11th December—the day of Magersfontein—many messages passed between Lord Methuen and Colonel Kekewich, they chiefly related to the proposed removal of the civil population from Kimberley to the coast. On the 5th Lord Methuen informed Kekewich that he was waiting till more troops reached him, "on the supposition that Kimberley was in no immediate danger"; Kekewich replied that Kimberley was not in any immediate danger. No other information at all about the General's plans was received from the 1st division until the morning of the 11th, when a despatch rider brought a message into Kimberley while the officers in the conning-tower were watching the British shells bursting over the heights of Magersfontein. After dealing at Communications between Kekewich and Methuen.

---

* An article in the *Diamond Fields Advertiser* pointed out that this order would entail financial ruin on a large number of the wage-earning class.

Dec. 11th. Warning received from Methuen of attack on Magersfontein, whilst it is actually going on.

length with questions relating to the supplies required by the garrison of the town, Lord Methuen said : " Now regarding my movements. I have been delayed two days by railway being destroyed near Enslin. First train crossed Modder river by seventh, and my additional men were crossed this morning. I bombard the enemy at Magersfontein this afternoon, assault to-morrow, and march to Abon's Farm, Hardings, Tuesday ; attack Scholtz Nek, Wednesday, at daybreak. Of course, my plan may have to be altered, but I hope to keep you daily informed as to my movements ; besides, I believe I can signal to Kimberley from Abon's Farm. Naturally I set great store on your valuable co-operation. After the fight I hope to see you, and may return to Kimberley with you." This despatch

Too late then for projected co-operation.

was received far too late to allow Kekewich to carry out the scheme which, with his staff, he had prepared to help Methuen in his advance northwards. When the relief column was due to make its final march from the Modder river he intended to sally out in force towards Alexandersfontein, in the hope of seriously disturbing the Boers at Spytfontein and possibly even causing them to loose their hold of that position. For this purpose he had saved his horses and men, and refrained from any movement towards Alexandersfontein which might have caused the Boers to strengthen their works in that direction.

On the night of the 11th a short message came from Methuen to the effect that he was checked and could not say until next day whether he could go forward. No definite news of the

News of result of Magersfontein received, 17th Dec., 1899.

result of the battle reached Kekewich until the 17th, when newspapers, giving details of the British losses, were brought in by native runners. Though on the 18th Kekewich received the significant order " to commence economising food to last till 30th January " (a date which was extended later to the end of February), it was not until the 26th December that it was made clear to him that the operations for the relief of Kimberley were indefinitely postponed. From this time, until the end of the siege, the husbanding of supplies became the chief anxiety of Colonel Kekewich and his staff. On 20th December all the remaining stocks of tea, coffee, and meal were purchased

THE SIEGE OF KIMBERLEY.

by the military authorities, and their administration was handed over to the Supply Committee. The issues of meat were further controlled by a proclamation prohibiting the slaughter of any cattle except on a military order, and the civilian inhabitants were now put on a fixed ration of half a pound of meat and fourteen ounces of bread daily, obtainable on production of a permit; a still lower scale was fixed for Asiatics and Kaffirs. Throughout the siege Kekewich made great efforts to carry off cattle from the enemy: he employed Kaffirs, to whom he paid a reward for every beast they captured. Several hundred cattle, from first to last, were thus obtained, and eked out the supply of meat for the population.

In Kimberley, as throughout the theatre of war, the Queen's message to her Army in South Africa: "I wish you and all my brave soldiers a happy Christmas; God bless and protect you all," touched the hearts of all who received it. On 1st January, 1900, the inhabitants of the town sent the following message to Her Majesty: "The inhabitants of Kimberley humbly beg to send Your Majesty New Year's greetings. The troubles they have passed through, and are still enduring, only tend to intensify their love and loyalty towards Your Majesty's Throne and Person." To this H.M. the Queen graciously replied: "Am deeply touched by your kind New Year's greetings. I watch with admiration your determined and gallant defence, though I regret the unavoidable loss of life incurred." The patience of the inhabitants during these weary months of waiting and hardship was indeed praiseworthy. Gradually the rations dwindled down. On 2nd January, 1900, the meat was reduced to a quarter of a pound, and by the middle of the month much horse-flesh had to be consumed. All luxuries had become extremely scarce, and milk was reserved for the children and the sick. But for the generosity and resourcefulness of Mr. Rhodes the privations of the siege would have pressed with overwhelming severity on the many whose incomes or wages had practically ceased. For the relief of Europeans a special committee was appointed at Mr. Rhodes' suggestion, under the presidency of the Mayor, and a fund formed, to which the De

Margin notes: Christmas message received from Queen has excellent effect. Reduction of rations. Rhodes organises measures for relief of poor inhabitants.

Beers Company contributed £10,000. During the last month of the siege, arrangements were made by Mr. Rhodes, and carried out by Capt. T. G. Tyson and the Hon. T. W. Smartt, M.L.A., for converting a large part of the daily ration into soup, of which 8,000 pints were distributed daily.

<small>Demonstrations of 9th Dec., 1899, and 17th Jan., 1900.</small>

After the fight of the 28th November the investment and defence of Kimberley were without incident, save for the occasional shelling, a demonstration in the direction of Kamfer's Dam carried out by a column under Lieut.-Colonel Chamier on the 9th December, and a sortie on 17th January to the south-east by the mounted troops under Lieut.-Colonel Peakman. The challenge of the "Long Cecil" produced a renewal of the bombardment by the enemy, whose shells, nevertheless, continued to do surprisingly little damage to the defenders. Early in February rumours reached the town that the Boers were about to bring a more formidable weapon into play, and on the 7th the 94-pr. gun, which had been injured in a sortie from Ladysmith and repaired at Pretoria, opened from the emplacement at Kamfer's Dam tailings heap. At a Krijgsraad held four days previously Colonel de Villebois Mareuil, an ex-officer of the French army who had placed his distinguished talents and restless energy at the service of the burghers, proposed that, after Kimberley had been vigorously shelled by the great siege gun, it should be closely attacked by the burghers. Under cover of feints from Alexandersfontein and the intermediate pumping station, de Villebois Mareuil was to lead the storming party. The plan was accepted, but the Boers had not yet learned to charge home on their enemy, as they did towards the end of the war, and the proposed assault was not delivered.

<small>Feb. 3rd, 1900. De Villebois Mareuil proposes to storm Kimberley. He gets no support.</small>

<small>Effect of 94-pr. gun.</small>

The fire of the 94-pr. gun proved a sore trial to the civilian population of the town, though it was partly kept in check by the shells of "Long Cecil," and by skirmishers, who were pushed forward to 1,800 yards from the emplacement. These men, who were picked shots from the various corps, volunteered for the work and, though exposed occasionally to the shells of the gun when the artillerymen, annoyed by their bullets, turned the piece upon them, returned day after day to this dangerous duty.

THE SIEGE OF KIMBERLEY.

On the 9th Mr. Rhodes desired to hold a public meeting to discuss the situation; but this was forbidden by the officer commanding the troops. Notwithstanding this prohibition, Mr. Rhodes and eleven others assembled at a private house and drew up a long remonstrance addressed to Lord Roberts. Kekewich had already reported* by signal to the Field Marshal the uneasiness with which the civil population viewed the continuance of the enemy's bombardment, and had been instructed to impress on the inhabitants "the disastrous and humiliating effect of surrendering," and the certainty of very early relief. On the 10th he sent the Chief of the Staff a summary of the remonstrance in the following flash message :— *Rhodes' remonstrance, Feb. 10th.*

> "Field Marshal's of February 9th and C. 85 this date communicated to leading inhabitants, I trust will have excellent effect. Mr. Rhodes and other leading inhabitants held private meeting to-day before Field-Marshal's two messages arrived. Rhodes called at my office this afternoon presenting lengthy document for communication by flash to you. Summary of same as follows :— 1st, Answer required whether immediate effort is being made to relieve Kimberley; 2nd, Duration siege, shortness of food, hardships endured, disease prevalent, strongly represented; 3rd, Consternation, destruction of life and property caused by enemy's siege guns pointed out; 4th, Their views military situation stated."

Its terms.

It has been already recorded† that these reports decided the Commander-in-Chief to begin the march of the cavalry division and army corps before the organisation of their units was complete. The tone of the remonstrance was, in fact, such as to cause grave anxiety, coming as it did from an invested town of so exceptional a character as Kimberley. Yet, disquieting as was the language of this remonstrance, those who signed it had no intention of suggesting surrender. They thought that the fate of Kimberley was being treated as a matter of secondary importance, and desired to force the authorities to make the immediate relief of the town their direct and primary object. To protect from the imminent peril threatened by the enemy's shells the lives and property of the inhabitants of Kimberley, and to secure for them the right to resume their normal occu- *C.-in-C. decides to relieve Kimberley at once.*

* See Chapter I.   † See Chapter I.

pations appeared to them a more pressing matter than the seizure of Bloemfontein, or even a great victory over the Boer field army. The urgent appeal to Lord Roberts, though it hastened his move, did not cause any serious alteration in the plan of action on which he had decided. The mode in which the town was relieved has been already described.*

Little remains to be said of the few days during which Kimberley was still cut off from the outer world. Throughout the 13th wagons and mounted men were seen trekking eastwards from Spytfontein. Early on the 14th it was ascertained that the Boers had evacuated Alexandersfontein, and Major Fraser, who commanded the section of the defence nearest to that place, immediately took possession of it. He was promptly reinforced by a squadron of mounted men, a company of the North Lancashire, and two guns of the Diamond Fields artillery, and, though the enemy assailed him vigorously with musketry and shell, he maintained his hold until the burghers drew off on the approach of the cavalry division. Kekewich was in heliographic communication with French's column by 4 p.m. on the 15th, and as the cavalry neared Kimberley he withdrew the troops from the southern defences and, with every man he could spare, hurried them northwards, under Lieut.-Colonel W. H. E. Murray, North Lancashire, to cut off the retreat of the Boer artillery. The part which the garrison of Kimberley played on the 16th merges into the general operations, and is described in Chapter VII. Until French's division began to appear on the afternoon of the 15th, the enemy exerted himself to make the town untenable by means of more or less constant shell fire; but the women and children, who had hitherto taken shelter in bomb-proof covers dug out of the débris heap, were, by Mr. Rhodes' care, placed in the still more secure protection of the Kimberley and De Beers mines.

The actual number of lives lost and the damage from bombardment throughout the investment were remarkably small. The enemy's guns shelled the town on forty days, and fired in all

---

* See Chapter III.

THE SIEGE OF KIMBERLEY.

over 8,000 projectiles, but the number of casualties from artillery fire, including women and children, amounted to only nine persons killed and twenty-two injured. On over twenty days of the bombardment no single person was hit. Yet although the mortality directly due to the guns of the enemy was very small, the indirect effects of the investment on the lives of the community were grave. For the first few weeks of the hundred and twenty-four days of its duration the health of the town remained normal, but from the middle of November onwards sickness rapidly increased amongst the 22,000 women and children (of whom 70 per cent. were of European descent) and the natives. The troops, owing to their out-door life, kept fairly well. The deaths from all causes per month were in November 133; in the following months, 302, 585, and 607 respectively. The aggregate was equal to the deaths during a complete year in normal times; the mortality of infants was as high as 500 per thousand for Europeans, and 935 per thousand for coloured races. The native population suffered a good deal from scurvy, which, in January, appeared for a time in an incipient form among the Town Guard.

From a military point of view, the history of the investment of Kimberley is remarkable for the extraordinary supineness of the attackers in not attempting a single assault upon the defences, the *enceinte* of which was of necessity out of all proportion to the strength of the garrison. It is equally remarkable as a proof of the ease with which the death-dealing effects of artillery fire can be evaded by those not compelled to be exposed to it. It is hardly possible that the position taken up could have been maintained against a determined assault by disciplined men.

In most sieges the military have formed a substantial, if not a preponderating, proportion of the besieged. In Kimberley the regular troops were a mere handful, and the whole armed force was less than a tenth of the population. The presence of a large number of native labourers was a danger to civil order, and, if they once got out of hand, to the lives and honour of the women. Among the white inhabitants not a few sympathised with the Boers, and sought to help them in every way in their

Conduct of population of Kimberley,

power. Had the European citizens been born in a Continental country they would have heard from their childhood tales of battles and sieges, and of the hardships which war inevitably brings to all within its grip. But the inhabitants of Kimberley were utterly ignorant of the meaning of war. The restrictions of martial law, though lightly enforced, galled this freeborn population. Their pride was wounded by the news of Magersfontein, Stormberg, and Colenso, and by the delay, to them inexplicable, in the operations for their relief. They saw trade at a standstill, industry partially paralysed. Their women and children were in danger not only from the enemy's shells but from hunger and disease. Yet, save in the matter of much discontent at the long duration of the siege, they behaved admirably, and showed a spirit and determination worthy of their race. The citizens looked to Rhodes for guidance, and to them he proved

and of Rhodes.

a tower of strength. To keep money in circulation, and to provide for the men thrown out of employment by the siege,

His great services.

he spent large sums on relief works. He started soup kitchens, and in every way did his utmost to grapple with the prevalent distress. But if to the citizens he was a tower of strength, to the responsible soldier he was a thorn in the flesh. Accustomed to be obeyed by all around him; wont to crash through difficulties in his own masterful way; despising, because he did not understand it, the routine necessary for the maintenance of discipline in a beleaguered town; stirred to his depths by the sight of the suffering around him; having as a politician made the mistake of predicting that the Boers would not declare war upon Britain; too ignorant of war to realise that Kimberley was but a piece, though undoubtedly an important piece, upon the chess-board of the campaign, it is not surprising that, as a colleague to Colonel Kekewich, which his position virtually made

His failings.

him, he was almost impossible to work with. Anxiety, and the confinement of the siege, told upon his health, his temper, and his judgment, and it is impossible to deny that, while his presence in Kimberley was of great value in many respects, in others it was a positive danger. His determination that Kimberley should be relieved at once, regardless of the general aspect of the cam-

THE SIEGE OF KIMBERLEY.

paign, induced him to do many things which, in calmer moments, he would have been the first to reprobate. Against the wish of the commanding officer, who, in the absolutely unique circumstances of this siege was powerless to enforce an order upon him, Rhodes sent by runners letters, often " in clear," to many personages in South Africa, describing the condition of the town, and clamouring for its instant relief. He opposed the project of transporting to the coast the non-combatant portion of the population. Towards the end of the siege, against the will of Col. Kekewich, he held a meeting of important citizens, who drew up a protest against the continuance of the siege. This was addressed to Lord Roberts and worded, as had been many of the previous communications, in such a way as to induce the idea that surrender was in the air. No such idea had ever entered into the head of Mr. Rhodes or any responsible inhabitant of Kimberley, but he thought that to obtain the immediate relief of the town all means were legitimate. To the judgment and good temper, tact and tenacity of purpose displayed by Colonel Kekewich, to the ability and zeal of his small staff, and to the fact that he succeeded in maintaining friendly relations with almost all the leading inhabitants throughout the siege, may largely be ascribed the successful defence of Kimberley, based upon the scheme drawn up by Colonel Trotter before the beginning of the war.

Nor is it possible to ignore the influence which the potent personage, once well-nigh the uncrowned ruler of South Africa, exercised upon all stages of the strategy of the campaign. This, as well as the extent to which public anxiety both at home and in the Colony had centred on the safety of Kimberley, made it impossible for Sir Redvers Buller to leave that town to work out its own salvation, and compelled him, in the hour of greatest strain, to launch Lord Methuen on the march to its relief. It was equally impossible for Lord Roberts and his staff to ignore all this when he started prematurely on his decisive march, and, in the hurry to get forward, both exposed himself to De Wet's damaging stroke against the convoy at Waterval and well-nigh sacrificed his splendid cavalry division by the trying marches

His great influence on the whole campaign.

and want of food which preceded and followed the surrender of Cronje. War is not waged *in vacuo*, and discussions of "strategy," which treat it as if it were, have about the same relation to facts as abstract mathematical calculations which ignore alike the presence of air, the strength of materials, and friction.

Casualties.

The casualties during the siege were few. Between the 13th October, 1899, and the 14th February, 1900, two officers were killed and twelve wounded; in the other ranks thirty-three were killed and eighty-seven wounded. Among the civilian population five were killed and twenty-four wounded.

CHAPTER VI.

PURSUIT OF CRONJE.*

DURING the cavalry movement, which had ended so success- Movements of infantry divisions during the cavalry advance. fully, much had occurred elsewhere. Though the obstinacy with which Cronje clung to his entrenchments at Magersfontein hourly improved the prospect that Lord Roberts would be able to achieve more than the mere relief of Kimberley, he as yet announced no change of plan. On the 15th, he issued no orders inconsistent with his avowed scheme for the gradual concentration on Kimberley of all the forces he could place near it. The VIth division, with two Naval 12-prs., remained at Klip Drift on the Modder, facing such of the enemy as had rallied after the charge of the cavalry division, for French was mistaken in reporting† that the road between the town and the Modder had been permanently opened by his action on the 15th. His brigades had, indeed, crashed through the centre of the position held by Froneman, but soon after French had reformed his column and started for Kimberley parties of Boers, who had returned, were seen entrenching a hill, about six thousand yards to the north of the kopjes on which the VIth division was then bivouacked. Hannay, with his mounted infantry, was to sweep these men before him on the 16th as he advanced to Abon's Dam, while a brigade of the VIth division, following in rear, was to secure the ground from which French had driven the enemy on the 15th. Tucker, from Wegdraai, with part of his

* See maps Nos. 22 (*a*) and 22 (*b*).   † See page 37.

division (VIIth), was to co-operate with Kelly-Kenny in the protection of the fords across the Modder, while the remainder of his troops were to march to Jacobsdal to establish close communication with Methuen at Modder River station, and thus open a direct line of supply to the army from the railway. To replace the VIIth division at Wegdraai, Colvile's division, the IXth, was to move from Waterval Drift at 1 a.m. on the 15th. It was of the utmost importance to replenish the brigade supplies actually accompanying the troops in their advance; and, therefore, that part of the cavalry division supply park which had halted on the night of the 14th at Waterval Drift, was to march on the morning of the 15th to Klip Drift, while the convoy was to move the same afternoon from Waterval Drift to Wegdraai.

Difficulties in crossing Waterval Drift.

At Waterval Drift the Riet runs in a deep channel, the banks of which are very steep. On the 14th the almost simultaneous arrival at the ford of the IXth division, the army convoy, and the ammunition park, while the whole of the cavalry supply park was still crossing, had caused a great block of vehicles of all kinds on the left bank. The passage was slow and difficult; thus, for instance, the two Naval 4.7-in. guns attached to the IXth division had to be lowered by hand into the bed of the river, then dragged by oxen across the drift, which, never a good one, became hourly worse under the stream of traffic, and again hauled by hand up the further bank. Mules stood the strain worse than oxen, so that the bullocks of the convoy wagons were worked unsparingly. By the strenuous exertions of all ranks and all arms, the remainder of the cavalry supply park, all the guns (a Field battery, a Howitzer battery, and the Naval 4.7-in.), and the greater part of the transport of the IXth division were taken over to the right bank before nightfall. Then the passage of the convoy began. By 3 a.m. on the 15th only twenty-four empty wagons remained on the left bank. Many of these were filled with sick and wounded and sent off to the railway line, which they reached in safety.

De Wet's whereabouts unknown.

When, on the 12th, after crossing the Riet at De Kiel's Drift, French had lost touch of De Wet's commando, he thought that

PURSUIT OF CRONJE.

General De Wet had retired northwards. Next day Lubbe, with a detachment of burghers, the strength of which was overestimated by our scouts, had hovered on the right flank of the cavalry division before he himself retreated across the Modder at Klip Kraal Drift. Several definite reports had come in on the 13th, all showing that about 1,000 Boers, with a gun, had retired towards Koffyfontein, or "to the hills east of Honey Nest Kloof"; yet the disappearance of the enemy after French's successful crossing induced the belief that no serious attack on the British right need be feared. This led to one of the most unfortunate incidents of the march. As the oxen of the convoy, exhausted by their long trek from Orange River bridge, and by the toil of the 14th, required a few hours to rest and graze, and therefore could not move directly in rear of the IXth division, some escort was needed for them. Under the impression that the Boers had been driven off, Headquarters decided that two hundred infantry, and about the same number of mounted infantry, would be sufficient for the purpose.

The army convoy, unable to march with IXth division,

The Highland brigade, with the divisional artillery and Naval guns, started for Wegdraai at 1 a.m. on the 15th. They were followed three hours later by the divisional mounted troops, the 19th brigade, the divisional transport and the ammunition park. The escort left with the convoy consisted of a company of Gordon Highlanders, a squadron of Kitchener's Horse, and some two hundred details of the 8th mounted infantry, under Lieut.-Colonel W. Ross. Colonel C. P. Ridley, who was on his way to assume command of a brigade of mounted infantry, was also present. At daybreak, all but ten of the wagons of the convoy were on the right bank of the Riet, with their oxen grazing to the eastward. The mounted part of the escort was still on the left bank, but the company of the Gordon Highlanders, with ten men of the Royal Canadian regiment unable to march with their corps, were bivouacked close to the main body of the convoy. The wagons had been formed into an irregular laager between the river and two kopjes, 1,800 and 2,200 yards respectively to the eastward. No officer had been detailed to command the convoy and its escort; but at 7 a.m., Colonel F. F.

is left to rest at Waterval Drift.

Johnson, Army Service Corps, who had remained to superintend the crossing of the convoy, rode round the position and gave orders that the oxen grazing on the right bank should be collected, as he wished to move the wagons to a safer spot. But whilst the cattle were being brought together, shots were heard to the east, and some of the natives in charge of the oxen ran in. By Colonel Johnson's direction, the Gordon Highlanders, under Captain K. Dingwall, lined a low ridge about four hundred yards to the east of the laager, and thence opened fire on the Boers, who were seen advancing towards the kopjes beyond. Colonel Ridley was instructed to prolong the Gordon Highlanders' line to the left, and thus keep open the road to Wegdraai. A section of the mounted infantry and the handful of Canadians were posted in the river bed below the drift. Attempts were still made to collect the oxen, but the enemy opened fire from the kopjes with shrapnel and with a pom-pom, and at once getting the range, swept down whole teams. A large number of the animals strayed towards the enemy and were captured. A few were driven in and placed under cover of the banks of the stream, but the native drivers refused, after a time, to face the fire.

Convoy attacked at Waterval Drift, 15th Feb., 1900.

Waterval Drift was still in telegraphic communication by field cable with Headquarters at Wegdraai, and at 8.40 a.m. Colonel Ridley, who for the moment conceived himself to be the senior on the ground, reported that an attack had been made "in our rear, nothing to show its strength at present." Lord Roberts thereupon ordered back three companies of the 7th mounted infantry, the 18th Field battery, and the 1st King's Own Scottish Borderers to help the convoy, and telegraphed that it should move on as soon as possible, and that assistance should be given to a small convoy then on its way from Enslin. These wagons contained boots and were under the escort of a party of about 32 officers and men. After a spirited resistance, in which nearly half their number were killed or wounded, this party surrendered to a largely superior force of burghers, who swooped down upon them from De Kiel's Drift. Between noon and 3 p.m., a series of further telegrams from Waterval informed

Escort to convoy reinforced by Lord Roberts.

A small convoy from Enslin is captured, Feb. 15th.

PURSUIT OF CRONJE.

Headquarters that the enemy at Waterval had been reinforced, and had now two Field guns and two pom-poms in action, and that the battery and mounted troops, which had reached the drift at 1.30 p.m., were not strong enough to beat off the attack. On receipt of these reports, Lieut.-General Tucker was ordered to hasten back to Waterval with the 62nd Field battery and the remainder of the 14th brigade.

<small>Tucker, sent to help the convoy with a battery and remainder of the 14th brigade,</small>

While General Tucker's troops were hurrying to their assistance, the original escort held their ground, helped by the non-commissioned officers and men of the 29th and 40th companies of the Army Service Corps, who rendered useful service as ammunition carriers to the front line. When the first reinforcements, the 18th battery and mounted infantry, arrived, an attempt was made to turn the enemy's right, but without success. The Scottish Borderers came up in time to repulse an attempt of the burghers to work down the river bed, but the accurate fire of the Boer guns and rifles made it quite impossible to carry out Lord Roberts' orders to move the convoy. Tucker, with the 62nd battery, five companies of the 2nd Norfolk, seven companies of the 2nd Lincolnshire, and seven companies of the 2nd Hampshire, reached the scene of action at sunset, and found the Boers holding a position about one and a half miles in length east of the drift. The enemy's strength had been increased by the arrival of further reinforcements from the east, and was now estimated to be 1,500 men, with two guns and two pom-poms. An attack on them could only be made over open ground. To assault immediately with tired troops appeared to be unwise. After consultation with Colonels Johnson and Ridley, General Tucker reported to the Commander-in-Chief that he could not be certain of success unless he was reinforced with at least two battalions and a battery. He stated that the remaining cattle of the convoy had been collected in the river bed, and were "fairly screened from fire."

<small>reports that he requires further troops,</small>

The Field-Marshal decided that, serious as the loss of the convoy with its supplies might prove, its abandonment would be a lesser evil than the dislocation of his plans by the entanglement of further troops in a fight at Waterval. He had arranged on the previous day that a second convoy of a hundred loaded wagons should be sent from Honey Nest Kloof to Jacobsdal, as soon as the latter village was secured. The Director of Supplies, Colonel W. D. Richardson, informed him that the troops could be rationed throughout the march, except that the issue of biscuit must be reduced. To make up for this, extra supplies of meat were to be served out. Satisfied upon this point, the Commander-in-Chief therefore sent off the following order in duplicate by telegram and messenger to Lieut.-General Tucker:—

<small>which the C.-in-C. cannot spare. Tucker is ordered back to camp.</small>

"15th February, 1900.

"If you find you cannot get the convoy away, leave it, destroying all you can, but bring the men back. I am most anxious that you should be in camp by daylight without further loss of life. General French was at the Club, Kimberley, this evening. Most important that you should return."

<small>16th Feb., 1900.</small>

This telegram reached General Tucker's hands soon after 11 p.m. A later order, dictated by the Commander-in-Chief after midnight, directed that the wagons should be destroyed "as well as you may be able." But as Tucker was ordered to be at Wegdraai by daylight, he had no time to destroy the wagons. It was only by starting as soon as possible that he was back in camp at the time appointed. Many of the mule carts, which had been placed for shelter in the bed of the river, were saved with their teams, but to the Boers were abandoned 176 wagons, containing approximately 70,200 rations of preserved meat, 180,000 rations of bread stuff and groceries, 38,792 grain rations, and eight wagon loads of medical comforts. The teams of the ox wagons and some 500 slaughter cattle were also lost.

<small>Convoy abandoned; its contents.</small>

<small>De Wet's stroke made from Winterhoek, where for three days he waited in concealment to effect surprise.</small>

This great success was achieved by De Wet, who, with his own and Andries Cronje's commandos, had lain at Winterhoek for three days awaiting an opportunity to strike at the British line of communications. The blow was a serious one, and had Lord Roberts been less resolute, might have impeded his plan of action. Yet it is open to question whether, having regard to the imminent peril of Cronje, De Wet might not have been better employed in assisting his comrades to hold the right bank of the Modder. The Boers marched the convoy at once to Winterhoek, capturing on the way the post dropped at Blaauwboschpan on the 13th by the cavalry division. From Winterhoek the convoy was sent, on the 17th, under escort to Koffyfontein.

During the afternoon of the 15th, Major-General A. G. Wavell had advanced on Jacobsdal with his brigade, the 15th (VIIth division), the 75th Field battery, and the mounted infantry of the City Imperial Volunteers, under Lieut.-Colonel H. C. Cholmondeley. The village was held by about 200 Boers, under Commandant Martins, but after some slight resistance it was carried by the British troops, at the cost of one man killed and eleven wounded. The Boer detachment retired to Bosjespan across the Modder, the passages of which, in the neighbourhood of Lord Methuen's camp, they continued to hold, although, as the Ist division ascertained that morning, their outposts had evacuated the ground between the Riet and the Modder. Jacobsdal occupied, 15th Feb

In the course of the day a Boer gun had fired from Magersfontein Hill, where a large laager still remained. Late in the afternoon of the 15th the Chief of the Staff telegraphed from Klip Drift to Lord Roberts that " Boers in considerable numbers are passing from Magersfontein across our front, whether to hold us or moving on is not known." From statements made by prisoners and Boer officials taken at Jacobsdal, it was evident that the greatest uneasiness now prevailed in Cronje's commandos. A deserter declared that the last order he had received was, " Every man for himself, we will meet the other side of Kimberley." But the best deduction that could be drawn was that Cronje would attempt to move on Bloemfontein by the nearest road which he could use with safety. One report asserted that reinforcements of 2,000 men and two guns from Natal had detrained at Brandfort, and another that a detachment of 800 men from the Colesberg commandos had reached Ferreira.

Having heard from French through Lord Kitchener by nighttime on the 15th of the relief of Kimberley, and decided if necessary to abandon the convoy and in any case recall General Tucker

80   THE WAR IN SOUTH AFRICA.

<small>C.-in-C.'s orders on hearing of relief of Kimberley.</small>

in order to take advantage of the intelligence that the Magersfontein position was still occupied by the enemy on the morning of the 15th, the Commander-in-Chief deemed it best now to concentrate a considerable force at Jacobsdal, so as to make certain of the new line of communications with Modder Camp, by which a fresh convoy with four days' supplies would, it was hoped, arrive on the following day. Lieut.-General Colvile (IXth division) was therefore directed to move on the morning of the 16th to that village, with his divisional troops, the 19th brigade, and the two Naval 4.7-in. guns under Commander W. L. Grant, R.N. Headquarters were also transferred thither. Lieut.-General Tucker (VIIth division), with one of his brigades (the 14th), and the Highland (3rd) brigade (IXth division), was to remain at Wegdraai awaiting orders. Lieut.-General Kelly-Kenny (VIth division) was to push through the Boer defensive line north of Klip Drift, and occupy Abon's Dam with one brigade, while his other brigade remained at the drifts; thus allowing Hannay's mounted infantry to join the cavalry division at Kimberley. No specific orders were sent to the commander of the cavalry division. Some anxiety was felt at Headquarters as to the possibility of further attacks against the lines of communication to the south, and officers commanding posts south of the Modder camp were warned to be on their guard. The General Officer Commanding lines of communication was desired to hasten to the front a brigade division of Royal Field artillery, and to despatch to Naauwpoort* another brigade division and a Militia battalion.

<small>Cronje (15th Feb.) decides to evacuate Magersfontein and move up Modder.</small>

While Lord Roberts was thus making his preparations for the 16th, Piet Cronje remained in his laagers at Magersfontein, but the news which reached him there was such as to break down at last even his stubborn determination. The piercing of the Boer line by French's charge, the relief of Kimberley, the occupation of Jacobsdal by over three thousand British troops, the reported presence of heavy columns to the south-east, all showed that his commandos were in extreme danger. Three courses were now open to him—either to fall back northward,

* See map No. 35.

PURSUIT OF CRONJE.

move round the west side of Kimberley and unite with Ferreira on the Vaal at Warrenton, as some of his burghers actually did do; to push past the east of Kimberley towards Boshof; or by rapid marches to try to escape to the eastward, and thus regain his communications with Bloemfontein. Strategically, either the first or the second of these courses would seem to have been the safest, but the Boer General considered that the deep sandy roads and lack of water to the north rendered quick movement in that direction impossible for his great train of wagons. He hoped, moreover, that Ferreira would still be able to assist him to the eastward. After a discussion, therefore, of the situation at a hastily-convened Krijgsraad, orders were issued to evacuate the works at Magersfontein and move up the right bank of the Modder. When the decision was announced the burghers fell into great confusion, which was increased by a vigorous bombardment by Lord Methuen's artillery at Modder River camp. This shell-fire continued throughout the day and greatly retarded the preparations, but about 10 p.m. the trek began, many Boers being obliged to go on foot from want of horses. A bright moon favoured their progress, and keeping about three miles to the north of Kelly-Kenny's outposts, the column had by daybreak marched across the British front. Cronje was joined by De Beer's men, whose energetic entrenching on the previous day had confined within narrow limits the reconnaissances of Hannay's mounted infantry, the greater part of whom consisted of infantry soldiers not yet trained in their mounted duties, and suffering from the long hours in the saddle to which they were quite unaccustomed. Later in the war they did excellent service, but in the middle of February, 1900, they were not able to manœuvre quickly under fire, and by their awkward riding galled both their horses and themselves. *His trek begins at 10 p.m. on 15th.*

At streak of dawn on the 16th, Hannay's brigade, now consisting of the 2nd, 4th, and 6th mounted infantry, New South Wales mounted infantry, and a detachment of Rimington's Guides, moved northward from Klip Drift, followed by the 81st Field battery and the 13th brigade, the whole under the command of Major-General C. Knox. The remainder of the VIth *16th Feb., 1900. Knox, moving northwards from Klip Drift at dawn,*

VOL. II. 6

division, including two Naval 12-prs., under Lieut. Dean, R.N., remained on the ground they had occupied during the night. The 6th mounted infantry, with a few of Rimington's Guides, and some scouts attached to the VIth division, furnished the advance guard to Knox's column. Moving rapidly, they found the ridge to the north of Kelly-Kenny's position abandoned, but in a valley beyond it great columns of dust rolling from west to east showed dimly through the morning haze. Pushing on at a gallop, the mounted infantry company of the Welsh regiment discerned through this cloud an immense line of wagons, trekking eastward, escorted by small parties of mounted men. Two stragglers were quickly captured, and from them it was learned that the rear of the transport of Cronje's commandos was in sight. Before the reports of the mounted infantry could reach divisional Headquarters, the movements of the enemy had already been observed by the officer commanding the Naval guns on the kopjes to the north of the river, and communicated to the Lieutenant-General. Kelly-Kenny, instantly realising the extreme importance of harassing and retarding Cronje's retirement, ordered the direction of the mounted infantry advance to be changed to the eastward, and every effort to be made by Major-General Knox's force to catch up, or at any rate keep touch with the Boer column, which, owing to the amount of transport accompanying it, was, in fact, a convoy to be caught in retreat. Both mounted infantry and the 13th brigade quickly carried out the change of direction, and the former speedily drove in the small parties left to protect the rearmost Boer wagons. Several of these were captured, and the pursuit was continued until the main body of the Boer rear-guard, under Commandants Froneman, Wolmarans and Roos, turned to bay on the eastern of the two ridges, by the occupation of which De Beer, on the previous day, had endeavoured to bar the cavalry advance on Kimberley. From the Nek across which French's brigades had charged, this ridge, called Drieputs Kopjes, stretches away in a south-easterly direction to within rifle-shot of the loop of the river. Its strength, as a rearguard position, was increased by the difficulty of crossing the

sees Cronje's force marching from west to east across his front.

Knox ordered to change direction and pursue Cronje.

Cronje's rearguard halts at Drieputs Kopjes.

Modder on its left flank, and by another ridge well adapted for defence, about three miles to the south-east, i.e., to its left rear. Behind this second ridge lay Klip Kraal Drift, the crossing of the Modder which Lubbe had occupied on the 13th. To gain this was now Cronje's immediate object, for either by this ford or by another further up the river he must needs reach the left bank if he was to recover his communication with Bloemfontein.

The 6th mounted infantry, which formed the advance guard of Hannay's brigade, ascertained that the enemy only held the southern knolls of Drieputs Kopjes. They at once seized the northern end of the ridge. The remainder of the brigade was received with so hot a fire from the southern end that they could make no progress, and were brought to a halt in the open plain. At this time the 13th brigade was two or three miles in rear, marching eastward parallel to the Modder. Major-General Knox sent the 81st Field battery on to support the mounted infantry, and, rightly judging that it was important to drive away the Boers from the drift towards which they were retiring, he determined to attack the left flank of the rear-guard which faced him, and ordered Hannay to push his way between the southern end of Drieputs Kopjes and the Modder. The attempt failed, because the accurate shooting of a field gun and a pom-pom drove the mounted infantry back in some degree of confusion to the shelter of the bank of the river. It became clear that the attack must be carried out by the 13th brigade, and Major-General Knox decided to demonstrate against the centre of the enemy's line with the 2nd battalion the Buffs, keeping the 2nd battalion Gloucestershire and the 1st battalion West Riding in reserve. The 1st battalion Oxfordshire Light Infantry, under Lieut.-Colonel the Hon. A. E. Dalzell, was to find a crossing to the left bank of the river, and work round the Boer flank. The 6th mounted infantry was brought down from the kopje it had gained on the left, and with the 2nd mounted infantry (Martyr) was to support Dalzell. As soon as the Oxfordshire Light Infantry had succeeded with difficulty in fording the muddy waters of the Modder, their Colonel distracted the enemy's attention by ostentatiously extending the greater part of his battalion, which advanced across the open veld. He himself, with two companies, meantime crept up the bed of the river. Whilst on the left bank the Oxfordshire Light Infantry under heavy fire was converging upon the enemy's left flank, the forces on the right bank—the Buffs, West Riding and Gloucester, supported by the 81st, and later also by the 76th battery, which Kelly-Kenny had sent up from Klip Drift—threatened his front by a slow but steady advance across the plain. The Boer rear-guard fell back to the second ridge, and by 9 a.m. the whole of the first position was in the possession of the British troops.

He is dislodged about 9 a.m. 16th Feb., and falls back to a second position.

At the instance of Lord Kitchener, who had now caught up the column, Major-General Knox prepared to attack the new line to which the burghers had retired. Their right and centre rested on a kopje about a mile to the west of Klip Drift and faced west and south; their left ran from this hill along a series of knolls, too small to be shewn on map No. 22 (*b*), until it reached Klip Kraal Drift. The Boer skirmishers found excellent cover in the bed of the Modder and the dongas which fell into it from each bank, while the guns posted on the highest part of the kopje commanded the approaches to the river. The tactics to be adopted in driving the Boers from this position, which was excellently adapted for a rear-guard action, were to be the same as Knox had employed in clearing the first ridge. The Oxfordshire Light Infantry was to push up the left bank of the Modder, and search for a crossing place. This found, the battalion was to pass over the river, and, supported by the 81st Field battery, *viâ* Klip Drift, and the 6th mounted infantry, make a flank attack upon the southern face of the kopje. The remainder of the mounted infantry, with the 76th Field battery, were to prolong the line on the left bank towards Klip Kraal Drift. The Gloucestershire, West Riding and the Buffs were to assault the western face of the right and centre of the position. The whole of the mounted troops crossed the Modder at Klip Drift. About noon the preliminary dispositions were complete, and the fresh attack was launched. The Oxfordshire Light Infantry succeeded once more in struggling across the river, at a spot where there was no drift, and where the banks had to be prepared for the passage of the 81st battery by hard pick and shovel work. While the gunners engaged the Boer artillery at about two thousand yards range, Dalzell selected for attack the southern front of a kopje which faced the 81st battery, but against the continuous fire which met him he could make no progress, though the 6th mounted infantry, leaving their horses in the bed of the river, moved to his right and brought every available rifle to bear in his support. A little later the West Riding, with the Gloucester in second line, began the frontal assault assigned to them. They worked up to close range of the Boers; they established touch with the left of the Oxfordshire, some of whom had crept forward to one hundred and fifty yards from the kopje they were attacking, and they carried a few outlying knolls, but the enemy was so little shaken that it was found impossible to assault the main ridge. *Rear-guard, though attacked at noon, hold their ground throughout the day.*

On the right things were equally unsatisfactory. While the mounted infantry brigade was attempting to carry out its duty of widely enveloping the enemy's left flank, it was joined by the 76th Field battery. This unit had already been in action in the latter part of the fight for the first ridge, and its horses, as well as those of the mounted infantry, were exhausted. Several had dropped dead; the majority could hardly be roused into a trot, and the teams in its ammunition wagons could not move. Under these conditions it seemed hopeless to push on, and the order was given to halt, water, and feed. Lt.-General Kelly-Kenny rode up from Klip Drift, and after he had discovered that the Boer convoy was laagered at no great distance from him near Klip Kraal (see map No. 22 (*b*)), he ordered the march to be resumed. Thanks to the short rest the horses were now in rather better fettle, and the column reached rising ground south-west of Klip Kraal Drift, beyond which the laager on the right bank was plainly visible. With mounted infantry guarding his flanks, Major R. A. G. Harrison led the 76th battery to the top of this rising ground, but even before his guns were unlimbered he came under so heavy a musketry fire from the bank of the river, eight hundred yards off, that he was obliged to retire to the foot of the rise. Then the guns were run by hand up the hither slope, and opened on the laager from a position far enough back from the crest to be screened from the fire of the riflemen in the river-bed. Their shells so annoyed the Boers that, at about 4 p.m., under cover of a dust storm, Roos' burghers made a vigorous counter attack, and drove in the escort. The guns, which had hardly any rounds left in the limbers, were assailed by two pieces of Boer artillery, and had to fall back, covered in their retirement by Hannay's mounted infantry.

Night was now falling; the troops had been fighting almost continuously since dawn, and they were tired out. Major-General Knox, therefore, ordered them to bivouac on the ground they held. The Oxfordshire Light Infantry lost ten men killed, and one officer and thirty-nine men wounded. The total casualties during the day were five officers wounded, and ninety-six of the other ranks killed, wounded and missing.

Casualties.

87

CHAPTER VII.

PURSUIT OF CRONJE (*continued*).*

THROUGHOUT the 16th, during the time the 13th brigade (Knox) was engaged, as described in the last chapter, with the Boer rear-guard, its sister brigade (18th, Stephenson), with Dean's Naval 12-pr. guns, occupied Rondeval and Klip Drifts. The general situation was not sufficiently clear to admit of these important fords being left without protection. From the 18th brigade the 1st Welsh was sent to gather everything they could bring away from Bosjespan, the main depôt from which supplies had been issued to the burghers who manned the works at Magersfontein. The camp of the depôt had been discovered early on the 16th by Captain R. Chester Master, Rimington's Guides, who, with a few of his men, rode back along the tracks left by Cronje's wagons to ascertain if any of the enemy still remained at Magersfontein. While employed in satisfying himself that all had trekked eastward, he found at Bosjespan a standing camp with tents, stores, a hospital, and seventy-eight wagons, which from want of oxen Cronje had abandoned in his flight. Two of these wagons were loaded with Mauser rifles, the remainder with stores, which to some extent made good the loss of the convoy at Waterval Drift.

Capture of Boer stores at Bosjespan, Feb. 16th., 1900.

Lord Roberts had moved his Headquarters at daybreak on the 16th February from Wegdraai to Jacobsdal, and about 8 a.m. a rumour reached him that Cronje's main body had

C.-in-C. hears of Cronje's evacuation of Magersfontein,

* See map No. 22 (*b*).

evacuated the Magersfontein position. He at once telegraphed to Lord Kitchener at Klip Drift :—

"I am afraid a good many Boers will escape unless French can send some of his cavalry, guns, and mounted infantry along the Bloemfontein trade road. The report here is that Magersfontein has been abandoned. I am enquiring."

and sends orders to French,

By 9 a.m. telegrams from Kelly-Kenny (VIth division) and from Lord Kitchener, Chief of the Staff, confirmed the report of Cronje's movement eastward. Later in the day the Commander-in-Chief addressed the following message to General French :—

"Kelly-Kenny's division is in touch with Boer convoy, supposed to be Cronje's, near Paardeberg Drift, and he and Kitchener think that if you would move in a south-easterly direction, *via* Boschvarkfontein, you might cut it off. You would be in a good position on that route for interrupting the enemy's troops recently at Kimberley, which, like Cronje's, are evidently making for Bloemfontein. Better not go farther east than Petrusburg, without orders from me. It would be a glorious finish if you can get the 6-inch gun which has punished Kimberley so severely, and if you could also catch Cronje. Reply to me here."

which are not received till late on night of 16th.

This and a somewhat similar order, despatched by telegraph to French by the Chief of the Staff from Klip Drift, did not reach the cavalry commander till late at night, after a written message from Lord Kitchener had been delivered by Captain Chester Master.*

Kelly-Kenny ordered to pursue Cronje.

To General Kelly-Kenny the Field-Marshal telegraphed from Jacobsdal :—

"Push pursuit all you can and try to get supplies from the country. I have told French to sweep round to the south-east. Every hour of pursuit now is worth days afterwards."

The Chief of the Staff was instructed by telegram to keep French informed of the situation.

Situation in western theatre of war, and estimated strength of enemy, 16th Feb.

The general situation in the western theatre of war, as it presented itself to the Commander-in-Chief at this moment, and the estimate then made of the strength of the various Boer

* See page 96.

forces in the field, will be seen from the following, submitted by Colonel G. F. R. Henderson, D.M.I., on the 16th February :—

"The disposition of the enemy appears to be roughly as follows :—Cronje's force (10,000 to 12,000) part N. of Kimberley, part N.N.E. of Klip Drift. Andries Cronje, Lubbe and De Wet near Waterval Drift, about 1,300 men and two guns ; near Goemansberg, forty miles east of Orange River station, probably, 300 ; coming from Ladysmith, possibly 3,000 to 5,000 (all the Free Staters) ; coming from Colesberg, 800 ; and probably more in a few days.

Summary.

Cronje	12,000	and 20 guns.
Andries Cronje	1,300	and 2 guns.
Goemansberg	300	and 1 gun.
Reinforcements from Ladysmith and Colesberg	5,000	(this is not yet certain).
Colesberg	8,000	and 10 guns.
Stormberg and Dordrecht ..	2,000	,, ,,

It will be observed that this report regards Ferreira's commandos as part of Cronje's force ; in reality it was a separate command. A telegram from Sir R. Buller, dated 21st February, confirmed the fact of the reinforcements from Natal, stating that "commandos from Bethlehem, Heilbron and Senekal went back from Spion Kop to Orange Free State by train last week."

This summing-up of the situation by the Intelligence Staff showed causes for anxiety which must be taken into account, if the orders now issued are to be seen in their true perspective. Subsequent events proved indeed that the strength of the enemy was somewhat exaggerated, but against this must be set the fact that the Field Intelligence Department had all through shown care and moderation in such estimates, and had never accepted the very high figures put forward by other authorities.[*] Moreover, the capture of the convoy at Waterval Drift had taught the lesson that at least a portion of the commandos was still active, mobile, and capable of striking a rapid blow. General Clements at Colesberg had reported to Headquarters on the previous day that he was being pressed by large numbers, and had been forced to fall back on Arundel.[†] Methuen's

[*] See Volume I., page 410.   [†] See Chapter XV.

reports, although they confirmed the evacuation of the Magersfontein position, left room for doubt whether a portion of Cronje's force might not have fallen back to the north towards Barkly West. Owing to the breakage of the cable line no communications had been received from French since the evening of the 15th.

<small>Movements of troops, other than French's and Kelly-Kenny's, during 16th Feb.</small>

Although the Field-Marshal had issued orders to Kelly-Kenny and French for the immediate pursuit of Cronje, he considered that until further definite information reached him, it would be unwise not to keep a firm grip of the crossings of the Modder which lay between the Ist and the VIth divisions. The 19th brigade, the Headquarters, and the divisional troops of the IXth division, including two Naval 4.7-in. guns, under Commander Grant, R.N., had marched in the early morning into Jacobsdal from Wegdraai; Tucker's divisional Headquarters remained at Wegdraai, although he had a brigade detached to Jacobsdal. The Field-Marshal determined that, as soon as the convoy of about a hundred wagons from Honey Nest Kloof, expected during the day, had reached Jacobsdal, he would push Generals Tucker (VIIth division) and Colvile (IXth division) forward to the Modder, concentrating the IXth division at Brown's Drift, and the VIIth at Klip Drift. He ordered these units to begin their march at 6 p.m., Kimberley being still their supposed destination. To Lord Methuen he telegraphed instructions to send to Jacobsdal his Naval guns—two 4.7-in. and two 12-pr., under Captain J. E. Bearcroft, R.N. The convoy, which carried four days' much-needed supplies, reached Jacobsdal without incident. Late in the afternoon the following despatch was received from Lord Kitchener, then at Klip Drift. It gives his appreciation of the situation to the eastward, towards the close of the Drieputs engagement:—

"16th February, 1900, 4 p.m.

"Have returned from Knox's brigade, which has been already held back by Boers, who fight an excellent rear-guard action. He has turned them out of three successive positions. I would propose that Knox's brigade should bivouac about Paardeberg, to which point I had hoped the mounted infantry and artillery would have gone early, only unfortunately they stopped short of it. Hannay with mounted infantry to continue pursuit and keep touch with enemy, who are reported to be inclining to the north and not to have crossed the river. The rest of the VIth division to join Knox's brigade about 1 a.m. to-morrow, and Colvile's division to follow evening of to-morrow, if they get in here at dawn. The enemy are very numerous and fight well and cleverly; I fear we have not done much damage to convoy, but we have hustled them all day. Telegraphic communication with French has been interrupted by convoy crossing the line. Break has now been found, and will be repaired very shortly. I will then try to get French to co-operate with us. If we only had time, I feel sure that we should make short work of convoy, but, with the troops we have, it is a very difficult operation. I am sending Chester Master to Kimberley to-night to ask French if he could meet me at Koodoos Drift. The supply question is becoming acute. Please tell Richardson to let me know at once when [and] what we may expect to have as regards supplies. I hope you will not send Smith-Dorrien's brigade to Brown's Drift, as it would be far longer to march, and there would be nothing now there for a brigade to do."

This report determined the Field-Marshal at once to order eastward Colvile's division, the men of which were fresher than Tucker's, owing to the heavy work done by the VIIth division on the previous day and night. The VIIth division was directed to concentrate at Jacobsdal early next morning. At 10 p.m., on the 16th, Lieut.-General Colvile left Jacobsdal with one of his brigades (19th), the 82nd Field battery, 65th Howitzer battery, ammunition column and 7th company R.E., and moving all night along a good track, reached Klip Drift at 4.30 a.m. on the 17th. On his arrival Colvile received verbal orders from the Chief of the Staff to march at 3 p.m. for Paardeberg. The remainder of his division (the Highland brigade), which lay at Wegdraai, left that place with the 7th and 8th mounted infantry at 11 p.m. on the night of the 16th, and after a sixteen miles' march arrived at its destination, Klip Kraal Drift, at 5.30 a.m. on the 17th. The supply convoy, after a few hours' halt at Jacobsdal, resumed at midnight its march to Klip Kraal Drift. Lord Methuen (Ist division), as soon as he had definitely ascertained by reconnaissance that the enemy had evacuated the Magersfontein position, had hoped to advance towards Kimberley that afternoon, but owing to lack of transport he found it necessary to be content with the occupation of Merton Siding.

Night marches on 16th-17th Feb., 1900.

Bearcroft's guns were despatched to Jacobsdal on the 17th, in accordance with orders.

<small>Movements of cavalry division after relief of Kimberley.</small>

The cavalry division, after it reached Kimberley on the afternoon of the 15th,* had moved as follows : On the night 15th–16th Broadwood's brigade, with the Carabiniers, bivouacked at Alexandersfontein, and the remainder of the force in the suburbs east of the town. Though the horses urgently needed rest after their severe work, Lt.-General French felt that it was necessary to sweep away any detachment of the enemy which might still linger in the neighbourhood, and he was not without hope of capturing the 94-pr. gun which from the site near Kamfer's Dam had alarmed the civil population during the last few days of the siege. That gun, moreover, not unnaturally, was much coveted by the Kimberley garrison ; it had been in action during the forenoon of the 15th, and later in the day, when the cavalry

<small>Sortie northwards of garrison of Kimberley in afternoon of 15th.</small>

division was seen nearing the town, Colonel Kekewich, by withdrawing all the troops from his southern and south-western defences, and combining them with his reserve, had made up about seven hundred of all arms and sent them north to try to cut off the retreat of the " Long Tom." The little column consisted of two companies 1st battalion, Loyal North Lancashire, three hundred mounted police and Diamond Fields Horse, four guns of the Diamond Fields artillery, and two hundred of the Kimberley regiment, with three Maxims. Murray's detachment seized two of the Boers' foremost redoubts, but towards sunset their further advance met with serious resistance. Murray was ordered to bivouac on the ground he had already occupied, pushing a mounted patrol of one hundred and twenty men up the railway towards Dronfield.

<small>French marches northwards from Kimberley on 16th Feb.</small>

About 6 a.m. on the 16th, having given orders to Broadwood to send the Carabiniers to rejoin Porter's brigade, and with his own brigade to reconnoitre from Alexandersfontein to the south and west, General French marched out with the remainder of his division along the Boshof road on the east side of the town. Murray's troops were already in action to the westward, and had found that the enemy during the night had evacuated the

* See Chapter III.

intermediate pumping station near Kamfer's Dam (see map No. 28), and were entrenched on a rocky ridge which runs east and west, near Dronfield station (see map No. 22 (b)), with their cattle grazing north of that station. The Boer force, which Murray's troops had discovered on the western end of the ridge, consisted of a small commando, under Commandant Van Aswegen, of some two hundred Griqualand West rebels with a field gun. Ferreira, with all the Free State burghers who had held the eastern section of the line of investment round Kimberley, had fallen back towards Boshof on the evening of the previous day, but the Transvaalers and the Free Staters of the western portions of the line of investment had moved northward under Du Toit and were now making for Warrenton.* Part of the Transvaal contingent which had been attached to Cronje's force had refused to follow that leader in his retreat up the Modder, and were also falling back on the Vaal by the west of Kimberley. If these various detachments had been left unmolested, they might have been rallied into a formidable body capable even of extricating Cronje from his dilemma. French's instinct to thrust the enemy further northward was, therefore, justified by the situation, although his information as to the actual movements of the enemy was lacking in detail. But about 8 a.m. news reached him that a strong force of the burghers was retiring towards the Vaal, and that a rear-guard held the western extremity of the Dronfield ridge, which lay about six miles north of the town. French accordingly directed Gordon's brigade to make a wide turning movement to the eastward to clear that flank, and then, crossing the Boshof road, to pivot towards the west. With Porter's and Alderson's brigades French moved northward towards the eastern end of the Dronfield ridge. On the Boshof road Gordon captured a few prisoners, who stated that their commando was retreating on Bloemfontein. The guns of the Diamond Fields artillery were now in action to the south-west of the Dronfield Siding, and as the 1st cavalry brigade (Porter) approached the eastern extremity of the ridge, that portion of the

<small>Cavalry operations during 16th.</small>

* See maps Nos. 35 and 36.

position was evacuated by the enemy, but it became apparent that he was holding in force the broken ground further to the north near Macfarlane Siding. The cavalry scouts soon afterwards reported the presence of a large laager (Du Toit's) near Droogfontein, to the westward (see map No. 28). The Boer strength near Macfarlane Siding was estimated at about two thousand men.

To meet this new development, General French desired Gordon to continue his turning movement, and cross the railway in rear of the enemy's second position. Porter was to envelop the south and south-west, clearing the hills in front of him as he advanced, while Alderson, with his mounted infantry, was to connect the two brigades and attack the centre of the Boer line. The enemy's left was found to extend some distance to the north-east, and the 3rd cavalry brigade (Gordon) was compelled to make a wide détour in carrying out its flanking movement. The absence of water, the great heat of the sun, the large number of barbed wire fences, and the sandy nature of the soil, told heavily against Gordon's horses, and his brigade division of Royal Horse artillery, unable to keep up, came into action against the knoll near Macfarlane Siding, facing which Alderson's men now lay dismounted, waiting to deliver their attack until Porter should appear from the south. But Porter, in his turning movement, had come under the fire of the Griqualand West commando, which still hung on tenaciously to the western end of the ridge near Dronfield. Porter was thus delayed, as he considered that his orders required him to deal with this outlying detachment before working northwards. Eventually the 3rd brigade could advance no further, and joined the mounted infantry in an attack on the Macfarlane knoll, which was carried about noon after a smart engagement, in which a detachment of the Kimberley Light Horse, under Major R. G. Scott, took part. The enemy's convoy could be seen labouring through the sand only five miles to the northward, trekking towards the Vaal. The 94-pr. gun, however, was not with the convoy, for it had been hurried to the north on the afternoon of the 15th, and had, during the night, been taken across the Vaal at Fourteen Streams near Warrenton.

French's horses were now utterly beat. No orders from Head- *French returns to Kimberley.* quarters had been received for twenty-four hours, and, not knowing what demands might at any moment be made upon him for immediate action to the south, the cavalry general realised that it would be imprudent to tax them further. He accordingly decided to leave the New Zealand and Queensland mounted infantry with two guns to hold Macfarlane Siding, and with the remainder of the division to return to Kimberley. To the Chief of the Staff he heliographed at 12.40 p.m. the following message :—

" My wire to Klip [Drift] has been either cut or disconnected since three this morning. Has Field-Marshal any orders for me ? I hold railway line north of Kimberley up to Macfarlane Station. Have been pursuing the enemy since daylight. All enemy's troops recently round Kimberley are now collected about Droogfontein, fifteen miles north of Kimberley. Prisoner states their intention is to march on Bloemfontein. My horses now very tired."

This heliogram reached Lord Roberts at Jacobsdal between 3 and 4 p.m., being signalled *viâ* Enslin.

On the way back to Kimberley an attempt was made to dislodge the commando still occupying the trenches on the Dronfield ridge. The 1st brigade held this detachment on the east and north, while the remainder of the division attacked it on the west and south-west. The Horse batteries shelled the works from three sides, and some dismounted squadrons were pushed forward to within six hundred yards of the ridge. But the Boers showed no signs of falling back, and General French considered that their entrenchments could not be carried without a loss which, in the circumstances, it would be unwise to incur. He accordingly withdrew his weary cavalry, leaving to Murray's troops the task of observing this commando. During the night the Griqualanders, who had made so stubborn a resistance, hastily evacuated the position, leaving behind them their Field gun and many killed and wounded. By 9 p.m. the cavalry division was back in Kimberley. The casualties for the day in officers and men were light ; two officers and three men had been killed, five officers and twenty-five men wounded.

Exhaustion of horses.

But the losses in horses were most serious. The 3rd brigade had left dead on the veld sixty-eight chargers. The majority of these had died from sheer exhaustion. Throughout the division the condition of the animals was pitiable in the extreme. One regiment, which had started with four hundred and twenty-two horses on the 11th, had now but one hundred and five fit for duty. Another corps had but twenty-eight which could be spurred into a trot.

French's orders for 17th, issued before news of Cronje's trek had reached him.

The detachments left by General French to guard the two watering places between Klip Drift and Kimberley had reported during the day that "a large force of Boers had left Magersfontein and moved eastward at dawn," but both these posts and the patrols sent southward by Broadwood's brigade failed to observe the British pursuit of the convoy. This incomplete reconnaissance, coupled with the breakage of the field cable, left the cavalry commander on the evening of the 16th in ignorance of the general situation, and uncertain whether Bloemfontein or the Vaal was now the object of the Boer main column. Orders were, therefore, issued that the 2nd cavalry brigade and the Carabiniers, the troops which had done least work that day, should on the morrow reconnoitre to the north, west, and south, and reopen definite communication with Klip Drift. The remainder of the division was to rest, so far as circumstances might permit. The supply arrangements were for the moment very inadequate. The food and forage carried by the troops were exhausted, and though forage had been drawn from the stores of the garrison of Kimberley, there was no means of conveying it to the troops on the night of the 16th, because the cavalry wagons had been left at Klip Drift when the division dashed forward to Kimberley on the 15th.*

Orders for pursuit of Cronje received from C.-in-C. at 10 p.m. on 16th.

At 10 p.m. Captain Chester Master, Rimington's Guides, who, accompanied by two of his men, had started from Klip Drift four hours earlier, arrived at the cavalry Headquarters with a written order from the Chief of the Staff, directing General French to move as rapidly as possible to intercept Cronje's retreat at Koodoos Drift. The Commander-in-Chief's detailed

* See Chapter III.

message, already quoted on page 88, was received immediately afterwards by flash signal. The plans for the 17th were at once recast. The two brigades, which had been engaged throughout the 16th, were unfit for immediate movement; Broadwood's brigade and the Carabiniers, some 1,500 mounted men in all, with twelve guns, were alone available. The orders from Headquarters admitted of no delay. French therefore determined to act on them at once with every man who had a horse still able to carry him, and to start as soon as the troops could get under way. Brigadier-General Porter was left in command at Kimberley with instructions to try to keep touch with the Boer force at Droogfontein, a squadron of the Carabiniers being detached for that purpose. This Boer force retired across the Vaal on the following day, the 17th, and took up a position on the north bank of that river, covering the road to Mafeking and Christiana. Gordon's brigade, with all colonial mounted troops which might then be available, was to follow General French twenty-four hours after his departure. The 1st cavalry brigade and the mounted infantry brigade were to remain at Kimberley until reinforcements should arrive from Modder River camp. *Fresh orders issued by French.*

Kitchener's intuition in assigning Koodoos Drift as French's destination was most happy. The conclusion of the action of the 16th left Drieputs Drift still in Cronje's possession. The vigorous attacks of Knox's infantry were not without effect, and had secured ground so close to that drift as to render dangerous any attempt to pass the Boer convoy over the river at Drieputs Drift. Cronje determined to strike eastward across the bend of the Modder for Vendutie Drift, from which a short march up the left bank of the river would place him on the main Kimberley-Bloemfontein road south of Koodoos Drift. The most dangerous part of his retreat seemed therefore to be safely over. No British troops lay between him and Bloemfontein, and he had little doubt that by steady trekking throughout the night of the 16th he would shake off his enemy and gain the Bloemfontein road without further molestation. Unobserved by the weary British outposts, Cronje with his burghers and wagons slipped away from Drieputs soon after dusk. *Cronje's march eastward.*

Two hundred of the wagons with a mounted escort pushed without halt to Paardeberg Drift, then crossed the Modder, and making south escaped the toils closing round them. Cronje himself rode on to the next drift—Vendutie, and slept for the rest of the night at Wolvekraal homestead, a house on the north bank, close to the ford. The main body of his convoy, hampered by women and children, and by the large number of dismounted men, halted at midnight on the 16th near Paardeberg Drift, where a rear-guard was posted, and, after a rest of four hours, followed Cronje to Wolvekraal; there they again outspanned at about 8 a.m. on the 17th to rest the oxen before crossing the river by the Vendutie Drift.

Knox's column marches in pursuit at 6 a.m., 17th Feb., 1900.

It was not until 6 a.m. on the 17th February that the 13th brigade could resume its march. Having bivouacked in the positions it held on the conclusion of the Drieputs action, it was somewhat dispersed on the right bank of the Modder. The 18th brigade, with the 38th company, Royal Engineers, and a Naval 12-pr., under Lieut. Dean, R.N., left Klip Drift three hours earlier. Marching by the left bank of the river and picking up at Drieputs the 1st Yorkshire, which had moved forward at 10 p.m. on the night of the 16th to support the mounted infantry, it reached at 1 p.m. Brandvallei, half way between Klip Kraal Drift and Paardeberg Drift, and nine miles below Vendutie Drift. At Brandvallei, Brigadier-General Stephenson's command was joined from the right bank of the river by Knox's brigade. The whole of the VIth division, thus reunited, halted for a few hours. Hannay's mounted infantry had been even more scattered than Knox's battalions during the fight of the 16th; but by 7.30 a.m. next morning his units were sufficiently collected to resume the march. Lord Kitchener, eager to recover touch with the enemy, personally accompanied this brigade, and at 10 a.m. came into contact with the Boer rear-guard, which had occupied a conical hill north of Paardeberg Drift. The sound of the firing which reached Cronje at the head of his convoy near Vendutie Drift four miles further up the river showed the Boer general that he had failed to out-march his pursuers. Still there seemed to him as yet no real cause for anxiety, for to the

Movements of other troops in support.

PURSUIT OF CRONJE.

north, south, and east the country was, he believed, still clear of his foes; moreover, on the north lay Ferreira's commando; from the east reinforcements might be expected from Bloemfontein, and to the south were De Wet and Andries Cronje, besides other Boer detachments.

General French and his staff had left Kimberley at 4.30 a.m. on the 17th, and by dawn had caught up Broadwood's column, which consisted of the Composite regiment of Household cavalry, 10th Hussars, 12th Lancers, and Colonel W. L. Davidson's brigade division of Horse artillery (G. and P. batteries). Two squadrons of the Carabiniers (6th Dragoon Guards) and the mounted troop Royal Engineers followed an hour later, marching *via* Oliphantsfontein. The shortest route across the veld, by Susanna and Boschvarkfontein Farms, was chosen for the main body; but, as on the previous days, the conditions were unfavourable to rapid movement, for the country was waterless and the heat became excessive. As the column advanced across Boschvarkfontein its left flanking squadron was teased at long range, but the mission of the cavalry was too urgent to permit of any investigation of the source of the fire. Really, the fact was important. Ferreira, on the evening of the 16th, had moved his commando south to Bothashoek, a farm on the north of Boschvarkfontein. His strength was at least equal to French's weak column, if not superior to it, and had he attacked Broadwood's regiments with vigour, he would have ensured Cronje's safety. But at this period of the war the Boers lacked the discipline necessary to assume the offensive against mounted troops in the open. At the sight of the British guns and squadrons, Ferreira's burghers became alarmed for their own safety, and fell back hurriedly to the north-east, leaving General French, unconscious of his good fortune, to press on to his goal. As early as 8 a.m. columns of dust began to be visible to the south-west. At 10.15 a.m. a Boer signalling post was captured at Kameelfontein Farm, a green oasis with good water supply, six miles north of Vendutie Drift. Reports from the cavalry scouts, who had been pushed out widely to the east and west, gave General French a clear idea of Cronje's situation. The head of

French marches from Kimberley on Koodoos Drift at dawn on 17th.

He ignores sniping fire from Ferreira's commando on the left of his column.

He captures a Boer signalling post, and ascertains situation.

the convoy was now beginning to inspan before crossing the river at Vendutie Drift; the remainder of the wagons stood stretched along the right bank and reached back nearly to Paardeberg, with their oxen still feeding in the plain. The Boer rear-guard held back Hannay's leading scouts; the advance guard under De Beer had already seized the rand which commands the left bank of the river at Koodoos Drift. Thus to an attack from the north Cronje could rapidly present a front of eight miles, both his flanks being secured by the river. French for the moment had under his hand a force of less than 1,300 men, for the Carabiniers marched more slowly than Broadwood's brigade, and did not reach Kameelfontein until 2.30 p.m. He was fully aware that his opponent had at least three, possibly four, times his own strength. He had however one point in his favour in carrying out the Field-Marshal's instructions; Cronje as yet knew nothing of the approach of the column from Kimberley. The cavalry was beyond the northern edge of a semi-circular plain, which, shut in on the west, north, and east by a ridge of high ground sweeping round from Paardeberg to Koodoosrand, slopes on the south gradually down to the bank of the Modder. Leaving his main body to water at Kameelfontein, and riding forward himself with a squadron pushed out to protect the front, French crossed the plain, discovered a good artillery position commanding Vendutie Drift at 2,100 yards range,

With his guns he surprises the convoy as it begins to cross Modder at Vendutie Drift.

and instantly ordered the Horse artillery batteries to occupy it. The ground over which they had to move was rough, the teams were fatigued by the twenty-six miles they had covered from Kimberley; yet Colonel W. L. Davidson brought his batteries rapidly into action, and at 11.15 a.m., just as the head of the Boer convoy was beginning to descend into the drift, British shells, bursting over the leading wagons, gave the burghers warning that their retreat was threatened from a fresh direction. Never was an attack more sudden or less expected. Cronje thought that French's cavalry were still north of Kimberley, and could only explain this sudden bombardment by supposing that he had been out-marched and out-flanked by Kelly-Kenny's division. For the moment there was a panic in the convoy. The oxen

PURSUIT OF CRONJE.

broke and scattered broadcast over the plain; the native drivers ran forward to the British guns holding up white rags, while their masters took cover in the bed of the river. Thanks to the discipline of the Orange Free State artillery, Major R. Albrecht rapidly unlimbered four guns to reply to those of the British, and, although they were silenced after a duel lasting only about ten minutes, the exertions of the Boer gunners enabled the burghers to recover from the effects of the surprise, and to take measures to drive back Davidson's batteries. A party under Field-Cornet Nieuwenholdt tried to work round the right flank of the Horse artillery by seizing, on the ridge to the north-west, a spur which commanded the ground on which French's batteries were posted. This attempt was frustrated by "A." squadron, the 10th Hussars, who, racing the enemy for the point of advantage, reached it first and succeeded in holding it with the help of "B." squadron of the same regiment, a squadron of the Household cavalry, and G. battery Royal Horse artillery. Later in the day, about 4 p.m., after Nieuwenholdt's men had fallen back towards the river, "A." squadron of the 10th Hussars was ordered by Broadwood to reconnoitre to the south-west, and made a bold attempt to seize a kopje (afterwards named Gun Hill), which overlooks the river-bed at a distance of only eight hundred yards (map No. 23). Riding forward with extended files, Lieut.-Colonel R. B. W. Fisher, who led the squadron, nearly reached the hill, but the fire from the kopje, with musketry and pom-pom shells from the river-bed and from Paardeberg, forced him to fall back with the loss of nineteen horses, and two men killed, nine men wounded. *The bombardment produces a temporary panic and a complete halt.*

Attempts by De Beer to turn the left of the British cavalry, and thus compel French to relinquish his hold of the coveted artillery position commanding the Vendutie Drift were unsuccessful. Though Boer detachments contrived to push up Koodoosrand near enough to Kameelfontein to shell with a pom-pom French's Headquarters at the homestead, this demonstration was quickly checked by a squadron of the 12th Lancers and two guns, which before nightfall forced the Boer advance guard back towards Koodoos Drift. The scouts of another *French holds his ground throughout the day and the following night till the infantry come up on the south of the river.*

squadron of the same regiment pushed down to the river between Koodoos and Vendutie Drifts, and examined the intermediate crossings which were neglected by the enemy. Meanwhile, as the afternoon wore on, Cronje's convoy still remained halted at Vendutie and to the westward, paralysed by the steady fire maintained by Davidson's guns. At 6 p.m. columns of dust, seen rising west of Paardeberg, showed that British reinforcements were at hand; but by sunset communication had not been established with the VIth division, nor even with the mounted infantry, the main body of which, after getting in touch with the Boer rear-guard on Paardeberg, had held the kopjes on the left bank of the river south and south-east of Paardeberg Drift. To attract attention to his position, as well as to annoy the Boers, French ordered Davidson to fire a round every half hour during the night. This signal, curiously enough, was not heard on the other side of the river. The enemy showed no signs of intending to move, and had already begun to entrench himself in the river bank and throw up an earthwork round the wagons, using, according to a Boer account, the Wallace entrenching tools which had been picked up on the field of Magersfontein. On the cavalry fell the anxious task of preventing any attempt at retreat, eastward or northward, during the night, and the troops under French's immediate command bivouacked on the ground they held at nightfall. Broadwood, with G. battery, the 10th Hussars, one squadron of the Household cavalry, and one squadron of the 12th Lancers, was ordered to occupy those kopjes which the 10th Hussars had seized. Another squadron of the same regiment with P. battery remained on the northern end of Koodoosrand. French's Headquarters, and the remainder of his column were near Kameelfontein homestead. No supplies had been issued either to the officers, the men, or their animals for forty-eight hours; the men had only for food a few captured sheep, and the horses such mouthfuls of withered grass as they could snatch from the veld. Both men and horses were weak from lack of food, and exhausted by the strain of their unceasing exertions. Yet that night was a memorable one for French's troops, for they had accomplished

PURSUIT OF CRONJE.

the mission assigned to them by Lord Roberts, and had demonstrated that the conditions of modern fighting still permit cavalry and Horse artillery to play a rôle of supreme importance in war. The action, having regard both to the skill and audacity displayed by General French and to the immediate strategic results thereby obtained, must be reckoned amongst the great achievements of British cavalry in war.

While French was thus successfully arresting Cronje's retreat at Vendutie Drift, the leading infantry divisions (VIth and IXth) of Lord Roberts' army were pressing up the left bank of the Modder in support of the mounted infantry, who remained in touch with the Boer rear-guard near Paardeberg. The VIth (Kelly-Kenny) after three or four hours' rest at Brandvallei Drift, marched again at 5 p.m. and about 10 p.m. finally halted two miles from Paardeberg Drift. The IXth (Colvile) had been distributed between Klip and Klip Kraal Drifts. MacDonald's brigade (the 3rd) leaving the Highland Light Infantry to hold the former of these fords, marched at 5 p.m. towards Koodoos Drift until orders from the Chief of the Staff turned it towards Paardeberg Drift, which the brigade reached about midnight. In the course of two or three hours MacDonald was joined by Colvile with his divisional troops and his other brigade, the 19th (Smith-Dorrien). Thus, by the early morning of the 18th February, Lord Kitchener had placed two divisions, as well as a brigade of mounted infantry, within striking distance of the laager which Cronje had formed when he was assailed by the shells of French's Horse artillery. Great as had been the exertions of the cavalry which headed off the Boers at Vendutie Drift, the efforts of the other arms were no whit inferior, for Hannay's, Kelly-Kenny's, and Colvile's men had made forced marches by day and night across the veld under conditions of heat and fatigue, hunger and thirst, uncertainty of their position, and expectation of an attack from any quarter, such as only those who have taken part in similar operations in Africa can appreciate. Nor must it be forgotten that the mounted infantry and a large party of Kelly-Kenny's division were warmly engaged on the 16th with the enemy's rear-guard. The dogged

Infantry marches on 17th and night of 17th-18th.

determination which sustained the infantry during their marches on the south of the Modder was a fitting complement to French's movement when, hastening from Kimberley with a small brigade of cavalry and two batteries of Horse artillery, he brought Cronje to a halt at Vendutie Drift. Each arm worthily supported the other and thus enabled Lord Roberts successfully to carry out his plans.

<small>Lord Kitchener's peculiar position with regard to the other generals.</small>

The Commander-in-Chief was detained by indisposition on the 17th at Jacobsdal, a mischance which made it necessary to strengthen the hands of his Chief of the Staff, who represented him at the front. Lord Kitchener's commission as Major-General was of earlier date than those held by Kelly-Kenny and Colvile, while French was in substantive rank merely a Colonel in the Army; but to all three of these divisional commanders the temporary rank of Lieut.-General had been granted in South Africa, thus making them senior to Kitchener for the purposes of command. In the capacity of Chief of the Staff, Kitchener while detached from Headquarters, had issued orders which had been promptly carried out, but these orders were based on Lord Roberts' instructions by telegraph; and it had become evident from the Chief of the Staff's reports that his position at the front, as a staff-officer separated from his chief, had become difficult. The Commander-in-Chief realised that in the critical situation now existing time might not permit of reference to him, and considered that, until he himself could resume the personal direction of the troops in touch with the enemy, it was desirable to make it quite clear that Lord Kitchener was empowered to give orders in his name. He therefore sent the following letter to the General Officer Commanding the VIth division :—

<small>Lord Roberts regulates this.</small>

" Jacobsdal,
" 17th February, 1900.

" My dear Kelly-Kenny—

" I hope you are pushing on with all possible speed to overtake Cronje's laager. It is of the utmost importance it should not get away. The bullocks drawing his wagons cannot go as fast as our mules, nor for so many consecutive days without breaking down. I hope to join you to-morrow; meanwhile, please consider that Lord Kitchener is with you for the purpose of communicating to you my orders, so that there may be no delay—such as references to and fro would entail. If we can deal Cronje a heavy blow, it is likely that there will be no more fighting in the Orange Free State.

"Yours very truly,
"ROBERTS."

General Kelly-Kenny's reply will be found in Appendix 1.

A note was at the same time sent by the Field-Marshal to the Chief of the Staff informing him of the authority with which he was entrusted, and stating—in reply to the representation that "the supply question is becoming very acute"—that a convoy with a month's groceries and a large quantity of biscuit was on its way to the front, and that the troops must obtain meat from the country they traversed.

Lord Kitchener, upon whom the responsibility for next day's operations now devolved, bivouacked on the night of the 17th with the mounted infantry, two miles south of Paardeberg Drift. Owing to the dispersion of the troops, it had not been possible for him to make precise arrangements with Kelly-Kenny and Colvile about the mode in which executive orders were to be issued, and beyond one officer of the Adjutant-General's department he had only his personal staff of Aides-de-camp with him. Thus, though in the divisions the commanders possessed the necessary staff for working their own commands, the officer in charge of the whole force was unsupplied with the machinery necessary for the organisation and direction of combined movements.

Inadequacy of Lord Kitchener's staff.

CHAPTER VIII.

THE BATTLE OF PAARDEBERG.*

<small>Cronje's situation night of 17th Feb., 1900.</small>

By the night of the 17th of February the plight of Cronje had again become critical. The road to Bloemfontein ran along the left or southern bank of the Modder, but his wagons, and nearly all his men lay on the right bank east and west of Vendutie Drift. This ford might still be used; for the fire of French's guns, which had denied him the passage during the day, would be ineffective at night. The other principal crossings over the Modder immediately above and below Vendutie, were held or threatened by British troops, and he did not know that the total strength of the detachments at these fords was little more than half that of his own commandos. A party of the "despatch riders,"† who had come again into favour, were now acting as links between him and the other Boer leaders in the west of the Free State. He was aware, therefore, that although the main body of the besiegers of Kimberley had retreated across the Vaal, Ferreira was still but a short march from him to the north, and that Ferreira had realised that it was incumbent on him not altogether to desert his colleague. An urgent appeal for help, which Cronje had sent to Bloemfontein before evacuating Magersfontein, had alarmed President Steyn, who was now diverting to the westward the reinforcements from Natal, originally destined to strengthen the commandos round Colesberg. To the south De Wet had been joined at Koffyfontein by the detachments sent from Bloemfontein to oppose a British advance on the capital. Thus it seemed not impossible that

<small>* See maps Nos. 22, 23 and 23 (a).   † See page 17.</small>

THE BATTLE OF PAARDEBERG. 107

another twenty-four hours might place at Cronje's disposal four or five thousand additional burghers, though for the moment he had under his hand only about five thousand men.

The gathering of his friends was known to Cronje. He could hardly be aware to how great an extent the numbers available for his release had been lessened by Lord Roberts' original success in imposing, not only on him himself, but on all the Boer leaders. President Steyn and De Wet had both been deceived as to the proposed plan of campaign. The delusion still had its effect. The earlier marches southward on Ramdam had actually achieved their purpose in keeping up the false impression that the blow was aimed at Bloemfontein *viâ* Koffyfontein and Petrusburg. Hence, when Cronje's danger was at last realised, much time had been lost by the movement of Boer forces in a wrong direction. As will be seen later, nervousness as to the safety of Bloemfontein made credible every rumour which reported a direct advance upon it. Up to the last De Wet, still fearing lest Roberts should swoop upon the capital, did not venture to strike with his full strength to the help of Cronje. He therefore greatly, perhaps for him fatally, reduced the forces which he ultimately led to the aid of his former chief.* *Reinforcements coming to him;*

Obviously, a crucial question pressed for Cronje's prompt decision. Should he attempt by a night march once more to shake himself clear of his pursuers, or should he give battle where he was, trusting to beat off their attack by the help of the outside aid which he might reasonably expect on the following day? With the exception of Commandant De Beer, who, from his post on Koodoosrand† urged him to move his laager thither, all his subordinates wished by a night march to avoid the risk of capture. They were supported by Ferreira, who sent an urgent message imploring Cronje to break out northward. If the Boer General had been content to abandon his wagons and their loads it would have been easy enough for the fighting men to slip away under cover of darkness. But besides the objection to this, which the presence in the laager of women and children forced home on men trained in the traditions of savage warfare, *he determines not to abandon his transport;*

* See page 135. † See page 100.

the loss of transport was in the eyes of the burghers a far more serious matter than it had been in those of Lord Roberts three days earlier. All the transport was the property, not of the State, but of the farmers themselves, and in many cases formed a large part of their capital and means of livelihood. Some of the Boer convoy might possibly have crossed to the left bank by Vendutie Drift during the night and thus escaped. But there were not enough oxen available for the whole of it; some had been shot, others had been scattered over the veld. Though Cronje had abandoned seventy-eight wagons at Bosjespan on the night of the 15th-16th, he now set his face against imposing any further loss on his followers. He refused to move, and resolved to repeat the tactics he had employed against Lord Methuen at Modder River by turning the bed of the stream into a fortification, of which a laager along the river east and west of Vendutie Drift was to be the central point.

and to hold the bed of the river.

The position. The laager lay at the bottom of a basin about nine miles long by six miles wide, the rim of which is formed by a series of well-defined kopjes, whence the ground slopes gently down towards the Modder. On hills, on the left or southern bank, the British artillery could be placed within easy range of the river, while to the north French's guns, whose shells had stopped the passage, were extended along the ridge near Kameelfontein. Across the plain thus enclosed the Modder winds its way, entering the basin at the east by a gorge under the southern slopes of Koodoosrand, and emerging at the west by a defile between Paardeberg and Signal Hills. The banks have here the same characteristics as those on the battle-field of "Modder River." *
The stream runs at the bottom of a channel about fifty yards wide, and thirty or forty feet deep. Its sloping sides are thickly covered with mimosa, thorn, and other bushes. In places thickets of these shrubs overlap the banks and spread for some distance into the plain, which is otherwise bare and shelterless. Into the Modder run numberless dongas which are a formidable series of natural defences. Difficult to search with shrapnel, and thickly covered with thorn, they present

* See Volume I., Chapter XV.

THE BATTLE OF PAARDEBERG. 109

successive lines of natural shelter trenches obstructing attacks along the course of the river. With one exception, that of the "big donga," south-west of Gun Hill, they are too small to be shown on the general map of Paardeberg (No. 23), but those on the eastern part of the battle-field are marked on map No. 24, which illustrates the work carried out by the Royal Engineers during the investment following the battle of the 18th. Within the basin there are several fords: the most eastern is Koodoos, then come in succession, Banks, Vanderberg, Vendutie and Paardeberg Drifts. Recent heavy rains had caused the stream to rise, and to make its passage, even at the fords, a matter of considerable difficulty. By two ponts near Vendutie Drift connection was kept up between the main body of the Boers on the right bank and four hundred men who were detached to the south of the river.

During the night a few hundred burghers who disapproved of Cronje's determination to hold his ground deserted the laager. Some joined De Beer on Koodoosrand, others made straight for their own homes. The remainder of Cronje's men worked incessantly to strengthen a naturally favourable fighting ground. So many of their picks and shovels had been abandoned at Magersfontein that digging was a matter of great difficulty, and, in the words of one of the defenders they "dug themselves in with their cleaning rods and their fingers." But by the morning they were well protected from fire in pits sunk into the soft earth of the river bank, and had made trenches running all along the top of the right bank, the higher of the two, for about a mile and a half above Vendutie Drift, and on the left bank for about half that distance. A mound of earth was thrown up to protect the wagons still on the open veld. The dongas and the patches of bush which project into the plain were lined with riflemen, some of whom climbed into the trees, tying themselves to the branches in order to obtain a steady aim. The guns were on the right bank. Thus the Boer position, though encircled and commanded by higher ground, formed a closed redoubt of considerable strength in the centre near Vendutie Drift, while for a much greater length the pits in the river banks

Cronje's men "dig themselves in."

brought an effective grazing fire to bear over the plain both north and south. This was flanked by fire, practically at right angles, from the dongas; and in particular the big donga on the north bank, with the pits in the river bank on either side of it, was a formidable outwork which must be captured before the laager could be approached from the west.

Lord Roberts' warning of counter-attack on 18th or 19th.

The actual knowledge which the Intelligence Staff with Lord Roberts at Jacobsdal had of the enemy's strength, dispositions, and intentions may be seen in the précis of information already quoted on page 89, and from the following telegram sent by Lord Roberts to the Chief of the Staff on the 17th.

"Jacobsdal,
"17th February, 1900.

"No. C 128. Cipher. A man who was with Cronje yesterday states that reinforcements of one thousand men are expected to join him to-morrow or next day from Colesberg, and the same number from Ladysmith. That Cronje's object is to go northward to invest Kimberley again from the north when joined by Bredenbach, who is some distance westwards. That the five thousand Orange Free State men with Cronje will go to Bloemfontein. That food with Cronje's convoy is scarce, and that many of his oxen are done up. He states that there is a depôt of supplies near Kalkfontein left behind by Cronje for want of cattle to draw the wagons. He states also that Cronje was very nearly surrounded by our troops yesterday and that he has to go through the night to Paardeberg Drift."

Kitchener's choice of plans;

To meet the situation with which, on the night of the 17th-18th, Lord Kitchener was confronted, two courses were open. One was to invest the enemy's position closely and shell him into surrender. The other was to assault the river fortress at once. To the first alternative the configuration of the Paardeberg basin was favourable, and when the guns of the VIth and IXth divisions were added to French's brigade division of Horse artillery, they would suffice for a heavy and sustained bombardment, which would enfilade the Boer works from various points. But, on the other hand, though it would have been comparatively easy to have encircled the laager during the day, there would not have been time to entrench the enveloping line so securely as to prevent a resolute and still partially mobile enemy from dashing through it in the night and joining hands with the reinforce-

THE BATTLE OF PAARDEBERG.

ments on the way to his assistance, while time would have been given to an enterprising commander to organise these into a formidable relieving force.

Lord Kitchener decided to attack. An immediate attack, even if it failed to carry the laager, would, by destroying or dispersing the remaining horses and oxen, dispirit the defenders, and chain them to the river bed; bombardment alone, without such an attack, could hardly achieve those decisive results, for the sake of which it is often necessary to face the heaviest losses. Unfortunately for the carrying out of Lord Kitchener's design much was wanting. Troops, perhaps in sufficient numbers for the purpose, were under his orders, but a General is in no efficient sense in command of an army because he can issue orders which must be obeyed when they are received. At this moment in particular unity of action was essential to success. Now unity could only be given by nerves connecting the brain of the man himself with every part of the great body which he had to direct, or, rather, to inspire. An army in modern fight needs to be an organism rather than a machine. It was that which, in the late war between Russia and Japan, gave to the smaller Empire most of its advantage. The Russian army was a machine, the Japanese army an organism. Exact verbal words of command could not possibly be applied at Paardeberg. Yet for success the purpose of the commander must be so consistently carried out everywhere that every part of the army should co-operate to the common end. Therefore there were needed everywhere those who could communicate, as nearly as possible at every period, to each unit the part it was at that time to play in the wide combination. Moreover, it was essential that those thus employed should have had the training by actual practice to catch quickly and interpret correctly the idea in the mind of their chief; that they should know one another, and know, at least, the most important of the leaders with whom they had to deal. Furthermore, it was especially to be wished that they should be aware of the limits of their own functions. For the whole method of army organisation is designed to facilitate the otherwise impossible task of one man in combining thousands

his decision.

Kitchener's lack of a staff and its effect on the action.

in a common purpose. The system of battalions, regiments, brigades, divisions, all tends to reduce the difficulty by limiting the number of those by whom the mind of the chief commander must be understood. His own staff, if long trained under him, is able to watch over the execution of his ideas ; but the cases are very rare and must be very important where they will not do mischief by interfering with the orders actually given by subordinate commanders, responsible to the chief for a special part in the general design. It is almost certain that they will do mischief if, for instance, they change, in the name of their master, orders given to some unit which has already been assigned a task by its own Brigadier or divisional General without informing such subordinate General of the change. Consequences that they cannot foresee may follow to much larger bodies because for an apparently wise purpose they have seized on a particular body of men. Now, from the circumstances detailed in the last chapter, Lord Kitchener entirely lacked any staff adequate to watch over for him the general scope of the action. Such staff as he had was not in itself an organised body accustomed to carry out with self-restraint and in unison his design. All of those consequences followed which have been suggested above. Their disastrous effect upon the day was conspicuous. Young staff officers did what was right in their own eyes to the shattering of combinations of the nature of which they were not aware. It was possibly also unfortunate that the character of the campaign in Egypt had not brought home to Lord Kitchener himself the evil effects of such intrusive action. All this tended to break up the battle into a series of isolated disconnected actions in which the design is lost in the detail. The interest of unity and the gradual working out of a definite scheme is wanting throughout ; but as an illustration of the kind of combination required in modern times, it is exceptionally valuable from the obvious results which followed from the very chaos. It was as far as Lord Kitchener was concerned a gallant attempt to substitute his own vigorous personality for the missing agency of command.

Yet another factor which influenced the results, not of this

THE BATTLE OF PAARDEBERG.

day only, but of many, must be understood before the detail can be intelligible. It was observed during the Franco-German war that the several units which came successively under the entirely novel experience created by the new weapons had, at least up to the battle of Gravelotte, each to pick up their own mode of meeting them for themselves. It was practically impossible for them to receive, soon enough, instruction in the modifications which had been adopted by others in the stress of fighting. Substantially the same thing occurred in South Africa. Lord Roberts had taken exceptional pains to impart to his army the deductions to be drawn from the earlier phase of the war. Of his anxiety to do so the papers published at the end of Volume I., under the heading of "Notes for Guidance in South African Warfare," are sufficient evidence. It may be doubted how far these had reached all those who would most have profited by them, and how far they had been read, marked, learned, and inwardly digested by those of the newly-arrived units who had received them. Yet they had been issued before he moved forward to the Riet. At any rate, it is certain that neither at Paardeberg nor elsewhere were the peculiarities of the new form of fighting recognised by those who had not been hitherto engaged. They, like the Germans in 1870, had to find out for themselves the special strength and weakness of their opponents, the conditions imposed by the new weapons, and the various artifices which after a few trials had already been applied by those who had become accustomed to the special tactics of the Boers. *The freshly arrived troops lack the experience acquired by those previously engaged in the new form of warfare.*

The intentions of Lord Kitchener are clear enough, and they were as simple as possible. He proposed from the south bank to engage and occupy the attention of the Boers whilst he attacked the laager from both west and east—that is, up stream and down stream. In general terms it was, as he telegraphed to Lord Roberts at 8 a.m., to the VIth division and General Kelly-Kenny that he entrusted the frontal action from the south against the Boers. For the movement down stream from the east it would be necessary for some force first to move up stream along the southern bank, and then cross the river high *Kitchener's plan of action.*

enough up to be clear of Boer opposition. He proposed to send for this purpose Hannay's mounted infantry, the most quickly moving troops at his disposal. He therefore required additional infantry support for them. It was easiest to obtain this from Stephenson's brigade* of the VIth division, which lay nearest to the Boers' outer flank up stream. Therefore, only one brigade, the 13th (Knox), with one battalion (the Yorkshire), of Stephenson's, out of the VIth division, were, in fact, to be employed in the frontal engagement from the south, whilst Hannay, supported by Stephenson with his other two battalions, the Welsh and Essex, was to form the attacking force down stream from the east. For the movement up stream from the west, where the greater part of the troops already were, much larger bodies were to be employed; in fact, all that remained to him, viz.: Lieut.-General Colvile's division. Of its two brigades, the whole of the 19th (Smith-Dorrien) was to cross the river at Paardeberg Drift, and work up stream along the right bank, making a wide turning movement, while the 3rd, the Highland brigade, marched eastward along the river. It seems to have been left to the discretion of the brigadier of the Highlanders, Major-General MacDonald, whether he should make his way along the left bank only or along both. In order that this movement from the west by General Colvile's division should not be without some mounted men, two of Hannay's six mounted infantry corps were to be left with it. Thus, according to the original intention, the laager was to be assailed simultaneously from east and west, down stream from the east by four mounted infantry corps and by two battalions of infantry, to whom were assigned the 81st battery and later the 76th. It was to be assailed up stream from the west by the whole of General Colvile's division (the IXth) and by two mounted infantry corps, to whom were attached the 82nd battery. The remainder of the artillery of both Lieut.-General Kelly-Kenny's and Lieut.-General Colvile's divisions was to take advantage of the hills on the south bank, so as to prepare the way for the infantry attack by a vigorous bombardment. Un-

* Bt.-Colonel T. E. Stephenson, 1st battalion Essex regiment, was acting Brigadier-General of the 18th brigade.

THE BATTLE OF PAARDEBERG. 115

fortunately the Boers in the river banks and dongas were quite invisible, and only the laager with its wagons and cattle was an object sufficiently conspicuous for artillery fire. Thus from the nature of the scheme the story of the fight divides itself into the following periods. Firstly, the period of preparation, during which Hannay was moving from west to east, so as to place himself on the extreme further flank from that whence he started, and was followed in that direction by Stephenson with his two battalions, the Welsh and Essex; while during the same period the larger part of the VIth division was closing in on the river, and on the west MacDonald with his brigade was moving up stream from Paardeberg Drift, so as to approach the laager from the west, while Smith-Dorrien's brigade was engaged in crossing to the right bank. Secondly, the period when Lord Kitchener, considering that the preparatory movements were sufficiently advanced, endeavoured to bring about simultaneous attacks on the laager from east and west. Both Cronje and his assailants had every reason to expect the coming of the outside Boers. These even when led by Steyn during the first period, that of preparation, had hampered both Stephenson and Hannay and made the attack from the east abortive. During the third period they assumed under De Wet a dangerously aggressive attitude, and so drew to themselves from the attack on the laager the attention of the Headquarter Staff. Fourth came the period of spasmodic attempts of small parties, started under orders given during the second period, and necessarily futile because the guiding hand was withdrawn. *Four phases of the battle. De Wet's attack to be expected both by Cronje and Kitchener.*

In all this it is clear that the real object of the attack was the laager and, though perhaps some outlying parties of Boers were expected, the movements along the stream were regarded as mere means of approaching the laager—Cronje's supposed stronghold. The dongas and river banks being covered with scrub, and therefore hardly visible, it was not realised that it was on them that the Boers mainly relied for their defence. Nor was this Lord Kitchener's idea alone. It may be seen, for instance, in the character of the formation adopted by MacDonald in his handling of the Highland brigade. This *The whole idea of the assailants was an attack on the laager; the danger from the river and dongas being only discovered later.*

VOL. II. 8*

116   THE WAR IN SOUTH AFRICA.

was admirably suited to enable him to take advantage of the river bank in order to move eastward, but quite unsuited for turning the enemy out of pits along the two banks and in the dongas.

<small>Kitchener's plan formed, and set in action without seeing Kelly-Kenny or Colvile who, before they hear from him, act.</small>

One other element in the circumstances of the battle must be taken into account. Lord Kitchener, with a most prompt grasp of the situation, had realised that the one thing that was essential was to capture Cronje's whole force. To do that either at once or later, and at least on this day to bend all his energies to the attainment of that end, was clearly his duty. Therefore he must act quickly. He formed his plan of action accordingly, and determined to put it into execution forthwith. At 3 a.m., the time when he issued his earliest orders to Hannay, he had seen neither General Kelly-Kenny nor General Colvile. Colvile himself had, in fact, only just arrived. Lord Roberts' warning, that Boers from outside were expected, tended to hasten Kitchener in pressing the attack. Unfortunately, from the weakness of his staff, both of his divisional generals, equally eager to deal quickly with the situation, and knowing nothing of what he intended to do, had already begun to act long before any instructions from him reached them. The peculiar relations of authority between him and General Kelly-Kenny made this matter the more serious.

<small>First period—preliminaries.</small>

Lord Kitchener, at about 3 a.m. on the 18th—nearly three hours before sunrise—sent for Colonel Hannay, and gave him the following verbal orders. Leaving two of the mounted infantry corps at Paardeberg Drift to reconnoitre the western part of the enemy's position, Hannay, with the remainder of his brigade, was to march eastward before dawn and cross to the right bank of the river, between Vendutie and Koodoos Drifts. These were the only two fords marked on the Staff map and, though the cavalry had discovered Vanderberg and Banks Drifts on the 17th, the Chief of the Staff had not yet received any report from Lieut.-General French, and therefore was not aware of their existence. When over the river Hannay was to wait until an attack from the west had developed. He then was to assault the laager from the east, and would be supported by

<small>Hannay receives his orders 3 a.m.</small>

THE BATTLE OF PAARDEBERG. 117

an infantry brigade. Artillery was to prepare the way. Meantime Hannay was to ascertain the exact places occupied by the enemy in the river bed and report them by signal so that they could be enfiladed by the British guns on both banks. The danger lest the eastern attack should suffer from the fire of the western was discussed, but it was agreed that the bending of the river made this improbable.

Hannay marched about 4 a.m. to carry out the movement from the east; he had with him the 4th, 5th, and 6th mounted infantry, and was shortly followed by the New South Wales mounted infantry. He detailed the 2nd and 7th mounted infantry to help in the western operations. A company of the 7th forded Paardeberg Drift and ascertained by dawn that the bend of the river immediately south of Gun Hill was held by the Boers in some strength. At sunrise the Chief of the Staff rode to the summit of Signal Hill, whence a good view could be obtained of the whole scene of action. He was there joined by Lieut.-General Kelly-Kenny, who was still in executive command of all troops, except French's cavalry. *[marginal: Hannay marches upstream 4 a.m. leaving 2nd and 7th mounted infantry at Paardeberg Drift.]*

Kelly-Kenny had already directed his brigades, the 13th (Knox) and 18th (Stephenson), the 18th leading, to move from their bivouac near Paardeberg Drift across the ford on to the right bank. The Yorkshire, acting as advance guard, was on the march, when, by Lord Kitchener's desire, these orders were cancelled, and those for his scheme issued. The 76th and 81st batteries, with a Naval 12-pr. gun (which broke down subsequently and was out of action all day), were sent to the long spur north-east of Signal Hill. Thence they fired against the laager at a range of 2,700 yards. Their shells set on fire many ox wagons, in which a certain amount of the Boers' small-arm ammunition was destroyed. Brigadier-General Stephenson next received his orders to take the Welsh and Essex, under cover of the artillery, up the left bank of the river. It is, however, important to realise that, whether from one of the many failures in the correct carrying of verbal orders or from some other cause, General Stephenson never understood that it was his particular duty to support Hannay, whose name was, he says, never *[marginal: Kelly-Kenny puts his division in motion to cross to right bank. 18th brigade, less Yorkshire, follows Hannay. Stephenson not informed of the intention that he is to join Hannay in attack on laager down stream.]*

mentioned to him. This, among other things, accounts for the fact that, as will be seen, he became engaged with the Boers at Vendutie Drift, the very point which Hannay was to avoid. Yet Hannay had been told that an infantry brigade was to support him, and Stephenson's brigade, small as it was, is the only one that could have been meant by Lord Kitchener. Stephenson seems to have understood that he was merely acting as the right flank of the VIth division along the river front.

A dramatic incident attended Stephenson's march, and the movement forward of the whole VIth division. The troops, weary from long marching and parched with thirst—there had been no opportunity to refill water-bottles since the afternoon of the 17th—were trudging on grimly. They began to descend into the valley, when suddenly the rising sun, glinting on the great mass of wagons about Vendutie Drift, and on French's Horse artillery batteries on the northern slopes beyond those wagons, disclosed both their evasive foe and the friendly force which barred his further progress. They thus for the first time became all at once aware that Cronje lay actually within their grasp. The joy of seeing with their own eyes that they had at last caught up the Boers, and that all their past toil was not in vain, showed itself on every face. Fatigue, hunger, thirst were forgotten. The men only asked to be allowed to close on their enemy. The elation caused by seeing the burghers reduced to immobility, and by the knowledge that they were forced to give battle, ran through all ranks and produced a desire for immediate attack which had an important effect on the conduct of the engagement. Nothing could be better than the spirit of the men, but the experiences at Modder River Bridge threatened to be repeated, and they largely were so.

The troops elated by sight of Boer laager and French's guns.

The Yorkshire regiment, under Kelly-Kenny's order to cross the Modder, had almost reached it under heavy fire before it was stopped. Retracing its steps, it deployed on the left front of the guns, about 1,500 yards from the stream, and lay down to await further orders. The trenches which faced it, with the exception of a few near Vendutie Drift, were all on the right bank, but for the moment it was almost impossible to ascertain from whence the

Yorkshire, recalled from crossing river, deploys; cattle concealing all view.

THE BATTLE OF PAARDEBERG. 119

enemy's bullets came, for the plain was covered with cattle. When the guns began to play upon the banks of the Modder, the Kaffir herdsmen in charge of a large number of trek oxen, concealed by the burghers in the bed of the river, took fright and drove the cattle before them into the British lines. Then it was seen by what extreme exertion Cronje had succeeded in evading the pursuit of the last three days. The animals were mere skin and bone, covered with sores, and utterly worn out. Major-General Knox (13th brigade), who had, meanwhile, been directed to hold the enemy in front without committing himself to a close attack, deployed on the left of the Yorkshire. The Oxfordshire Light Infantry and the West Riding formed his first line. Each battalion had two companies in the firing line extended to ten paces interval, with the other companies as local supports and reserves. Between the firing line, supports, and reserves, there were distances of about eighty yards. Four hundred yards further back was the brigade reserve, half a battalion of the Buffs, the remainder of which battalion, and the Gloucester, less two companies escorting the guns, guarded the divisional transport. *13th brigade, with Yorkshire, deploys along the front.*

Though the 3rd (Highland) brigade reached the neighbourhood of Paardeberg Drift shortly before midnight on the 17th, it was not until the small hours of the 18th that the whole of the IXth division (Colvile) had assembled there. As neither the divisional commander nor his staff had any knowledge of the local situation, Colonel J. S. Ewart, A.A.G., was directed to reconnoitre. After an abortive attempt to cross Paardeberg Drift, he worked up the left bank of the Modder, discovered the site of Cronje's laager, and ascertained that parties of Boers were making their way from it down the river bed. Soon after Ewart had brought back this information to his General, Lieut.-Colonel Martyr, about 5 a.m., reported that the 2nd mounted infantry, one of the corps left by Hannay at the drift, was under fire from the enemy in the bush near the ford. He added that the river was high, hardly passable by infantry, and that several of his horses had been drowned in crossing the drift. The division at once stood to their arms, while Colvile rode off to *Laager and position of Boers along river ascertained by Colvile.*

Colvile, on long spur, has Paardeberg Drift prepared for passage.

the long spur to study the ground. In the dim light of earliest dawn he saw the importance of the ridge on which he stood, and, not having received any orders from Kelly-Kenny or Kitchener, sent for the 65th Howitzer battery, with an escort of half a battalion of Highlanders. His divisional transport, guarded by the Duke of Cornwall's Light Infantry, was ordered to move sufficiently far south of Paardeberg Drift to be sheltered from the enemy's projectiles. Colonel J. C. Barker, Royal Engineers, of the IXth division, was told to make provision for the passage of troops across the river near Paardeberg Drift. As the pontoons had been left at Jacobsdal from lack of transport, the only bridging material immediately at hand was one section of a James' collapsible boat. In this the Royal Engineers carried a rope across the Modder, and then ran some wagons into the ford to break the force of the current. While these various movements were being executed, the burghers attempted to drive the 2nd and 7th mounted infantry from their post in the river bed near Paardeberg Drift. To meet this development Colvile ordered MacDonald (3rd brigade) to clear the enemy out of the scrub and thickets which fringed the left bank above the ford. Hardly had the Highland brigade, less the Highland Light Infantry still at Klip Drift, been set in motion, when an officer brought a verbal message to Colvile from the Chief of the Staff. It was so conveyed that while Kitchener intended it merely to order Colvile to prolong Kelly-Kenny's line of guns with his divisional artillery, Colvile understood it to mean that he was to reinforce Kelly-Kenny with the whole of his troops. He at once ordered the 65th Howitzer and the 82nd Field batteries to the eastward, and sent to Lord Kitchener to say that the infantry brigades would follow as soon as they had driven the enemy out of the bush on the left bank.

Burghers threaten Paardeberg Drift.

Colvile sends Highlanders to drive enemy from banks of river above Paardeberg Drift.

A misunderstanding.

MacDonald moves up the left bank.

The counter-attack on the mounted infantry at Paardeberg Drift was increasing in strength. MacDonald, thinking that he could best deal with it if he placed his brigade further to the east before engaging the burghers in the bush, moved up the river in three parallel columns, each in single file, with four paces between the men. Nearest the river marched the Argyll and

THE BATTLE OF PAARDEBERG.   121

Sutherland Highlanders, followed by the Black Watch; six companies of the Seaforth formed the second column, the remaining two companies of that battalion the third. The 82nd Field battery was recalled at 7.30 a.m. from the eastward by Colvile, and took post on the left of the Howitzer and 76th Field batteries.

Since daybreak, Colvile had been anxious to throw a portion of his force across the river, but he did not know whether such a movement would harmonise with Lord Kitchener's plans until 8.30 a.m., when an explicit order reached him to push the 19th brigade and the 82nd Field battery across Paardeberg Drift to the north bank. The execution of this order began about 9 a.m. Movements on the east (*i.e.*, the right) and in the centre of the line had preceded it by several hours. *19th brigade and a battery sent to right bank 8.30 a.m.*

The march of Hannay's mounted infantry towards Koodoos Drift had been interrupted in the grey of the morning by heavy musketry from trenches south of Vendutie Drift, which, falling unexpectedly upon Kitchener's Horse, then acting as a flanking guard, threw the corps into some confusion. Hannay left part of the regiment to face the burghers in these trenches and rode on with the remainder of his brigade till he came level with the large kopje, now known as Kitchener's Kopje, which, rising some three hundred feet above the plain, commands the river and the plain on either side of it, and is the key to the whole battlefield. Here he dropped the 4th mounted infantry and a squadron of Kitchener's Horse, to occupy the kopje, and to hold the little homestead of Osfontein which lies to the east of the hill. This detachment soon became engaged with parties of burghers, who suddenly appeared from the eastward and seized Stinkfontein and the hill to the south of that farm. Soon after 6.30 a.m., two staff officers, one from Lieut.-General Kelly-Kenny, the other from the Chief of the Staff, brought Hannay instructions to occupy any fords he might find between Vendutie and Koodoos Drifts. Exchanging shots with the enemy across the river as he marched, he reached Vanderberg Drift; and, halting on the left bank, sent a company of the 6th mounted infantry across the Modder, where they obtained touch with a squadron of the 12th Lancers from French's force. Two other companies of the 6th *Hannay under fire on his march to Koodoos Drift. Hannay occupies Kitchener's Kopje and Vanderberg Drift; and joins hands with French.*

mounted infantry protected Hannay's right flank from De Beer's commando on Koodoosrand, and seized the crossing at Banks Drift. When Brigadier-General Stephenson with the Welsh and Essex, following Hannay's movement up the river from west to east, reached the ground held by the party of Kitchener's Horse which was engaging the Boers at Vendutie Drift, he reinforced them with two companies of the Welsh. Then, attracted by the musketry of the parties of Boers who from the east of Kitchener's Kopje were firing at the 4th mounted infantry, he deployed facing towards Stinkfontein. Not long after this deployment had been completed the Chief of the Staff sent him orders to collect his two battalions and to "push in on the laager." Stephenson accordingly turned his men about and marched towards the river.

To check parties of Boers 18th brigade faces Stinkfontein, but is ordered to move on laager.

It was not until 7.15 a.m., while these various movements were in progress, that Lord Kitchener's signallers succeeded in opening communication with Lieut.-General French, who shortly afterwards heliographed as follows:—

Communication opened with French by heliograph.

"Koodoos Drift was found about noon yesterday strongly held. I at once occupied Kameelfontein Farm, pushed left out towards the river, and my right is on the hill. Have shelled the enemy since noon yesterday. He has not moved a wagon since our arrival. Enemy appears to be in force along edge of laager facing north. My horses and men are nearly worn out."

This heliogram crossed a message from Kelly-Kenny asking French to prevent the Boers from escaping northwards. A squadron of the 12th Lancers was accordingly sent to reconnoitre towards Koodoos Drift, and cleared the north of the Koodoosrand of the enemy. Two squadrons of the Carabiniers were also sent to examine the ground north of the drift, but the fire from the detachment of De Beer's commando on the south of the ridge compelled them to remain in the plain half way between Banks Drift and Kameelfontein, watching the Koodoosrand throughout the day. By 8 a.m. the manœuvres of the infantry and guns on the south bank could be seen by French's divisional staff, who became aware that the troops were hotly engaged. The Horse artillery of the cavalry division shelled the laager

THE BATTLE OF PAARDEBERG. 123

during the action from the position it had occupied since the 17th.

The Chief of the Staff's appreciation of the tactical situation at this hour was set forth in the following telegram to Lord Roberts :— *8 a.m. Kitchener describes situation.*

" From Lord Kitchener,
    " Cable Cart, Front.
" To Lord Roberts.
                            " 18th February, 1900. 8 a.m.
" We have stopped the enemy's convoy on the river here. General Kelly-Kenny's division is holding them to the south, enemy lining bank of Modder, convoy stationary in our immediate front. General Colvile's division has arrived and they are putting one brigade and one battery on the north side of the river, and one brigade and one Howitzer battery on the south side and will march eastward, up stream. The mounted infantry have gone round, and hold the river on our right flank. I have been in heliographic communication with General French, who is opposite to us, in rear of the enemy's position; he is now moving down on opposite bank on our right flank. The enemy is thus completely surrounded and I think it must be a case of complete surrender. Will keep you informed as events occur."

To this telegram the Commander-in-Chief replied :—

" To Major-General Lord Kitchener,
    " *viâ* Klip Drift.
                            " Jacobsdal,
                            " 18th February, 1900.
" Your news is most satisfactory; I am sending off at once Chermside's brigade and the brigade of Guards and will be at Klip Drift myself early to-morrow. These troops can push on should reinforcements reach Cronje before you have defeated him. Ask Kenny and Colvile to tell their troops that I count on them to make this business a brilliant success."

Thus by 8 a.m. preparations were everywhere in hand for a combined assault on the Boer entrenchments from the east and west, while Knox's brigade (13th) and the Yorkshire were ready to move towards the works on the south bank, and engage the enemy's attention while his flanks were being enveloped. The Yorkshire, with four companies extended as firing line and supports, and the remainder in reserve, advanced towards the river by rushes of alternate sections, covered at first by section *8 a.m. 13th brigade and Yorkshire advance towards river.*

volleys and afterwards by individual firing. No Boers could be seen, though their bullets caused many casualties, including Lieut.-Colonel H. Bowles, who was severely wounded. In the absence of any definite target, the musketry of the Yorkshire was turned on the edge of the bushes fringing the river, amongst which it was supposed that the enemy lay in rifle pits. Gradually reinforced by the supports and the reserve, by 9 a.m. the attack was carried to within two hundred yards of the river bank. A party of five officers and about sixty men then dashed forward, and reached the river, but found it impassable. One officer and many of the men of this detachment were killed, when the rest took cover in the dongas.* While this was taking place, the main body of the Yorkshire had received orders from divisional Headquarters to halt in the position which it had reached at 9 a.m. There it remained till nightfall. The West Riding, in very extended lines, reached the broken ground near the long spur, where they obtained a certain amount of cover. Here their commanding officer, Lieut.-Colonel G. E. Lloyd, who had been warned not to press the attack home, halted for orders. The Oxfordshire Light Infantry followed on the left of the West Riding, until its right flank joined the left of that battalion. Then the greater part of the West Riding, with a detachment of the Oxfordshire, worked their way towards the river, and at 11.45, by a charge, drove the Boers out of the trenches. A definite message was then received from Lieut.-General Kelly-Kenny, forbidding them to cross the river, as he was fully convinced that any such attempt at this point would result in disaster. The West Riding, therefore, took cover in the dongas. About noon Major-General Knox was wounded.

On the left, the main body of the Oxfordshire Light Infantry succeeded in reaching within four hundred yards of the Modder, but could then make no further progress. Thus Knox's brigade (13th), with the help of the Yorkshire, very thoroughly carried out, if it did not indeed exceed, the duty of holding the enemy

---

* Sergt. A. Atkinson here was mortally wounded while carrying water to his wounded comrades. He was awarded the Victoria Cross (posthumous) for his gallantry on this occasion.

THE BATTLE OF PAARDEBERG.

on the left bank.* Towards evening many of the men, desperate from want of water, left cover and dashed down to the river, to drink and to fill their water-bottles. At first not a few were shot down, but when the Boers realised that they were not coming on with any aggressive purpose, but only to satisfy their thirst, they were chivalrous enough to allow them to do so unharmed. <small>A war courtesy.</small>

The Highland brigade was also engaged on Knox's left. MacDonald in his march eastward up the river had arrived near to the 13th brigade, when about 8 a.m. he came under such heavy musketry from the banks that he was obliged to turn to the left and face the enemy. He thus committed himself to a direct attack across open and coverless ground against the southern face of the Boers' position. Marching as he had been in his three straggling columns, his formation when he now fronted the river was ill adapted for an advance against a well-entrenched enemy. The attack, delivered in a formation which lacked the depth necessary for success against a strong position, could not be forced home. The Argyll and Sutherland Highlanders overlapped the left of Knox's brigade, and many of them gradually thrust their way into its ranks. The Black Watch and Seaforth Highlanders attacked more to the west, and did not intermingle to any large extent with the 13th brigade. The Black Watch, and some of the Argyll and Sutherland, partially reinforced by the Seaforth, pushed to within four hundred yards of the river, but then, about 9 a.m., were completely checked by the heavy fire from the trenches. When the Highland brigade was thus brought to a standstill, MacDonald's troops extended further down the Modder than did the right of the Boer works, and the Major-General determined to work up the river bed and attack these trenches in flank. The first step was to collect such of his brigade as were not pinned fast to the ground by the enemy's musketry. Two companies and a half of the Black Watch and two companies of the Seaforth were led by Major E. B. Urmston, brigade-major, to the river, several hundred yards below the big donga. Under heavy fire the <small>Highland brigade advances on river, 8 a.m.</small> <small>Detachments of Highland brigade attempt to work up stream on right bank towards the laager.</small>

* See Kitchener's telegram, page 123.

two companies of the Black Watch and one of the Seaforth succeeded in crossing, by joining hands and so making a chain to stem the force of the current. They were supported by parties of the 7th mounted infantry already on the right bank, and reinforced by a mixed body of Black Watch and Seaforth, who forded the river lower down. On the left bank other parties of mounted infantry joined in the fight. Through broken ground, covered with bush, the men on both banks pushed eastwards against the big donga. They had gained some ground, and were within a few hundred yards of it when the attack gradually withered up. Most of the officers with Urmston had been killed or wounded; the casualties among the men had been heavy, and those still uninjured were tired out. Urmston did not know that the 19th brigade had been ordered to cross the river, and in the bush in which he found himself it was impossible to see any of Smith-Dorrien's troops. Thus, checked on both sides of the river, and without adequate reinforcements, the 3rd brigade could do no more than remain until nightfall extended within effective range of the enemy's position. During the day the Black Watch lost about twenty, and the Seaforth about twenty-six per cent. of their strength. Major-General MacDonald was wounded, and the command devolved on Lieut.-Colonel J. W. Hughes-Hallett.

19th brigade on the right bank. Before Lieut.-General Colvile received Lord Kitchener's order to throw the 19th brigade (Smith Dorrien) across the Modder, the Royal Engineers had done their best to render Paardeberg Drift passable for infantry. At 9 a.m. the troops began to cross, the 2nd Shropshire Light Infantry leading, followed by the 82nd Field battery, the 1st Gordon Highlanders, and the Royal Canadian regiment. The water was waist-high, and the current was strong. Each section of fours linked arms together and the right-hand men steadied themselves by the rope stretched by the Engineers across the ford. By 10.15 a.m. the column had reached the right bank without casualties. The three machine guns which accompanied it were carried across in the James' boat. No specific instructions had been given to Major-General Smith-Dorrien, but he soon observed that Gun Hill

THE BATTLE OF PAARDEBERG.

commanded the valley and would, if not held by us, enable the Boers to flank and enfilade an attack on the laager from the westward. Seeing that the occupation of this hill was therefore essential, he directed the five leading companies of the 2nd Shropshire, under Lieut.-Colonel J. Spens, to advance to the north-east until they could move forward against the north-western slopes of the hill. The 82nd battery and the Gordon Highlanders followed on the left flank of the Shropshire. Immediately after they had crossed the drift two companies of the Shropshire Light Infantry and the whole of the Canadian regiment had been ordered to wheel to the right and support and prolong the attack which was being made by the detachments of the Highland brigade against the big donga. These troops were for many hours separated from the rest of the 19th brigade and had to act on their own initiative. Each worked independently. The detachment of the Shropshire dashed into the bush which fringed the right bank, and pushed forward under its cover, while the Canadians, under Lieut.-Colonel W. D. Otter, moved straight across the open veld towards the donga, in extended order, with two companies in the firing line, two in support, and four in reserve. The line of skirmishers soon came within range of the Boer trenches, and by 10 a.m. were forced to halt in the open, their left some eight hundred yards from the donga, and their right about half that distance from the bed of the river. The Boers met them with a fire of varying volume; they were well concealed; they had the exact range; their aim was accurate, and their shooting extremely galling. In the next two hours Lieut.-Colonel Otter found it necessary to reinforce his firing line gradually with the two supporting companies and half a company from the reserve. The discipline of his battalion, thus rudely tested, proved excellent. On the right the detachment of the Shropshire Light Infantry succeeded in working its way up the river, and virtually prolonged the line of the Canadians to the river, though connection was not established between them. The Canadians were not in touch with the Highlanders, a few hundred yards higher up the river, and neither Lieut.-Colonel Otter nor the officer in command of the party of Shropshire Light Infantry knew that the attack of the

Separate movements of Canadians and part of the Shropshire. General want of unity in this attack.

THE WAR IN SOUTH AFRICA.

Highlanders on the big donga, which they had been ordered to support, had come to a stop. The confusion was worse because of the fact that Major Urmston, who led the Highlanders, was not even aware that the 19th brigade was on the right bank.

Headquarters of Shropshire L.I. occupy Gun Hill.

The two battalions and the battery which Smith-Dorrien kept in his own hands made their way slowly northwards, till about 11 a.m. the Shropshire Light Infantry drove a small number of Boers from the crest of Gun Hill and occupied it. Spens was then ordered by his Brigadier to halt pending further instructions. The Gordon Highlanders were in support of his left rear, but were not in touch with him. The 82nd battery, except that it fired a few rounds from near Paardeberg Hill, was not seriously employed in the attack until 1.30 p.m., when it came into action on Gun Hill against the donga. The battery might have much aided the assailants, but unfortunately its commander, seeing a few of his shells burst near the Highlanders, and not knowing that the western attack was being made against the donga, diverted his fire to the main laager further to the eastward.

Second period of action— Kitchener orders western attack to be forced home.

The Chief of the Staff and Lieut.-General Kelly-Kenny watched these operations throughout the forenoon from a point a little to the east of Signal Hill, while Lieut.-General Colvile established his Headquarters on Signal Hill itself. Soon after 1 p.m. Lord Kitchener judged that Smith-Dorrien's turning movement had sufficiently developed to permit of the western attack being forced home, and ordered Colvile to send across the river all his spare men to rush the donga. The Headquarters and three companies of the Cornwall Light Infantry, then acting as divisional baggage guard, were the only troops of the IXth division available, as three companies of the Cornwall had already been sent to reinforce the Highland brigade, and one company was on outpost.* Colvile reported this to the Chief of the Staff,

---

* It should be remembered that some of the battalions had furnished entire companies to the mounted infantry corps; and thus had only seven companies at Headquarters. Other battalions, though providing the same number of men for the mounted infantry, drew men from all their companies, and thus retained their original organisation.

THE BATTLE OF PAARDEBERG.

and was told to call up the three companies from the baggage guard. He accordingly summoned the commanding officer of the battalion, Lieut.-Colonel W. Aldworth, and gave him Lord Kitchener's orders. It was left to Aldworth's judgment to decide how his mission could best be carried out, and he was not instructed to report his arrival on the right bank to his Brigadier, Smith-Dorrien. Efforts were made both by Lord Kitchener and the staff of the IXth division to communicate to Smith-Dorrien the orders given to Aldworth. Unfortunately heavy rain and a dull sky had both interrupted communication by heliograph, and had made the river temporarily impassable for messengers. Thus Smith-Dorrien was still unaware that an assault had been ordered. This was the more unfortunate because on Gun Hill Smith-Dorrien had outflanked the Boers manning the big donga, and a move from Gun Hill, combined with the frontal attacks actually being made, if the whole had been worked together under his orders, would almost certainly have driven the enemy out of the big donga and prepared the way for assault on the laager itself, into which it is not impossible that the Boers might have been followed as they fled from the donga. As it was, no real progress had yet been made on this side of the battlefield.

Meantime affairs on the right of the British line had developed. Colonel Hannay received from the Chief of the Staff an order, sent off about 8 a.m., to cross the Modder at Vanderberg Drift and push down stream. He recalled the 6th mounted infantry from Banks Drift, and on its arrival led part of his brigade across the river, and then worked down the stream along both banks. To support him, the 81st battery, which had been sent to Stephenson from the long spur, and was posted about one thousand yards south-west of Vanderberg Drift, came into action against the laager. But hardly had the gunners found the range, when shells dropped amongst them from a kopje lying to their right rear. The first of the Boer reinforcements from Natal—two guns and a few hundred of the Bethlehem commando—which, under Commandant Steyn, had pushed ahead of their main body by forced marches and seized the ridge lying to the north of Stinkfontein, thus announced their arrival.

Hannay on both banks begins to work down stream.

Boer guns open behind him. Steyn has arrived.

The commander of the battery promptly replied. Reversing the whole of his guns, he concentrated so heavy a fire on Steyn's artillery as to kill the greater part of the mule teams and drive away the gunners from their pieces. A detachment of mounted infantry at the same time occupied Stinkfontein and threatened to envelop the Boers, who fell back on the kopjes to the eastward, leaving their guns on the hill. These guns never actually fell into the hands of the troops, and, when later De Wet occupied Kitchener's Kopje, they were carried away in safety by the Boers.

<small>18th brigade ordered to advance on the laager.</small>

The effect of this counter-attack was to delay Hannay's crossing of Vanderberg Drift, and to draw Stephenson's battalions further to the eastward. Lieut.-General Kelly-Kenny, about 10 a.m., sent his A.D.C. to Brigadier-General Stephenson, telling him not to allow himself to be detained by the Boers on the east, but to advance on the laager; the 76th battery was at the same time ordered to reinforce the artillery engaged on the eastern flank. It was found necessary to employ the 81st battery, the 4th mounted infantry, and the squadron of Kitchener's Horse in keeping back Steyn's men, who continued to threaten and harass with long-range fire the right and right rear of the British line; but the 76th battery came into action against the laager from a site between Kitchener's Kopje and the Modder. The two companies on the extreme left of the Welsh regiment, after some hours' fighting near Vendutie Drift, finding that their flank was turned by the enemy, who was creeping up a small donga from the river, had fallen back with the detachments of Kitchener's Horse to the ridge immediately to the south of that drift. The rest of the battalion, quitting the skirmish with Steyn, moved towards the river, and facing northward, at first occupied a slight depression in the veld, a little to the east of Vendutie Drift. After remaining here for a short time, four companies, under the immediate command of Lieut.-Colonel R. J. F. Banfield, took ground to the right and occupied a deep donga about a mile to the west of Vanderberg Drift. The remaining two companies of the battalion escorted the 81st battery. The Essex regiment meanwhile concentrated at Vanderberg Drift, two companies being extended

THE BATTLE OF PAARDEBERG. 131

on the left bank covering the drift. The rest were near them in quarter column under the bank. Notwithstanding the pressure of Hannay's mounted infantry on the right bank, some of the burghers still clung to the dongas on that side, and fired with effect upon the Essex.

So placed, Stephenson's battalions were able to give little assistance to Hannay's advance. The regimental commanders, although acting under orders from one authority for a common object, worked quite independently, and the commander of the 18th brigade, because of the failure to convey to him any conception of the purpose for which he was sent up river,* took no steps to combine with Hannay in his operations down stream. Hannay, on the other hand, was well aware that it was his mission to attack the main laager. On de Lisle's arrival from the eastern drift Hannay had informed him that the 6th mounted infantry was to assault the laager, and had consented with reluctance to an attempt being made by de Lisle to work round the eastern face of the Boer works. De Lisle reconnoitred to the north, coming into touch with French's Horse batteries, which, escorted by part of the Household cavalry, were in action on the left front of the Gordon Highlanders, about two thousand yards from the river. Nowhere in the Boer entrenchments could an opening be seen such as appeared to offer any chance of success to an assault by a few weak companies of mounted infantry. Hannay, before de Lisle could return with a report to this effect, had arrived at a similar conclusion, and at 1.30 p.m. sent a written message to the Chief of the Staff that he could advance no further. This message reached Headquarters soon after the issue of the order to Colvile that the attack was to be pushed home on the western flank. Lord Kitchener, resolving that the enemy should be pressed on both sides simultaneously, determined on a general advance. Unfortunately, this order was not addressed to the senior officer of the eastern attack—Brigadier-General Stephenson—directing him to assume command of all the troops in the neighbourhood and to carry

_{The attempt is made to push in on east.}

_{Hannay reports he cannot advance further;}

* See page 117.

out a combined assault, but to Colonel Hannay in the following terms :—

but is ordered to push on, the purpose of the order being to bring about a simultaneous attack on the laager from east and west.

"The time has now come for a final effort. All troops have been warned that the laager must be rushed at all costs. Try and carry Stephenson's brigade on with you. But if they cannot go the mounted infantry should do it. Gallop up if necessary and fire into the laager."

These instructions must have represented what was passing through Lord Kitchener's mind, not any orders actually issued. Kelly-Kenny knew nothing of his brigades (the 13th and 18th) having been so warned. No directions to aid the assault had been given to the 18th brigade. Of Colvile's division, the only available men, three companies of the Cornwall Light Infantry, had not even begun to cross the river at Paardeberg Drift. Hannay, who received Lord Kitchener's message

His reading of the order, 3 p.m.

at about 3 p.m., read it as a direct personal order to charge immediately with such men as he could collect. He thought that his instructions were so urgent that time would not permit of his making any arrangements for joint action with Stephenson, who was two miles away from him on the opposite side of the river. He regarded his mission as a forlorn hope, and determined to carry it out in that spirit. Sending one of his gallopers to tell the 4th mounted infantry to cross to the right bank, and another with directions to de Lisle to charge the laager—a message which did not reach that officer until next morning—Hannay, without further pause, called to a party of his men who lay in support of the skirmishers, to mount and form line. With the brief order to this handful of men, "We are going to charge the laager, follow me," he

He charges the laager, and is killed.

galloped forward. The men, led by Captain H. M. A. Hankey, Royal Warwickshire regiment, followed. Passing through the intervals of the firing line, Hannay shouted to the nearest officer to support him, and rode straight for the Boer trenches, some five hundred yards distant. A little more than half way Hannay's horse was killed under him; but having disentangled himself, he pressed forward on foot until, some two hundred yards from the position, he again fell, pierced by many bullets, while Hankey

THE BATTLE OF PAARDEBERG. 133

was also killed almost on the same spot. Of the troops which took part in this gallant but ill-considered charge two officers—Captains O. G. Godfrey-Faussett, 1st Essex, and W. E. Cramer-Roberts, 1st Norfolk—and a few men actually reached the laager, where they were taken prisoners. Some of the soldiers swerved off to the right, and thus escaped, the remainder were shot down. Under cover of this movement the firing line had dashed forward; a company of mounted infantry reached a good position only three hundred and fifty yards from the entrenchments and there remained until dark, though later in the afternoon they suffered slightly from musketry from the south of the river.

Although the premature movement of Hannay's troops had achieved nothing, Lord Kitchener still hoped to arrange a combined attack simultaneously from east and west. The 4th mounted infantry, in obedience to Hannay's last message, had left the ground to the east of Kitchener's Kopje in charge of Kitchener's Horse, and at 3.30 p.m. passed over the drift, worked down stream and reinforced the right of the mounted infantry firing line. Half an hour later—at 4 p.m.—Stephenson led the Headquarters and three of the companies of the Welsh and four companies of the Essex over Vanderberg Drift. Here, as at other drifts, the water was up to the men's armpits and the current strong, but by holding each other's rifles, the crossing was effected without accident in about half an hour. The ammunition carts and machine guns followed, although with some difficulty. A half-battalion of the Essex remained on the left bank guarding the drift; two companies of the Welsh were still with the 81st battery, and the other two companies were to the westward, on the ridge between Kitchener's Kopje and the Modder. After crossing the river Stephenson brought his seven companies clear of the bank and dongas and then launched them westward, against the eastern flank of the Boer trenches about a mile and a half lower down the stream. The Welsh led across open ground in successive lines of companies with ten paces interval between the men; the Essex followed on the left rear, taking advantage of the shelter of the bushes

The first attempt on the east having failed, a second is made. 18th brigade ordered to advance on the laager.

Stephenson crosses Vanderberg Drift;

and attacks down stream.

on the river bank. After a few hundred yards a slight change of front to the right became necessary to get round the bend in the river, and from the crest of an undulation in the ground, some half a mile further on, the Boer laager could be seen about a thousand yards off. Along this crest mounted infantry were in action with the burghers. The first line of the Welsh now came under a heavy fire, and Brigadier-General Stephenson ordered his own troops and the mounted infantry in front of him to attack the Boer position. The Welsh firing line, gradually reinforced by its supports, pushed across the plain, by short rushes of alternate half-companies, but the clouds had cleared away, and the setting sun, blazing straight in the men's eyes rendered their fire ineffective, while that of the enemy caused many casualties. Thus, although the Welsh had fixed bayonets for the charge, they could get no nearer to the Boer trenches than five hundred yards, and, therefore, failed to give any substantial impetus to the mounted infantry firing line. Meanwhile, the left of the Welsh had been prolonged by the four companies of the Essex, who, under the command of Major F. J. Brown, worked on a narrow front through the bushes on the river bank to within four hundred yards from the laager. Lieut.-Colonel R. J. F. Banfield, who commanded the Welsh, had been severely wounded, and from the right it was reported that the companies there could advance no further. On hearing this, Major Brown, the senior officer on this part of the field, judged that the troops were too far from the enemy's position, and the fire too intense, to permit of a successful attack with the bayonet, and on his own authority directed both battalions to fall back slowly, carrying their wounded and dead with them. At this moment Brigadier-General Stephenson was not with the front line; he had received a message to say that a detachment of Royal Engineers had been sent to him by Lieut.-General Kelly-Kenny, and gone back to give instructions about the works he wished to be thrown up. As Stephenson was returning to the firing line he met the infantry after they had retired a short distance. Halting them, he at once set all the available men to dig trenches on the ground upon which they stood.

<small>18th brigade entrenches.</small>

THE BATTLE OF PAARDEBERG. 135

While Cronje's commandos, save for the local counter-attack in the early morning towards Paardeberg Drift, had remained strictly on the defensive all day, and while there was for the moment something very like a "stalemate" on both sides, an offensive stroke by a master hand was being prepared altogether outside the circle of the combat. This now suddenly changed the whole aspect of affairs, and by distracting attention from the measures for a combined attack on the laager, upset all Lord Kitchener's arrangements and made the further efforts of his troops spasmodic and fruitless. The spirited and partially successful attempt of Commandant Steyn to create a diversion on the south-eastern flank during the forenoon, had come to an end when General C. De Wet delivered this new and far more formidable counter-stroke. *Third period —De Wet's attack.*

The movements of the Boer reinforcements outside the laager.

De Wet had continued to gather at Koffyfontein, where he was when last mentioned,* reinforcements from various quarters. On the afternoon of the 17th Lubbe, who had left Cronje on the march to Paardeberg, had joined him with some hundred burghers. That evening further reinforcements under General Jacobs, of Fauresmith, and Commandant Hertzog, of Philippolis, reached him. This concentration, so far to the south, was due to the impression still prevailing at Bloemfontein that Koffyfontein and Petrusburg were the real objects of Lord Roberts' movement. De Wet, still imposed upon by the old idea and the direction of Lord Roberts' earlier marches, despatched Jacobs and Hertzog to the westward to meet a rumoured British advance from Belmont station, while a small escort was assigned to the convoy captured on the 15th at Waterval Drift. This was ordered to push on to Edenburg, probably to place its supplies at the disposal of the Boer forces at Colesberg. There still remained under De Wet's command six hundred burghers and a couple of guns, and with this force he hastened to Cronje's assistance. Marching through the night he assembled his commando six miles south-east of Paardeberg on the afternoon of the 18th, at a time when the only troops left near Kitchener's Kopje were the 81st battery, its escort, and

* See page 106.

part of Kitchener's Horse. Steyn, who had been reinforced by small parties of Boers, was just held in check and no more, and the skirmishing on this part of the field had almost died away when De Wet's arrival decided the issue at this point.

Why Kitchener's Kopje was an easy prey.

Lieut.-General Kelly-Kenny had proposed to detail four companies of the Essex to hold Kitchener's Kopje, but at the Chief of the Staff's suggestion, he had only sent two companies. Without Kelly-Kenny's knowledge, these had been called away by one of Kitchener's Staff officers to meet an emergency on some other part of the field. They had been replaced on the hill by some of Kitchener's Horse. A party of about sixty of that corps had been thrown forward to hold the farm buildings of Osfontein. Both detachments appear to have regarded their share in the day's operations as practically over, and to have neglected the ordinary measures of security. De Wet determined by a rapid advance to seize both Osfontein and the kopje. Sending half his men, under P. Botha, against the farm, he galloped with the remainder straight for the kopje. In each case the surprise was complete. Most of the detachment at Osfontein were taken prisoners; the kopje was captured with little opposition; guns were hastily dragged to the summit. About 4.30 p.m. shrapnel and rifle-fire was suddenly opened on the baggage of the VIth division, and on the 76th and 81st Field batteries. The 81st was now limbering up, for Lord Kitchener, considering that it was no longer necessary to keep it in action against Steyn's party on the kopje north-east of Osfontein farm, had sent an Aide-de-camp to order it to move closer to the laager. The battery commander, Captain A. M. A. Lennox, before the storm burst upon his guns, had galloped off to look for a suitable position from which to shell the entrenchments. In a very short time the battery had to turn its fire in three directions. Two guns engaged a party of adventurous Boers who, concealed by a herd of cattle, crept within eight hundred yards of the battery itself. Two more resumed the combat with the enemy on the kopje north-east of Osfontein farm. The two remaining tried to beat down the fire of a pom-pom which from the northern slopes of Kitchener's Kopje played on some twenty-five mounted

De Wet captures Kitchener's Kopje.

Thence he fires on baggage and batteries.

THE BATTLE OF PAARDEBERG. 137

infantry who had been rallied in the bed of the river, and were now attacking the Boer marksmen lining the cactus hedges of Osfontein Farm. These burghers were driven off, but not before the pom-pom had killed or wounded nine men and sixteen horses of the party of mounted infantry.

When the attack of the 18th brigade down the right bank halted, the four companies of the Essex, on the left of its line, were opposite the 81st battery. An appeal was now made to them to assist. The river proved impassable at this point, but a message to Lieut. F. N. Parsons* brought him to the guns with part of the detachment of the Essex left to guard the drift. Thrusting in on the exposed flank and supported by the two companies of the Welsh regiment, he covered the battery's retirement to the long spur. The only troops available as a general reserve to meet this counter-attack were the Gloucester and a half battalion of the Buffs not yet thrown into the firing line. Sending the VIth divisional transport, under an escort of two companies of the Gloucester, back to join the wagons of the IXth division south of Paardeberg Drift, Kelly-Kenny ordered the remaining five companies of the Gloucester, with two companies of the Buffs, to advance towards Kitchener's Kopje. Towards nightfall the firing line of these units reached the foot of the hill and there entrenched. On their left, prolonging the line to Vanderberg Drift, lay those four Welsh companies which had been kept on the south side of the river. These dispositions, coupled with the fire of the 76th and Howitzer batteries, sufficed to protect the right rear of Kelly-Kenny's division from further attack. But De Wet drove back all attempts to regain any of the ground he had won. A party of the 8th mounted infantry tried before sunset to work round the north of Kitchener's Kopje towards Osfontein, but were repelled with the loss of nearly all their horses and half their men.

Parsons aids 81st battery.

The real importance of De Wet's sudden stroke was that it was delivered at the very moment when the whole attention, both of Lord Kitchener, of Lieut.-General Kelly-Kenny, and of

Effect of De Wet's stroke.

---

* For gallantry during the battle Lieut. F. N. Parsons, Essex regiment, was awarded the Victoria Cross.

the staff, would have been concentrated on the development of the final stages of the attack on Cronje. As it was, just at the crucial moment for the general advance it became necessary to deal with an entirely different subject. The threads, for the time being dropped, could not be picked up again. But for De Wet's daring swoop upon the key of the position it is possible that Lord Kitchener's determination to assault the Boers in their laager might have been rewarded by ultimate success that evening.

It is true that before De Wet's arrival the troops both on the west and east were much scattered, and that for the moment Aldworth's three companies were all that were available on either side for attack on donga or laager, but the whole of Colvile's division was near at hand to support Aldworth, and for that purpose needed merely to be drawn together and combined. Though the case was not so favourable on the east the number of men lost in Hannay's premature assault had not been large. The greater part of the force originally designed to move down river was intact, though for the moment its impetus was expended. With a little patience and method both on east and west, enough remained to carry the laager under the protection of the guns, which had been altogether undisturbed and had a clear range. De Wet's stroke made all this impossible both because most of the troops in hand, whether on the east or in the centre, had to be turned off to meet him, and because there was no one who could give attention to the organisation required on both flanks to drive home the blows simultaneously.

<small>Fourth period—Movements on the right bank. Spens, from Gun Hill, attacks big donga.</small>

While De Wet's attack on Kitchener's Kopje was beginning to develop, further efforts were made by the troops on the right bank to capture the big donga. About 3.30 p.m. the officer commanding the Shropshire Light Infantry obtained leave from Major-General Smith-Dorrien to move from the crest of Gun Hill down to its lower slopes, and pushed the first line of his five companies to within eight hundred yards of the donga, which appeared to be open to an assault in flank. But the head of the donga, which splayed outwards, was so stoutly defended that Spens without support could make no further progress. No support was forth-

THE BATTLE OF PAARDEBERG. 139

coming, as the Gordon Highlanders, less one company escorting guns, were extended towards French's Horse artillery batteries, out of sight of the Shropshire, and the frontal attack on the donga had died away.

About 4 p.m., that is nearly at the same time that Stephenson was crossing at Vanderberg Drift, the three companies of the Cornwall Light Infantry, which, under Lieut.-Colonel Aldworth had been ordered to the right bank, succeeded in crossing the river, now swollen with the recent rain. Then in a column of extended lines each one hundred and fifty yards behind the other, they turned eastward, and somewhat later Aldworth with the leading company joined the front line of the Canadians. Otter's men still held the ground they had reached at 10 a.m. This was separated from the donga by a perfectly open space of seven or eight hundred yards. Aldworth informed Otter that he had "been sent to finish this business, and meant to do it with the bayonet." He then asked for and obtained information respecting the situation both of the Canadians and of the enemy. The two rear companies of the Cornwall Light Infantry gradually closed upon the leading company, each échelon as it came up being received by hot fire. About 5 p.m. Colonel Aldworth told Lieut.-Colonel Otter that a general advance was to be made. Both corps now fixed bayonets, and Aldworth, placing himself in front of his three companies, ordered a charge. With a tremendous shout the Cornishmen, and all the Canadians, with the exception of one and a half companies of the latter held in reserve, dashed forward. A party of nearly a hundred Highlanders, chiefly of the Seaforth, also joined in the assault on the extreme right. A storm of bullets, pom-pom shells, and shrapnel immediately burst on the advancing line. Though men fell rapidly, at first things promised well, and the soldiers on the south of the river, watching the charge with breathless interest, could see some of the enemy beginning to slip away. When a little more than half the distance had been covered, and the Boer trenches were but three hundred yards distant, Aldworth, struck by a bullet, plunged forward on his face. Raising himself, he gave a last cheering cry to his men—" Come on, Dukes ! Come on, Corn-

4 p.m. Attempt to carry the big donga by Cornwall Light Infantry and Canadians.

140   THE WAR IN SOUTH AFRICA.

It fails.

walls!" and then dropped back dead. The line behind him, weakened in strength by over twenty per cent. of casualties, now staggered under the concentrated fire of the Boers and threw itself on the ground. Neither the Canadians nor the Cornwall Light Infantry could push on any further.

A typical instance of causes of failure.

This gallant but unsuccessful assault is typical of the numerous attacks made during the 18th. They were not organised by superior authority. They were not prepared by artillery fire. They were never in sufficient strength, and they were not supported by simultaneous flanking attacks. Hence Spens' flanking attack, made separately, became merely a frontal attack. The value of long-range covering fire appears to have been ignored. Except in this instance they were usually delivered without combination between the senior officers of the units actually engaged. Had the general officer commanding the 19th brigade received notice from Headquarters, which, in spite of the temporary failure of the heliograph, could have been brought by hand when Aldworth crossed the river, he could have arranged for a united effort of all the troops scattered on the west of the laager.

The cavalry division during the action.

Throughout the day Lieut.-General French, with only a weak brigade and twelve guns, had closed Cronje's line of retreat to the northward. It was not until late in the afternoon that the 3rd cavalry brigade (Gordon), consisting of the 9th and 16th Lancers,

Gordon's brigade arrives in the afternoon.

O. and R. batteries, Royal Horse artillery, with a squadron of Roberts' Horse attached, joined in the action. Gordon had left Kimberley at 7 a.m. on the 18th with orders to join General French at Koodoos Drift. His total strength, exclusive of the squadron of Roberts' Horse, was 43 officers, 735 men and 751 horses, of which about a hundred were remounts, obtained from the De Beers Company. The guide assigned to the brigade led by the direct Bloemfontein road, but after following it for eight miles, he quitted that track, and swung more to the north, crossing the bushy ground of Mostershoek and Bothashoek Farms. Seven derelict ammunition wagons of the Boers were found on the former and destroyed. The left flank of the column was occasionally "sniped" by Ferreira's patrols, as Broadwood's

THE BATTLE OF PAARDEBERG. 141

brigade had been on the previous day, but, as in the former case, this interruption was ignored. Owing to the weakness of the majority of the horses, the whole march was made at a walk, and it was not until nearly 5 p.m. that Gordon's advance guard reached the eastern side of Koodoosrand, about three miles from the drift. Pushing on parallel to the ridge they soon came into collision with De Beer's commando, which, in danger of being enveloped by the fire of Gordon's Horse batteries and of his advance guard, fell back across the Modder to the south bank, followed as far as Koodoos Drift by a squadron of the 16th Lancers. On the left a squadron of the 9th Lancers also reached Makauw's Drift, although somewhat harassed on their left flank by parties of the enemy on kopjes to the north-east. At sunset, Gordon, deeming it unwise to commit his brigade further in the dark on unreconnoitred ground, concentrated his main body about four miles from the river on the east side of the ridge, and recalled his advance squadrons. In the darkness they could not find him and bivouacked together on the veld some two miles from his Headquarters. The 3rd cavalry brigade had done useful work; not only had it manœuvred De Beer across the river, but its march, like that of French on the 17th, had afforded Ferreira's commando a pretext for not entering the battle area. The absence of this commando much reduced the numbers of the enemy available for counter-attacks on the troops which surrounded Cronje's laager. Throughout the night touch was not established between the Headquarters of the cavalry division and the 3rd cavalry brigade, although in the afternoon of the 18th the movements of a large column, north-east of French's bivouac, had been observed.

With the loss of Kitchener's Kopje on the south, and the repulse of the Cornwall Light Infantry and the Canadians on the north of the Modder, the battle virtually came to an end. There were no reserves left. The troops who went into action, already tired by forced marches and want of food and sleep, were now exhausted by the long day's fighting. It was imperative that men and horses should be rested and fed, and about dusk orders were issued for the withdrawal of part of the troops from the

Engagement broken off.

advanced positions, leaving some detachments in close contact with the enemy. Colvile directed Smith-Dorrien to retain his foothold on the right bank, and if possible to entrench. Five companies of the Shropshire were accordingly ordered to hold Gun Hill, while five companies of the Highland brigade remained clinging to the river bed till morning. The Shropshire, during the night, reconnoitred the big donga and found it evacuated. By midnight, the Canadians, Gordon Highlanders, half a battalion of the Cornwall Light Infantry, and two companies of Shropshire Light Infantry, were concentrated at Paardeberg Drift. The 82nd battery recrossed it. On the left bank the West Riding regiment held its advanced station until daylight, but the 1st Oxfordshire Light Infantry and 1st Yorkshire were drawn back on to the brow of the long spur. The main body of the Highland brigade and the 65th Howitzer battery were bivouacked on Signal Hill. The troops further to the east retained through the night the ground they occupied at sunset.*

The Chief of the Staff's final report to the Field-Marshal on the battle was worded as follows :—

" From Lord Kitchener,
    " Cable Cart, E. of Paardeberg.
" To Lord Roberts.
    (Received at 7.40 p.m.)

" 18th February, 1900.

" We did not succeed in getting into the enemy's convoy, though we drove the Boers back a considerable distance along the river bed. The troops are maintaining their position and I hope to-morrow we shall be able to do something more definite. Late this afternoon the Boers developed an attack on our right, which is still going on, but is kept under control by our artillery. Our casualties have, I fear, been severe. Owing to the bush fighting near the river I have not been able to get lists yet, but will send them as soon as possible."

The Commander-in-Chief telegraphed the following reply, showing that he intended to resume personal control of the operations on the morrow :—

" Jacobsdal,
" 18th February, 1900.

" We must not let Cronje escape now or be able to hold out until reinforcements can reach him. I have warned Chermside's and the Guards' brigade

* See map No. 23 (a).

THE BATTLE OF PAARDEBERG. 143

that they may have to push on to your assistance on reaching Klip Drift, where they ought to be by daylight to-morrow. We shall have three Field batteries and eight Naval guns, and about four hundred mounted infantry. Have information waiting for me at Klip Drift.

"ROBERTS."

The British casualties during the day were 24 officers and 279 men killed, 59 officers and 847 men wounded, and 2 officers and 59 men missing—a total of 1,270.* Casualties.

The battle of Paardeberg had thus failed to achieve the success which Lord Kitchener had hoped to gain.

This failure may in part be attributed to the nature of the enemy's position, to his stubborn resistance and to the diversions effected by Steyn and De Wet, but, notwithstanding these factors, it would seem probable that Cronje's main laager might have been carried during the afternoon of the 18th had the attacks from east and west been better synchronised, and had they been delivered by a combined effort of all the troops available on each flank. These defects in execution appear to have been largely due to the peculiar circumstances under which the executive direction of the troops in the action was carried out. The Chief of the Staff's position, as well as that of Lieut.-General Kelly-Kenny, was an unusual one, and over no other battle during the war did the lack of a trained General Staff and of clearly expressed operation orders exercise a more marked influence. Few of the subordinate leaders appear to have been aware that Lord Kitchener had formulated a plan of attack, and the verbal instructions delivered to them, or to those under them, failed to convey explicitly his intentions. The inherent defects of a force, whose organisation had only sprung into existence a few days earlier and whose commander and units had never had the advantage of previously working together, were very apparent. All these causes, no doubt, greatly affected the result, but, had it not been for De Wet's counter-attack at the precise hour at which it came, the presumption is that they would not have actually decided it. If that reading of the situation be correct, it is a strong proof of the value of even a small force brought in to a decisive Causes of failure.

* See Appendix 2.

position by an active leader at the right moment, and of the necessity for a general reserve retained in hand to the last in order to meet the unforeseen. The effect of De Wet's attack is the more noteworthy because it was certainly not unexpected. It will be seen from Lord Roberts' telegram, given on page 110, that Lord Kitchener was warned to expect, either on the 18th or 19th, that two thousand men would attempt to join Cronje. Half that number are the most that can have been engaged against him in the counter-attack, adding Steyn's men to those whom De Wet brought with him. Yet the battle was creditable to the British infantry, who though weary from forced marches and weakened by want of food and sleep, responded heartily to every call made upon them. These qualities were not displayed in vain. Cronje's mobility was destroyed, his oxen and horses killed or scattered, the spirit of his burghers crushed. The Boer commandos imprisoned in the bed of the Modder were, in fact, doomed.

Yet a battle fatal for Boers.

CHAPTER IX.

THE INVESTMENT OF CRONJE'S LAAGER.*

WHILE the divisions near Paardeberg Drift, with the help of French's cavalry, were engaged in arresting Cronje's retreat and bringing him to bay, Lord Roberts was completing his arrangements for protecting Kimberley, and for bringing up reinforcements to the army at present under Lord Kitchener. On the 17th of February, Lord Methuen was placed in command of the troops on the railway between Kimberley and the Orange River bridge, and was directed to take up his quarters in Kimberley as soon as the railway north of the Modder was restored. He had at hand the 20th and 38th batteries, Royal Field artillery, and the 9th brigade, to the command of which Colonel C. W. H. Douglas had recently been appointed with the local rank of Major-General. One New South Wales and two Canadian field batteries and about one thousand Imperial Yeomanry were to join him as soon as they landed in South Africa, as was also a brigade to be composed of militia battalions still on the sea. The Guards' brigade (Pole-Carew), and Lieut.-Colonel E. M. Flint's recently-arrived brigade division of Field artillery (83rd, 84th, and 85th batteries), were to march up the left bank of the Modder. Flint's batteries formed part of the IXth division, but did not actually join it till the 9th March.

_{Lord Roberts arranges for holding Kimberley and the railway to it, while he pushes on Guards and Artillery.}

* See map No. 23. [In order not to increase the number of maps of Vol. II. the map illustrating the first phase of the battle of Paardeberg is used in this chapter. The reader will understand that the dispositions of the troops thereon in no way refer to the operations of the 19th-27th February.]

His information about Boer strength.

Lord Roberts' staff, during the halt at Jacobsdal, had gathered further information as to the enemy's dispositions and as to the terrain on which the British army was now entering. On the morning of February 18th, before the news of the battle of Paardeberg had come in, the following report was presented to the Commander-in-Chief by Lieut.-Colonel C. J. Mackenzie, who, owing to the illness of Colonel G. F. R. Henderson, had become acting Director of Military Intelligence in South Africa.

"The result of the recent combined operations having for their object the relief of Kimberley has been the complete disruption for the time being of the enemy's forces at Magersfontein and investing Kimberley.

"The distribution of the forces in the western theatre of war is estimated as follows:—

Cronje	5,000 and 8 guns.
Koffyfontein	3,000 and 3 guns.
Wolve Kraal } Goemansberg }	800 and 1 gun.
Reinforcements en route from Ladysmith	3,000.
At Bloemfontein	1,000 and 6 guns.
North of Kimberley	3,000.
Rebels west of Kimberley-Hopetown line	1,500.
Stormberg	3,000 and 4 guns.
Dordrecht	800 and 2 guns.
Colesberg	7,000 and 17 guns.
Total	28,100 with 41 guns.

"The occupation of Kimberley will make the rebels less of a menace than they already are.

"The forces north of Kimberley are melting rapidly away."

After suggesting that Cronje's commandos and those from Natal might unite to defend Bloemfontein, the memorandum continued thus:—

"The Colesberg force, being largely composed of rebels, who will not all be prepared to leave their own country, if retired *en masse* to Bloemfontein, will on arrival there be reduced in strength by desertions possibly to one-half of its present number. The same applies to the Stormberg force.

"If the effect of threatening the enemy's rear and communications acts on the southern portion of the theatre of war in any measure approaching that of the recent operations, it may be assumed that if we are able to take and hold on to Bloemfontein, it will paralyse all the enemy's forces now south of that place."

THE INVESTMENT OF CRONJE'S LAAGER.

The paper then ended by comparing the various possible routes, laying stress on the difficulties of water supply, and recommending that the line from Abraham's Kraal Drift* on the Modder, *viâ* Kaal Spruit, should be chosen. This spruit had been reconnoitred in the month of February, 1897, and at that time of year contained plenty of water.

Lord Kitchener's telegrams from the battlefield, received on the 18th, showed Lord Roberts that his first step must be to concentrate all available strength against Cronje. The Commander-in-Chief therefore ordered Lieut.-General C. Tucker, whose division (the VIIth) was at Jacobsdal, to push to the front with all speed, taking with him the Naval guns, increased to four 4.7-in. and two 12-prs. by the arrival from the Modder of the Headquarters of the Naval brigade under Captain J. E. Bearcroft, R.N., the mounted infantry of the City Imperial Volunteers, Lt.-Colonel F. H. Hall's brigade division Royal Field artillery (18th, 62nd, and 75th batteries), the 9th company Royal Engineers, and the 14th brigade (Chermside). Major-General Wavell, with the remaining brigade (15th), was to hold Jacobsdal and to cover the line of supply from the Modder, while the Guards' brigade and the Highland Light Infantry watched the Klip and Klip Kraal Drifts.†

<small>VIIth division ordered to Paardeberg.</small>

These orders reached Tucker at 4 p.m. on the 18th. He started at 9 p.m., and by 6 a.m. on the 19th reached Klip Kraal Drift, sixteen miles from Jacobsdal. After a rest of three hours his troops were again on the march, though without the Naval brigade and the divisional transport, the oxen of which could go no further without a day's rest. Hall's Field batteries pushed on to Paardeberg Drift and arriving about noon, were by 3 p.m. in action against the Boer entrenchments from the neighbourhood of Signal Hill, where, three hours later, they were joined by Chermside's brigade (14th). The battalions composing this unit (2nd Norfolk, 2nd Lincoln, 1st King's Own Scottish Borderers and 2nd Hampshire), had marched on half rations rather more than thirty miles in less than twenty hours, a fine performance considering the great

<small>19th Feb. 1900.</small>

<small>Reinforcements reach Kitchener.</small>

---

* See map No. 25.   † See map No. 22.

VOL. II.   10*

heat, the lack of water, and the thick clouds of dust, which choked and parched the throats of the men.

Roberts arrives at Paardeberg 10 a.m. 19th Feb. The situation.

Lord Roberts, with his staff, left Jacobsdal at 4 a.m. on the 19th, and six hours later joined the Chief of the Staff at Paardeberg Drift, where he found that fighting had ceased, as it was believed that Cronje was about to surrender. In the early morning the Boer General had sent into the British lines a letter asking for an armistice to bury his dead and for leave to send away his wounded. Lieut.-General French, who received it, replied :—

"I have the honour to acknowledge the receipt of your communication of to-day, and have sent your letter to the G.O.C. of the British forces. As soon as I receive his reply, I shall inform you thereof. In the meantime I shall not attack your laager. Seeing that your troops are completely surrounded, I would advise you to surrender your force, and then peace will again reign in the land."

Cronje's proposal for an armistice refused.

Lord Roberts refused the request and demanded an unconditional surrender. To this Cronje, at 1 p.m., replied :—

"If you are so unreasonable as to refuse me time to bury my dead, you must do as you please."

The final sentence of this message was erroneously translated "I must do as you please." This was understood to mean that he yielded. The Commander-in-Chief, therefore, sent a reply accepting the surrender, and requesting the Boer General to return with the bearer of the flag of truce. The answer was :—

"It appears as if you entirely misunderstood my reply. I said, if you are so uncharitable as to refuse me a truce as requested, then you may do as you please. I shall not surrender alive. Therefore bombard as you please."

Feb. 19th. Positions on morning after battle.

During the time taken by these fruitless negotiations, Lord Roberts made himself acquainted with the general situation. It had not, since the battle had been broken off the night before, materially changed, except to the west of the laager. Smith-Dorrien, after calling up from their bivouac near the drift the Royal Canadians and three companies of the Gordon Highlanders, with two companies of the Shropshire Light Infantry, had recon-

THE INVESTMENT OF CRONJE'S LAAGER. 149

noitred the big donga, which the Boers had so successfully defended on the 18th. On ascertaining that the burghers had evacuated it during the night, and had fallen back to their main entrenchments, he placed the Shropshire detachment, with its right on the river, as a line of outposts eight hundred yards from the most western of the trenches now held by the enemy. In support of this advanced party the Gordon Highlanders and Canadians were extended in a semi-circle about a mile behind them.

To the east of Cronje's works the Essex and Welsh (18th brigade) still held their trenches on both sides of the river, near Vanderberg Drift, but the 4th mounted infantry, which through the night had remained in front of these battalions, was sent back to the ford. At daybreak the Boers were busily engaged in throwing up cover on the edge of the brushwood to the east of the laager. Thence, as well as from a donga running down to the river, a desultory fire was soon opened on Stephenson's infantry. This "sniping" was quickly silenced by two Maxims which searched out the trees and bushes. Of the 13th brigade, now under the temporary command of Colonel R. A. Hickson, the Buffs, the West Riding, and the Yorkshire (18th brigade, for the time attached to the 13th), were withdrawn at daybreak to the rising ground in rear.

From Kitchener's Kopje De Wet threatened the south (or rear) of the British investment of Cronje's works, impeded communication with French by the eastern fords, and formed a rallying point, both for fugitives from the laager and for reinforcements from the eastward. In the night Commandants F. J. Potgieter, of Wolmaranstad, and C. C. Froneman, slipping with eighty or ninety others between the outposts of the 13th and 18th brigades, had joined their comrades outside the laager. In order to manœuvre De Wet off the hill the Chief of the Staff, during the night of the 18th, had directed Lieut.-General French to send a cavalry brigade and a Horse artillery battery to the left bank of the Modder. The 10th Hussars, 12th Lancers, two squadrons of the Carabiniers and G. battery Royal Horse artillery, under Broadwood, leaving Kameelfontein at 5 a.m.

De Wet still holds Kitchener's Kopje.

on the 19th, passed along the north of the Boer position, crossed Paardeberg Drift, and there drew rations for men and horses for the first time since the 15th. When Broadwood marched off, Gordon's brigade had not yet rejoined cavalry Headquarters, and thus, during four hours, the only troops remaining under French's hand were the Household cavalry regiment and a battery of Horse artillery.

<small>Bombardment begun.</small>

Cronje's defiant answer to Lord Roberts' acceptance of his imaginary surrender promptly received a vigorous reply from the guns south of the Modder. Dean's 12-pr., Hall's brigade division, the 76th and 82nd Field batteries, and the 65th Howitzer battery, at once began to bombard the laager. The 81st battery crossed to the right bank at Paardeberg Drift, and from Gun Hill maintained a continuous fire at a range of 2,700 yards throughout the afternoon. The Chief of the Staff proposed to assault the laager at once, but the Commander-in-Chief decided not to do so until he had been able thoroughly to study the ground and to judge of the state of his troops, though he ordered that De Wet's detachment at Kitchener's Kopje should be attacked.

<small>Cavalry demonstration against Kitchener's Kopje</small>

As soon as Broadwood's horses and men had fed at Paardeberg Drift, the column swung round to the south-east of Kitchener's Kopje. The shells of G. battery drove a detachment of the enemy from a small outlyer to the south-east, but De Wet, with his main body, clung to the hill, which, with Broadwood's weak force, it would have been useless to attack. The 2nd cavalry brigade therefore fell back to Paardeberg Drift. Later in the afternoon, Lieut.-Colonel the Hon. A. E. Dalzell,

<small>is followed by an infantry attack,</small>

Oxfordshire Light Infantry, was ordered to assault De Wet's position with his own battalion, the Gloucestershire (both of the 13th brigade), and the Yorkshire (18th brigade). The Gloucestershire were still facing Kitchener's Kopje behind their sangars on the plain to the north-west of the hill; the other two battalions were bivouacked some distance off. By the time the latter had come up, only an hour of daylight remained; and to guard against the risk of his men becoming scattered in the dark, Dalzell kept his command well together. He sent the

THE INVESTMENT OF CRONJE'S LAAGER. 151

Gloucestershire straight to its front, with the Yorkshire in support, while the Oxfordshire, on the right, was to turn the burghers' left flank. The brunt of the affair fell upon the Gloucestershire, the actual strength of which, reduced by an escort to the 76th Field battery then co-operating with Dalzell, and by fatigue parties searching for water, was only about four hundred of all ranks. Moving steadily across the plain it reached the foot of a spur of the hill just as twilight came on. Then the commanding officer, Lieut.-Colonel R. F. Lindsell, fixed bayonets and led a charge up the slope. After a brisk fusilade, the enemy fell back rapidly to the main position, abandoning a number of rifles and some ammunition. Lindsell, who, though severely wounded during the charge, still remained in command, now ordered his men to entrench themselves, and sent back a message asking for reinforcements, water, food, and ammunition, the last being urgently needed, as barely a round was left. Dalzell gave him a plentiful supply of cartridges and told him to hold his ground till daylight, when he would be reinforced and supported by artillery. Then, drawing off the two other battalions of his command, Dalzell sought for the Chief of the Staff, to report his movements and to ask for artillery. By the time Lord Kitchener had taken him to Lord Roberts it was nearly dawn on the 20th. The Commander-in-Chief decided to gain his object without further loss of life by menacing De Wet's rear with mounted troops, as had been Lord Kitchener's intention when he sent for Broadwood's detachment, and the Gloucestershire battalion was at once recalled from the spur it had captured. *[margin: which nightfall, 19th Feb. 1900, delays. Lord Roberts, wishing to menace De Wet's rear, recalls infantry.]*

Throughout the 19th, De Wet had been in heliograph communication with Cronje, and repeatedly urged him to break loose from the toils closing round him; but Cronje thought that the loss of his transport and horses made movement impossible. He still hoped that a few days' passive resistance would give time for so large a number of reinforcements to mass in the neighbourhood of Paardeberg that the British Commander-in-Chief would be obliged to relinquish his investment of the laager. *[margin: Cronje rejects De Wet's advice to break out.]*

To the north of the Modder the only change of importance

152   THE WAR IN SOUTH AFRICA.

<small>Cavalry occupies fords south of Kameelfontein.</small> was the concentration of Gordon's brigade (3rd) at Kameelfontein, to replace the troops sent under Broadwood against De Wet on Kitchener's Kopje. During the afternoon it was reported that the Boers had evacuated Makauw's Drift, and Gordon sent a detachment, of a squadron 16th Lancers, part of Roberts' Horse, and two guns R. battery, Royal Horse artillery thither, with orders to hold it and watch the approaches from the south and east. Porter's brigade (1st), which was still at Kimberley, was ordered to rejoin the Headquarters of the cavalry division. The heliogram did not reach him, a mischance which compelled Lord Roberts to postpone the execution of his plan for manœuvring De Wet from his position.

<small>Night of 19th-20th Feb., 1900. News from inside laager.</small> During the night of the 19th–20th February, the Shropshire Light Infantry pushed their trenches closer to the western side of the laager, and the 81st battery on Gun Hill shelled the enemy at intervals of ten minutes. A few deserters who crept out to the British lines, reported that the Free Staters were in favour of immediate surrender, and that ammunition was running short. Cronje was said to be awaiting assistance from De Wet, from the Colesberg commandos, and from the burghers who had retreated northward from Kimberley.

<small>The gathering storm outside.</small> Information about the movements of the enemy outside the laager was conflicting. On the 14th, General Clements had fallen back from Rensburg to Arundel,* and had since telegraphed that the enemy in front of him was increasing rather than diminishing in strength. On the other hand the Headquarters staff were convinced by reports from other sources that commandos, estimated at from one thousand to three thousand men, had been withdrawn from Colesberg, and were on their way to Cronje's assistance. The staff had also heard positively that a large Free State detachment had been recalled from Natal. The main body of burghers, pushed northward from Kimberley by French on the 16th, was known to be still near Fourteen Streams. Dordrecht on the far east had been evacuated; but in the extreme west the occupation of Prieska by a party of malcontents from Griqualand West was causing a good deal of anxiety to the

* See Chapter XV. and map No. 35.

THE INVESTMENT OF CRONJE'S LAAGER. 153

High Commissioner at Cape Town, since this band might become a nucleus for the discontented in those thinly populated regions.

A quick and decisive success at Paardeberg was much to be desired, yet there were serious reasons against forcing an action at once. The troops who invested Cronje, although full of spirit, were not as yet in hard condition or capable of the endurance they showed later in the campaign. They were physically exhausted by the trying marches, prolonged fighting, and want of rations which had been their lot since they left the Modder camp. Not only had the casualties on the 16th and 18th somewhat weakened the strength of the units engaged, but the large numbers of all ranks withdrawn from regimental duty for staff work, for newly-raised mounted infantry and irregular corps, had weakened the battalions, especially in officers and non-commissioned officers. To replace the private soldiers and non-commissioned officers drafts must arrive from England, while the gaps in the commissioned ranks could only be filled by lads partially or even wholly untrained, for the members of the Reserve of Officers, not already employed, were almost entirely of field rank, retired from active service, most of them on account of age. If another day's heavy fighting should reduce units of this army to the verge of inefficiency there were not, even at home, any organised cadres to replace them except the VIIIth division, the Militia, and the improvised corps of Imperial Yeomanry.

<small>Roberts' reasons for not assaulting the laager.</small>

In addition to the necessity of husbanding the strength of the comparatively small number of troops under his immediate command, Lord Roberts was met by the difficulty of dealing with the men wounded in the fighting on the 16th and 18th. These now filled the field hospitals to overflowing. If he assaulted Cronje's entrenchments before the sick and wounded had been sent off to the railway, the casualties, inevitable in such an operation, would overwhelm the surgeons and wholly disorganise the medical service. It was therefore essential to evacuate the field hospitals before the next general engagement took place, but to do this rapidly was out of the question, because, as has been stated in Volume I., Chapter XXV., in order to supply adequate transport for the relief of Kimberley, the vehicles allotted to the Royal Army Medical Corps had been considerably reduced. Another factor in the situation was that neither the transport nor the supplies of food and ammunition actually at hand were adequate for an immediate march on Bloemfontein by the whole army. Thus, whether Lord Roberts stormed the laager, or reduced it by sap, bombardment, and starvation, he would be equally obliged to remain some days near Paardeberg, until he had sent off his wounded and renewed his stock of supplies from the railway. The first alternative would certainly have involved heavy losses, which might have impaired the efficiency of the units engaged. The second, though undoubtedly a slower process, seemed certain of success in a few days, unless the various bodies of Boers in the western theatre of war should combine under a common leader in sufficient strength to defeat the investing line, while Cronje escaped from the trap in which he had been caught. But the imperfect organisation and want of discipline of the burghers and the previous experience of the campaign showed that the risk of such a combination was small. After weighing all these considerations the Commander-in-Chief decided that the enemy's position was to be approached by sap carried out by night, and that by day a bombardment as steady as the supply of ammunition permitted was to be maintained. While the siege was being pressed on, the forces gathering for the relief of Cronje were to be dispersed.

Projected advance of cavalry division on Bloemfontein.

Bloemfontein was known to be practically unfortified. If, as soon as Christian De Wet had been shouldered off Kitchener's Kopje, Bloemfontein could be occupied by French's cavalry, President Steyn's efforts to organise into an army the reinforcements now concentrating at the Free State capital would be frustrated, and the commandos facing Clements at Colesberg would be obliged to retire. The Field-Marshal believed that two or three days would suffice to bring up from the Riet and Kimberley the limited amount of transport and supplies needed for the cavalry raid, and hoped soon to be able again to thrust the cavalry division far in advance of his main army. One

THE INVESTMENT OF CRONJE'S LAAGER.

of the chief objects of the scheme of campaign had been to draw towards the invading army a part of the forces opposing Sir Redvers Buller and Major-General Clements. This had been successfully accomplished, but as the operations against Cronje were likely to take some time it was important that both Buller and Clements should take advantage of the reduction of the enemy's strength and press him hard, to prevent further reinforcements reaching De Wet. Lord Roberts therefore telegraphed to General Buller :— *Orders to Buller,*

"Paardeberg,
"20th February, 1900.

"From a reliable source I hear that lots of special trains have been running from Natal and Transvaal Republic with strong reinforcements, and that Boers are hastening from all parts to offer determined opposition to our advance in the Orange Free State. Now is your time to push on to Ladysmith. Do all that is possible to effect the relief of White's garrison."

To Major-General Clements on the same day a telegram was sent to say that, according to trustworthy information, a large Boer force had left Colesberg. "It is most desirable," Lord Roberts added, "that no time should be lost in pressing the enemy back north of the Orange river, so that the railway may be repaired without delay, as our line of communication will have to be changed to that route very shortly." *and to Clements to push on, Feb. 20th.*

To prepare this new line of communication the Director of Railways, Lieut.-Colonel Girouard, as soon as the Boers had been driven north of the Orange river, was to make good the damage done by the burghers to the railways leading from the eastern ports of Cape Colony to the Orange Free State. He was also to arrange for the future reorganisation of the railway system from the Orange river to Bloemfontein. These instructions intercepted Girouard at Klip Kraal Drift while on his way to join Lord Roberts with detachments of Royal Engineers, civilian railway employés, and half a battalion of the Railway Pioneer regiment. *Preparations for change of line of communication.*

Such bombardment was maintained as the deficiency of ammunition allowed. Three 4.7-in. and one 12-pr., under Commander W. L. Grant, R.N., the 76th and 82nd Field batteries, *20th Feb. 1900.*

Operations: the bombardment.

and the 65th Howitzer battery crossed to the right bank at Paardeberg Drift, and joining the 81st Field battery on Gun Hill, came into action at a range of about three thousand yards. On the left bank Hall's brigade division, and one Naval 12-pr., under Lieut. Dean, R.N., reinforced about midday by another Naval 4.7-in. and two 12-prs. from Jacobsdal, were posted to the east of Signal Hill, within 1,200 yards of the river bed, in which were concealed Boer sharpshooters, whose fire, though annoying, did little harm. The effect of the fire of these forty-four guns and six howitzers, concentrated on a narrow strip of the river bed little more than a mile in length, appeared to be great. The lyddite shells seemed to fill the bed of the Modder with their fragments, while the shrapnel bullets searched every donga and every bush. The wagons lying deserted on the right bank frequently burst into flame. The Boer guns made no reply. Yet, although the moral influence of the bombardment tended to hasten the surrender, the material results were small. The attractive target of the wagons drew to it most of the shells of the British guns, while the burghers crouched in safety in well-made shelters, dug under the overhanging bank of the river. At dusk all the British batteries, with one exception, were withdrawn under cover, to enable men and horses to obtain food and rest; the 76th remained in action on Gun Hill, and kept up a slow fire throughout the night. The trails of two Naval 12-prs. were damaged. At first they were ordered back to Simon's Town for repairs. Thanks to the energy of Lieut.-Commander W. J. Colquhoun, Royal Victorian Navy, who was in charge of them, they were made good in Kimberley, and the guns were back at the front by the 3rd March.

French's cavalry occupy drifts east of laager.

While the artillery was thus employed, French strengthened the net which was now closing round Cronje by moving the small body of cavalry under his immediate command from Kameelfontein to Koodoos Drift. Gordon, with part of the 16th Lancers, R. battery, and Roberts' Horse, crossed the river and after a sharp skirmish cleared the kopjes on the left bank between Makauw's and Koodoos Drifts. At nightfall a detachment of the 16th Lancers held the ford at Makauw's

THE INVESTMENT OF CRONJE'S LAAGER. 157

and Roberts' Horse guarded the kopjes south of Koodoos Drift, to the north of which the remainder of French's troops bivouacked. No progress was made in the attack against the flanks of Cronje's entrenchments, though the Shropshire Light Infantry, Gordon Highlanders and Canadians to the west, and the Essex and Welsh to the east, maintained their positions with small loss. On the south bank the Highland and the 13th brigades made a demonstration towards the main laager, chiefly in order to keep down the " sniping " against the Naval guns and Hall's batteries. Late in the afternoon Major-General Chermside was directed, with two of his battalions, to continue the line of investment across the plain from the foot-slopes of Signal Hill to the neighbourhood of Vanderberg Drift. Leaving the Norfolk and the Hampshire, Chermside started at 7 p.m. with the Lincoln, King's Own Scottish Borderers, and 9th company Royal Engineers, marching in extended order with a line of men on either side of the wagons, ready to form front in any direction. There had been no time to reconnoitre the ground. Bearings had been taken for a march by compass and stars, but as the route followed was necessarily circuitous to avoid the kopjes and trenches held by the Boers, these bearings were of little or no use. After a time, owing to the darkness and the clouds which obscured the stars, the direction was lost, and a halt was ordered while an officer's patrol, sent forward to reconnoitre, drew the fire of a Boer piquet and found that the column had been moving straight on Cronje's laager, and was close to the left bank of the river. Chermside halted and decided not to start again until daylight.

Infantry make no progress against the flanks of the laager.

Chermside's night march towards Vanderberg Drift.

On the 19th and 20th reports of Boer reinforcements from Natal, Colesberg, Aliwal North, and the Basuto border had poured into Headquarters; Lord Roberts felt that before these fresh troops were organised he must manœuvre Christian De Wet from Kitchener's Kopje, not only to rid himself of the menacing presence of the Free State commander, but also to prepare the way for the proposed cavalry raid on Bloemfontein. General French, to whom this task was assigned for the 21st, resolved to repeat the tactics of the 19th, and to threaten the south of

21st Feb. 1900.

The cavalry attack on Kitchener's Kopje, Feb. 21st.

Kitchener's Kopje with Broadwood's brigade from Paardeberg while he himself shelled the kopje from the north with O. and P. batteries, escorted by two squadrons of the Household cavalry (150 strong), the 9th Lancers, which could only mount eighty-eight men, and a detachment of forty men of Roberts' Horse. As it was thought probable that De Wet would retire to the eastward, the Headquarters and two squadrons of the 16th Lancers, and two sections of R. battery, Royal Horse artillery were sent to reinforce the post at Makauw's Drift. Broadwood's brigade, which, beside the 10th Hussars, 12th Lancers, two squadrons of the Carabiniers, and G. battery, had with it for the day the 75th Field battery and the 4th and 8th mounted infantry, started from Paardeberg Drift at daybreak, making for that south-easterly outlying kopje which for a time it had held on the 19th. French, who was still without Porter's brigade and Alderson's mounted infantry, which did not arrive from Kimberley until dusk, formed his small column in line of masses on the left bank of Koodoos Drift at 5.30 a.m. and moved south-west between the low hills C and D, about two miles south of the drift (see map 23) still occupied by the outposts furnished by Roberts' Horse. As the column emerged from the Nek between the hills detachments of De Wet's burghers were found posted to the south-west on the kopjes marked A and B on the map. De Wet had selected these hills to guard his right flank; and had placed on them his guns, now very short of ammunition. French brought his batteries into action against the more southern of the hills, from about 2,500 yards to the north-east. The shells drove the burghers back to kopje A; the guns were therefore diverted to that target, but the boulders with which the hill was strewn afforded excellent cover from shrapnel, and the Horse artillery failed to dislodge the Boers. On this, French changed his plan. He moved south-east in order to turn the enemy's right flank and join hands with Broadwood. Swinging well clear of the eastern end of B kopje, the squadrons and batteries gradually brought up their left shoulders until they marched westwards. As they cleared Banks Drift Farm three vehicles could be seen retiring hurriedly southward

THE INVESTMENT OF CRONJE'S LAAGER. 159

along the Petrusburg road. They were two Boer guns, which had now no ammunition, and a Royal Engineer wagon previously captured. The Household cavalry, supported by the batteries, started in pursuit, but their horses were so weak that their best pace was a slow trot. The Boer guns escaped; the wagon was retaken.

French now opened communications with Broadwood, whose batteries, some four miles to the westward, were engaged against the southern slopes of Kitchener's Kopje. The 18th and 62nd Field batteries were also in action on the north. Whether this artillery and cavalry demonstration alone would have sufficed cannot now be determined, for it happily chanced that infantry were able to take part in it.

Before daylight on the 21st of February, Major-General Chermside (14th brigade) had resumed his march to Vanderberg Drift, from the bivouac close to the main laager to which the loss of direction of the night before had led him.* Hardly were his troops in motion when they came under fire from three quarters. Guns and rifles played upon them from the Boer entrenchments, De Wet's men opened a slow fusilade from Kitchener's Kop, and a little later they were shelled from the Stinkfontein hills. The situation was an impossible one, and Chermside retired to the southward in order to get out of dangerous range of the laager. Then he pushed on to Vanderberg Drift, which he reached with thirty-eight casualties and some losses in his first line transport. On his arrival he noticed Boer movements on Kitchener's Kopje, and he sent the Lincoln, supported by a half battalion of the King's Own Scottish Borderers, to reconnoitre in that direction. The former battalion went up the northern slopes of the kopje, while the King's Own Scottish Borderers remained at the foot of the hill. *The attack is joined by Chermside's brigade.*

De Wet saw that he was in danger of being surrounded. "It was a hard thing," he has since declared, "to be thus forced to abandon the key to General Cronje's escape," but his men were pressing him to go, and it could not be helped.† On his *De Wet abandons Kitchener's Kopje,*

---

* See page 157.   † "Three Years' War," by C. R. De Wet, page 60.

order, the main body, mounting their ponies, galloped, apparently without much definite guidance, towards French's column, which after its pursuit of the guns had halted to the south-east of Stinkfontein. As the Boers, retreating from Kitchener's Kopje, drew near, some of them dismounted and fired on French's troops, at the moment when the cavalry were hampered by a wire fence. The batteries were instantly brought into action and the troopers dismounted. The burghers could not face in the open the shrapnel and carbine bullets which now smote them. De Wet drew back northward towards the hills A and B, but the commando, pursued at the best pace which the cavalry horses could muster, lost all cohesion, and fled past the outpost line on hill D to Makauw's Drift. Major S. Frewen, 16th Lancers, in command at this crossing, had placed two guns of R. battery and a squadron of his regiment on high ground on the right bank, close to the river, the remainder of his detachment, including two Maxims, being on the left bank. The British guns opened at a range of about three thousand yards on the burghers as they streamed across the plain. The first half-dozen shells diverted the flight to the south-east towards " Table Mountain " (see map No. 23), and the battery continued a rapid fire with accurate aim, but the effect on the scattered horsemen was not great. As the horses of the cavalry were quite unfit for further exertion, the captures were only two or three prisoners and an ammunition wagon. Field-Cornet T. Spiller, of Wepener, and forty-five burghers, had clung to Kitchener's Kopje, and there surrendered to the Lincolnshire battalion. Horses in some number, arms and ammunition in some quantity, were taken. Besides these prisoners, fifteen dead and twenty-eight wounded Boers were picked up on the field. The casualties of the mounted troops in this engagement were only one man killed and two officers and four men wounded. The arrival of the Lincoln and King's Own Scottish Borderers contributed much to the success of French's skilful manœuvring, but De Wet was fortunate to extricate his small party—probably about 1,500 men in all—with such slight losses. Had the horses of the cavalry been fit to gallop, the

but escapes from the net.

THE INVESTMENT OF CRONJE'S LAAGER.

kopje would have been enclosed on all sides and his escape would have been difficult.

A reconnaissance, which was carried out by Captain G. F. Milne, of the Intelligence Staff, on the afternoon of the 21st, showed that De Wet had retreated to the rising ground extending " from a flat-topped hill " (" Table Mountain " on map No. 23) " south-east of Makauw's Drift to a point on the Bloemfontein road, some three miles above the drift." The length of this position was stated to be roughly from three to four miles ; the force holding it was estimated to be two thousand. Therefore, the danger of a counter-attack had not passed away, since reinforcements from Bloemfontein and Colesberg were forming up behind De Wet, and Sir Redvers Buller had reported that three commandos had left Natal.* In addition to the investing line already drawn round Cronje, it became necessary to provide a complete system of defence against possible attacks by the relieving army which De Wet and President Steyn were striving to collect. The VIth division was placed in charge of Kitchener's Kopje, and the Yorkshire, still attached to Knox's brigade (13th), was detailed to hold it, while the King's Own Scottish Borderers occupied Stinkfontein Farm, and joined hands with the cavalry division. French continued the line of observation through Banks Drift, where he had a strong advanced post, and his line of outposts on the right bank of the Modder prevented any attempt by the besieged Boers to break out northwards. As soon as Kitchener's Kopje had fallen into Lord Roberts' hands, arrangements were made for the resumption of Chermside's interrupted march. Calling up the Norfolk and Hampshire from the bivouac near Signal Hill, where they had been left on the evening of the 20th, he led them and the Lincoln during the night of the 21st–22nd to Vanderberg Drift. There he relieved Stephenson's brigade (18th). That brigade moved to the west of Kitchener's Kopje. Then facing south-west it completed the outer line, the perimeter of which was about twenty-four miles.

Margin notes: De Wet, holding Table Mountain, threatens fresh attack. The investment takes a double form. 1. To enclose Cronje. 2. To ward off external attack.

* No. 206 Cipher telegram, 21st February, 1900.

CHAPTER X.

THE SURRENDER OF CRONJE.

The investment completed.

THE inner line of investment now consisted of MacDonald's Highland brigade (3rd) and the 13th brigade (Knox) on the left bank; Smith-Dorrien's brigade (19th) on the right bank, west of the laager, and Chermside's brigade (14th) astride of the river to the east of the laager.

Progress of 19th brigade on west, Feb. 21st.

During the night of the 20th–21st, and while the engagement with De Wet was taking place, the troops on the inner circle had made some progress towards the reduction of Cronje's works. On the east of the laager Stephenson's brigade (18th) continued to work upon the system of trenches they had begun on the night of the 19th. To the west the Shropshire Light Infantry, at daybreak on the 21st, pushed forward under heavy musketry to within six hundred yards of the enemy's works. Not long after the battalion had established itself a series of messages under flags of truce began to pass between Lord Roberts and the Boer General, respecting the disposal of the wounded, and the women and children who accompanied the besieged commandos.

Roberts' offer of help to Boer wounded.

The Field-Marshal spontaneously offered to send surgeons and medicines into the laager, and to allow safe conduct for the women and children to a place of safety. Cronje declined the safe conduct, but accepted the surgeons and medicines on the understanding that he should be free to detain the medical officers. Lord Roberts replied, regretting that he could not dispense with his surgeons for an indefinite time. Then Cronje suggested the establishment of a neutral hospital for the Boer wounded, one thousand yards to the west of the laager; this proposal, if accepted, would have protected one of

THE SURRENDER OF CRONJE.

its two most exposed sides from attack. The Commander-in-Chief felt compelled to reject this suggestion, and replied: "I regret that I do not possess sufficient hospital equipment for my own men. If my original offer be not accepted, I am not in a position to make another." An exchange of wounded prisoners was, however, arranged on the 24th, the British being sent out of the laager and the Boer wounded in British hands being transferred to a German hospital at Jacobsdal.

<small>No agreement.</small>

The lull in the firing caused by the transmission of these messages enabled Major-General Smith-Dorrien to obtain a better view of the Boer defences, and convinced him that he ought to add to his approaches some trenches on the left bank. At dusk, after the temporary truce was over, fifty men of the Shropshire were ferried across the river in a James' boat, and by 11 p.m. they had entrenched themselves on ground selected by the Brigadier. Smith-Dorrien was now given the assistance of the divisional company, Royal Engineers for the construction of regular approaches against the western side of the laager. Before daybreak of the 22nd, the Gordon Highlanders relieved the Shropshire in the advanced trenches on both banks, and pushed forward on the north bank another fifty yards towards the laager.

<small>Smith-Dorrien opens trenches on left bank during night of Feb. 21st.</small>

Throughout the 21st the artillery fire was very slow, and drew only occasional replies from the Boer guns. Owing to heavy rain the tracks across the veld were almost impassable; the first convoy from the railway was not due until the 25th of February, and it became necessary to warn artillery officers to economize ammunition, and to call their attention to the labour of its transport in a country such as that in which the troops were operating. Not only was the supply of shells for the moment inadequate; that of food for man and beast caused much anxiety. It was not until the 23rd that the forage ration of 4lbs. a day—issued very irregularly—could be increased to 8lbs. The men were on half rations of biscuit until the 25th. The deficient bread-stuff was usually replaced by double issues of meat rations, as a considerable number of sheep and cattle had been captured from the enemy.

<small>Necessity for reducing artillery fire, 21st Feb., 1900.</small>

<small>The question of supplies.</small>

VOL. II.

Salvoes were fired from time to time during the night—21st to 22nd—by single batteries detailed for that purpose on each bank. Deserters slipping away in the darkness from the laager stated that there was still sufficient food; that Cronje considered himself safe from assault and had hopes of being relieved, but that he could not break out for want of horses. On the other hand, it was reported that the number of human beings and dead animals crowded in a small space had produced very insanitary conditions. Unfortunately for those of the besiegers who were bivouacked below the Boer camp, they were obliged to draw water poisoned by what was washed down from it. When the river rose after a heavy storm on the 22nd, dead horses in various stages of decomposition floated down at the rate of more than a hundred an hour, and many of them caught in the bushes and trees in the bed of the river and remained there until pushed back into the stream by parties detailed for the purpose. The consequence was a terrible outbreak of enteric fever when the army reached Bloemfontein. The malady, once contracted, attended the army long afterwards.

Insanitary laager.

Water from it carries disease to British Army.

French's success in driving De Wet from Kitchener's Kopje encouraged the Commander-in-Chief to hope that, without waiting for Cronje to surrender, it might be possible to send the cavalry division eastward to brush aside the commandos gathering at Poplar Grove and to seize Bloemfontein. That it might be more easily handled in any such operation, the cavalry was reorganised on 22nd February into two brigades, under Gordon and Broadwood. The detached force commanded by Broadwood had returned to Paardeberg Drift after De Wet's expulsion, but was ordered to rejoin French on the 23rd, convoying to him three days' supplies for the whole division.

Lord Roberts' first scheme for sending cavalry on to Bloemfontein.

There was much to be done outside the area of the raid against Bloemfontein if that stroke, as Lord Roberts hoped, was to open up a fresh line of supply by the Norval's Pont railway.* The forces under Clements and Gatacre and the troops stationed along the present line of communication must be brought under

* See map No. 35.

THE SURRENDER OF CRONJE.

one directing hand. The change involved in shifting the whole machinery required for moving forward the vast tonnage of food and warlike stores necessary for the army was in itself a very serious undertaking. The materials for repairing the bridges and other damaged parts of the railway had to be brought up to the front, whilst the needs of the army in the field must at the same time be met. For this all-important duty Lord Roberts selected Lord Kitchener, who started for Modder River station on the afternoon of the 22nd February, with the following instructions from the Commander-in-Chief:— *Kitchener sent to superintend arrangements for change of line of communication, Feb. 22nd, 1900.*

> "Paardeberg,
> "22nd February, 1900.
>
> "You are to proceed to Naauwpoort in view to assisting Lieut.-Colonel Girouard in pushing the railway across the Orange river as soon as the enemy vacate the country in the south. The Norval's Pont bridge is reported to be so strongly fortified, and the ground immediately north of the river in that direction to be so difficult, that the Bethulie bridge would appear to be the one we could secure the more easily. This would require assistance from General Gatacre's troops, and you are authorised to call upon him for such assistance as he may be able to afford. As Brabant pushes forward, and the enemy's numbers decrease, Gatacre will doubtless be able to occupy Stormberg.
> "ROBERTS."

Kitchener's Kopje had rightly been regarded by De Wet as "the key to General Cronje's escape," and he was too able a leader not to try to recover it. The good fortune which had attended his withdrawal on the 21st was somewhat deceptive, for if he could have clung to the kopje until the afternoon of that day he might have been reinforced by the Winburg and Senekal commandos, which reached Poplar Grove from Natal that morning. The Winburg commando, conveyed by special trains, is shown by the railway records to have been about one thousand strong, exclusive of a large number of natives, arms, horses and transport. President Steyn had striven hard to save Cronje. From Colesberg, a large body arrived at Poplar Grove on the 22nd, raising to about five thousand men the total strength under Christian De Wet, who had now supreme command of all the Free State forces. But, though the Free Staters responded readily to the calls made on them in this emergency, they *De Wet gathers strength at Poplar Grove. Transvaalers hold aloof.*

received little aid from their allies of the Transvaal. Most of the Transvaal commandos which had invested Kimberley remained sullenly at Fourteen Streams on the right bank of the Vaal, under General Du Toit, apparently expecting an attack from the Kimberley garrison, now reinforced by the 9th brigade (Douglas) and by Lord Methuen's divisional troops. One detachment had fled to Christiana, and thence telegraphed an appeal to Kruger to make peace. Another, under Kolbe, had retraced its steps from Boshof and on the 18th joined General J. S. Ferreira's contingent to the north of Koodoosrand. Ferreira himself was accidentally shot that night by one of his own sentries, and his death left his immediate following without leadership. He had succeeded General C. J. Wessels as Commander-in-Chief of the Free State forces in the western theatre in January, 1900. His loss led to C. De Wet's appointment to that position. It was not the fault of the Transvaal President or of the Commandant-General that their burghers were thus backward. They both sent urgent telegrams, directing every exertion to be made to relieve Cronje. The later phases of the campaign prove that the disregard shown to these orders was due neither to cowardice nor to lack of patriotism, but to the disintegration produced by want of discipline and of proper military organisation. Even though the besieged were chiefly Transvaal men, each group of burghers deemed the protection of their own homes of more importance than the defeat of the enemy. Steyn, therefore, became more and more anxious as to the future, and on the 21st he telegraphed to Pretoria to arrange for the transmission thither of all surplus ammunition from Bloemfontein.

Boers project a raid against the rail near De Aar, and strive to rouse Cape Colony to revolt.

On the same day Mr. Grobelaar (a member of the War Commission at Pretoria) telegraphed to Mr. A. Fischer, who held a similar position at Bloemfontein, to suggest that De la Rey with a commando of 1,000 to 1,200 and two guns should be sent from Colesberg to raid the railway between De Aar and the Orange river, and, if possible to destroy bridges and culverts. President Steyn referred this suggestion to De la Rey, but replied to Pretoria that he did not think it was practicable, as the Coles-

THE SURRENDER OF CRONJE.

berg commandos had been reduced in strength and De la Rey's horses were weak. The plan came to nothing. A leader like C. De Wet might have carried it out, but he was otherwise employed. Foiled in this respect, the Free State President hoped to create a diversion by other means. On the 22nd, he telegraphed to Judge Hertzog at Petrusburg :—

"Confidential. It is deemed desirable that an immediate movement be started, under the leadership of their chief men, among Cape Colonial friends, for the establishment of a republic, or at the least of self-government there, to be supported at the outset with money and arms by this State. It is necessary that somebody with the required authority should proceed from here to call and superintend a meeting at Burghersdorp, select a leader, and assist in arranging matters ; I would gladly see you take this upon yourself. If you are agreeable kindly come over here at once to discuss matters. . . . Someone from the Colony is waiting here."

Kruger was asked on the same day if he could supply ten thousand rifles which the secret agent from Cape Colony required for the projected "movement." The movement proved abortive.

Little need be said about the operations of the troops forming the inner line on the 22nd. When Chermside relieved Stephenson in the trenches east of the laager, he arranged for steady sapping towards Cronje's works. As the 14th brigade did not leave its position on the right bank until the surrender of the laager, it is convenient now to summarise its action up to the end of the siege. The trenches dug by the brigade, with the help of the 9th company Royal Engineers, were deep and narrow, like those of the Turks in the war of 1878-9. Every evening before sunset Lieut.-Colonel R. C. Maxwell, C.R.E., of the VIIth division, and his staff, reconnoitred to the front and were thus able to give precise orders for the capture during the night of sites which, under the protection of covering parties, were entrenched before sunrise. The details of the progress made from day to day are shown on map No. 24, and the diary of the work done is given in Appendix 3.

Chermside's operations from the east, Feb. 22nd to 27th.

During the days and nights in which the 14th brigade thus dug itself forward few casualties occurred, but the troops here, as elsewhere, suffered much from lack of sleep and food. Rations could only be brought up after dark, and the covering parties were frequently without other food than a half, and in some cases, a quarter ration of biscuit. Frequent downpours of rain filled the trenches with water and greatly increased the hardships of the soldiers.

<small>Artillery closes in.</small>

The recapture of Kitchener's Kopje on the 21st enabled the artillery on the south of the river to move a mile to the east and thus obtain better positions for shelling the Boer entrenchments, but the scant supply of ammunition still restricted the guns to an occasional round during the day. On the night of 22nd–23rd nearly the whole of the artillery, including the Naval guns, fired hourly into the laager.

<small>Night of 22nd-23rd Feb., 1900.</small>

<small>Balloon detachment.</small>

A balloon detachment, which reached Paardeberg on the 22nd, under command of Lieut. A. H. W. Grubb, R.E., observed and signalled the effect of the fire, but the exchange of messages between the car and the batteries left much to be desired. The signallers with the balloon repeatedly failed to attract the attention of those with the guns.

<small>Boers plan a fresh attack on Kitchener's Kopje.</small>

Meanwhile Christian De Wet was reorganising his burghers at Poplar Grove, and arranging for a fresh attempt to recover Kitchener's Kopje. It was decided at a Krijgsraad held on the 22nd that the main body, about three thousand strong, led by De Wet and A. Cronje, should attack on the following morning the hills A and B (see map No. 23), now held by the King's Own Scottish Borderers, and that Froneman, with four hundred men, should seize Banks Drift Farm, occupied by a squadron of the 9th Lancers, under Captain F. T. Lund, while Commandant Philip Botha with the rest of the commandos stormed Kitchener's Kopje. The actual strength of the detachments which embarked upon these various enterprises is doubtful; for the majority of the burghers had neither the discipline nor the determination needed for offensive action, and not a few lingered at Poplar Grove when their comrades moved off in the grey of the early morning of the 23rd.

<small>The execution of the plan, Feb. 23rd.</small>

De Wet's and Froneman's attacks began at dawn, but were never pressed home. Kelly-Kenny, on hearing the firing, sent the 62nd Field battery to support the King's Own Scottish

THE SURRENDER OF CRONJE. 169

Borderers; while Colonel Porter, with a Horse artillery battery, a squadron of the Scots Greys, another of the Carabiniers and a company of mounted infantry, was ordered by French to assist Lund. Porter, on arrival on the scene of action, found De Wet's and Froneman's commandos in possession of kopje B. Directing his battery to come into action against the enemy's left, he sent the Scots Greys to turn that flank, and a little later menaced the enemy's right with the Carabiniers, while the mounted infantry reinforced Lund. This threat of envelopment, although by an inferior force, was enough; the Boer right attack broke up, and retired in haste across the veld to the eastward. Porter being unable to pursue, only eight prisoners were taken. Not a single casualty occurred in the British cavalry; one officer and three men of the King's Own Scottish Borderers had been wounded in the earlier part of the skirmish. On the withdrawal of De Wet, the 62nd battery remained at Osfontein as part of the outpost line; the company of the mounted infantry stayed with Lund at Banks Drift Farm. *De Wet and Froneman driven back.*

Botha's attack proved to be a somewhat more serious affair, and his leading detachment showed no lack of enterprise. Major J. A. Fearon, who was in command of the Yorkshire, had detailed four of his companies for outpost duty. These, with their piquets, were on the southern spur of Kitchener's Kopje; the rest of the battalion bivouacked in a fold of the ground in rear. Part of the Winburg commando, under Commandant H. Theunissen, crept forward just before dawn, drove in a small post thrown out from the advanced piquet and seized a bush-covered under-feature, which marks the end of the southern spur. A hot musketry duel ensued, and as dawn broke, a long loose line of dismounted Boers could be seen in the plain below moving towards the bush. Volleys fired at a range of 1,500 yards failed to stop them, and Botha, with little loss, succeeded in bringing his men into the scrub already occupied by Theunissen. The main body of the Yorkshire had reinforced the outpost line, and at 8.30 a.m. the 75th Field battery, the Buffs, and Essex regiment, under Colonel R. A. Hickson, the Buffs, who had been sent up by Lieutenant-General Kelly-Kenny, *Botha also repulsed.*

arrived on the scene of action. As these further reinforcements pushed forward, and began to act against the flanks of the attack, Botha lost heart, withdrew his main body, and remounting retired at a gallop across the veld. But Theunissen's men, with much gallantry, remained and defended the under-feature until noon, when, their horses having been all lost or killed, they were compelled to surrender. The British casualties in this part of the fight amounted to nine men killed, five officers and twenty-three men wounded, and two men missing. Eight or nine dead Boers were found on the field, and there were many wounded amongst the eighty-seven prisoners. The conduct of Theunissen's followers was in marked contrast to that of the rest of their comrades in this boldly conceived but timidly executed enterprise.

De Wet urges Cronje to cut his way out. During the progress of the fight Cronje had signalled from the laager that he could defend himself for two days more, and De Wet had answered: "Hold out, we hope to cut our way through." But the failure of the day's operations and the increased depression it had produced among his already disheartened burghers now convinced De Wet that he was not strong enough to break through Lord Roberts' line of investment. The only chance left for Cronje was to cut his way out at night. De Wet was anxious to impress this upon the Transvaal leader, and to explain to him that when once out of the laager his retreat would be protected. Daniel Theron, the leader of the Boer Intelligence scouts, volunteered for the dangerous task of conveying De Wet's views to the laager. He succeeded in reaching Cronje on February 24th, and returned in safety, but failed to induce the burghers to respond to De Wet's appeal. Their attitude of passive despair is well portrayed in a telegram from Petrusburg, sent on the 26th to President Kruger by the intrepid scout :—

Report on condition in laager. "Your Honour, the night before last I took a report to General Cronje, and got back safely again last night, thanks to God's guidance. The English piquets are stationed around the laager about ten paces apart, and consequently it took a long time and was difficult to creep through them. My knees are bleeding. The state of affairs in the laager is indescribably miserable and dreadful.

THE SURRENDER OF CRONJE.

General Cronje and his wife are well. There are about twenty-five dead and fifty wounded. It is heartrending to see how men who have been comparatively slightly wounded perish and die owing to want of nursing and proper food. General Cronje said there was hardly sufficient food for to-day. There are still about one hundred horses in the laager in a critical state owing to want of food, for as soon as they go one hundred yards from the laager they run the risk of being shot. The Lee-Metford bullets whistle over our heads the whole day long. The English seem to have stationed sharpshooters in the immediate neighbourhood of the laager, who, throughout the whole day, make our lives unsafe. They have now even dug trenches in some places. The laager is completely surrounded, is being enfiladed by a number of guns which are bombarding it from all sides. Our people are seeking protection in trenches, holes, and in the banks of the river, and when it rains like it did the night before last one can only with the greatest difficulty get from one place to another. There does not seem to be much sickness among our people. This is surprising, for the putrefying and pestilential dead horses are lying in hundreds among the people, and the stench is almost unbearable. Most of the wagons and other things have been burnt. I went to propose to General Cronje a plan to break through—how, where and when. He agrees with it, but most of his officers and men are unwilling. The General, I, and a few others yesterday went about among the men and did everything to encourage them and to make them willing, but half of them are so disheartened and depressed that they really no longer mind falling into the enemy's hands. Very many of them say straight out that they are not going to leave the trenches, but are going to surrender to the English as soon as General Cronje makes a dash out. God grant that they may change their minds, should one man force a way out for himself. The plan was to come out the night before last, but during the day the river became deeper and the bridge and pont could not be worked. The attempt therefore must be made this evening. They have more than enough ammunition to take with them, but naturally a large amount and also their goods will have to be left in the lurch. The distance which they will have to go is about one hour on horseback. I also heard there that quite a large number of our men from time to time make their escape from the laager and that they have all fallen into the hands of the English. President, I do not send you this telegram to depress you, but to let you know exactly how things are there, so that you may not have a false impression about the peril of our position. Please urge President Steyn to well provide Bloemfontein with food, and to have trenches and forts made. The women and children also intend to come out with the men; they do not want to remain behind."

While Botha's attack on Kitchener's Kopje was going on, Broadwood's brigade had escorted a supply column from Paardeberg Drift to Koodoosrand. The concentration of the cavalry division for an advance on Bloemfontein was thus completed; but the state of the horses made the enterprise im-

23rd Feb., 1900. The cavalry raid on Bloemfontein impossible, from state of horses.

possible. The total strength of the division on the 24th amounted to 4,510 officers and men, 4,221 horses, 42 Horse artillery guns and 6 Maxims. The condition of the animals still at work may be judged from the fact that they had all been suffering from the same causes which had killed nearly a third of those which started from Ramdam. Hardly any were fit for a charge or for a long and rapid march. On the evening of the 23rd Lieut.-General French reported to the Field-Marshal that neither the cavalry nor the artillery horses of the units under his command were equal to a great effort and that rest and good feeding were an absolute necessity. To miss the opportunity for this great stroke was an even harder blow to the cavalry leader than to the Commander-in-Chief.

Meantime, the reported arrival at Poplar Grove of Boer reinforcements, believed to include a commando two thousand strong, under General J. H. Olivier from Stormberg, had changed the situation since Lord Roberts first thought of sending French on to Bloemfontein. The enemy were collecting nearer than the capital. Poplar Grove was only twelve miles from Paardeberg. Forage and remounts were beginning to arrive from Kimberley and from Modder River station. There seemed reason to hope that a few days' delay would bring about the surrender of Cronje, and that a heavy blow might then be struck at the other body of the enemy without so great a strain on the cavalry horses as the original scheme would have involved. Lord Roberts therefore cancelled the orders for the cavalry march, informing the Chief of the Staff, who had now reached Naauwpoort, of this change in his plans.

Consequent change of orders, Feb. 25th.

Clements' instructions were also modified. For those orders of the 20th, in which he had been urged to press the Boers back north of the Orange river, and for those to the Chief of the Staff of the 22nd which suggested Bethulie as the best point for the passage of the Orange river, were now (February 25th) substituted directions to Clements through Lord Kitchener that " he should confine himself to protecting Naauwpoort." Lord Roberts saw that Norval's Pont would be evacuated as soon as Piet De Wet's rear was menaced by the advance of the main

THE SURRENDER OF CRONJE. 173

army on Bloemfontein, and that therefore no good would result from a direct attack on the strong natural positions which covered the road and railway crossings of the Orange river. General Buller was warned to be prepared to send one of his divisions to East London as soon as Ladysmith had been relieved.

For the next three days the work of the army consisted in digging trenches at night, guarding them by day, and watching the movements of the Boers who hovered round the outer line of defence. A complete change in the situation came about on February 26th. On the morning of that day the 19th brigade, with Lieut.-Colonel W. F. H. S. Kincaid's company (the 7th) Royal Engineers, by dint of strenuous work had finished entrenching the ground first won by the Shropshire Light Infantry and the Gordon Highlanders. On the right bank they had made a trench 460 yards in length, which first ran northwards, and then turning gradually to the north-east towards the enemy, cleared a patch of scrub which had hitherto given shelter to Boer sharpshooters. On the left bank of the Modder they had continued the trench about 280 yards to the southward. Thus they were astride of the river. The officer in the balloon had reported that the enemy's main position consisted of a series of entrenchments parallel with the right bank, covered by a short flanking trench which ran northwards from the river for thirty-five yards. Between this flanking trench and the north-east end of that excavated by the 19th brigade the ground was open, and when once this space was crossed and the Boer flanking trench had been captured, the enemy's main position could be enfiladed at close range. After inspecting the British works, Lieut.-General Colvile became convinced that a more rapid advance was now possible. He discussed the situation with Major-General Smith-Dorrien and Major-General Elliott Wood, E.-in-C., and then obtained leave from Lord Roberts to make on the flanking trench a night attack, the orders for which were issued in the course of the afternoon.

The battalions of the 19th brigade took their turn by roster for manning the front trenches on both banks. On the night

23rd-25th Feb.

Situation on 26th. 19th brigade's works on both banks.

An assault sanctioned. The orders.

of the 26th–27th it was the turn of the Royal Canadian regiment, to whom thus fell the honour of leading the assault. Six companies of Canadians, about 480 men in all, were to advance, extended at one pace interval and formed in two lines, with fifteen paces distance between the lines. The front rank, or first line, of each company, was to march with fixed bayonets, the second line following with shovels and picks, their rifles slung. All had orders not to fire till the enemy opened. Lieut.-Colonel Kincaid, with Captain F. R. F. Boileau, R.E., and thirty Sappers were to accompany the right of the second line. To protect the outer flank of the Canadians three companies of the Gordon Highlanders were detailed to hold the left of the main British trench. This protecting line was prolonged to the left by the Shropshire, who, as soon as they heard firing, were to pour long-range volleys upon the laager. A company of the Canadians was held as a local reserve in a work behind the main trench. The remaining five companies of the Gordon Highlanders were extended five hundred yards behind them, and still further back the Cornwall Light Infantry, Argyll and Sutherland Highlanders, and two companies of the Black Watch formed a general reserve. A company of the Canadians was in the trench on the left bank. While preparations for this advance were in progress, the artillery on both banks shelled the main laager for two hours. The guns to the south of the river had this day been reinforced by four 6-in. Howitzers and three 1-in. Vickers-Maxim quick-firers (pom-poms). At nightfall Lord Roberts issued orders for a general bombardment next morning.

The advance begins, 27th Feb., 1900. The advance of the Canadians and Royal Engineers began at 2.15 on the morning of the 27th. Major-General Smith-Dorrien was on the right of the line ; the Commanding Officer of the Canadians—Lieut.-Colonel W. D. Otter—moved in rear of the front rank on the left. Of the two regimental majors, one, Lieut.-Colonel L. Buchan, was posted on the left, the other, Lieut.-Colonel O. C. C. Pelletier, on the right. A fine night favoured the enterprise, but the moon was not due above the horizon for more than an hour, and, though the stars shone out brightly, the

THE SURRENDER OF CRONJE. 175

men found some difficulty in keeping touch while passing through the bush on the right. When once clear of this scrub progress was steady and silent until at 2.50 a.m. the assailants were within sixty-five to one hundred yards of the Boer flanking trench, from which two shots suddenly rang out, followed almost immediately by the flame of a fierce fusilade. For a moment the troops slightly recoiled, but the premature discharge of the two rifles had served as a warning, and gave time to many of the Canadians to throw themselves on the ground. The enemy's fire was at once vigorously returned, chiefly by volleys. A slight fold in the ground, only eighteen inches high, gave partial cover to the troops on the right; the remainder lay entirely in the open, but there were not many casualties. Screened by the musketry of the front rank, the rear rank and the Royal Engineers set to work to make a trench within about one hundred yards of the enemy.

On the right rapid progress was made, but on the left an unfortunate mishap occurred. An authoritative voice, the identity of which was never discovered, was heard calling out "Retire and bring back your wounded." The four companies on the left obeyed and fell back. Regardless, however, of this miscarriage of his plans, Smith-Dorrien held on to the right with Kincaid's Sappers and "H." and "G." companies of the Canadians (commanded respectively by Captain H. B. Stairs and Lieut. A. H. Macdonell), and by 5 a.m. had made an entrenchment, thoroughly revetted and loop-holed with sandbags. The Shropshire meanwhile kept the main Boer laager occupied by continuous long-range fire, and a party from the reserve was told by Smith-Dorrien to make use of two stone huts on the left bank of the Modder to protect the new trench on the right bank from enfilade. As daylight broke, the Boer flanking trench, sunk almost level with the ground, could be seen about one hundred yards away. At this close range firing was kept up for a quarter of an hour. Then suddenly a white flag fluttered from the Boer trench. Some parleying ensued. About 6 a.m. another white flag could be seen flying over the main laager and it became known that Cronje had surrendered unconditionally.

An unlucky mistake.

Boers raise the white flag.

The cost of Smith-Dorrien's attack was but twelve men killed, and three officers (including Lieut.-Colonel Pelletier) and thirty men wounded.

As long as Smith-Dorrien's musketry was enfilading the line of trenches along the river bank, not a man was to be seen. The laager looked absolutely deserted. But when the surrender was announced and firing ceased, the burghers rose from their trenches, and the plain suddenly swarmed with hundreds of men. In the words of an eye-witness, "It was like the Day of Judgment. The graves gave forth their dead."

The true cause of surrender.

Nothing could have been better than the completeness with which all the arrangements for the attack were made nor, despite the unfortunate incident which allowed success to be achieved by only part of the companies engaged, better than its execution, but it would not be historically true to say that this led to the surrender of the Boers. It did not even determine that the surrender should be on Majuba Day. The order for the hoisting of the white flag at the hour when it appeared had been given on the previous evening. Theron's despatch to Kruger shows that by the 25th February—that Sunday which the Boer scout had spent in the laager—the majority of Cronje's burghers had lost all heart and cherished little hope of further resistance. Cronje himself was well aware that his hold on his men had slackened. A plot had been discovered amongst the faint-hearted to cross over in a body to the British lines without their Head Commandant's consent. Nevertheless, the Boer General's resolution continued unbroken. On the morning of the 26th, determined to do his duty to the last, he formally laid before a Krijgsraad De Wet's appeal, and exhorted the burghers to fight their way out, but hardly a hand was held up in favourable response. With much difficulty Cronje persuaded his Council of War to postpone formal surrender until the 28th, so as at least to tide over the anniversary of Majuba. This resolution was broken down by the two hours' bombardment of the big 6-in. shells of the four Howitzers, and by the projectiles of the Naval 4.7-in. guns. The Krijgsraad, cowed by the effect of the fire, decreed that a surrender must be made at 6 a.m. on

THE SURRENDER OF CRONJE.

the 27th. At that hour a flag of truce with the following despatch, written during the night by Cronje, was sent out to Lord Roberts :—

<blockquote>
"Headquarter Laager,
"Modder River.
"February 27th, 1900.

"HONOURED SIR,

"Hereby I have the honour to acquaint you that the Council of War resolved last night, being compelled to do so under the existing circumstances, to surrender themselves with the forces here unconditionally, throwing themselves on the clemency of Her Britannic Majesty. As a sign of surrender, a white flag will be hoisted from 6 o'clock this morning. The Council of War further desires that you will give immediate orders that all further hostilities shall be stopped in order that further loss of life may be prevented.

"I have the honour to be,
Sir,
"Your most obedient servant,
"P. A. CRONJE, GENERAL."
</blockquote>

Surrender of Cronje's force, Feb. 27th., 1900.

The Commander-in-Chief replied :—

<blockquote>
"HONOURED SIR,

"Your letter of this date is to hand. It gives me great pleasure to accept your unconditional surrender. I shall be glad to receive you here in person and to take care of you. Your burghers will, if you please, come out on to the plain without arms, which must be left in the laager under supervision of a guard. The officer who takes this letter will conduct you to my camp. Please accompany him."
</blockquote>

General Cronje, conducted by Major-General G. T. Pretyman, appeared shortly after 7 a.m. at the Commander-in-Chief's quarters, and the details of the surrender of the Boer force were arranged. The Boers, each carrying a bundle of clothing, then waded across the Drift and were received by Lieut.-General Kelly-Kenny, who, as soon as they had been counted, marched them to Headquarters under an escort of the Buffs. By noon the laager was in the occupation of the 19th brigade, to which three representative companies of the 3rd brigade had been attached in order that the Highland regiments might share the distinction. During the afternoon the burghers marched under guard of the Gloucestershire to Klip Drift, and were thence on the following day, escorted by the 3rd Grenadier and 2nd Coldstream Guards, to Modder River station for transport by rail to Cape Town. They were preceded by General Cronje and his wife, who were taken immediately to Cape Town by Major-General Pretyman. From the return to be found in Appendix 4, it will be seen that 3,919 fighting men, of whom 2,592 were Transvaalers, surrendered on the 27th. To this total must be added the men who had dribbled into the British lines day by day during the investment of the laager. Four field guns, one pom-pom, and a large quantity of rifles and ammunition were also captured. In addition to this ammunition, ten or eleven tons weight of Mauser cartridges, a good number of field-gun shells and some 6-in. projectiles were dug up from the laager by a search party sent, two or three months later, to Paardeberg by the Military Governor of Bloemfontein.

<small>Prisoners taken.</small>

The surrender of Cronje was in itself a mere incident. His fate was decided when, arrested by French's audacity at the moment of his attempt to cross Vendutie Drift, his hesitation allowed Kelly-Kenny's and Colvile's hard-driven divisions to close with him, and destroy his power of further movement. Cronje had previously been outwitted and imposed upon by his opponent. The vacillation at the drift was a fatal and final blunder. Yet the grim determination with which the old Boer leader compelled his disheartened subordinates to resist superior forces for ten days in a hopeless position, merited to the full Lord Roberts' first greeting to him: "You have made a gallant defence, sir." That respectful sympathy, which Joubert had shown to the vanquished at Majuba, became now the just due of Cronje and his burghers, and was gladly repaid.

<small>Feb. 28th. The changed aspect of affairs.</small>

The British Commander-in-Chief had in truth ample reason to be generous to his vanquished foe. Sound strategy and a well-equipped and sufficient army, combined with the gallantry, energy, and endurance of the troops alike in the western and eastern theatres of war, had in less than three weeks completely changed the whole aspect of the campaign. The end of the investment of Paardeberg on February 27th and Buller's entry into Ladysmith on March 3rd were events of importance very different from the mere capture of four thousand men. The

THE SURRENDER OF CRONJE.

whole of the enemy's plan of campaign was destroyed, and the prizes for which the Boers had fought for five months were wrested from their grasp. A few days later not only was Cape Colony practically clear of the main body of its invaders, but the southern half of the Free State lay open to Lord Roberts. The struggle, it is true, lingered on for another two years, but the hoisting of the signal of surrender in Cronje's laager and the victory of the 27th February on the Tugela mark the final disappearance of Kruger's and Steyn's power for offence and ensured the triumph of the British flag in South Africa. Henceforth no other design inspired the Boer strategy than to save, if it were possible, from the wreck of their ambitions the independence of the two Republics.

A summary of the casualties in Lord Roberts' operations on the Modder will be found in Appendix 2.

CHAPTER XI.

FROM PAARDEBERG TO POPLAR GROVE.*

<small>Halt now enforced by weakness of horses,</small>

THE Commander-in-Chief, much as he wished after Cronje's surrender to push on for Bloemfontein at once, found that the condition of the cavalry and artillery horses obliged him to give them a week's rest, during which the more ample forage now obtainable might partially at least enable them to recover from the long strain of work on empty stomachs which had reduced them to inefficiency. Unfortunately adequate forage did not come up in time to restore the horses to efficiency, and the whole story of Poplar Grove turned on that fact. Moreover, he was about to break loose from the Kimberley railway, on which he had hitherto drawn, intending to open a fresh line *via* Norval's Pont and Bethulie on his arrival at Bloemfontein. To carry out

<small>and the need of supplies for march.</small>

this plan a few days were needed to accumulate the supplies necessary for the advance eastward, and to clear up and close the old line of communications from the Modder Camp. Orders were, therefore, issued on the 28th of February that the main body of the army should vacate the tainted ground round Paardeberg for fresh bivouacs near Osfontein. Advantage was

<small>Restoration of regular organisation.</small>

taken of this move to restore the displaced units to their proper corps. The IXth division (Colvile) remained on the right bank of the river, but was moved forward to a site near Vanderberg Drift. The cavalry division still bivouacked close to Koodoos Drift. On the 3rd March further orders were issued for the concentration at Osfontein of the Guards' brigade from Klip Drift and Klip Kraal, of the 15th brigade and Lieut.-Colonel

---

* See maps Nos. 25 and 26.

E. M. Flint's brigade division, Royal Field artillery, from Jacobsdal, and of various mounted infantry details from the Modder Camp.

The Guards' brigade reached Headquarters on the 6th, and, until the arrival of the army at Bloemfontein, was retained under the direct orders of the Commander-in-Chief as corps troops. The 15th brigade rejoined its division, the VIIth, on the 9th at Waaihoek after the action of Poplar Grove. Flint's brigade division Royal Field artillery marched in to Osfontein on the 6th, but was not actually united to Colvile's division, of which it formed the divisional artillery, until the 9th. The arrival on the 6th at Osfontein of the additional mounted infantry permitted of the redistribution of that arm into four brigades, under Colonel C. P. Ridley and the following Lieut.-Colonels: E. A. H. Alderson, P. W. J. Le Gallais, C. G. Martyr.* Mounted infantry formed in four brigades.

On February 28th, Lord Roberts appointed Lieut.-Colonel J. M. Grierson as A.A.G., on the Staff of the Army, to be responsible for the movement and distribution of the troops—a much needed improvement. Hitherto these duties had not been assigned to any particular section of the Staff.† The losses due to De Wet's exploit at Waterval Drift had been partly made good by the convoy from Modder River, partly by the captures made at Bosjespan, partly by transport supplied by the De Beers Company at Kimberley. By the 4th March, twenty-five days' biscuit rations and twenty days' groceries for the whole force had reached Osfontein, or were close at hand. Of forage there were only 30,000 lbs. unissued, but 300,000 lbs. (35,000 rations) were en route from Kimberley or the Modder Camp, and another 900,000 lbs. were to follow. Heavy storms of rain still made the ground soft, and the drifts in many cases impassable. The movements of convoys were impeded not only by the absence of roads and the condition to which the tracks were reduced, State of supplies.
Peculiar difficulties of transport.

---

* For composition, see Appendix 5.

† For the working of the British Staff system prior to 1888 and the history of the changes then made, see the evidence given by Lieut.-General Sir W. Nicholson before the War Commission.—Minutes of Evidence, Volume II., pages 344-6.

but by the perpetual passage of narrow drifts over petty streams, which had been converted in a few hours into raging torrents, so that often it was necessary to wait till the water had run down and then carry the contents of the wagons across by hand. As a set-off to this, the young grass, which the rain, in that semi-tropical climate brought up almost at once, helped to revive the starved horses and mules. Of slaughter cattle there were present with the main army on the 4th March only three days' rations, but just as these had been nearly all eaten, anxiety was relieved by a further capture of cattle enough for two or three days longer. Afterwards meat could be obtained from the farms as the troops marched eastward. Good progress had been made in the evacuation of the Field Hospitals. In the week from the 25th February to the 4th March, convoys of sick and wounded, amounting in all to 742 all ranks, were removed to the Modder Camp and Kimberley. The sudden demand of the medical authorities for 100 wagons for this purpose, withdrew transport badly needed for the feeding of the troops. Had the accumulation of sick been gradually relieved by using the empty wagons on their return journeys, this would not have been required.

March 1st. Lord Roberts visits Kimberley.

The Field-Marshal himself, in order to discuss with Lord Methuen the situation to the northward, rode on March 1st to Kimberley. There he was joined by the Chief of the Staff. Clements had on 28th February been warned "to act strictly on the defensive until further orders."

Lord Kitchener sends three columns to clear country round Prieska.

Lord Kitchener, leaving Naauwpoort, had spent a day at De Aar, and there arranged with Brigadier-General H. H. Settle, commanding the section of the line of communications to the south of the Orange river, for the despatch westward of three small flying columns, under the respective commands of General Settle himself, Colonel J. Adye, R.A., and Colonel Sir Charles Parsons, R.A., to deal with the hostile bands assembling in the direction of Prieska and Van Wyk's Vlei.*

On the arrival of the Commander-in-Chief and Chief of the Staff at Kimberley the possibility of raising a local force to

* These operations will be described in Volume III.

effect the immediate relief of Mafeking was considered, but for this events were not yet ripe. Lord Roberts, returning to Osfontein on the 2nd, sent Lord Methuen orders to clear Boshof of the enemy, and when a force of Imperial Yeomanry and other mounted troops sufficient for that purpose should have joined him, to assume the offensive. He was then to cross the Vaal by a flanking movement, and push towards Mafeking. Orders were accordingly given for the despatch to Kimberley of a mounted brigade, under the command of Colonel Lord Chesham, consisting of the newly arrived 3rd, 5th, and 10th battalions of Imperial Yeomanry.

Methuen to seize Boshof, and with Chesham's Yeomanry push on to Mafeking.

The welcome news of the victory of Pieters Hill reached Lord Roberts on 28th February. He telegraphed at once to General Buller :—

Feb. 28th. Lord Roberts congratulates Buller and White on relief of Ladysmith.

"Paardeberg,
"28th February, 1900.

"Your telegram 0428 of to-day has given everyone in this force the greatest pleasure. We rejoice to think that your goal is so nearly reached, and that the courage and endurance, so conspicuously displayed by your troops, are about to be rewarded by their having the great honour and proud satisfaction of relieving Sir George White and the beleaguered garrison at Ladysmith."

To Sir George White the Field-Marshal telegraphed from Kimberley on the following day :—

"It is impossible for me to express my delight on hearing that Dundonald had reached Ladysmith. The prayers that have been offered up throughout the Empire have been heard, and from one end of it to the other there will be general rejoicing. I wish I could personally congratulate you and your gallant troops on the splendid defence that has been made. Please convey to one and all my high sense of their conduct as soldiers worthy of the best traditions of the British Army."

The distribution and future action of the four divisions in the eastern theatre, including the Ladysmith garrison, had now to be determined. In reply to Lord Roberts' warning of February 25th that the despatch of one of these divisions to East London would probably prove necessary, General Buller had telegraphed : " I will send every man I can spare as soon as I get to Ladysmith." On the 3rd March he reported :—

<small>Sir Redvers' proposals, March 3rd.</small>

"I find that the defeat of the Boers is more complete than I had dared to anticipate. . . . My troops want a week's rest, boots, and clothes. The Ladysmith garrison wants a fortnight's food and exercise. I do not think there is any chance of the enemy making a stand this side of Laing's Nek. . . . Will you advise me as to what course you wish pursued. My own view would be that we should send three brigades to occupy Northern Natal, to restore order and repair the railway, and with two divisions attack the three passes, Tintwa, Van Reenen's and Bezuidenhout, and pass through one of them the division you wish sent to your side, or, in the alternative of your not wanting a division, that the force here should reoccupy Northern Natal and the Wakkerstroom-Vryheid district of the Transvaal. The latter is the alternative I. incline to, as likely to be most objectionable to the enemy . . ."

<small>Lord Roberts' plans for Natal and Cape.</small>

The Commander-in-Chief deemed it unwise to embark on extensive operations in a country so favourable for the tactics of the Boers as the passes of the Drakensberg. He had, moreover, resolved to strengthen the military situation in the eastern portion of Cape Colony, which had been weak ever since the beginning of the war. He meant to place one of Buller's divisions and General Gatacre's force under the command of Sir George White. He replied at once, therefore, in this sense to Sir R. Buller's telegram, directing him to despatch a division to East London, and with the troops remaining with him " to act strictly on the defensive until such time as the operations of this column (i.e., the army under Lord Roberts' personal command) have caused the enemy to withdraw altogether from or considerably reduce their numbers in the Drakensberg passes."

<small>C.-in-C. orders Buller to send a division to Cape Colony.</small>

<small>These orders changed, March 10th, because of Boer rally and Sir G. White's health.</small>

The Vth division was selected by Sir Redvers Buller for transfer to East London, but for two distinct reasons the scheme for Eastern Cape Colony was not carried out. First, the embarkation of the Vth division at Durban was, with Lord Roberts' sanction, suspended on March 10th in consequence of a representation from Sir Redvers Buller that the enemy had rallied on the Biggarsberg, that a purely passive attitude would allow of the resumption of Boer raids, and that the occupation of Dundee,

FROM PAARDEBERG TO POPLAR GROVE. 185

was, therefore, desirable. Secondly, Sir George White's health had suffered from the hardships of the long siege, and he was obliged to return to England.

So close had been the net round Cronje's laager during the last few days of the investment, that definite information as to the surrender did not reach Christian De Wet until 1st March, though native reports, which he did not believe, had come in on February 28th. Telegraphing this disastrous intelligence to Bloemfontein, on the day he had it confirmed, the Free State Commandant-General added :— March 1st. De Wet hears of Cronje's surrender.

> "We will bow under this trial and trust that the Lord will strengthen our officers and burghers in this trial, so that they may better appreciate their duties towards Him, our Government, our country, and our people."

On the 3rd the further disheartening news filtered through Bloemfontein to De Wet's commandos that "the burghers have given up their positions around Ladysmith in order to occupy other positions in the Biggarsberg and on the frontier of the Orange Free State, and by so doing to effectively withstand the overwhelming force of the enemy." To soldiers so intelligent as the Boers such messages bore no equivocal meaning. March 3rd. He hears of relief of Ladysmith.

De Wet, one of those born leaders who show their mettle best when tried by disaster, was not a man to lose courage under this accumulation of misfortune. He at once set to work to reanimate his burghers and to strengthen the ground to which he had fallen back from Kitchener's Kopje on the 21st of February. His main line ran north and south, taking in Table Mountain, and across Nooitgedacht Farm to the southward. On that side its left flank ended at a distance of about six miles from the river in an open plain (see map 26). The right flank was prolonged by an underfeature of Table Mountain, which, flung back to the north-east, stretched down to the Poplar Grove Drift. Thence it was continued across the river due northward by Leeuw Kop, a steep sugar-loaf hill, commanding the drift at a range of about 4,500 yards. Beyond Leeuw Kop a series of kopjes, bending round to the north-west towards Pan- De Wet's action thereon.

The position he takes up.

fontein (see map 25), offered good posts, from which an attack on Leeuw Kop could be outflanked, if the numerical strength of the defenders should suffice for their occupation.

Its character. The vital point of this great line of defence was the Poplar Grove Drift, known to the Boers as Modder-rivier-poort. Its seizure by the enemy would not only cut the position in two, but, since the road to Bloemfontein passed close to its southern bank, would also imperil the line of retreat of the whole of the defenders who lay on the northern side of the river. To a direct attack against the drift along the southern bank from the westward, the Table Mountain ridge with its gentle slopes presented a barrier. An advance against this ridge in the face of magazine rifles would prove costly. Nevertheless, its southern end was dangerously *en l'air*, and exposed to a turning movement. On the other hand the northern part, although guarded by the Panfontein Kopjes from being locally outflanked, was not so strong as the southern against frontal attack, for the bush-covered broken bed of the river led to the heart of it, and it was further weakened by three kopjes, Three Stone Hill and the Cactus Knolls (see map 26), which were artillery sites favourable to the attack. There was for the defenders, faced by superior forces, this danger also that the country in rear as far eastward as Abraham's Kraal was open and ill-adapted to defence.

On receiving reinforcements he extends it. The paucity of burghers with De Wet had at first obliged him to restrict himself to the ground on the south side of the river. But on the 2nd March his strength had been increased by the arrival of men from Bloemfontein and Colesberg, and he sent to Leeuw Kop 1,000 to 1,500 men. On the following day he even reported to Steyn that he had been considering the possibility of seizing Koodoosrand and attacking the British troops lying on the north side of the river, but had come to the conclusion that "a little rest will do the burghers good," and that such an attack would be too risky, as it would weaken his defence. He said he was doubtful whether the burghers had enough picks and shovels " to entrench properly the long stretch of ground which we now occupy." On the night of the

6th, De Wet's right flank was made more secure by the arrival from Fourteen Streams of about 1,000 men, a Free State commando, under Kolbe, chiefly drawn from the Boshof district. They had with them a Krupp field gun, and two smaller pieces. Kolbe at once settled his burghers on the Panfontein ridges, which were separated by a valley, some three miles wide, from Leeuw Kop, the right of the main position. On Leeuw Kop and between it and Poplar Grove Drift lay the Senekal, Bethlehem and Potchefstroom commandos. Another Krupp gun had been dragged by hand over the boulders which covered the almost precipitous sides of the kop. It was mounted on the summit. The section of the defence from the drift to Table Mountain was assigned to detachments of Heidelberg, Bloemfontein, Edenburg, and Ladybrand burghers, three guns being posted on the mountain. Special care had been devoted to the thorough entrenchment of this section. The southern section, including the Seven Kopjes, held by commandos from Ficksburg and Philippolis, assisted by a Bloemfontein detachment, had three guns. Eastward of the Poplar Grove Drift the Winburg commando with two guns was posted on Slaag Kraal Hill as a central reserve and *point d'appui* in case of retreat. De Wet made the Poplar Grove homestead his Headquarters. He was able to send his orders by heliograph to all his commanders. His whole strength, including Kolbe's commando, is estimated by Colonel de Villebois Mareuil, a French officer attached to his staff, at 9,000 men. On the *moral* of this force the same officer records in his diary for March 4th the following notes :—

Moral of the burghers.

"Desertion is universal, just as there is utter demoralisation. Those who are frank anxiously question you about the end of the war, whilst those who still pose are generally men who are trying to assume an attitude which will act as a corrective to their cowardice."*

Steyn and Kruger strive to rouse them.

Steyn had on the 27th February spent the day in De Wet's laager, exhorting the commandos. Kruger was equally in-

* "War Notes: the Diary of Colonel de Villebois Mareuil": authorised translation from the Paris *Liberté*, page 264.

defatigable in his efforts to revive the national spirit of the two Republics. On the news of Botha's withdrawal from Ladysmith he had issued a proclamation to all his burghers, in which, after recalling to their remembrance the difficulties the Israelites of old successfully overcame in their march from Egypt to the Promised Land, he implored them " to stand fast in the faith and continue to fight." * Nor was he content with this. Hurrying south by train to Joubert's Headquarters at Dundee, he was able by the influence of his presence to prevent the abandonment of the Biggarsberg by the disheartened commandos in Natal. Thence he again hastened northward, travelled down through the Free State, and, after a brief conference on 6th March with President Steyn at Bloemfontein, started across the veld in a Cape cart, hoping to arrive at Poplar Grove in time to inspire De Wet's burghers with the fire of his zeal and induce them to resist to the last.

Estimated strength and distribution of Boers, March 5th.

Throughout the week's pause after Cronje's surrender Lord Roberts' and De Wet's forces were in sight of each other, separated only by five miles of open plain. The movements and dispositions of the enemy were therefore constantly watched by the cavalry; from their reports and from those of Major the Hon. H. A. Lawrence and Captain G. F. Milne, Intelligence Staff, assisted by Mr. F. R. Burnham, the American scout, a fairly accurate plan of the Boer position was prepared on the 5th March. The following estimate of the numbers and general distribution of the Boer forces was submitted by the Director of Military Intelligence to Lord Roberts :—

---

* This proclamation, in which Biblical quotations figure very largely, was published in the *Standard and Digger's News* of the 2nd March, but had already been transmitted by telegram to all the Transvaal commandos in the field.

		Men.	Guns.
Poplar Grove	De Wet / De la Rey / Englebrecht / Botha	5,000—6,000	8
About Petrusburg	(A. Cronje)	500—1,000	2
Left Colesberg at end of February and not since located—say		4,000	3—10
Reinforcements which left Ladysmith third week in February and not since located—say		5,000	
		16,000	20
Norval's Pont	(Grobelaar)	700—1000	2
Colesberg Bridge		500	2
Stormberg—say		500	2
North of Dordrecht		500—1,000	2
About Boshof		500	2
Warrenton	Ferreira / Du Toit / Bredenbach	4,000	6
Prieska—Griquatown—Kenhardt		1,000	3
		24,500	39
Mafeking	(Snyman)—say	1,500	3
O. F. Staters left Van Reenen's Pass for West 1st March		2,000	
Joubert's main force, retreating northward		8,000	44
	TOTAL	36,000	86

It will be seen from the above that, while the commandos immediately facing the Osfontein Camp were known to consist of not less than 5,000 burghers and eight guns, it seemed possible that these numbers might ere long be trebled by the arrival of reinforcements. De la Rey was then believed to be in supreme command at Poplar Grove, though he did not actually join De Wet until after the retirement to Abraham's Kraal. The importance of De Wet's presence was recognised. In a précis of Intelligence, dated Osfontein, 6th March, he is described as "a strong, determined man, good disciplinarian, popular and respected, but not greatly trusted as a leader." Two deserters had reported that the men in the Poplar Grove laagers were thoroughly tired of the

Views at Headquarters.

190   THE WAR IN SOUTH AFRICA.

war, but the fact that there were no other desertions and that the enemy were full of activity led the British Staff to expect strong opposition to the march on Bloemfontein.

Lord Roberts details his scheme of attack, March 6th.

Assisted by this information and by observations made by himself of the enemy's position, the Commander-in-Chief assembled the whole of his General Officers at Osfontein in the afternoon of the 6th March, and read to them the following written instructions, a copy of which, together with a sketch, was handed to each Commander on the conclusion of the conference :—

"I have asked you to meet me here this afternoon in order to communicate to you the proposed plan of operations for to-morrow. The enemy, as you know, occupy a strong but somewhat extended position in our immediate front. Their object, of course, is to block the road to Bloemfontein, and so far as the information we can procure goes, it is apparently the only place between here and Bloemfontein where our progress could be checked. It is difficult to calculate the exact strength of the enemy, but, allowing that the troops withdrawn from Colesberg, Stormberg, and Natal have joined, it seems scarcely possible that it can number more than 14,000 at the outside, with perhaps 20 guns. To meet this number we have some 30,000 men and 116 guns.* My intention is to send the cavalry division with Alderson's and Ridley's mounted infantry, and seven batteries Royal Horse artillery, to threaten the enemy's line of communication with Bloemfontein. To avoid coming under the enemy's fire throughout this distance the cavalry will have to make a détour of about 17 miles. This would bring them to the south bank of the Modder river, probably some two miles above

---

* The field state of the 6th March showed the following to be the effective strength of the troops under Lord Roberts' personal command on that day :—

	Officers.	Men.
Cavalry	108	2,694
Mounted Infantry	230	4,652
Royal Horse Artillery and Royal Field Artillery	115	3,100
Royal Engineers	37	770
Infantry	455	16,530
Naval Brigade, etc.	39	634
Headquarters Staff	49	73
Total on parade ..	1,033	28,453
15th Brigade (at Brand Vlei)	85	2,909
Non-Combatants	89	935
GRAND TOTAL ..	1,207	32,297

FROM PAARDEBERG TO POPLAR GROVE.

the Poplar Grove Drift. It is very likely, however, that General French may find some vulnerable points which it would be desirable for him to attack before he reaches the river. The destruction of their laagers practically cripples the Boers, as we have learnt from experience. There are three or four laagers reported to be on the places marked on the plan,* a copy of which has been supplied to all officers in command, and it would be well worth General French's while to bring the fire of his 42 guns to bear on them. The Boers are very clever at taking cover themselves, but they cannot hide their wagons, transport animals, and riding ponies, and the destruction of these must in time bring them to terms, the more especially as they will be cut off from their supplies at Bloemfontein. It is intended that the VIth division, with its brigade division of artillery, and the Howitzer battery, and also Martyr's mounted troops (except those ordered to join the VIIth division), will follow the route to be taken by the cavalry division for about six miles. It will then be on the south-east of the 'Seven Kopjes,' the southernmost limit of the Boer position. General Kelly-Kenny will not, I think, have much difficulty in driving the enemy off these kopjes. They will be shaken by knowing that the cavalry has passed round their rear, and a judicious use of mounted infantry, and a combined bombardment of 24 guns will further dishearten them. The first position to which the Boers can retire from the 'Seven Kopjes' is 'Table Mountain,' distant four and three quarter miles. They should be followed up by the VIth division, which will be assisted in its attack on 'Table Mountain' by the brigade of Guards, the four 4.7-in. Naval guns, Flint's brigade division of artillery, and Le Gallais' mounted troops. This latter force will assemble at daybreak at the posts now held by Le Gallais' and Martyr's mounted troops, distant nearly two miles from the Headquarters camp. The 'Table Mountain' is the key of the enemy's position, and with that in our possession they will have to retire into the Modder River, as Cronje did, or force their way across it. The VIIth division (14th brigade only) is occupying the ground hitherto held by the 2nd and 3rd brigades of cavalry. It will have with it its brigade division of artillery, Nesbitt's Horse, New South Wales and Queensland mounted infantry. The duty of the VIIth division is to threaten the enemy as best it can, and draw their attention from the main attack on the 'Table Mountain.' Should they show signs of retiring across the river, the VIIth division should move eastwards towards the drift, and endeavour to harass them as much as possible. The IXth division will act in the same way on the north bank of the river. It will have to look out for the hill on its left front, on which the Boers had a gun a day or two ago. This division will be accompanied by three Naval 12-pr. guns, and its left flank will be protected by two regiments of mounted infantry under Lieut.-Colonels de Lisle and Henry. Lieut.-Colonel Rhodes will be good enough to arrange that signalling may be carried on throughout the day between the Headquarters and the several infantry divisions. My Headquarters will be with the Guards' brigade, at the post now occupied by Le Gallais' mounted troops. The P.M.O. will be pleased to see that medical arrangements are made

---

* Seven laagers were shown in the plan, but the three or four specially referred to in these orders appear to have been those near Poplar Grove Farm.

suitable for the movements of the several divisions, as above indicated. General officers in command will issue orders that their troops are to take cooked food with them, and that a supply of water is to be arranged for as well as circumstances will admit of. All baggage should be left in camp.

"ROBERTS."

Misunderstanding about hour of marching.

It will be observed that no hours for starting are given in these instructions. These were mentioned verbally afterwards. It was probably due to this fact that it was not realised that General French had left the conference under the impression that he was to move at 3 a.m., a fact of which his written orders issued shortly afterwards, are a clear proof (see page 195), whilst General Kelly-Kenny, whose division was to follow the cavalry, understood that they would move off at 2 a.m. He, starting at the hour named for him, found the cavalry division blocking his way, so that, having impassable ground on either side of him, he was obliged to halt. It may also be noticed that as no orders had been previously issued for the packing of the baggage, this caused great delay when it had to be subsequently collected and sent forward by Lieut.-Colonel Grierson.

Summary of the C.-in-C.'s plan.

Although the form in which these orders are cast is not that usually adopted, they present a perfectly clear picture of the Field-Marshal's plan for the overthrow of the enemy. To summarise the orders: The cavalry division is to swing round the Boers' left flank, making a détour of 17 miles, seize the position above Poplar Grove Drift, where the Winburg commando was guarding that crossing, and thus cut De Wet from Bloemfontein. Kelly-Kenny, after the cavalry has arrived in rear of the enemy's main position, is to deliver a flank attack, and gradually roll the left up from Seven Kopjes to Table Mountain, and from Table Mountain to the river bed; the Guards' brigade is to support the attack on Table Mountain. The 14th brigade, having its left close to the south bank of the Modder, is "to threaten" the enemy. The IXth division is to perform a similar rôle on the north bank. In this manner Lord Roberts "calculated on cutting the enemy from the Bloemfontein roads and forcing him to get entangled in the difficult drifts of the

Modder." * He conceived in fact that the cavalry division would be able by audacious demonstration and a skilful use of its Horse batteries to paralyse De Wet, as French had paralysed Cronje on 17th February; this being done, Lord Roberts hoped that the infantry would find no difficulty in manœuvring the commandos into the river bed, and would so bring about a second Paardeberg. March 7th was fixed as the date when the scheme was to be put in operation.

* See Volume I., page 465, Minutes of Evidence before the War Commission.

CHAPTER XII.

POPLAR GROVE.

March 5th and 6th, 1900. Preliminary movements.
ON March 5th and 6th, the IXth division without its divisional artillery, but with three Naval 12-prs. moved up to Makauw's Drift, the Highland brigade on the 5th relieving the cavalry division outposts on the hill to the east of Koodoosrand, named Ferdinand's Kraal. The 4th and 6th mounted infantry, with two squadrons of Roberts' Horse, the whole under the command of Lieut.-Colonel St. G. C. Henry, took over the line of observation on the kopjes to the north-east. Two pontoons had been brought up from Klip Drift and Paardeberg on February 28th by the Royal Engineers' Field troop and formed into a ferry, and over this, during the afternoon of the 5th, the brigade division of the 1st cavalry brigade passed. The crossing began at 2.30 p.m. The artillery was not all over the river till 6.30 p.m. The cavalry crossed by the drift. On the afternoon of the 6th the whole of French's division with Alderson's and Ridley's mounted infantry concentrated at Osfontein, and there bivouacked for the night in column of brigade masses facing south. The VIth division, with Martyr's mounted infantry, bivouacked in rear of the cavalry. The Guards' brigade marched in from Klip Kraal just before sunset on March 6th, and halted for the first part of the night near at hand. At 1 p.m. the rest of the Naval brigade, with four 4.7-in. and one 12-pr. moved towards Le Gallais Kopje, and after dark took up the position selected for them. The VIIth division (14th brigade), under Lieut.-General Tucker, with the detachments assigned to it in Lord Roberts' operation-order, was by that

POPLAR GROVE.

evening assembled on the left bank of the river close to Makauw's Drift, where it came under fire from guns posted on Table Mountain.

The route to be followed by the cavalry division had been reconnoitred by Major the Hon. H. A. Lawrence and Mr. Burnham, who were to act as guides. General French issued the following march order to his command :—

> "Headquarters,
> "Osfontein,
> "6.III.oo., 6.30 p.m.
>
> "1. The division will march at 3 a.m. to-morrow in column of regimental masses in the order in which brigades are bivouacked.
> "Bearer companies and mounted infantry in rear of the cavalry, Royal Horse artillery in line of battery columns on the left of brigades.
> "2. The leading brigade (Broadwood) will send forward one troop as advance guard. The direction of the march will be about south-east by south (magnetic).
> "3. Major Lawrence, D.A.A.G., will direct the march.
> "4. General Officers commanding brigades will arrange to give their men a hot meal before starting; horses will also be fed.
> "5. Baggage wagons, ammunition columns and supply columns will remain at Osfontein until further orders.
> "6. Dismounted men and spare saddles to be sent to the supply park to-morrow.
> "7. The General Officer commanding will march at the head of the 2nd brigade (Broadwood).
>
> "By Order,
> "D. HAIG,
> "Lieut.-Colonel, A.A.G."

French's orders to cavalry division, 6.30 p.m. March 6th.

The moon, now in its first quarter, set at 10 p.m. Although the stars shone out, the light was but scanty when the column started. The delays in drawing out a large body of mounted men in the darkness did not allow the front of the VIth division, which had moved off, to be cleared by the time it reached the cavalry rendezvous. The VIth division, completely blocked, remained halted. Moving forward at a slow pace French's command reached Damfontein at 5 a.m., and there awaited daylight. Kelly-Kenny's division, with Martyr's mounted infantry, conformed, halting about a mile to the north-west. As soon as the first signs of dawn appeared on the horizon,

Cavalry and VIth division march off, 7th March, 1900.

French moved on so as to pass at a distance of two or three miles to the south of the southern extremity of Seven Kopjes, bending round the enemy's left. On arriving at Damfontein, General French had pushed forward a squadron of the 10th Hussars eastwards and one of the 12th Lancers northwards. The main body remained in column of masses. At 6.30 a.m. a gun from the extreme left flank of the enemy opened with shrapnel, but the distance was so great that, although several men were hit by the bullets, no real wound was inflicted. A report of this development was despatched at once by field telegraph to Headquarters. A section of the telegraph division, Royal Engineers, was attached to the cavalry and maintained good communication with Headquarters throughout the day. The division took ground somewhat to the right, and, making for Kalkfontein Farm, there watered at a dam. Meanwhile the left flank guard, strengthened by a battery and a second squadron, turned north and began to threaten the rear of the enemy's left flank. The advance guard, also increased to two squadrons, was at the same time ordered to continue its march and seize Drie Kopjes, three little hillocks rising out of the plain about three miles to the north-east of Kalkfontein. While his main body was watering, French himself, accompanied by his Staff, rode up the valley towards Nooitgedacht to reconnoitre. At

7.30 a.m. French south-east of Seven Kopjes.

7.30 a.m., from a point two miles south-east of Seven Kopjes, he dictated the following report to the Chief of the Staff :—

"Enemy has withdrawn gun and is leaving the south end of Seven Kopjes. I have quite turned enemy's left flank, and am following his retreat with Horse artillery fire. Seven Kopjes should now be quite open to Kelly-Kenny's advance. I am moving round to attack laager in rear of flat-topped hill" (*i.e., Table Mountain,* map No. 26).

8 a.m. French reports: 1. Boer flight; 2. His pursuit with artillery fire.

Half an hour later this message was followed by another written at the same place :—

"Long line of wagons moving towards river from laager in rear of flat-topped hill. Am following them with artillery fire. They are too well protected by riflemen in neighbouring kopjes and positions to enable me to attack them mounted or dismounted. I am watching for every opportunity. I do not believe enemy means to defend flat-topped hill (*Table Mountain*, map No. 26) longer than is necessary to cover his retirement over river."

Meantime at dawn, about 5.45 a.m., Lord Roberts, with his Staff, had gone to the top of the hill marked "Le Gallais Kopje" on map 26. Thence the cavalry division could be seen halted, and the VIth division close behind, and also halted. Everyone realised that there was no hope of the intercepting action of the cavalry now taking effect. When General French's second message arrived, it was clear that instead of cutting off the enemy, he was in fact, pursuing them. The idea, understood by all who were present, of effecting large captures was now unattainable. It was a bitter disappointment. The further movement of the cavalry made the certainty of not gaining what had been hoped even more obvious. In order to realise the sequence of events, it must, however, be understood that it was not the cavalry in their original bivouac that was seen from Le Gallais Kopje, but the cavalry halted at Kalkfontein, for watering, and the VIth division waiting till the cavalry had turned the enemy's left, which was to be the signal for their attack. The difficulties of struggling with emaciated horses in the darkness for a mile and a half had convinced General French that he could not safely, with what was not a body fit for active offence, move on without more light, and that his time would be better employed in preparing the horses for a long day by watering them.
5.45 a.m. Lord Roberts on Le Gallais Kopje realises the failure of his hopes.

French, although a direct attack on the retreating enemy appeared to be for the moment impracticable, hoped that by striking north-east he would still be able to place himself across their line of retreat. The whole cavalry division was therefore now ordered to advance to the low ridge on Middelpunt Farm to the north of Drie Kopjes.
French still hopeful.

The VIth division had moved in an easterly direction in the track of the cavalry, but without following their diversion to Kalkfontein. At 7.55 a.m. Lord Roberts, from Le Gallais Kopje, repeated French's report of 7.30 a.m. to Kelly-Kenny, adding: " Please push on, and, as soon as we see you advancing on the ridge, we will co-operate with you."
Roberts urges on VIth division, 7.55 a.m.

This order crossed the following message, timed 8 a.m., from Lieut.-General Kelly-Kenny, whose mounted infantry had been engaged in reconnoitring the position:—

Kelly-Kenny, 8 a.m., reports,
"I am 3 to 4,000 yards south-east of Seven Kopjes. Enemy has reoccupied Seven Kopjes. I send report from mounted infantry. I am going to shell enemy south of kopjes. When I can get on with safety, I will, but at present the enemy appears pretty thick along south of hill, 1,000 yards east of Seven Kopjes. I waited till French moved."

and attacks; but at 9.45 a.m. is still not on the Kopjes.
Kelly-Kenny now deployed his brigades, the 13th on the right, the 18th on the left; the divisional artillery came into action in the interval between the brigades. Each brigade had two battalions in first line and two in support; the companies of the battalions were extended, one behind the other, at an interval of three paces between each man; the distance between companies being about 100 yards. An interval of 300 yards was preserved between battalions in each line, the second line being deployed 400 yards in rear of the first. Each brigade, therefore, thus formed a double column of extended companies, the two columns having a total frontage of about half a mile, and a total depth of over a mile. The deployment, although out of range of the enemy, took time to carry out. More than one message was sent from Headquarters to hasten matters, but Lieut.-General Kelly-Kenny at 9.45 a.m. could only state that his brigades were "pushing on as fast as they can," and that the hill, 1,000 yards east of Seven Kopjes, was still occupied "by a large number of Boers," the reports from his mounted infantry being explicit on the subject, while General French's détour had been so wide that he had not passed near enough to reconnoitre the hill closely. The impression of artillery that they have cleared a hill is always very uncertain, because, as has happened in all wars, and often happened in South Africa, distant artillery fire may be evaded by infantry remaining out of action till the shelling is over and then taking their places again. The Naval brigade, under Captain Bearcroft, whose 4.7-in. guns, placed on Le Gallais Kopje, had come into action against the western face of Seven Kopjes, began shelling it at 8 a.m.,

POPLAR GROVE.

"as the VIth division seemed to be approaching its objective." Tucker's column, with the Guards' brigade immediately on its right, had since daylight remained halted near a house 500 yards east of Makauw's Drift. All understood that they were held in leash until the cavalry should be in position to intercept the enemy when driven out by them. Lieut.-General Tucker in particular, the most naturally eager by temperament of all commanders, was chafing at the delay, but he had been warned to restrain himself, and his left was exposed to the river bed, the very ground of which recent experience had made everyone in the army cautious. The brigade on his left (the 3rd or Highland) was in its turn waiting for its right to be covered by the 14th brigade. But at 9.30 a.m., in obedience to orders from the Commander-in-Chief, the 14th brigade began to move forward slowly in the direction of Table Mountain, followed by the artillery of the VIIth division. The Guards' brigade, écheloned back on the right, conformed. At 10 a.m. one battery of the VIIth division shelled Table Mountain for an hour until the approach of Martyr's mounted infantry from the south obliged them to cease. Martyr's scouts, preceding the VIth division, were thus able by 11 a.m. to cross Table Mountain and to report to Kelly-Kenny that this portion of the position was clear of the enemy. Kelly-Kenny meanwhile had occupied Seven Kopjes without further opposition. Tucker, with the 14th brigade, now pushed on cautiously to Poplar Grove, which was reached at 3 p.m., the Guards' brigade arriving soon after 5 p.m. The VIth division, after a halt on Seven Kopjes, struck to the north across the plain, arriving at the river by 2.30 p.m. to the west of Poplar Grove. Throughout the day none of the infantry on the left bank of the Modder appear to have come within effective rifle range of the enemy.

Rest of army await cavalry.

Tucker with 14th brigade moves at 9.30 a.m.

Scouts of VIth division cross Table Mountain at 11 a.m.

Tucker reaches Poplar Grove 3 p.m. Guards at 5 p.m.

Colvile's division (IXth) and the two mounted infantry regiments under Henry on the right bank had carried out with similar caution their orders to threaten the enemy's right flank. Colonel Henry's patrols, pushing slowly northward an hour before daybreak, did not come into contact with Kolbe's commando on the Panfontein ridges until 10 a.m. Kolbe showed no

Movements on north or right bank.

disposition either to retire or to attack, and as Colonel Henry did not feel himself strong enough to advance, he was content with protecting the flank of the IXth division throughout the day. The 19th brigade, under Major-General Smith-Dorrien, moved forward at daybreak, and passing through the Highlanders' outposts reached Three Stone Hill at 7 a.m. The Boer wagons could be seen retiring up the valley which ran between Leeuw Kop and the kopje to the north-west, which formed the left of Kolbe's position; but, having regard to his orders, and the considerable number of the enemy apparently on Leeuw Kop, Smith-Dorrien did not as yet feel justified in attempting any further advance. Meanwhile the 3rd (Highland) brigade, commanded by Lieut.-Colonel Hughes-Hallett, at 6.30 a.m. seized the ridge to the south of Cactus Knoll, and three Naval 12-prs., under Lieutenant Dean, R.N., came by Lieut.-General Colvile's direction into action on the ridge. On this a gun on Table Mountain began a gallant duel with the Naval pieces. At 10 a.m. Dean's guns were moved forward to Cactus Knoll. Thence they next engaged a Krupp gun on Leeuw Kop, at the same time keeping up an enfilade fire on the trenches south of the river. Soon after 9 a.m. Sir Henry Colvile received a message from the Commander-in-Chief, ordering the IXth division "to harass and, if possible, intercept the retreating enemy." Hughes-Hallett accordingly was ordered to push on to the eastward. His brigade at the same time was strengthened by the arrival of the Royal Canadians from the 19th brigade, but, aware of the presence of the enemy in the river bed, the Brigadier moved with great deliberation, and did not reach the houses half way between Cactus Knoll and Poplar Grove until 2 p.m. Not a shot was fired by this brigade, and they suffered no casualties.

The movements of the 19th brigade, which was covered on its otherwise exposed left flank by the mounted infantry, were more rapid. Smith-Dorrien, at 11.30 a.m., observing the general retirement on the left bank of the river, determined to turn the Leeuw Kop by the valley passing its north side; it seemed possible that a rapid envelopment of the kop might secure the gun, which still continued firing. Smith-Dorrien, therefore, informing Colonel Henry of his intention, extended the Shropshire Light Infantry and sent them up the valley. The Gordon Highlanders and Cornwall Light Infantry followed the Shropshire. The movement was carried out with skill and success. The Shropshire was led on by Lieut.-Colonel Spens at a great pace, being at first kept well out of rifle range of the kop. Then they swung round the farm in rear. The enemy hurriedly retired, leaving the gun on the summit of the kop where at 2 p.m. it was captured, and a signalling station established. The Royal Canadians reached Slaagslaagte, a little later in the afternoon. *and takes it, 2 p.m.*

Ammunition, cooking utensils, cooked food and tents were found in large quantities in the Boer entrenchments on both sides of the river. The sudden appearance of French's division at dawn on their flank had in fact created a panic, and the main body of the commandos on the Seven Kopjes and Table Mountain withdrew hastily to the eastward. Between Table Mountain and Poplar Grove the Heidelberg burghers held out for a time and delayed with desultory artillery fire the advance of Tucker's infantry into the heart of the position. The resistance on the right of the Boer line at Leeuw Kop was not so well maintained. On the left disaster was only warded off by the gallantry of small groups of the bolder burghers, who, making for the Middelpunt ridge, there checked the cavalry division, which after quitting Kalkfontein had moved eastward in column nearly as far as Drie Kopjes. As soon as it deployed and took ground to the left, it found that the northern side of the ridge was held by this rear-guard. By 9 a.m. Broadwood's brigade and one battery, Royal Horse artillery, with Alderson's mounted infantry in rear in support, was engaged on the western slopes a little to the north of Middelpunt homestead. Gordon's and Porter's brigades were similarly stopped on the left. Escorted by Ridley's mounted infantry, the remainder of the Horse artillery batteries had come into action on the Nek between the Middelpunt ridge and Nooitgedacht, engaging two of the enemy's guns to the north-east. *Boer panic when French appeared.*

A detachment of the Boer rear-guard on Middelpunt ridge now

French is checked by Boer rear-guard.

with audacious skill crept round Broadwood's right, and seizing Middelpunt Farm, enfiladed the right of the British line. This farm had originally been occupied by Broadwood as a pivot of manœuvre, but, owing to orders from the divisional commander, it had been evacuated. This counter-attack induced General French to withdraw Broadwood's men from the ridge, and taking that brigade, Alderson's mounted infantry, and a battery under his personal command he enveloped the enemy's left, forcing him at about 11.30 a.m. to relinquish not only the farmhouse but the whole of the Middelpunt position. A simultaneous attempt made by a squadron of the 9th Lancers, under Captain F. T. Lund, to turn the right flank of the enemy had failed a little earlier, the squadron losing 11 men and 25 horses. The Boer rear-guard now retired at a gallop across the plain, part towards Schuinshoek, the rest north-east towards the river. "The horses of the cavalry division," the Staff diary records, "were very tired," but in spite of this one of the batteries pushed eastward and pursued the enemy with rapid fire. Broadwood's brigade advanced towards Slaag Kraal Hill, the occupation of which would have cut the enemy's retreat, but De Wet's untiring energy had organised a fresh rear-guard, which held the line from Slaag Kraal to Schuinshoek. The 2nd cavalry brigade was thus repulsed, while the enemy's long-range musketry from Bosch Kop was now felt. French on this reassembled his force, and at 3 p.m. began another turning movement. Broadwood's brigade moved south of Bosch Kop so as to envelop the new left flank. The remainder of the division menaced the front. Bosch Kop itself appears to have been held by a detachment of only 40 burghers, summoned by heliograph from Petrusburg.* This brave little band ultimately gave way, after losing half its numbers, and Broadwood turning northward took the whole of the enemy's rear-guard in reverse. The main body of De Wet's commandos, including its long lines of wagons, had escaped to the eastward; the Boer rear-guard, therefore, having done its work, broke up

---

* See Report of Captain Reichman, United States Attaché, on the operations of the Boer army, page 192.

POPLAR GROVE.

into small parties and scattered to the north, east and southeast. The Winburg commando, with its two guns, still held on to Slaag Kraal Hill. Porter's and Gordon's brigades, with five batteries, caused this final position to be evacuated at 5 p.m. The enemy was pursued for a short distance, but French's horses could do no more. The division, therefore, except Broadwood's brigade, settled down in a bivouac a mile east of the hill. Broadwood was still at Bosch Kop, where he desired to remain for the night; but on an order signalled to him, he eventually rejoined at 11 p.m.

In this action Lord Roberts' army had 4 officers and 4 men killed and 3 officers and 46 men wounded, almost all in the cavalry division, which also lost 213 horses. The Boer casualties were estimated at 50 men. No prisoners were taken by the British troops.

The Commander-in-Chief, both in his despatch describing the action of Poplar Grove, and in his subsequent evidence before the War Commission, did not conceal his disappointment at these results, a disappointment which was sharpened by the information which reached him after the engagement that, if he had succeeded in surrounding De Wet's forces, the President of the South African Republic would have been included in the captures. Kruger had in fact reached the Boer Headquarters at Poplar Grove with a tired team of horses at dawn, about the time that the cavalry division resumed its advance from Damfontein. Threatening the fugitives with his heavy stick, and even with the rifles of his escort of Mounted Police, Kruger did his utmost to stem the flight, but fortunately for himself, unfortunately for Lord Roberts' plans, he failed to stay the bulk of the burghers. He at last gave up the attempt in despair, and retired to Bloemfontein. *Lord Roberts dissatisfied with result.*

If, as Lord Roberts had hoped, the Boer commandos at Poplar Grove could have been forced into the river-bed, and there surrounded, the fruits of victory would have been so ample as to have done much to end the war. De Wet, it is true, had not to cross the river to make good his retreat, as Cronje wished, but failed, to do at Paardeberg. In other respects the situation of *De Wet's advantages for safe escape.*

De Wet on the night of the 6th of March was not unlike that of Cronje on the morning of the 17th of February; in some respects it was even more critical, for, whereas Cronje had for 12 hours to deal only with one weak cavalry brigade, De Wet was within easy striking distance of an army of more than three times his own strength, and greatly superior to him in artillery power. Yet De Wet had for the purposes of mere escape advantages both in his superior mobility and in that trained habit of his burghers which, as has been shown in the study of their past history,* had made the art of evasion one of the most carefully perfected weapons in the Boer armoury. Every one of his burghers was mounted, and comparatively well mounted. Only part of Lord Roberts' army was on horses, and those horses were still weak from lack of food and overstrain of work on empty stomachs with heavy loads. As soon, therefore, as De Wet had escaped from the grip of the British infantry divisions, he had only to keep back the pursuit of French's brigades, inferior both in mobility and strength to his own commandos.

Other causes leading to result. There were other causes which prevented the day of Poplar Grove from being as decisive as Lord Roberts had hoped that it might have been. The British Army in 1899–1900 was dealing, as no European army had yet done, with the new conditions of war. The weapons in the hands of the opposed forces were in point of efficiency about in the same proportion to those with which thirty years earlier the contest between France and Germany had been fought out as these stood to the " Brown Bess " of Waterloo. That some change in the handling of troops must be made to meet these novel circumstances had long been recognised by all those who in every army of the world had thought upon the subject. So it had been in Germany prior to the great war of 1870–71. Yet the German army, highly trained as it was, had then during the actual stress of fighting to adapt itself to facts regardless of all the maxims taught in the schools up to the very eve of war. With the British Army abstract discussions had not led to any fixed principles suitable to the

* Volume I., Chapter IV.

POPLAR GROVE.

new conditions becoming engrained in the habits and traditions of all parts of it. It was inevitable therefore that the actual experiences of the war itself should produce great effect on the thoughts with which, after the capture of Paardeberg, all ranks, from the Commander-in-Chief downwards, started on a new movement. Not to refer to the incidents in Natal which, known only by report, practically exercised less influence than those in the western theatre itself, Modder River, Magersfontein, Paardeberg could not be forgotten. At Paardeberg more especially a General decked with fresh laurels from a contest in which he had used the new implements of war to shatter barbarian hosts in the open field had not realised the resisting power which such weapons might confer on trained sharpshooters of the veld holding a strong position even against a well-disciplined and properly equipped army. The reaction produced by the failure of the imperfectly organised attack could not but be operative for some time afterwards. The army and the Commander-in-Chief himself were feeling their way just as the Germans had been forced to do in 1870. For the moment the tendency was to produce extreme caution. This tendency had certainly been aggravated by two other causes. On the one hand that perpetual variety of experience and consequent change in the theories of umpires at manœuvres and of instruction at field-days, which has been recorded in the chapter on the British Army* had in its last phase encouraged such frontal attacks as had not been successful in the war. The reaction could not but be all the more severe. Again the great mass of the public at home had naturally not closely observed the changes that were taking place both in armament and in the mode of fighting imposed thereby. It would have been as reasonable to suppose that the public should have closely followed either the latest development of legal wisdom or the latest phase of philosophical or scientific discussion. In no other profession but that of arms would this have mattered in the least. But " England expects," " What will they say in England ? " are necessarily operative powers over the minds of those who on sea or land have the

<small>Disastrous effect on this day of popular ignorance at home.</small>

* Volume I., Chapter V.

responsibility for upholding the good name of a mighty nation. That we were in the earlier stages of the war necessarily fronting with far inferior forces two nations highly trained in the peculiar mode of warfare adapted to their conditions and to the country, and well accustomed to apply them in actual warfare, both being organised more completely than almost any others on earth as "nations in arms," was hardly anywhere taken into account. That European factories had for years been supplying them amply with the most perfect weapons was absolutely unknown to all but a very few outside the Government offices. It was much more popular to ignore all this and to throw the whole blame upon our "ignorant generals" and our "stupid soldiers." Those whose sole duty it was to be popular necessarily gave loud voice to these impressions. A Boer "farmer" was taken as the exact equivalent of an English agriculturist, untrained to arms, unaccustomed to warfare, enclosed in no organisation. When a cry of horror and astonishment burst from a myriad mouths as to the losses inflicted by " a set of farmers " during the earlier actions upon the heirs of those who had defeated the best troops of great powers, this view of the case tended much to emphasise the impression produced by the losses themselves on the army itself.

So complex are the influences which act on an army that, despite this sense of the need to move warily on ground unbeaten by the tread of past tradition, there was undoubtedly also no little elation at the actual success of Paardeberg and at the change in the whole aspect of the campaign produced by that and the relief of Ladysmith and Kimberley. In many minds this sense overrode the other, and the one anxiety was lest the Boers should be scared away by a too early advance before the cavalry could intercept them. It was rather as to the mechanism of advance necessary after recent experiences than in the zeal for attack that there was any doubt. Each division was instructed to conform to that which was on its right, and the right had been checked both by the cavalry blocking it at first, and subsequently by the delay of the cavalry in turning the enemy's left.

It was peculiarly unfortunate that this should be the dominant impression made by past events at a moment when the efficient fighting power of the Boers had been reduced well-nigh to nothing by the depression produced by their defeats. There are moments in war when the exact gauging of the state of mind of the enemy is the most important factor in securing victory and its results. According to Lord Roberts' original scheme his purpose was to have planted the cavalry division completely in rear of the whole line taken up by De Wet whilst the infantry divisions closed in on it. This could only be done by a difficult and somewhat hazardous night march. General French had had more, and more successful experiences than any then living cavalry leader in dealing with the particular foes against whom he was on this occasion to act. When he, taking account of the loss of striking power in his division, due to the condition of the horses, made up his mind most unwillingly that he could not venture to deal with such a leader as De Wet in this way, and that he must wait for daylight before he placed himself in the proposed position, it is safe to say that there is in the world no living authority who can pronounce a decision against him. Thirty years of European peace, and circumstances wholly changed, have destroyed the judicial value of the decision of those whose view in 1870 would have been accepted as decisive. Yet from the moment when French formed this resolution it was certain that the great prize on which Lord Roberts had counted could not be won. The caution which is so obvious a feature in the handling of the infantry columns throughout the day only contributed indirectly to the result. Smith-Dorrien alone seems to have as yet realised that the Boers had been morally shattered by the very struggles which had impressed the need of caution on the victors. His success, small as its scale was, enforces the truth of a favourite principle of General Grant, the man who brought to an end the great American war, that the time for pressing boldly on, is that when you feel that your own men have had about enough, because it is certain that the enemy will be in the same state and then the side that goes in wins.

Extreme Boer depression makes them hard to catch under these conditions.

CHAPTER XIII.

DRIEFONTEIN.*

THE evening of the 7th March found De Wet at Abraham's Kraal, much disheartened by the demoralisation of his commandos. In his efforts to stay the retreat, during which he had ridden two horses to a standstill, he had been oppressed by the conviction that, if the British troops pushed through the weak rear-guard which screened the flight of his burghers, all would be lost. Nevertheless, on the morrow his determination to continue to oppose Lord Roberts' advance remained unshaken.

<small>De Wet chooses kopjes near Abraham's Kraal on which to reorganise.</small>

The task before De Wet was a hard one. He had to delay Lord Roberts' march on Bloemfontein, to rally his own scattered commandos, and to gain time to enable the burghers, collected by the President round the capital, to complete their preparations for its defence. The occupation of the kopjes round Abraham's Kraal Farm, a homestead on the Modder about eighteen miles above Poplar Grove, appeared to promise well for these purposes. Some twelve miles east of Poplar Grove the Boshof-Bloemfontein road crosses the Modder at Oertel's Drift. The track from Kimberley to Bloemfontein runs along the left or south bank of the river, having at Poplar Grove an offshoot, which joins the Boshof-Bloemfontein road about twelve miles south of Oertel's Drift (see map No. 25). Though the veld was so open that an army could move freely in any direction across it, water could only be obtained away from the Modder at the dams and wells of the farms. The situation of these alone determined the course of the roads. Thus an army advancing from Poplar Grove on Bloemfontein was virtually obliged to follow the tracks, the guarding of which therefore became a

<small>Reasons for his choice.</small>

* See maps Nos. 25 and 27.

DRIEFONTEIN.

matter of great moment to the Boers. The occupation of Abraham's Kraal menaced them all.

Nor was this De Wet's only reason for his choice. His right flank would rest on the Modder, and owing to the open nature of the ground any attempt at a turning movement on that side would be instantly visible unless a very wide détour was made. His left flank, it is true, would be exposed, but the further south his adversary was compelled to march, the more chance was there of his being opposed by the reinforcements hurrying up from Colesberg. The selected site was as a whole fairly defensible. Three groups of kopjes (see map No. 27), the one on Abraham's Kraal Farm, the second on Driefontein and Boschrand some five miles to the south, and the third on Damvallei, commanding a little to the eastward the gap between the first and second groups, supplied the means for opposing a column marching on Bloemfontein by the Kimberley route to Bain's Vlei (map 25). These three groups of kopjes lie in the angle formed by the junction of the Kaal Spruit with the Modder; this was not in itself a disadvantage to a force unencumbered by transport; for the spruit, although running in a deep bed between steep banks, is, when not in flood, passable in many places by mounted men. *The position.*

The panic on the 7th had carried many of De Wet's followers past the green poplars of the Abraham's Kraal homestead, well on their way to their own farms or to Bloemfontein. Those who, on the morning of the 8th, were still within hail of De Wet, were equally bent on pursuing their flight. De Wet promptly called together a Krijgsraad. His vigour and the good news that reinforcements—a strong party of Transvaal Police, and commandos under De la Rey and Piet De Wet from Colesberg—were at hand, induced the burghers to accept the following resolutions, proposed by Commandant Kolbe, who with Commandant Roos had handled the Boer rear-guard so skilfully at Drieputs on 16th February:— *De Wet obtains a decision from Krijgsraad for defence of Abraham's Kraal.*

1. That, as the wagons have up to the present proved an embarrassment to the commandos, they should be sent back to Bain's Vlei.

2. That the commandants should be instructed to concentrate their men at Abraham's Kraal.

3. That the Government should be requested to put Bloemfontein in a state of defence under the supervision of an officer chosen by the Krijgsraad for that purpose.

He visits Bloemfontein, March 8th, to organise its defence.

These decisions were at once telegraphed to President Steyn, who approved them. Later in the day, at Steyn's request, De Wet rode into Bloemfontein to confer with Judge Hertzog as to the details of the defence of the town. The 9th of March was spent in hurriedly selecting positions, giving orders for their entrenchment, and directing the organisation, under Commandant Fourie, of a defence force, to be composed of the fugitives who were now crowding into Bloemfontein from the front. Having done what he could in these matters, De Wet by the morning of March 10th was back at Abraham's Kraal, where he found a large column of British troops once more threatening him. During his absence much confusion and doubt had prevailed amongst the burghers. No arrangements had been made for the commissariat after the transport had started for Bain's Vlei. Food was running short. The resolutions of the Krijgsraad had failed to stem the tide of retreat. A telegram, despatched by Andries Cronje on the 9th March, reported to Bloemfontein that 265 out of 380 men of the Ladybrand commando had "gone home," and that of 163 of another unit but seventeen were left. The actual arrival of the Transvaal Police and of De la Rey and Piet De Wet's commandos from Colesberg put heart into those who had not fled. Out of the scenes of chaos which he found, De la Rey, who, in Christian De Wet's absence, assumed command, soon, by his personal influence, evolved something like order. His dispositions were these: The Abraham's Kraal group of kopjes, between which and the river passes the northern road to Bloemfontein, were prepared for defence by the construction of strong lines of stone walls, connecting with the dongas running down to the river. For the occupation of this position De la Rey kept under his personal orders the Johannesburg part of the Police detachment, together with his own and

On his return, March 10th, finds De la Rey has restored order and made preparation.

De la Rey's dispositions.

DRIEFONTEIN.

Piet De Wet's commandos. Some burghers, under Andries Cronje, were sent into the river bed, and lay hidden there, hoping thus to enfilade the attack and throw it into confusion. De la Rey at first fixed his left flank on the Damvallei kopjes, assigning to them the main body of De Wet's commandos, the Pretoria contingent of the Police, two Krupp guns, and two of the 15-prs. captured at Colenso. Subsequently it was decided to take in the Driefontein group of hills, and to post thereon three or four guns, detachments of the Senekal and Winburg commandos under Commandants Vilonel and Kolbe, and a small foreign corps of forty Frenchmen, commanded by Colonel de Villebois Mareuil. A telegram, dated 10th March, 1900, from the Commandant-General, Pretoria, conferred on Colonel de Villebois Mareuil the rank of "Vecht-General," but he does not appear to have actually assumed that title. The numbers of the burghers were, after the action of Driefontein, estimated by the British Intelligence Staff at from four thousand to seven thousand men with six to ten guns. Christian De Wet, on the morning of the 10th, took over command of the left wing. Commandant P. Fourie was responsible for the Damvallei kopjes.

Since the flight from Poplar Grove the burghers had been in little mood for scouting. Touch with the British army had, therefore, been lost, and De la Rey, seeing that Lord Roberts might decline to oblige him with a frontal attack, had telegraphed on the evening of the 9th to President Steyn:— *De la Rey fears that Lord Roberts will avoid Abraham's Kraal.*

> "After taking into consideration how difficult it is to hold this position, and that it is in vain to occupy it if the enemy should simply select another road, we have agreed to divide our commandos, to trek down right and left of the Modder to attack the enemy in flank or in rear when opportunity presents itself, and thus in future to work with flying columns. We think this is the only way to keep the enemy back. Chief Commandant De Wet is also present."

The De Wet referred to was Piet De Wet, not to be confused with his more famous brother Christian.

On the night of the 7th Lord Roberts' Headquarters were at Poplar Grove. They were covered by the VIIth and VIth divisions and the Guards' brigade, which in the order named *Lord Roberts' movements.*

212   THE WAR IN SOUTH AFRICA.

bivouacked on the south bank of the Modder. The cavalry division passed the night about a mile east of Slaag Kraal Hill. The Naval guns lay a little in rear. The IXth division, with three of the Naval 12-pr. guns, was still on the right bank of the river. As early as 2 p.m. that afternoon orders had been issued to the baggage and supply trains to push on from Osfontein ; but, although the distance by road was only thirteen miles, and the wagons trekked across the veld in column, some six abreast, yet owing to the heavy ground the greater portion did not reach Poplar Grove that night. Thus, on the morning of the 8th, the cavalry division found itself without forage, and it was not until 3 p.m. that French could push on, and then only with his 1st brigade (Porter's) and Alderson's mounted infantry. This small column marched some twelve miles up the river, following the northern of the two roads leading from Poplar Grove to Bloemfontein, but without sight of the enemy ; at dusk it halted for the night close to the river bank at Waaihoek. Kelly-Kenny's division moved the same afternoon in support to Rooipoort, four miles west of French's bivouac.

Situation in north-west of Cape Colony induces Roberts to send Kitchener thither, March 8th.

Meanwhile, at the British Headquarters news had been received of a check sustained in Cape Colony by Adye's small column, one of the three which had moved out at the end of February to stem the advance of raiding parties from Prieska and Van Wyk's Vlei.* Though this small affair was in itself insignificant, its effect on the general situation might be serious. Except for the three columns under Settle, Adye, and Parsons, and the immobile troops guarding the railway, the whole of Cape Colony west of a line drawn from Cape Town to Kimberley was without military protection, and this vast region teemed with waverers whom any Boer success might in a moment bring over to the Republican side. On the 8th, therefore, when Lord Roberts received the intelligence, he sent the Chief of the Staff to De Aar to take charge of the western operations.

11.20 a.m. March 9th. Lord Roberts hears of occupation of

To return to the campaign against Bloemfontein. At 11.20 a.m. on the 9th, French, who had previously reported all clear in the direction of Bloemfontein, informed Headquarters that

* See page 182.

the Boers held "a position at Abraham's Kraal Drift and kopjes to the south; strength uncertain." At noon, Colonel Martyr, who, with the 2nd mounted infantry brigade, had covered during the morning the laying of a field telegraph to the front, reported from Katdoorn, a farm on the southern road to Bloemfontein, eight miles to the south-east of Poplar Grove (see map No. 25), that there was no sign of the enemy for three miles further to the east. About the same time a telegram from Basutoland reached the Intelligence Staff that "reports are being continuously received to the effect that Spitz Kop, near Bain's Vlei, is being heavily entrenched and will be held by ten thousand Free Staters." This was but a repetition of the contents of a telegram from the same source on the 5th March. Spitz Kop, which lies about six miles north-west of Bloemfontein (see map No. 25), had as a matter of fact, been chosen, and was being entrenched. Telegrams from Burghersdorp, which had been occupied by Lieut.-General Gatacre on the 7th, stated that the enemy was falling back in the direction of Bethulie and Aliwal North. The whole of the Colesberg commandos were now known to be on the north bank of the Orange river, and had blown up Norval's Pont bridge on the 6th. Major-General Clements held the south bank, and reported that no great force was facing him. Abraham's Kraal, and on same day that Spitz Kop, north-west of Bloemfontein, is being prepared for defence.

From all this Lord Roberts judged that the Boers were gathering for a final stand west of Bloemfontein, leaving a rear-guard at Abraham's Kraal. He thereupon matured a plan of moving his army forward for the next two or three marches in three parallel columns, intending subsequently to concentrate the whole on one road, out of reach of the enemy, and then strike for a point south of Bloemfontein, so turning the left flank of the position defending the town. His deduction. His decision to march in three columns, slipping past Abraham's Kraal and turning Spitz Kop.

The 15th brigade, less the North Stafford, had rejoined the VIIth division early on the 9th. The same morning Colvile's division (IXth) crossed at Poplar Grove Drift to the left bank, picking up there its divisional field batteries. That afternoon the following orders were issued:— Orders for March 10th.

1. The force will advance on Bloemfontein in three columns, composed as follows:—

Left Column.—Lieut.-General French—VIth division, 1st cavalry brigade, Alderson's mounted infantry.

Centre Column.—The Field-Marshal Commanding-in-Chief—IXth division, Guards' brigade, 2nd cavalry brigade, Martyr's and Le Gallais' mounted infantry, 65th Howitzer battery, heavy artillery, Naval brigade, ammunition reserve supply park, 9th Field company Royal Engineers.

Right Column.—Lieut.-General Tucker—VIIth division, 3rd cavalry brigade, Ridley's mounted infantry.

2. The movement will commence to-morrow morning, 10th instant, and the points to be reached each day will be as follows :—

Date.	Left Column.	Centre Column.	Right Column.
10th	Baberspan	Driefontein	Petrusburg
11th	Doornboom	Aasvogel Kop	Driekop
12th	Venter's Vallei	Venter's Vallei	Panfontein
	(cavalry to Leeuwberg)	(cavalry to Leeuwberg)	
13th	Leeuwberg	Leeuwberg	Venter's Vallei

3. The General Officers commanding left and right columns will be responsible for keeping up communication during the march with the centre column.

4. On Saturday—10th—the right column will march at 5 a.m., the centre and left at 6 a.m.

5. Army Headquarters will march with the centre column, and the Director of Telegraphs will arrange for keeping up telegraphic communication between it and the rear.

By Order,
W. F. KELLY, Major-General,
D.A.G. for C. of Staff.

A march on Bloemfontein, northern flank guarded by French's column.

The idea of these orders is clearly that while the left column guards that flank against any enemy there may be at Abraham's Kraal, it pushes on without being delayed by him while the army as a whole marches for the south of Bloemfontein, thus avoiding Spitz Kop. By the 12th the main body of the army was to be assembled on the Kaal Spruit, while a large mounted force would, it was hoped, have seized Leeuwberg, an isolated hill commanding the railway about eight miles south of Bloemfontein. By the 13th the whole army, save the VIIth division and two mounted brigades, would be concentrated at that point. The country between Leeuwberg and the capital was known to be practically open, and there was within it no position suitable for prolonged defence. Everything looked as if Steyn's seat of Government might be seized without much fighting, and a blood-

DRIEFONTEIN.

less occupation of Bloemfontein would, it was hoped, go far to convince the Free State at least of the uselessness of further resistance.

At 5 a.m. on the 10th, the right column duly moved off for Petrusburg, thus clearing the front of the central column, to which special orders were issued. The 2nd cavalry brigade and Le Gallais' mounted infantry marched at 6 a.m., followed by the IXth division, the Guards' brigade, the 9th company Royal Engineers, and the 65th Howitzer battery. The Naval brigade, heavy artillery, ammunition and supply parks were not to start until 3 p.m., four companies of mounted infantry being assigned to them as escort. The Field-Marshal rode at the head of the IXth division.

General French's orders ran as follows :—

March Order—Left Column.
Headquarters, Waaihoek Farm,
9.III.00, 6 p.m.

1. The army marches eastwards in three columns to-morrow. The Left Column, composition as per margin, under Lieutenant-General French, marches on Baberspan.   *1st Cav. brig. Alderson's M. I.*

2. The VIth Infantry division will march at 6 a.m. along the main road to Abraham's Kraal in accordance with orders already issued.   *VIth division.*

3. The detachment as per margin (under Major Scobell) will march at 4.30 a.m. and reconnoitre towards Baberspan. The Officer Commanding will report as early as possible whether the hills about Abraham's Kraal are still held by the enemy.   *1 squadron Cavalry. 1 company M. Infantry.*

4. The 1st brigade (less 1 squadron) will assemble at 6.45 a.m. at the point where the road from Waaihoek Farm joins the main road to Abraham's Kraal. One squadron will be detailed as Advance Guard.

5. (a) Colonel Alderson will detail two companies of mounted infantry to report to Colonel Porter for orders and accompany the 1st cavalry brigade.

(b). Alderson's mounted infantry (less three companies) will act as rear-guard and will join the column on the main road to Abraham's Kraal at a point south of Waaihoek Farm at 7 a.m.

6. The baggage, ammunition and supply columns will join the column on the main road at 7 a.m., following the Infantry at quarter mile distance.

7. Reports to be sent to the head of the Infantry.

By Order,
D. HAIG, Lieut.-Colonel, C.S.O.

The left column, starting from a point twelve miles to the eastward of the centre column, marched like it at 6 a.m., and was guided towards Baberspan. The three columns were thus advancing in échelon from the left, and the respective halting places assigned to each for the next night's bivouac—Baberspan, Driefontein, and Petrusburg—would leave them in that relative position at the end of the first day's march.

<small>At sunrise, March 10th, Scobell obtains touch of Boers.</small>

At 4.30 a.m. on the 10th, Major H. J. Scobell, with a squadron of the Scots Greys and a company of mounted infantry, moved out from the cavalry bivouac, and before sunrise reached a point two miles west of Abraham's Kraal. His scouts pushed forward, but as soon as they were within three hundred yards of the main cluster of kopjes they were greeted with rifle-fire. Scobell thereupon occupied the little knoll marked **a** in map No. 27, and after a scrutiny of the ridges facing him, sent back a report to General French that they were held in force, that the enemy could be seen on the hills to the south and south-east, and that two or three guns had been observed. This report was handed in at 7 a.m. at the junction of the branch Waaihoek track with the main road, the point of assembly of the column. French at once decided to outflank the enemy, and with that object changed to the south-east the direction of his march. Sending orders to Scobell to hold the enemy in front, he rode forward with his staff to the rising ground marked **b** (map No. 27), about two and a half miles south of Scobell's knoll, from whence there was an excellent view of the whole position taken up by the Boers. The parties of the enemy already reported by Scobell could be seen plainly on Abraham's Kraal and Damvallei kopjes. In the long grass of the valley stretching up to the latter a large group of springbok were roving uneasily, as if recently disturbed; but to the south-east the presence of Scobell's patrols on the lower slopes of the extreme western spur of the Driefontein kopjes seemed to prove that these were as yet vacant.

<small>French turns off south-east to outflank them.</small>

<small>From **b** he reconnoitres.</small>

<small>9.30 a.m. VIth division halts for food.</small>

About 9.30 a.m., when the head of French's main body was about a mile to the north-west of **b**, it was decided to let the men of the VIth division breakfast. The following order was issued to Colonel Porter:—

"The infantry are about to halt for one hour. Dispose your force as march outposts about two miles ahead of the infantry. With about two squadrons of your command reconnoitre to Baberspan. Report the best road for this column to follow to Baberspan out of range of positions held by the enemy. Also the amount and position of water at, or near, Baberspan, with a view to bivouacking the column there."

Colonel Alderson was at the same time ordered to send two companies of mounted infantry to relieve Scobell's detachment, which was to rejoin the cavalry brigade.

The head of the central column was now in heliographic communication with the left, and the following message was signalled to Broadwood, the Brigadier of the Field-Marshal's cavalry, by French :— *French signals to Broadwood, and receives at 12.30 message from Lord Roberts to "avoid kopjes and guard baggage."*

"I am now, ten o'clock, four miles south of Abraham's Kraal; enemy occupies in some strength position on my left front. I am trying on south and reconnoitring towards Baberspan. Infantry halted in rear one hour."

Half an hour after noon Lord Roberts asked French whether he was yet in communication with Broadwood. General French replied :—

"I have been, but have told him that I do not want support."

To a message from Lord Roberts directing him "to avoid the kopjes and protect baggage," French replied at 12.45 p.m. by signal :—

"Field-Marshal's telegram received. Enemy barring my way to camp at Baberspan. I am therefore obliged to engage him, and move round his flank."

While the infantry was resting, Porter advanced his brigade, as he had been ordered to do, to the western edge of the dam due south of Abraham's Kraal, and sent two squadrons of the Scots Greys eastward to reconnoitre the proposed bivouac at Baberspan. But the Scots Greys soon found that the enemy, entrenched on Damvallei ridge, barred the way. Porter therefore called up his brigade division of Royal Horse artillery. They were escorted by a squadron of the Carabiniers and a company of mounted infantry. T. and Q. batteries came into action to the eastward of the dam against the Damvallei kopjes, taking as *Enemy at Damvallei block road to Baberspan. Artillery engage guns on Damvallei.*

their targets the centre and southern extremity of that ridge, where the enemy now disclosed guns in position. U. battery, somewhat to the northward, engaged two Boer pieces on the southern end of Abraham's Kraal kopjes.

<small>10.35 a.m. Kelly-Kenny resumes his march.</small>

About 10.35 a.m. the VIth division started again. Its commander, with Lieut.-General French's approval, purposed to outflank the Boers by bearing well to the south-east, hoping thus to carry out the Commander-in-Chief's wishes and reach Baberspan without serious contest. A strong rear-guard was, as the Field-Marshal had suggested, obviously needed, seeing that the march would take the division across the front of the enemy. Lieut.-General Kelly-Kenny, therefore, now determining to be on the safe side, added to Alderson's mounted infantry the 82nd Field battery, 1st West Riding regiment, and 1st Oxford Light Infantry, and directed Major-General Charles Knox, who had recovered from his wound and rejoined for duty on the 6th, to take command of the whole. There were thus left at his own disposal only the 76th and 81st Field batteries and five battalions, viz., 2nd The Buffs and 2nd Gloucester, under Colonel R. A. Hickson, and Stephenson's brigade, the 1st Yorkshire, 1st Welsh and 1st Essex.

<small>De la Rey, finding his defences at Abraham's Kraal turned and useless, gallops for Driefontein kopjes, whence De Wet had moved to Boschrand.</small>

Porter's cavalry now pushed forward towards Driefontein to prepare the way for the infantry. Hardly had they moved when five hundred to six hundred Boers, in regular formation, were seen to gallop from the back of Damvallei ridge to the Driefontein kopjes. De la Rey had seen that he must give up his hope of luring his opponents into delivering a frontal attack against the Abraham's Kraal group of kopjes. He suddenly found himself forced to conform instead to the movements of his adversary, and was quick to perceive that thereby the action was already half lost. Telegraphing hurriedly to Bloemfontein reporting the situation, he wrote: "We shall try to hold them back as long as possible, but the positions here are untenable." Then, placing himself at the head of the Johannesburg "Zarps" (South African Republic Police), he led them at full speed towards his menaced left wing. Their arrival was opportune; for De Wet, with the burghers originally assigned to that part of the field, had been drawn away to the Boschrand by the approach of the mounted troops of the centre British column. The total frontage, therefore, now occupied by the Boers—although not continuously—was not less than ten miles, measuring from the extreme left on the Boschrand to the right on the river. The cause of De Wet's evacuation of the Driefontein kopjes and movement to the Boschrand must now be more fully explained.

Martyr's mounted infantry, with the field telegraph section, had marched from Katdoorn in the early morning, before Broadwood's cavalry had reached that farm, and the leading company of the mounted infantry brigade (the Burma mounted infantry, so called because it consisted of officers and men drawn from British corps in Burma), having been fired at from the Driefontein ridges, occupied the kopjes (180 on map) west of Draaibosch pan at 9 a.m. Two hours later, observing Porter's cavalry moving south and Broadwood's brigade approaching from the westward, Martyr, taking forward two of his companies, dismounted them near the small detached hill (200) in which the south-western spur of the Boschrand comes to an end, a mile north-east of the pan, and seized it with a rush. Broadwood meanwhile, notwithstanding French's message that he required "no assistance," had decided to menace the enemy's left flank, and, detaching to his left Le Gallais' mounted infantry to reinforce Martyr, moved eastward with his own brigade. De Wet's burghers, observing this, had promptly left Driefontein, and concentrated on the southern edge of the Boschrand.
De Wet's transfer to Boschrand due to seizure by Martyr of south-west end of that ridge.

Before this De la Rey's men, having reached the Driefontein ridge, had already opened fire on Porter's cavalry. The VIth division therefore again halted until the situation could be cleared up. The 82nd Field battery was, by Lieut.-General French's orders, now summoned from the rear-guard to relieve U. battery in its task of shelling the Abraham's Kraal ridge, and the latter unit, together with T. battery, Royal Horse artillery, came into action against Vieh Kraal Hill. Q. battery, escorted by a squadron of the Carabiniers, remained in its original position engaged with the Damvallei ridge guns. The other two squadrons of the Carabiniers, under Major A. Sprot, dismounting,
Arrival of De la Rey causes a pause in advance of VIth division, while U. and T. shell Vieh Kraal Hill and Carabiniers seize part of Yorkshire Kopje.

seized under a heavy fire the under-feature on the south-west spur of Yorkshire Kopje. The rest of Porter's brigade halted in support near the guns in the valley to the westward.

<small>11.30 a.m. Kelly-Kenny supports T. and U. with 76th and 81st batteries, reconnoitres, and sends 18th brigade to attack Vieh Kraal and Yorkshire Kopje.</small>

It was now 11.30 a.m., and Kelly-Kenny was anxious to push on. Ordering the 76th and 81st Field batteries to assist the Horse artillery in their bombardment of the position, he himself rode forward to reconnoitre and to consult with French; but French could not be found, as he had moved southward towards the Driefontein homestead and the Headquarters Staff. The ridge by which the VIth division was confronted presented one of those double positions not uncommon on the high veld. The Driefontein and Boschrand kopjes combined to form a horn-shaped plateau, the base of which ended near Draaibosch pan, while the main stem curved northward for three miles, till it ended at Yorkshire Kopje (map No. 27). From this an arm projected towards the north at right angles to the main plateau. On this was the round-topped hill, called Vieh Kraal—beyond which the plateau sloped gently down into the plain below. This Vieh Kraal Hill, with the ridge, which joined it to Yorkshire Kopje, formed therefore an advanced line of defence covering and concealing the main position on the arc of the plateau in rear. The approach to both the advanced and main positions was enfiladed by the Boer guns on the Damvallei ridge. The plateau and the plain with which it was surrounded were covered with a luxuriant growth of long, coarse grass, which hid many boulders on the kopjes. Kelly-Kenny closely studied the situation and then determined to clear the enemy off the nearer ground held by the foremost parties of Boers. Some delay had occurred in bringing up the batteries which, by a mistake, had halted with Knox's rear-guard, and could not get on quickly from the state of the horses; but, as soon as the artillery had prepared the way, he ordered the 18th brigade to deploy for attack, the leading battalion, the Welsh, against the Vieh Kraal Hill, and the Yorkshire against the kopje to the south, which thereafter bore their name. The Essex was detailed as second line on the left rear of the Welsh, while the two battalions of the 13th brigade formed the reserve.

DRIEFONTEIN.

About noon Brigadier-General Stephenson moved forward his battalions, all being widely extended in attack formation, across the plain. As the Welsh approached the ridge artillery and musketry opened on them, but they pressed on, supported by the shells of the British batteries in rear, and carried the Vieh Kraal. The Yorkshire, on the right, in two lines of half battalions, extended at four paces, reached their kopje with but little opposition. The Essex regiment, extended at four paces interval in three lines, two companies in first line, two in support, and the remainder in reserve, now moved up to the ridge on the left of the Welsh. The enemy had fallen back to the kopje marked **o**. Holding it in force, they checked any immediate further advance with brisk rifle and pom-pom fire. Two long-range field guns made excellent practice on the two battalions, at first from Damvallei ridge, and later from a site on the open veld somewhat nearer. To enable the Essex to obtain some cover behind the boulders on the plateau, the Welsh were ordered to pass off to their right, and the leading companies of both battalions went two hundred yards down the south-eastern slopes of Vieh Kraal Hill to within 1,200 yards of kopje **o**. The 81st battery, to engage more closely the Damvallei guns, came into action a little to the north of Vieh Kraal. It was met by such a concentrated fire of shrapnel and pom-pom shells, that the onlookers on the Boer side thought that the battery was overwhelmed. Few of the shells burst however, and only two of the British gunners were wounded.

Stephenson carries Vieh Kraal with Welsh and the other hill with Yorkshire.

French, who had watched the advance of the infantry from the south-west, now saw that the time was ripe to turn the enemy's left. Porter, the commander of the 1st cavalry brigade, had already moved T. and U. batteries from their second position to the low ground immediately to the south of Yorkshire Kopje, in order to give closer support. The squadrons of Porter's brigade were organised at this time into two regiments, composed as under :—

French wishes with 1st brigade of cavalry to outflank and turn left.

> 1st regiment, under command of Major A. Sprot, Carabiniers. 3 squadrons Carabiniers; 1 squadron 14th Hussars.

2nd regiment, under command of Lieut.-Colonel the Hon. W. P. Alexander. 3 squadrons Scots Greys; Composite squadron of Inniskillings and New South Wales Lancers; 1 squadron Australian Horse.

<small>Porter sends Sprot to Broadwood at **x**.</small>

He now reinforced "A." and "C." squadrons of the Carabiniers, which were still on the under-feature to the south-west of Yorkshire Kopje, with the squadron of the 14th Hussars, a squadron of the Scots Greys, the composite squadron of the Inniskillings and New South Wales Lancers, and the squadron of Australian Horse. He sent verbal orders to Major Sprot, the senior cavalry officer present, to leave one squadron on the under-feature, and with his remaining five squadrons to push round the enemy's left flank and co-operate with Brig.-General Broadwood. Sprot accordingly led his column across the dry edge of the Driefontein pan, to the south of the kopje held by Martyr's mounted infantry, and thence eastward, parallel to the southern edge of the Boschrand, from whence the long-range rifle fire of De Wet's burghers caused a few casualties amongst the horses. Two miles eastwards of Martyr's Kopje, a small isolated hill (marked **x** on map No. 27), roughly one hundred feet high, rises out of the plain. Broadwood, who was without orders, and in doubt as to the actual situation, had occupied this hill with dismounted men of the 10th Hussars and 12th Lancers. Davidson's Horse batteries, G. and P., were in action on Broadwood's right against a Boer field gun and pom-pom in the plain to the north near a solitary house, "the shop," on the Bloemfontein road (map No. 27). Sprot, on seeing where Broadwood was, rode up to the hill to report personally to him, meanwhile sending his squadrons to water at Surrey Farm, a mile to the south. From the kopje occupied by the 2nd cavalry brigade a broad open plain stretches northward towards the river. The entrance is closed to the west by the Boschrand, and to the east by a detached hill on Vaalbank Farm. After consultation with Sprot, Broadwood desired him to lead his five squadrons up this valley. Major Sprot therefore rejoined his men at Surrey Farm, and led them thence into the valley. A few Boers could be seen on the slopes of the Vaalbank Hill as the squadrons passed to the westward, but they allowed

DRIEFONTEIN.

the British cavalry to ride by them unmolested. Pushing on towards the Bloemfontein road, Sprot came under fire from the gun and pom-pom near the shop. A wire fence crossed his line of march, and beyond this, on his right front, could be seen the marshy ground of Vlaaklaagte, but neither of these obstacles seemed to him to be sufficient to stop him if he were supported by the 2nd brigade. He thought that he could, in that case, have captured the Boer guns now standing on the open veld. At this moment, however, a galloper came up from Broadwood with an order to stop the advance. Sprot accordingly fell back on kopje **x**, detaching a squadron in extended formation to the eastward to cover his retirement from the party of Boers on Vaalbank Hill, who had now opened fire. Broadwood's brigade had meanwhile been opposing the Boers on the Boschrand, and in this task was assisted by Porter, who, about 3.30 p.m. had, with the rest of his squadrons, escorted T. and U. batteries to a site a little to the north-west of the kopje held by Martyr; thence the Horse artillery shelled the western face of the Boschrand hills. {Sprot is stopped by Broadwood, who with the Horse artillery and Porter is engaged against the Boschrand.}

Kelly-Kenny had remained on the Vieh Kraal and Yorkshire hills awaiting the result of the turning movement of the mounted troops. As the afternoon drew on, he saw that, whether the VIth division was to advance to Baberspan as ordered, or to stay for the night near Driefontein, in either case it was impossible to leave the enemy undisturbed on the main ridge of the Driefontein kopjes. No other orders had been received from French, and there were no signs that the Boers were being pressed on their left flank. Further delay would leave his battalions at nightfall at a great disadvantage. He therefore decided about 2 p.m. to act on his own initiative, and at once directed Stephenson to attack the main ridge. The two divisional field batteries at hand, the 76th and 81st, were sent up the Nek between Vieh Kraal and Yorkshire Kopje to support the infantry. The Buffs and Gloucester at first remained in reserve. {Kelly-Kenny finds himself obliged to force his way. At 2 p.m. he orders Stephenson to attack the main ridge, and sends forward 76th and 81st batteries to support attack.}

Brigadier-General Stephenson chose the highest point held by the enemy, kopje **c** (map No. 27) for the attack of his central battalion, the Welsh, which lay extended in one long line across {Stephenson} the plateau. The Essex, which was still in its original attack formation, was to deal with the Boer right flank, while the Yorkshire from Yorkshire Kopje was to envelop the left. The Welsh was thus the directing battalion, and had to deliver the frontal blow. Almost from the first a biting and accurate rifle fire from the kopje began to take toll of the ranks of this battalion. The companies on the left were under continual shelling from the Damvallei guns, and those on the right harassed by a pom-pom placed near Alexandra Berg (map No. 27). Yet the men gained ground by rushes of some forty to fifty yards at a time, and by 3 p.m. the left half-battalion, supported by the advance of the Essex on its left flank, was within three hundred yards of the centre of the main position. The infantry had begun to move before the field batteries were ready to assist them; but the guns now came into action, and their well-placed shells, concentrated on the western edge of kopje o, enabled the Welsh to carry it at 3.30 p.m. The enemy fell back to the eastern side of the kopje, and the battalion, being exposed to severe enfilade from Alexandra Berg, was compelled to pause. Of the Yorkshire, one company had been detached, and advanced in échelon on the right rear of the Welsh, much aiding them by long-range volleys. The rest of the Yorkshire, in the course of their attack on the enemy's left, had been drawn off by a flanking fire from the Boschrand into that valley, up which the Driefontein—Bloemfontein road runs towards the Nek. Pushing through this valley, never free from fire from both front and right flank, the Yorkshire drove a Boer detachment from a red farmhouse on the road. There for a while they were stayed by a fusilade from Alexandra Berg. The ammunition of both Welsh and Essex was beginning to run short. Their carts had earlier in the day been shelled by the Boer guns, and, having been sent to the rear for cover, were not available. Moreover, as the orders for the day were not issued in anticipation of a serious engagement, the men had left their bivouac with only the normal hundred rounds in their pouches.

Stephenson's advance had been watched by Kelly-Kenny and his staff at first from Vieh Kraal, but, when driven thence

at 3.30 p.m. captures **o** *with Welsh.*

DRIEFONTEIN.

by shell fire, from Yorkshire Kopje. Shortly after the VIth division had been committed to this attack, touch had been regained with French, who sent news that the flanking movement of the mounted troops was progressing. Kelly-Kenny on receipt of this, ordered his first line to halt as soon as the western crest of kopje **c** was gained, and, seeing that that position was on the point of being carried, replied to French as follows :— *Stephenson, detained for a short time on western crest of* **o** *in hopes of turning movement taking effect, is after a message at 3.30 p.m. from Lord Roberts sent on.*

"I have now (3 p.m.) ordered my infantry not to press forward the advance beyond the crest of the hill, but to await turning movement of your mounted troops on the left."

At 3.30 p.m., however, just as the Welsh had carried the western edge of the kopje, Kelly-Kenny received the following order from the Field-Marshal, who had reached some high ground above Driefontein homestead :—

"I believe enemy in front of you to be in no great strength. Push on to the camping-ground."

The Buffs and two companies of the Gloucester now lay at the foot of the western slope of kopje **o**, in close support of the first line. It was clear that the situation could not be known to Lord Roberts. Yet, as only two hours of daylight remained and there was no sign that the Boers were yielding ground because of pressure by the cavalry, orders were sent to Stephenson to push the attack home, and to Colonel Hickson, commanding the Buffs, to reinforce the first line.

The Buffs, led by Hickson, who shortly afterwards fell wounded, climbed the steep western slope of kopje **o**, and reinforced the Welsh, overlapping their left companies. The attackers, with this impetus, quickly cleared the whole kopje; but the fight was not over. On the key of the position—kopje **d**—five hundred yards to the eastward, the Johannesburg Police, who alone of the Boer forces added discipline to courage, still presented a determined front. The left of the enemy was here protected by the burghers on Alexandra Berg, their right by the two Damvallei guns, which had come in to nearer range and were raking, from open ground, the whole of the Essex and the left of the Welsh. *He clears kopje* **o**.

VOL. II. 15

The 76th and 81st batteries shell **d.**

The 76th and 81st batteries were now ordered forward to a point between Vieh Kraal and kopje **c**, from whence they bore on this, the last stronghold of the defenders. Here they remained in action until the final assault was delivered, co-operating admirably. The two companies of the Gloucester had already thrust themselves into the first line of Welsh and Buffs. All three regiments were therefore intermingled; but the front, if confused, was strong and eager, inspirited alike by the prospect of battle, and by the well-arranged system of successive support which had replenished it. On the right the Yorkshire had resumed its advance, and was now five hundred yards behind and to the north-west of the farmhouse. On the left the firing line of the Essex had been reinforced at the right moment by its support, and, having swung to the north of kopje **c**, was menacing kopje **d**. The British rifle fire now began definitely to master that of the Boers, the Yorkshire regiment assisting the leading battalions by long-range volleys. The burghers could be seen slipping to the rear by twos and threes across the plain to the north-east. The pom-pom had disappeared, although the raking fire from the Damvallei guns continued. Five hundred yards of open veld separated the British line from the still unbeaten enemy. There was only one more hour of daylight. The moment for the assault had come. Stephenson, throwing the remaining six companies of the Gloucester forward into the fight, gave the word, "The enemy are retreating; the line will advance." The left half-battalion of the Welsh rose up, and, with Buffs mingled in its ranks, and Gloucesters close behind, marched steadily forward, fixing bayonets on the move. To their left were the four leading companies of the Essex, level with them in one long, irregular line. A hail of rifle bullets issued from the boulders and schanzes, but the enemy's aim was flurried and their shooting too high. Still the guns on the Boer right

The Essex, Welsh and Buffs, with one company of the Gloucester, carry it.

made admirable practice, and many fell. When the foot of the kopje was reached, only three of the Essex company leaders were untouched. The advance had up to this point been continuous, without break or check. Many of the Boers had already gone, but the stalwarts still stood, and at close range the rapid

DRIEFONTEIN.

fire of even a few is deadly. A short pause was made at the foot of the kopje, whence every rifle poured in its bullets on the enemy. Then the Essex rushed in with the bayonet. The Welsh and Buffs, and a company of the Gloucester on the right, simultaneously swept over the crest of the kopje. The Welsh had suffered even more severely than the Essex; six officers were down; and of the Buffs, four officers. As for the enemy, a few brave men of the Johannesburg Zarps waited to be bayoneted with face to foe. The rest made a dash for their horses behind the eastern slopes of the kopje, and sought to escape. Many were brought down by rapid fire from the top of the ridge. About a dozen held up their hands. The rest fled to the north-east, favoured by the twilight now closing in.

The fight, during its later stages, had been watched by the Headquarters Staff from ground on Driefontein Farm. As the head of the infantry of the centre column approached Driefontein, about 5 p.m., orders were sent both to Colvile's troops and the Guards' brigade in rear to push on and support the VIth division. These instructions were, however, soon cancelled. Victory was won by Kelly-Kenny's battalions before aid could reach them. Broadwood, with his own brigade and Sprot's squadrons, had been left throughout the infantry action without orders. He continued to occupy kopje x, to the south-east of the Boschrand, and, although the sounds of heavy firing three miles to the north-west reached his ears, he had no knowledge of the exact situation. Meantime on the Boschrand De Wet's men had learnt that the fine stand of the Police on the Driefontein kopjes had been vain. Who would remain where they had failed? Yet since the Abraham's Kraal group of kopjes was held by the enemy at nightfall, and the Damvallei ridge and the Boschrand plateau were also intact, De la Rey was hot to continue their defence. But De Wet, with his quick perception of his men's feeling, thought otherwise, and issued orders to his burghers to fall back gradually from the plateau to the ridge on Strydomspan Farm, about two miles to the eastward of Damvallei. Broadwood, now seeing that the enemy was everywhere retreating, at once ordered his regiments to pursue.

Kelly-Kenny carries Driefontein before supports ordered forward by Lord Roberts reach him.

De Wet decides to yield.

Broadwood pursues,

They were accompanied by the mixed squadron of Inniskillings and New South Wales Lancers, and the Australian squadron. The horses of the rest of Sprot's five squadrons were incapable of further exertion. The 10th Hussars led, and, pushing northward towards the shop, came into contact with the enemy, whose rear-guard turned and opened a smart fire. Four men were wounded in the British ranks, and, the horses of the cavalry being unfit to charge, a squadron of the 10th Hussars dismounted and fired volleys at the enemy. On this the Boer rear-guard fell back so fast as to defy pursuit by the exhausted cavalry, for whom a slow trot was the fastest possible pace. Darkness came on and Broadwood, finding himself no longer in touch with the Boers, called in his squadrons to the shop, and there bivouacked. Porter's brigade assembled at Surrey Farm. The VIth division re-formed and passed the night near Yorkshire Kopje, covered by outposts thrown out to the north and eastward by Martyr's and Le Gallais' mounted infantry. Many of the wounded still lay where they fell, and it was nearly daylight before, by diligent search amongst the long grass and broken ground, all were collected and cared for. Army Headquarters remained at Driefontein homestead, with the Guards' brigade lying to the north of the Bloemfontein main road, the IXth division to the south. The rear portion of the centre column, including the Naval brigade and heavy guns, did not reach Driefontein until 3 a.m. the 11th. Lieut.-General Tucker's column had marched to Petrusburg during the 10th without incident, and there halted for that night.

The total British casualties in the action of Driefontein amounted to 7 officers 80 men killed, 18 officers 329 men wounded, and 4 men missing, 438 in all. Most of this loss fell on the Welsh, Essex, and Buffs. Of these units the first had 2 officers, 28 men killed, and 5 officers, 107 men wounded, or about 17.5 per cent. of the effective strength of the battalion. The casualties of the Essex were made up of 2 officers, 17 men killed, 4 officers, 73 men wounded, 11.25 per cent. of its strength. Of the Buffs, 1 officer and 21 men died on the battlefield, 3 officers and 77 men were wounded, over 15 per cent. The cavalry had in all 17 men

DRIEFONTEIN.

wounded. The casualties of the artillery were remarkably small, considering the close support given through the day to the infantry by the 76th and 81st batteries. They were only 1 officer and 3 men killed, and 2 officers and 9 men wounded.

In the official report of the action the Boer authorities alleged that they had only had 7 men killed and 18 wounded. This was doubtless done in order not to cause alarm in the country, but in falsely minimising their losses they minimised also their own gallantry, for men do not fall in numbers from the ranks of cravens. The British troops buried on the battlefield 102 Boers, and the owner of a neighbouring farm, who subsequently visited the scene of action soon after the army had gone forward, reported that "a great number" of dead Boers were still unburied. Some thirty prisoners were also taken.

Boer casualties.

CHAPTER XIV.

THE OCCUPATION OF BLOEMFONTEIN.*

Boers retreat towards Bloemfontein.

THE severe punishment which the Boers had received at the hands of Kelly-Kenny's battalions at Driefontein on the 10th March, once more spread panic throughout the commandos. They fell back that night towards Bloemfontein "a disorderly crowd of terrified men blindly flying before the enemy." † Yet De Wet still cherished the hope of making another stand before the capital, and induced his men on the night of the 11th-12th March to occupy the entrenched position at Spitz Kop, with a detachment on a ridge to the south of the town. The prospect of success was, nevertheless, but faint, and the Government officials, ever the gauge of fortune in the field, hastily transferred themselves by train northward to Kroonstad.

British estimate of Boer strength on 11th March, 1900.

The appreciation of the enemy's dispositions submitted by the Intelligence Staff to the Field-Marshal on the day following the Driefontein fight was as follows:—

	Men.	Guns.
On line running south from Bain's Vlei (De Wet and De la Rey)	5,000 to 6,000	10
Further reinforcements possibly arrived from Colesberg and Stormberg	4,000	8
Left Ladysmith end of February, not since located, but may have been north of the Modder yesterday	2,000	—
Add for recent and final commandeered men, say	1,000	—
Approximate total between this and Bloemfontein	13,000	18

* See map No. 25. † "Three Years' War," page 70, by C. De Wet.

THE OCCUPATION OF BLOEMFONTEIN. 231

It was further estimated that two thousand men and four guns were still distributed under Olivier between Bethulie and Aliwal North, that two thousand men and two guns faced Clements at Norval's Pont, that one thousand men and two guns lay at Boshof, and three thousand men and six guns at Fourteen Streams. The total Boer forces in the field, including thirteen thousand in Natal, were held at this time to amount to 37,000 men and fifty-seven guns.

As regards the fighting spirit of the commandos immediately opposing Lord Roberts' main army, the Intelligence report stated that "the demoralisation of the Free Staters and their disinclination to continue the war are again repeated, but, generally speaking, the burghers still seem to be fairly within the control of the various officials. The Transvaalers seem determined to fight the matter out to the end."

The deflection of the left column on the 10th from Abraham's Kraal had brought it across the front of the centre column. The two now lay on one road, and the Commander-in-Chief directed both to carry out the next march thus concentrated. On the morning of the 11th French's column was ordered to move due east along the Bloemfontein road to Doornboom on the Kaal Spruit. The centre column followed, halting three miles in rear on Aasvogel Kop Farm. The start in the morning was delayed by the time needed for searching the field of yesterday's action and burying the dead. As the transport was insufficient to carry the wounded forward with the army, they were left in hospitals at Driefontein, their arms being made over to the ammunition park. The day's march of the two columns was without incident, the cavalry reporting that parties of the enemy were retiring in front of them. Thus, on the afternoon of the 11th, the left and centre columns duly reached the points assigned to them for that date in the original march orders of the 9th.*

Lieut.-General Tucker's column was ordered to halt at Driekop, where, according to the programme, it had arrived on the 11th

Lord Roberts marches towards Bloemfontein, 11th March, 1900.

---

* See pages 213, 214.

from Petrusburg. It was there to wait for a final convoy coming through Poplar Grove.

The bulk of Lord Roberts' army was thus, on the afternoon of the 11th, only twenty-five miles due west of Bloemfontein. But it was known from a sketch made in 1897 that the western approaches to that town were crossed by a low range of hills, running for some eight to ten miles from north to south, and "suitable for Boer defensive tactics." The reports previously received at Poplar Grove, that these were being prepared for defence, were reiterated. Lord Roberts therefore adhered to his programme of the 9th, according to which the cavalry of the left and centre columns were to seize the railway to the south of Bloemfontein on the 12th, the other arms moving in their support to Venter's Vallei. So far as that place the mounted brigades were to move with their respective columns.

His plans for the capture of the railway south of Bloemfontein.

The following orders were issued by Lieut.-General French to the left column :—

March Orders, Left Column.
Headquarters, Doornboom.
5 p.m., 11.III.00.

1. The "Left Column" will march in the order as per margin to Venter's Vallei at 5.15 a.m. to-morrow (the mounted troops only bivouac at Leeuwberg).

2. The baggage, ammunition, and supply columns of the cavalry and mounted infantry will follow the cavalry, escorted by two companies mounted infantry.

Porter's brigade. Alderson's M.I. VIth Infy. division.

3. The General Officer Commanding the VIth division will be good enough to make his own dispositions for the march of his division and baggage. The Centre Column follows the Left Column to-morrow to Venter's Vallei.

4. The General Officer Commanding will march with the main body of Porter's brigade.

By Order,
D. HAIG, Lieut.-Colonel, A.A.G.

The march orders for the Centre Column were issued at 5 p.m., and ran as follows :—

1. The enemy has retired on Bloemfontein.

2. The column will march to-morrow to Venter's Vallei. The right column halts to-day at Driekop, and the left moves also to Venter's Vallei. Particular

THE OCCUPATION OF BLOEMFONTEIN. 233

attention is to be paid during the march to scouting and covering the march of the troops on their left flank.

3. The column will march at 5.30 a.m., headed by the 2nd cavalry brigade and Colonel Martyr's mounted infantry. The order of march of the remainder will be—IXth division and 9th Field company Royal Engineers (latter with the advance guard), Guards' brigade, 65th battery, Naval brigade. The head of the IXth division will move off from the level of Aasvogel Farm at the above hour.

4. The heavy artillery, ammunition reserve, balloon section and supply column, under Lieut.-Colonel T. Perrott, R.A., escorted by Colonel Le Gallais' brigade of mounted infantry, will march at 3 p.m. for Venter's Vallei.

5. The baggage of the units named in para. 3 will march at 6.30 a.m. in the same order as the corps, Headquarters baggage leading, under Major R. M. Poore, Provost-Marshal, with an escort of four companies Colonel Martyr's mounted infantry, and one battalion Guards' brigade.

6. The outposts will join their units as these move through the outpost line.

7. The Field-Marshal Commander-in-Chief will march at the head of the IXth division.

By Order,
J. M. GRIERSON, Lieut.-Colonel,
A.A.G. for Chief of Staff.

The two columns, moving on parallel roads, marched on the morning of the 12th to Venter's Vallei in conformity with these instructions, save that at 5 a.m. the Guards' brigade was ordered to remain with Lieut.-Colonel Perrott's command until the hour fixed for its start. There was no opposition, although bodies of the enemy could be seen on the hills to the east. The Field-Marshal had heard a rumour that the Free Staters were expecting reinforcements from the Transvaal. In fact, the only support actually given by Pretoria was an order sent by Kruger to De la Rey that "in case the burghers are compelled to retire, he must remain with his men with the O. F. S. burghers so long as they stand fast." Both, however, because of this report and because he wished to seize as much rolling stock as possible, Lord Roberts sent forward the cavalry that afternoon a little nearer to the town. He desired General French, after a short rest at Venter's Vallei, to take the 1st and 2nd cavalry brigades, with Alderson's mounted infantry, on to Brand Kop, a hill near the railway four miles north of Leeuwberg, and only five miles south of Bloemfontein. French was supplied with copies of

The C.-in-C. sends cavalry close to Bloemfontein, 12th March, 1900.

Proclamations for distribution in Bloemfontein. the following proclamation for distribution to the inhabitants of Bloemfontein :—

"Aasvogel Kop.
"11th March, 1900.

"Her Majesty's troops are within a short distance of Bloemfontein, and will enter the town in a few days. If no opposition is encountered, the town will be protected and peaceful inhabitants remain unmolested.

"If opposition is met with, the Field-Marshal Commanding-in-Chief will be compelled to take such steps as may seem to him best to overcome it. This may result in damage to the town and loss of life, which the Field-Marshal would regret.

"The inhabitants of Bloemfontein are hereby warned to take such measures as will, in the event of opposition being offered, tend to the security of their own safety.

"ROBERTS."

Movements of the mounted troops. The main bodies of the left and centre columns were to remain for the night of March 12th on the banks of the Kaal Spruit at Venter's Vallei. General Tucker, under a telegraphic order, sent the 3rd cavalry brigade from Driekop to join Army Headquarters at Venter's Vallei that evening. French, after giving his men and horses a rest of two and a half hours, moved forward from Venter's Vallei at 1 p.m., with Porter's cavalry brigade, Alderson's mounted infantry, Nos. 2 and 3 sections of the field troop, Royal Engineers, and No. 4 section of the telegraph division, Royal Engineers. Broadwood's brigade, which had left Aasvogel Kop in the morning before drawing its supplies, was to follow as soon as it had obtained forage and rations from the supply column.

French's progress. French moved parallel to the right bank of Kaal Spruit as far as Sterkfontein, and there struck north-east, following the line of Ferreira Spruit. At Sterkfontein copies of Lord Roberts' proclamation were given to a farmer to deliver to the Mayor of Bloemfontein. A squadron pushed eastward with No. 3 section field troop, Royal Engineers to cut the railway and telegraph line two miles south of Ferreira Siding. Another, under Major E. H. H. Allenby, scouted to the north-east, and a third on the northward. About 4 p.m. Allenby reported that he had occupied Brand Kop, but that about two thousand yards to his front the

THE OCCUPATION OF BLOEMFONTEIN. 235

railway and main road crossed a ridge of ground running from west to east, and that this was held by the enemy. Sending a company of mounted infantry to reinforce Allenby, French pushed forward towards the centre of the ridge with his other squadrons, but was checked by rifle fire. It was now 3 p.m. The Horse artillery, unable to trot, was still some distance in rear. It was important to seize the ridge before nightfall, for a few hours' delay might give time for the arrival of large Boer reinforcements. He directed Porter to despatch a squadron to turn the enemy's left flank, and sent Alderson's mounted infantry over the railway to hold a kopje just north of the Leper hospital (see map No. 25). Porter detailed a squadron of the Scots Greys for the turning mission. Major Scobell, its commander, led his men to the railway, but was at first stopped by a fence, the wire of which resisted all attempts to sever it. Nine of his horses were shot down, but at length, finding a weaker place, he passed over the line and advanced at a gallop, with the sixty-five men still left mounted, to the eastern extremity of the ridge. He found it unoccupied, dismounted his squadron, and pushed forward on foot over the crest of the rise to the northern edge, to encounter on the far side a party of two hundred to three hundred Boers riding up from the north-west to seize this very ground. The burghers, taken by surprise, halted, but the volleys of the Scots Greys quickly drove them back in some confusion, leaving nine of their men dead on the veld. The sun was setting, and twilight was rapidly coming on; the west of the ridge was still in the hands of the enemy, who had been reinforced by a pom-pom. In the few minutes of daylight left, one of the Horse artillery batteries struggled up and at once engaged the Boer gun. The latter, however, continued its fire until after 10 p.m.

Scobell, reinforced by a company of Alderson's mounted infantry, and a detachment of Rimington's Guides, was told to hold the ridge east of the line throughout the night. Allenby was still on Brand Kop. Porter's brigade bivouacked in rear. Two squadrons remained as outposts on the left flank. French took up his quarters at Ferreira Farm, the homestead of President

Steyn's brother. There Broadwood's brigade arrived at 9 p.m. During the afternoon No. 3 field troop, Royal Engineers, commanded by Major A. G. Hunter-Weston, had broken the railway in two places—to the south of Ferreira Siding and to the north of Brand Kop. Hunter-Weston now offered to carry out a suggestion that the line to the north of Bloemfontein should also be cut during the night. Calling for volunteers from his troop and from the cavalry pioneers attached to it, he selected Lieut. E. M. S. Charles, R.E., and seven men, and obtained as guides Mr. Hogg and Private Penny of French's Scouts. The party started at 1 a.m. on the 13th, supplied with gun-cotton and mounted on picked horses. They rode north-east until they struck the Thabanchu road, and the embankment for the proposed railway to Wepener near Bloemspruit Farm. Then they turned to the westward, making for the main line to Pretoria. The veld was seamed with deep and steep-banked spruits, difficult to cross even in the moonlight. At 3 a.m. the moon set, and the night became pitch dark. The party succeeded in evading two patrols of burghers, and by 4.20 a.m. Hunter-Weston, after cutting the Reddersburg-Bethulie telegraph line, reached the railway. After a short search the Sappers found a double-spanned culvert, and in twenty minutes one of its iron girders had been destroyed by two charges of gun-cotton, both of 10lb. weight, placed at each end clear of the abutments. The telegraph line running northward to Pretoria was also cut. The party now turned back, and on their way in the dim light of dawn came suddenly on a strong Boer piquet entrenched in one of the deep sluits, which had to be re-crossed. To hesitate meant destruction, for only thirty yards separated the British patrol from the hostile piquet, and there was no cover to be had. Hunter-Weston, therefore, followed by the rest of the party in single file, galloped straight at the donga, and forced his horse to jump down into its bed. The enemy, though in greatly superior strength, rushed to their horses and retired on a neighbouring support, from whence a heavy rifle and shell fire quickly opened on the British patrol. Fortunately the light was still bad, and although three more deep sluits were

R. E. cut the railway south of Bloemfontein,

and to the north, also capturing much railway plant.

THE OCCUPATION OF BLOEMFONTEIN. 237

crossed under fire, the party, moving in extended order at ten paces interval, was not touched. At the fourth spruit Sapper Webb's horse failed to scramble up the bank, and he was thus left in a critical position. Sergeant H. Engleheart, 10th Hussars, went back to help him, while the rest of the patrol were ordered by Hunter-Weston to go on at a slow trot under command of Lieut. Charles. The Boers on this advanced, but ultimately Engleheart succeeded in rescuing his comrade, and both rejoined the party.* Major Hunter-Weston from this point kept well to the eastward, and reached the foremost scouts of the 2nd cavalry brigade by 6 a.m. His exploit led to the capture at Bloemfontein of valuable railway plant—twenty-five engines and one hundred and eight coaches and trucks, fifty of the latter being loaded with coal.

The sound of the explosions had been very audible to French's Staff, who anxiously awaited it at Ferreira Farm; it was reported at 4.55 a.m. on the 13th March by telegraph to the Field-Marshal at Venter's Vallei. Half an hour later Lord Roberts started for the front with the 3rd cavalry brigade, leaving orders for the artillery of the IXth division to follow at once, the VIth division (with the Naval and Guards' brigades) to move on Brand Kop, and the remainder of the troops at Venter's Vallei to march to Ferreira Siding, where they would be able to meet any attack from the Boer forces still to the south. French was in the saddle before sunrise, and on reaching his outpost line found the situation unchanged, and the ridge west of the railway still in the enemy's occupation. The 2nd cavalry brigade, under Broadwood, was now ordered to push out to the plain to the east of the town, and circle round to the northward. Two of Porter's batteries were placed to shell the ridge and the hills to the north-west. The audacity of the forward move of French's cavalry on the previous afternoon had had its effect on De Wet's commandos, already seriously shaken by their losses at Driefontein. All through the night the bulk of the burghers had been falling back northward. The few left as a rear-guard gradually trickled away in small parties as the morning wore on. About 11 a.m.

13th March. Movement of the troops.

* Sergeant Engleheart was awarded the Victoria Cross for this act of gallantry.

Bloemfontein surrenders, 13th March, 1900.

on the 13th the Mayor of Bloemfontein, accompanied by three of the principal inhabitants, drove over the ridge and made a formal surrender of the town to the Field-Marshal. Two hours later Lord Roberts rode to the President's house at the head of the 3rd cavalry brigade (Gordon), and with all due ceremony the Union Jack was officially hoisted in the capital of the Free State. At 2.30 p.m. General French threw out a circle of outposts to protect the town. Before sunset the Guards' brigade marched into Bloemfontein, having covered forty miles in twenty-six hours. The VIth division bivouacked at Brand Kop, the IXth at Ferreira. Tucker's column moved forward the same day to Panfontein, as the water at Driekop had run short. It was joined by the convoy from Poplar Grove on the 15th, and was close to Bloemfontein on the following day.

Situation throughout South Africa.

Wonderfully had the operations of a single month changed the military aspect of the war. In the western theatre of war the thirty days from 11th February to 13th March had seen Kimberley relieved, Cronje's army defeated and captured, Bloemfontein occupied, and Cape Colony, except for the raiders in the Prieska district, freed from the enemy's presence: in the eastern area the natural fortress of the Tugela heights had been reduced, Buller's troops had joined hands with the Ladysmith garrison, and Botha's disheartened burghers, deserted by their Free State comrades, had fallen back to the Biggarsberg. Lord Roberts, writing from the Government House at Bloemfontein, congratulated his troops in the following terms :—

> Government House,
> Bloemfontein, 14th March, 1900.
>
> It affords the Field-Marshal Commanding-in-Chief the greatest pleasure in congratulating the Army in South Africa on the various events that have occurred during the past few weeks, and he would especially offer his sincere thanks to that portion of the army which, under his immediate command, have taken part in the operations resulting yesterday in the capture of Bloemfontein.
>
> On the 12th February, this force crossed the boundary which divided the Orange Free State from British territory. Three days later Kimberley was relieved. On the 15th day the bulk of the Boer army in this State, under one of their most trusted generals, were made prisoners.

THE OCCUPATION OF BLOEMFONTEIN. 239

On the seventeenth day the news of the relief of Ladysmith was received, and on the 13th March, twenty-nine days from the commencement of the operations, the Capital of the Orange Free State was occupied.

This is a record of which any army may well be proud, a record which could only have been achieved by earnest, well-disciplined men, determined to do their duty, and to surmount whatever difficulties or dangers might be encountered.

Exposed to extreme heat by day, bivouacking under heavy rain, marching long distances (not infrequently with reduced rations), the endurance, cheerfulness, and gallantry displayed by all ranks are beyond praise, and Lord Roberts feels sure that neither Her Majesty the Queen nor the British nation will be unmindful of the efforts made by this force to uphold the honour of their country.

The Field-Marshal desires especially to refer to the fortitude and heroic spirit with which the wounded have borne their sufferings. Owing to the great extent of country over which modern battles have to be fought, it is not always possible to afford immediate aid to those who are struck down ; many hours have, indeed, at times, elapsed before some of the wounded could be attended to, but not a word of murmur or complaint has been uttered ; the anxiety of all, when succour came, was that their comrades should be cared for first.

In assuring every officer and man how much he appreciates their effort in the past, Lord Roberts is confident that in the future, they will continue to show the same resolution and soldierly qualities, and to lay down their lives if need be (as so many brave men have already done), in order to ensure that the war in South Africa may be brought to a satisfactory conclusion.

The four anxious months of the first phase of the war, the course of which, though not lacking in bright spots and gallant deeds, had been steadily overshadowed for the British troops by a sense of failure, were thus succeeded by a fifth of unbroken sunshine, during which the advantage was wrested permanently from the enemy's hands. To what causes was this remarkable and complete change due ? The primary and most important was the assembly in South Africa of forces adequate in strength to deal with the tasks confronting them. At the outbreak of war the inferiority both in numbers and mobility of the British troops in Natal and Cape Colony had rendered it impossible for the British commanders to take the initiative, and after a three weeks' struggle had compelled them to surrender that advantage to the enemy. The arrival of the first Army Corps was insufficient to compensate for this loss. The disembarkation in South Africa of the VIth and VIIth divisions, and the assistance of the Colonial contingents, both South African and oversea, was needed to turn the scale and swing to the British side the pendulum of victory. The VIIIth division did not reach Cape Town until after the occupation of Bloemfontein. The IXth had been formed by taking a brigade from the Ist and organising another from line of communication battalions. Thus this new division was composed of troops already in the country and did not add to the forces at the disposal of Lord Roberts. Yet it was not merely the weight of numbers which so completely changed in a month the balance of power in South Africa. An adequate strength was indeed essential to the fulfilment of Lord Roberts' mission, but the moral element is a far more potent factor in war than the material. The final causes, therefore, to which the relief and defence of Ladysmith and Kimberley and the victory of Paardeberg must be ascribed, are the sound strategy of the Commander-in-Chief, the implicit confidence which his soldiers placed in him, and the devotion and gallantry with which the troops, both Regular and Volunteer, carried out his designs and imposed his will on the enemy.*

The return of the troops, as they marched into Bloemfontein, will be found in Appendix 6.

* The losses which Lord Roberts' main army suffered in accomplishing this task are summarised in Appendix 2.

CHAPTER XV.

GATACRE AND CLEMENTS FROM CAPE COLONY JOIN HANDS WITH THE MAIN ARMY.*

ON March 13th, 1900, when Lord Roberts occupied Bloemfontein, the British forces at Headquarters consisted of the Naval brigade, the 1st, 2nd and 3rd cavalry brigades, four corps of mounted infantry, the VIth and IXth infantry divisions and the Guards' brigade, which were encamped in and around the Free State capital. The VIIth division had been halted at Panfontein to await and escort convoys of supplies from Osfontein. It arrived with the convoys seven miles west of Bloemfontein on the 16th of March. These convoys were escorted into the town next day, but, owing to difficulties of water supply at Bloemfontein, the division itself was halted at Poundisford until the 22nd March. The Ist division (Lieut.-General Lord Methuen) was at Kimberley, now the advanced depôt on the west. The IIIrd division (Lieut.-General Gatacre), the 12th infantry brigade (Major-General Clements) and the Colonial division (Brigadier-General Brabant) were still south of the Orange river.

Composition of army at Headquarters, March 13th, 1900.

Of the Boer forces which had opposed Lord Roberts at Driefontein, numbers had gone from the battlefield straight to their homes. The remainder were retreating in hot haste through Brandfort to Kroonstad, where the seat of the Free State Government had been transferred by President Steyn, when on the 12th of March he fled from Bloemfontein. The commandos were utterly demoralised. Their leaders had found it impossible to induce them to make a stand for the defence of

* See map No. 35.

242   THE WAR IN SOUTH AFRICA.

Furlough granted to Boers, demoralised by defeat.

the capital, and Generals De Wet and De la Rey had granted furlough to their commandos till the 25th of March, when they were to reassemble at Kroonstad. In explaining his action, De Wet said: "I cannot catch a hare with unwilling dogs; and whatever I had said or done, the burghers would have gone home." He hoped that during this period of rest they would recover from their panic and would come back ready to fight.

Positions of other commandos.

On Cronje's surrender the commandos which had occupied Stormberg and Colesberg began to retire, and orders were subsequently sent to them to fall back over the Orange river in the direction of Thabanchu and Ladybrand. On the frontier of Natal General Prinsloo continued to hold the Drakensberg passes, while L. Botha faced the British on the Biggarsberg. On the west, Snyman still invested Mafeking, and a detachment under Du Toit lay about Fourteen Streams to resist movement in that direction.

Lord Roberts unable to follow up his success—causes of his delay.

Had the Commander-in-Chief been able to take advantage of the existing state of demoralisation and disorganisation of the enemy and to follow up his victories by a general pursuit, probably the war would have been brought to a speedy termination. Unfortunately for the present such operations were out of the question. The advance on Bloemfontein had been made under trying conditions. The heat had been severe. Water had been both scarce and impure, and frequently, owing to the difficulties of supply and transport, reduced rations only had been available, so that men and horses had been sorely tried. Many animals had died on the way from the exertions of forced marches over the veld, very heavy under the semi-tropical rains. Those that survived were little more than alive, and remounts were urgently required. The troops had been called upon to drive the enemy from one position after another, and both cavalry and infantry in making wide turning movements had covered long distances. Like the horses, a number of the men were exhausted and in need of rest. Moreover, even had the troops been in condition to pursue the enemy, it was indispensable, before moving again, to open up the new line of communication from Bloemfontein to Springfontein, and thence over the Orange

GATACRE AND CLEMENTS JOIN MAIN ARMY.

river to the seaports. Cape Town, the base and the main depôt of supplies, was 750 miles from Bloemfontein. The intended march on Johannesburg and Pretoria was at right angles to the previous route taken from Modder Camp, and this, the only available line of communication, was uncovered and exposed throughout its length to attack by a most mobile foe. The movement, which had turned Cronje out of his old position at Magersfontein, had made the relief of Kimberley possible and had ended in the surrender at Paardeberg and the occupation of Bloemfontein, had been immediately dependent on wheeled transport. This could only be used as a special resource for these particular objects, and because it made possible a blow for which the enemy was unprepared. For the supply of an army such as Lord Roberts commanded a railway was by far the best means of communication with the sea, and the whole idea of the campaign had been that of changing the main line of supply from the Orange river—Kimberley railway to the Free State railway as soon as Bloemfontein had been occupied. This transfer could not be effected at once, and a halt was therefore inevitable.

The lines of railway to be dealt with were the two which, crossing the Orange river from Cape Colony at Norval's Pont and Bethulie respectively, join at Springfontein, and the one line thence to Bloemfontein. It must be borne in mind that the termini on the coast of the eastern and central lines are East London and Port Elizabeth, and that cross lines connect these two railways with each other and with the Cape Town—Kimberley line at Stormberg, Middleburg, Naauwpoort and De Aar. A number of store and supply ships had been ordered from Cape Town to East London, both to relieve the congestion of the docks at Cape Town itself, and to take advantage of as many lines of railway as possible directly the change was made; but neither the eastern and central railways nor the Orange Free State line could be considered safe till the commandos, then on the Orange river, had been swept from the south of the Free State and forced to the north of the Bloemfontein—Ladybrand road. The movements of the columns in Cape Colony under the command of Generals Gatacre and

Railway system in Orange Free State and Cape Colony.

Clements, up to the 15th March, when they simultaneously crossed the Orange river and invaded the territory of the Free State, formed the first stage in the process of driving back these commandos and making secure the communications with the sea.

Gatacre's column.

After Lieut.-General Sir W. F. Gatacre's retreat from Stormberg* on the 10th December, 1899, he established his Headquarters at Sterkstroom with advanced posts between himself and the Boers, who, apparently incapable of profiting by their victory, remained inactive in their positions. Reinforcements reached him soon after the battle. On the 12th the 79th battery, Royal Field artillery joined him; and five days later the 1st battalion, Derbyshire regiment, over one thousand strong, arrived from East London. As the 2nd Northumberland Fusiliers had been withdrawn from the front and sent to East London to wait for drafts of officers and men from England to make good its losses in the engagement, these reinforcements did not materially add to his strength; and even had his orders not debarred him from resuming active operations, his numerical weakness would certainly have tied him to the defensive. Beyond a few affairs in which British mounted patrols engaged scouting parties of the enemy, there were no military operations of importance in this part of the theatre of war during the remainder of December, 1899, or in January, 1900.

Brabant's mission.

Lord Roberts, on his arrival at Cape Town,† had ordered that a Colonial division of mounted troops, about three thousand strong, should be formed under the command of Colonel E. Y. Brabant, who was given the rank of Brigadier-General. He was placed under Gatacre's orders, but with permission, when necessary, to communicate direct with the Chief of the Staff. His division was to consist of the Cape Mounted Rifles, the Kaffrarian Rifles, the Queenstown and East London Volunteers, the regiment of Brabant's Horse he had already formed, and a second regiment of the same name, which was to be raised at once. Brabant was to work on Gatacre's right flank, in the first place to occupy Dordrecht, and then to move on to Jamestown.

* Volume I., Chapter XVIII.   † Volume I., Chapter XXV.

GATACRE AND CLEMENTS JOIN MAIN ARMY. 245

It was hoped that these operations would make the Boers fear for their communications, and therefore cause them to evacuate Stormberg. General Gatacre was to place a garrison in Dordrecht, but was to confine himself generally to the strict defensive until the effect of the advance on Jamestown became known.

On the 16th February Brigadier-General Brabant, with the whole available strength of his division, 1,600 men, with two 15-pr. and four 2.5-in. guns manned by a detachment of the Cape Mounted Rifles, marched towards Dordrecht from Penhoek, where his command had concentrated. Next morning he was in action at Bird river against the enemy, who were posted to the north of the main road; at the end of the day's skirmishing the Boers abandoned their wagons and their laager, and disappeared during the night. In this affair the Colonial division, especially the 2nd Brabant's Horse, commanded by Bt. Major (local Lieut.-Colonel) H. M. Grenfell, 1st Life Guards, did good service. After occupying Dordrecht, Brabant hoped to be able to push on to Jamestown at once, but he found his division not strong enough; the authorised numbers had not been reached, many time-expired men were leaving him, and recruits were not coming in fast. The Royal Scots and a section of the 79th battery, Royal Field artillery were sent to reinforce him, and on the 3rd March he moved with about 1,400 men against a detachment of the Boers, said to be 1,200 strong, posted on Labuschagne's Nek between Dordrecht and Jamestown. On the 4th March an attack was delivered by two columns, that on the left under Major V. M. Birkbeck, Royal Scots, and that on the right under Major Cedric Maxwell, R.E. The duty of the left column was confined to threatening the Nek in front, and thus preventing the burghers from reinforcing those of their comrades who were attacked by Maxwell. After a long day of desultory fighting, in which the guns of the Cape Mounted Rifles and the section of the 79th battery, Royal Field artillery were well served, Maxwell carried the part of the position which he had assailed and held it throughout the night, and on the 5th the Boers retired all along the line. The British losses were

Occupation of Dordrecht.

Affair at Bird river, Feb. 17th.

Capture of Labuschagne's Nek, 4th March, 1900.

small; those of the enemy were, as usual, unknown, but their laager, with wagons and a large number of cattle, was captured. The effect produced in the east of Cape Colony by the forcing of Labuschagne's Nek was very great. It had not been believed that the Boers could be driven out of such strong ground by a column little superior in numbers to their own. The Colonial troops were also much encouraged by their success, and rapidly acquired confidence in their officers and in themselves.

Aliwal North occupied, 11th March, 1900.

After the action at Labuschagne's Nek, General Brabant seized Jamestown. There he remained till the 10th, when he marched towards Aliwal North. On the 11th, his advance guard, the 1st Brabant's Horse, under Major J. A. Henderson, 8th Hussars, caught up the enemy, who was retreating across the river, captured the hindmost of his wagons, and took possession of Aliwal North bridge. It had been prepared for demolition, but was saved by the energetic movement of the Colonial troops, who galloped in a body across the bridge, and followed the enemy until they found him with two guns posted some distance back from the river. The position was too strong to be attacked by the troops at hand, and Brabant was compelled to draw off his men. He fell back to the Orange, and to protect the bridge entrenched himself on the Free State bank, covering his working parties with his 15-pr. guns, which had just arrived, and with riflemen extended on the Cape Colony bank. The bridge did not again fall into the hands of the Boers, who retired northwards. In this affair Brabant lost five rank and file killed, and nineteen wounded. Since the formation of his division, his casualties had amounted to two officers killed, two wounded; twenty-six non-commissioned officers and men killed, fifty wounded and seven missing.

Gatacre's reconnaissance on 23rd Feb., 1900.

While the Colonial division was thus employed on the right front of the IIIrd division, which on the 11th February numbered approximately 5,300 officers and men, Lieut.-General Gatacre ordered a reconnaissance on the 23rd February, to ascertain the truth of rumours that, in consequence of Lord Roberts' invasion of the Free State, the Boers were falling back from Stormberg. Five companies of the Derbyshire with one machine gun, and the 74th and 77th batteries, Royal Field artillery (four guns each), were posted north of Pienaar's Farm, while the mounted troops, numbering about 450, and consisting of De Montmorency's Scouts, four companies mounted infantry, and a party of Cape Mounted Rifles, were ordered to scout to the front as far as the height overlooking Van Goosen's Farm,* and to try to lure the enemy towards the position occupied by the guns and the infantry. The scouts were fired on from a ridge held by the burghers; their advance was checked, and General Gatacre, finding that the Boers were not to be tempted forward, ordered a general withdrawal. The reconnaissance was not effected without loss. About 10.30 a.m. Captain the Hon. R. H. L. J. De Montmorency, V.C., 21st Lancers, had mounted a small kopje, accompanied by Lieut.-Colonel F. H. Hoskier, 3rd Middlesex Volunteer artillery, Mr. Vice, a civilian, and a corporal, when sudden fire at short range was poured into the little party, and De Montmorency, Hoskier and Vice were killed. This was not at once known to those behind, who for a time were left without orders. The enemy's fire was so heavy that until 3.30 p.m. it was impossible to extricate the remainder of the scouts. The losses in De Montmorency's small corps were two officers and four rank and file killed, two rank and file wounded, one officer and five other ranks missing, of whom two were known to have been wounded. The result of the day's operations, in Lieut.-General Gatacre's opinion, tended to show that the enemy's force at Stormberg had diminished.

By another reconnaissance on the 5th March, Gatacre ascertained that the Boers had just evacuated Stormberg and were retreating northward. On the 6th March he took possession of Stormberg and on the 8th of Burghersdorp, the enemy falling back slowly before him. The deliberation of Gatacre's movements surprised his younger officers, who did not know that the divisional General had received orders from the Commander-in-Chief not to commit himself seriously until reinforcements had reached him, and, if possible, to repair the railway which connects Stormberg with Naauwpoort Junction. On the 9th

Gatacre advances, 6th March, 1900.

* See map No. 14, Volume I.

the advance guard, under Bt. Lieut.-Colonel W. H. Sitwell, Northumberland Fusiliers, consisting of four companies of mounted infantry, a detachment of Cape Police, the 74th battery, Royal Field artillery, and De Montmorency's Scouts, marched twelve miles to Osfontein, where, by Lieut.-General Gatacre's order, they were to halt until he should join them next day. In the early afternoon news reached Sitwell that the Boers were mining the bridges across the Orange at Bethulie, thirty-seven miles off, and he accordingly sent Lieut. (local Captain) A. J. McNeill, Seaforth Highlanders, who, on De Montmorency's death had been selected for the command of the scouts, to reconnoitre in that direction, and to get touch of the enemy.

Scouts reach Bethulie on 10th March, 1900,

With thirty of the best mounted of his men, McNeill reached the river at Bethulie at dawn on the 10th, and remained hidden on the left bank, watching the Boers swarming over the railway and road bridges, and making ready to destroy them. This handful of De Montmorency's Scouts was too weak and too far from the nearest support to attempt by day to interfere with the work of demolition, and at 4.30 p.m. they had the mortification of seeing the railway bridge blown up. Just before dark the preparations to wreck the road bridge, four hundred yards in length, were nearly finished, and it was clear to McNeill that if nothing was done to save it, this second avenue of approach to the Free State would also shortly be lost. Trusting to the failing light to conceal the weakness of his force, McNeill, with about a dozen men, crawled down the open slope to within long range of a party of Boers, who were then crowding over the bridge, and opened fire upon them. Surprised by this sudden musketry and ignorant of the strength of their assailants, the burghers fled in panic. The fire of McNeill's party was returned from rifle pits on the right bank, but the enemy did not venture again on the bridge, though two days later, a brave Boer crept down to one of its stone abutments to light the fuse of a charge of dynamite. His gallant attempt was unsuccessful and cost him his life. McNeill's action undoubtedly saved the bridge, and compelled the enemy to disclose the positions they had prepared to defend the passage. In the early morning of

and save the road bridge.

GATACRE AND CLEMENTS JOIN MAIN ARMY. 249

the 11th, the scouts were reinforced by a party of Cape Police under Major J. N. Neylan, and at dawn they occupied Hollams' Farm, a house close to the southern end of the bridge. At about 9 a.m. the remainder of Sitwell's advance guard began to arrive. The battery came into action about a mile from the bridge; the mounted infantry moved up to within five hundred yards of it, and engaged the enemy, about 1,500 strong, entrenched along the northern bank. Of the two Boer guns, both of which out-ranged those of the 74th battery, one was posted between the railway station and Bethulie town, and fired on the farm; the other was on a hill to the north-east, whence it shelled the battery at extreme range. During the night the garrison of Hollams' Farm was subjected to much cannonading and to many outbursts of musketry from the far bank. At 11 p.m. the enemy made a determined attempt to force the bridge, in order to reach the wires connecting the charges prepared for explosion, but they were driven back by the fire which the British poured upon it throughout the night. Early on the 12th the Derbyshire came up and joined Lieut.-Colonel Sitwell's command. After nightfall, Second Lieut. R. S. Popham, Derbyshire regiment, with four men, crept across the bridge and examined the abutment at the north end for explosives. He removed the wires to the mines, discovered a large quantity of dynamite, and under a heavy fire brought it across the river. The work begun by this exploit was finished on the night of the 13th by Captain P. G. Grant, R.E., who, in order to remove all the charges of dynamite which had been placed among the girders of the bridge, was lowered by a rope round his waist through holes broken in the roadway. He was accompanied by a small party of the 2nd Royal Irish Rifles. This battalion and the 1st Royal Scots had reached the left bank of the river during the day. On the 14th it was reported by patrols that bodies of Boers were moving off in a northerly direction. On the morning of the 15th March the mounted troops passed over the river and found that the burghers had disappeared. The main body followed, and by noon had occupied Bethulie.

Artillery and mounted infantry arrive, 11th March, 1900.

Infantry begin to come up, 12th March, 1900.

Gatacre crosses the Orange on 15th March, 1900.

When Lieut.-General French, on the 6th February, was

250   THE WAR IN SOUTH AFRICA.

Clements' task at Rensburg.

summoned by Lord Roberts to lead the cavalry division of the main army,* Colonel (local Major-General) R. A. P. Clements remained in charge of the detachment left at Rensburg. His was no easy task. With a force almost denuded of regular cavalry, and numerically weaker than that which French had commanded, every man and gun of which had been employed to the uttermost, he had to detain the Boers at Colesberg and prevent them from swooping upon the lines of communication south of the Orange—a movement which, if successful, would have caused an outbreak of active disloyalty in large districts of Cape Colony, hitherto sullenly quiescent. By maintaining himself between Rensburg and Arundel he fulfilled his chief function, as well as the hardly less important duties of guarding the right rear of the main army, of securing the safety of the important railway junction at Naauwpoort, and incidentally of keeping under his fire a body of the enemy, who might otherwise have joined in the opposition to Lord Roberts' march.

Profiting by the experience they had gained in the fighting of the last six weeks, the Boers round Colesberg had strengthened the weak points in their system of works ; they had recently been reinforced by a considerable body of burghers under General De la Rey, and were now said to number nearly eleven thousand men. Their artillery consisted of a 40-pr., five field guns, and five Vickers-Maxims, or pom-poms. The line of front to which Clements had succeeded was about twenty-five miles in length ; his Headquarters were at Rensburg, with two wings thrust widely out to the front and flanks. The right wing was commanded by Lieut.-Colonel G. W. Hackett Pain, 2nd Worcestershire regiment, the left by Lieut.-Colonel H. M. Carter, 2nd Wiltshire regiment.

Boer attacks on Clements, 6th-12th Feb., 1900.

On discovering that the numbers of the British facing them had perceptibly diminished, the Boers began a series of attempts to cut Clements' communications by circling round his flanks, and fighting in various degrees of severity was continuous all along his line from the 6th to the 12th of February.† A serious effort was made on the 9th against his extreme right at Slingers-

* See Volume I., Chapter XXIV.   † See map No. 16, Volume I.

GATACRE AND CLEMENTS JOIN MAIN ARMY. 251

fontein. This was checked by a squadron of the Inniskilling Dragoons, the West Australians, and J. battery, Royal Horse artillery. The West Australians, who were in action for the first time, played their part well; and a body of twenty of them, under Captain H. G. Moor, R.A., attached to the corps, distinguished themselves by holding a kopje all day against very superior forces. On the 10th the left of Clements' system of entrenchments was attacked. The burghers drove in the Cossack posts, occupied Bastard's Nek, and, after a long firefight with a squadron of the Inniskilling Dragoons and the Victorians, succeeded in ousting them from Hobkirk's Farm. Yet Clements' artillery denied it to the Boers; and for the time being it remained unoccupied. On the 12th both flanks were simultaneously and strongly assailed. On the right the brunt of the fighting was borne by four companies of the Worcestershire, about four hundred strong, who defended an isolated range of kopjes, three miles to the east of Slingersfontein. At about 4 a.m. the attack on these kopjes began, and was carried on all day with both artillery and rifle fire. The Worcestershire were supported by four guns, Royal Horse artillery, and later by two Howitzers. The burghers are believed to have suffered considerably, while the Worcestershire sustained serious loss; Lieut.-Colonel C. Coningham was killed; Major A. K. Stubbs fell while making a gallant attempt to re-take a position with the bayonet; three other officers were wounded, one mortally; sixteen rank and file were killed, twenty-eight rank and file wounded, and nineteen missing. In the machine gun detachment all were killed or wounded.

While the Worcestershire were struggling valiantly, but not altogether with success, to hold the kopjes on the right, Lieut.-Colonel Carter, at the other end of the line, was already hard pressed, two miles from Bastard's Nek, where a body of about seven hundred burghers assaulted the post near Hobkirk's Farm, which marked Clements' extreme left flank. The garrison consisted of two troops of the Inniskilling Dragoons, half a company of the Wiltshire and a hundred mounted Victorians under Major G. E. Eddy. After a spirited resistance, in which

252   THE WAR IN SOUTH AFRICA.

the fighting was almost hand to hand, the detachment was driven back to the Windmill Camp. In the retreat the Wiltshire were helped in every way by the mounted troops; the conduct of the Victorians on this occasion is described by the Colonel of the Wiltshire as "heroic." Their losses were considerable; Major Eddy and another officer were killed; all but one of the surviving officers of the Victorians were wounded; twelve of the rank and file were killed. In the half company of the Wiltshire there were fifteen casualties.

<small>Clements falls back on Rensburg, 13th Feb., 1900,</small>

When the post at Hobkirk's Farm was driven in, Major-General Clements realised that the situation had become perilous. His left flank was forced, his extreme right was hotly engaged, and the Boers had made good a lodgment on part of the position on which it rested. Owing to the great extension of his troops, rendered necessary by the length of front which he guarded, he had no reserves with which to regain the ground thus lost. He decided to fall back under cover of darkness to Rensburg, and issued his orders for a concentration there during the night. While Colonel Carter so impressed the burghers that they did not attempt actively to follow up their success on the left, and the Worcestershire continued their struggle for the possession of the kopjes on the right, the 15-pr. guns, so laboriously mounted on Coleskop a month before,* were hastily brought down from the top of the mountain; the garrisons of Kloof Camp and McCracken's Hill were warned, stores were collected, and such preparations for retreat, as could be made without attracting the Boers' attention, were carried out. By 6 a.m. on the 13th the whole of the troops and nearly all the stores had safely reached Rensburg. The ground was ill suited for defence, and the burghers had occupied the heights of Taaiboschlaagte, commanding the railway to Arundel and Naauwpoort. Clements,

<small>and then on Arundel.</small>

therefore, determined to retire on Arundel; the baggage was to move at 3 a.m. on the 14th, to be followed two hours later by the troops. In the evening he decided to march his baggage off at midnight, with the troops immediately behind it. The necessary orders for the earlier start were issued. After all

* Volume I., page 401, and freehand sketch in the map case of Volume II.

GATACRE AND CLEMENTS JOIN MAIN ARMY. 253

units were reported present at the point of assembly, the column moved off in dense darkness, and reached Arundel in safety at 5 a.m. on the 14th. Then it was discovered that two companies of the Wiltshire, which had been on outpost, were missing; the matter was reported to Major-General Clements, who at once sent all available mounted men and Horse artillery guns to their help. The rescue party had arrived within four miles of Rensburg when they met a few stragglers, who stated that the remainder of their comrades had fallen into the enemy's hands. The order for the change in the hour had duly reached the Headquarters of the Wiltshire, but by a regimental blunder it had not been passed on to Major F. R. MacMullen, who commanded the two companies, which formed the reserve to the outposts. He therefore continued under the belief that the general retirement from Rensburg would be at 5 a.m. and at the time appointed fell back upon the camp, which he found deserted. He instantly marched towards Arundel, but his detachment, which numbered only 151 officers and men, was soon assailed by strong parties of the enemy, who encircled it in front, in rear and in flank. Seizing some low kopjes he defended himself with a skill and courage for which the Boers expressed their admiration. He fell mortally wounded; the men became broken up into small isolated groups, and resistance gradually became impossible. Besides MacMullen, one officer was wounded; of the other ranks twelve were killed and forty-four wounded. Thus thirty-eight per cent. of these two companies of the Wiltshire were killed or wounded before, finding rescue to be impossible, they laid down their arms.

_{Two companies of the Wiltshire cut off.}

For the next few days Clements remained on the defensive, awaiting reinforcements. On the 20th he was attacked in front and on both flanks by the enemy, whose strength disproved the information, received that day from Headquarters, that Schoeman, with a large number of men, had left Colesberg to oppose the advance of the main army. Two days later the promised reinforcements arrived:—the 2nd and the 39th batteries, Royal Field artillery, two 5-in. guns, Royal Garrison artillery, about 520 Cape Volunteers, viz.: two companies of the

Uitenhage Volunteers, one of the Eastern Province Horse, two of the Prince Alfred's Guard, and one of the 1st City Mounted Volunteers; and an Australian contingent, composed of a detachment of Victorian Mounted Rifles, and of infantry companies from New South Wales, Victoria, South Australia, Tasmania, and West Australia, recently mounted. After these reinforcements joined him, Clements had under his orders about 6,500 troops of all arms, not including the 4th Derbyshire, 660 strong, which came up a few days later. Clements, thus strengthened, struck hard at the burghers who had now worked round to his left rear. He forced them back to Kuilfontein, a farm to the north-west of Rensburg. Lord Roberts' instructions to him were to lose no time in pressing the Boers towards the Orange, so that the railway, which would very soon be wanted for the new line of communication, could be at once made fit for use.* Acting on these orders he gradually regained ground, shelling the enemy out of successive positions, the flanks of which he threatened with his mounted troops.† On the 25th, fresh instructions were received from the Commander-in-Chief, through Lord Kitchener, who was then at Arundel. " There is no necessity for Clements to push on in the direction of Norval's Pont; that position could not be forced by any troops we could send for the purpose. He should confine himself to protecting Naauwpoort. Norval's Pont will be evacuated as soon as we are able to advance towards Bethulie, and this we shall be able to do the moment our cavalry reach the railway south of Bloemfontein."

Clements, reinforced, advances again;

Judging that the best way to protect Naauwpoort was to edge the enemy away from it back to the river, Clements without difficulty re-occupied Rensburg and the Taaiboschlaagte heights. On the 28th, ascertaining that the Boers had recrossed the Orange at Norval's Pont, he entered Colesberg with an advanced detachment. On that day he received the following telegram from Lord Roberts, dated 28th February: " It is now, I think, quite unnecessary for you to make any forward move-

and entering Colesberg on the 28th Feb., 1900,

---

* See page 155.

† For gallantry in a skirmish on the 24th Sergeant J. Firth, 1st battalion West Riding regiment, was awarded the Victoria Cross.

GATACRE AND CLEMENTS JOIN MAIN ARMY.

ment likely to involve casualties to your force. Act, therefore, strictly on the defensive till further orders." Finding that there was no opposition to be encountered, and therefore no risk of casualties to his column, Clements gradually pushed towards the Orange, and repaired the railway on his march. By the 7th-8th March he had occupied the hills above Norval's Pont bridge, the three centre spans of which had been blown up, and had posted detachments to cover the Stockenstroom and Alleman's Drifts. The enemy, in unascertained strength, were seen on the right bank, but even had his instructions not forbidden him to do so, it was impossible to attempt a passage as the river was in flood, and continued impassable for several days. Lord Roberts, on the 10th March, telegraphed to Clements from Driefontein : " Do not attempt to force the passage of river at Norval's Pont until you hear from me, or are certain that the enemy have considerably loosened their hold over the heights on the north bank. This they are sure to do when we reach Bloemfontein, and it is better that the repair of the bridge be delayed a few days than that lives be lost unnecessarily." *[is near Norval's Pont on 7th-8th March, 1900.]*

On the 12th the Pontoon troop and the 47th company, Royal Engineers arrived : two days were spent in preparing material, and on the morning of the 15th a covering party was ferried across the Orange to hold the right bank while the bridge was being built. Eight of the pontoons proved to be so old and defective that they could not be used ;* and the structure, 260 yards in length, was supported partly on pontoons and partly on piers extemporised from casks. Later in the day two battalions of infantry, a squadron of cavalry, and six hundred mounted infantry crossed over and established themselves without opposition on Free State territory. Between the 6th February and the 15th March the casualties in General Clements' column were five officers killed, twelve wounded and three missing ; of the other ranks forty-six were killed, seventy-six wounded, and 185 made prisoners. *[Clements enters Free State, 15th March, 1900.]*

Thus, on the 15th March, the Orange had been crossed by the heads of Gatacre's and Clements' columns. From

* See Volume I., pages 27, 28.

Bethulie, Gatacre pushed mounted troops to the north. After advancing some six miles they were recalled, with the exception of De Montmorency's Scouts. In the course of the afternoon a small party of this corps, under Captains H. G. Turner (De Montmorency's Scouts) and G. P. Hennessey (Cape Police), seized a railway trolly and "trollied" to Springfontein, where they captured an engine and some trucks, in which a few armed Boers were asleep. They brought the engine, trucks, and prisoners into Bethulie at 4 a.m. on the 16th. A little later Clements' advance guard from Norval's Pont occupied Donker Poort.

Russell-Brown's reconnaissance, March 14th and 15th.

Meanwhile, Lord Roberts had taken measures to establish touch with his Lieutenants on the Orange. Immediately after his occupation of Bloemfontein the cavalry and mounted infantry had encircled the town with outposts, and reconnaissances were made to the north and east without meeting the enemy. To the north of Bloemfontein the bridge over the Modder River at Glen Siding was reported to be intact, but not till some days later was any movement made to ascertain the fact. On March 14th Lieut. C. Russell-Brown, R.E., was sent with a small party on a truck attached to one of the engines captured at Bloemfontein, to discover how far to the south of Bloemfontein the rail was unbroken. He reached Bethanie station about 10 p.m., seized the telegraph office and by telegraphing in the name of the station-master to his colleague at Edenburg, ascertained, during the night of the 14th-15th, that advanced bodies of the Fauresmith commando had arrived at Edenburg on their way to Ladybrand. This news was immediately sent back to Bloemfontein. Russell-Brown then ran down the line to the Riet River bridge, which was found to be intact. Here he left the train and marched his men to within sight of Edenburg. From an inhabitant he learnt that the Landrost and chief burghers had decided to surrender on the first appearance of the British in strength, but that the members of the Fauresmith commando, who proposed to start for Ladybrand on the 15th, were inclined to show fight.

Acting on the information thus obtained, Lord Roberts despatched a column down the line, towards the Orange river.

GATACRE AND CLEMENTS JOIN MAIN ARMY. 257

At 10 a.m. on the 15th, Major-General Pole-Carew, with two sections of the 84th Field battery, one section, 9th company, Royal Engineers, the 3rd Grenadier Guards, the 1st Scots Guards, twenty-six mounted infantry, a field hospital, a bearer company, and a supply column, left Bloemfontein to open up railway communication to the south. Dropping detachments to guard the bridges over the Riet and the Kaffir rivers, he reached Edenburg at 6 p.m., where the local commando surrendered. He secured much ammunition, many rifles, and some of the oxen and wagons captured at Waterval Drift on the 15th February. He here heard that a considerable number of the enemy, with guns and many wagons, were trekking from the extreme south of the Free State towards Ladybrand and Thabanchu. This information was at once telegraphed to Headquarters. Next morning (March 16th) the column, leaving a garrison in Edenburg, entrained for Springfontein, where more news of the north-easterly movement of the burghers was obtained and immediately reported to the Commander-in-Chief. After a conference with Lieut.-General Gatacre, who arrived from Bethulie about 11 a.m., Major-General Pole-Carew took train for Norval's Pont, where, about 3 p.m. he was in communication with Major-General Clements. Then leaving a detachment at Jagersfontein to collect arms and ammunition, he railed his column back to Edenburg, where the troops halted, while he himself returned to Bloemfontein, to confirm the reports respecting the trek of the burghers towards the north-east, which several times during the day he had telegraphed to the Commander-in-Chief. The news brought back by Pole-Carew, and personally communicated by him to Lord Roberts on March 17th appeared to be satisfactory. The burghers were retiring from the south of the Free State in a north-easterly direction. No enemy now remained on the left, or Cape Colony bank of the Orange. Gatacre had received Lord Roberts' orders to take charge of the country along the Orange river, but not to go beyond Springfontein. He was leaving two battalions of infantry and a company, Royal Engineers, to guard Bethulie; the rest of the IIIrd division would arrive at Spring-

Pole-Carew sent to join hands with Gatacre and Clements, March 15th.

Situation on the Orange river—night of 16th March.

fontein during the 17th. The railway, safely held by the troops écheloned along it from the river to the capital, was fit for traffic. The damage done by the Boers to the lines south of the Orange had been made good. A road bridge at Bethulie had been secured; a pontoon bridge at Norval's Pont had been made; Aliwal North bridge was intact and held. To restore the railway bridges at Norval's Pont and Bethulie would take some time, but meanwhile the rails could be laid upon, and the traffic diverted over, the road bridge at Bethulie.

Railway reopened to Cape Town, 19th March, 1900.

On March 19th, two days after Pole-Carew's return, the first regular train left Bloemfontein for Cape Town. Lord Roberts might congratulate himself on having carried out his purpose of reopening communication by the new line to the coast, the essential condition of the success of his whole scheme of campaign. It would be some time before reinforcements and supplies could flow in freely to his Headquarters, but in the meantime the ample resources of the capital and the surrounding districts were in his hands, and these would be sufficient to tide over the interval before the trains ran without interruption. To such communication the broken bridges at Norval's Pont and Bethulie soon formed the only obstacles. A temporary railway bridge was completed at Norval's Pont on the 30th of March, but trucks had been worked over by hand on the 27th. At Bethulie the line was diverted over the road bridge, which was 1,400 yards below the railway bridge, the length of deviation necessary being two and a half miles. This work was accomplished by the 29th of March. As this bridge was not considered safe for engines the trucks were pushed across by hand, not more than one truck being allowed upon any single span at a time. Each train was then made up again on the other bank, and an engine from Springfontein took it on. The river being here over four hundred yards wide, delays were caused by this necessary precaution, but the crossing was a valuable addition to that at Norval's Pont.

The casualties, etc., of Gatacre's and Clements' columns will be found in Appendix 2.

CHAPTER XVI.

LORD ROBERTS SEIZES THE WATERWORKS, DESPATCHES FRENCH TO THABANCHU, AND BY AN ACTION AT KAREE SIDING IS ENABLED TO RESTORE THE RAILWAY BRIDGE NORTHWARDS OVER THE MODDER.*

On the 13th March, the date of his arrival at Bloemfontein, Lord Roberts found that the supply of pure water, which the town obtained from waterworks on the Modder, twenty-one miles east of Bloemfontein, had been cut off. The army was compelled to draw water from the old wells in the town, which had long been out of use. Thus it was most important to obtain possession of the waterworks as early as possible. Major C. G. Amphlett, with three companies of mounted infantry, was at once sent to occupy them. He was to leave half a company at Boesman's Kop as a connecting post with Headquarters. On the 15th Lord Roberts learned that the commandos facing Gatacre and Clements had retired, and that it was believed they were to concentrate at Dewetsdorp. Subsequent reports stated that these commandos had broken up into small parties, and that their wagons were making their way along the Basuto border.

<small>Waterworks occupied.</small>

The actual movements of the burghers will be given more in detail later. For the present it will be enough to say that on evacuating their position south of the Orange river, the commandos from the neighbourhood of Colesberg went north-east, and near Smithfield joined with those from the Stormberg district. In all, they numbered about six thousand men, nearly

---

* See map No. 35.

all mounted, and with them were more than seven hundred wagons. The Generals in command were Grobelaar, Lemmer and Olivier. It was obvious that any actual or potential concentration at Dewetsdorp threatened the security of the connection with the waterworks, and that it was well to cover the occupation by a detachment stronger than Amphlett's. There were, moreover, other reasons why as effective and as mobile a body as possible should be sent into the district between Bloemfontein and the Caledon.

In the first place, on the 15th of March Lord Roberts had issued the following proclamation :—

Lord Roberts issues proclamation ;

PROCLAMATION III. OF 15TH MARCH, 1900.

To the Burghers of the Orange Free State.

In continuation of the proclamation which I issued when the British troops under my command entered the Orange Free State, in which I warned all Burghers to desist from any further hostility, and undertook that those of them who might so desist and were staying in their homes and quietly pursuing their ordinary occupations, would not be made to suffer in their persons or property on account of their having taken up arms in obedience to the order of their Government, I now make known to all Burghers that I have been authorised by the Government of Her Most Gracious Majesty the Queen to offer the following terms to those of them who have been engaged in the present war :—

All Burghers who have not taken a prominent part in the policy which has led to the war between Her Majesty and the Orange Free State, or commanded any forces of the Republics or commandeered or used violence to any British subjects, and who are willing to lay down their arms at once and to bind themselves by an oath to abstain from further participation in the war, will be given passes to allow them to return to their homes and will not be made prisoners of war nor will their property be taken from them.

ROBERTS, Field Marshal,
Commanding in Chief Her Majesty's Forces in South Africa.

Government House,
  Bloemfontein,
    15th March, 1900.

Now though there was no doubt that many would be willing to lay down their arms if these conditions became known to them, it was difficult to ensure that the proclamation would reach them. To spread the news of peace throughout the south-east of the Free State, and open it up as a source of supplies; to protect the waterworks; and to intercept, if possible, such of the Colesberg and Stormberg commandos as had not yet crossed the Bloemfontein—Ladybrand road, Lord Roberts sent into the Ladybrand district a flying column, 1,700 strong, under Lieut.- General French. As the news from the Basuto border was that the commandos were breaking up, it was hoped that French's appearance would induce all who had not already done so to start for their homes. The composition of the flying column will be more conveniently detailed in the next chapter.* The day after Pole-Carew's interview with Lord Roberts (i.e., on March 18th), it assembled with five days' supplies at Springfield Farm, eight miles east of Bloemfontein, and bivouacked at Boesman's Kop that night. The next day French crossed the Modder, and halted about six miles east of the river. Meanwhile, further reports had come to Headquarters as to the movements of the Colesberg and Stormberg commandos, and an orderly from Bloemfontein reached French at 7 a.m. on the 20th with information that these commandos were moving by the Wepener—Ladybrand road, and would probably arrive at Ladybrand that afternoon. The column continued its march at 9 a.m., and met no enemy except a few men who fired at a flanking patrol near Israel's Poort. At Thabanchu the Landrost came out to receive the troops, and the attitude of the inhabitants of the town was apparently friendly. At 1 p.m. the main body bivouacked on a slope two miles west of the town. A guard of a squadron of cavalry and one section Royal Horse artillery was placed in charge of the town and detachments were posted to hold the Neks on the two roads leading to Ladybrand and on the road to Dewetsdorp.

sends French's flying column to Thabanchu, 18th March, 1900.

Thabanchu occupied, 20th March.

The following orders were issued confidentially at 4.30 p.m. on the 20th for the next day :—

French's orders for 21st March.

" 1. A considerable force of Boers (some 3,000 or 4,000) with guns, are reported moving on the Wepener—Ladybrand road. At ordinary rate of march they should reach Ladybrand this afternoon.

* See page 275.

"2. The detachments (one squadron cavalry, two companies mounted infantry and two machine guns) under Lieut.-Colonel Pilcher will march at 6 a.m. to-morrow for Newberry's Flour Mills on the Leeuw river. A defensive position will be occupied near the Mills to prevent enemy getting supplies, and reconnaissances pushed towards Wepener—Ladybrand road, especially towards Commissie Poort, with the object of discovering whether any movement of the enemy is in progress in the direction of Ladybrand, and if he is getting supplies from the Mills.

"Report by helio and through relay posts. Supplies for two days to be taken on horses. 5 per cent. led horses.

"By Order,

D. HAIG, Lieut.-Colonel, A.A.G."

Pilcher at Leeuw River Mills, 21st March, 1900.

Lieut.-Colonel T. D. Pilcher, with about two hundred men marched from Thabanchu at 6 a.m. on the 21st; he reached the Mills, twenty-one miles distant, at about 4.30 p.m., and to secure them entrenched a strong position. From information gathered that day, he reported that General Grobelaar was at Ladybrand, that the enemy's main body was on the way to Clocolan, and that a detachment, apparently a flank guard, was at Modder Poort. This message was received at Thabanchu shortly before midnight on the 21st of March. Communications by telegraph and signal were opened with Bloemfontein on the 21st, and on the 22nd with Pilcher's force. During the next four days Lieut.-Colonel Pilcher strengthened the ground he occupied, and reconnoitred actively in all directions. On March 26th, having strong reasons for wishing to arrest the Landrost of Ladybrand, and having been led to believe that the task would not be difficult, he marched, with a hundred men and a Maxim, upon the village, which is eighteen miles from the Mills, and about forty miles from Thabanchu. When he drew near to Ladybrand, he posted half his men and the Maxim in reserve, and entered it with the remainder. He was received with open arms by the inhabitants. He then arrested the Landrost and a Field Cornet, and had just obtained, with some difficulty, a conveyance in which to transport them, when he was told that about a thousand Boers were rapidly approaching. He succeeded in carrying off his prisoners and in withdrawing safely, pursued by the fire of the Boers and of the inhabitants, who had now

Pilcher's raid on Ladybrand, 26th March, 1900.

exchanged the white flag, with which they originally welcomed him, for rifles. His retreat was covered by the Maxim gun. The Boers did not pursue, and Lieut.-Colonel Pilcher reached the Mills that evening, with the loss of one man wounded and a sergeant and four men missing.

Meanwhile the late invaders of Cape Colony had carried out their march from the south unmolested. The Colesberg commandos had started from the neighbourhood of Norval's Pont on the evening of the 12th March, and, leaving four hundred mounted men to demonstrate along the northern bank and cover their retirement, moved in the direction of Smithfield, in order to join the Stormberg commandos from Bethulie. These, sending their wagons on ahead, evacuated Bethulie on the 14th. The two forces eventually joined hands about the Commissie Drift just east of Smithfield. *[Retreat of the Boers from the Orange river.]*

The retreating commandos had not much to fear from the south, for their wagons had covered a long distance from the Orange river by the 14th March, while the British troops were still on the Cape Colony side of the stream. The only danger was that of being cut off by a column from Bloemfontein before they succeeded in passing to the northward of the Thabanchu—Ladybrand road, where they would be in safety. Their object, therefore, was to move their convoy rapidly by a route as remote as possible from Bloemfontein. They decided that it should work up the Basuto border *viâ* Wepener. With numerous drifts to cross, and an indifferent road some 140 miles long, there was no time to waste if they were to preserve their 750 ox wagons. For the driving of these a thousand Kaffirs were employed, and the burghers from the outset formed an effective screen moving wide to north, south and west of the convoy, which covered some fifteen miles of road. Cyclists did most of the orderly duty, keeping up communication between the different parts of the column. The march of the convoy began at 2 a.m. each day and continued till 5 a.m., when, after resting for two hours, the journey was continued till 11 a.m. In the afternoon they did another stage, from 2 until 5, and one more in the evening from 7 until 9.30 or 10 p.m. A remarkable feature of the trek was *[March of the commandos.]*

the rapidity with which the order to inspan was carried out. According to Boer accounts, in fifteen minutes from the time that the order was given for the collection of horses, mules and oxen, everything was ready and the march had been resumed. This retreat was most successfully accomplished under conditions of very great difficulty. But few wagons broke down, and notwithstanding the wretched tracks and difficult drifts which had to be passed, the losses in oxen and horses were light. Soon after the convoy started from Commissie Drift, most of the mounted men left it and went to Leeuwkop, evidently in order to watch any movement from Bloemfontein. Here President Steyn met and addressed them, encouraging them to carry on hostilities. They rested their horses there for a day and a half before returning to the convoy, which had continued on its way. The long column of wagons crossed the Caledon at Jammersberg bridge, close to Wepener, and as announced by Lieut.-Colonel Pilcher, was trekking from Commissie Poort (west of Maseru) to Ladybrand on the 21st and on the 22nd towards Clocolan.

Information at Headquarters about movements of Boers.

Various reports of the proceedings of the commandos and of the convoy had reached Headquarters. The movement of wagons from Bethulie and Norval's Pont had been noted on the 13th, and on the 15th news was received that a considerable number of the Colesberg and Stormberg commandos had gone to their homes, and that the remainder were making northwards intending to unite at Dewetsdorp. Information continued to come in to the effect that the enemy had been seen in small bodies, and on the 18th the impression at Headquarters was that the commandos had broken up into such parties. It was not till the 18th that the Commander-in-Chief obtained accurate knowledge about the huge convoy of wagons. On that day it was believed to have set out from Smithfield on the 17th, and on the 20th it was definitely ascertained to be at Bokpoort, eighteen miles from Wepener. On the same day General French, at Thabanchu, was informed of the news which had reached Lord Roberts.*

* See page 261.

LORD ROBERTS SEIZES THE WATERWORKS.

When Lieut.-Colonel Pilcher reported the presence of the Boers about Commissie Poort and Ladybrand on the 21st of March, General French at Thabanchu was forty miles distant. The enemy was known to be at least six thousand strong, so that any aggressive action, with horses such as the cavalry had, could not be attempted, and it was evident that the convoy of wagons had already passed. This large detachment of burghers, although they doubtless shared in the present depression caused by the successes of the main British army, had suffered no demoralising defeat, and it was at all events possible that, as soon as they were aware of the presence of such a small isolated column, they might attack it. Apart from the news of this march gained by General French on the spot, later information as to the enemy's real strength had by this date reached Headquarters. If the southern commandos had at one time dispersed, as previously supposed, it was evident that they were once more concentrated in greatly superior numbers. On the 28th, by Lord Roberts' orders, Lieut.-Colonel Pilcher's party was recalled from the Mills to Thabanchu, where it arrived on the morning of the 29th March.

Soon after De Wet had allowed his burghers to disperse to their homes on the occupation of Bloemfontein, a Council of War was summoned. It was held at Kroonstad on the 17th March, and the Presidents and many officers of both Republics attended it in order to decide on their future course of action. President Steyn discussed the situation, and stated that he had ascertained from reliable sources that if they could continue the struggle for another six or eight weeks, Russian action against India would compel England to make peace in South Africa. He exhorted the officers present to do all in their power to instil courage into the burghers, and to induce them again to take the field. Then Generals Joubert, De Wet, and Botha spoke, and it was unanimously resolved that, although Bloemfontein had been occupied by the British, the burghers should not sacrifice the independence of the two Republics, but should continue hostilities. In the course of the discussion which followed, General De la Rey attributed their previous failures

Krijgsraad at Kroonstad, 17th March, 1900.

to the large size of the commandos. President Kruger agreed that the forces should be divided into several flying columns, of which he proposed that one should go towards Bloemfontein and entice the enemy out of it, while another should pass Bloemfontein and collect and bring up the commandos which still remained in the southern part of the Free State. It was also resolved that, as soon as the commandos were concentrated, the whole should be organised in various bodies, which, moving out in different directions, were to endeavour to cut the enemy's communications. These parties should be without wagons, should not occupy positions and await attack, but should act aggressively. It was further agreed that the Commandants of districts should order their Field Cornets to appoint to every twenty-five men a corporal, who would be held responsible that his section was equipped with necessaries and ammunition. Reports sent by Liebenberg from Britstown and by Steenkamp from Prieska were read, and in view of the importance of cutting the British communications in the neighbourhood of Victoria West, it was decided to send the money and ammunition asked for by these Generals *viâ* Klerksdorp and the Vaal river. General Du Toit at Fourteen Streams was to furnish an escort to the ammunition, which General Steenkamp was to meet half way and conduct to Prieska.

Steyn's counterblast to Roberts' proclamation.

Among those present no voice was raised against carrying on the war to the bitter end, but there was evident anxiety as to the willingness of the burghers again to take the field. The Presidents feared the effect of Lord Roberts' proclamation, and that same day President Steyn issued the following manifesto, sending it by despatch riders and by telegraph all through the country :—

From State President.

At a full meeting of the Council of War, at which were present Presidents Kruger and Steyn, Commandant General Joubert, Chief Commandant C. R. De Wet, and thirty Commandants and fighting Generals of the Transvaal, Free State, and Colony, it was resolved that taking into consideration the difficult circumstances under which the country is suffering, although Bloemfontein is occupied by the enemy our independence must still be prized, and the Government must still be supported with all strength and power ; and considering the willingness of the burghers, who are coming in from all sides and with fresh courage, all officers in both States are notified that strong and active measures will be taken to fight the enemy in every possible way, and for that purpose to call up all officers and burghers in terms of martial law. Encourage then all the burghers to continue the fight. All officers and burghers here are full of courage and hope, determined to fight to the end. Fresh military plans have been made and with God's help we hope to win our cause. From the north and north-west a large laager will be formed here in the course of a couple of days, and from all other parts we hear of burghers who are hastening here, whilst from Europe and the Colony our news is no less favourable. Bring it home to the burghers everywhere that the proclamation spread by the English Field-Marshal, Lord Roberts, is a subterfuge to cause the burghers to forget their duty to their country and people, and to put them off their guard. That this proclamation is unlawful and of no value. A counter-proclamation will be issued before long and published. Those who now lay down their arms make themselves guilty of the blood of their fellow-citizens, and if they do not remain true to their oath and their calling they may have to live through many bitter days of repentance, and will have to give a heavy account to their children and posterity for their lost birthright. Our cause is as justifiable to-day as it was six months ago, and the duty of the burghers to their country is not an iota less. They must thus persevere, in spite of the fine promises of the crafty enemy which will never be fulfilled, and come to our aid.

Whilst this cloud was gathering at Kroonstad the attention of the British Headquarters Staff was directed to the railway line northward, and to the bridge by which it crossed the Modder. In order to understand the importance of this bridge, it must be realised that carts and wagons were now pouring into Bloemfontein with country produce. They were a tempting prey for mounted raiders; but to the south, east and west there appeared at present to be little danger. The course of the campaign had swept the Boers from the south and west, and as yet French's cavalry, pushed out to Thabanchu with Pilcher close to Ladybrand, seemed an adequate protection for the eastern district and for those passages over the Modder which lay to the north-east between Thabanchu and Bloemfontein. The nature of the ground to the west of the capital made it easy to guard on that side, and Clements was marching up west of the railway line whilst Gatacre's detachments were stretching over all the south-east. To the north, on the other hand, the Modder flowed through a wide plain, and if any parties of raiders should come

Importance of the bridge over the Modder at the Glen.

south of the river they might spread out in all directions and find rich spoils everywhere. Lord Roberts therefore felt it to be necessary to hold the line of the Modder, and on March 19th, the day when the first train passed south (see *ante*, page 258), a company of the 2nd Coldstream Guards was sent up by rail to the Glen, fourteen miles north of Bloemfontein, to protect the bridge. They arrived just too late, as the enemy had blown it up during the night of the 18th. The immediate danger of a raid from the north was thus removed; but it would have been very unsafe to leave the river in the hands of the Boers as a screen to cover their movements, and as the bridge must be restored before an advance to the north, dependent on the railway for supplies, could be made, its rebuilding by the Royal Engineers under adequate protection became necessary. Therefore, on the 20th, the 1st battalion Coldstream Guards was sent to the Glen to reinforce the detachment and on the 22nd the 3rd battalion Grenadier Guards followed it. As yet there were no mounted troops at this post, and hostile patrols had been reported in the neighbourhood. On the evening of the 23rd, Boer scouting parties, growing bolder, had fired on and wounded several officers of the Guards, who had wandered a short distance to the north of the river, and on the 24th of March the 3rd cavalry brigade, with O. and R. batteries, Royal Horse artillery marched to join the Guards battalions at the Glen bridge. Next morning, the 25th, a squadron from each of the 9th and the 16th Lancers, were pushed forward to reconnoitre the railway line as far north as Brandfort (eighteen miles), and, if possible, to search that town. They had nearly reached it without meeting the enemy, when a heavy fire was opened upon the cavalry patrols from the kopjes to the east and from the direction of Brandfort itself. The two squadrons were then attacked by about four hundred Boers from the town, while the burghers on the kopjes tried to work round their right flank. As the enemy pressed on vigorously and were causing some casualties, the squadron of the 9th Lancers charged, while that of the 16th Lancers aided it by dismounted fire. The enemy was at once checked, and the squadrons then retired, rendering each other

LORD ROBERTS SEIZES THE WATERWORKS.

mutual support. The Boers followed them for some two miles from Brandfort, and then desisted from further pursuit, though their patrols, evidently supported by a strong force, still showed vigour. The cavalry reached camp about 4 p.m., having had about ten casualties.

This skirmish showed Lord Roberts that the Boers on the right bank of the Modder were in sufficient strength to prevent the restoration of the railway bridge. He decided to drive them away, and to occupy Karee Siding, a little station eight miles north of the Glen, and, as a preliminary measure, ordered Lieut.-General Tucker with his division, the VIIth, and Colonel P. W. J. Le Gallais' mounted infantry to the Glen, where they bivouacked on both banks of the river. To rid himself of his immediate enemy with the least loss, Lord Roberts, as usual, proposed to employ the mounted arms in a wide turning movement. As usual, also, he wished to keep his plan a secret, and at the same time to have French at hand to execute it. He therefore sanctioned French's proposal to return from Thabanchu to superintend the remounting of the cavalry, and as soon as the cavalry General arrived at Bloemfontein on the 27th, Lord Roberts unfolded to him his plans for the capture of Karee Siding. Broadwood took over command at Thabanchu. *Roberts decides to occupy Karee Siding*

On the 28th Lieut.-General Tucker was directed by the Commander-in-Chief to dislodge the enemy from Karee Siding, and informed that Lieut.-General French would explain to him how the Field-Marshal thought the operation should be carried out. *with Tucker's division.*

The same day the cavalry outposts round Bloemfontein were taken over by Colonel C. P. Ridley's mounted infantry, while French, with nearly all the mounted men still with Headquarters, marched to the Glen. The wear and tear of war had greatly reduced the strength of the troops concentrated there. The cavalry, which consisted of the Scots Greys, Carabiniers, and 1st Australian Horse of the 1st brigade (Porter), the 9th and 16th Lancers of the 3rd brigade (Gordon), and the 12th Lancers of the 2nd brigade (Broadwood), could only find mounts for 650 men, while the four Horse artillery batteries could bring but *Concentration at the Glen, 28th March, 1900.*

four guns each into the field. There were 880 mounted infantry. The VIIth division numbered 6,400, with twelve Field artillery guns. Throughout the mounted arms the horses were weak and in poor condition.

When French reached the Glen the two Generals settled on the details for the next day. The Boers were known to have entrenched themselves astride of the railway near Karee Siding, about eight miles north of the Glen, on a line of kopjes four or five miles in length. Their main position was on the hills east of the railway; their centre, on the Nek crossed by the line, was not entrenched, but afforded good natural cover; their right rested on Hondenbeck Hill, a kopje about a mile and a half west of the station. French was to swing round to the west and threaten the burghers' communications north of Karee Siding. Le Gallais' mounted infantry were to circle eastward and bear upon the Siding. While the mounted troops were working against the enemy's flanks and rear, the VIIth division, in échelon of brigades, the 14th (Chermside) leading, was to march northwest from its bivouac against the line of kopjes held by the burghers. Soon after 8 a.m. on the 29th the cavalry brigades were set in motion and by 10 a.m. they had occupied Kalkfontein. On learning that this farm was in French's hands and that Le Gallais, on his side, reported his front to be clear of the enemy, Tucker advanced. His artillery marched behind the leading brigade (14th) of his division. His front and right flank were covered by a mounted infantry detachment of the City Imperial Volunteers, which was later to take its place as escort to the guns, when the arrival of mounted infantry from Le Gallais' force enabled the City Imperial Volunteers to return to this, their original duty.

About noon French, from the left, informed Tucker that he had turned the enemy's right flank, and that he was about to halt, covering himself to the eastward with scouts. Le Gallais also reported from the right that about two hundred Boers with a gun were retiring northward before him. The 14th brigade (Chermside) was now moving up the foot-hills east of the railway, and the 15th brigade (Wavell), in échelon to the left rear, had occupied the kopjes west of the station, when, about 12.40 p.m., shortly after the scouts had announced that there were no burghers on the kopjes south of Karee, fire was suddenly opened on the foremost infantry from north, east and west. The guns first came into action from a Nek about a thousand yards south-west of the station, against Boers visible on Hondenbeck Hill, about 2,300 yards off. On the right the 14th brigade, covered by the fire of the guns, continued its advance, the 2nd Norfolk regiment leading. The enemy fell back, and the Norfolk, with the 1st King's Own Scottish Borderers on their left, halted along a line of kopjes about a mile and a half east of Karee Siding. The two battalions were reinforced by the 2nd Hampshire, while the 2nd Lincoln was held in reserve on the right rear, where it was joined later by a section of field guns which were manhandled up to a steep ridge within short range of the Boer position. Here they gave Chermside's brigade great assistance at a time when all the Boer guns were directed upon it. The burghers held the outlying spurs with skirmishers, and had entrenched themselves on the far side of the summit, some few hundred yards back.

Action of VIIth division.

It was now about 2 p.m. A considerable number of reinforcements, including guns, were seen to join the enemy, and in this part of the field a long fire-fight took place, in which the King's Own Scottish Borderers did good service and lost considerably. After a time the 15th brigade was ordered to push further to the north. In this brigade the Cheshire and East Lancashire were in front, the North Staffordshire was in reserve, while the South Wales Borderers were sent to prolong the left of the 14th brigade. This battalion was exposed to a heavy cross fire from its front and left. During these infantry movements the artillery pushed closer to Karee and once more came into action against the high hill west of the Siding.

Soon after 3 p.m. French resumed his march towards the east, threatening the enemy's line of retreat, and the burghers who faced him began to withdraw. When the 14th brigade was again able to advance, the South Wales Borderers on its left became separated from it. About 3.30 p.m. Major-General Wavell sent the Cheshire from the 15th brigade to fill the gap thus caused, and these two battalions became a mark for the Boer cross fire. Wavell saw that progress was checked by this cross fire, and to beat it down directed the East Lancashire to carry the south-eastern flank of Hondenbeck Hill, which seemed to be the enemy's stronghold, and then to push on to the eastern end of the summit.

The officer commanding the East Lancashire, Lieut.-Colonel A. J. A. Wright, ordered forward three of his companies, supported by three more in second line. The remaining company he sent westward to threaten the enemy's right flank. Under a sharp fusilade, the main body worked across open ground to a deep donga, some five hundred yards from the foot of the ridge they were to attack. From the shelter of this donga they advanced in short rushes, under a hail of fortunately ill-aimed bullets, to within two hundred yards of the base of the hill. They then lay down and fired at the skyline, while the British guns swept the crest and summit of the ridge with shrapnel. The Boers, so well concealed that even at this short distance not one of them could be seen, kept up a hot fire and showed no signs of retiring. At this moment Lieut. E. J. Wolseley dashed forward, and by successive rushes led a section, numbering twenty-three men, towards the ridge, but this gallant, though ill-advised, attempt to storm completely failed. After losing five men killed and ten wounded he was driven back to the donga. The firing line was then reinforced from the supports, bayonets were fixed, and a properly organised advance began. By a series of well-timed rushes the East Lancashire passed over the danger zone between the donga and the foot of the hill. Then followed a steep climb up the boulder-strewn slope, but when the summit was gained it was found that the enemy had disappeared. At the same time the South Wales Borderers swung round to the east, in support of the 14th brigade. The Boers were now everywhere falling back, but the cavalry movement against the enemy's line of retreat had been checked. The enemy had been seen retiring near the railway to the north-east of the hill

LORD ROBERTS SEIZES THE WATERWORKS.

attacked by the East Lancashire, and O. and R. batteries Horse artillery were brought into action. The burghers replied with two heavy pieces from the east of the railway, and a commando lined the hills to keep back the cavalry, which then pushed forward and dismounted to the right and left front of the Horse batteries, where they were forced to remain for the rest of the day.

The main body of the Boers, covered by the fire of their guns and the riflemen, made for Brandfort. Pursuit was out of the question, for the teams of the Horse artillery could hardly move out of a walk, and the cavalry horses were also thoroughly exhausted.

On the eastern flank Colonel Le Gallais' mounted infantry was opposed by a comparatively small force of the enemy, Le Gallais pushed the Boers back some three miles from ridge to ridge, but did not succeed in more than effectually covering the right flank of the 14th brigade. The Boers on this flank made one attempt at a counter-attack, but this was at once brought to a standstill by the fire of the pom-poms.

In the evening the cavalry, which had covered about forty miles of ground during the day, fell back by Karee Siding to their previous bivouac, while the infantry spent the night on the position from which the enemy had been driven, and which he had occupied with about four or five thousand men and four guns.

The British casualties were :— Casualties.

	Killed.	Wounded.	Missing.
Officers	1	11	—
N.C.O.'s and men	18	155	3

Of these losses thirty-six per cent. fell on the King's Own Scottish Borderers. In this battalion one officer was killed and five wounded, one mortally ; in the other ranks eleven were killed and fifty-three wounded.

On the 30th the VIIth division remained in bivouac at Karee Siding, while the cavalry division returned to Bloemfontein.

CHAPTER XVII.

OPERATIONS IN THE ORANGE FREE STATE DURING THE HALT AT BLOEMFONTEIN.

SANNAH'S POST.*

IN the plan of campaign to which the Boer leaders agreed at Kroonstad on the 17th March (see page 265), it was decided that some of the commandos were to march direct upon Bloemfontein, and "entice the enemy out of it," while others struck at the British line of communication from the capital to the Orange river. As the first group of commandos moved southward along the railway line, they had encountered at Karee Siding, with the result already described, a large detachment of Lord Roberts' main army, which he was pushing forward to secure a foothold on the right bank of the Modder. This he required for the protection of the working parties engaged in the restoration of the bridge at the Glen, and for the prevention of a possible foray over the river. The success of the engagement gave Lord Roberts the advantages he desired; yet the concentration to the north of Bloemfontein of troops, and especially of cavalry, necessary to obtain the requisite strength for his blow, greatly helped the operations of the second group of commandos, selected to act from the east against his communications. The escape of the three last commandos across the Bloemfontein—Ladybrand road had allayed the anxiety as to their fate which had been expressed in the Krijgsraad on 17th March. Beyond weak garrisons along the railway line, the communications

* See maps Nos. 33 and 35.

OPERATIONS IN THE ORANGE FREE STATE.

and the country to the east of the capital were protected by Broadwood's detachment at Thabanchu, forty miles from Bloemfontein, to which it was linked by two posts of no great strength. Broadwood was the main obstacle to a descent from the east of the Orange Free State upon the railway. Once he had been crushed or brushed aside, the burghers could pour southward, with a long start of any considerable body of mounted troops that could be sent against them. For this work their best leader, De Wet, was available. The world was soon to learn how he seized the opportunity.

On the 30th March Lord Roberts heard that his eastern flank guard at Thabanchu was threatened. The detachment, about 1,700 strong, commanded by Brigadier-General Broadwood, consisted of the composite regiment of Household cavalry, the 10th Hussars (with only 332 horses between them), and Q. and U. batteries, Royal Horse artillery; parties of Royal Engineers, Army Service Corps and Royal Army Medical Corps, and Lieut.-Colonel E. A. H. Alderson's brigade of mounted infantry, 835 strong. This brigade was composed of the 1st battalion mounted infantry under Major C. G. Amphlett, who with two companies was guarding the Waterworks; a company of the 2nd battalion mounted infantry; the 3rd battalion mounted infantry (Lieut.-Colonel T. D. Pilcher, Bedfordshire regiment); Rimington's Guides (Major M. F. Rimington, Inniskilling Dragoons); the 1st New Zealand contingent of mounted rifles (Major A. W. Robin); the Burma mounted infantry (Major D. T. Cruickshank, Essex regiment), and Roberts' Horse (Lieut.-Colonel H. L. Dawson, Indian Army).

Broadwood at Thabanchu

At 11 a.m. on March 30th Broadwood's outposts ascertained that three thousand to four thousand Boers were on the march from Ladybrand. At the same time, natives reported that a force from the north was coming towards the left flank. The outposts on the Ladybrand road were reinforced; three squadrons were sent to meet the turning movement; the town was evacuated, and the baggage drawn up in column of route along the Bloemfontein road. The convoy thus formed consisted of ninety-two wagons and carts, some of which contained women

is threatened from Ladybrand,

and children, British refugees from the disturbed sections of the Free State, while in others were carried the sick and wounded. With it marched about a hundred men, whose horses had broken down. Brigadier-General Broadwood telegraphed to the Chief of the Staff at Bloemfontein that, if the enemy was really about to turn his flank, he would be compelled to retire to the Waterworks, where he would be in open country and near enough to Bloemfontein to be supported from Headquarters. He warned Major Amphlett, who had ridden out to Thabanchu to see him, that the column might have to retreat, and urged him to patrol vigilantly, especially to the north, from his post at the Waterworks. At about 3 p.m. the enemy attacked the Nek on the Thabanchu—Leeuw River Mills road. General Broadwood then ordered the baggage, escorted by Lieut.-Colonel Pilcher's battalion of mounted infantry (the 3rd), to Israel's Poort, where he was to bivouac, but later in the day, when the reports of the enemy's turning movements were confirmed, he told Pilcher to push straight through to the Waterworks. The convoy arrived there about midnight, and the wagons were parked five or six hundred yards west of the Modder, and protected by a chain of small posts not more than two or three hundred yards distant

and falls back to the Waterworks during night of 30th-31st March, 1900.

from the vehicles. The main body of Broadwood's column remained near Thabanchu till nightfall, and then followed the convoy. At about 3.30 a.m. on the 31st March, it reached the Modder, crossed it by the Waterworks Drift and bivouacked close to the spot where the baggage was parked.

The terrain between the Waterworks and Boesman's Kop.

The Waterworks are about twenty-three miles east of Bloemfontein. They lie on the left or western bank of the Modder, which in this part of its course runs, though with many windings, from south-east to north-west. On the early morning of March 31st the river was in flood, and could only be crossed by the drifts, of which two became important during the next three days. The southern ford is that at the Waterworks; the northern, five miles down stream, is called the Waterval Drift. The approaches to these passages are commanded by clusters of rugged, broken kopjes on the right bank. From the valley of the Modder a vast plain stretches towards Bloemfontein, its monotony only broken

OPERATIONS IN THE ORANGE FREE STATE.

by the outline of Boesman's Kop, a grim pile of boulders about eight miles west of the Waterworks. At the north end of this kopje the tracks from the various drifts across the river join the main road to the capital. Between Boesman's Kop and the Waterworks several spruits run northwards into the Modder; the roads pass them by drifts, one of which, that over the Korn Spruit, two miles and a quarter from the Waterworks, is of considerable difficulty. The bed of this spruit is here about fifteen feet below the plain, and the sides of the watercourse are very steep. Between the Korn Spruit and the next watercourse to the westward, the Mealie Spruit, is a slight ridge commanding the ground where the road crosses the Korn Spruit. About four miles to the south of the Waterworks rises a kopje, called Sannah's Post, which has given the name to an engagement that would be more correctly described as that of the Korn Spruit. *The Korn Spruit.*

When the news of the enemy's attempt against Thabanchu and of Broadwood's intention to retreat was confirmed, orders were at once issued by Headquarters for the IXth division, under Lieut.-General Sir H. Colvile, to march at daybreak on the 31st from its bivouac, two or three miles east of Bloemfontein, to the Waterval Drift. Lieut.-General Colvile was informed that he would be joined at Boesman's Kop by Lieut.-Colonel C. G. Martyr's mounted infantry, who on the 30th were supplying the outposts to the east of the town. *Reinforcements for Broadwood to leave Bloemfontein at daybreak on 31st March.*

The Waterworks were held by Amphlett's two companies of mounted infantry, in all about two hundred strong. During the apparent collapse of the Boers after the occupation of the capital of the Orange Free State, this had seemed an adequate garrison. Two posts connected the main army with Amphlett. The first was at Springfield,* a farm about eleven miles from Bloemfontein, where a number of troops were encamped; the second, four miles east of Springfield, was at Boesman's Kop, the natural strength of which had been increased by entrenchments. It was held by forty mounted infantry, under Capt. N. Bainbridge, West Riding regiment. The commander of the Waterworks was responsible for the communications westward to *Connecting links between Bloemfontein and Waterworks.*

* See map No. 35.

278   THE WAR IN SOUTH AFRICA.

Boesman's Kop, while Captain Bainbridge was charged with those between that post and Springfield.

<small>Patrol between Waterworks and Boesman's Kop</small>

In accordance with his usual practice, Major Amphlett, in the early part of the night of the 30th, i.e., before the arrival of Broadwood's baggage, sent out a non-commissioned officer and three men to patrol to Boesman's Kop. He did not take this opportunity to warn Bainbridge of Broadwood's probable retirement from Thabanchu. The movements of the patrol, and those of a reinforcement it received later from the party at Boesman's Kop, largely influenced the events of the 31st, which can only be understood by following their doings in detail. The patrol reached Boesman's Kop soon after midnight and reported that the road was all clear. Shortly after 3 a.m. on the 31st they started on the return journey, but at about 4.30 a.m. they reappeared at Boesman's Kop, bringing with them a Boer farmer who lived in the neighbourhood. This man had met the patrol on the road and told them that he was on his way to inform Bainbridge of the presence of a force under De Wet, who intended

<small>is warned that De Wet is in the neighbourhood,</small>

to attack the Kop at daybreak. The farmer also warned the patrol that if they went on towards the Waterworks they would surely be captured. Captain Bainbridge, though he did not believe in the truth of this story, sent the Boer under escort to Springfield, *en route* for Bloemfontein, with the request that the news should be at once forwarded to Headquarters. About 5 a.m. Bainbridge detailed a section of sixteen or seventeen of his own men, under a sergeant, to accompany Amphlett's patrol, and ordered them to reconnoitre towards the Waterworks and to the north-east, to verify the information which the Boer farmer had supplied and to enable the patrol to make its way back to its Headquarters. The remainder of his men manned the entrenchments. An hour later the sound of guns was heard from the neighbourhood of the Waterworks; this Bainbridge at once reported by orderly to Springfield. He could not leave Boesman's Kop unoccupied, and remained anxiously awaiting the return of his men, who came back at 6.45 a.m. to announce that they had been fired at from a spot they could not describe, and that they had failed to discover the strength of the enemy

Though the non-commissioned officer in command of the patrol had about twenty men with him, he neither opened fire in reply to that of the Boers, nor tried to send messengers either to Boesman's Kop or to the Waterworks to warn the garrisons. Bainbridge had trusted that with the help of his own section the patrol from the Waterworks would be able to reach Amphlett, and, disbelieving the statement of the Boer farmer, had not sent any orderly to make his way by another track to the Waterworks, and thus neither by message nor burst of musketry was Amphlett warned of the presence of the Boers between the Waterworks and Boesman's Kop. *but does not report the news.*

From the Waterworks patrols had also been sent out before daylight, towards Waterval Drift on the north, and across the plain to the south of the bivouac, and an officer's patrol had gone by the Waterworks Drift across the Modder. In the grey of the morning Amphlett informed Broadwood that the country to the north was reported clear of the enemy, but that the officer's patrol had been driven back with loss by Boers on the kopjes about a mile to the east of the river. The party sent to Boesman's Kop had not yet returned, but those sent there usually came back about daybreak, and though this detachment was rather late he did not see anything suspicious in that fact. Broadwood's troops, tired with the long night march, had hardly begun to stir in their bivouac, when first musketry and then a heavy shell fire opened upon them from the east of the Modder. The enemy's guns were posted upon the kopjes, which from the north overhang the road from Thabanchu to the Waterworks over which the column had marched but three or four hours earlier. *Measures for security at the Waterworks.*

31st March, 1900. Broadwood surprised by enemy and shelled from right bank,

At this time General Broadwood believed that, with the exception of the mounted infantry detachment on Boesman's Kop, the nearest British troops were at Springfield, nearly twelve miles away. He decided to withdraw to Boesman's Kop. It was a strong position, and could be held either to cover his further retreat, should this prove necessary, or to delay the enemy until reinforcements from Headquarters joined him. If he remained where he was, he was liable to have his flank turned and possibly *decides to withdraw to Boesman's Kop.*

might be cut off from Bloemfontein. At Boesman's Kop he would be safe. The reported movement of a considerable number of the enemy close to Waterval Drift led him to think that the Boers also realised the importance of Boesman's Kop, and, if he was to forestall them and render timely assistance to the small mounted infantry post there, not a moment was to be lost. He, therefore, gave orders for the withdrawal of his whole force from the Waterworks to Boesman's Kop. Roberts' Horse was to act as escort to the convoy and to the artillery, which were to march at once. Instructions, which had already been anticipated by Colonel Alderson, were issued to the mounted infantry brigade to continue to act as rear-guard as they had done during the march from Thabanchu. Since the Modder was unfordable, except at the drifts, the holding of these drifts was the chief duty of the rear-guard. The directions to the convoy were merely to withdraw out of the range of the shell fire from the further side of the Modder, and it started in good order, though without waiting for troops to head its march and to guard its flanks. In passing a small stream, a few hundred yards east of the railway station, several wagons stuck hopelessly in the muddy bottom. To avoid the obstruction thus caused the convoy spread out right and left, and many of the Kaffir drivers urged their teams at their greatest speed towards the drift over the Korn Spruit. Then in four or five columns they converged again upon the Korn Spruit Drift, where a crowd of wagons soon formed a helpless, almost impenetrable block at the steep descent into the ford. The convoy, inspanning on the first alarm, had started before the Horse artillery was ready to move, and the batteries followed it in line, under the impression that the ground in the immediate neighbourhood of the bivouac had been adequately patrolled. They had just moved off, when Colonel A. N. Rochfort, commanding the Horse artillery brigade division, was told by General Broadwood to push Roberts' Horse and a battery to the far side of the spruit to protect the retreat of the convoy, U. battery accordingly trotted on, forcing its way in battery column as best it could through the turmoil, while Q. battery followed at a walk. A terrible surprise awaited them.

Hasty retreat of the convoy.

Confusion near Korn Spruit Drift.

OPERATIONS IN THE ORANGE FREE STATE.

In accordance with the decision of the Krijgsraad of March 17th, Lemmer and De Villiers were called up from Clocolan* to attack Broadwood at Thabanchu, while C. De Wet left Brandfort on March the 28th, intending to surprise the guard of the Waterworks, and to cut off the supply of water from Bloemfontein. He marched towards Winburg, and, carefully concealing his commandos during the 29th and 30th, sent out patrols to obtain news. On the 30th he held a council of war at a farm three hours' ride from the Waterworks. It was decided that Chief Commandant Piet De Wet, Commandants G. Theron of Bethlehem, and M. G. Van der Merwe of Winburg, with about 1,100 men, six guns, a pom-pom and a Maxim, should occupy the ridges east of the Modder, while De Wet himself, with Commandants Fourie and Nel and four hundred men, should line the bed of the Korn Spruit, so as to intercept the convoy which they had just heard was retreating from Thabanchu towards Bloemfontein. The party under De Wet reached the spruit about 4 a.m. on March 31st. It was their arrival that was reported by the farmer at 4.30 a.m. to Bainbridge at Boesman's Kop. It was they who had fired on the sergeant's patrol, which returned to Boesman's Kop at 6.45 a.m. Soon after he posted his men, De Wet heard from natives that not only the convoy, but Broadwood's whole column had crossed the Modder and was bivouacked near the Waterworks.

De Wet's ambush.

He reaches Korn Spruit, 4 a.m. on March 31st, and hears that all Broadwood's column is at the Waterworks.

Broadwood's unexpected retirement had altogether changed the conditions under which De Wet's scheme was devised. De Wet had proposed to lie in wait for the convoy and its escort; he had by no means reckoned on an encounter with the column of some seventeen hundred mounted men and two Horse artillery batteries which now lay between him and the main body of his comrades concealed in the ridges to the east of Waterworks Drift. The British presumably had occupied the passages over the Modder; and consequently, while denying the fords to the main or eastern force of burghers, they might be able to crush his detachment before it could be helped to escape by Piet De Wet's men. Such were the dangers of De Wet's situation.

* See map No. 35.

On the other hand, the troops bivouacked round the Waterworks had not discovered his presence in the spruit. For an ambuscade his position was ideal. There was no immediate hurry for a decision, and he resolved for the present to await events. Two hours later he heard the guns of his friends across the river, as they began to shell Broadwood's bivouac. Soon afterwards he observed with satisfaction that the column in its retreat was preceded, not by quick-sighted and skilful scouts, but by panic-stricken native drivers and civilian refugees, whose wagons were in a state of utter disorder. The artillery, the arm that he dreaded most, as with his party he had no guns, was following these wagons so closely as to be already involved in the confusion. For so capable a man, it did not take long to make arrangements for securing the prize which his own skill, good fortune, and the mistakes of his opponents had combined to throw into his hands. As the first wagons of the refugees struggled down the steep slope into the spruit, and thus became invisible to the drivers and troops following in rear, there suddenly appeared among them armed Boers, who at once imposed silence, seized the animals and led their prisoners to a spot in the bed of the watercourse, where they could be easily guarded, and were out of sight of everyone to the east of the spruit. Thus there was nothing to arouse the suspicions of the gun drivers and detachments who were forcing their way through the tangle of transport which blocked the approach to the drift from the east. When the guns were within a few yards of the spruit, a Boer officer suddenly emerged from the bed of the stream and demanded the surrender of U., the leading battery. At the same moment a long line of burghers appeared upon the banks, and covered the artillerymen with their rifles, while others sprang upon them from behind the wagons of the convoy. The gunners were scattered, unarmed, defenceless. The guns, though limbered up, being hemmed in by transport wagons, were powerless even to retire. With the exception of the battery commander and Sergeant-Major J. Martin, the whole of the *personnel* of U. battery was captured and hurried into the bed of the Korn Spruit. Their escort, Roberts' Horse, which,

OPERATIONS IN THE ORANGE FREE STATE. 283

as has already been said, was hastening after the guns, narrowly escaped the same fate. The regiment, in extended order, was within two hundred yards of the spruit, when a number of Boers stood up and made signs to the troopers to go to the drift. Colonel H. L. Dawson (Indian Army), who commanded Roberts' Horse, instantly grasped the situation, and giving the word to turn about, galloped back under very heavy fire to the buildings at the station. He lost considerably in his retreat, not only in killed and wounded, but also in prisoners, for the men whose horses were shot under them were in most cases captured. Very nearly all the soldiers who were marching with the convoy shared the fate of the men of U. battery; but Lieut. B. T. Buckley, Northumberland Fusiliers, and a few of the men who were leading sick horses succeeded in making their escape. *Roberts' Horse escapes,*

Major E. J. Phipps-Hornby, with Q. battery, was then some two or three hundred yards from the spruit, and, imagining that the block and confusion was only due to the crowd of wagons waiting to get over the drift, he was bringing his battery quietly along, when a soldier who had escaped from the Boers, gave him the alarm. Phipps-Hornby inclined off to the left, so as to have between his guns and the drift the great mass of the convoy wagons and the stream of fugitives, and then wheeling his sub-divisions to the left gave the word to gallop. It was at this very moment that Colonel H. L. Dawson, commanding Roberts' Horse, ordered his men to retire, and the Boers, seeing that they were discovered, poured a hail of bullets into both guns and horsemen as they dashed away. The horses of U. battery, which till then had stood quietly on the bank, began to stampede with the guns. The teams of five of them were shot down by the Boers to prevent their following the horses of Q. battery, and thus escaping. These five guns were captured, but when the stampede began the horses of the sixth gun broke away from the Boers who held their heads, and galloping a long distance between the still unbroken troops, finally came to a standstill. Later in the day Sergt.-Major Martin, with the help of two men in charge of a water-cart, brought the gun to the column when it had reformed near Boesman's Kop. Q. battery had covered *and Q. battery, R.H.A. also.*

some three hundred yards, when several horses in one gun team were hit, the piece was overturned and had to be left behind, while in a wagon team three horses were knocked over and the wagon brought to a standstill. The rest of the battery galloped on to the station buildings, near which the guns were brought into action against the eastern edge of the spruit, 1,100 yards distant; but the only target was the heads of the Boers appearing above the bank, and directly the burghers saw a flash they took cover and were practically safe. As the bed of the spruit was fifteen feet below the plain, and the banks steep, the guns could do them little damage; yet the shells sufficed to reduce, though not to silence, the musketry of the enemy.

Broadwood's dispositions;   When the Boers disclosed their admirable ambush the main body of the cavalry was about half a mile in rear of the artillery. They at once took cover behind the railway station buildings. The Burma mounted infantry battalion was facing the Modder in column of companies when the firing broke out in the Korn Spruit. Colonel Alderson at once sent the Durham Light Infantry company to the assistance of Q. battery. They galloped to the station buildings through a mob of loose horses, dismounted, and extended to the right and left of the guns. The two other companies of the battalion, with a company of the 2nd mounted infantry, moved on to the south of the unfinished railway.

and his situation.   The situation had now become one of great difficulty for Broadwood. He was on a bare, featureless plain. To the west, sheltered in the Korn Spruit, across the track leading to Boesman's Kop, were an unknown number of burghers, who had already taken one of his batteries and the greater part of his convoy, had inflicted some loss on Roberts' Horse, and were then engaging his remaining guns, which stood in the open within effective rifle range of the perfectly concealed occupants of the spruit. Behind him, the eastern bank of the Modder was held by the enemy, also in unknown numbers, with several guns which outranged such as he still possessed. He was thus taken between two fires.

After the Boers on the right bank of the Modder saw the disaster to the convoy they came down from the hills to the

OPERATIONS IN THE ORANGE FREE STATE. 285

stream, and kept up a heavy fire upon the rear-guard of mounted infantry who faced them on the left bank. Under cover of this fusilade, parties of burghers gradually worked their way along the river. They occupied the ground near the Waterval Drift on the north, and reached about a mile above the Waterworks Drift on the south. *Boers extend along the right bank of the Modder.*

Brigadier-General Broadwood knew nothing of the measures taken by Lord Roberts to support him. He did not know that Colonel Martyr's force of mounted infantry was close to Boesman's Kop, nor that Colvile's division was on the march from Bloemfontein to his assistance. He now ordered Colonel Alderson to hold in check the attack from the east as long as possible; while Captain N. R. Radcliffe's company of mounted infantry, part of Amphlett's original garrison, was sent to hold a kopje near Waterval Drift. The Household cavalry moved up the Korn Spruit to a point about two thousand yards above the drift, to prevent De Wet's men from extending to the south; the company of the 2nd mounted infantry crossed the spruit and occupied the ridge on its far side, thus prolonging the line of the Household cavalry to the west; the 10th Hussars were to pass round this company of mounted infantry and act against the rear of the enemy in the spruit. The Household cavalry, when shortly afterwards relieved by a company of the Burma mounted infantry from the south of the railway embankment, were directed to co-operate with the 10th Hussars. *Broadwood's fresh dispositions.*

It may appear that these measures should have sufficed, not only to extricate the column, but to change the whole aspect of affairs. The situation of the Boers in the spruit at this time seemed most perilous. They were but four hundred strong, without artillery, and isolated from their main body, from which they were separated by a river, passable only at a few drifts on which the British still maintained some hold. Five guns, supported by an escort, were in action against them from the east, two companies of mounted infantry were engaging them from the south and south-west, while a force of cavalry, nearly equal to them in numbers, had started to attack them in rear from the west. Added to this, they were in a spruit which was com- *Situation of the Boers in the Korn Spruit.*

manded by a ridge running along their rear at about one thousand yards range.

The turning movement. Everything now depended on the execution of the turning movement. But Broadwood did not obtain the relief he expected from the action of the cavalry, and even when strengthened, as they were later in the morning by part of Martyr's mounted infantry, neither they nor their reinforcements made any headway against De Wet's burghers, weak as the defenders' position seemed to be. The small strength of the Boers was greatly reduced by the numbers required to guard the prisoners, and to prevent the animals of the captured wagons from bolting in every direction. The dread of seeing a strong British force on the ridge behind them was ever in their minds, for, if once it was lost to them, the Korn Spruit, both in their opinion and in that of the captive officers, would become untenable. *De Wet's danger.* So few burghers were available to deny this ridge to their assailants and to face at the same time the fire from the party of mounted infantry established athwart the spruit to the south, and that of the guns with their escort to the east, that De Wet could only push out to the westward a few detached posts, each consisting of a handful of picked men, whose steady fire held back the far superior numbers of the cavalry and mounted infantry. No one seems to have been specifically placed by Broadwood in command of the various units detailed for the turning movement. Though Lieut.-Colonel R. B. W. Fisher, 10th Hussars, was the senior officer on this part of the field, he did not take charge of the operation—probably because he was unaware of his responsibility. The Boers on the ridge, few as they were, were exactly in the kind of position to give ample scope to practised riflemen. The ground before them lay open to the full range of their weapons, while they were completely hidden from the view of the British.

Martyr reaches Boesman's Kop at 7 a.m. When Lieut.-Colonel Martyr received orders on the 30th to march at daybreak next day to Waterval Drift, he was informed that the enemy was advancing from the direction of Thabanchu, but of Brigadier-General Broadwood's movements he was told nothing. His brigade consisted of three companies of the 2nd

OPERATIONS IN THE ORANGE FREE STATE.

battalion mounted infantry, the remaining company of which was with Broadwood; the 4th battalion mounted infantry, and the Queensland mounted infantry. The 4th battalion of mounted infantry had only three companies. His departure was somewhat delayed by the necessity of collecting his brigade, which was spread over a wide front, and also by the time lost in obtaining rations and forage from the supply depôt, two miles in rear of the line of outposts which he was holding. On arriving at Boesman's Kop about 7 a.m., Colonel Martyr heard the sound of heavy firing at the Waterworks, and judged that Amphlett's two companies, which he knew to be posted there, were in danger. After reporting this by heliograph to Head- *His* quarters and despatching a messenger to meet General Colvile, *dispositions.* commanding the IXth division, he divided his column into two detachments. He sent the three companies of the 2nd mounted infantry under Major C. M. Dobell along the road which leads across the Korn Spruit to the Waterworks. Colonel St. G. C. Henry, with the 4th battalion mounted infantry and the Queenslanders, was despatched to Waterval Drift, five miles distant, with orders to work up the Modder towards the Waterworks.

The 10th Hussars, as they marched westward to get behind the Boers in the Korn Spruit, had seen figures moving on Boesman's Kop. Colonel Fisher sent on a patrol to discover whether these were friends or foes, while, after following to the rising ground between the Kop and the Mealie Spruit, he halted at Klein Klipkraal. When the patrol returned, with the news that Colonel Martyr's mounted infantry had reached the field, Fisher turned eastward, and worked back to the western slopes of the down which separates the Mealie and the Korn Spruits. Here he *Fisher in* obtained touch of the 2nd mounted infantry. Dobell was ready *touch with* to co-operate with him, for Martyr, who before 10 a.m. had *mounted* received a message from Fisher asking for support, had directed *infantry, but* him to help the cavalry in every way. Dobell dismounted his *impression.* men and advanced with the cavalry on his right, but the combined attack failed to push back the enemy posted on the ridge.

While matters were thus undecided in the valleys of the Mealie and the Korn Spruits, the situation on the eastern part of the field was not improving. All Broadwood's mounted infantry were heavily engaged; and the casualties among them were already considerable. For about four hours Q. battery had been in action on the open plain against the burghers in the Korn Spruit. A party of Boers, issuing from a point on this spruit some distance below the drift, attempted to close on the right flank of the artillery, and reached within 1,200 yards of the gun nearest to them, when the musketry of the escort drove them backwards. Phipps-Hornby, at the same time, opened upon them with one gun, but the fire from the Korn Spruit so quickly increased that he was soon obliged to turn the piece on its original target. The officers were nearly all disabled. Lieuts. E. B. Ashmore and D. J. Murch were severely wounded early in the day, and Lieut. H. R. Peck was hit later in the engagement; the sergeants who had taken the officers' places and the corporals on whom the duties of the sergeants had devolved were all shot down. At one gun every man had been hit; with two other guns but one man for each was left, and the ammunition for both was brought up by one gunner. The doctor, Lieut. F. S. Irvine, R.A.M.C., was killed while bandaging the leg of one of the sergeants. Colonel Rochfort had been shot through the arm while pulling a limber towards the guns in order that the gunners should not have so far to run for the ammunition. At the last one sergeant, one corporal, eight gunners and Phipps-Hornby himself were the only unwounded men left to fight the guns, for Captain C. Humphreys was then engaged in bringing up ammunition. Broadwood's cavalry had failed to produce any impression on the Boers in the spruit; and as they had not even gained any information about the enemy, the General was still ignorant of the strength of his immediate antagonists, and did not know how far up and down the spruit they extended. As Colonel Martyr, though he had reached Boesman's Kop at 7 a.m., had omitted to report himself, Brigadier-General Broadwood did not know that a fresh brigade of mounted infantry had arrived upon the battlefield. In the circumstances, he decided to continue the retirement on Boesman's Kop, which De Wet's ambush had so completely arrested. The battery, with its

OPERATIONS IN THE ORANGE FREE STATE.

escort, passing in rear of the pivot formed by the company of the Burma mounted infantry and part of Roberts' Horse, was to cross the Korn Spruit and make for Boesman's Kop, while Colonel Alderson supported, and then followed, the retreat. When Broadwood gave the order for the battery to retire he did not consider that it would be feasible to get the guns away under the very heavy fire to which they were exposed. But Phipps-Hornby had no intention of abandoning them without a desperate struggle. He saw that it would be impossible to bring the horses up to the guns under the storm of bullets which was falling around him, so he determined to man-handle the guns to the railway station, about seventy yards in his rear, where behind the shelter of a few iron huts and of a low stone wall, the horses could be hooked into the limbers. Telling his plan to the officer commanding the escort, Major D. T. Cruickshank, Essex regiment, he gave the order to run back the pieces. The eight unwounded gunners managed to drag two of the guns about forty yards, but were then quite exhausted. Major Phipps-Hornby now called on the escort for volunteers. Lieut. G. M. H. Stirling and Private Bright of the Essex regiment; Lieuts. W. J. Ainsworth, L. F. Ashburner and A. S. Way, Corporal Steele, Privates Pickford and Horton of the Durham Light Infantry; Lieut. P. C. Grover, Shropshire Light Infantry; Private Parry, West Riding regiment; and Lieut. F. A. Maxwell, 18th Bengal Lancers, sprang forward, and with one or two of the gunners brought four out of the five guns back to a spot where they were under fair cover. Captain Humphreys, Lieut. Stirling and some drivers and gunners then dashed forward with pairs of horses and brought back four of the limbers. There still remained in the open a gun and a limber, and several determined efforts were made to save them, but in vain. The burghers shot so well that on each attempt the horses were killed, and Humphreys was severely wounded. Phipps-Hornby was now the only officer of the battery uninjured. A large number of the men were dead or wounded, and many of the horses were killed or so severely wounded as to be useless. He decided to abandon the remaining gun and three limbers, and retired at a walk with four guns, one

Withdrawal of Q. battery

with help of mounted infantry.

290   THE WAR IN SOUTH AFRICA.

wagon and one wagon limber. These had been saved from the enemy by the stern devotion to duty of the officers and men of Q. battery and the mounted infantry who helped them in their bitter need. Among the officers of the escort Lieut. Grover fell mortally wounded, and Major Cruickshank was blinded by a bullet. For their conduct on this occasion the Victoria Cross was awarded to Major E. J. Phipps-Hornby, Q. battery Royal Horse artillery, and to Lieut. F. A. Maxwell, 18th Bengal Lancers. The non-commissioned officers and men of Q. battery were allowed to select by vote the recipients of three Victoria Crosses, which were allotted to the unit for collective gallantry. Their choice fell upon Sergeant C. Parker, Gunner Isaac Lodge, and Driver H. H. Glasock.

Alderson covers retreat of Q. battery.

At about 10.30 a.m. Alderson, who was exchanging hot fire with the burghers across the Modder, received orders from Broadwood to cover the retreat of the guns, and that done, to reassemble his brigade close to Boesman's Kop. He formed a second line from his reserve to cover the first line as it fell back westward. When the guns, loudly cheered by the mounted infantry, had filed in column of route past the left of his force, he gave the command for his front line to retire through the second, and reform at some distance to the rear. Directly the front line began to retire the Boers swarmed over the Waterworks Drift; and while a large number of them reinforced De Wet in the Korn Spruit, the Winburg and Bethlehem commandos followed Alderson in pursuit, either shooting from the saddle, or dismounting to fire, but ever pressing vigorously on. As soon as the first line had reformed behind the second, the latter fell back, and thus, each detachment covering the retreat of the other, the mounted infantry reached the upper part of the Korn Spruit, and crossed it about a mile and a half south of the drift. Here the burghers halted and contented themselves with annoying the retreating British with long-range fire. Alderson's movements were well conducted; the men were exceedingly steady, and showed absolute reliance, not only on their officers, but on their comrades in the supporting corps. But the company officers and the rank and file, in their determination to save

OPERATIONS IN THE ORANGE FREE STATE. 291

the guns of Q. battery, occasionally held their ground too long and thus suffered considerable loss in killed, in wounded and in prisoners—men whose horses were shot and who could not get back to the supporting line before they were captured by the enemy. To the New Zealanders and Pilcher's battalion of mounted infantry, which had covered the retreat of Alderson's brigade, fell the honour of bringing up the rear-guard.

Not until Broadwood had begun to retire did he hear that Dobell's mounted infantry were in the Mealie Spruit valley. He at once sent Dobell orders to push forward to the ridge to the west of the Korn Spruit and ascertain if there was hope of recovering the guns and the convoy. Dobell advanced a short distance, but the fire of the Boers posted on the rise stopped him. Later on, he heard from a patrol that the enemy in the spruit had been reinforced to a strength of about 1,500 rifles. After reporting this, he saw that the various units of Broadwood's force had fallen back, and that small parties of Boers were beginning to move about his flanks. At about 1 p.m. he withdrew to Boesman's Kop, being shelled by the Boer guns until he was out of range. Later in the day he followed the IXth division towards Waterval Drift. Dobell unable to approach Korn Spruit.

As soon as Alderson had retired De Wet determined to run no risk of losing his valuable prizes; he rapidly harnessed every available horse and mule to the guns and wagons, and before midday had passed his prisoners and his spoils of war through the Waterworks Drift. Two of the guns were brought back across the river about 2 p.m., and from the west of the Korn Spruit came into action against those mounted infantry, who, as will be seen, were still clinging to Waterval Drift.

By 11.15 a.m. the greater part of General Broadwood's force had been withdrawn into a position of safety, and formed up between the Korn Spruit and Boesman's Kop; but there was still fighting on the banks of the Modder between the Waterworks and Waterval Drift. It has already been said that at 7 a.m. (see page 287), Colonel Martyr reached Boesman's Kop and sent the larger portion of his troops, under Colonel Henry, to Waterval Drift, four miles from the ford across the Korn Spruit, which The mounted infantry at Waterval Drift.

Henry at Waterval Drift crosses to right bank,

VOL. II. 19*

Phipps-Hornby's guns were then shelling vigorously. Two companies and a half of mounted infantry made good their footing on the eastern side of Waterval Drift, but they soon came under heavy infantry fire and were shelled by guns and a pom-pom from the plateau north-east of the ford. Their right flank was protected to some extent by Captain Radcliffe's company of mounted infantry, which had occupied a kopje on the left bank about a mile east of the drift. Radcliffe's position *relieves Radcliffe,* was a serious one, for the Boers had surrounded him with a ring of musketry, and played upon him with two guns. With the Queenslanders Colonel Henry relieved Radcliffe, who lost several men and many horses; but as soon as Broadwood's mounted infantry had retired across the Korn Spruit the Boers turned upon Henry and pushed him backwards to Waterval Drift. He clung to it till about 2 p.m., when the pressure became so great that *but has to retire to left bank.* he recalled from the right bank the mounted infantry, and the Queenslanders who had joined them, and gradually fell back to the westward, watching the ford till, at about 4 p.m., the IXth division arrived. In his retreat several of the rear-guard were captured.

Colvile's march from Bloemfontein. The IXth division had started from Bloemfontein at 5.30 a.m. by the road to Waterval Drift through Springfield. Colvile's infantry was about five thousand strong. His troops had not marched five miles before heavy and continuous firing was heard to the eastward. At Springfield news was received that the Thabanchu column was hard pressed between Sannah's Post and Boesman's Kop.

Colvile reaches Boesman's Kop at 11.15 a.m. From Springfield Lieut.-General Colvile rode with his staff to Boesman's Kop, ordering the artillery to come on as quickly as possible and the infantry to follow them. Colvile joined Martyr on the kopje at 11.15 a.m.; the artillery was not far behind him, and by noon the infantry, who had stepped out well on hearing the guns, had come up. Here he received from Martyr, who during the last four hours had been an eye-witness of the engagement, some account of its progress. The action was not yet completely over. The last of Broadwood's rear-guard could be seen hastening across the plain to join the column,

OPERATIONS IN THE ORANGE FREE STATE. 293

which had formed up some two miles from Boesman's Kop. A long string of stragglers, protected by the fire of the remaining guns of Q. battery, were flying before the pursuing Boers. The shells were bursting on the east of the Korn Spruit. At the Waterworks there was great activity, and through field-glasses it was possible to make out that wheeled vehicles were being passed across the ford. Colvile sent a staff officer to Broadwood to tell him of his arrival at Boesman's Kop and to direct him to come there forthwith. This order reached Broadwood about noon, when he had shaken himself clear of the enemy and was engaged in reforming his men. Realising that if the guns were to be recovered no time was to be lost, he decided to remain with his command and, according to his official report, he suggested a direct advance of the fresh troops against the Korn Spruit as the best means of saving the artillery. The staff officer who took back his reply does not confirm Broadwood's recollection of the terms of the message, which Colvile did not receive. After his interview with Broadwood, the staff officer collected information about the events of the morning, and heard that the enemy had recently reinforced the defenders of the Korn Spruit, which, as he could see, was strongly held. Before his messenger returned to Boesman's Kop, Colvile was joined there by his Brigadiers, MacDonald and Smith-Dorrien, who, after he had explained to them the situation as he knew it, urged him, but in vain, to go off and discuss matters with Broadwood personally. A ten minutes' canter would have taken him to the spot, and it was clear to them that Broadwood could not at the moment leave his command.

Until 2 p.m. Broadwood remained near Boesman's Kop in the expectation that some attempt would be made to recover the guns and convoy. Then he learned that the IXth division had moved off towards Waterval Drift, and, realising that the guns and convoy, baggage, stores and prisoners were completely lost, he withdrew his men to Springfield, where they bivouacked for the night. Broadwood marches to Springfield.

The problem before Colvile was in fact this: Was he to march straight after the enemy to Waterworks Drift, or to adhere to the Colvile's problem.

letter of his orders and move to Waterval Drift? Before he could approach the former ford he would have to cross various spruits, presumably still held by the Boers; and the experiences of the battles of Modder River and Paardeberg proved that the burghers were never more formidable than when defending the bed of a stream against a direct attack. He was not in strength to make a combined frontal and flank assault upon their positions. His orders to march upon Waterval Drift were clear, but many things had happened since they were issued. He had reason to think that the ford was still held by Colonel Henry's mounted infantry. He believed that by crossing the Modder at that drift he would be able to act effectively against the enemy's right flank. After weighing the arguments of his brigadiers and his staff officers, whom he called into council on the point, he decided, against the opinion of the former, to move to Waterval Drift, and on his march there received a heliograph message from Lord Roberts which not only informed him that reinforcements were at hand, but convinced him that in making for Waterval Drift he had anticipated the wishes of the Commander-in-Chief.

His decision to march on Waterval Drift.

In the course of the morning news of the successful ambuscade at the Korn Spruit had reached Bloemfontein, and soon after 10 a.m. Lieut.-General French had been ordered to hasten with every available man of the cavalry division to Waterval Drift and rescue Broadwood's column.

Cavalry division ordered to Waterval Drift.

Lord Roberts' message, sent to Colvile at 3.28 p.m., was thus worded:—

"The enemy will endeavour to delay you on the spruit in order to give themselves time for carrying off the guns. It is very desirable, therefore, that you should, if possible, make a turning movement which will enable you to act on their line of retreat. French's cavalry brigades, which should shortly be with you, will help to this end. Acknowledge receipt."

Operations at Waterval Drift.

At about 4 p.m. the IXth division approached Waterval Drift, where the enemy, now reinforced by Lemmer's and De Villiers' men from Thabanchu, held on the right bank high ground, which commanded the ford from the north-east. The Highland brigade was deployed and the artillery was brought into action against the Boer guns, while the 19th brigade made a wide turning movement and threatened the enemy's right flank. So slow were the burghers to give up the drift that, as the prisoners from Henry's mounted infantry were being marched away, they could see one of MacDonald's battalions advance towards the ford and open fire upon the Boers who formed their escort. A gun which had harassed Radcliffe on his kopje was still in its place on the right bank of the Modder, about half a mile up stream from Waterval Drift. Not long after they were taken away from the ford the prisoners passed the guns and wagons captured from U. battery, collected in a hollow about three miles east of Waterval Drift. About dusk MacDonald's infantry had established their outposts on the right bank; but, even had they known that the captured guns were near them, the men were so tired out that they were incapable of further effort. It was not until late at night that all the wagons of the division had crossed the ford. Soon after sunset Lieut.-General Colvile received a message from Lieut.-General French to say that the cavalry division would be with him by 6 a.m. on the 1st April.

When Lord Roberts' orders were received at the cavalry Headquarters, instructions were at once sent by helio to the 1st and 3rd cavalry brigades, encamped four and a half and two and a half miles respectively from Bloemfontein, and to the 12th Lancers at Bloemspruit, four miles east of Bloemfontein, to concentrate at Boesman's Kop as soon as possible, taking with them two days' supplies. By 2 p.m. the cavalry was at Springfield. The 3rd cavalry brigade moved on to Boesman's Kop and opened communication with the IXth division, while the remainder halted to reconnoitre to the south and south-east, owing to a report that a hostile column, some miles south of Boesman's Kop, was then marching westward. Valuable time was lost in ascertaining that this report was unfounded, and the division, which had been rejoined by Broadwood's brigade, bivouacked at Springfield and Boesman's Kop. The fatigue of Karee Siding and of the march which had followed it had further developed the weakness of the cavalry and Horse artillery

Movements of cavalry division.

horses, which had been sufficiently conspicuous in the action itself.

13th brigade sent to Krantz Kraal.

From Headquarters orders had also been sent on the 31st to Major-General C. Knox, who held the north-western outposts round Bloemfontein with the 13th brigade, to try to intercept the enemy, who would probably retire by the Krantz Kraal Drift. He marched at 2.30 p.m. and by 10 a.m. on the 1st April he had occupied Krantz Kraal.

The movements of De Wet after his victory are described in the next chapter.

Colvile's views, April 1st.

The IXth division bivouacked on the night of the 31st on the right bank of the Modder, Henry with the 4th and the Queensland mounted infantry holding a line of hills to the north-east of the Waterval Drift. Early on the morning of the 1st April Colvile heliographed to the Chief of the Staff that French had not yet appeared, and added: "Enemy has been reinforced during the night. Four laagers are now visible. He shows no disposition to move and is probably waiting to see what I do. My division is numerically equal to a strong brigade and I am not strong enough to leave a containing force and make a flank movement which seriously threatens his communication. I shall thoroughly reconnoitre his position to-day, but, unless I find him much weaker than I imagine, I propose, unless I receive orders to the contrary, to withdraw transport over the drift at dusk, and retire on Boesman's Kop station."

Cavalry division join Colvile 11 a.m. on 1st April.

French, with the cavalry division, less the 1st brigade, which moved direct towards the Waterworks, joined Colvile at 11 a.m., but did not assume command of the combined forces. The appearance of the cavalry caused the enemy apparently to retire, and after a consultation between the two divisional Generals, it was decided that the cavalry should remain at Waterval Drift, while Colvile with a brigade of infantry on the left bank reconnoitred the Waterworks, with the intention of recapturing them if they were but lightly held. At noon the 19th brigade (Smith-Dorrien), with the Field artillery brigade division, moved towards the Waterworks, while the Highland brigade (MacDonald) marched straight to

OPERATIONS IN THE ORANGE FREE STATE. 297

Boesman's Kop. Colvile had not gone far when, ascertaining that the enemy still occupied the Waterworks, he sent to French to point out that a demonstration on his left flank by the cavalry would greatly help him. The cavalry accordingly crossed to the right bank of the Modder and worked up stream; but French soon noticed that the 19th brigade was retiring, and at 4 p.m. he received a message, timed 3.20 p.m., from Colvile, to say that the enemy held the Waterworks and river bed lightly; that about 1,200 men occupied the hills to the east; that the remainder of their forces had divided to threaten the British flanks, and that he was consequently retiring to Boesman's Kop. French at once replied that as far as the left was concerned he had himself been out on that flank and had observed no movement of the enemy. Colvile, nevertheless, abandoned all idea of retaking the Waterworks, and fell back to Boesman's Kop, where the IXth division halted for the night. *Colvile reconnoitres Waterworks and retires to Boesman's Kop.*

The Headquarters Staff at Bloemfontein were kept fully informed by Lieut.-General Colvile of all movements near the Waterworks. At 1.45 p.m. Colvile reported to D.A.G. Headquarters that, being relieved by French he was advancing on the Waterworks. A short time afterwards he received a reply to the message already quoted, which he had addressed to the Chief of the Staff early in the day, before the cavalry division had arrived. The answer was thus worded :— *Colvile's reports to Headquarters.*

"No. C. 787—1-iv.-'00, 12.10 p.m. In reply to yours of this date to the Chief of Staff, your proposed action approved. Do not engage enemy, as you are not strong enough to do so with advantage. Act as you propose by sending transport across the drift after dusk and retire to Boesman's Kop. Keep Knox informed accordingly. Acknowledge receipt. Military Secretary."

He replied to it at 2.20 p.m. as follows :—

"Regarding your 787, am now passing transport to west of river and shall proceed to Waterworks as I advised you in mine of 1.45. If I find myself likely to become seriously engaged will retire on Boesman's Kop; present arrangements are that Knox takes my place here and French holds line of hills to the east."

In the course of the evening Colvile received from the Chief of the Staff the following telegram approving of the retirement to Boesman's Kop of the IXth division :—

"A. 640. If the enemy are as strong as you have reason to believe at Likhatlong, it would be better for you with your whole division to fall back on Boesman's Kop, otherwise it is not improbable that they may try to cut off your communications with Bloemfontein by turning your right flank. Communicate this to French and acknowledge receipt. The force with which Broadwood has been engaged is under De Wet, who came from Brandfort, and crossing the Modder river at Krantz Kraal, got right in his rear during the night. He will probably try the same game with you, when you will probably be between two fires. Acknowledge receipt."

The 1st cavalry brigade had remained about Klipkraal till dusk to cover the withdrawal of the infantry and the removal of the wounded men of Broadwood's force to Boesman's Kop. They then joined the remainder of the division at Waterval, leaving a squadron to watch Klipkraal. The cavalry division bivouacked on either side of Waterval Drift, the 3rd brigade on the right bank, the remainder, with all the guns, on the left bank. The 13th brigade (C. Knox) marched from Krantz Kraal in the afternoon of the 1st April, and halted two miles north of Waterval Drift.

The troops ordered to fall back towards Bloemfontein. The next day, April 2nd, orders were received from Headquarters, at 1.30 p.m., for the cavalry, the IXth division and the 13th brigade to retire on Springfield. That night the infantry and Broadwood's (2nd cavalry) brigade bivouacked at Springfield, and the remainder of the cavalry division at Boesman's Kop; and by nightfall on the 3rd all the troops which had taken part in the Thabanchu and Sannah's Post operations were reassembled in Bloemfontein and its immediate neighbourhood.

Material and moral effects of De Wet's success. The material result of De Wet's achievements at Sannah's Post was the acquisition of seven guns, much ammunition, many horses and wagons, and a large number of prisoners. By occupying the Waterworks, which did not again pass into Lord Roberts' hands until the 23rd April, he inflicted great injury on the health of the troops in Bloemfontein. The moral effect of his success was enormous. It confirmed the resolution of those of the Free State burghers who still remained in arms ; it encouraged the

OPERATIONS IN THE ORANGE FREE STATE.

waverers; it afforded De Wet the occasion for putting strong pressure upon the considerable numbers of his fellow countrymen who, declaring themselves tired of the war, had given in their rifles to the British troops, and had been allowed to return to their farms as peaceful non-combatants; and it gave those who followed him good heart for his next stroke.

The total casualties in Broadwood's engagement at Sannah's Post on the 31st March were 571. The principal losses in units will be found in Appendix 2.

Casualties.

CHAPTER XVIII.

OPERATIONS IN THE ORANGE FREE STATE DURING THE HALT AT BLOEMFONTEIN (*continued*).

REDDERSBURG.*

De Wet after Sannah's Post strikes south.

SUCCESSFUL as the stroke at Sannah's Post had been, it was only an incident in the scheme which had been designed at Kroonstad. Fortune had favoured De Wet, and he had swept aside the only troops which interposed between him and his task in the south. He was thus able to take the next step. He now might hope to place himself between Bloemfontein and the Orange river, and by striking at the communications with the sea to hamper the advance northwards of Lord Roberts' main army. The withdrawal towards Bloemfontein first of Broadwood's brigade and then of Colvile's and French's divisions opened for him the larger prospect. Opposed to him were only a series of detachments, neither firmly established in their posts nor adequately connected with the railway or with each other. These he might hope to capture or drive headlong before him. The disposition of these detachments was consequent on movements in the south of the Free State since the 15th of March, the day when Gatacre (IIIrd division) and Clements (12th brigade) crossed the Orange river at Bethulie and Norval's Pont and joined hands with Pole-Carew's column from Bloemfontein.†

His quarry.

How the situation was prepared for him.

On March the 17th the bulk of the IIIrd division was concentrated about Springfontein; two battalions remained at Bethulie to guard the railway and to help in passing stores over

* See maps Nos. 34 and 35.   † See page 257.

OPERATIONS IN THE ORANGE FREE STATE. 301

the river. From Springfontein Gatacre sent out patrols in every direction. On the 19th he received the following telegram from Lord Roberts : " Could you manage to take a small force, say two battalions, one battery and some mounted infantry, as far as Smithfield ? It is very desirable British troops should be seen all over the country, and opportunity given to burghers to surrender and deliver up their arms under the conditions of the Proclamation of the 15th March." Gatacre replied that he could not spare more than one battalion (the 2nd Royal Irish Rifles), a Field battery, a company of the mounted infantry of the Royal Scots and a section of that of the Royal Irish Rifles. His suggested reduction was approved, and the troops started for Smithfield on the 20th. Following the spirit of his instructions Gatacre at the same time ordered Brabant, whose Headquarters were at Aliwal North, to send detachments to Rouxville and Zastron ; and on the 21st Gatacre himself, with a small escort, rode to Philippolis, took over the keys from the Landrost, and returned the same day to Springfontein. Clements had meanwhile received orders to march with the 12th infantry brigade, two Field batteries and a force of mounted infantry, principally Australians, from Norval's Pont, through Philippolis and Fauresmith, to Bloemfontein ; and, after concentrating at Donker Poort, he started on the 20th March. Gatacre was advised of this movement, and was also told to take charge of the country along the Orange river as Clements advanced northward.* On March the 26th the Commander-in-Chief directed that two squadrons of the Colonial division from Aliwal North and the Royal Scots company of mounted infantry from Smithfield should push forward to Wepener. Next day he summoned to Bloemfontein the 1st battalion Derby regiment and the 11th brigade division Royal Field artillery. The battery at Smithfield, which formed part of this brigade division, was brought back, and the two battalions left at Bethulie (1st Royal Scots and 2nd Northumberland Fusiliers) were called up to Springfontein.

British detachments sent to Smithfield, Rouxville and Zastron, March 20th, 1900.

Clements moves on towards Bloemfontein.

Detachment ordered to Wepener, March 26th.

On the 27th Gatacre reported to Headquarters a rumour

* See page 257.

that the Boers were returning from Clocolan in force, and had occupied Stateberg and Modder Poort. He mentioned that he had already ordered a detachment of Brabant's Horse to hold Bushman's Kop, " at the junction of the Rouxville-Zastron roads," and asked if he should reinforce the troops which were then moving on Wepener. The reply was that, though the Commander-in-Chief did not anticipate a return of the enemy to Wepener, it would be better to strengthen the party there. On the next day, March 28th, Lord Roberts sent the following telegram to General Gatacre : " If you have enough troops at your disposal I should like you to occupy Dewetsdorp. It would make the road from this to Maseru safe and prevent the enemy from using the telegraph to the south. Let me know what you can do to this end." Gatacre replied : " Following moves are in progress in view to covering whole country east of railway : Three squadrons Brabant's moving from Rouxville to Wepener ; two of them reach Wepener Sunday next, the third one on Tuesday. One squadron Brabant's is moving to Bushman's Kop, half way between Rouxville and Wepener. One company Royal Scots mounted infantry reaches Wepener Sunday. Two companies Royal Irish Rifles reach Dewetsdorp Sunday. One company Royal Irish Rifles and one section mounted infantry Royal Irish Rifles reach Helvetia to-morrow. Two companies Royal Irish Rifles remain at Smithfield, with one squadron Brabant's Horse." To carry out Lord Roberts' wishes Gatacre next day ordered a concentration at Dewetsdorp of the mounted infantry companies of the Northumberland Fusiliers and of the Royal Irish Rifles from Springfontein, and three, instead of two, companies of the Royal Irish Rifles from Smithfield. He telegraphed these changes in his dispositions to Headquarters on the 30th March.

C.-in-C. orders Dewetsdorp to be occupied, March 28th.

Gatacre orders concentration at Dewetsdorp.

Although on March 26th the Intelligence department had reported to the Commander-in-Chief that there was reason to believe that the Boers were collecting in the neighbourhood of Ladybrand and Modder Poort, the march of the various detachments on Dewetsdorp was not countermanded until the 31st March, the day of Sannah's Post, when two important telegrams were sent to Gatacre from Headquarters. The first

OPERATIONS IN THE ORANGE FREE STATE. 303

directed him to support and reinforce the Colonial division in the south-east of the Free State, whereupon Gatacre at once told Brabant to send the Cape Mounted Rifles, with their guns and the 2nd Brabant's Horse, to Wepener. The second message informed Gatacre of Broadwood's misfortune, ordered the concentration of the small outlying parties and the protection of the line of railway, and expressed the opinion that Dewetsdorp was too far advanced to be safely held. On receipt of the second message Gatacre telegraphed orders that the garrison of Dewetsdorp must fall back on Reddersburg. A still later telegram desired General Gatacre to send a battalion and a battery to Leeuwberg Kopje, eight miles south of Bloemfontein, to be there at daybreak on the 1st April. This was done.

C.-in-C.'s orders to Gatacre on March 31st. Wepener reinforced.

Dewetsdorp garrison recalled 31st March.

With the IIIrd division there were two battalions of mounted infantry, each of four companies, and another company, used as divisional troops. Two companies had been sent on detachment to Dewetsdorp, and on April 1st Lieut.-General Gatacre ordered that the remainder should furnish posts along the railway from Springfontein to Bloemfontein. Single companies were stationed at Springfontein, Jagersfontein, Kruger's Siding, Edenburg, and two companies at Bethanie. On April 2nd the distribution of the troops along the railway was rearranged by Headquarters; the Guards' battalions were brought into Bloemfontein, while the garrisons of the railway posts were supplied by the Royal Scots, Derbyshire, and Northumberland Fusiliers, with sections of the 5th Field battery at Ferreira Siding and the Kaffir and Riet bridges. When, on April 3rd, the troops returned to Bloemfontein from their fruitless expedition to the Waterworks, the 1st cavalry brigade was ordered to Springfield, the 2nd cavalry brigade to Bloemspruit, and the 3rd cavalry brigade to Rustfontein. The IXth division and 13th infantry brigade marched into Bloemfontein, from whence the VIth division had not moved. The VIIth division (Tucker) held Karee Siding to the north and Clements' brigade, the 12th, was within a day's march of Headquarters from the south. The IIIrd division (Gatacre) was écheloned along the line from Bloemfontein to Springfontein. But though the greater part of Lord

April 1st, 1900.

Distribution along railway at beginning of April.

Roberts' force was thus once more collected under his hand, many troops continued scattered throughout the villages in the south-east of the Orange Free State. There were detachments at Smithfield and Helvetia. Dewetsdorp had been evacuated, and its former garrison was moving towards Reddersburg. Two squadrons of the Colonial division, with a mounted infantry company of the Royal Scots, held the distant Wepener, linked with Aliwal North by small bodies of Brabant's Horse at Rouxville and Zastron. A reinforcement of the 2nd regiment of Brabant's Horse, the Cape Mounted Rifles, and part of the Kaffrarian Rifles was on its way to Wepener from Aliwal North, which was for the moment the Headquarters of Brabant's Colonial division, and served as the base for its operations in the south-east of the Free State. The Intelligence department at Headquarters at this time reported that on the Ladybrand—Thabanchu line were concentrated between thirteen thousand and twenty thousand Boers, of whom about one thousand were moving south, with advanced patrols twelve miles south-east of Bloemfontein at Leeuw Kop Farm, where it was said that a concentration of all burghers in the Dewetsdorp district was to take place on the 5th April.

The general distribution of the troops south-east of Bloemfontein had been made when from the facts then known it was inferred that the spirit of the Boers had been thoroughly broken. Those who had seen the retreat along the Basuto borders had announced that the burghers were "in a complete state of demoralisation and collapse, and were retiring in hot haste, leaving the road strewn with men, baggage and ammunition." To Lord Roberts it appeared that the best way to profit by this collapse and to restore peace to the southern portion of the Free State was to show small detachments of troops all over the country. By this means he hoped to encourage the farmers to throw off the influence of such of their fellow countrymen as were bent on continuing the war, and, accepting the terms of his Proclamation, to surrender their rifles and return quietly to their homes. The sturdy defence of the kopjes at Karee Siding no doubt showed that there were men still in arms who intended to

OPERATIONS IN THE ORANGE FREE STATE.

oppose the march on Johannesburg and Pretoria, but this the Commander-in-Chief had been led to expect. It was well known that Kruger, Steyn, De Wet, and a few more of the leaders would fight to the last, and that they were gathering round them at Kroonstad all the warlike force they could muster. Some opposition to the march to Pretoria, with its long and difficult line of communications had, therefore, been anticipated. Suddenly like a bolt out of the blue came De Wet's success at Sannah's Post. It had been achieved by only a fraction, fifteen hundred out of the thirteen thousand, now reported to be mustering in the Ladybrand region. For resistance to so large a body of mounted men, under a leader such as De Wet had shown himself, the dispositions of the troops, designed to restore peace, were not merely inadequate, they were altogether inappropriate. The importance of this offensive return, formidable in itself, was doubled by the fact that it at once attracted recruits to De Wet's commandos. As long as the organised armed forces of the Republics were flying, almost without showing fight, before Lord Roberts' victorious arms, and while the "Rooineks" seemed to be flooding the country in every direction, the temptations of a quiet life and the blessings of neutrality seemed irresistible to a large number of burghers. On the other hand, when De Wet had captured more than half of the artillery opposed to him, and was coming south with swarms of mounted men, and with some of the captured weapons to be used against their former owners; when, armed with the authority of both Republics, he was proclaiming vengeance against all traitors and appealing to the patriotism of the people—things presented a very different appearance alike to the farmers and to the petty detachments of soldiery scattered among them. At a moment's notice all the existing dispositions of troops had to be changed by Headquarters. The railway was necessarily the first care; if that was seriously broken, the army in Bloemfontein, if it did not actually starve, must be injuriously affected, and the northward march, the one hope of quickly ending the war, postponed for a considerable, if not an indefinite time. Next, the many outlying detachments must be drawn in, and, in particular Dewetsdorp,

Sannah's Post affair changes whole situation.

Peaceful burghers become active enemies.

Hurried redistribution inevitable.

which, for administrative purposes, it had seemed desirable to hold, must be abandoned.

<small>Effect on *moral* of changed orders,</small>

There are few things which tell more on the fighting quality of soldiers than the harassing effect of changing and uncertain orders. A vigorous march towards the enemy, under severe conditions of soil and weather, is exciting and inspiring, but a rapid retreat over the same ground, even to men accustomed to victory, is a trying experience. Unhappily the garrison of Dewetsdorp knew war chiefly in failure. Overdriven by the zeal of an energetic commander, they had, through no fault of their own, been defeated with much loss at Stormberg. Now came the order for them to flee before De Wet, who was armed with the very guns which were supposed to have been covering their peaceful mission. They had no cavalry to scout for them, and no artillery.

<small>particularly on Dewetsdorp troops.</small>

<small>Assembly at Dewetsdorp, April 1st.</small>

On the 1st April the troops which had been ordered to assemble at Dewetsdorp, now the most exposed outpost in the Free State, began to arrive there. The first to reach their rendezvous were three companies of the 2nd Irish Rifles. Four companies of this battalion and a section of mounted infantry had marched under Captain W. J. McWhinnie on March 28th from Smithfield. McWhinnie had dropped a company and the section of mounted infantry at Helvetia, to serve as a connecting link with the railway. On reaching Dewetsdorp, he was greeted with information from local sources that a Boer commando was expected soon to appear before the village and, selecting ground which commanded the place, he began to strengthen his position, which he covered by outposts. In the evening a patrol to the north of Dewetsdorp was fired upon. He informed the Headquarters, IIIrd division, of this by telegram, and also of the rumoured approach of the commando, which, however, was not credited by the Intelligence officer who accompanied his detachment. During the day two companies of mounted infantry from Springfontein had joined him, after a march of about a hundred miles in ninety-six hours.

<small>McWhinnie in touch with Boers on evening of 1st April;</small>

At midnight arrived Gatacre's telegram of the 31st March, which directed McWhinnie to be ready to return to Redders-

OPERATIONS IN THE ORANGE FREE STATE. 307

burg on receipt of further instructions. These were brought by a messenger from Springfontein, who rode into Dewetsdorp at 3.30 a.m. on April 2nd. The troops moved off at 5 a.m. in a downpour of rain. The tracks were heavy, and greatly delayed the wagons, especially those of the mounted infantry transport, the teams of which were much exhausted by the toil of the past four days. McWhinnie pushed on without interruption till 9.15 a.m., when the mounted infantry were ordered to feed their horses and give them a short rest. The animals were tired out. One had already died on the road from exhaustion. The three companies on foot now found their own advance and flank guards, and trudged on till noon, when they halted, and were rejoined by the mounted troops, who meantime had lost more horses from fatigue. Soon all were again on the march until, about 6 p.m., the little column bivouacked for the night. *he is recalled to Reddersburg, April 2nd. A heavy and exhausting march.*

By dawn on the 3rd it was once more in movement. The road along which McWhinnie's troops were plodding ran for miles almost due east and west over an open plain seamed with many dongas. At about nine o'clock, when a little way east of Reddersburg, the leading scouts came in sight of a rough boulder-covered ridge parallel to the track and a few hundred yards to the north of it. This feature was about a thousand yards in length, and about a hundred feet higher than the surrounding level; from its southern flank jutted out three spurs, each higher than the parent hill. As Captain McWhinnie, at the head of the main body, was nearing the ridge he learned from his right flank guard that a cloud of dust had been seen to the north. At the same time the leading scouts came under fire from the western end of the main ridge, on which a party of the enemy was concealed. He thereupon ordered two companies to seize two isolated kopjes, and with the mounted infantry moved up the eastern spur. From this higher ground he saw that he must hold the western spur, as it commanded the whole system of kopjes around it; he accordingly sent the mounted infantry there, and, bringing up all his infantry, occupied the eastern and central spurs and the part of the ridge which connected them. The hospital was established on level ground *The march of the 3rd April. McWhinnie attacked near Reddersburg about 9 a.m., April 3rd.*

VOL. II. 20*

between the ridge and the road, and the transport placed under cover. The troops were hardly in position when Captain McWhinnie received a message from General C. De Wet, in which the Boer guerilla leader informed him that his opponents numbered more than two thousand men with four guns, and called upon him "for the sake of humanity" to surrender.

De Wet calls on him to surrender.

De Wet's movements, after he defeated Broadwood on the 31st March, must now be described.

De Wet's scheme as reported to Steyn on the night of 31st March.

Before midnight on the 31st, from Klip Kraal, a little south of the Waterworks, he had sent a despatch to the President at Kroonstad to report that, with a small escort, he was on his way to Dewetsdorp. "Our commandos will join this evening with those of Chief-Commandants Lemmer and Olivier, and I shall march out to-morrow with two thousand men to cut off railway communication between Bloemfontein and Bethanie. Lemmer and Grobelaar, with 2,500 men, will remain between here and Bloemfontein and do whatever their hands find to do. We go to Dewetsdorp with Commandant Fourie to gather together the burghers of that district, and also to obtain dynamite for our operations."

De Wet's movements between 1st April and the morning of the 3rd.

On the morning of the 1st April De Wet learned that Dewetsdorp was occupied by a British detachment. After sending back peremptory orders to his Lieutenants, Wessels, Froneman and De Villiers, to meet him with all speed, he visited the neighbouring farms in order to rally the spirits of the burghers who had taken the oath of neutrality and been permitted by Lord Roberts to return to their homes. He persuaded or coerced more than a hundred of them to join his commando. Next morning his scouts informed him that the British had recently evacuated Dewetsdorp. He then directed the main body of his men, who were still some distance in rear, to ride towards Reddersburg, where he hoped to attack McWhinnie on ground of his own choosing, while he himself, dogging the march of the British column, halted for the night a little to the north of its bivouac. Early on the 3rd, burghers had arrived in sufficient numbers to enable him to bring the British to a halt, and no sooner had McWhinnie's refusal to surrender reached De Wet than with two guns he began to

OPERATIONS IN THE ORANGE FREE STATE. 309

shell them at a range of two thousand yards. At this distance the infantry were able to annoy the artillerymen, and the guns were drawn back out of reach of musketry. Soon afterwards two more pieces were brought into action and four guns now harassed the troops, one from the north-east, one from the east and two from the south. Nor did the burghers limit their attack to a cannonade. Taking advantage of the cover afforded by the dongas, they gradually closed in and practically ringed the British with a continuous rifle fire, which was maintained until nightfall. The ground which McWhinnie held was extensive; his men were worn out by the long marches of the last few days; they suffered from the depression produced by a bombardment to which they could not reply. Never was the controlling influence of officers more required to keep the rank and file steady and in good heart, to maintain discipline, to ensure watchfulness and vigilance in patrolling during the trying hours of the night. In the fighting on the 3rd the casualties among the rank and file were inconsiderable, but of the twelve officers in the column two were killed and two severely wounded. Thus by the end of the afternoon there were but eight, one for every seventy soldiers, left fit for duty. In the days when men fought shoulder to shoulder this number might have sufficed. On the kopjes of Reddersburg, where the troops were necessarily greatly scattered behind rocks, boulders and improvised shelters, it was wholly inadequate. To this loss in officers was largely due the disastrous result which followed next day, April 4th. *On McWhinnie's refusal to surrender De Wet opens fire with artillery, and encircles the British with rifle fire.* *Effect on troops of loss of officers on April 3rd.*

As soon as it was dusk the Intelligence officer sent a messenger to Bethanie for assistance. Creeping along the dongas, this man succeeded in passing through the Boer lines, and eventually reached the railway, but not till the news which he brought had already been forestalled. When darkness set in sentries were pushed out in every direction. The mounted infantry on the western spur were reinforced before dawn by some twenty infantrymen, and a company was pushed forward to occupy the part of the ridge between the western and the central spur. The anxieties of the commanding officer were not confined to his dispositions for defence. The spot where, to use the soldier's *Urgent message for help sent to Bethanie.* *British dispositions for the night.*

310 THE WAR IN SOUTH AFRICA.

Want of water.

term, the Boers "had held him up," was waterless, and when during the evening water was issued from the carts there was only enough to fill about one-third of each man's bottle.

Throughout the night the Boers kept up steady rifle fire, and at dawn on the 4th they renewed the attack. Then, to McWhinnie's dismay, he realised that under cover of the darkness some burghers had crept up the side of the hill and had settled themselves within thirty yards of the top of the ridge, just east of the ground held by the mounted infantry. Soon after eight o'clock the Boers forced their way upwards to the ridge itself, and made a determined rush for the spur held by the mounted infantry, who capitulated. The enemy now held the key of the position. McWhinnie first lined the central spur, but, under fire from three sides, his men were soon obliged to retire to the eastern spur. Here they were still worse off: they were bombarded by four guns and scourged by musketry at short range from every side.

During night Boers establish themselves advantageously, and at 8 a.m., 4th April, carry the key of the position.

Surrender of the detachment, 9 a.m., April 4th.

Soon after 9 a.m. the white flag was hoisted, and eight unwounded officers and five hundred and thirty-eight unwounded non-commissioned officers and men of the regular army laid down their arms, after a total loss of two officers and eight men killed, two officers and thirty-three men wounded. All that can explain this surrender has been recorded.

De Wet lost not a moment in securing his prisoners. In little more than two hours after their capture they were being hurried off to Winburg, *viâ* Thabanchu, at the moment when his rear-guard was skirmishing with the leading mounted troops of the force which had been hastily collected from various quarters and sent to the rescue of the Dewetsdorp detachment.

News of attack reaches the railway.

The first news of the engagement was brought to Edenburg at 7 p.m. on the 3rd April by one of De Montmorency's scouts, who had been reconnoitring towards Dewetsdorp. The village, he said, was now in the hands of the Boers, who were shelling McWhinnie's column near Reddersburg, at a spot about fourteen miles from Edenburg. The scout under-estimated the distance, but in other respects his information was correct. It was at once telegraphed to Headquarters and to Gatacre.

OPERATIONS IN THE ORANGE FREE STATE. 311

Lord Roberts directed Gatacre to hasten with all speed to the help of the detachment with such troops as he could collect, and he himself sent five companies of the Cameron Highlanders by rail from Bloemfontein to Bethanie. Gatacre ordered two batteries and the mounted infantry at Edenburg to rendezvous at Bethanie, whither, with a party of scouts and mounted infantry, he himself hurried from Springfontein. On his way he received a telegram from the Commander-in-Chief warning him not to move against the Boers until he had satisfied himself that their strength and position warranted his doing so with success. When Gatacre reached Bethanie he learnt that the enemy's guns were still in action; and, arguing that if the British column, weak in numbers and without artillery, was still holding out, the Boers could not be in very great force, he decided to attempt the relief of the detachment.

<small>Lord Roberts' directions to Gatacre.</small>

At 6.15 a.m., April 4th, De Montmorency's scouts and the company of the Derbyshire mounted infantry started from Bethanie to reconnoitre towards Reddersburg, twelve miles distant, and an hour later they reported that the action was still going on. When the five companies of the Cameron Highlanders, which had left Bloemfontein at 11 p.m. on the 3rd, and the mounted infantry from Edenburg had joined him at Bethanie, Gatacre marched towards Reddersburg. At 9.30 a.m. came a disquieting message from the officer commanding De Montmorency's scouts to say that firing had ceased for half an hour. Gatacre pushed on till he reached a ridge to the west of the village, five or six miles from the kopje which McWhinnie had defended. Here he was met by rumours that the British had surrendered, and at 10.30 a.m. he halted—as is now known, about half an hour before De Wet began to march his prisoners towards Thabanchu. The mounted troops, pushing on, drove before them a few of the enemy's rear-guard scouts; but General Gatacre decided that, as firing had ceased about two hours earlier, it would be useless to advance further, and ordered his whole force to retire on Bethanie. He had marched four miles when directions were received to occupy Reddersburg, and there he remained till midnight, when a telegram from Lord Roberts

<small>Gatacre's action thereon; he marches from Bethanie early on 4th April,</small>

<small>but hearing of the surrender, halts about 10.30 a.m.,</small>

<small>and retires towards Bethanie.</small>

ordered his immediate return to Bethanie, which he reached on the morning of the 5th.

<small>De Wet dashes off to Wepener, sending Froneman against Smithfield.</small>

As soon as De Wet was satisfied that there was no danger of his prisoners being rescued, he turned his attention to the other British posts east of the railway. On the night of the 4th he himself rode towards Wepener, and detached General Froneman with five hundred men to deal with the troops at Smithfield. These consisted of the Headquarters and one company of the 2nd battalion Royal Irish Rifles, and about eighty mounted men of the Queenstown Rifle Volunteers, who had recently arrived from Aliwal North. On the 3rd of April, Major E. Allen, who commanded the Royal Irish Rifles at Smithfield, was directed by telegram to recall the mounted and dismounted detachments of his battalion from Helvetia, twenty-eight miles from Smithfield. Starting at 4 p.m. on the 4th, they joined him at 1.30 a.m. on the 5th. During the night of the 4th-5th Allen received orders from Bloemfontein for the immediate evacuation of his post. He was to retire at his own discretion either to Aliwal North (forty-five miles) or Bethulie (forty-two miles), and, knowing that twenty-three miles off, at Rouxville, a post of Kaffrarian Rifles was in telegraphic communication with the Headquarters of the Colonial division at Aliwal North, he chose the longer route.

<small>Smithfield garrison, evading the stroke, reach Besters Kraal.</small>

By 8.30 a.m. on the 5th he was on the march, and had placed the Caledon River between himself and the Boers before he halted for the day, five miles south of the Commissie bridge. So far he had seen or heard nothing of the enemy, but at 9.30 p.m. Major H. L. Hallowell, commanding the Queenstown Volunteers, which had been left as rear-guard at the river, warned him that the burghers were at Smithfield, and that two commandos, one of which had guns, had passed through the town during the afternoon, apparently making for the drifts above and below Commissie bridge. Allen decided to retire at once, and calling in the Queenstown Volunteers, started at 11 p.m., and at 3.15 a.m. on the 6th arrived at Rouxville. He at once telegraphed to Aliwal North for help, and, in reply, General Brabant promised to send two hundred of the Border Horse to meet him at Besters Kraal, a strong position about twelve miles north of Aliwal. At

OPERATIONS IN THE ORANGE FREE STATE. 313

daybreak on the 7th the mounted patrols reported that there was no sign of the enemy within five miles of the camp, and at 8 a.m. his weary troops, accompanied by the detachment of Kaffrarian Rifles, were once more on the move, and reached Besters Kraal at noon. Here the Border Horse, which had been so opportunely sent out by General Brabant, took up the rear-guard. An hour after Allen marched for Aliwal, the Border Horse were attacked, but gradually falling back, they effectually checked the burghers, who, finding that their prey had escaped them, drew off to the north. With the Border Horse Brabant had sent a number of empty bullock wagons, in which to carry the infantry, whom he knew would be footsore and exhausted by their forced marches. When, between 8 and 9 p.m., he went to the bridge at Aliwal to welcome the Irish Rifles, he found them almost barefoot, and reeling with fatigue, but still keeping in the ranks. They had refused to ride on the wagons, urging that if they did so the good name of the regiment would suffer. *Border Horse cover the retreat to Aliwal, April 7th.*

The distances covered by Allen's troops were :—

> Helvetia to Smithfield, 28 miles.
> Smithfield to Rouxville, 23 miles.
> Rouxville to Aliwal North, 22 miles.

The detachment from Helvetia marched seventy-three miles in fifty-two hours, and that from Smithfield forty-five miles in thirty-six hours.

CHAPTER XIX.

DEFENCE OF WEPENER.*

<small>Results of Boers' offensive movement between 30th March and 7th April.</small>
WHEN, at the end of March, the Boers assumed the offensive, four British detachments lay east of the railway, at Thabanchu, Dewetsdorp, Smithfield and Wepener. Of these, the first had escaped only after a severe reverse at Sannah's Post on the 31st; the second had been taken prisoners at Reddersburg on April 4th; the third, by dint of extremely hard marching, had barely succeeded in reaching Aliwal North on April 7th. Only one outpost, that of Wepener, still remained intact. With the exception of Lord Methuen's column at Boshof, in the west of the Orange Free State, the garrison of Wepener was for the moment the only British force which did not appear to be tied to the railway, and against this garrison De Wet, postponing or abandoning his intention to harry the line of communication south of Bloemfontein, now prepared to concentrate his energies.

<small>Kruger wishes De Wet recalled.</small>
Yet, brilliantly successful as had been De Wet's operations, his policy of adventure was viewed with great anxiety at Pretoria. In a telegram to President Steyn, President Kruger said that, while he did not wish to interfere with the plans of the Free State Generals, he must point out that it was undesirable that De Wet

> "Should be so far south while the great movement of the enemy is northward. The danger in this is that a difficulty may arise similar to that after the retreat from Magersfontein. I think that as soon as he has broken up the railway beyond Bloemfontein, or if this takes too much time without doing so, he must join the forces north of Bloemfontein. Further, I think that the burghers to the east of Bloemfontein towards Winburg and Thabanchu should, or at least some of them, come over to the west side."

<small>* See maps Nos. 34 and 35.</small>

DEFENCE OF WEPENER.

The troops which De Wet was now hastening to attack had at first been under the orders of Major Cedric Maxwell, R.E., but on April 5th they had passed to the command of Lieut.-Colonel E. H. Dalgety, Cape Mounted Rifles. On that date their strength and composition was as follows :— Garrison of Wepener.

Units.	Officers.	Other Ranks.	Horses.
Royal Engineers..	1	10	1
Royal Scots mounted infantry..	3	78	81
Cape Mounted Rifles	18	409	420
1st Brabant's Horse	25	320	340
2nd ,, ,, ..	29	430	450
Kaffrarian Rifles..	23	370	400
Driscoll's Scouts..	3	53	56
Cape Mounted Rifles artillery ..	3	90	50
Royal Army Medical Corps	6	27	6
Total	111	1,787	1,804

The artillery, under Captain H. T. Lukin, Cape Mounted Rifles, consisted of two 15-pr. B.L., two Naval 12-pr. 8 cwt. guns, which had been taken over by the Cape Mounted Rifles from the Royal Garrison artillery on the 22nd March; two 7-pr. R.M.L. mounted on field carriages, and a Hotchkiss 14-pr. Q.F. gun of French manufacture, which had been presented to the 2nd Brabant's Horse by Mr. A. Beit.

When Maxwell with his detachment first reached Wepener, he encamped about a mile to the north of it, but after a careful study of the country on April 3rd, he decided not to attempt to hold the village itself, but to occupy a series of kopjes which surround an oval-shaped basin between six and seven miles in circumference. Though these kopjes are dominated by an outer ring of heights, the position was a strong one; it had a good water supply, and it commanded the Jammersberg bridge over the Caledon River, three miles north-west of Wepener, and the numerous roads which converge upon it. On April 4th, soon after reaching this ground, the troops were summoned to surrender by the bearer of a flag of truce who came from the direction of Ladybrand; but it was not until the 9th that Maxwell's choice of a defensive position near Wepener.

The position.

Maxwell called upon to surrender by the Boers.

hostilities began. By that time De Wet had gathered around him about six thousand burghers, whose numbers were soon raised by reinforcements to eight thousand, or possibly even ten thousand men. This respite was used in digging shelter trenches, throwing up stone breastworks, preparing gun emplacements, and bringing up stores from Wepener. On the 7th Dalgety established his men in the sections of the defence to which they had been allotted. Brabant's Horse and the Kaffrarian Rifles held the northern and the Cape Mounted Rifles the southern half of the position. During the first day's fighting they were permanently reinforced by the mounted infantry of the Royal Scots and Driscoll's Scouts, who, by the original scheme of defence, were detailed as a reserve to be sent to the part of the line where help was most needed.

April 9th. Siege of Wepener begins.

Early on the 9th De Wet opened the siege with a heavy and well-sustained fire from ten or twelve guns, supported by the musketry of large numbers of riflemen, who, undetected by the piquets, had crept during the night towards the southern works. The fight continued throughout the day, and revealed in some of the defences weak spots which could not be made good until darkness put an end to the combat. Then the defects were repaired; but many casualties had occurred and this, the first day's fighting, was the most costly of the investment. The ground allotted to the Cape Mounted Rifles was hard to fortify. There was but an inch or two of earth above solid rock, so that it was impossible to dig trenches, and the scarcity of loose stones made the building of sangars very difficult. Later in the siege sandbags, improvised out of mealie sacks, were used to strengthen this part of the line. After a steady bombardment all through the 10th the Boers made a determined attack during the night of the 10th-11th on the section held by the Cape Mounted Rifles; they forced their way up a spruit to within forty yards of the defences, when, on hearing the order given to fix bayonets, their resolution failed them, and they fell back with loss.

Siege continues.

That the burghers did not renew their attempt to storm the British works was due to no want of energy in their leader.

DEFENCE OF WEPENER.

De Wet urged them to close on their enemy, but without success. On the night of the 12th he made emplacements for a battery of four guns with which he proposed—to quote the words in which he telegraphed to President Steyn—" to shell with all our power the most important point of their forts from which they fire on us most heavily with rifles. Then we shall try to take this point by storm. If we succeed in getting hold of it, there is every hope that they must surrender at once." Later in the siege, on the 22nd, he again telegraphed to Steyn: " Yesterday we could not get the storming carried out, but it will be done to-morrow certainly." Though the Boers were indisposed to join in a forlorn hope they were very willing to fight in their own way. For sixteen days their riflemen were constantly in action; and at night their "snipers" harassed the working parties as they threw up new traverses to meet the ever-varying direction from which the enemy's guns played upon them, or made good the damage done by the bombardment of the previous day. In this task the skilled labour and technical knowledge of the Royal Engineer detachment was of great value. So heavy and ceaseless was the enemy's fire that the garrison were kept continuously in their works. To add to the discomfort of the troops rain fell without intermission for three days and nights, the trenches were flooded, and in some places men in the firing line had to kneel in water a foot deep, while so shot-swept was the ground behind the works that rations could only be brought up and distributed under cover of darkness. The severity of the bombardment varied from day to day. Sometimes two or three hundred shells were fired in the course of a few hours into the *enceinte* held by the Colonial division; then for two or three days there would be a lull, owing to the absence of the greater part of the Boer guns, which were temporarily sent to the assistance of the burghers at Dewetsdorp, and were brought back to resume the attack on the Jammersberg position.

De Wet hopes to storm the works.

Not the least of Colonel Dalgety's anxieties was his limited amount of ammunition. He had to husband every round, while De Wet received large supplies from Brandfort, and was thus able to keep every gun and rifle fully employed. The following

Dalgety's ammunition

table shows the ammunition expended by the besieged during the sixteen days that the investment lasted :—

	In possession at the beginning of the siege. Rounds.	Expended. Rounds.	In hand at the end of the siege. Rounds.
Per rifle	500	250	250
,, 15-pr.	850	750	100
,, 12-pr.	250	200	50
,, 7-pr.	250	100	150
,, Hotchkiss	350	342	8

Towards the end of the defence the British could only afford to fire about four shells an hour; but, notwithstanding their lack of ammunition, all Dalgety's guns continued in action to the last and were frequently moved from one prepared position to another. Communication with the outer world was kept up by heliograph to Mafeteng in Basutoland, whence messages were received from time to time to report the progress of the columns sent by the Commander-in-Chief for the relief of Dalgety's com-

Relieving column under Hart and Brabant.

mand. On the 14th April, Brigadier-General Brabant, with the remainder of the Colonial division, about 1,200 strong, left Aliwal North for Rouxville. His force consisted of a company of mounted infantry from Malta, the Border Horse, Queenstown Volunteers, New Zealand Rough Riders, and detachments of Brabant's Horse and Kaffrarian Rifles, with two 15-prs., manned by the Cape Volunteer artillery. He was followed next day by Major-General Hart, who, in addition to part of the 5th brigade from Natal—the 2nd battalion, Somerset Light Infantry, the 1st battalion, Border regiment—had with him three companies of the 2nd Royal Irish Rifles, and the 8th battery, Royal Field artillery, in all about 2,840 officers and men. Hart and Brabant remained at Rouxville until the 18th awaiting orders from Bloemfontein. On the 19th they marched towards Wepener, and, after a couple of skirmishes, in which the burghers were manœuvred out of their positions by wide turning move-

April 25th, Wepener relieved.

ments combined with direct attacks covered by artillery fire, they joined hands with Dalgety on the afternoon of the 25th.

That morning De Wet had retreated northwards and was far out of range of any possible pursuit.

During the sixteen days which the siege lasted three officers were killed and eleven wounded; of the other ranks twenty-five were killed and a hundred and thirty wounded. These casualties chiefly occurred during the first two or three days, before all the men had thoroughly realised the value of defensive works. But soon they had "dug themselves in" so skilfully that very few were hit in the trenches, and the losses generally fell among those whose duty called them to leave their shelters. The horses, for which the ground afforded no cover, suffered greatly; nearly fifty per cent. of the animals were hit, a loss which seriously weakened the fighting strength of the Colonial division. The successful defence of the Jammersberg bridge position by 1,800 men against four or five times as many of the enemy, whose artillery was far better than their own, did credit both to the courage and staunchness of the Colonial division, and to the skill with which Major Maxwell designed the works held by Colonel Dalgety's troops. *Casualties during siege.*

When De Wet abandoned his original scheme of harrying the railway line between Bloemfontein and the Orange river, and devoted his energies to the investment of Dalgety, he played into the hands of the British Commander-in-Chief. By leaving the line of communication with Cape Colony unbroken he permitted an uninterrupted stream of trains to enter Bloemfontein with reinforcements of animals and men, food and ammunition. The arrival of these much aided Lord Roberts' preparations for his advance on Pretoria, so that by the middle of April he was nearly ready to start. But before the march to the north could begin Wepener must be relieved and the Free State cleared of the commandos which threatened the railway. *Whilst De Wet is occupied at Wepener, trains pour into Bloemfontein from the coast.*

Lord Roberts, when now taking in hand this double task, hoped not only to rescue Colonel Dalgety, but to surround and capture many of the enemy. As the numbers and positions of the Boers became better known the scheme gradually took definite shape. Whilst Brabant's division and Hart's brigade *Lord Roberts proceeds to clear the Boers out of the south-east.*

were carrying out the mission assigned them, the VIIIth division, which had been destined originally for Kimberley, was now, as fast as its units landed from England, to concentrate at Edenburg under Lieut.-General Sir Leslie Rundle, who was then to march to Dewetsdorp, get into touch with Brabant, and when the burghers besieging Wepener had been driven north, endeavour to cut them off.

Rundle's division was composed of the 16th brigade (Major-General B. B. D. Campbell), consisting of the second battalions of the Grenadier Guards, the Scots Guards, and the East Yorkshire regiment (the 1st Leinster, though nominally part of the 16th brigade, did not join till June). The 17th brigade (Major-General J. E. Boyes) was formed of the first battalions of the Worcestershire and South Staffordshire, and the second battalions of the Royal West Kent and Manchester regiments. The divisional artillery consisted of the 74th, 77th and 79th batteries Royal Field artillery; and as mounted troops there were the 4th and 7th battalions of Imperial Yeomanry.

Major-General Sir Herbert Chermside, who had relieved Lieut.-General Gatacre in the command of the IIIrd division,* was to guard the railway from the Orange river to Bethanie with one of his two brigades (the 23rd, W. G. Knox), and with the other (the 22nd, R. E. Allen) to co-operate with Rundle. On the 16th April a new division, under Major-General R. Pole-Carew, had been formed of the Guards' brigade (Inigo Jones), and the 18th brigade (Stephenson), the place of which in the VIth division was now filled by the 12th brigade (Clements), which had not been under its divisional commander (Kelly-Kenny) since the beginning of February. From Bloemfontein this new division, the XIth, with the 3rd (Gordon) and 4th (Dickson) cavalry brigades, was to march on Dewetsdorp. Ian Hamilton's† mounted infantry was to reconnoitre towards the Waterworks and if possible to occupy them; the VIth division was to remain

* For the circumstances connected with General Gatacre's removal from his command, see Appendix 7.

† Colonel (local Major-General) Ian Hamilton on the relief of Ladysmith was summoned to Bloemfontein to join the main army.

DEFENCE OF WEPENER.

at Bloemfontein, the VIIth division at Karee Siding and the Glen.

On the 18th of April Lieut.-General Rundle, after many delays from want of transport, had concentrated his division (the VIIIth) at Rosendal. With him was Major-General Chermside and the 22nd infantry brigade (IIIrd division), four batteries Royal Field artillery, the mounted infantry belonging to the IIIrd division under Lieut.-Colonel W. H. Sitwell (Northumberland Fusiliers), and six companies of Imperial Yeomanry under Major-General J. P. Brabazon. Rundle moved next day as far as Oorlog's Poort, and on the 20th, soon after he resumed his march, his scouts were met by Boer patrols. The enemy's advanced posts were found near Wakkerstroom, on the edge of a high plateau from which rises a long ridge that proved to be his main position. Attempts on the 20th and the 21st to turn the flanks of this ridge were unsuccessful, but on the information obtained during the engagement, Rundle based a scheme for an attack on the 22nd which he submitted by telegraph to the Commander-in-Chief. In his answer, Lord Roberts told him that French was advancing *via* Leeuwkop on Dewetsdorp with the 3rd and 4th cavalry brigades and the XIth division (Pole-Carew), and desired that he should not commit himself to a definite assault until he was in touch with them. The reason for this order was that Lord Roberts hoped, if no strong attack was made upon the burghers who faced the VIIIth division at Wakkerstroom, that they might hold their ground until the columns from Bloemfontein were near enough to prevent their escape. Rundle accordingly halted for the next three days; he pushed mounted reconnaissances round the enemy's right flank, and kept up a desultory shell and rifle fire against the front of the Boers' main position until the 24th, when he established connection with Pole-Carew.

On the 21st April the XIth division, with which were Alderson's mounted infantry, and the 4th cavalry brigade, was concentrated at Springfield. On the 22nd Pole-Carew engaged the enemy at Paardekraal, a spur of Leeuwkop, and by 6 p.m. had driven him back at the cost of about twenty casualties. A little

The several columns detailed for this purpose concentrate.

Rundle's operations near Wakkerstroom.

322   THE WAR IN SOUTH AFRICA.

French with cavalry division and XIth division moves towards Dewetsdorp, 21st-22nd April.

later in the evening General French, with the 3rd cavalry brigade arrived at the bivouac of the XIth divison and took command of the whole force, which halted on the 23rd, the cavalry at Tweede Geluk, and the infantry four miles to the west of them at Erste Geluk. Here news was received from Rundle, who reported by signal that the enemy was covering Dewetsdorp from an entrenched position five or six miles in length, held, as far as he could estimate, by six thousand men with six guns.

The cavalry started at 6 a.m. on the 24th, and to the west of Vlakfontein encountered a detachment of the enemy, 1,200 to 1,500 strong, which had been pushed forward to secure the right flank of the main body, under Piet De Wet, in front of Dewetsdorp. Reinforcing the advance guard, to enable it to hold the burghers in front, Lieut.-General French moved the rest of the cavalry rapidly to the Roodekop ridge, and forced the burghers to retire to the north. At about 11 a.m. a staff officer from Rundle reached French and reported that in the neighbourhood of the VIIIth division the situation was unchanged. French then determined to surround the remainder of the Boers near Dewetsdorp, and issued the following orders :—

He joins hands with Rundle on 24th.

No. 3 Field Force Order.
Roode Kop,
24th April, 12 noon.

1. The enemy, estimated at about 6,000 with six guns, is reported to hold a position covering Dewetsdorp on the west, his right near Nieuwjaarsfontein and left near Bultfontein.

General Rundle's Headquarters are near Constantia.

2. It is the intention of the G.O.C. to surround the enemy's position and cut their line of retreat towards Thabanchu.

3. (a) The 3rd and 4th cavalry brigades, under General Dickson, will march at 1 p.m. to gain a passage over the Modder in the direction of Logageng (near where road to Thabanchu crosses) and extend his left flank southward.

(b) General Carew, with the XIth division and Alderson's mounted infantry and supply columns, will halt near Damfontein Farm to-night, and will hold the hills between that place and Rietfontein.

(c) General Rundle will bar the enemy's escape to the west, south, and southwest, and will detach a sufficient force to hold Roodepoort Hill, which will be entrenched. He will also detach a body of mounted troops eastwards to cross the Modder south of, and join hands with, the 3rd and 4th cavalry brigades if possible.

DEFENCE OF WEPENER.

In the event of this threat causing the enemy to withdraw, General Rundle will at once close in and pursue. Communication by helio and lamp to be arranged between the posts held.

General French will march with the 3rd and 4th cavalry brigades.

By Order,

D. HAIG, Lieut.-Col.,
C.S.O. Field Force.

Copies of this were sent to General Rundle, General Pole-Carew, and General Dickson.

The following instructions were issued to General Pole-Carew:—

General French hopes to occupy to-night a passage over the Modder River near where the road to Thabanchu crosses.

He desires you to send forward about 300 mounted infantry at 5 a.m. to-morrow to hold the passage over the river, and enable the 3rd and 4th cavalry brigades to operate southwards and south-eastwards.

Your further action will depend on whether the enemy—(a) withdraws from or (b) remains in, his present position. (a) In the case of the enemy withdrawing eastwards, you will follow the cavalry to the Modder. (b) In the case of the enemy holding on to his position (indicated in No. 3 Field Force Order), your task is to hem him in on the north, and to extend your left across the Modder to support the cavalry. General French is of opinion that a movement in échelon from the left of your force towards the river crossing would enable you to reach suitable positions from which to turn southwards to complete the circuit of investment.

By Order,

Roode Kop,
24th April, 1900, 2 p.m.

D. HAIG, Lieut.-Col.,
C.S.O. Field Force.

Owing to the vigorous opposition of the Boers, Dickson's brigades did not accomplish the task allotted to them; they failed to gain a passage over the river before nightfall, though they occupied the heights commanding the valley of the Modder, and bivouacked within forty minutes' ride of the drift they were to have taken. The casualties during the affair of the 24th were all in the cavalry division; they amounted to four officers and thirty other ranks killed or wounded; forty-five horses were killed or died of exhaustion, while twenty-seven became useless from other causes.

Early next morning Dickson crossed the Modder, driving before him a rear-guard of about two hundred men. But,

Boers escape from the net, night of 24th-25th.

before he had fairly established himself at the ford, it was discovered that during the night the enemy had slipped away from his main position, and that all hope of bringing him to bay at Dewetsdorp was at an end.

It was not only from Dewetsdorp that the Boers had retired. The retreat was a general one along the whole of the Dewetsdorp—Wepener line. Christian De Wet had been warned by Steyn that from Delagoa Bay had come a rumour that the British meant to surround him. Piet De Wet, who commanded at Dewetsdorp, had reported that one of his lieutenants, Commandant Fourie, had been so severely handled that he had retreated to the northwards, and that he himself could no longer withstand the pressure on his front and flanks. Froneman, who had attempted to stop Hart and Brabant on the way to Wepener, had been brushed aside. Ian Hamilton's movements were known to Christian De Wet, who saw the net closing in upon him, and lost not a moment in escaping from it. By his orders, as soon as night fell on the 24th, the various commandos sent off all their wagons to a rendezvous, to which a few hours later their mounted men followed. By the morning of the 25th the Boers were concentrating to the south-east of Thabanchu, at a spot well out of danger of any immediate pursuit.

French, unaware of Hamilton's mission, abandons pursuit.

Such information as French's patrols obtained convinced him that the Boers had gained so long a start that it would be useless to pursue them. He had not been told that any British detachment was operating to the north of his own troops; much less did he know that Ian Hamilton had re-occupied the Waterworks Drift on the 24th, and that on the morning of the 25th he was marching towards Israel's Poort. Neither was he aware that De Wet had raised the siege of Wepener the night before. The verbal instructions given to him at Bloemfontein led him to believe that he was to assist Rundle, to ensure the relief of Wepener, and, this done, to return to Headquarters. After a consultation with Rundle, who had now occupied Dewetsdorp, he called in the cavalry; sent Brabazon with the Yeomanry and four companies of mounted infantry towards Wepener, with the 3rd cavalry brigade following in support; ordered Pole-

DEFENCE OF WEPENER.

Carew to hold his ground until Wepener was relieved, and then telegraphed to Headquarters to report the steps he had taken. On the 22nd April, Major-General Ian Hamilton had left Springfield with three corps, the 2nd, 5th, and 7th of mounted infantry, and P. battery, Royal Horse artillery to re-occupy the Waterworks, and he had authority, if necessary, to call upon General Colvile (IXth division) for the support of the 19th brigade (Smith-Dorrien). Next day (the 23rd), though shelled from the kopjes on the right bank of the Modder, he made good the left bank from Klip Kraal Drift to Waterworks Drift. On the morning of the 24th the 19th brigade crossed Waterworks Drift, while the mounted infantry turned the Boers' right flank by passing the Modder at Waterval Drift. The enemy, who was not in strength, fell back before them. In the evening the Highland brigade (of the IXth division), which had been sent up by Lord Roberts, reached Hamilton, who was also promised reinforcements of mounted troops. *[Ian Hamilton occupies Waterworks Drift on 24th April.]*

On the 25th, after refilling his supply wagons, Hamilton marched eastwards. Very soon he learned that the enemy was astride of the road at Israel's Poort, on an irregular chain of strong kopjes which form a horse-shoe, through which the road runs from Bloemfontein to Thabanchu. After a careful reconnaissance, he decided to attack; one battalion was to hold the Boers in the right centre of their position; two battalions and a half were to assault the right flank, while the mounted infantry circled widely to the right and threatened the line of retreat. The Horse artillery battery was to engage the right centre and the left of the enemy's line, while the guns of the 2nd battery, Royal Field artillery covered the main attack. This was delivered by the 2nd Duke of Cornwall's, the 2nd Shropshire, and half a battalion of the 1st Gordon Highlanders, while the Royal Canadian regiment, extended on a front of nearly two thousand yards, advanced to within eight hundred yards of the right centre. As soon as the turning movement of the mounted infantry made itself felt, the enemy, after a stout resistance, drew off. Twice during the 25th Lord Roberts telegraphed to Hamilton to give him details of the Boer *[Boers driven from Israel's Poort, April 25th, 1900.]*

retirement from Dewetsdorp, and to say that, in the hope he might be able to cut off the enemy's retreat to the north, reinforcements of mounted infantry and two pom-poms had been sent to him.

To the Commander-in-Chief, the telegram in which Lieut.-General French had announced his return to Dewetsdorp had been a very disagreeable surprise. Lord Roberts knew of the plan which French had formed for surrounding Dewetsdorp, and at 11 a.m. on the 25th, after he had learned that the Boers had evacuated their position in the night, had telegraphed to urge French to attempt the capture of their guns and wagons; and at 3.45 p.m. he again telegraphed that Dalgety's force was no longer invested. By one of the mischances of war neither of these messages was delivered until late in the night, and it was not until 8 p.m. that General French received a telegram from Headquarters, in which Lord Roberts expressed his surprise that French was not pursuing towards Thabanchu, and explained Hamilton's situation, which, in his opinion, required immediate assistance. This was the first news French received of Hamilton's movements.

Miscarriage of Lord Roberts' messages, 25th April, 1900.

French moves towards Thabanchu, 26th April, 1900.

As soon as French learned that Wepener had been relieved, he sent messengers to recall the mounted infantry, Yeomanry, and the 3rd cavalry brigade, whom he had despatched many hours before to Dalgety's assistance; and on the morning of the 26th he set the cavalry division and the VIIIth and XIth divisions in motion towards Thabanchu, leaving Chermside to hold Dewetsdorp with the 22nd brigade and the Yeomanry and mounted infantry, which, for the time being, were to be under his orders. After the XIth division had been some hours on the march, Pole-Carew was ordered by Headquarters to return to Bloemfontein, which he reached on the 29th. The remainder of French's column bivouacked a few miles south of Thabanchu, where Hamilton had already arrived. On the 27th, both commands joined hands, and strengthened by the VIIIth division, which came up during the afternoon, they manœuvred the Boers from the mountain which overhangs Thabanchu from the west. Next day (the 28th), by a series of turning movements the Boers, who still numbered five or six thousand men, were driven off the high hills which dominate the Thabanchu valley from the east. The day's operations cost the cavalry one officer killed and nine wounded; in the other ranks there were twenty-seven casualties. Among the horses the losses were heavy: sixteen were killed or wounded, twenty-five died from fatigue, and a hundred and thirty-seven were broken down, unfit for immediate use. On the 29th there were skirmishes to the east of Thabanchu, and on the 30th April, Ian Hamilton, with his mounted infantry and Smith-Dorrien's brigade, turned northwards and marched towards Hout Nek, a formidable pass crossed by the road from Thabanchu to Winburg. From Wepener, Brabant, whose division, reinforced by Dalgety's detachment, now numbered more than 2,700 men, was marching to Leeuw River Mills, to guard Hamilton's rear. Hart's brigade (the remainder of the relieving column) was hastening to Bethulie, to take train for Kimberley, where it was to join the Headquarters of the Xth division (Hunter). This new division had been formed after Buller's and White's forces joined hands at Ladysmith. Major-General (local Lieut.-General) Sir A. Hunter's troops consisted of the 5th and 6th brigades as enumerated on page 429, with this exception: the Inniskilling Fusiliers were replaced in the 5th brigade by the 2nd battalion Somerset Light Infantry. *Skirmishing round Thabanchu, April 27th, 28th, 29th. Movements of troops which had relieved Wepener.*

By the 30th the main army under Lord Roberts was thus disposed. The VIth division garrisoned Bloemfontein, and in the immediate neighbourhood the XIth division and Major-General E. T. H. Hutton's mounted infantry were preparing for the march to Pretoria. Chermside's division (the IIIrd) was charged with the double duty of defending Dewetsdorp and of guarding the railway from Bloemfontein to the Orange. The newly-formed 21st infantry brigade, under Major-General Bruce Hamilton, lay round the Glen. Tucker was at Karee Siding with the Headquarters of his division (VIIth) and the 15th brigade (Wavell); the 14th brigade (Maxwell) watched the fords near Krantz Kraal. Higher up the river, Waterval Drift was held by the 2nd cavalry brigade (Broadwood); Colvile (IXth division) occupied the Drift at the Waterworks with *Dispositions of troops.*

the 3rd (Highland) brigade, his other brigade (19th, Smith-Dorrien), being at Thabanchu, attached to the column with which Ian Hamilton had entered that village a day or two before. Rundle's division (the VIIIth) was also concentrated around Thabanchu, as was French's cavalry division, less Broadwood's brigade at Waterval Drift, and Porter's brigade at Springfield. Thus the whole line of the Modder from Karee Siding to Thabanchu was held in strength, preparatory to the advance of Ian Hamilton's column, which with other movements was to begin on the 30th. Ian Hamilton was to act as the eastern flank guard to Lord Roberts' march along the railway, and to clear away the burghers who were known to have gathered round Winburg. He was to be joined at Jacobsrust, a farm fifteen or sixteen miles north of Thabanchu, by Broadwood's cavalry brigade, Bruce Hamilton's infantry brigade, a battery of Horse and two of Field artillery and two 5-in. guns of the Royal Garrison artillery.

The engagement at Hout Nek begins, April 30th. Accordingly at daybreak on April 30th Ian Hamilton set his troops in motion towards Winburg, where the Commander-in-Chief desired him to arrive on the 5th of May. His column consisted of Smith-Dorrien's infantry brigade (19th), Ridley's brigade of three mounted infantry corps, and two batteries of artillery. For some hours the enemy made no sign, but at 8.30 a.m. the mounted infantry, which formed the right flank guard, came under the distant fire of guns and pom-poms posted on a range of hills, four or five miles in length, which crosses the Winburg road from west to east and then turns sharply to the south. The right of the Boer position rested on the most western hill, a high flat-topped kopje, named Thaba mountain; the centre occupied a series of sharp rocky knolls which stretch about three miles eastwards from Thaba; the left held the kopjes which run from north to south. In front of the centre of the position is a bare shallow valley, about two thousand yards in width. The Winburg road crosses Hout Nek between Thaba mountain and the sharp, rocky knolls; it is dominated in every direction by these heights. The officers commanding the advanced troops at once took measures for the safety of the column.

DEFENCE OF WEPENER.

Bainbridge with the 7th mounted infantry kept back the enemy on the right flank and right rear. De Lisle led the 6th mounted infantry and the New Zealanders at a gallop to the southern edge of the broad valley and occupied it. Major N. Legge, 20th Hussars, who with Kitchener's Horse was on the left front, noticed that Thaba mountain was but lightly held, and instantly directed his corps against it. These various movements, made on the initiative of the officers commanding units, exactly anticipated the orders issued by Major-General Hamilton.

After reconnoitring the ground Hamilton realised that a frontal attack on such a position, especially as it was strengthened with well-placed stone breastworks, was impossible. Equally impossible did it seem to turn it by the east. He therefore determined to seize Thaba mountain and then, passing his mounted troops round its western flank, to assail the enemy from the rear. During the time occupied in the reconnaissance, Smith-Dorrien, dropping the Duke of Cornwall's Light Infantry as rear and baggage guard, had reinforced de Lisle. As soon as Hamilton was satisfied that Kitchener's Horse had made good their footing on Thaba mountain, he ordered the 19th brigade to support them. Smith-Dorrien, leaving himself only six companies of the Shropshire Light Infantry to hold the southern edge of the valley, sent the remainder of the Shropshire, the Gordon Highlanders, and the Royal Canadian regiment against Thaba mountain. As they marched in the open across the enemy's front these troops came under heavy artillery fire, but it was remarkable that, though the shells fell fast among their ranks, only one man was killed, though many were knocked down by the explosions, stunned, or slightly injured. *[Attack on Thaba mountain.]*

As soon as the Boers saw that Thaba was threatened, they began to reinforce the burghers on the mountain, and before long they had become so strong there that the 19th brigade could gain no further ground. About 2 p.m. the enemy began to take the offensive, and advanced in several long lines from the northern end of the mountain to thrust back those of the British who had reached the southern crest. So regular were the formations, so soldierly the bearing of these men—European adventurers

Counter-attack by foreign adventurers repulsed.

who had served in the armies of their own countries—that it was hard to believe they were not British troops. Until the General through a telescope saw that each time they raised their rifles to the shoulder they pointed them to the south he refused to allow his artillery to play upon them. Though the shells seemed to burst accurately over them, about 150 of the enemy pushed steadily forward towards a knoll, to which Captain E. B. Towse, Gordon Highlanders, was leading a dozen of his men and a handful of Kitchener's Horse. Owing to the lie of the ground neither side could see the movements of the other, until they were little more than fifty yards apart. Then Towse caught sight of the foe, dashed forward and opened a very rapid fire. The surprise was complete, and the enemy recoiled before him, just as he fell to the earth, struck by a bullet which totally destroyed his sight. The success of this unexpected stroke was great, for it enabled Ian Hamilton to keep his hold upon the southern crest of the mountain, though he was unable to make headway across the plateau on the summit. For his gallantry and initiative on this occasion Captain Towse was awarded the Victoria Cross.

Boers make counter-attack on the right and right rear.

To prevent further Boer reinforcements reaching Thaba, Smith-Dorrien and de Lisle kept up a hot fusilade against the centre of the enemy's position. In this they were successful, but the burghers, seeing that their comrades had not been driven from the mountain, took heart and gathered in threatening masses upon the right flank and right rear of Smith-Dorrien, and from the kopjes running north and south hotly engaged the mounted infantry and shelled the transport and the rear-

At nightfall the action is broken off,

guard which escorted it. Until darkness put an end to the combat the situation remained unchanged. Then the General ordered that every man should stay during the night on the ground he had occupied by day, in readiness to resume the battle at earliest dawn; and as his mounted infantry were so fully employed in holding back the enemy that none were available for the turning of Thaba mountain, which was essential to the success of his plan, he called upon Lieut.-General French at Thabanchu for assistance.

At daylight on May 1st firing began again all along the

DEFENCE OF WEPENER. 331

line, and Smith-Dorrien renewed his efforts to possess himself of Thaba mountain. Fortunately the enemy was slow in reinforcing its defenders, and the knolls on its western crest were gradually over-run by detachments of Gordon Highlanders, Canadians, and Shropshire Light Infantry. A half company of the latter, well handled by their Colour-sergeant, Scouse, worked their way across part of the plateau and maintained their position under a heavy cross fire which killed or wounded twenty-five per cent. of their numbers. Lower down the western slopes the Victorian Mounted infantry under Major K. E. Lean did useful work in co-operation with these movements. In the course of the morning, Lieut.-Colonel P. L. Clowes, 8th Hussars, arrived from Thabanchu with reinforcements consisting of his own regiment, a composite Lancer regiment, the East Yorkshire and a Field battery. The guns and the infantry were sent off to strengthen the right rear, which at that time was very hard pressed, while Clowes, with his mounted men and Hamilton's Horse battery, was directed to move eastward, if possible circle right round Thaba, and threaten the enemy from the rear. *(and resumed at dawn on 1st May. British reinforcements arrive.)*

At about 10 a.m. some of the Boer guns, after shelling the summit of Thaba with great vigour for nearly an hour, began to retire; but this movement by no means heralded a general retreat, for the fire on the right rear between Bainbridge's mounted infantry and the Boers continued to be heavy, and the burghers on Thaba held its northern crest with great tenacity. About noon the 21st infantry brigade (Bruce Hamilton) and the 2nd cavalry brigade (Broadwood) could be seen about five miles away on the plain to the north-west of Thaba. Smith-Dorrien, who, since early morning had watched the combat from the southern crest, saw that the time had come to sweep the enemy off the top of Thaba, and thus, by securing the Nek, enable the troops and baggage to cross it in broad daylight. He therefore arranged for a general advance across the plateau, so as to drive the Boers from it, and then to rake with musketry the centre of their position. A line of the Shropshire Light Infantry and the Gordon Highlanders dashed forward by rushes under a heavy fusilade from the northern edge, and when the troops *(Thaba cleared of enemy.)*

THE WAR IN SOUTH AFRICA.

charged, the Boers broke into headlong flight. The pressure of Broadwood's and Bruce Hamilton's advance in the north-west and of Clowes' turning movement round the mountain had already made themselves felt, and when Thaba was lost, the Boers abandoned the whole of their position, and retired towards Clocolan. By 3.30 all the transport was safely through the Nek, at the northern end of which Colonel Clowes, having completely encircled Thaba mountain after a sharp encounter, had halted. Ian Hamilton marched on that afternoon to Jacobsrust, where he was joined by Broadwood's and Bruce Hamilton's brigades. On the morning of the 30th these troops had skirmished with a considerable number of Boers, who had drawn off towards Winburg. Next day (May 2nd) the column thus reinforced bivouacked at Isabellafontein, which it reached without molestation by the enemy.

Boers retire.

Movements along the east of the railway.

To the east, along the railway, the XIth division, consisting of the Guards' brigade, 18th brigade (Stephenson), a brigade division, Royal Field artillery, two 4.7-in., two 12-prs., and two 5-in. guns, the West Australian mounted infantry, and the Prince Alfred's Guard, marched from Bloemfontein to Karee Siding. The VIIth division remained at Krantz Kraal and Karee Siding, as its march towards Brandfort was postponed. No other movements took place. French, with the 3rd and 4th cavalry brigades remained at Thabanchu, and the 1st cavalry brigade was at Springfield.

Events on the west of the line.

During these operations to the east of the railway, certain events had taken place to the west of the line. From Kimberley, which since its relief he had held with the Ist division, Lord Methuen had repaired the railway northward towards Mafeking as far as Warrenton, a village on the south bank of the Vaal, which is there spanned by a bridge at a point known as Fourteen Streams. The Boers had destroyed this bridge and held the further bank in strength. After he had seized Barkly West on March 26th, Methuen was ordered, whilst providing for the safety of Kimberley, to secure Boshof, in the Free State, as a stepping-stone to Hoopstad. The move on Boshof was for two purposes. It would turn the left flank of the Boers at Fourteen

DEFENCE OF WEPENER.

Streams, and perhaps cause them to leave that place, so that the repairs to the bridge could be at once begun; it would also threaten Kroonstad, and thus draw off part of the enemy from the direct line of advance of the main army along the railway through the Free State. By April 4th Lord Methuen, with a large part of the Ist division, had occupied Boshof, and next day he learned that a commando, led by Colonel de Villebois Mareuil, and largely composed of Continental adventurers, was at Tweefontein, five miles to the south-east of Boshof. A detachment of Imperial Yeomanry, the Kimberley Mounted Corps, and the 4th battery, Royal Field artillery, surrounded the kopje upon which this commando was posted, and attacked it from two sides. The adventurers fought gallantly, and did not surrender until the troops, with bayonets fixed, were within thirty yards of their position. De Villebois Mareuil and eight men were killed; eleven wounded and fifty-one unwounded men, chiefly French and Germans, were taken prisoners. To their leader's memory every possible respect was paid; his funeral was a military one, and was attended by Lord Methuen in person. The French prisoners pronounced that the attitude of the English towards their dead chief had been *d'une correction parfaite*.

Methuen at Boshof, 4th April, 1900.

Affair at Tweefontein. 5th April, 1900.

Two days later Methuen, leaving the 4th battalion Scottish Rifles to garrison Boshof, pushed on to Zwart Kopje Fontein,* where he halted until the VIIIth division should begin to arrive from the coast to guard Kimberley and hold the lines of communication. But when Rundle's division was diverted to the east of the railway, Lord Methuen was warned to act with great caution; and, though during the remainder of April his presence near Boshof and the vigilance of his patrols kept in check many of the enemy, he was unable to penetrate further into the Free State, especially as part of his mounted men were required elsewhere.

Methuen's employment to end of April.

Thus, by the beginning of May, De Wet's raid had been brought to an end, and the preparations for the march against the Transvaal completed. All was ready for the next great stage of the war.

* Fourteen miles north-east of Boshof.

CHAPTER XX.

THE SPION KOP CAMPAIGN.*

THE FIRST STAGE.

HITHERTO this volume has dealt with the operations in the western theatre of war. The campaign on the Tugela and the relief of Ladysmith have now to be described.

After the battle of Colenso,† Sir R. Buller's position may be summed up as follows. His communications with the Government had made it plain that in their view the relief of Ladysmith was the chief military object of the moment. This view he welcomed, as it appeared to him to justify his own presence in Natal, and his task, though heavy enough, was clear, and far more hopeful than it had seemed when he had misunderstood the order as to Sir C. Warren to apply to that General's division.‡ Until the arrival of the reinforcements, there was nothing for it but to wait, holding the enemy north of the Tugela, and carrying out what reconnaissance was possible to assist the next advance.

Owing to want of water, Buller withdraws part of his army from Chieveley to Frere, 16th-17th Dec., 1899.

To keep the force united at Chieveley was impossible owing to the scarcity, almost the absence, of water. On the night of December 16th, the 4th and 5th brigades, the Royal Dragoons and six Naval 12-pr. guns were withdrawn to Frere, Sir R. Buller himself making that place his Headquarters. The camps of the troops left at Chieveley under Clery, consisting of the 2nd and 6th brigades, the rest of the mounted brigade, two

---

* See maps Nos. 18, 19 and the freehand sketches.
† Volume I., Chapter XXII.
‡ See Volume I., pages 377–379.

brigade divisions, Royal Field artillery, two 4.7-in. and six 12-pr. Naval guns, were also slightly retired, near to the station, where henceforward they depended for water on a somewhat precarious supply drawn from the Bushman's river at Estcourt, and forwarded by rail. From this date, until the end of the month, few events of any importance occurred at the front. An occasional reconnaissance on a small scale, a cattle raid on the 22nd, a few trifling affairs of outposts, and a slow bombardment of the Colenso trenches and road bridge, one span of which was destroyed by a shell from a Naval gun on the 19th, made up the daily diary of the troops at Chieveley. Thus, as described in Volume I., over the whole theatre of war the British forces had relapsed into temporary immobility, Methuen on the Modder river, Gatacre at Sterkstroom, the Natal armies at Chieveley and in Ladysmith. Only at Colesberg, where French, by his incessant and skilful manœuvring was more than holding his own against Schoeman, was there any activity and actual conflict with the enemy. Pending the arrival of Field-Marshal Lord Roberts, Buller still exercised complete control over the vast area and widely separated units. There was much cause for close and anxious supervision. At any moment the enemy, flushed by success, might assume the offensive. On the east there were signs of a Boer concentration on the Zulu borders, with grave risk that they might set aflame that impulsive and warlike people: from the west came rumours of wavering amongst the Pondos and Griquas. Amongst the Dutch in Cape Colony disaffection was spreading so rapidly that the High Commissioner thought it his duty to protest against even the smallest withdrawal of force from the Colony. "The Dutch population," telegraphed Sir A. Milner, "are at boiling point, and it will be something like a miracle if we can keep the west line open till VIth division arrives." * Nor did his anxiety seem unreasonable, since Sir R. Buller had himself received from London a warning of an intended insurrection of the Cape Dutch, aimed at the communications near the seaports.† Sir

Difficulties of Buller's situation between Colenso and the arrival of Lord Roberts.

* Telegram from High Commissioner, December 26th, 1899.
† Telegram from Secretary of State, No. 66 Cipher, December 25th.

A. Milner's fears were further aroused by a rumour that the Boers were about to surround and isolate Lord Methuen just as they had penned Sir G. White in Ladysmith. Though fully alive to the moral disadvantages of retreat, he suggested that as the lesser of two evils, Lord Methuen should be ordered to retire if possible to the Orange river.* Had the report proved correct, nothing, it is true, could have prevented the rising, or saved the Colony from a combined onslaught both from within and without. Sir R. Buller, however, was unmoved by these alarms. He had a clear understanding of the military situation in the west, and had little fear for Methuen, whom he refused to withdraw from the only position in which he could minimise the pressure on Kimberley and at the same time react on the rebellious element in Cape Colony.† Until all the measures for reinforcement were completed, the safest course was to wait, a policy in which Lord Roberts, telegraphing from Funchal, on December 28th, 1899, concurred. Except at one spot, which, from their President downwards, they had made the *crux* of the whole campaign, the Boers, too, appeared to acquiesce in that policy. Early on the morning of January 6th, the troops at Chieveley were aroused by the sound of prolonged and heavy firing coming from the direction of Ladysmith. All the morning the distant uproar continued, rising sometimes to a clamour in which even the sound of fierce musketry could be distinguished, at others falling to silence, or to the occasional heavy discharge of a single cannon. Two messages, sent from Ladysmith at 9 a.m. and 11 a.m., informed Sir R. Buller that Cæsar's Camp had been assaulted at 2.45 a.m.; that the attack, after being once repulsed, had been renewed in increased strength, and that all the British reserves were in action. In the second of these messages, which was received at 1 p.m., Sir G. White signalled that he thought that the enemy, having been reinforced from the south, must have weakened his force in front of Chieveley. Sir R. Buller immediately ordered Clery to take out

Boers attack Ladysmith at Cæsar's Camp and Wagon Hill, 6th Jan., 1900.

White signals to Buller.

---

* Telegram from High Commissioner, December 23rd.

† Telegram from Sir R. Buller to High Commissioner, Cipher 199, December 27th.

THE SPION KOP CAMPAIGN.   337

all his available troops and make a demonstration in front of Clery demonstrates from Chieveley.
Colenso, at the same time informing Sir G. White of his action.
At 2 p.m., Clery left camp, and moving in battle formation,
the 6th brigade on the east of the railway, the 2nd brigade on
the west, down to within 3,000 yards of the river, opened a
bombardment against the whole line of trenches. Although
only a few stray shots were drawn in reply, the scouts discovered that the trenches were fully manned, and no attack
was delivered. After remaining out until dark, Clery withdrew to camp, and the troops prepared to carry out on
the morrow the first stage of a series of operations for
which Sir R. Buller had now everything ready. A heliogram received from Sir G. White (sent at 12.45 p.m.) at
4 p.m. gave some inkling of the danger to which Ladysmith
had been exposed:

"Have beaten enemy off at present, but they are still round me in great numbers, especially to south, and I think renewed attack very probable."

The sun then failed, and further signalling was impossible. Not
until 12.40 p.m. on the next day (January 7th) did the message
come to hand, despatched at a moment when the fate of Ladysmith had trembled in the balance:

"Ladysmith, 3.15 p.m.—Attack renewed, very hard pressed."

What effect such a communication might have had on the
action of Sir R. Buller's force on the 6th can only be surmised. A whole day of anxiety followed at Frere and
Chieveley before the news of Sir G. White's victory reached
Headquarters. Sir R. Buller immediately signalled his congratulations, and asked Sir G. White to assure his troops
that his own men would "strain every nerve to be with them
soon." *

His arrangements for the second attempt to relieve Ladysmith Buller's plans for a flank march.
had now been completed by the arrival of the Vth division

* No. 145 Cipher heliogram, January 8th.

under Lieut.-General Sir Charles Warren,* and some additional batteries of artillery. The mountainous barrier which intervened between his own and Sir G. White's forces has been described in Volume I., Chapter XXI., and is shown upon the accompanying maps. For the new phase, a further brief description is, however, necessary to present more fully the complex topographical problem, of which many of the features were, it must be remembered, unfamiliar to the General, or, indeed, as a whole, to anyone in his army.

<small>The scene of operations.</small>

Southward, through a defile penetrating the great spur of Tintwa (a projection of the Drakensberg), flowed the Venter's Spruit. It is convenient to start from this stream, the western limit of the operations upon the Upper Tugela, in picturing the district. Two converging ranges of heights, both of them broken by many watercourses, met one another along the eastern bank of the Venter's Spruit. One, running northeast, parallel to the Drakensberg, by Blaauwbank, Nicholson's Nek, Intintanyoni, and Jonono's Kop, touched the Sundays river to the north of Ladysmith, all but merging there into the cross barrier of the Biggarsberg. The other, with a south-south-easterly direction, clung closely to the course of the Tugela along its left bank, past Colenso, to a lower point on the Sundays river, and beyond that stream to the Buffalo. Within the fork bounded by these two ranges lay an undulating plain, studded by kopjes, seamed by the beds of many spruits; and in the centre thereof, guarded on all sides by the converging heights, by three broad rivers, and now by a ring of Boer cannon and riflemen, stood Ladysmith. Since the general level of this plain exceeded by 200-300 feet that of the ground south of the Tugela, the reduction of the fortress, of which Ladysmith may be compared to the Keep, involved great topographical difficulties for Sir R. Buller's army operating from the lower ground. Almost everywhere were the troops to be confronted by either a precipice or a glacis, and the passage of a river, for the most part within rifle range, everywhere within cannon shot, of the alternately steep and sloping northern banks.

* For the composition of the Vth division, see Volume I., pages 490-1.

THE SPION KOP CAMPAIGN. 339

From Acton Homes to the Buffalo the positions stretched almost without a break. At two spots alone were they commanded from the southern bank, namely, at Mount Alice—Zwart Kop above Potgieter's Drift, and Hlangwhane—Monte Cristo in a loop of the river east of Colenso.

Reinforced by the Vth division, Sir R. Buller now felt himself to be strong enough to revert to his original plan of campaign, that which he had abandoned but two days before the action of Colenso, on receipt of the news of Magersfontein.* Briefly, this was to leave a small retaining force upon the railway opposite to the enemy posted at Colenso, whilst the bulk of the army, moving westward, would force the Tugela at Potgieter's Drift, sixteen miles from Colenso. In such a country as has been described no scheme of offence could be easy, and the difficulties of this one were fully foreseen by the General. On January 2nd he signalled to Sir G. White that he expected to have to fight at least three battles before he could break his way through to Lancer's Hill. For rapid movement was as impossible as its concealment from the enemy. The army, quitting its lines of communication, must be hampered by vast numbers of wagons, and its march along the south bank of the Tugela would be visible from almost any point of the commanding northern bank, from every ridge and peak of which the enemy's vedettes and patrols watched from the Drakensberg well nigh to the Zulu border. Little as was known of the details of the country north of Potgieter's Drift, this was a drawback common to any projected line of advance. There was only one map, and that a bad one, a work which, at one inch to the mile, was concerned with farm boundaries rather than with hill features, these, where intelligibly depicted, being commonly wrong, and as often unintelligible as omitted entirely. The manipulation of large forces, even in well-remembered localities, bestows a new aspect on ground; and Sir R. Buller, though he was no stranger to Natal, knew that a little known country, as well as a bold and numerous enemy, confronted his army and himself, should he succeed in forcing the river. Of that, however, he had little doubt. The Potgieter's

Buller's scheme and its difficulties.

* See Volume I., page 339.

scheme seemed to him at that time to have more advantages than any other. The northern bank once gained, the fifteen mile advance to Ladysmith was obviously less rugged than that *viâ* Colenso; indeed, it was reported to be actually easy. The approaches to Potgieter's Drift from the present camp had been well reconnoitred preparatory to Sir R. Buller's original, and subsequently abandoned, designs in this same direction. They were found to present no difficulties, and Springfield, a village on the Little Tugela, promised well as an auxiliary base, where stores could be collected for the campaign. There was little likelihood that Springfield would be held by the Boers, for the river, with its few and uncertain drifts, would be behind them; there was no good position, and retreat would be dangerous from the fact that here the right (southern) bank commanded the left. At any rate, the place had been unoccupied as lately as the 30th December, when patrols had visited it without coming upon the enemy; and though Mount Alice, a height rising immediately from the south bank at Potgieter's Drift upon the Springfield-Dewdrop road, was reported to be held in strength, it was probable, for the aforesaid reasons, that this was merely the temporary occupation of an advanced post, or of the guard to a bridge or passage-head at the drift.

Buller issues orders for his advance, Jan. 8th and 9th, 1900.

On the 8th and 9th January, therefore, Sir R. Buller issued his orders* for an advance to Springfield. An Organisation Memorandum (see Appendix 8 (C)) was issued with the orders. This made many changes in the distribution of units. Thus the 5th brigade went to the IInd division, and the 6th brigade remained at Chieveley. The 4th brigade was transferred from the IInd to the Vth division, the 10th brigade being taken from the Vth division for duty with the corps troops. The consequent changes of staff were also numerous. The orders themselves are noteworthy for their minuteness of detail, especially as to supply. Except for a brief reference to Potgieter's Drift, they did not extend beyond the concentration at Springfield. No mention was made of the enemy's positions, since these were too distant to affect the march. Beyond the fact that the Boers

* See Appendix 8 (A) and 8 (B).

THE SPION KOP CAMPAIGN.

had begun to entrench north of the Potgieter's Drift road, little was known of any westward extension of the enemy. Reconnaissance north of the river had been impossible, and the Kaffir spies, the only ones available, were suspected of being neither accurate nor faithful.

At dawn on January 10th the army was in motion, Hildyard's troops, with Thorneycroft's mounted infantry marching from Chieveley (where the 6th brigade was left to hold the enemy), and Hart's brigade with the 1st Royal Dragoons from Frere, both columns pointing on Pretorius Farm, some nine and six miles from the respective camps. The heavy rains of the previous three days and nights had flooded the spruits and converted the tracks into morasses. The march proved to be a long struggle with the heavy transport wagons. To extricate these from the drifts and mud, the soldiers themselves had continually to assist the over-matched teams, double, and often treble-spanned though they were. This, combined with the tropical sun which beat upon the steaming country, made the rate of progress phenomenally slow—but one mile an hour. *The army of Natal marches, Jan. 10th, 1900; its slow progress.*

Colonel the Earl of Dundonald, commanding the mounted brigade,* had, at 8.30 a.m., received special orders that, when he should have followed General Clery into camp at Pretorius Farm, he was to take his command, with a battery of artillery, on to Springfield, and to hold that place until the arrival next day of Sir C. Warren's division.† The mounted troops, accordingly, had left Chieveley as escort to Clery's baggage, but Lord Dundonald, when but a few miles out, obtained leave to go on at once, away ahead of the weary march. Pushing past the infantry *Dundonald, ordered to occupy Springfield,*

```
* Composition :—1st Royal Dragoons (detached)..      ..      ..   514
               Thorneycroft's mounted infantry (detached)..  420
               Bethune's mounted infantry  ..      ..      ..   500
               South African Light Horse   ..      ..      ..   300
               Composite Regt. mounted infantry   ..      ..   301
                                                              -----
                                                              2,035
```

† See Appendix 8 (D).

columns, he was soon far to the front. After resting his men and horses for an hour at Pretorius Farm, Dundonald, starting again at midday, entered Springfield in the early afternoon. There was no sign of the enemy in the place; the fine masonry bridge over the Little Tugela was standing intact; the scouts, who had gone out in every direction, returned reporting the country clear for some distance ahead. Dundonald at once saw his opportunity. After the incessant rains the Tugela must be in high flood; the Boers would have no strong bodies south of the river, with their line of retreat, their constant care, barred by that broad and turbulent stream. The commanding heights upon the south bank, points which would be invaluable in the coming operations, might therefore be seized by a rapid stroke, and Dundonald, though only ordered to Springfield, instantly decided to make the attempt. Leaving 300 men of the Composite mounted infantry, a company of Bethune's mounted infantry, and two guns at Springfield, both for the protection of the place and as a base for his own manœuvre,

pushes on to the heights above Potgieter's and seizes them.

he pressed on with the remainder (700 men and 4 guns of the 64th battery, R.F.A.) for Potgieter's, and by nightfall was in safe possession of the wooded heights, called Spearman's Hill and Mount Alice, dominating the drift from the southern bank. With the exception of a small piquet guarding the ferry-head on the northern bank, not a Boer was to be seen, and Dundonald, reporting his success to General Clery, disposed his troops for the night.

March of Warren's command.

Meanwhile, Sir C. Warren's command (4th, 10th, and 11th brigades) had left Frere at 5.30 p.m., and following in the wake of Hart's column arrived near Pretorius Farm about midnight. The march in the darkness, along the road badly cut up by the previous troops, hampered, moreover, by an immense train of pontoon, ammunition, and supply wagons,* was toilsome out of all proportion to its mileage, and when,

---

* See Appendix 8 (E). The statistics found therein, dealing as they do with the wagons (324 in number) for supply only, detail perhaps about half of the vast accumulation of vehicles which encumbered the army as it moved away from its line of communication.

THE SPION KOP CAMPAIGN. 343

on the vanguard approaching the farm, it was found that an intervening drift had become flooded and impassable, all hope of pitching camp was abandoned, and Warren's battalions bivouacked wherever each had happened to halt on the marshy road.

Early on the morning of the 11th, Hildyard took Thorneycroft's mounted infantry, a battery Royal Field artillery, the 2nd Devonshire and 2nd West Yorkshire from Pretorius Farm to demonstrate towards Porrit's and Deel Drifts, in order, as was hoped, to deceive the enemy as to the true point of crossing.* The operation, carried out in great heat, had no result. By midday the detachment was back at the farm, having seen but few Boers, and drawn the fire of none. Meanwhile, Warren's division had marched to Springfield bridge, the 4th brigade going on to Springfield in support of Dundonald. That officer, after a somewhat anxious night, had, in the early morning, improved his command of Potgieter's Drift by the capture of the ferry boat from under the very eyes of the enemy. The boat had been moored to the northern bank of the river, and though parties of Boers were to be seen riding down towards it, some troopers of the South African Light Horse volunteered to swim across and capture it. The enemy detected the attempt; but the adventurous swimmers safely reached the boat, cut it adrift, and brought it rapidly back amid a shower of bullets. On the afternoon of the 12th, the 4th brigade was close at hand at Spearman's Hill. On the 13th the 4.7-in. guns were mounted on the same height, and the drift was safe. On the 12th Sir R. Buller issued an inspiriting general order to the troops.† During this and the two following days, the concentration of troops at Springfield, and the formation of a base there, continued without interruption. Progress was unavoidably slow. The roads and drifts, bad at the outset, became hourly more difficult from the constant passage of the double stream of ox wagons, which laboured heavily laden from Frere, and having discharged their

<small>Hildyard demonstrates.</small>

<small>Warren reaches Springfield.</small>

<small>Dundonald seizes Potgieter's Drift.</small>

<small>Base formed at Springfield.</small>

---

* See paragraph 4, General Buller's orders of January 9th, Appendix 8 (B).

† See Appendix 8 (F).

loads at the magazine at Springfield, returned again for fresh supplies. The IInd division, which had remained at Pretorius Farm, was usefully engaged in assisting the forward movement of the transport. By the 15th Springfield was stocked with sixteen days' provisions and forage for the whole army, over 600,000 rations in all.* The IInd division, therefore, its work at Pretorius Farm ended, followed the rest of the army to Springfield, not by the main bridge, but by a trestle bridge and rafts, rapidly constructed by half of the 17th field company, Royal Engineers, at Sand Drift on the Little Tugela, a mile and a half below Springfield bridge itself. The trestle bridge was begun at 9.15 p.m. on January 11th and finished by 8 a.m. on January 12th. Timber had been hauled to the spot by steam-sappers. The bridge consisted of eleven trestles, with spans of twelve feet between each. The river at this point was some forty yards wide, five and a half feet deep, the current running at about three miles an hour.

<small>Buller's army concentrated.</small>

<small>Movements of the Boers.</small>

It had thus taken the army six days from the time of leaving the railway to concentrate at the spot whence actual operations would begin against an enemy little prone to remain quiescent whilst a hostile body trailed across his front. From the very inception of the march from Chieveley on the 10th, the Boers, to whom on their heights much of the movement was actually visible, were riding on a parallel line westward, easily keeping abreast of the slow British columns on the other side of the river. Therefore Sir R. Buller's concentration at Springfield and Spearman's did but coincide with a corresponding massing of commandos opposite to him, Viljoen's Johannesburgers occupying Vaal Krantz, and the Carolina, Ermelo, Vryheid, Lydenburg, and Free State commandos entrenching a strong line between Vaal Krantz and Spion Kop. Of the whole British manœuvre, indeed, the dash by the cavalry upon Potgieter's Drift alone had surprised the enemy. All else was not only known to him, but had been fully expected for some time. The Boers had never been blind to the exposure of their right

* See Appendix 8 (E) for statistics of numbers and weight of rations, and of wagons employed in transporting them.

flank, prolonged as it was by ground even more commanding than that which they occupied at Colenso, and they had been reminded of their weakness by the reconnaissance to Springfield a month earlier. Whilst anticipating that a move towards Potgieter's, at least, would certainly be forced upon them, they felt by no means secure from a wider flank movement from still further to the westward. The country beyond Spion Kop was, therefore, well watched by patrols, to whom after a few days it became evident that the blow was indeed about to fall there, and not at Potgieter's.

Three days before his concentration was completed, Sir R. Buller had changed his plans. A very brief survey from the lofty summit of Mount Alice had convinced him of the tremendous strength of the position across the river. Along an arc some ten miles in length rolled a magnificent amphitheatre of heights, whose flanks, curling southward, overhung the river at the great wooded mass of Doorn Kop* to the eastward, and to the westward where the Twin Peaks (or Sugar Loaf Hill) of Spion Kop twisted with its rugged projection the course of the Tugela into two remarkable northward bends, in the angle between which was situated the object of the operations—Potgieter's Drift. From flank to flank this range stretched unbroken. East of the Twin Peaks, Brakfontein, running level like the curtain of a fortress, joined the one bastion on the right to another on the left. This, a hill called Vaal Krantz, jutting as suddenly as its larger counterpart, pushed the river sharply southward once more past Doorn Kop, which lay a little back, down to Skiet's Drift, the only other passage in the section. Except at the two high flanks, and the central salient of Vaal Krantz, which all but touched the river, a strip of open ground, devoid of any cover but that afforded by a few dongas, rose with a gentle gradient from the river bank and ran as a perfect glacis, to the foot of the heights behind. Nor was the prospect

<small>Buller's fresh plan. His reasons for the change.</small>

---

* This is beyond the limits of map 19. It will be found on maps 18 and 21. This height is not to be confused with another of similar name, which lies a few miles west of Chieveley, upon the route taken by Hildyard from Chieveley to Pretorius Farm on January 10th. It was often known as Doorn Kloof.

on the British side of the river much more propitious for an attack. The road from Mount Alice to Potgieter's Drift, descending the northern face of the mountain by a steep zig-zag, was exposed to the enemy's view and fire throughout its length; and though a natural bridge-head position, called "The Kopjes," more or less safeguarded the re-entrant of the river at Potgieter's from actual assault, these kopjes were so low, so completely dominated by the whole arc of heights to the northward, and so dangerously enfiladed by the protruding flanks, as to be of little more than local value for defence. The alternative route to Ladysmith, that quitting the Potgieter's road about three miles south of Mount Alice, was no more favourable. Though Mount Alice and Zwart Kop afforded it some protection in front, the road itself was bad, and its passages over the river, i.e., Maritz Ferry and Skiet's Drift, difficult and dangerous. Moreover, by this route, the ground on the left bank of the river was even more awkward than that across Potgieter's, for here no less than three miles of open plain would have to be crossed under the fire of Doorn Kop.

Such was the distant spectacle which was unfolded to Sir R. Buller when, on January 12th, he first ascended Mount Alice to gather the nature of the task he proposed to set his army, namely, the forcing of the Tugela at Potgieter's Drift. He quickly decided it to be impossible, and as quickly formulated *He informs White and the War Office of his new scheme.* a new scheme, which he communicated to the Secretary of State for War next day,* and to Sir G. White by signal on the 14th. This, briefly, was to hold Potgieter's with a portion of his army, and with the remainder to cross the Tugela at Trickhardt's Drift, five miles up stream, thence to turn Spion Kop and the Twin Peaks, the mountains which formed the right flank of the enemy's position. Little opposition was anticipated at this point. Bastion Hill, above Venter's Spruit, seemed to be the extreme Boer right. Up to January 15th Sir R. Buller's information was that it was but thinly held—only 400 men were said to be stationed between this height and Brakfontein. Of the remainder of the 7,000 burghers known to be upon the line

* See Appendix 8 (G).

THE SPION KOP CAMPAIGN. 347

of the Tugela, the bulk were supposed to be still opposite Colenso, with a weak right flank upon Brakfontein; and though, on January 16th, news reached the Intelligence Department that a "general move westward"* was in progress, there seemed to be nothing to show that the strength of the enemy so far to the west as Trickhardt's Drift was being much increased. Of a commander's best ally—reconnaissance—Sir R. Buller was almost denied the aid. Except with the telescope it was impossible against an enemy so swift and sleepless, posted on commanding heights, protected by a river, and skilled in the use of weapons of high precision. On January 13th, Captain H. Gough (16th Lancers, Intelligence Officer to Lord Dundonald's mounted brigade) had ridden to Trickhardt's Drift, and on the next day some three miles to the westward, where, from a high bluff called Endangwe Hill, commanding a good view of the road from Acton Homes to Spion Kop, he observed parties of the enemy apparently employed in building gun epaulments between Bastion Hill and Spion Kop. On the 15th Sir R. Buller himself rode to the same spot with Captain Gough, but saw nothing to cause him to alter his new plan. Later in the day he issued secret orders on the subject† to Sir Charles Warren, to whom he had deputed the conduct of the whole flanking movement.

<small>Buller's knowledge of Boer movements.</small>

<small>His secret orders to Warren, 15th Jan., 1900;</small>

These orders, which merit the closest attention, embodied a broad and bold conception. Though Warren, taking with him the larger portion of the army‡ was to force his way by Trickhardt's Drift up to the westward of Spion Kop, it was still the Boer position behind Potgieter's Drift at which the blow was really aimed. All Warren's manœuvres were to be directed to passing to the rear of the enemy in that stronghold (paragraph 4, secret orders), and opposite it Sir R. Buller himself would remain with the rest of the force.§ With these troops he intended to create diversions in Warren's favour, to threaten Spion Kop

<small>their purport.</small>

* Intelligence Report, 16th January, 1900.
† See Appendix 8 (H).
‡ Composition. See Appendix 8 (I).
§ Composition. See Appendix 8 (J).

and Brakfontein, and even to attempt a crossing at Skict's Drift (paragraph 5, secret orders) under the shadow of Doorn Kop. Beyond the recommendation contained in paragraph 4 of the orders, i.e., to push forward continually the left flank and refuse the right, the movements of Sir C. Warren, when once he should gain the north bank of the river, were left entirely to that officer's discretion.

<small>Buller's advice to Warren.</small>

Nevertheless, Sir R. Buller, apparently convinced that the enemy's right flank rested on Bastion Hill, when discussing the impending operations with his subordinate, did enter into details so far as to advise him to "swing round his line from the west of Spion Kop, as a centre, and envelop Bastion Hill, so as to roll up the Boers." As to the resistance to be anticipated, the Generals differed from the outset. Sir C. Warren, after reconnoitring Trickhardt's Drift on the 15th, had reported that hard fighting was likely to follow the crossing, basing his opinion, doubtless, more upon the immense visible strength of the ground north of the river than upon the numbers of the enemy who actually allowed themselves to be seen. Sir R. Buller, on the other hand, not only believed that no more than 400 Boers were in front of the British left (paragraph 6, secret orders), but showed his confidence that the detached force would be able to seize and hold the heights, by desiring Sir C. Warren to return the Pontoon troop to Potgieter's Drift after he had crossed the river (paragraph 9, secret orders). As for the Boers themselves, seldom has an enemy of superior mobility been more favourably circumstanced than were Botha's well-mounted commandos operating by a shorter route against the cumbrous British columns. Here, however, speed was unnecessary, so near were the vital points, and so secure from observation the approaches to them from the laagers at Colenso and Ladysmith. Good scouting itself, at which the burghers were past masters, was scarcely needed, for who, in that clear air, could fail to see the marches of an army dragging behind it fifteen miles of transport upon open and lower ground, at five miles distance, and often less?

Sir R. Buller's estimate of the Boer strength, which, up to the

13th had been fairly accurate, was falsified almost as soon as made. Before Warren had issued his orders for the march, his designs on Trickhardt's Drift were suspected, causing such uneasiness at the Boer Headquarters, that even from the laagers at Ladysmith men were drawn to extend the front in the threatened direction. From the lines of investment rode the Pretoria District, Pretoria Town, Krugersdorp, and some Free State commandos, to the west of Spion Kop. Nor were these considered to suffice in prolonging the defences, for a little later a portion of the Ermelo commando, and more men of the Free State took up the line from Spion Kop westward to Bastion Hill, until, by January 16th, a strong body lay upon the ridges north of Trickhardt's Drift watching the preparations of the British army across the river.

Boers reinforce their right wing strongly.

CHAPTER XXI.

THE SPION KOP CAMPAIGN.

THE FLANK MARCH TO TRICKHARDT'S DRIFT.*

<small>The heights from which Warren was to drive the Boers.</small>

IN order to understand the operations which followed the movements recorded in the last chapter the nature of the Boer stronghold which on the west barred the way to Ladysmith must be realised. If scarcely as strong against attack as those at Colenso, the positions opposite Trickhardt's Drift were even more imposing in appearance. Facing westward, from the defile of the Acton Homes–Ladysmith road to the southern point of Bastion Hill, rose a steep rocky scarp, some 600 feet in height, forming the western end of the Tabanyama plateau, or Rangeworthy Heights. From Bastion Hill the ridge turned eastward, and ran almost level for about two miles, narrowing during its easterly course from a mile and a half to half a mile in breadth. Just below Sol. de Jager's Farm, a long knoll, about fifty feet higher than the rest, ran east and west athwart the plateau, blocking it at its narrowest point. Beyond this the heights trended southeasterly, rising again at Green Hill, their eastern limit. Green Hill marked the centre of the enemy's position, the western section of which was thus some three miles long, and of fairly even height. From the southern front of Tabanyama, that which faced the Tugela and the British advance, bold spurs, divided by narrow gorges, flung themselves out towards the river, falling sharply to the mealie fields along the Venter's Spruit. On the west, Bastion Hill, its sides as steep and as regular as

<small>* See maps 18, 19, and the freehand sketches.</small>

those of the "tip heap" of a mine, cut the sky with its knife-edged summit; eastward of Bastion Hill two small steep under-features ran out from Tabanyama, and next a long narrow spur pointed like a finger southward to Fairview Farm, which lay close at its base. This spur sank with a gentle slope to the southward, but on the eastward dropped suddenly to a profound chasm, crowned by a deeply-recessed, triple re-entrant, from which a stream of good water flowed past the farm to join the Venter's Spruit. Eastward of this again, yet another spur, longer, of greater breadth, and more broken than the others, ran from Green Hill down to the Tugela, splaying out more widely as it fell to the river and broken by many watercourses and minor elevations. Amongst the latter, Three Tree Hill and Piquet Hill, on west and east respectively, interrupted the feature about half way down its slope. Between them ran the road from Trickhardt's Drift to Ladysmith, *viâ* the farms named Fairview and Rosalie. A spruit, bounding the steep eastern side of this great spur, flowed past Wright's Farm to the Tugela near Trickhardt's Drift. Together with its parent, Green Hill, it marked off the western section of the Boers' position from the very different eastern portion. Of the former, which has thus been described in detail, the peculiar strength lay in the fact that everywhere the rearward crest of the plateau slightly commanded the forward crest, the intervening ground being destitute of cover. These conditions were precisely such as the Boers needed for their defence. Not only so, but from the nature of the approaches this rearward crest, the true position, was quite invisible from the northern bank of the Tugela. Only the bold serrated outline of the southern face of Tabanyama stood in relief against the sky-line, hiding all behind it. From Three Tree Hill alone could anything of the summit be descried, and of that nothing more than the top of Long Kopje, and the heights eastward of it. From the Acton Homes road, therefore, to Long Kopje, the Boer line of defence, secure from view, from reconnaissance, and from direct artillery fire, was only to be unmasked when the crest-line above the Venter's Spruit should be won, and an attempt made to push on therefrom. The weak points of the ground held by the Boer right were, first, at the right flank, which was in the air, and, secondly, perhaps, in the very steepness and brokenness of the southern face of Tabanyama, offering both cover and dead ground, and, therefore, protection to the assailants from fire till the top of the lower and nearer crest was reached. East of the above-described section the left of the Boer line was posted amidst country of wild and noble irregularity. Nine hundred yards from Green Hill, and separated from it by a low saddle barely 200 yards wide, rose the precipitous Conical Hill, a peak some 1,350 feet high. At this point the watershed turned suddenly southward for about half a mile and then as suddenly eastward. At the angle thus formed, and projecting like an advanced ravelin from the watershed, towered the great mass of Spion Kop ("Look-out Hill"), so named by a party of Voortrekkers, the first white men to stand upon its lofty summit, who had seemed to see all Natal rolling at their feet, so magnificent the view in all directions. From this mountain the ground fell to the eastward along a narrow saddle, swelling once more into two knobs where the hills most nearly touched the river. These, called the Twin Peaks, stood a mile and a half and a mile and three-quarters respectively from the top of Spion Kop, the nearer being of 230 feet, the further of 360 feet less elevation. Below, the first of those two great loops of the Tugela, described in the previous chapter, curled northward to meet these eminences, and together with them and a spruit which flowed into the apex of the loop, in a measure divided the whole Spion Kop position from the amphitheatre which curved to the eastward from Brakfontein to the Vaal Krantz Ridge and Doorn Kloof. To effect the passage of the river, to force the five and a half miles of heights which everywhere commanded by 1,200 feet the points of crossing, and to find a way through to the easier country behind were the tasks imposed upon Sir C. Warren by the secret orders of January 15th.

<small>Strength of Warren's column.</small>

His preparations were speedily completed. He had at his disposal six batteries, Royal Field artillery (7th, 73rd, 78th, 19th, 28th, and 63rd), 12,000 infantry with 14 machine guns, and,

THE SPION KOP CAMPAIGN. 353

after the junction with Lord Dundonald's mounted brigade, at Trickhardt's Drift, about 2,000 mounted troops, with Royal Engineers and details.*

At 5 p.m. on January 16th the troops allotted to him were suddenly ordered from their camps at Springfield. So secret had the plans been kept, that even the senior officers had learned nothing of the hour of setting out, and when the order came,† almost every soldier thought that Potgieter's Drift and a direct advance on Ladysmith were before him. In the hopes of equally mystifying the enemy every tent was left standing, and small parties of soldiers remained behind, with instructions to wander conspicuously about the lines, to blow the usual bugle calls, and generally to counterfeit the normal camp life of the army which had departed to give battle.

The secrecy of his plan.

The column itself took with it little transport. Only three wagons, one containing the men's great coats, another one day's rations, the third the 20 lb. kits of the officers, were allowed to each battalion. The men themselves carried one day's ration, the usual "emergency ration," 150 rounds of ammunition, and, strapped to their belts, jersey and waterproof sheet; "light" marching order truly compared with the regular infantry scale, yet a burden imposing a severe handicap on soldiers whose enemy, on his swift and sturdy pony, knew nothing of the chief toil of war—the march afoot. The baggage train was to follow later.

Burden carried by the troops.

The night was dark, though occasionally a brilliant moon, breaking through the clouds, illuminated the long columns, which moved on either side of the roadway, leaving the centre for the guns, pontoons and transport. Except for the rumbling of these vehicles, and the dull sound of the trampling of the battalions upon the grass, silence pervaded the line of march, no talking or smoking being permitted. Some three miles north of Springfield, the head of the column was deflected to the left, and it dawned on the troops that Trickhardt's and not Potgieter's was to be the goal. Thereafter progress was slow, but the river bank was reached before light, and on the high ground above the drift the force bivouacked at 2 a.m. on the

Warren's night march from Springfield to Trickhardt's Drift, 16th-17th Jan., 1900.

* For full state see Appendix 8 (I). † See Appendix 9 (A).

VOL. II.

17th. Meanwhile the contingent under Major-General Lyttelton, designed to operate at Potgieter's and Skiet's Drift, had also moved out earlier in the afternoon of the 16th. It consisted of eight 12-pr. Naval guns, 64th battery and 61st Howitzer battery, Bethune's mounted infantry, and 8,000 infantry.* First the Dorset, with a squadron of Bethune's mounted infantry, and the 64th battery marched from Spearman's at 3 p.m., with orders to occupy a position on Zwart Kop, thereby covering Skiet's Drift, and denying it to the enemy for purposes of a counter-stroke. Owing to a mistake on the part of the guide detailed to lead this detachment, Zwart Kop was not reached by nightfall. Nevertheless, a position sufficiently good to command the drift was taken up for the night, the enemy only firing a few ineffectual shots from across the river. At Potgieter's Drift a section of the 37th company, Royal Engineers and a party of bluejackets busied themselves in re-establishing the tackle, and restoring the "pont" to working order. This work was completed by 5.15 p.m., and six hours later the 1st Rifle Brigade, the Scottish Rifles with their transport, and the 61st Howitzer battery with its train complete, had been ferried across and safely disembarked, the first body of troops to stand upon the northern bank of the Tugela. The bridge-head position, called "The Kopjes," known afterwards to the troops as "Maconochie's Kopjes," from the name of the manufacturer of a preserved meat ration which was there issued to the soldiers, was at once occupied. The horses and ammunition wagons accompanying the detachment were ferried at 1.30 a.m. on the 17th back to the southern bank, where the Naval 12-prs. were already in position.

As an instance of the already described hazards attending warfare in a country where both the rivers and the information concerning them were equally unreliable,† the stream at Potgieter's Drift proved to be so deep and swift, that many who tried to ford were swept away. A pontoon raft was, therefore, constructed by another section of the 37th company Royal Engineers to supplement the "pont," and it greatly facilitated the passage of troops and vehicles.

* See Appendix 8 (J). † See Volume I., Chapter III.

THE SPION KOP CAMPAIGN. 355

The difficulties confronting Sir C. Warren at Trickhardt's Drift were of a more serious nature. The river at that point was about eighty yards wide. The banks, rising some thirty feet above the water, were not only exceedingly steep, and here and there interspersed with bushes, but composed of rock so hard that it almost defied tools. The reports of the Intelligence Department pointed to the probability of the passage being under the fire of three or four Boer guns, and that of an advanced party of 300-400 riflemen said to be posted about Wright's Farm. This information seemed to be justified when, shortly after dawn on January 17th, a patrol of the Imperial Light Horse, which forded the river and rode up the left bank, came under a smart fusilade from the farm and from the foot-hills beyond. Before the construction of bridges could be taken in hand, it was therefore necessary to arrange for a covering fire, and, as on the morning of the 17th a thick mist enshrouded the country, it was with great difficulty that positions for the artillery were found and taken up. This was effected by 5 a.m., and a little later Hildyard, to whose brigade fell the duty of guarding the passage, had disposed the 2nd Queen's on the Nek by the drift road, and the 2nd East Surrey on a hill to the eastward. The remaining two battalions, the 2nd Devonshire and 2nd West Yorkshire, were detailed for work at the drift and pontoons.

Warren's difficulties at Trickhardt's Drift.

Positions taken up to cover the crossing, 5 a.m., Jan. 17th,

As four companies of the former battalion marched down to the water side as escort to the pontoons, a volley from the left bank, which killed one of the soldiers, seemed to presage opposition to the crossing. But the mist having lifted, the artillery quickly shelled the enemy out of the plantations in which he was ensconced, and thereafter the bridging party worked on unmolested. At 9 a.m. four companies of the 2nd West Yorkshire regiment were rowed across the stream in the pontoons of A. troop bridging battalion Royal Engineers, and took up a position on the opposite bank to protect the bridge building and the passage of the troops. The work then began. It was carried on with the utmost skill and rapidity. In two hours the Royal Engineers, commanded by Major J. L. Irvine, R.E., notwithstanding the difficulties of the banks and swiftly running

which is effected with little opposition from the enemy.

Troops ferried across Tugela at 9 a.m., Jan. 17th.

One bridge thrown for the troops,

stream, had completed a bridge of twelve pontoons. The approaches were more troublesome than the bridge itself. It was only possible to dig during that day a track suitable for infantry and led horses in the steep and rocky face of the right bank, down which it was necessary to lower by ropes the regimental carts and wheeled machine guns, which were then manhandled across the bridge. For the wagons another passage was needed. A little higher up, where an island lay in mid-stream, and the confluence of a watercourse cleft the rocky bank, forming a natural ramp, a site was found for a second bridge. This consisted of three trestles between the right bank and the island, and of five pontoons between the island and the left bank, which proved to be of soft earth, easy for digging. These works, with the smoothing of a road across the island, took the whole day. It was not until 7.30 p.m. that the first of the train of wagons crossed the bridge. Nor were the difficulties then over. The mules and oxen, terrified at the swaying of the structure, and by the ringing of their hoofs upon the wooden " chesses," or planks which formed the roadway, refused to move. Some of the mules even flung themselves into the river in a panic, and were swept away and drowned. Rushes and tussocks of coarse grass were then mixed with sand and strewn upon the roadways of both bridges, and the animals, still suspicious and troublesome, were then slowly induced to cross over. Difficulty of this kind is inevitable in the passage of a river by a temporary bridge, even though the stream be of moderate width and the enemy refrain from interruption.

At 9.30 a.m. Lord Dundonald had received orders to move his mounted troops to the further bank. After waiting several hours for the completion of the bridges, he made up his mind to go by a ford about half a mile below the lower pontoon, both in order to leave the bridges free, and because his horses, like the mules and oxen, were shy of the pontoons. Here, also, there were difficulties. The river, which was in half flood, ran deep and rapid; the bed of the drift was rough with boulders, and complicated by a sharp bend in mid-stream. Several of the horses were carried off their feet, and a trooper of the 13th

Hussars was drowned.* It was late in the afternoon, nearly twelve hours after their arrival at the river bank, and some time after a large portion of the infantry, that the whole of the mounted troops had struggled through, and there was then no choice but to bivouac close to the drift. The officer commanding the Royal artillery, who was to have used the same ford, declined to risk his guns and went by a bridge. The infantry marched over rapidly and without trouble. As it was now certain that the enemy was holding the high ground between Bastion Hill and Spion Kop it was needful to show a front in that direction; the 11th brigade (Woodgate), therefore, supported by the 5th (Hart), were immediately pushed towards the ridges, some two thousand yards to the north of the left bank, moving in attack formation on either side of the watercourse which descended from Piquet Hill.† The artillery and infantry cross later.

Infantry advance to heights on left bank.

It happened that Major-General E. R. P. Woodgate, during his advance, showed a momentary tendency to trend north-eastward, that is, towards the enemy's centre and left, fronting Green Hill and Spion Kop. This was at once noticed by Sir R. Buller, who had ridden over to Trickhardt's Drift to watch the bridging operations, and it seemed to him to show that Woodgate had not grasped the objects of the movement. He therefore sent to Sir C. Warren a letter in which, in the plainest terms, he suggested the tactics he wished carried out. "The one thing," he wrote, "if we mean to succeed is to keep our left clear. . . . If your direct road is blocked we must go forward by moving off to the left . . . consequently the left flank must always be thrown outward. . . . Until you have so far encircled the enemy that you can wheel to the east, pray always try to overlap their right with your left."‡ Buller reiterates his plan of attack. His letter to Warren.

Neither Hart nor Woodgate met with any opposition, though

---

* Captain J. H. Tremayne, 13th Hussars, made a gallant attempt to save this man, and was himself rescued in a state of unconsciousness by Trooper Llander, Natal Carbineers.

† See map No. 19 (a).

‡ For the full letter, see Appendix 9 (B).

the enemy was plainly seen upon the heights, busily entrenching. Both brigades bivouacked for the night upon the foothills, a few scattered rifle shots coming into the lines just before sunset.

<small>Buller, though in possession of Potgieter's and Trickhardt's Drifts on 17th Jan.,</small>

Thus, before the evening of January 17th, Sir R. Buller had the satisfaction of seeing both Potgieter's and Trickhardt's Drifts in his possession, and his widely separated wings in safe occupation of ground upon the enemy's side of the Tugela. Already Lyttelton, whose guns had sounded from Potgieter's and Mount Alice all day, had signalled to Sir C. Warren that he was prepared to help him with his heavy artillery and to demonstrate strongly with his infantry at any moment, to distract the enemy's attention from Warren's next advance.

<small>has still a heavy task before him.</small>

Although Sir R. Buller had thus good hopes of success, he did not disguise from himself the formidable nature of the task he had set his army. Close in front, the enemy's stronghold itself, rearing its rampart of heights, now dotted with groups of busy diggers, above the valley, gave unmistakable warning of the lions lying across the path to Ladysmith. The passage of Sir C. Warren's transport was painfully slow, and every hour must increase the strength of the position towering before him. Nor was the news from the besieged town itself encouraging. A message received from Sir G. White on the previous day (January 17th) painted in no bright colours the condition of the defending troops. Sickness was rife and increasing daily; there were already 2,400 in hospital, and many of the men on duty were weakly; the force had lost the services of no less than 230 officers in three months, and, to use Sir G. White's expression, " was much played out." Such a communication could not but strengthen Sir R. Buller's already half-formed impression that Sir G. White did not think himself able to sally from Ladysmith to co-operate in his advance, an impression indeed conveyed to him by Sir G. White himself, who, on January 7th, and then for the first time, had informed Sir R. Buller that his powers of co-operation were fast

<small>News from Ladysmith; condition of the besieged troops</small>

<small>will not permit White to co-operate with Buller.</small>

dwindling.* Sir R. Buller had already forwarded this to Lord Roberts, who had just arrived at Cape Town, and whilst now sending on this fresh corroboration to the Commander-in-Chief, he added his own views as to the consequences which followed from it.† Success, he said, depended upon Sir C. Warren's being able to turn the flank of the Boers upon the Rangeworthy Heights. Should that fail, the relief of Ladysmith was doubtful—nor would a larger force be of much avail, so enormous would be the difficulty of keeping it supplied. Sir C. Warren (he continued) agreed that, despite Sir G. White's confessed incapacity to co-operate, the operation so well begun should be persevered in. Sending, therefore, an encouraging message to Sir G. White,‡ Sir R. Buller adhered to his plans and the slow passage of the transport continued. Throughout the night of the 17th and the whole of the next day the spans of shy and clumsy oxen, dragging the apparently interminable train of wagons, were coaxed or flogged across the bridges, whilst the infantry brigades lay idle upon the north bank, and the enemy improved his defences upon the heights, 2,500 yards away, in the sight of all. Not until 10 p.m. on the 18th was the last wagon hauled up the ramp of the north bank, twenty-six hours after the first, a length of time indicating both the strenuous labour involved and the incubus of transport with which Sir C. Warren was burdened.

<small>Buller's plan dependent on Warren turning the Boer right.</small>

<small>Though White cannot co-operate, Buller adheres to his plan,</small>

<small>and his transport crosses the Tugela on 17th-18th Jan.</small>

Of all the rest of Warren's force only the cavalry had been active this day (the 18th), and their manœuvres resulted in a feat notable from its being the first success to attend the arms of the Relief Column.

* See Chapter XXXII. Heliogram No. 44P, January 7th.
Previously to that, Sir G. White, though he had pointed out the impossibility of his actually "cutting his way out" to Sir R. Buller's force (heliogram of Dec. 16th replying to Sir R. Buller's No. 88), had invariably expressed his willingness to co-operate to the extent of his power. See Chapter XXXI., messages of November 28th and 30th, and heliograms No. 33P, December 18th, and 39P, January 2nd.

† Sir R. Buller to Lord Roberts, 17th January, 1900.

‡ See Chapter XXXII. Heliogram No. 159, January 17th: "I somehow think we are going to be successful this time. . . . . I hope to be knocking at Lancer's Hill in six days from now."

THE WAR IN SOUTH AFRICA.

The mounted troops move west and north-west, 18th Jan.,

Early in the morning Sir C. Warren, who feared for the safety of his vast herd of transport oxen, had sent instructions* to Lord Dundonald to detach 500 mounted men† for piquet duty around the camp. A later message (11.45 a.m.) to the cavalry leader requested him to scout to the front with the remainder of his command, "and to send patrols about ten miles to the west and north-west." Moving cautiously under cover of the low hills north of the Tugela, Dundonald crossed the Venter's Spruit, and reconnoitred the approaches to the Rangeworthy Heights, of which he caused sketches to be made. At 2 p.m., having completed his reconnaissance, he sent back to Sir C. Warren a report, in which he detailed the only practicable line of advance for a flank attack upon the heights, i.e., by the right bank of the Venter's Spruit, and not by the left, which was closely commanded by the foot-hills.‡ Then, becoming aware that, contrary to his expectations, he was not followed by the main body of the army, Dundonald, after securing with small dismounted parties all the tactical points of the route which he had

and patrol towards Acton Homes.

followed, pushed out patrols in the direction of Acton Homes, and made arrangements for bivouacking at Erthcote, a post which safeguarded all the western or right bank of the Venter's Spruit. The object of the patrols was to ascertain if the enemy was making use of the Ladysmith—Acton Homes—Orange Free State road.§ Whilst advancing in observation, the scouts reported to the officer in command (Major H. W. G. Graham, 5th Lancers) that a strong body of Boers was riding down from Tabanyama towards the road. A brief scrutiny of this party

---

* See Appendix 9 (C).

† Dundonald's strength at this time was approximately as follows :—

Royal Dragoons	412 men
Squadron 13th Hussars	260 ,,
Composite mounted infantry regiment ..	270 ,,
South African Light Horse	300 ,,
Thorneycroft's mounted infantry ..	300 ,,
	1,542 ,,

‡ See map 19, and Appendix 9 (C).

§ See map No. 18.

THE SPION KOP CAMPAIGN. 361

satisfied Graham that they knew nothing of the presence of the British cavalry, and, noticing that further on, about two miles south-west of Frere's Store, the track which the Boers were following would lead them into a defile between two kopjes, he at once decided to attempt an ambuscade, and ordered his two squadrons to advance. Skilfully guided by the commander of the Natal Carbineers (Major D. McKenzie), who contrived, whilst moving forward at speed for two miles and more, to keep the force invisible behind the undulations of the ground, the squadrons crossed the Venter's Spruit by a drift which brought them out directly behind the two kopjes which imprisoned the road. But the enemy, still unaware of what was going forward, was by this time also near to the kopjes, and Graham's men had to gallop their hardest to set the trap instead of being themselves entrapped. In this they just succeeded, the Natal Carbineers dashing up to the left-hand kopje and the Imperial Light Horse to that on the right, as the enemy, some 300 in number, approached them closely from the other side. So unsuspicious of danger were the advancing Boers that they, usually the wariest of horsemen, were riding carelessly in close formation, their scouts but a few yards in front of the main body. Just as they came within seventy yards of the British rifles, and the capture of the whole seemed certain, a shot was accidentally discharged by one of the impatient troopers, and was immediately followed by a general fusilade from both kopjes. The Boers thereupon turned and broke, the majority escaping into safety, some falling dead from the saddle, and many, whose ponies were killed, running for shelter behind the boulders which strewed the kopjes, whence for some time they replied vigorously to the fire of the cavalry. Graham then sent back for his supports, the mounted infantry of the King's Royal Rifles and a squadron of the South African Light Horse, and these, hurrying into the firing line, soon assisted to overcome the resistance amongst the rocks of the outnumbered Boers, who rose to their feet and surrendered. In all some fifty burghers, killed, wounded and captured, were lost to the enemy, the British casualties numbering but three.

A patrol surprises 300 Boers,

and does them much damage.

Meanwhile, Lord Dundonald, before ascertaining the nature of this combat and its successful issue, had sent a message to Sir C. Warren, which considerably alarmed that officer, when he received it at sunset.* In it Dundonald announced that his advanced squadrons were engaged with the enemy, that he had sent support to them, and that he would like the Royal Dragoons to be restored to him. The very brevity of this message misled the General, whose doubt as to the extent of Dundonald's commitment with the enemy was little cleared by another telegram,† received at 9 p.m., in which the cavalry leader, in giving a few details of his action, ended by saying that he was "holding the position and kopjes commanding the west of your (Sir C. Warren's) line." Two hours earlier three squadrons of the Royal Dragoons had been ordered to rejoin Dundonald, and Hildyard's brigade to march to Venter's Spruit at 4.30 a.m. next morning to support the cavalry. The affair at Acton Homes, therefore, which was in reality nothing more than a normal incident in the work of cavalry covering an advance, by no means pleased Sir C. Warren, because he had no opportunity of properly realising what had happened. Misled as to its importance by Dundonald's hurried request for reinforcements, it seemed to him that in accepting an engagement the cavalry leader had unduly forced his hand, and that not only Hildyard's brigade, but the whole column must now be moved towards Venter's Spruit to support the—as he imagined—involved cavalry.‡ The restoration of the Royal Dragoons to Dundonald had indeed dangerously deprived the main body of scouts and cattle guards, and once more Sir C. Warren became anxious for the safety of the multitude of wagons which were massed around Wright's Farm, where the available grazing for the 15,000 oxen was also rapidly disappearing. In pursuance of these ideas, at 7.30 p.m., and again later in the evening, he despatched messages to Dundonald complaining of his having "forced on an action," and ordering him to retire upon the

Marginal notes: Warren, not fully acquainted with the nature of this affair, believes himself to be committed to an advance to disengage Dundonald, and orders him to retire,

---

* See Appendix 9 (C). † See Appendix 9 (C).

‡ See Appendix 9 (D).

THE SPION KOP CAMPAIGN. 363

main camp unless he were sure of success.* Nor did Lord Dundonald take steps during the night to remove the impression his reports had created. At 7 a.m., January 19th, therefore, Sir C. Warren, who had already apprised Dundonald of the movement of the infantry to his support, thought it necessary to address a strongly-worded message to his subordinate, in which he pointed out that the cavalry commander was evidently mistaking the whole operation, and by detaching his command was hampering the movements of the main body, and forcing the General to change his plans.† Only then did Dundonald assure Sir C. Warren of his safety, and his reasons for the action he had taken,‡ but the latter, dissatisfied with the remoteness of the cavalry and the apparent independence of its commander, despatched at noon a message in which he reiterated his complaints, and directed Dundonald to come in person to receive his orders. At the interview which followed Dundonald endeavoured to obtain permission to continue his progress around the Boer right; but these tactics, for reasons which will appear later, no longer suited the general scheme of advance which Sir C. Warren had been formulating during the day. Before considering this plan the movements of the rest of the force during January 19th must be briefly detailed. At 6 a.m., General Hildyard's brigade marched to Venter's Spruit in accordance with the design of supporting the cavalry to the northwest. The wagons, in six parallel columns, accompanied the brigade, and once more emphasised the great possibilities of delay which their use entailed. The road was indifferent, and had to be repaired during the march; the drift proved so difficult that it ended by baulking altogether the whole proceeding. By 4 p.m., ten hours after leaving camp, so few wagons had crossed the obstacle that it was obvious the movement could scarcely be begun before nightfall, and an order arrived cancelling the march. Accordingly, Hildyard's brigade, which had gone forward two miles, to spend an idle day awaiting the trans-

<small>and not to continue his movement round the Boer right.</small>

<small>Movements of 2nd brigade and the transport on 19th Jan.</small>

* See Appendix 9 (C).   † See Appendix 9 (C).
‡ See Appendix 9 (C).

364   THE WAR IN SOUTH AFRICA.

port, retraced its steps and went into bivouac in the midst of the transport on the east of the Venter's Spruit.

<small>Movements of 5th and 11th brigades on 19th Jan.</small>

Meanwhile Hart's and Woodgate's brigades, quitting at daybreak the positions in which they had lain since sunset on the 17th—that is, for about thirty-six hours—had followed Hildyard towards the Venter's Spruit. Woodgate's brigade, moving along the lower slopes of the Rangeworthy Heights, as a right flank-guard to the transport, halted for the night near Fairview Farm. Hart, crossing the Venter's Spruit, held the passage for the baggage, withdrawing all but one battalion—the Connaught Rangers—which remained on guard over the wagons on the western side, to the eastern bank of the spruit at night. Thus ended January the 19th. With the Boers, beyond a general strengthening of their position, the chief event had been the emplacing of a heavy gun, brought from Ladysmith, upon a height about two miles north of the Acton Homes road, which it commanded.*

<small>Warren, established on north bank of the Tugela, has to decide by which road he will advance.</small>

Sir C. Warren had now held a footing on the north bank of the Tugela for sixty hours, the other wing of the army, Lyttelton's force at Potgieter's, for some nine hours longer. Except for Dundonald's skirmish at Acton Homes there had been no contact with the enemy, who had had ample time in which to entrench and bring up reinforcements. The question of the line of advance to be taken against the enemy from Trickhardt's Drift, pressed for immediate decision. Briefly the problem was as follows. Two roads led into the enemy's position; one by

<small>Description of the routes at his disposal.</small>

Fairview and Rosalie Farms, 22 miles to Ladysmith, the other, skirting the Rangeworthy Heights by Acton Homes, 30 miles to the besieged town. A third road from Potgieter's Drift (18 miles to Ladysmith) was at Lyttelton's disposal, and all three united at Dewdrop (see map 18) some three miles from Lancer's Hill, one of the positions of the Boers around Ladysmith. This junction, therefore, was obviously the point to be aimed at, both for the purpose of joining hands with Lyttelton, and for reaching Sir G. White. The assistance of that General could be counted upon for a distance of at least six miles from

* See map No. 19 (c).

his base, thereby reducing the mileage to be covered by Sir R. Buller's forces in effecting his relief. At Dewdrop, where a strong position called Roodepoort would be available, the plan went that Warren should swing eastward, his right pivoted on the river, his left, prolonged by Dundonald's cavalry, overlapping the right of the Boers, who would be pushed eastwards, their flank exposed to Lyttelton, who, by that time, it was hoped, would be securely posted upon Brakfontein. Sir C. Warren had a free choice in selecting between the roads. Nothing in Sir R. Buller's secret or other orders bound him to one or the other. Nor on the evening of the 19th did he, as might be gathered from his messages and orders, consider himself committed to the Acton Homes route by Dundonald's action in that direction, for at that very time he discarded it. Having inspected the road in question during the day, he came to the conclusion that, owing to its narrowness, his multitude of wagons could only move along it in single file; it was also eight miles longer than the other track, and would consequently doubly delay the advance. Finally, he received from Sir G. White a report that the Boers were assembling in force (1,500 to 2,000) in this direction.* Only the Fairview road remained, and to secure it, it was first necessary to capture the hills either to the east or the west of it, i.e., either the Spion Kop—Green Hill positions, or the Rangeworthy Heights. To an assault on the former he understood Sir R. Buller to be averse. He decided, therefore, that nothing remained but to attack the Rangeworthy Heights, to send his wagons back across the Tugela when those were captured, and to push on for Ladysmith without transport, with three or four days' rations in the soldiers' haversacks. At a Council of War held on the evening of the 19th he made known his plans to his General Officers. At the same time he informed Sir R. Buller by letter of this choice of roads, saying nothing more of the details of his scheme than that he was about to " adopt some special arrangements " which would involve his staying at Venter's Laager for two or three days."†

He decides on the road by Fairview and Rosalie Farms,

and informs Buller of his choice.

---

* See Appendix 9 (E). † See Appendix 9 (F).

Sir R. Buller asked no questions, merely promising in reply supplies for the period named, and Sir C. Warren issued his preliminary orders* the same night. Briefly summarised, they contained directions for the clearance of the enemy from the spurs and re-entrants which formed the southern crest of the Rangeworthy Heights from Bastion Hill to the westward to Three Tree Hill on the east, with the special object of finding artillery positions whence to shell the strongly posted Boers left at Green Hill and Spion Kop. This duty was assigned to Lieutenant-General Sir C. F. Clery, under whom the following troops were placed : Hart's (5th) and Woodgate's (11th) infantry brigades, six batteries, Royal Field artillery, and three squadrons of cavalry. At 3 a.m., whilst Hildyard remained in reserve with the wagons at Venter's Spruit Drift, Clery pushed forward two of Woodgate's battalions (2nd King's Own (Royal Lancaster) and 1st South Lancashire regiments) to capture Three Tree Hill, and the other two (2nd Lancashire Fusiliers and the 1st York and Lancaster regiment) to seize the long spur previously described as falling towards Fairview Farm, close to the westward. These movements were accomplished without fighting, and the whole of the artillery was sent on to Three Tree Hill, the range from which to the main Boer trench was some 2,300 yards, Bastion Hill lying at about 3,000 yards to the westward. But Three Tree Hill was found to be too small for six batteries. It was shaped roughly in three terraces, each of an area to hold one battery in close order, but all so difficult of approach owing to the rocks and steepness of the gradients, that the guns of the 7th, 63rd and 73rd batteries which were posted thereon had to be man-handled into position, and their wagons left below. A site for the other three batteries, the 78th, 19th, and 28th, was found in a mealie field to the east. These positions, the best available, were by no means good. The restricted view from Three Tree Hill has been described ; the southern, not the true, crest-line of the Rangeworthy Heights, with a portion of the actual top of Long Kopje were alone visible from the hill itself, whilst the batteries placed to the eastward could

* See Appendix 9 (G).

THE SPION KOP CAMPAIGN. 367

only direct a fire at a steep upward angle upon Spion Kop and a portion of Green Hill. For the rest, the position had the great disadvantage that the further forward and westward the infantry attack inclined, the less support would it obtain from the artillery, which, moreover, could hardly be sure enough of the true site of the Boer guns posted with so superior a command, and in rear of the crest-line, to engage them effectually. Hart's brigade, changing formation, as the ground served, from column of route to mass of quarter columns, and finally to line of quarter columns, moved north from its bivouac, and at 9 a.m. reached the spur to the westward of Three Tree Hill, where it absorbed Woodgate's two battalions. Hart thus had five battalions under his command.* Then, whilst all the artillery bombarded the hills in front, the advance began, the honour of leading being accorded to the troops who had been first on the ground, Woodgate's two battalions. On the right the 2nd Lancashire Fusiliers, on the left the 1st York and Lancaster regiment in extended order, supported by the 2nd Royal Dublin Fusiliers and the 1st Border regiment in " rank entire,"† pressed forward up the spurs lying between Bastion and Three Tree Hills, Hart's intention being to push the enemy from the successive crest-lines which appeared to rise before him in a long series. The attack was an inspiriting spectacle. The soldiers, burning to efface the memory of what seemed to them their unaccountable rebuff at Colenso, forced their way forward with great speed, yet skilfully using the advantages of the ground, whilst the enemy fired so constantly, and at times so hotly, down upon them that the supports had quickly to be extended like the firing line, and it became impossible to advance save by short rushes across the bullet-swept ground. Over the heads of the infantry, the artillery launched a continuous stream of shrapnel, which beat upon the hillsides, and soon covered them with blazing grass, the heavy smoke rising like a wall before the assault.

Hart, with five battalions, arrives near Three Tree Hill at 9 a.m., 20th Jan. The advance begins.

* The 1st Connaught Rangers, of Hart's brigade, having been detailed to guard the general right rear, were posted south of Three Tree Hill, and formed no part of the attacking column.

† i.e., in single line, the men shoulder to shoulder.

Hart occupies the first line of Boer trenches,	Pressing forward without a check, Hart's men rapidly cleared the lower ground, and before long were in the trenches upon the southern crest of Rangeworthy, the Boers falling back to the true crest about a thousand yards to the northward. Thence they continued their unremitting fusilade, which now became in large measure a cross fire upon the attacking lines. But Hart was sanguine of success; his men were in high spirit, and he was on the point of ordering them to close and sweep the enemy from the hill, when a peremptory message arrived from General Clery to stop all further advance. Clery, in fact, who had kept a keen watch on the proceedings, perceived that the glacis, which lay between the northern and southern crests of Rangeworthy, had
but as his attack must be frontal, is recalled by Clery.	yet to be crossed, and that by a frontal attack which could be little supported by the artillery. With Sir C. Warren's full concurrence.* therefore, he declined to risk the final stage of the attack, and Hart, by his orders, had to rest contented with entrenching himself on the captured crest, with the enemy's main position still before him.†
The operations of the mounted troops on Jan. 20th;	Whilst this was in progress, the cavalry on the left had not been idle. Early in the morning, Sir C. Warren had sent on to Lord Dundonald the information he had received from Ladysmith as to the enemy's concentration on the Acton Homes road,‡ once more accompanying it by an order for the cavalry to keep closer touch with the main body. In compliance, Dundonald, leaving a party conspicuously posted to deceive the Boers, whilst continuing to threaten the road with the Composite regiment, moved eastward from his Headquarters at Erthcote, and at 11 a.m. set about the capture of Bastion Hill. This
they capture Bastion Hill at 2.50 p.m.	was easily effected at 2.50 p.m. by a dismounted squadron of the South African Light Horse, supported by Thorneycroft's mounted infantry, the enemy giving up the advanced trenches with little resistance. No sooner was the cavalry in possession of the hill, however, than the Boers endeavoured to dislodge them by heavy shell fire from their main position in rear and to the eastward, causing the cavalry some losses. The fire was so

* See Appendix 9 (H). † See map No. 19 (d).
‡ See Appendix 9 (E).

THE SPION KOP CAMPAIGN.

hot that the flag of the signaller, who immediately communicated with Hart, was perforated by eight shots in a brief time. Hearing the uproar, not only from Bastion Hill, but from Hart's attack on the right, Hildyard moved forward his reserve brigade (2nd) at 1 p.m., ready to support either flank. The 2nd Queen's (Royal West Surrey) regiment first went a mile and a half to the front in order to be near Dundonald, followed at 3.30 p.m. by a company of the 2nd East Surrey regiment, the two parties uniting between 4 p.m. and 6 p.m., whilst at 5.30 p.m. the 2nd West Yorkshire regiment was sent to strengthen Hart upon the spurs immediately east of Bastion Hill. The remainder of the brigade, consisting of the rest of the East Surrey and the 2nd Devonshire regiments, continued on guard over the wagons at Venter's Spruit Laager, which they surrounded with outposts. The casualties on January 20th were, from all causes, 8 officers and 108 men. *[The 2nd brigade supports Dundonald and Hart.]*

A night of great uneasiness followed. The Boers, momentarily expecting an attack, sent spasmodic bursts of musketry across the narrow plateau which divided them from the troops on the crest, and star shell, bursting above the lines, brilliantly illuminated at intervals the darkness which was already ruddy with the sombre glow of the smouldering grass fires. Throughout the night the Boers and their Kaffir servants laboured hard at their entrenchments, which by daylight had grown well nigh impregnable. *[The night of 20th-21st Jan.]*

Dawn of the 21st January broke in silence, each combatant waiting for a movement on the part of the other. On the British side the first stir occurred on the left, where, at 4.10 a.m., three companies of the East Surrey regiment, followed at 8 a.m. by the remaining three, reinforced the Queen's regiment upon Bastion Hill, the cavalry relinquishing this position to the infantry and retiring to Venter's Spruit, where they came under Hildyard's command. All the infantry of the 2nd brigade which were now in the front line, viz., the Queen's, West Yorkshire and East Surrey regiments, were then brigaded under Brevet Colonel F. W. Kitchener of the West Yorkshire regiment and added to General Hart's command. East of Bastion Hill, that *[21st Jan. Clery makes new dispositions. The infantry relieve the mounted troops,]* is, to Hart's left and front, ran a stretch of crest-line which had not been occupied during the previous day's operations, and Hart was now ordered to make this good, whilst Kitchener endeavoured to turn the enemy's flank by the west of Bastion Hill. The two movements began simultaneously, under a general discharge from every gun and rifle in the Boer lines. Hart, sending the Dublin Fusiliers and the Border regiment around the head of the long donga which ran down from Long Kopje, and the York and Lancaster regiment and the Inniskilling Fusiliers across the donga lower down,* gained his point with few casualties, and was soon secure along the crest on Kitchener's right. The latter was less fortunate in his enterprise. It had been planned that whilst four companies of the East Surrey regiment worked around the west of Bastion Hill, covered by the fire of the Queen's regiment from the Nek east of the hill, two companies of the Queen's regiment on the right, and two of the West Yorkshire on the left would push across the top of the plateau, covered by the remainder of the latter battalion. Artillery support was provided by the arrival of the 19th and 28th batteries, Royal Field artillery, which came into action with their left on the Venter's Spruit, whence they could send shrapnel past the left side of Bastion Hill. But the movement was too fragmentary for success. The companies of the East Surrey were soon brought to a standstill on the western face of Bastion Hill, and the troops on the top of the plateau, who had made good progress in spite of a fierce fire, had to be withdrawn from their frontal attack, the flank movement having failed. One company of the West Yorkshire remained out in front in a donga until the evening, to avoid heavy losses in retiring. By 11 a.m. the attempt, which had cost 123 casualties, was discontinued. Soon afterwards a rumour reached the wide-thrown line of battle that the siege of Ladysmith had been raised, and a roar of cheering ran along the ragged crests held by the fighting line, and rose from the deep gorges beneath, wherein the supports lay crowded together. It was silenced as quickly as it had

* His other battalion, the Lancashire Fusiliers, was detached as escort to the 19th and 28th batteries R.F.A.

THE SPION KOP CAMPAIGN.

arisen, and the shooting, which had paused a moment, continued without intermission. Although all these movements were over early in the day, no further offence was attempted throughout the rest of the 21st January. The enemy in his main position across the glacis-like plateau remained unshaken, practically untouched by the artillery, and at no time mastered by the musketry and Maxim-gun fire* of the infantry, which, continuous and heavy as it was, never failed to be answered in equal volume from the Boer schanzes. Indeed, an accurate cross fire from the enemy's field guns, pom-poms and Maxims, which the artillery never succeeded in silencing, inclined the balance all day against the troops of the attack, who neither in the front line nor in the deep resting-places of the supports, were secure from the bursting of shrapnel or the strings of little projectiles from the automatic pieces. The casualties on January 21st were: killed, 1 officer, 13 men; wounded, 8 officers, 131 men; missing, 5 men. Towards evening Sir C. Warren, who had been visited by Sir R. Buller during the day, rode out to the west of Bastion Hill to survey the situation. From a brief report which he had received, describing a considerable movement of wagons towards the Orange Free State passes, he had formed an impression that the enemy was preparing for a general retirement westward, and was now fighting less to bar the way to Ladysmith than by a delaying action to keep intact his lines of communication and retreat,† until the transport in question should get clear. At these lines he determined to strike, and his present force being already fully engaged, he despatched (6.30 p.m.) an urgent message to Sir R. Buller, requesting that Talbot Coke's brigade (10th) (composed of the 2nd Somersetshire Light infantry, 2nd Dorsetshire, and 2nd Middlesex regiments), should be sent from Spearman's Camp to reinforce him as speedily as possible. He also asked for four Howitzers, since indirect fire alone seemed likely to be of any service against the enemy's concealed positions and sunken

No further attack on Jan. 21st.

Casualties on Jan. 21st.

Warren believes the Boers are fighting a rearguard action,

and determines to strike at their lines of communication.

He asks for reinforcements of infantry and for Howitzers.

---

* The Maxim guns expended from 7,000–8,000 rounds apiece during the day.

† See Appendices 9 (I) and 9 (J).

communications. Except that on Bastion Hill the 2nd Queen's regiment was relieved by the 2nd Devon and the 2nd East Surrey regiment by the Lancashire Fusiliers, which had come to this part of the field with the two field batteries, night fell without further movement.

Jan. 22nd. The action continues.

Daybreak next morning (January 22nd) was greeted with a universal outburst of fire from the whole line, and the clamour rolled round the great amphitheatre from Acton Homes to Doorn Kloof, a distance of over twelve miles. Both combatants were by this time so well covered that this imposing display, though wearing to the spirit, proved almost harmless. Throughout the long day the casualties were trifling. They were: killed, one man; wounded, one officer and twenty men; missing one man.

The Howitzers arrive.

The Howitzers, arriving early, were posted, two with the artillery on Three Tree Hill, and two on the left by Venter's Spruit, and immediately joined in the attack. Still there was no advance. Sir C. Warren was awaiting the 10th brigade, which had left Spearman's Camp at 3 a.m. Before it appeared, Sir R. Buller again rode across from Spearman's. Sir C. Warren had already received a message from him, warning him of a possible counter-attack on the left, and impressing the necessity of caution in attempting "any enterprise further to the left at present."*

Warren and Buller confer at 10 a.m., Jan. 22nd.

At 10 a.m. an interview between the two Generals took place. In the course of the discussion on the situation Sir C. Warren, adhering to his plan of forcing the Fairview—Rosalie road, now declared the impossibility of doing so unless Spion Kop, which lay over it to the eastward, were first taken. To this Sir R. Buller did not disagree, though he continually preferred an attempt at the other flank, i.e., at Bastion Hill and beyond, and this, despite his message of the early morning. At the conclusion of the meeting he returned to his own Headquarters, leaving Sir C. Warren under the impression that he was to adopt one of the following four courses, viz., to retire altogether; to attack the Boer right either east or west of Bastion Hill, or their left at Spion Kop. Sir C. Warren once more pronounced in favour of the fourth alternative, and Talbot

Impression produced on Warren by conference.

* See Appendix 9 (K).

THE SPION KOP CAMPAIGN. 373

Coke having come in with his brigade at noon, he summoned some of his General Officers and invited their views.* The meeting resulted in a decision that both the westerly movements, entailing as they did a frontal attack across the open against an enemy strongly posted and, if the reports were true,† in equal or superior numbers, were too hazardous. Although the report from Ladysmith quoted was mistaken, Sir C. Warren had no information in disproof of it, other than the negative messages of Dundonald's scouts, who sighted no large bodies of Boers in the direction of Acton Homes. The Boer right flank, instead of resting on a point opposite Bastion Hill, seemed now to overlap it considerably to the westward, so that an advance from the hill would be subject to an enveloping fire from the outset. Discarding these alternatives, then, Sir C. Warren forthwith decided to adopt the last of those among which he was to choose, the capture of Spion Kop. *He decides to attack Spion Kop and invites the views of his subordinate Generals. Reasons for his decision.*

That mountain, whose bold outline, arresting the eye even in this grand theatre of highlands, soared high above those of the surrounding heights, seemed to command them all, including Tabanyama. If it could be won, and artillery placed upon its summit, the enemy along the Rangeworthy Heights, invulnerable to a frontal attack, would be probably as thoroughly outflanked, and more thoroughly dominated than from the other flank, Acton Homes itself. This, though not certain, was at least as likely as any other theory of the little known and ill-mapped district whose problems confronted the British Generals at every turn. Farmers were present with the force who had long driven their cattle to and from grazing on the slopes, but the topographical descriptions of such men, seemingly accurate, but in reality vague for military use, seldom throw much light on the dark places of commanders who project operations in a strange terrain. Spion Kop lay about three miles north-east from Trickhardt's Drift, from which the ground rose towards it easily at first, then more steeply, but still practicable, as it merged into the *Spion Kop, once crowned with artillery, would appear to dominate and outflank the Boer position. Uncertainty of topography of the surrounding country.*

---

* Present—Generals Clery, Hildyard, Talbot Coke and Woodgate.

† See Appendix 9 (E).

long spur of the southern extremity. Its western flank, exposed to view from the British bivouacs, fell rapidly, in parts precipitously, to the ravine dividing it from Three Tree Hill. The eastern sides, imperfectly seen from Lyttelton's position, dropped almost sheer from the crest, and below were nearly everywhere excessively steep and broken. The summit was reported to be flat, of rocky soil, and covered with boulders. From Sir C. Warren's positions the mountain could be approached by two tracks, one from Three Tree Hill, the other, and longer, from Trickhardt's Drift up the northern spur. Thus much, with the fact of its being held by the enemy in uncertain strength, was known of Spion Kop. The dimensions of the top, its relation to the surrounding eminences, and the nature of the country immediately beyond it to the north, north-east and north-west, were only to be discovered when the mountain should be in British possession. Determining now to effect this without further delay, Sir C. Warren detailed two of Talbot Coke's battalions to seize the hill that very night. But Coke, having examined the ground, which he saw for the first time, asked for time to reconnoitre more fully. To this Sir C. Warren assented, and the assault was postponed until the following night. Although on the eve of operations which would require mutual familiarity between units and staff, orders were issued at 1.20 p.m. for a temporary re-organisation of the forces, which were divided into two distinct tactical commands, the "right" and "left" attacks,* the left being given to Clery, the right to Talbot Coke. So passed January the 22nd.

Approaches to Spion Kop from Warren's position.

Warren details two battalions to seize the hill on night of 22nd,

but postpones the assault until the 23rd.

He re-organises his forces.

Jan. 23rd. Warren reconnoitres the mountain,

and discusses the situation with Buller,

At 4 a.m. on the morning of the 23rd, whilst along all the ridges the rifles and cannon of both combatants re-awakened, Sir C. Warren rode out to reconnoitre for himself the approaches to Spion Kop, which he did as thoroughly as circumstances permitted. On his return he was met by Sir R. Buller, and again a discussion took place regarding the position of affairs. On this occasion the Commander-in-Chief, desirous of immediate action of some sort, reduced the former four alternatives to two —attack or retirement—advocating once more, however, an

* See Appendix 9 (L).

advance from the left.* That course Warren had already rejected, partly on account of Sir R. Buller's own warning of the day before. He now showed the Commander-in-Chief his orders for the attack on Spion Kop, which, but for the postponement at Talbot Coke's request, would have been already in course of execution. In these orders Sir R. Buller made no alteration beyond desiring that Woodgate should replace Coke in command of the actual assault, the latter officer being still lame from the effects of a lately broken leg, and therefore at a disadvantage in leading over ground so steep as Spion Kop. Sir R. Buller then returned to Headquarters, and Sir C. Warren immediately issued to Coke his orders for the attack.† The force, under command of Woodgate, would consist of two battalions of infantry, Thorneycroft's mounted infantry, and half a company of Royal Engineers. A start was to be made before midnight. Coke would make all necessary arrangements for the place of assembly, for the carriage by mules of extra ammunition, for the provision of one day's complete ration to be carried by each soldier; he was further to arrange that all natives in the neighbourhood of the operation were confined to their kraals. The Imperial Light Infantry, a Colonial battalion which had arrived at Trickhardt's Drift from Frere at 9 a.m., were attached to Coke's command, and he was instructed to post them upon the heights above Wright's Farm to act as a support to Woodgate, for whom also a Mountain battery, which was still on the road behind the Imperial Light Infantry, was intended as soon as it should arrive. Coke was further ordered to provide means for the entrenching of the top of Spion Kop, for the establishment thence of signalling communication, and, finally, for the general support of the assaulting column by all the troops of the right attack.

[margin: who acquiesces in the scheme for the attack, and places Woodgate in charge of the assault.]

[margin: Woodgate's troops.]

[margin: Coke to take measures for supply and secrecy.]

[margin: Supports detailed to Woodgate.]

On receipt of the above, Coke, in turn, issued his attack orders,‡ wherein Woodgate was desired to select two battalions of his brigade (11th) to accompany him. The place of assembly

[margin: Coke's orders for Jan. 24th.]

* See South African Despatches.
† See Appendix 9 (M).
‡ See Appendix 9 (N).

was fixed at a point immediately east of the Royal Engineers' bivouac, in rear of the artillery positions on Three Tree Hill; the time of forming up to be 7 p.m. Each man would carry 150 rounds of ammunition, one day's rations, and a filled water-bottle. Mules were allotted to carry extra ammunition and a supply of water in tin biscuit-boxes; the stretchers would be utilised to transport the entrenching tools. In order to watch the natives, the Royal Dragoons were to piquet the kraals.

<small>Woodgate issues orders for the actual attack.</small>

Woodgate's brigade-orders followed shortly,* detailing the following force for the attack—2nd Royal Lancaster regiment (six companies), 2nd Lancashire Fusiliers, two companies 1st South Lancashire regiment, Thorneycroft's mounted infantry (180 men), and half the 17th company Royal Engineers. Water was to be borne in waterproof sheets on pack mules; the stretchers would carry twenty picks and twenty shovels. The wagons containing the men's great coats, the water carts, and the machine guns would follow the troops as soon as possible. An alteration was at first made in the rendezvous. Woodgate knew nothing of the track leading from Three Tree Hill up the mountain side. He therefore appointed Wright's Farm as the place of assembly, whence the route from Trickhardt's Drift, with which he was acquainted, could be picked up. The effect of this was that later a portion of the column had already almost reached the farm when Woodgate was made aware of the superiority of the spot selected by Coke, which considerably shortened the march, and changed his rendezvous accordingly.

<small>Warren, at 7 p.m. on the 23rd, notifies all his troops of the attack, and arranges for supporting fire.</small>

At 7 p.m. Sir C. Warren, in Field Force orders,† informed the whole of his troops that Spion Kop was to be attacked that night, and instructed them how to act should opposition be encountered. The battalions and batteries near Three Tree Hill were to be prepared to support, directing their fire especially towards the line of advance of the enemy's reinforcements which would be illuminated by the star shell of the artillery. It was left to the discretion of Clery, in command of the left attack—which still lay where it had been since January 20th—to create a diversion (by fire only) against the enemy on his front. During

* See Appendix 9.(O). † See Appendix 9 (P).

THE SPION KOP CAMPAIGN. 377

the 23rd the 2nd Devon regiment had been withdrawn from Bastion Hill, moving next day to Three Tree Hill; the 19th battery, Royal Field artillery, also brought across from the left, was to be placed upon a ridge north of Wright's Farm, whence it could command the Nek between Green Hill and Conical Hill. The guns of this, and all the other batteries, were carefully laid on various points in the Boer line, and all arrangements made for firing in the dark. As night fell Woodgate's troops moved unseen towards their place of assembly, and thereafter the stir of expectancy disturbed the widely dispersed bivouacs of the rest of the army. *[Movements of troops to support Woodgate.]*

To complete the account of the position of the army on the night of the assault on Spion Kop, the doings of General Lyttelton, since he, at daybreak on January 17th, had secured both banks of Potgieter's Drift,* must be now recorded. Since that date Lyttelton had never ceased to communicate with Sir C. Warren, informing him of his readiness to co-operate by day or night, as might seem most advantageous. Though Sir C. Warren had at no time gained ground enough to render such co-operation necessary, nevertheless Lyttelton, having entrenched his force, rather than remain inactive, made attempts to draw as many as possible of the enemy to his own front and away from Sir C. Warren's. In rear of his position at the drift the two 4.7-in. Naval guns had been emplaced on Mount Alice, and the eight 12-prs. on the plateau to its north. On the night of January 19th Lyttelton sent two 12-prs. across the river to the bridgehead position. Early next morning the 1st Durham Light Infantry relieved the 3rd King's Royal Rifles on The Kopjes, and at 10.30 a.m. the last-named battalion left cover and began a demonstration against the Brakfontein ridges. Advancing by half-battalions, which diverged on either side of the Ladysmith road, the battalion approached sufficiently near to the Boer trenches to draw from them a warm fire. As no useful purpose could be served by pressing the reconnaissance more closely, the Rifles, having played with the enemy all day, retired, still briskly fired upon, and regained The Kopjes with a loss of *[Lyttelton's movements and dispositions from 17th to 23rd Jan.]*

* See map No. 19 (a).

seventeen casualties. Next day, the 21st, the remaining six 12-prs. were withdrawn from beneath Mount Alice and established about The Kopjes, the King's Royal Rifles recrossing the river to replace a battalion of Coke's departed brigade as escort to the 4.7-in. guns. Beyond this, and the constant practice of their heavy artillery, the troops at Potgieter's, despite the eagerness of their commander, had hitherto been forced to remain almost out of sight of the long battle to the westward, close at hand as it was. Events now suddenly called upon them for an active and honourable share therein.

CHAPTER XXII.

THE SPION KOP CAMPAIGN.

THE CAPTURE AND EVACUATION OF SPION KOP.*

SHORTLY after 9 p.m. Woodgate's detachment left the rendezvous and, headed by the Lancashire Fusiliers, moved up the long gully which led towards Spion Kop. At the Brigadier's request, an officer from the Headquarters Staff, Lieut.-Colonel C. à Court, accompanied the force. It was a cloudy and oppressive night; at intervals a warm drizzle of rain fell, clearing now and again to brief periods of dim starlight. Little or nothing would have been known of the route to be followed had not Colonel Thorneycroft, who was present in command of a part of his own regiment of mounted infantry, fortunately used the last few moments of light to note and roughly sketch a few landmarks on the mountain side. After about half a mile of the march he went to the General and offered his services as guide. Thereupon Woodgate halted and desired Thorneycroft to take his men to the front and lead the column, which then resumed the advance in the following order :— Woodgate starts; he selects Thorneycroft to lead the column.

> Thorneycroft's mounted infantry, dismounted (18 officers 180 men). Order of march.
> 2nd Lancashire Fusiliers.
> Half company 17th company Royal Engineers.
> 2nd Royal Lancaster regiment (six companies).
> 1st South Lancashire regiment (two companies).

Thorneycroft himself, accompanied by two officers and two

* See map No. 20.

soldiers of his corps, moved a short distance ahead. His task would have been one of great difficulty even to a man intimately acquainted with the ground; yet, though periodical halts were necessary to enable him to verify his position, neither the darkness, nor the broken and ever-changing contours of the mountain were able to lure him from the few marks which, from a long distance, and in the waning light of the evening, he had photographed upon his mind. At midnight the column reached the first of these, a group of Kaffir kraals about one-third of the way up the ascent. Thence the hillside increased in difficulty at every yard. The long grass, in itself an obstacle at night, concealed boulders and crevices over which a way had actually to be felt by the hands of the climbing soldiers. The advance became a slow scramble. The grinding of nailed boots upon the stones, the clatter of accoutrements and entrenching tools, seemed to banish all hopes of secrecy, and the burst of firing which would show the movement to have been detected by the Boer piquet was momentarily expected. But a head wind favoured the movement, and the column reached undetected all Thorneycroft's points in succession; first a clump of trees, next a ledge of steep rocks, and finally a grassy slope fringed with trees, which had been marked as leading directly to the summit. The climb was over; the enemy, if, indeed, he were still on the hill, lay close ahead, hidden in the dense fog which wrapped the mountain top. Arrived at the edge of the open plateau, Thorneycroft's men, who had been climbing in double files, halted, and having formed line, stole forward again over the crest with fixed bayonets, expectant of a volley, which they had been previously ordered to receive by flinging themselves to the ground. Behind them, the Lancashire Fusiliers followed closely in column of double companies, single rank, about one hundred yards intervening between the companies. Suddenly a loud challenge, twice repeated in Dutch, rang out from the depths of the mist, followed by a burst of fire from a surprised Boer piquet, whose position was revealed by a line of dancing flashes from a dozen rifles. Flat upon the grass dropped the soldiers, and lay motionless in accordance with their orders, suffering few casualties whilst the bullets whistled close above them for two or three minutes. Then, when the magazines of the Mausers were nearly exhausted, and the fire slackened, the word was given, and the men, leaping to their feet, charged down upon the piquet, which disappeared into the protecting fog, escaping with the loss of one man only. The rest of the Boer outposts upon the mountain, numbering some seventy men, vanished without offering opposition, and undiscovered. Thus, at 4 a.m., by skill and good fortune, the summit of Spion Kop was almost bloodlessly delivered into Woodgate's hands. The troops, congratulating themselves that in these commanding crests, which they had often eyed from far below, they had now the key of a strong position, needed little encouragement to raise a loud cheer to acquaint those in the valley of their success.

is driven off.

The summit occupied at 4 a.m. on Jan. 24th, 1900.

The gunners of the batteries, who had stood long at their pieces waiting for that distant shout, instantly acknowledged it with the pre-arranged star shell, this signal sending the news of the capture to all the scattered bivouacs, and to the fighting lines still clinging to the verge of Rangeworthy.

The artillery guns announce this success to the remainder of the army.

Woodgate at once gave orders to entrench. But though he thought he stood upon the summit, since the ground seemed to fall gently away to the northward, what that summit was like in form and surface, how it stood with respect to the enemy, where indeed the enemy was, all this the impenetrable fog rendered purely conjectural. Nevertheless, in a few minutes the Royal Engineers had laid down the trace of a defence work the front of which, some three hundred yards long, faced northward, with a blunt salient, shorter arms being thrown slightly back on the right and left. The men then set to work. But both spade and pick were soon foiled by the nature of the ground. The removal of a few inches of soil uncovered a bed of rock; the stones upon the surface proved too massive and too deeply imbedded to be handled, or too small for useful cover. When eighteen inches of trench and parapet combined had been with much toil completed, the work came to a standstill, and almost immediately, the mist, lifting a little from the mountain, revealed the fact that the paltry cover had been constructed

Woodgate entrenches in the fog,

on very difficult ground in which to dig.

382 THE WAR IN SOUTH AFRICA.

Owing to the fog, the works are wrongly placed.

in the wrong place. Truly, it traversed the top of the hill, but this, shelving downward in front, dropped so suddenly and steeply less than two hundred yards away that the ground below was invisible or "dead." There, then, was the tactical crest of the plateau, below which the enemy was free to assemble unseen, within decisive range of the trench which had been made upon the natural crest. No time was lost in sending forward parties of Royal Engineers, covered by outposts, to entrench also this outer edge, but both workmen and tools were again baffled by the immovable boulders and the adamantine ground. As the Sappers laboured here, a few flights of bullets came amongst them, to which the covering parties replied. Then the mist descended again, and in the silence which returned, the sentries, standing on the forward ridge line, became conscious of a stir and a low buzz of voices on the invisible slopes below them. A little later, spasmodic bursts of firing again broke from various points in the ring of vapour which encircled Spion Kop. It was evident that the enemy was close at hand and alert, and Woodgate organised his troops for defence. On the right of the main trench he posted four companies of the Lancashire Fusiliers, supported by the other four in a smaller sangar écheloned in rear. Thorneycroft's mounted infantry were stationed in the obtuse angle of the centre. On their left the Royal Lancaster regiment took post, and beyond them again the two companies of the South Lancashire regiment occupied a short sangar thrown back on the left. About 7.15 a.m., whilst these dispositions were being made, Woodgate despatched à Court with a letter to Sir C. Warren, informing him of his success. Half an hour later the fog began to disperse, and as it rolled away from the mountain, a steady fire broke from each neighbouring feature as it emerged within range, until the air was clear, and Spion Kop stood disclosed, a target to them all. From Green Hill and Conical Hill, and from trenches in the rolling ground between, a stream of musketry at medium ranges began to pour upon the front and left front of Woodgate's defences, which, moreover, soon shook and splintered under the shells from three field guns and a pom-pom coming from

The Boers rally and return.

Woodgate's dispositions.

He reports by letter to Warren, 7.15 a.m.

The fog lifts, and discloses Woodgate to the Boers,

THE SPION KOP CAMPAIGN. 383

the same quarter. A mile to the eastward, no excessive range for the accurate Mausers and the well-sheltered marksmen who levelled them, Boers posted on the Twin Peaks sent a fusilade which searched the British trench from flank to flank. Close to the right front, only four hundred yards away, a body of the enemy, securely ensconced on a kopje which crowned a spur of Spion Kop itself, shot point-blank into the flank of the main trench and into the rear of the piquets and parties working upon the forward crest-line. These troops, who were practically without cover, were thus almost surrounded by fire, and were speedily forced to fall back upon the main trench, leaving sentries scattered among the rocks. In this manner the plateau, so quietly won, became in a few moments the focus of a severe fire, resounding with the bursting of shells and crack of musketry. Soon the 4.7-in. guns on Mount Alice endeavoured to blow the enemy from the kopje close to the flank. But the Boers there, creeping to the northern side, were safe from the lyddite shells, and continued to shoot with deadly rapidity, still having the whole length of Woodgate's line in full view. To one acquainted with the Boer tactics, such steady shooting from a distance, and the presence of a band of the enemy so near and so venturesome, might well indicate a settled purpose. Nicholson's Nek, Colesberg, and Wagon Hill, had shown what was the type of a Boer attack, and exemplified the dangers which so often seemed to lie in wait for British detachments on the tops of isolated South African kopjes. If there had been any man upon the summit of Spion Kop with leisure to examine the hill, he had perceived that the Boers, to whom entrenchment was an instinct, had nevertheless raised no schanzes thereon, a fact suggesting their conviction that it was untenable by friend or foe. A glance northward, and on either side, the noting of the angles at which the shells and clouds of bullets were arriving would have shown that Spion Kop was but a cape projecting into the enemy's positions. As such, indeed, had the Republican Generals recognised it. The loss of the hill dismayed them little; they had never seriously provided against its occupation, for, retake it or not as they might, they knew that it could

[Marginal notes: who search the summit with fire. The troops on the forward crest withdrawn. Boer reasons for not holding Spion Kop in strength.]

not gravely threaten their own commanding and enveloping positions. Scarcely had the cheers of its captors died away, when General Schalk Burger, whose men had provided the outposts, sent back to the laagers for reinforcements. Shortly after daybreak, when the fog was still thick, over five hundred burghers, responding to the call, had gathered at the foot of the northern slopes of Spion Kop, ready to storm the hill. Following their invariable custom, to rely less on a frontal attack than on the effects of a flanking and converging fire, small detachments then pushed out to right and left, as Pohlmann's Policemen and the Free Staters had done at Nicholson's Nek, and before the mist rose, were in positions on either side of the British trench. Then, the gunners on the heights behind having been warned to co-operate, the advance began; not in the impetuous fashion of European soldiery, emulous as much of personal glory as of victory, but in the slow and cautious manner of men who, valuing their lives, stalk dangerous game; stealing unseen from boulder to boulder, from crevice to crevice; firing rapidly, but never at random, the more formidable because they never intended to close with an enemy who fixed his hopes upon the bayonet. Soon after 8 a.m. some of the boldest, having crept up under the north-eastern crest, covered by the fire of the Boers on the kopje to the east, were within fifty yards of the main trench. About that time Woodgate, seeing the inefficiency of the field of fire from this main trench, decided to reinforce the sentries on the edge of the plateau. In the face of severe fire some sixty men of Thorneycroft's mounted infantry ran out to the front, detachments of the Lancashire Fusiliers going forward to the right and left respectively, thus occupying in a thin semi-circle the outer crest-line of the summit.* At 8.30 a.m., Woodgate, whilst walking calmly around the hill supervising the defences, was mortally wounded by a shrapnel ball in the head. The command then fell upon Colonel M. Crofton, Royal Lancaster regiment. This officer immediately sent to Headquarters a message which, however dictated—and with regard to this there is doubt,

* See map No. 20.

THE SPION KOP CAMPAIGN. 385

the sentence being only verbally given to the signaller—Sir C. Warren received at 9.50 a.m. in the following form :—

"Reinforce at once or all is lost. General dead."*

This communication much astonished Sir C. Warren. Repeating it immediately to Sir R. Buller and Lyttelton, he replied at 10.5 a.m. to Crofton that reinforcements were on the way up, and that there must be no surrender. The reinforcements referred to consisted of the 2nd Dorset and 2nd Middlesex regiments from Coke's brigade, and the Imperial Light Infantry. From the moment when Woodgate had begun to climb the hill these had been held in readiness, and two of the units had, in fact, actually started for Spion Kop before the receipt of Crofton's signal. When, at 9.25 a.m., the severity of the engagement became apparent to Sir C. Warren, he instructed Coke to send a battalion to assist. Coke first despatched the Imperial Light Infantry, which had reached the foot of Spion Kop from Wright's Farm before dawn, and next, at 9.40 a.m., the Middlesex regiment, the Dorset replacing the Imperial Light Infantry in reserve. Ten minutes later came Crofton's alarming signal. Sir C. Warren then moved the 2nd Somerset Light Infantry to a convenient position on Piquet Hill, and having thus provided for support from his side, telegraphed at 9.53 a.m. to Lyttelton asking him to assist from Potgieter's.† That General had already been active since 4 a.m. endeavouring to draw the enemy from Spion Kop by means of a feint against Brakfontein, carried out by the 1st Durham Light Infantry and the 1st Rifle Brigade, covered by the fire of the Naval guns. The demonstration was withdrawn by Sir R. Buller before much progress had been made. In five minutes from the receipt of Sir C. Warren's message, two squadrons of Bethune's mounted infantry and the 2nd Scottish Rifles received orders to go to the help of their comrades viâ Kaffir Drift.‡ At the same time, in response to

Warren's action in reply to the message.

Lyttelton, who had demonstrated since 4 a.m., sends reinforcements.

---

* For correspondence regarding this message, see South African Despatches. Also Appendix 10 (A).

† See Appendix 10 (B).

‡ See map No. 19.

VOL. II. 25

further messages from Sir C. Warren, Lyttelton caused the Naval 12-pr. guns to turn their fire on to the eastern slopes of the contested hill. At 10.15 a.m. an urgent appeal for aid reached Lyttelton directed from the kop,* just as he had sent word to the 3rd King's Royal Rifles to get under arms and move towards it. Some hours had necessarily to elapse before these troops could reach the distant scene of the fighting, and in that interval matters on the summit grew critical. Upon the plateau, which was now exposed in every part in the clear air and the full glare of the sun, the Boer fire from far and near was concentrated with ever-increasing effect. Under cover of it, and shooting fast themselves, the attacking burghers were, by 10 a.m., almost amongst the foremost British sangars, which were pestered from so many directions at once that the men behind them sometimes leaped from side to side of the low walls, uncertain as to which side afforded most cover. Whilst so doing many were killed; for to move was to become the target of rifles held, within a few yards, by adepts in snap-shooting. Here and there the Boers were actually in possession of parts of the outer crest-line, where the fall of the ground behind them, their flat hats, which, unlike the British helmets, did not show above the rocks, their cunning in taking shelter, and in lying quietly behind it until certain that they were undetected, all combining to keep them invisible until their bitter fire at close quarters suddenly threatened to empty every trench within their view. At about 10.30 a.m. the damage from such a band upon the right front became so intolerable that a party of twenty of Thorneycroft's mounted infantry, led by an officer, charged out of the main trench, and attempted to oust them. But though the soldiers won the rocks, a deadly fire converged upon them from other Boers lurking to the right and left, and they had to fall back with the loss of half their number. The enemy then closed in still nearer, and shooting across the plateau, aimed into the backs of the men in the small sangars on the other side. Thereupon Thorneycroft himself, who was still in the centre angle of the main defence, calling upon all near him to follow,

* See Appendix 10 (C).

THE SPION KOP CAMPAIGN. 387

dashed out of the trench, and bore down on the outer crest-line; about twenty men of his own corps—all that were left in the main work—and the same number of the Lancashire Fusiliers charging in his wake. Seeing this, every Boer turned his rifle in that direction, and so terrible a discharge met the party that they were almost destroyed within a few yards. The survivors then crawled back behind the shelter they had quitted. Nevertheless, in some parts, small detachments of troops did contrive, with many losses of men and officers, to reach the outer crest, which, though every moment in extreme jeopardy, never fell altogether into the hands of the enemy. Before long, too, the reinforcements sent by Coke, viz., the Middlesex regiment and the Imperial Light Infantry, began to arrive irregularly on the summit, the steepness of the climb, and other circumstances, preventing their reaching the battlefield together. About noon four companies of the first-named battalion were in the firing line, thrusting themselves in wherever they seemed to be required, for by this time the whole front resounded with shouts for reinforcements, and the new-comers in response hurried forward in all directions to stiffen the melting defence. In this respect the situation was peculiar, and in favour of the British. Whilst their line of communication was so far clear, and they could be reinforced at any time, the Boers who were actually on the hill could expect no addition to their numbers. The saddle intervening between them and their main body at Conical Hill was swept by the fire of the artillery at Three Tree Hill, whilst, on the other side, the heavy guns at Mount Alice shelled all the ground between Spion Kop and the Twin Peaks, and practically isolated both. Thus the eastern and western flanks of the kop were alike secure from an assault in strength, the rear remaining free. But assault would have been but a minor risk compared to that which momentarily threatened to clear the hill of its defenders. The intense rifle fire, coming from and falling at all angles and ranges, the long-range bullets dropping over the low walls, those fired from a few yards tearing a way through the interstices of the stones, or sweeping from end to end of the trenches, the shrapnel

Reinforcements begin to arrive on Spion Kop,

and are hurried into the firing line.

The British advantages of ground

which rained incessantly upon every quarter and sought out every nook, the flights of little shells from the pom-poms racing in procession of explosions across the plateau, these were dangers which the soldiers would willingly have exchanged for close combat, for these it was impossible to avoid, to deal with in return, or for long to survive. The enemy remained almost invisible, suffering instantaneous losses, however, when at rare intervals exposure became unavoidable; for the troops were watching as keenly as they were watched, and their shooting was not inferior. So cunningly placed were the Boer guns that, though visible to the men whom they punished, neither the Field artillerymen nor those serving the heavy guns were able to locate, much less to silence them, though they searched earnestly every likely crevice within view. Under such disadvantages the defence of Spion Kop was maintained with fine tenacity for many hours.

<small>counteracted by those of the Boers.</small>

To the troops engaged the struggle seemed to be by no means without hope. Every moment that movement in another part of the field was looked for which would divert the fire from Spion Kop, and throw the whole Boer line of battle on the defensive. Especially towards the Rangeworthy Heights were eyes continually turned throughout the fight, for there Hart's and Hildyard's brigades were still extended along the crests, in formation ready to obey an order to attack. But no such order reached them; the troops on Rangeworthy remained immobile, and Spion Kop continued to be the scene instead of the pivot of a battle.

<small>The troops on Spion Kop expect some support by Clery,</small>

<small>who, however, makes no sign.</small>

Sir R. Buller, watching the action through a telescope from Mount Alice, had early realised the gravity of the situation. Many of the incidents on the summit were plainly visible to him, and even at that distance, the energetic and courageous movements of a single officer—Thorneycroft—a man of great stature, were to be singled out from the swaying knots of figures. At 11.40 a.m. Sir C. Warren received from the Commander-in-Chief the following telegram:—

<small>Buller, seeing Thorneycroft's activity through a telescope,</small>

<small>suggests to Warren that Thorneycroft should be placed in command on the top of the hill.</small>

"Unless you put some really good hard fighting man in command on the top, you will lose the hill. I suggest Thorneycroft."

At 11.50 a.m., therefore, Sir C. Warren heliographed to

Crofton, who, since Woodgate's mortal wound, had exercised command, as follows :—

"With the approval of the Commander-in-Chief, I place Lieut.-Colonel Thorneycroft in command of the summit, with the local rank of Brigadier-General." _{Warren gives him command at 11.50 a.m.}

To this no answer was received, then, or at any time. Forty minutes earlier, General Talbot Coke, in command of the "Right Attack," had, by Sir C. Warren's instructions, proceeded to Spion Kop in order to be in closer touch with that portion of his command which was engaged. At 12.50 p.m., having arrived near the summit, Coke despatched a message to Sir C. Warren (received at 2.20 p.m.) in which he informed the General that the top of the hill was reported to be crowded with men who were holding out well, that he had stopped the movement of further reinforcements beyond the point where he himself was, but that the troops in front knew that help was close at hand. Though in general charge of the Right Attack he was not told of Thorneycroft's appointment as commander of the summit. Thorneycroft himself only heard it from the lips of his orderly officer, who had seen the message soon after it had reached the signalling station. Though the responsibility for action thereafter devolved upon the Colonel, his appointment could make but little change in his immediate duties. His presence had long been urgently necessary in the actual trenches, where his voice and example succeeded in maintaining spirits which every moment were being more sorely tried. For Coke's report, which he did not personally verify, was, as has been seen, over-sanguine. By 1 p.m. the situation on Spion Kop was in reality critical. Most of the officers and very many men had been killed or wounded, and the long exposure to a destructive fire, under a blazing sun, without food or water, had all but exhausted the endurance of the survivors, though their numbers had been maintained by the previous reinforcements at a strength of about 1,800 men. The Boer fire had, if anything, increased in intensity, and even the path by which the reinforcements must arrive was now swept by shrapnel.

_{Coke goes to Spion Kop at 11.10 a.m., and at 12.50 p.m. describes the situation to Warren.}

_{Thorneycroft hears of his appointment, but cannot leave fighting line to supervise.}

_{The situation at 1 p.m. becomes very serious.}

Thorneycroft rallies part of the troops, temporarily broken.

Soon after 1 p.m. a party of about 170 men in one of the exposed trenches on the right front, fired at from all directions, and deprived of their officers, suddenly abandoned hope, leaped to their feet and surrendered to the enemy, who were within a few yards. The Boers were amongst them in a moment, and having secured their prisoners, made as if to advance further across the plateau, waving handkerchiefs and shouting to the troops in rear to lay down their arms. At once that dangerous confusion began to arise in which, from pure misunderstanding, disaster may easily ensue with scattered and exhausted troops. But Thorneycroft, who was at hand, instantly grasped the situation. Dashing out towards the Boers, he shouted that there was no surrender, and that they must go back. Then, calling to the soldiers about him, he led them back to a line of rocks which bounded the rear of the plateau. Thence fire was opened on the adventurous enemy, who dropped to the ground and replied hotly at first, then fell back to the cover of the captured trench. At this moment a company of the second half of the Middlesex regiment arrived at the summit close to the rocks. Seizing the opportunity, Thorneycroft immediately ordered a charge, and heading the rush across the plateau, drove the Boers from the trench and re-established the line of defence along the crest. Having thus retrieved a situation of extreme danger, Thorneycroft posted himself in a central position in rear of the main trench. Thence he directed the movements of the remainder of the reinforcements which came up soon after, pushing them into the firing-line to the right or left as occasion demanded. Although his actual assumption of command was evident to all, it must be noted that at this period none except himself and his orderly officer knew of his appointment from Headquarters.

He posts his reinforcements.

Situation at 2.30 p.m.

For the next hour, from 1.30 p.m. to 2.30 p.m., the situation remained unchanged, excepting that the enemy, convinced of the futility of assault, appeared no more on the plateau, but placed his hopes on the rain of shells and bullets which he poured unceasingly into the half a square mile of exposed area crowded with British troops. During that period Sir C. Warren, who, since Crofton's appeal, had had literally no news from the

Warren's efforts to obtain information.

battlefield, made many attempts to communicate with the summit, but without avail. The heliograph on Spion Kop had long since been blown to pieces by a shell, and there was as little chance of replying to messages as of delivering them on a field where no man could move for any distance and remain alive. The first intelligence received by the General was therefore at 2.20 p.m.—Coke's message sent off at 12.50 p.m.— and, as has been seen, it was rather reassuring than otherwise. Nothing further reached him for an hour and a half, when a second message from Coke, and one from Sir R. Buller, acquainted him more nearly with the true situation on Spion Kop. On the kop itself Thorneycroft, having disposed all his available troops, wrote, at 2.30 p.m., a letter to Sir C. Warren which depicted affairs still more fully; but many things happened before this and the two above-mentioned messages were in the hands of Sir C. Warren. Thorneycroft had not long finished his despatch when the Scottish Rifles, whose approach from Potgieter's had been seen from afar, arrived on the summit and joined in the fight.* Since the forenoon (see page 385) the march of Lyttelton's contingent had been uninterrupted. The Scottish Rifles, the first to receive orders, passing through the Durham Light Infantry, and the 1st Rifle Brigade, which held the bridge-head at The Kopjes, moved to the south bank of the Tugela, and thence across the neck of the great river loop to Kaffir Drift, two miles to the north-eastward.† Here the battalion re-crossed to the northern bank, and made for the southern spur of Spion Kop. The ascent was toilsome in the extreme. The track, which was both steep and narrow, was congested by ascending and descending stretcher-bearers, by carriers of water, by wounded men, by soldiers wandering down, dazed by the fighting and fatigue, by others pressing upward to join the battle. It was possible to advance only in single file, and in this tedious formation six companies and a half pushed on to the summit, whilst one company and a half were detailed to carry up water, for which there was urgent need in the trenches. A heavy shrapnel fire burst over the van of the

At 2.30 p.m. he receives Coke's message of 12.50 p.m.

Lyttelton's reinforcements; the Scottish Rifles arrive,

* See map No. 20 (a). † See map 19.

battalion as it emerged to the top of the pathway, necessitating instant deployment. As the companies prepared to cross the plateau, a hot fusilade was suddenly encountered at close quarters from a band of the enemy ensconced on the left front. These were fiercely charged by a detachment of fifteen officers and men, and though four times as strong as their assailants, fled from the bayonets. But the fifteen Scottish Riflemen had rushed into a trap; a murderous flank fire from another party of the enemy struck them, and all were destroyed. The rest of the battalion, working skilfully forward in small bodies, with considerable loss but without a check, were soon (about

and about 4 p.m. are in the front line. 4 p.m.) in the forefront, filling the many gaps and encouraging the defence with their presence.

The 3rd King's Royal Rifles Very different were the route and adventures of the other troops from Potgieter's, the 3rd King's Royal Rifles, the battalion which had received orders to advance some fifteen minutes later than the Scottish Rifles. As they moved off, Lyttelton, looking across to Spion Kop, noticed the arrival of reinforcements (i.e., the first half of the Middlesex regiment) on the summit, which seemed to be crowded with troops.* It appeared unnecessary, therefore, to send two battalions to the spot, and the General, scanning the country for a more effective position

ordered to attack the Twin Peaks; of support, settled on the Twin Peaks, and ordered the King's Royal Rifles to attack them. The idea was as bold as it was certain to be useful. The Peaks were more than three miles in a direct line—more than five miles *viâ* Kaffir Drift—from his base at Potgieter's Drift. The enemy was probably holding them in strength, for two Field guns and a pom-pom were firing from the northern slopes, and an incessant musketry could be heard assisting the artillery to thresh the troops on Spion

the importance of these kopjes. Kop. The capture of the Peaks would silence this fire, which was raking Thorneycroft's trenches, and Lyttelton determined to attempt it. Fully recognising the attendant risks, he enjoined extreme caution on the commanding officer of the Rifles.

Attack on Twin Peaks begins at 2 p.m. About 2 p.m. the battalion, leaving great coats by the river bank, so as to move unimpeded, forded the river at Kaffir Drift,

* See South African Despatches.

THE SPION KOP CAMPAIGN.   393

and advanced in attack formation, the right half battalion against the eastern Peak, the left against the western.* Each half battalion was thus formed: 1*st Line*—Halves of two companies in firing line at eighteen paces extension, supported at 200 yards distance by their complementary half companies at fifteen paces extension. 2*nd Line*—200 yards in rear of 1st line, two companies similarly disposed, at twelve paces extension. Upon the long undulating slopes which led from the river to the uplands, a smart fire, increasing at every yard in volume and accuracy, fell amongst the ranks. The occupants of the Peaks, consisting of over 200 men of the Carolina commando and Edwardes' Scouts, feared little for the safety of their almost inaccessible positions. A donga, at the foot of the hills, in which the soldiers took temporary cover, was heavily raked. Beyond it the ground rose at once, and though almost precipitous, there was at first little shelter from the rapid cross-fire which the enemy brought to bear on the clambering lines. Soon, however, the bulging sides of the kopjes, and little hollows which here and there indented them, afforded some dead ground, which was used to regain breath and re-form the trailing companies. Covered by heavy fire from the Naval guns, and pressing upward with such speed that the supports, which had opened a covering fire, had to desist almost as soon as they had begun, the Riflemen had all but gained the top when a difficulty was encountered on the right which caused a momentary check in that part. Here, as at Talana, a flat and open shelf skirted the hill in full view and within decisive range of the defenders on the crest, who poured down a destructive fire when the soldiers appeared upon it. In other parts, where the shelf was narrower, or some slight cover sheltered it, the troops rushed across with many casualties but without a pause. But the front of the company on the extreme right, essaying to do the same, was destroyed at the first attempt, and the rest had to file to the left where the passage was more easy. By 5.15 p.m. both Peaks were triumphantly carried, and immediately entrenched. The loss of these outworks struck a heavy blow

_{Twin Peaks held by about 200 Boers.}

_{Twin Peaks carried at 5.15 p.m.}

* See map 20 (a).

at the enemy, not only in this part of the field, but on and around Spion Kop itself. For, of the real attack on the hill, the factor most relied upon—the converging covering fire—was thus largely diminished, and that in its most effective quarter, the British right flank. As for the defenders of the Peaks themselves, they fled incontinently no less than eight miles north-eastward, their flight spreading consternation along the whole rear of the Boer army, which immediately began to stir uneasily and prepare for retreat.

Meanwhile the pressure on Spion Kop had relaxed but little, the Boer fire, indeed, increasing from the front and left front as the attack on the Twin Peaks caused it to dwindle from the right. Still Sir C. Warren, by a train of unfortunate circumstances, could gather no true idea of the situation, for his messages remained unanswered, and those he received, if confusing, were still not of an alarmist nature. At 4 p.m. Coke's second message, heliographed at 3.50 from the lower slopes, arrived, saying that, though the troops were suffering much from shell-fire, the hill was being cleared of Boers, the Scottish Rifles had reached the top, and that further reinforcements had been ordered up. A quarter of an hour after receipt of the above Thorneycroft's despatch was placed in his hands. It bore an addition, written by Coke as it passed him, and ran as follows:—

Warren can obtain no clear idea of the situation.

At 4.15 p.m. he receives letter sent at 2.30 p.m. by Thorneycroft,

"Spion Kop,
"24th January, 1900. 2.30 p.m.

"To Sir C. Warren.

"Hung on till last extremity with old force. Some of Middlesex here now and I hear Dorsets coming up, but force really inadequate to hold such a large perimeter. The enemy's guns on north-west sweep the whole of the top of the hill. They have also guns east; cannot you bring artillery fire to bear on north-west guns? What reinforcements can you send to hold the hill to-night? We are badly in need of water. There are many killed and wounded.
"ALEX. THORNEYCROFT."

"If you wish to really make a certainty of hill for night, you must send more infantry and attack enemy's guns."

on which Coke at 3 p.m. had written his own views.

"Spion Kop,
"24th January, 1900. 3 p.m.

"I have seen the above, and have ordered the Scottish Rifles and King's Royal Rifles to reinforce. The Middlesex regiment, Dorsetshire regiment, and

Imperial Light Infantry have also gone up, Bethune's mounted infantry (120 strong) also reinforce. We appear to be holding our own at present.

"J. TALBOT COKE, Major-General."

Thorneycroft's information and views, in themselves sufficiently grave, were thus, in a measure, discounted by the addendum of Coke, who Sir C. Warren had no reason to suppose was not—as, in fact, he was not—in closest touch with the events transpiring in his command on the summit of the mountain. A comparison of the times at which the above documents had been written still further tended to allay any fears which might have arisen in his mind. Coke's second message was timed fifty minutes later than his addendum to Thorneycroft's letter, and one hour and twenty minutes later than that letter itself, which thus appeared to depict a situation of the past. If a dangerous crisis had arisen, all that could be done in the way of reinforcements had, he thought, been done, and was still being done. So, too, in the matters of water, tools, and sandbags for the troops engaged, and guns with which to reply to the enemy's overmastering artillery. As for water, the Royal Engineers had been occupied since dawn, damming the spruit which flowed from Green Hill, and sending the water thus obtained up the hill in biscuit tins slung upon the backs of mules. They had also found and developed a small spring of turbid water about three-fourths of the way up the mountain. That the water, thus forwarded, could never pass through the fire and through crowds of men parched with their exertions or their wounds, and reach the firing-line was unknown to Sir C. Warren. Tools, he knew, had been taken up by Woodgate's original storming party, supplemented by others carried by the reinforcements. He was unaware that the stormers, clambering in the dark, had dropped half of the implements on the hillside, and that the rocky nature of the soil on the summit rendered difficult the employment of the remainder. In short, he had little evidence of the true needs and shortcomings of the defence other than that of his own eyes. Staff officers to acquaint him further, to see to the despatch and the proper delivery and distribution of necessaries, to take orders, to report on the

Thorneycroft's report discounted by Coke's memorandum.

Measures already taken by Warren to help the troops on Spion Kop.

varying phases of the action, to suggest or relieve him of details, such a staff was not so much defective as deficient, for it did not exist. As for guns, Sir C. Warren intended, and had prepared to do much during the coming night. On the steep slopes of Spion Kop slides had already been levelled by the Royal Engineers and drag-ropes laid by them in readiness for use. A rough road down the gorge by which the first advance had been made had also been constructed. True, an artillery officer, who had been sent up the mountain to try to find out the true position of the enemy's artillery, returned with the report that heavy guns would not be able to reach the top before dawn next morning, and that in any case the nature of the soil would almost prohibit the construction of proper emplacements. Nevertheless, Sir C. Warren, once more not realising the conditions—the extreme difficulty of getting heavy weapons on to the summit, the comparative inutility of lighter pieces, and, indeed, the practical impossibility of serving either in the contracted area which was swept incessantly by converging shot and shell—decided that the attempt should be made. Two Naval 12-prs. from The Kopjes, and the No. 4 Mountain battery from Frere, were already on their way, both batteries arriving at Trickhardt's Drift between 4 p.m. and 6 p.m.

Guns to be placed there during the night.

Meanwhile Spion Kop was being stubbornly maintained. The shallow trenches were full of dead and wounded; but the living, crouching amongst them, overwrought as they were with fatigue and heat, with hunger and thirst, and the continual bursting of the shells amongst their crowded shelters, yielded no ground, and endured their unanswerable punishment in silence. But it was plain that the efficiency of the defence was fast dwindling. Many of the soldiers were so exhausted that they fell asleep in the sangars, and were shot as they slept. Towards sunset the enemy redoubled the shell-fire and swept the plateau from end to end, and from side to side, with a searching stream of projectiles. At 5.50 p.m. Coke himself, who was still on the shelf below the summit where he had been all day, wrote to Sir C. Warren that the situation was extremely critical, that the men could not stand another day's

About sunset the summit is still staunchly held.

Coke at 5.50 p.m. reports the gravity of the situation.

THE SPION KOP CAMPAIGN. 397

repetition of such an experience; and that he had troops in hand to cover a withdrawal, should the General decide upon that step.* About an hour later Thorneycroft, in his turn, wrote to Headquarters describing the situation, and asking for orders.† But, as he wrote, the Boer fire grew hotter every moment, and Thorneycroft, looking about him on the stricken plateau, came to the conclusion that nothing but retirement could save the force entrusted to him. From the moment of his arrival on the kop he had perceived, and many with him, that the mountain of itself gained no military end, but could only be the means to an end. Without diversions in other parts of the field, without artillery with which to meet the hostile guns, the kop was as untenable as it was tactically useless. No diversions except the local attack on the Twin Peaks, which had no effect on the rifle or shell-fire from the north, had occurred; he had not been told that guns were being sent to him, and were they to come, he foresaw that they could only share his difficulties, not remove them. Support itself would not save the situation. There are junctures in a battle when reinforcements, to be useful, must be sent, not to the threatened, but to the free points, and this seemed to be such an occasion. As Brigadier-General the right of decision was his, and he determined to exercise it in favour of retreat. Before issuing orders to that effect he decided to confer with the regimental commanding officers on the hill. Proceeding to do so, the question as to who was really in command immediately arose amongst the officers. All were still unaware of Thorneycroft's appointment, and Coke, who shared the prevailing ignorance, had actually delegated the direction of affairs to Lieut.-Colonel A. W. Hill, Middlesex regiment. That officer was nowhere to be found. Darkness fell, and Thorneycroft, after consulting with the other commanding and senior officers, issued orders for an evacuation a little before 10 p.m., informing Sir C. Warren of his action by a note which only reached the General at 2 a.m. the next

marginalia: About 7 p.m. Thorneycroft asks Warren for orders.

marginalia: Thorneycroft decides to retire,

marginalia: issues necessary orders at 10 p.m., and writes to Warren.

---

* See Appendix 10 (D). This message reached Sir C. Warren at 7.50 p.m.

† See Appendix 10 (E). This message did not reach the General for over two hours.

morning.* The losses on Spion Kop itself during the day, out of a total of about 4,500 men (including the unengaged reserve) were as follows :—68 officers and 976 men killed, wounded, and missing ; or roughly, 23 per cent.

Casualties.

Whilst these events were in progress on Spion Kop, the King's Royal Rifles received orders to abandon the Twin Peaks. Sir R. Buller, who from Mount Alice had full view of Lyttelton's proceedings, had from the first doubted the advisability of splitting up a force upon the integrity of which much of the value of Sir C. Warren's operations might depend. By the detachment of the Scottish and King's Royal Rifles, Lyttelton's command became widely separated, part being at The Kopjes and Mount Alice, part upon the Twin Peaks, and part upon Spion Kop itself. There, at least, his help was scarcely required, for the proper reserve to the fighting line, the Dorset regiment, had itself not yet been drawn upon. Sir R. Buller had early attempted to stop the King's Royal Rifles, but with such speed had they launched their successful attack, that the order for recall was outpaced, and only reached the battalion when it had all but carried the positions. Retreat was at that time impossible. Waiting for the cover of darkness, the Rifles withdrew in perfect order, re-crossing the Tugela about midnight by a light bridge, which had been especially constructed under Mount Alice for their passage. Their efforts, though they seemed to be wasted, had been in reality as useful as they were brilliant. By the capture of the Twin Peaks the troops on Spion Kop had been largely relieved of the gun and rifle fire which had raked their right flank. Still more important were the effects on the enemy. The long day's battle had worn out the spirit of the Boers. Their utmost efforts, the skill of their gunners, and of their long-range riflemen, the bravery of the burghers clinging to the rocks upon the fringe of the plateau, all had failed to recapture Spion Kop. Before sunset they had abandoned all hopes of doing so, and it only needed such a blow as the sight of the Carolina men fleeing from the Twin Peaks to shatter their crumbling opposition. By nightfall every laager and most of

King's Royal Rifles ordered to abandon the Twin Peaks.

They withdraw at night.

Effect on Boers of the capture of the Twin Peaks.

* See Appendix 10 (F). and *post*.

THE SPION KOP CAMPAIGN. 399

the guns were on the move to the rear, the stormers of Spion Kop, utterly exhausted, slipped away one by one, four of the commandos from the actual front were riding for the passes, and there arose signs of a panic throughout the whole federal forces. But General Louis Botha, here, as at Colenso, the sole link of the incoherent units of the Republican armies, strove hard to prevent disintegration. Hastily summoning a council of war, he urged the impossibility of retreat, since so many dismounted burghers were present with the commandos. By this and other arguments he succeeded in prevailing upon many to return, pledging them to a last desperate attempt to storm Spion Kop in the morning. One objection he was unable to answer, and it chilled even those who agreed to stand by him. The Twin Peaks were in the hands of the British on the flank of the kop, the prospects of retaining which, even if they could retake it, seemed therefore remote. Nevertheless, many stayed in the trenches, so strongly impressed that the day had gone against them, that they lay awake under arms all night, fearful of pursuit. L. Botha, by his energy and determination, rallies the Boers.

Whilst Thorneycroft was writing his message as to giving up the hill, whilst the King's Royal Rifles were on the one side retiring in good order, and on the other the enemy was melting away disorganised, Sir C. Warren, who knew nothing of any of these events, except that at 8.35 p.m. he had heard of the evacuation of the Twin Peaks, was considering only how the contest could be renewed next day.* The Naval 12-prs. and the Mountain battery had both arrived from Trickhardt's Drift by 7.30 p.m. After a rest, one gun of the former and four of the latter were ordered to Spion Kop at 9 p.m., the heavy gun being placed under the guidance of a Natal colonist, who knew of a practicable way up the mountain. To construct cover for these, strong working parties were detailed from the Somersetshire Light Infantry, and 1,200 men were ordered to be drawn from Coke's reserves, which, it must be noted, did not in reality amount to much more than half this number. At 7.50 p.m., before these measures were in operation, Coke's message of Warren, ignorant of the retirement, prepares for the next day's fighting,

* See Appendices 10 (G, H, and I).

5.50 p.m.* reached the General. From Thorneycroft himself he had received nothing since 4.15 p.m. (see page 394). At 8.20 p.m. he therefore sent a note to that officer, asking for his views on the situation, and what measures he proposed to take. This was not received by Thorneycroft till 10.30 p.m.† Fifty minutes later, weary of the indecision caused by the paucity of news, and the confusing nature of the little which had reached him, Sir C. Warren by signal desired Coke to come down and see him in person. Coke was unwilling to quit the hill, knowing that his journey in the dark would take so long as to render his presence impossible should, after all, a withdrawal be ordered; and he tried to reply to this effect by lamp signal. But misfortune, which had attended the signal station all day, persisted to the last. The oil supply for the lamp failed, and the message could not be sent. Coke, therefore, after arranging for the Dorset regiment to cover a retirement, went down the hill at 9.30 p.m. in search of Sir C. Warren. Once more ill-luck intervened. During the day the General's Headquarters, coming under fire from the Boer shells, had been moved into shelter only some 200 yards from its former position. No less than five hours elapsed, and Spion Kop had been evacuated, before Coke, wandering in the darkness over the broken ground, discovered the General's camp.

At 10 p.m. the Middlesex regiment and Imperial Light Infantry, with a rear-guard of the Scottish Rifles, began to withdraw from Spion Kop. At 10.30 p.m., when the leading troops were some way down the hill, Sir C. Warren's message, written at 8.20 p.m.‡ was delivered to Thorneycroft, who handed to the bearer a reply which, as related, was not to reach the General for three hours.§ The retreat was made in good order, though the steep path was encumbered with wounded, and with many who had fallen exhausted out of the ranks to sleep by the wayside. As the rear-guard passed the shelf on which Coke and his staff had been all the day, Capt. H. G. C. Phillips, the

---

* See Appendix 10 (D).   † See Appendix 10 (J).   ‡ See Appendix 10 (J).

§ See Appendix 10 (F). The bearer left the hill with Thorneycroft at 11.30 p.m.

THE SPION KOP CAMPAIGN.   401

D.A.A.G. of the right attack, was awakened about 11.30 p.m. by the noise. Thinking that all this was contrary to his own absent General's wishes and intentions, and unaware of Thorneycroft's appointment as Brigadier, he issued to the regimental commanding officers a memorandum* in which he protested against the evacuation of the hill, which by that time was almost completed. Shortly after midnight Thorneycroft himself reached the foot of the mountain. Here he was met by the Mountain battery and the working party of the Royal Engineers. The commander of the latter handed him a note from Sir C. Warren, which told him that the guns and working parties were on the way, and urged him to hold on to the hill. Thorneycroft then went to find Sir C. Warren, to whom, after much searching, he reported at 2 a.m., the 25th January, arriving before his own last message, and about the same time that Coke succeeded in discovering the General's whereabouts. Sir C. Warren was amazed at the news. Despatching the Royal Dragoons to reconnoitre, with a view to the reoccupation of the mountain, he telegraphed to Sir R. Buller, who rode over at once, and arriving at 6 a.m., once more assumed command of the whole army. *(Thorneycroft, at foot of hill, meets guns and R.E., and receives a message from Warren to hold on. Warren, Coke and Thorneycroft meet, 2 a.m. 25th.)*

At about that hour the enemy, reconnoitring cautiously Spion Kop and the Twin Peaks, found to his surprise and relief that both were deserted, and immediately reoccupied them. So many dead lay upon the former that the Boer General requested an armistice to bury them, which being agreed to the troops remained immobile until the evening. Then orders for a general retreat were issued, and preparations begun. For Sir R. Buller had decided to abandon the attempt to break through to Ladysmith by this route, hoping to find elsewhere a weaker point in the enemy's defences. At dusk the Royal Lancaster regiment withdrew across the Tugela at Trickhardt's Drift, and took up a covering position on the south bank, where two Naval 12-prs. had been in readiness since 9 a.m. Once more the wagons had to cross the river. But the burden which the army had borne to the front in daylight with toil and delay, was carried back with so much skill and expedition during the *(Jan. 25th, 6 a.m. Boers reoccupy Spion Kop. Buller decides to retire.)*

* See South African Despatches.

hours of darkness, that by dawn on the 26th most of the transport was safely on the south bank, and later in the day the bridge was free. In order to divert the enemy's attention from this movement, the battalions on the Rangeworthy ridges, where for seven days they had lain under fire, and during the last of these had been spectators of the scene on Spion Kop, checking and checked by the enemy across the glacis, kept up a brisk fire all day. At 6 p.m. the Dorset withdrew to the bridge-head, covering the passage of the troops who had been engaged on Spion Kop. Then at nightfall, amid wind and rain, the left attack retired, firing to the last, and finally, about 1 a.m. on the 27th, the troops on Three Tree Hill were also withdrawn. Before the latter quitted their position the enemy, who lay to arms on all his hills, hearing the stir in the British lines, became suddenly alarmed by fears of a night attack, and a heavy outburst of musketry pealed along the entire front, revealing in the darkness the strength and extent of his positions by line upon line of flame from the rifles. The firing lasted so brief a time, that though the men of the Devonshire regiment, which formed the rear-guard on Three Tree Hill, dropped on their knees with fixed bayonets, in their turn fully expecting attack, the general retirement continued without interruption and with the utmost smoothness. The arrangements were admirable. At intervals of fifty yards cavalry vedettes had been posted to show the tracks, the boundaries of the whole area being marked out with stones and empty biscuit tins, so that no man might wander outside them, whilst a fire blazing at the bridge showed its position to the most distant. As dawn broke on the 27th January the last troops of the column crossed the worn chesses of the pontoons, a single shell from a Boer gun falling close by into the water. The dismantling of the bridge, an operation covered by the Dorset regiment, was then effected without molestation. By the afternoon the army was in camp at Hatting's Farm, between Trickhardt's and Potgieter's Drift, eighteen days after its departure from Frere and Chieveley, having suffered in that period more than 1,750 casualties.*

* For details of losses see Appendix 2.

CHAPTER XXIII.

VAAL KRANTZ.*

WHILST his troops were yet in the act of withdrawing from the Spion Kop zone, Sir R. Buller was revolving another plan for the relief of Ladysmith. The difficulties confronting him were now as plain as they were serious. Beyond the Tugela, in itself a continual embarrassment to offence, the wall of mountains which divided the two British forces was manned, not by contemptible guerillas, but by an army as mobile as a squadron of cavalry. It was composed of warriors skilled in all the arts which could be employed against them, adepts in many unknown to any regular soldiery; men in whom patriotism, the exhilaration of invasion, and signal successes were supplying the place of discipline, causing them neither to be browbeaten by superior artillery, nor to melt before the attack of highly trained regular infantry. Though many unforeseen obstacles had arisen before the British forces in Natal, none, it may be averred, had been more unexpected than the power and steadfastness of their opponents, whom no strategic errors had prevented from becoming, as they now seemed, tactically almost invincible. The choice left to Sir R. Buller, therefore, seemed to lie only between evils. The rampart before him had nowhere a breach, and was nowhere ungarrisoned. Even on January 23rd, when, having apparently drawn the bulk of the Boer forces in that direction, he was in full battle on the Rangeworthy ridges, Barton, reconnoitring in force from Chieveley (where he had

<small>Buller's new plan.</small>

<small>The mountain barrier, unbroken and well guarded, between his army and Ladysmith,</small>

* See map No. 21.

appears passable at Vaal Krantz.

been since December 13th, 1899) found the enemy still in strength at Colenso, Hlangwhane and Cingolo, thirty miles to the eastward. Nevertheless, it was necessary to make another effort, and that at once. Delay was equivalent to defeat. The Ladysmith garrison was weakening daily, and both Sir G. White and the authorities at home had already mooted, as a desperate resort, the project of abandoning the sick and wounded, the stores, railway stock and heavy guns in Ladysmith, in an attempt to cut a way out, an expedient considered impossible both by Lord Roberts and Sir R. Buller.* Once more surveying the heights across the river, this time from the summit of Zwart Kop, Sir R. Buller could perceive but one point which offered any likelihood of success, namely, the Vaal Krantz Ridge.† The barrier here was at its narrowest, open ground lying close behind it. The ridge itself came down to the river banks, which impinging its flank, offered an approach in some measure covered. Although it was of no great height, yet any Boer guns which might be trained upon it would apparently be themselves dominated from Mount Alice or Zwart Kop, on both of which Sir R. Buller intended to establish heavy batteries. Though he had no information on the subject, the top of Vaal Krantz itself appeared practicable for artillery, which would thence command the plain and tracks leading to Ladysmith. Whilst noting these advantages, Sir R. Buller did not disguise from himself or Sir G. White‡ the counterbalancing drawbacks of an advance by Vaal Krantz. Assuming the capture of the ridge, of which he had little doubt, the Boers would still be in strength

---

* See Royal Commission on the War in South Africa, Minutes of Evidence, Vol. II., p. 164. Heliogram No. 55P, January 27th, 1900, Sir G. White to Sir R. Buller; also Telegram No. 97, Cipher, 26th January, 1900, from Commander-in-Chief, London, to Sir R. Buller; same to same, No. 101 Cipher, 27th January, 1900; Telegram No. 171 Cipher, 27th January, 1900, from Sir R. Buller to Commander-in-Chief, London; Telegram No. 29 Cipher, 27th January, 1900, Lord Roberts to Sir R. Buller; reply thereto, No. 172 Cipher, 27th January, 1900; Heliogram No. 173 Cipher, 28th January, 1900, from Sir R. Buller to Sir G. White.

† For a description of the relative situation of this feature, see Chapter XX.

‡ Heliogram No. 173 Cipher, 28th January, 1900, from Sir R. Buller to Sir G. White.

on the left of the successful force, that is, upon the Spion Kop—Brakfontein positions, whence they might or might not retire. Nor was Vaal Krantz by any means the door into Ladysmith. Not only did twelve miles still intervene, but behind Vaal Krantz, Roodepoort* was now reported to be heavily entrenched; it commanded the plain, a bar to Sir R. Buller's further advance, as its sister eminence, Lancer's Hill, was to a sally by Sir G. White.

Between January 27th and February 2nd, whilst reinforcements arrived,† the troops rested in their camps at Springfield, Spearman's Hollow, Hatting's Farm, and the bridge-head at The Kopjes. Their inexhaustible spirit went far to lighten a time of anxiety. Not bad news from other quarters, nor their own two rebuffs, neither long days and nights of fighting, nor the hardships of lack of rest, continual exposure by day and night, and finally of a bitter retreat, had left upon a single battalion or company any mark which a few hours' repose would not remove. On January 29th, the whole force paraded by brigades to be addressed by Sir R. Buller, and the thunderous cheers which answered his hopeful words might have come from soldiers who had not yet been engaged, instead of from men who, in a few weeks, had encountered many of the misfortunes and none of the rewards of war. With such troops, the possibility, which had been taken into account both by the War Office and by Lord Roberts, of being forced to abandon active measures for the relief of Ladysmith, and, pending developments elsewhere, sheltering the force in an entrenched position,‡ covering South Natal, seemed remote. *High spirit of Buller's army unshaken by reverse.*

Preparations for the projected battle had been begun on the 27th. They involved heavy work at Zwart Kop, up whose *Preparations for the attempt to pierce the line at Vaal Krantz.*

---

* See Chapter XXI.

† Including two 5-inch guns (16th company southern division R.G.A.); A. battery R.H.A.; two squadrons 14th Hussars, and considerable drafts of infantry.

‡ See the following telegrams from Lord Roberts to Sir R. Buller: No. 26 Cipher, January 26th, 1900; No. 32 Cipher, 27th January, 1900; No. 35 Cipher, 28th January, 1900; and letter of same date.

steep and wooded southern slopes a slide was smoothed for the haulage of the Naval ordnance, for the movement of which one and a half miles of road had also to be made through bad country. Stormy weather seriously hampered these labours, the difficulty of which was further increased by the necessity of endeavouring to keep them invisible from the enemy. By February 2nd all was ready. Fourteen guns (six Naval 12-prs., two of the 64th Field battery, and six of No. 4 Mountain battery) lay concealed amongst the trees on the top of Zwart Kop. The two 5-inch guns, which it had been found impossible to drag up the steep and slippery gradients, were placed below a spur to the westward of the kop. The above, with a 4.7-in. gun on Naval Gun (Signal) Hill, another on Mount Alice, and two Naval 12-prs. on the plateau north of Mount Alice, were the guns of position (i.e., not intended to be moved about) at Sir R. Buller's disposal. Against them, on the enemy's side, only seven pieces could at present be certainly observed; two to the west (hill 694) and two to the east (hill 630) of Brakfontein, one on a spur in front of Krantz Kloof, one on Vaal Krantz itself, and one behind Skiet's Drift. The Boers themselves were plainly to be seen entrenching the heights, which curved like a vast lunette from the Twin Peaks clear round to Munger's Farm. A detached post held Skiet's Drift, where it was watched by Bethune's mounted infantry.

On the 28th Colonel A. S. Wynne was appointed to command the 11th brigade in succession to Major-General Woodgate, mortally wounded at Spion Kop. He was succeeded by Colonel H. S. G. Miles as Chief of the Staff in the Natal army.

Organisation of mounted troops into two brigades.

The mounted arms had been reorganised on February 1st: The *1st Cavalry brigade* (Burn-Murdoch) consisted of the following regular troops, viz., Royal Dragoons; 13th Hussars; 14th Hussars (2 squadrons); and A. battery R.H.A. The *2nd Mounted brigade* (Dundonald) was almost entirely composed of volunteers. Under Dundonald's command were the South African Light Horse, Thorneycroft's mounted infantry, Bethune's mounted infantry, Imperial Light Horse (1 squadron), Natal

VAAL KRANTZ.

Carbineers (1 squadron), detachment Natal Mounted Police, 1 company mounted infantry King's Royal Rifles, and 1 section mounted infantry Royal Dublin Fusiliers.

On the 3rd February, Sir R. Buller, after meeting his officers in conference, issued orders for the operations.* Vaal Krantz, presumed to be the extreme left of the Boer position, was to be the object of attack. For its capture the 4th brigade (Lyttelton), supported by the 2nd (Hildyard) and 5th (Hart) brigades, were detailed, the whole to be commanded by Sir C. F. Clery. To lure the enemy from the real point of attack, a feint on a large scale was arranged to be delivered against Brakfontein between the two great loops of the Tugela. This was to be carried out by six batteries, Royal Field artillery, the 61st Howitzer battery, and the 11th brigade (Wynne), which on this day was in process of relieving the 4th brigade at The Kopjes. The fire of the Naval guns on and under Mount Alice, and of the remainder of the heavy artillery, except the pieces on Zwart Kop, was to cover the movement. It was hoped that the massing of the brigades for the true attack close to the eastward of No. 2 pontoon bridge would look as if they were about to cross to join in the assault of Brakfontein. When the enemy had been thus drawn into the threatened trenches, a pontoon bridge, No. 3, would be thrown at a point in the eastward loop of the Tugela opposite to No. 2 pontoon. The Sappers were to be covered whilst making it by the 4th brigade, by the remaining four guns 64th battery, and by the left battery of the false attack, which for this purpose would come across to the right by No. 2 pontoon. This third bridge was necessary because Munger's Drift was now unfordable, even had an advance so far up the exposed river loop, and a passage so close under the enemy's rifles been practicable. At the same moment the batteries on and below Zwart Kop would unmask for the first time, and shell Vaal Krantz. As soon as the bridge should be completed, the remaining five batteries in front of Brakfontein, and the 61st Howitzer battery, crossing also by No. 2 pontoon, would come over to the right and join in the bombardment of Vaal Krantz, which would then

Buller's plan of attack.

* For text of orders, see Appendix 11 (A).

be assaulted by the infantry. Immediately the ridge should be captured, the artillery was to push forward to the summit, and thence attack Brakfontein, whilst the 1st cavalry brigade, watching a favourable opportunity, would pass Vaal Krantz, and get out into the open ground behind. Such was the plan; its fruition, it will be noticed, dependent both upon the success of the feint in deception, and the suitability of Vaal Krantz for the establishment of artillery.

By the night of February 4th the preliminary movements had been nearly effected; the 11th brigade had relieved the 4th at The Kopjes, behind which the six Field and the Howitzer batteries had gathered in readiness. The brigades detailed for the real attack moved down into bivouacs near the bases of Mount Alice and Zwart Kop. The enemy showed no sign; all his hills had relapsed into quiet, and beyond the scanty data gathered from distant observation, his dispositions, and the issue of the coming battle, seemed inscrutable.

A feint attack on Brakfontein begun at 6 a.m. on Feb. 5th.

At 6 a.m. on the 5th Wynne emerged from The Kopjes, and deployed as if for the attack of Brakfontein, with the 1st South Lancashire and 1st York and Lancaster on right and left in front line, the 2nd Royal Lancaster in second line, the 2nd Lancashire Fusiliers holding the bridge-head in reserve. The six Field batteries, commanded by Lieut.-Colonel L. W. Parsons, Royal artillery, moving out a little beyond The Kopjes, came into action in short échelon from the left, in the following order from left to right—63rd, 28th, 19th, 78th, 73rd and 7th; the 61st Howitzer battery was posted on the left rear at the western extremity of The Kopjes.

Covered by the practice of this array of artillery, which at 7 a.m. was swelled by that of every gun of position except those concealed on Zwart Kop, Wynne then advanced. His broad lines, forging steadily to the front, bore an imposing and menacing aspect as they striped the whole width of the flats between the river loops. But Brakfontein awaited them in silence. Behind its crest, which now smoked from end to end with bursting shell, lay the Senekal, Vrede and other Free State commandos,

Hidden in deep and narrow trenches, they had been commanded by their General, Prinsloo, to fire no shot until the British were within 400 yards. At 9.35 a.m. the 63rd battery on the left of the artillery retired slowly through The Kopjes, so as to deceive the enemy as to its destination, and made its way rapidly thence to cover the construction of No. 3 bridge. Its leisurely departure awoke no sound from the western heights. Nearer marched the infantry, until it seemed as if the demonstration were about to develop perforce into a serious attack. It was not until 11.45 a.m., when they had drawn to within 1,000 yards of the trenches, that three Boer guns and a pom-pom, in position between Spion Kop and Brakfontein, began to shell vigorously the batteries exposed on the plain. Thereupon the ranks halted and lay down, projectiles from the left falling amongst them also, though still not a rifle was discharged from Brakfontein. Thus situated, for the next hour and a half the 11th brigade and the artillery, heavily but almost harmlessly shelled, played with the enemy in full hopes that by attracting him to their own front, they were opening a joint in his armour for the unaccountably delayed stroke on the right. *Boer guns do not open fire till 11.45 a.m.*

At 12.20 p.m., just as Parsons had on his own responsibility ordered the 28th battery to lead off the pre-arranged flank movement to join in the bombardment of Vaal Krantz, the signal, "Bridge completed," was received, and all the batteries prepared to leave. The change of position was attended with much danger. Every detail was plainly visible to the Boer gunners. From their lofty eyries, which were beyond the range of the field guns, and skilfully defiladed from the heavier artillery behind, they poured down shell upon each unsheltered gun team and wagon, as, limbering up in succession from the left, the batteries quitted the line and moved calmly upon the bridge. The 7th battery, on the right, which was under orders to cover the retirement of the infantry, finally remained alone on the plain, the target of a concentrated fire which, though in reality almost ineffective, seemed to be blowing it to pieces. At 1.30 p.m., Wynne, considering his mission accomplished, *On the completion of pontoon bridge Wynne's artillery move off to bombard Vaal Krantz*

410   THE WAR IN SOUTH AFRICA.

and Wynne, having done his work, falls back.

gave the word to retire. As the men rose and faced about, Brakfontein at last burst into life, with an immense discharge of rifles, the Boers, weary of their long inaction, even quitting their shelter to empty their magazines at utmost speed. But Wynne's files were widely extended; a few steps carried them out of the medium zone, and the 11th brigade and the 7th battery, retiring with unconcern, regained the shelter of The Kopjes with little loss in men and none in order. The infantry had one man killed, 27 wounded; the artillery, two officers and eight men wounded.

Preparation for the real attack.

Meanwhile preparations for the main operations on the right had been going forward. Setting out at 7 a.m., an hour after Wynne's deployment in front of The Kopjes, the three brigades destined for the attack filed down from their bivouacs under the guns on Mount Alice and Signal Hill, and, following the road by Harding's Farm, halted in the neck of the river loop to the eastward of No. 2 pontoon and north of Zwart Kop.

The heavy guns open at 9.15 a.m.

At 9.15 a.m. the 5-in. guns, and a little later the united batteries on Zwart Kop, unmasked and opened an overwhelming bombardment over the heads of the infantry upon Vaal Krantz. The 63rd battery, the first from Wynne's side, arrived an hour later, its appearance being the signal for the Royal Engineers to start work upon the third pontoon. At 10.25 a.m. A. Pontoon Troop, the 17th and half the 37th companies, Royal Engineers, commanded by Major J. L. Irvine, Royal Engineers,

Pontoon bridge built.

began to build at a point 1,500 yards to the south of Munger's Drift. A Maxim gun near Munger's Farm, and a brisk " sniping " from the dongas and mealie fields to the eastward, as well as from the kopjes above Skiet's Drift, greatly pestered the workers, nor could the fire of the two covering batteries (63rd and 64th) nor that of the escort (2nd Scottish Rifles) appreciably diminish the annoyance. Neither their danger, however, nor their losses (some 10 men), delayed the Sappers an instant, and in fifty minutes the bridge was finished. A somewhat protracted pause followed. The attacking columns were ready, but an unfortunate delay of over an hour occurred in the transmission of the signal announcing to Parsons the completion of the pontoon. At length the artillery of the feint attack was seen to be coming across, the whole army watching with anxiety and admiration the deliberate execution of the dangerous manœuvre of withdrawal. On their arrival the batteries were at once pushed into action, the 28th joining the 63rd and 64th in dealing with the rifle fire from the eastward of the bridge. Fifty guns converged upon Vaal Krantz itself. That low hill was scarcely to be seen through the thick fumes and earthy eruptions of the shells which burst upon its crest. Its garrison, about 100 men of the Johannesburg commando, with a pom-pom, under a bold officer, Commandant B. Viljoen, crushed by the devastating tempest, suffered severely. At 2 p.m. two of Lyttelton's battalions, the 1st Durham Light Infantry and 1st Rifle Brigade, descended to the pontoon. The severity of the musketry and pom-pom fire which still swept the structure was minimised by the speed of the troops in crossing by rushes of companies, though a few casualties occurred. Under the left bank, here some twenty feet high, the units reformed, then pushed on in single file along a narrow path straight up-stream from Vaal Krantz. For half a mile the bank gave shelter from the "snipers" scattered along the right, and from a gun which, endeavouring to drop shell into the defile, dashed up at intervals the waters of the Tugela. Thereafter the protection ceased, and the battalions, clambering out into the mealie fields which fringed the river, extended, the 1st Rifle Brigade on the right of the Durham Light Infantry. Men were struck down by fire from all directions, even from the survivors on Vaal Krantz, where half of the defenders had already been put out of action. The Boer garrison had 29 killed, 24 wounded. Breaking through Munger's Farm, Lyttelton's troops stormed the southern end of the ridge at the bayonet's point, swept right across the double-peaked summit, and were soon in possession of the whole hill, and of five prisoners from Viljoen's flying remnant. The pom-pom gun, extricated by the gallant example of the Commandant himself, barely avoided capture. In the wake of the storming party now followed the 2nd Scottish Rifles and 3rd King's Royal Rifles of Lyttelton's brigade, and the 2nd Devonshire of Hildyard's brigade, the two first-named corps to reinforce Vaal Krantz. The Devonshire had received special orders, namely, to attack Green Hill to the eastward of Vaal Krantz, and were setting out with this intention, when a message arrived directing the battalion to conform to the movements of the 4th brigade. The rifle fire from east and south-east, which had harassed the bridge builders and the troops of the assault, now beat upon the supporting corps as they crossed the pontoon, and in spite of the fire from the Field artillery below Zwart Kop, which had never ceased, the Boer shooting from this quarter appeared inextinguishable, until the massing of the Maxim guns of the 4th brigade near the mouth of the bridge on the right bank greatly diminished its volume. The progress under the river bank and the emergence into the open mealies, save for the silence of Vaal Krantz itself, repeated the experiences of the previous troops. Not without losses, Lyttelton's two regiments joined him upon Vaal Krantz, and were placed in support, the King's Royal Rifles behind the left of the hill, the Scottish Rifles in the centre. Of the Devonshire, two companies prolonged Lyttelton's right down the southern shoulder, one remained in a donga running out to the river bed, whilst the Headquarters occupied Munger's Farm, where they lined the low stone walls, and fired into the cloud of sharpshooters which hung about Green Hill.

Doubtful value of Vaal Krantz as a position.

Before 4 p.m. the specific object of the day's operations, the seizure of the Vaal Krantz Ridge, was in this manner attained. A very brief occupation, however, sufficed to arouse doubts in its captors, not only as to its value, but also as to its actual security. Immediately to the northward, and separated only by a deep and narrow saddle, the grassy downs of Brakfontein and Krantz Kloof ended in a bold hill (marked 360 on map). This was seamed with trenches, and though it had been early set ablaze by shells, was still strongly held. The musketry from it, and from the arc of heights curving westward, searched the flank and reverse of Vaal Krantz, which was subject also to a cross fire of artillery from Spion Kop, Brakfontein and Green Hill. Especially exposed was the dividing depression, the only approach, a defile not to be entered whilst filled with such a fire. Furthermore, neither a safe road to, nor any practicable position on, Vaal Krantz for the artillery, the ultimate purpose of the capture of the kopje, could as yet be found. Nothing more, therefore, could be done immediately, although Lyttelton had at once seen the dangers of hill No. 360, which would be greatly increased by the appearance of guns upon its close and unfortunately-situated slopes. Disposing his men to the best advantage along the rocky crest, he ordered them to entrench, and the soldiers, weary as they were with the day's fighting, began a long night's toil to secure what they had won. They were often interrupted; at first by quick strings of pompom shells, which in the early hours of darkness pitched with wonderful accuracy amongst them, and later by a series of outbursts of Mausers discharged at close quarters from behind a veil of smoke rising from the saddle, which the enemy had set alight.* These fusilades, the nearness and intensity of which showed that they were attempts to recapture the hill, were one and all quenched by prompt responses from the growing sangars of the 4th brigade. Infantry entrench on Vaal Krantz, night of Feb. 5th, under fire.

As regards the artillery, the broadside of Zwart Kop was strengthened before morning by the addition of the two Naval 12-prs., which moved from Potgieter's to a spur north of the Kop, being joined there by the two 5-in. guns. The enemy himself took little more rest. General Louis Botha, who had visited Pretoria after Spion Kop, returned to his army after dark and took over command from Prinsloo. As usual, for he alone commanded so much confidence as to be obeyed, an activity full of purpose marked his arrival amongst the burghers, whose numbers were promptly swelled considerably by the reappearance of many who had avoided battle under less trusted leadership. The aim of the wedge which had been driven in by Sir R. Buller during the day was unmistakable. The commandos and guns were therefore called in towards the spot from near Spion Kop; a Field gun and a pom-pom were moved thence to Green Hill, leaving two heavy pieces still commanding the left Botha resumes command of Boers; his activity and new dispositions.

* The positions of the rest of the army at nightfall are shown on map 21 (a).

rear of Vaal Krantz; other guns on Brakfontein closed further to the eastward, whilst on the lofty Doorn Kop,* far to the right, the 94-pr. (Creusot) cannon, which had been lately duelling with the Ladysmith Howitzers from Telegraph Ridge, was mounted in a shell-proof work. The skirmishers near Skiet's Drift then fell back beneath it. Thus, before morning came, the enemy was firmly posted, no small portion of his strength, which numbered about 5,000 men with ten guns, clustering about Vaal Krantz itself.

Buller, wishing to use Vaal Krantz as a pivot of attack,

Sir R. Buller was now anxious to utilise Vaal Krantz as the pivot of further operations. As indicated in his orders, he believed that the sole value of this ridge depended upon the possibility of there establishing an artillery position which would serve to cover a further advance. The strength and proximity of the height 360 made the success of the previous day disappointingly incomplete. Before all else it was necessary to possess it. At 4.30 a.m. on 6th February, whilst it was still dark, Sir Redvers sent a message to Lyttelton, acquainting

brings artillery to bear upon hill 360.

him with his intention of clearing, with artillery fire, the way to an attack on this hill. Should the attempt prove a failure, and Lyttelton be feeling no relief by 10 a.m., he was then to retire. Half an hour later dawn broke, and the battle was

Boer bombardment of Vaal Krantz.

renewed with heavy interchanges of artillery. The Boer gunners, looking down on the field as from a series of towers, had, in full view beneath them, the brown oval of Vaal Krantz, streaked with its half-finished defences, of which the front, rear and both flanks were each exposed to some portions of the hostile fire, and parts to all. From every angle shells dropped amongst the troops thereon, the men of the firing line often receiving in their backs those aimed at the reserves, the right of the line those which overshot the left, and the reserves all which cleared the crest; there was no corner unsearched, and but for the shelters the hill would have been untenable. The British artillerists, on the other hand, puzzled by the distance, the invisibility, and the superiority of command of the opposing guns, had only vague

* Variously called Doorn Kop or Doorn Kloof.

spots, or even uncertain and echoing reports, by which to guess at their targets.

At 5.15 a.m. the 94-pr. on Doorn Kop fired its first shot. This gun dominated not only Vaal Krantz, but Zwart Kop and all the ground within the river loop, which was crowded with battalions and batteries throughout the space. It was immediately engaged by the 5-in. guns, the Naval 12-prs. and the 4.7-in. guns on Signal Hill and Zwart Kop, which for the rest of the day never ceased to batter the earthwork which shielded the cannon. Although they did not succeed in finally silencing it, their missiles, exploding constantly close to the embrasure, and even among the reserve ammunition behind, allowed the Boer artillerymen to serve their gun only at long and irregular intervals, between which the weapon was hauled back for reloading out of sight. At 6.40 a.m. Lyttelton signalled that, in spite of the assistance of the artillery, it was still impossible to attempt the seizure of hill 360. He had previously urged the removal of No. 2 pontoon to a spot close under Vaal Krantz, in order to make the retreat easier, should it be necessary to abandon the hill. At 7.10 a.m. he heard that this was being done. A few minutes later he was asked by Sir R. Buller what chance there was of success in an attack by a brigade west of Vaal Krantz. To this Lyttelton replied that there could be but little. Krantz Kloof, which the British guns could not touch at present, was unshaken, and two camps visible to the northward proved that it was held in force. He thought that an advance by the east of Vaal Krantz would probably fare better. About an hour later Lyttelton was asked if he could maintain his position until relieved at sundown, as Sir R. Buller wished to "watch developments." Lyttelton answered that he could do so if the enemy mounted no fresh guns on his left rear. Sir R. Buller's hopes of placing artillery on Vaal Krantz were then finally quenched by a definite statement by Lyttelton that the mounting of even two field guns was impossible. Such was certainly the case, so steep, so encumbered with boulders, and so searched by shot and shell were the sides of the ridge. The capture of Vaal Krantz had therefore lost all its value. The wedge, its

6.40 a.m., Feb. 6th. Lyttelton reports that, even with artillery help an attack on hill 360 is impracticable.

Impossibility of mounting guns on Vaal Krantz.

chief means of ingress unserviceable, could be driven in no further here, but merely lay imbedded in the enemy's lines on right and left. Sir R. Buller estimated that an attempt to force back these lines would cost 2,000 or 3,000 men, with even then no certainty of success. He, this day, telegraphed these views to Lord Roberts, of whom he inquired whether he thought the possible relief of Ladysmith worth the certain risk. At the same time Sir R. Buller admitted that, were this attempt given up, he could devise no other. The Commander-in-Chief, it will be remembered, had already suggested that offensive measures for the relief, if their issue seemed doubtful, should await the effect on the Boers of the pressure of his own army. He now replied decisively in favour of perseverance. Even at the loss named Ladysmith must be relieved. The Field-Marshal finished his telegram with a message to the troops, reminding them that the honour of the Empire was in their hands, and expressing his confidence in their ultimate success.

<small>Buller, thinking that an attempt to force his way would entail heavy loss, telegraphs to Lord Roberts,</small>

<small>who replies that Ladysmith must be relieved.</small>

With scarcely any change on either side the day wore on. The shell-fire neither ceased nor decreased for a moment. Whilst Vaal Krantz continued to be the focus of the bombardment, occasional shells from the 94-pr. on Doorn Kop fell upon the troops and batteries in the river loop, or shattered the trees which concealed the guns on Zwart Kop. During the afternoon the enemy made a determined attempt to recapture Vaal Krantz, approaching close to the defences, and firing hotly from behind a curtain of burning grass. The Durham Light Infantry, reinforced by the King's Royal Rifles, soon drove them down the hill again by their fire; after which the Boers contented themselves once more with maintaining a constant discharge from guns and rifles at a distance. Towards evening, No. 2 bridge being now rebuilt (shown as No. 4 on the map) under Vaal Krantz, Hildyard's brigade crossed the river by it, and released the 4th brigade from their fatiguing service of twenty-six hours on the ridge.

<small>In afternoon of 6th Boers attempt to recapture Vaal Krantz.</small>

<small>The garrison of Vaal Krantz relieved.</small>

Up on the crest, the 2nd Queen's (Royal West Surrey) regiment replaced the Durham Light Infantry on the left, the 2nd East Surrey prolonging the line, whilst the 2nd West Yorkshire

VAAL KRANTZ. 417

manned the sangars of the 1st Rifle Brigade on the southern knoll and shoulder of the hill. The 2nd Devonshire regiment, its Headquarters having been relieved at Munger's Farm by the 1st Connaught Rangers, took post as a general reserve in slightly separated half battalions behind the northern hummock of Vaal Krantz. A spasmodic shell-fire, which did not cease with the fall of darkness, harassed the process of relief. That accomplished, the troops of the 2nd brigade set themselves to improve the defences, working as Lyttelton's men had done, far into the night. They, too, were disturbed by demonstrations of musketry at close quarters, which more than once obliged the men to exchange pick and crowbar for the rifle.

Daylight (February 7th) once more was ushered in by an artillery combat. The enemy's guns, paying but intermittent attention to the British batteries, which still searched vainly for their hiding places, concentrated their fire from the first upon Vaal Krantz, around which they had closed yet nearer. The new occupants of the ridge profited greatly by their night's labour. Strong sangars, barred gridiron-wise with traverses, afforded fair cover, and though losses occurred steadily, they were few in proportion to the number of shells which burst amongst the crowded walls. Nevertheless, during the long hours of the day the soldiers were kept pinned to their shelters; the heat was intense, and food and water obtainable only at the risk of life. Any movement at once brought not only an increased visitation of projectiles, but also a sniping fire on the northern side from the hill 360, which was still strongly held by the enemy. The urgency of the capture of this annoying feature had never been lost sight of. In the course of the morning, Hildyard made a personal reconnaissance of it, and forwarded a report to Sir R. Buller. The hill, he said, might be seized at dusk by two battalions. Their tenure, however, would be more than doubtful; fortification would be difficult; both flanks would be enfiladed next day, and that at ranges a thousand yards less than those which already rendered Vaal Krantz an easy target to the enemy. The attempt, therefore, was not made, and the operations seemed to have come to a deadlock.

Boers resume the bombardment of Vaal Krantz at daylight, Feb. 7th.

A fresh attempt to capture hill 360 discussed, but considered impossible.

Sir R. Buller, accompanied by Sir C. Warren, had himself ridden forward and inspected the positions. He returned to his Headquarters convinced of the inutility of Vaal Krantz, which could neither enable him to establish the dominion of his own guns, nor be relieved of its subjection to those of the enemy; nor, indeed, though the hill was lined with his rifles, could he even rid it of the sharpshooters who on hill 360 and the neighbourhood clung on tenaciously and were not to be shaken off. The bombardment continued without intermission. Once a lyddite shell from a 4.7-in. gun, falling into the work which sheltered the cannon on Doorn Kop, blew up some of its ammunition, a vast column of smoke ascending after the explosion. Yet the weapon was undamaged, and after an interval resumed its practice. Throughout the action, indeed, the artillery strength of the enemy diminished by not so much as a single piece, although seventy guns expended nearly ten thousand rounds of shell during the three days of battle upon only ten of his. The Field batteries, Mountain battery and 5-inch guns fired 7,206 rounds; the Naval 4.7-in. and 12-prs. fired 2,393; in all, 9,599 rounds.

Buller becomes convinced of the uselessness of Vaal Krantz.

Such is the value of the concealment and dispersion of artillery in action; devices, nevertheless, which unless in very exceptional circumstances, are rather to be suspected of fruitlessly safeguarding guns than of enabling them to win victory for an army. Certainly that was the case on this day. The Boer gunners, turning their metal now upon Vaal Krantz, now into the wooded recesses of Zwart Kop, now upon the pontoons, now over the river loop, left no part of the field untouched, but crushed none, causing losses only slightly less trifling than those they suffered. Nevertheless, from the topographical conditions, their fire completely dominated the British sphere of operations, and emphasised, though it did not determine, the failure of this line of advance.

At 4 p.m. Sir R. Buller called together his generals, and after hearing their various suggestions, announced his intention of abandoning the present attempt, and of seeking some more practicable point at which to pierce the hostile lines. Overlooked

Buller decides to abandon his attempt and to try again elsewhere.

VAAL KRANTZ.

everywhere by the enemy's invisible artillery, confronted, as it was reported to him, by an army of 16,000 men, convinced that even success here would not open to him the road to Ladysmith, he considered that persistence would entail useless waste of life. He proposed now to throw his divisions by a forced march across to Chieveley, and from that base to aim straight across Hlangwhane at Umbulwana, the heart of the investment. This decision he at once telegraphed to the Secretary of State, to Lord Roberts and to Sir G. White,* and at 5.45 p.m. issued orders for all to withdraw. Meanwhile the artillery fire on both sides had never slackened, the bombardment of Vaal Krantz perceptibly increasing in severity about the time when Sir Redvers assembled his generals and gave his orders. At nightfall it ceased, and the troops, issuing for the first time from their shelters, prepared for retreat. The evacuation of Vaal Krantz was a delicate operation.† The enemy lurked close in front of the defences, listening to every sound. Only with the profoundest secrecy would the widely-spread units of the 2nd brigade be able to abandon the crest and converge down the steep and rocky hillside upon the single bridge (No. 4) at the foot. An attack in rear whilst so doing would delay, if not altogether confuse, the whole movement; an attack on the pontoon itself, which was not impossible, might block it altogether.

His new scheme.

Vaal Krantz evacuated on night of the 7th Feb.

Hildyard, therefore, secured the crest with a skeleton line (one section per company of the defence), and the bridge with a half battalion of the Devonshire regiment on either bank of the river, and at 9 p.m. the infantry began to cross in silence. At this moment the Boers, either fearing or making an attack, opened a heavy fire against the top of Vaal Krantz. The thin array of troops left behind replied vigorously, and for about fifteen minutes a lively interchange continued, which then

---

* Telegrams from Sir R. Buller to Secretary of State for War and Lord Roberts, No. 189 Cipher, 7th February, 1900; and from Sir R. Buller to Sir G. White, No. 190 Cipher, of same date, see page 425.

† For orders of 2nd brigade, which well illustrate the nature of this difficult and instructive manœuvre, see Appendix 11 (B).

ceased as suddenly as it had opened. Soon afterwards the skeleton line faded undetected from the front, and by 9.55 p.m., the passage of the main body being effected, the covering half battalion on the left bank withdrew across the bridge, which the Royal Engineers, still covered by the half battalion on the right bank, then demolished. No further incident occurred. The pontoons were rapidly drawn ashore and packed, and were soon on their way southward. Meanwhile the Connaught Rangers had safely retired from Munger's Farm by No. 3 bridge, and before midnight on February 7th no British soldier remained on this flank on the left bank of the Tugela.

Before evening General Clery was placed on the sick list and General Lyttelton took over command of the IInd division, Colonel Norcott succeeding to the 2nd brigade.

The whole army in retreat, dawn of Feb. 8th. Dawn of February 8th revealed to the enemy the whole army in motion. The head of the column was already buried in the gorges below Mount Alice, but the rear still lingered on the narrow track leading past Harding's Farm, and the gunners on Doorn Kop threw shell in chase clear over Zwart Kop, and though given no rest by the 4.7-in. gun, shooting as usual with accuracy as surprising as its harmlessness. By 8 a.m. the rear-guard (5th brigade) had withdrawn out of range, following the main body to Springfield, where it went into bivouac at 4.30 p.m. Sir R. Buller had his Headquarters at the bridge. There still remained to be effected the evacuation of The Kopjes, the removal of No. 1 pontoon from Potgieter's Drift, the withdrawal of the heavy artillery from Zwart Kop, and the clearance from Spearman's Camp of the stores and ammunition, all of which were to be forwarded with speed to Springfield and Chieveley. These heavy duties were assigned to Sir C. Warren and the Vth division,* and by the evening of February 9th they were successfully accomplished. The enemy, exhausted by the strain of three weeks' almost continuous fighting, made no effort to interfere, beyond shelling languidly the two battalions (2nd Somerset and 2nd Dorset), which had reinforced the bridge-head at The Kopjes. During the night of the 8th the

* For Sir R. Buller's order, see Appendix 11 (C).

12-prs. were sent down from Zwart Kop, the 4.7-in. guns following next evening, the lowering of these ponderous pieces down the precipitous slopes proving almost more toilsome and dangerous than their previous elevation had done. The 2nd Royal Lancaster regiment and 2nd Royal Scots Fusiliers meanwhile garrisoned Zwart Kop, and afterwards escorted the artillery to Springfield. At 1.30 p.m. on the 9th, No. 1 pontoon was broken up, and withdrawn to Spearman's, whence, on the 10th, Sir C. Warren, with the last pound of stores safely on his wagons, marched with all his units for Springfield Bridge. Five hundred and fifty-nine wagon loads had been cleared from Spearman's in seventeen hours. The main army had already left that place, pushing on for Pretorius Farm, where it lay on the night of the 10th. Thence next day it moved to Chieveley, beyond which, in a pleasant valley watered by the Blaauwkrantz river, and shaded by luxuriant mimosas, the soldiers went into bivouac. Warren, leaving a small mixed force under Lieut.-Colonel J. F. Burn-Murdoch at Springfield Bridge, made a short march to Pretorius Farm on the 11th, and on the 12th joined the main body around Chieveley. Thus the army of Natal found itself once more concentrated opposite the Colenso heights after a month's absence, of which few days had passed without fighting, and none without hardship. During that time the casualties had numbered nearly two thousand. *Army reaches Chieveley Feb. 11th.*

Nevertheless, further losses and exposure had weakened the body of the army as little as repeated failure had damaged its spirit. The casualties, with the exception of those of Vaal Krantz (under 350 in number*), had been nearly made good by reinforcements received at Spearman's. The bronzed and active appearance of the soldiers, their undeteriorated endurance and discipline, which, even on marches of retreat, caused straggling to be more rare than on peace manœuvres, their unabated cheerfulness and resource in bivouac, in short, their utter disregard of fatigue and defeat in the determination to achieve their seemingly impossible purpose, all these testified once more that the

* For summary of casualties and approximate strength of troops engaged, see Appendix 2.

leader of such troops, aided by a fine climate, had nothing to fear either from the rigour or the disappointments of campaigning. So little was Sir R. Buller's army affected by either, that the briefest of rests at Chieveley sufficed to invigorate it for the longest, the most hotly-contested, and the most exhausting battle of the whole campaign in Natal.

423

CHAPTER XXIV.

RELIEF OF LADYSMITH.

THE CAPTURE OF CINGOLO.*

[Throughout the chapters describing the relief of Ladysmith, the heights of the hills are given, not with relation to sea level, but to that of the Colenso railway station, which is 3,156 feet above sea level.]

DURING the operations at Spion Kop and Vaal Krantz, described in the last four chapters, Major-General G. Barton was left at Chieveley† to guard the rail-head and to watch the Boers in the works about Colenso. He had with him at first the Royal Fusiliers, half a battalion of the Royal Scots Fusiliers, the Royal Welsh Fusiliers, and the Royal Irish Fusiliers, all of his own brigade—the 6th. Towards the end of January he was called upon to send a battalion and a half to reinforce Buller's army, receiving in their stead three hundred of the Royal Fusiliers from Maritzburg and the Rifle Reserve battalion‡, 700 strong, from Frere. His artillery consisted of four Naval 12-prs., under Lieut. S. R. S. Richards, R.N., to which later was added a part-worn 4.7-in. gun, mounted on a railway truck. For a few days he had also a Mountain battery, soon called away to Head-quarters. As mounted infantry he had two hundred of the South African Light Horse. After making strong entrenchments, he devoted himself to harassing the enemy as far as his limited means would permit. He frequently demonstrated against the works at Colenso. From gun positions which he prepared on

<small>Barton with 6th brigade at Chieveley.</small>

---

* See map No. 30 and the freehand sketches for this and the following chapters.

† See page 340.

‡ A corps improvised out of drafts, chiefly of Reserve men, recently arrived from England for the Rifle regiments besieged in Ladysmith.

a knoll two thousand yards north of his camp, two of his 12-prs. daily, and often very heavily, shelled the Boers as they improved their existing trenches or excavated new ones. When the 4.7-in. arrived, Barton greatly disturbed the burghers by bringing it into action during the night. He patrolled vigorously to the east and west. He so impressed the burghers in his front that their general, Lukas Meyer, hesitated to comply with Louis Botha's reiterated and strongly-worded appeals for help on the Upper Tugela. From captured telegrams it seems clear that Barton succeeded in thus keeping inert considerably more than three thousand of the enemy around Colenso.

Difficulties of Buller's fresh attempt to force Tugela. When Sir Redvers Buller decided to withdraw his troops from Vaal Krantz and to try once more to force the passage of the Tugela near Colenso, he did so with a full knowledge of the difficulties of the task. The battle of December 15th had shown him the impossibility of crossing the river close to the village; before he marched to Springfield it was known that the enemy had strengthened himself to the north of Colenso; since then Barton had ascertained that there were hostile posts on Cingolo, and that Hlangwhane was strongly held.

The Boer leaders had acted on their firm belief that, on the 15th December, it would have been impossible for them to have maintained their hold upon the Tugela, if the British, instead of attacking the centre of their carefully-prepared system of entrenchments, had thrown their strength against Hlangwhane—isolated as it was on the further side of the river, and, in their *Boer works on the right bank of the Tugela.* judgment, essential to the safety of their left. A series of trenches and sangars now stretched from Hlangwhane to Green Hill, and defended the northern slopes of the valley of the Gomba from direct attack. From Green Hill, the line of works was flung back to the southern end of Monte Cristo, to guard against a turning movement on the extreme left of their position. Every span of the railway bridge had been demolished by the Boers before the 15th December. After the battle, the Naval guns were turned upon the road bridge, and by their shell-fire threw down one span, one hundred feet in length, besides greatly straining the whole structure, and throwing a large part of it out of the perpendicular. Thus, neither the railway nor the road bridges at Colenso could be used. The Boers had established communication between their right and left wings by a bridge thrown over the Tugela under the slopes of Naval Hill. It was made of material taken from the railway. On a series of rocks, which stretched across the stream, were laid beams, and on this foundation were placed rails, with sleepers as chesses and rails as ribands. To supplement it, the Boers had built an aerial tramway for the passage of supplies to the right bank, and had also arranged a ferry.

On Wednesday, February 7th, General Buller decided that his fresh effort to relieve Ladysmith should begin by the capture of Hlangwhane and the other hills occupied by the Boers on the right bank. He heliographed his intention to General White in the following words :— Buller's plan, in brief, 7th Feb., 1900.

"No 190 Cipher. 7th February. The enemy is too strong for me here, and though I could force the position it would be at a great loss. The Bulwana big gun is here and a large force. My plan is to slip back to Chieveley, take Hlangwhane, the Boer position south of Tugela and east of Colenso, and the next night try to take Bulwana from the south. Can you think of anything better ? I find I cannot get my guns and trains through these mountains. I hope to be at Hlangwhane on Saturday."*

At first, the Boers were not a little perplexed by Sir Redvers' movements, and General Louis Botha, in a telegram of the 10th to General Lukas Meyer, said : "It is not impossible they will now entrench themselves on some place or another, and that the greater part of them are going to Cape Colony." Two days later, however, General Fourie, who was in charge of the burghers at Monte Cristo on the extreme left of their line, divined General Buller's plan, and in a message demanding reinforcements, stated that the British appeared to intend to seize the heights on which the Boer left wing rested. Boers, at first puzzled, divine Buller's plan.

By the 12th the new dispositions of the army of Natal were completed. The main body lay concentrated round the railway station at Chieveley, where Sir Redvers Buller established his Headquarters. The left flank was protected by a mixed force, which, as has been mentioned in Chapter XXIII., on the retire- Disposition and composition of Buller's army, 12th Feb., 1900.

* Corrected next day to "Monday" (12th February).

ment from Vaal Krantz had been left under the command of Lieut.-Colonel Burn-Murdoch, Royal Dragoons, at Springfield, sixteen miles to the west of Chieveley. The detachment consisted of the 1st cavalry brigade (Burn-Murdoch),* with A. battery R.H.A., two Naval 12-prs. under Lieut. C. R. N. Burne, R.N., and two infantry battalions, the 1st York and Lancaster and the Imperial Light Infantry. It numbered about 106 officers and 2,680 men of other ranks. The right flank was watched at Greytown by Lieut.-Colonel E. C. Bethune, 16th Lancers, with a party about 460 strong, composed of Bethune's mounted infantry, Natal Police, the Umvoti Mounted Rifles, and two 7-pr. Field guns, manned by the Natal Field artillery. Still further to the east, a small body of mounted infantry, with two light Naval 12-pr. 8-cwt. guns from H.M.S. *Terrible*, policed Zululand, and prevented the natives from attacking such commandos of the enemy as approached the frontier.

The main body at Chieveley was thus composed :—

HEADQUARTERS STAFF.

Naval Brigade (Captain E. P. Jones, R.N.) :—
    One 6-in. gun.
    Three 4.7-in. guns. (It must, however, be noted that on the 13th three more 4.7-in., with all the gear necessary for mounting them on platforms, arrived at Chieveley by train. These were left on the railway trucks until the 19th, when one was mounted at Gun Hill, Chieveley. The other two were not detrained until the 25th, when they were dragged to the Hlangwhane plateau, and took part in the action of the 27th.)
    Ten 12-pr. 12-cwt. guns.
Strength : 30 officers, 305 other ranks.

Corps Troops :—
    19th battery R.F.A.
    61st Howitzer battery R.F.A.

---

* The Royal Dragoons, the 13th Hussars, and the Headquarters and two squadrons of the 14th Hussars. The 3rd squadron of the 14th Hussars was with Lord Roberts' army.

RELIEF OF LADYSMITH. 427

Two 5-in. guns, 16th company southern division R.G.A.
(The other two guns of this company reached Chieveley from Cape Colony on the 15th.)
No. 4 Mountain battery R.G.A.
Ammunition column.
Telegraph detachment R.E.
A. Pontoon Troop R.E.
Balloon Section R.E.

Strength, including Headquarters Staff : 69 officers, 1,105 other ranks.

2nd *Mounted Brigade* (Colonel the Earl of Dundonald) :—
Composite regiment of mounted infantry (Captain H. De la P. Gough, 16th Lancers).
South African Light Horse (Lieut.-Colonel the Hon. J. H. G. Byng, 10th Hussars).
Thorneycroft's mounted infantry (Lieut.-Colonel A. Thorneycroft, Royal Scots Fusiliers).

Strength : 53 officers, 1,033 other ranks.

IIND INFANTRY DIVISION (MAJOR-GENERAL THE HON. N. G. LYTTELTON).

Divisional Troops :—
1 troop 13th Hussars.
7th battery R.F.A. ⎫
63rd battery R.F.A. ⎬ Brigade division R. F. A.
64th battery R.F.A. ⎭ Major W. L. H. Paget.
Ammunition column.
17th company R.E.

Strength : 53 officers, 977 other ranks.

2nd *Brigade* (Major-General H. J. T. Hildyard) :—
2nd Bn. "Queen's" regiment (Lieut.-Colonel E. O. F. Hamilton).
2nd Bn. Devonshire regiment (Major H. Batson).
2nd Bn. West Yorkshire regiment (Colonel F. W. Kitchener).
2nd Bn. East Surrey regiment (Lieut.-Colonel R. H. W. H. Harris).

Strength : 110 officers, 3,647 other ranks.

4th Brigade (Colonel C. H. B. Norcott, vice Major-General the Hon. N. G. Lyttelton) :—
 2nd Bn. Scottish Rifles (Lieut.-Colonel E. Cooke).
 3rd Bn. King's Royal Rifle Corps (Major R. C. A. B. Bewicke-Copley).
 1st Bn. Durham Light Infantry (Lieut.-Colonel A. L. Woodland).
 1st Bn. Rifle Brigade (Major C. A. Lamb).
Strength : 97 officers, 3,341 other ranks.
Total strength of the Division*: 260 officers, 7,965 other ranks.

VTH INFANTRY DIVISION (LIEUT.-GENERAL SIR C. WARREN).
Divisional Troops :—
 1 troop Royal Dragoons.
 Colonial Scouts.
 28th battery R.F.A. ⎫ Brigade division R.F.A.
 73rd battery R.F.A. ⎬ Major W. Apsley Smith.
 78th battery R.F.A. ⎭
 Ammunition column.
 37th company R.E.
Strength : 56 officers, 1,025 other ranks.

10th Brigade (Major-General J. Talbot Coke) :—
 2nd Bn. Somerset Light Infantry (Lieut.-Colonel E. J. Gallwey).
 2nd Bn. Dorset regiment (Lieut.-Colonel C. H. Law).
 2nd Bn. Middlesex regiment (Lieut.-Colonel A. W. Hill).
Strength : 81 officers, 3,041 other ranks.

11th Brigade† (Major-General A. S. Wynne) :—
 2nd Bn. King's Own (Royal Lancaster) regiment (Colonel M. E. Crofton).
 1st Bn. South Lancashire regiment (Lieut.-Colonel W. McCarthy-O'Leary).

---

* Includes 29 officers and 326 other ranks of Army Service Corps and Royal Army Medical Corps, already reckoned in the brigades.

† The York and Lancaster regiment had been detached from the brigade on the 11th February, and the Lancashire Fusiliers on the 12th February.

Rifle Reserve battalion (Major the Hon. E. J. Montagu-Stuart-Wortley, King's Royal Rifle Corps).
Strength : 60 officers, 2,350 other ranks.

6*th Brigade* (*temporarily attached to Vth Division*) (Major-General G. Barton) :—
    2nd Bn. Royal Fusiliers (Lieut.-Colonel C. G. Donald).
    2nd Bn. Royal Scots Fusiliers (Lieut.-Colonel E. E. Carr).
    1st Bn. Royal Welsh Fusiliers (Lieut.-Colonel C. C. H. Thorold).
    2nd Bn. Royal Irish Fusiliers (Colonel J. Reeves).
Strength : 130 officers, 4,074 other ranks.

Total strength of the Division* : 327 officers, 10,490 other ranks.

5*th Brigade* (*unattached*) (Major-General A. F. Hart) :—
    1st Bn. Royal Inniskilling Fusiliers (Lieut.-Colonel T. M. G. Thackeray).
    1st Bn. Border regiment (Major J. S. Pelly).
    1st Bn. Connaught Rangers (Colonel L. G. Brooke).
    2nd Bn. Royal Dublin Fusiliers (Colonel C. D. Cooper).
Strength : 92 officers, 3,609 other ranks.

Thus, irrespective of Burn-Murdoch's and Bethune's flanking detachments, General Buller had concentrated round his Headquarters at Chieveley a force of 831 officers and 24,507 non-commissioned officers and men, with 42 Field guns, 6 Howitzers, 6 mountain guns, two 5-in. guns of the Royal Artillery, 22 machine guns, and the formidable array of Naval guns enumerated above.

The railway line from Chieveley to Pietermaritzburg was held at Frere by the 2nd Lancashire Fusiliers, reduced by their losses at Spion Kop to 8 officers and 662 of other ranks, and two Naval 12-pr. guns; and thence southward by detachments of 1st Royal Dublin Fusiliers, Natal Royal Rifles, Colonial Scouts, Durban Light Infantry, four Naval 12-pr. guns, and Natal Field artillery. Pietermaritzburg was guarded by the depôts

* Includes 40 officers and 529 other ranks of Army Service Corps and Royal Army Medical Corps, already reckoned in the brigades.

of battalions, the convalescents, and details of various corps, while Durban lay secure under the guns of the fleet.

The terrain. The terrain from which Buller's army was about to attempt to drive the Boers is a portion of the great natural redoubt protecting Ladysmith from the south, the general features of which have already been discussed in Volume I., Chapter XXI. The length of the battlefield in which the troops under Sir Redvers Buller's immediate command took part between February the 14th and the 27th, is about ten miles, and stretches from Cingolo Mountain to Vertnek Mountain; its breadth, from the valley of the Gomba to Pieters Station, is a little more than six miles. This area is cut in two by the Tugela, which after flowing in an easterly direction from its source to Colenso, turns sharply to the north-west a mile to the east of that village. This course it follows for about two miles and a half, till it reaches the first waterfall, and then runs eastward for a mile and a half. For the next three miles the Tugela flows to the north-east, and then again changes its direction to the eastward. Its bed gradually deepens until, below the first waterfall, the river runs through a deep and rocky gorge with sides several hundred feet in depth, and so steep that men scale them with difficulty.

On the right bank the mountains rise in a well-defined horse-shoe, the western heel of which is formed by Hlangwhane, 544 feet in height. From Hlangwhane, a spur, only 200 feet lower than the parent hill, runs parallel to the river in its northern course for nearly two miles, at first in a sharp and narrow ridge, but then broadening out into the comparatively level ground now called Naval Hill, to commemorate the concentration of Naval guns upon it during the fighting of February 26th-27th. The toe is marked by a further series of heights, named Fuzzy Hill and Clump Hill, which are respectively 444 feet and 894 feet high; they overhang the Tugela as it heads to the north-east and east, and face Terrace, Railway, and Pieters Hills. Then the horse-shoe, sweeping southward in the long mountain of Monte Cristo (1,044 feet), ends at Green Hill, its eastern heel. The plateau enclosed by this system of hills is about four miles in length from north to south, by three miles and a half from east to west; its surface is broken and undulating, and in places covered by a thick growth of thornbush and low trees. To the south-east of Monte Cristo, with which it is connected by a high Nek, rises a rocky and isolated hill, Cingolo, 844 feet in height, the lower slopes of which are covered with dense scrub. At the foot of Hlangwhane, Green Hill and Cingolo, is the bed of the Gomba stream, which falls into the Blaauwkrantz river, two miles and a half to the southeast of Cingolo. The Blaauwkrantz runs through Frere, passes two miles south of Chieveley, and joins the Tugela eight miles to the east of Cingolo. Between the Blaauwkrantz and the Gomba is a rolling upland, the western portion of which was called Hussar Hill, while the eastern was named Moord Kraal.

On the left bank of the Tugela the country is even more hilly, and more difficult for the operations of regular troops, than it is to the east of Colenso. Three hills stand out prominently among the sea of kopjes, through which wind the roads from Colenso to Ladysmith.* The rising ground between the valley of the Tugela and the Onderbrook reaches its greatest height in Vertnek, 874 feet above Colenso, and five miles west of Hlangwhane. Two miles to the north-east stands Grobelaar Mountain, a flat-topped, steep-sided kopje, 150 feet lower; two miles further north frowns the loftiest eminence of the series, Onderbrook Mountain, 1,314 feet. From its slopes rises the Langewacht Spruit, which, in its eastward course to the Tugela, is commanded alike by Onderbrook and Grobelaar Mountains. South of the latter, the Onderbrook Spruit runs roughly parallel to, and about a mile south of, the Langewacht, dominated throughout its length by Grobelaar. Between the three mountains just described a mass of subsidiary ridges stretch eastward towards the river. The north side of the valley of the Langewacht is formed by a belt of country, a mile and a half in width, seamed with dongas, and bristling with kopjes. The eastern boundary of this difficult piece of ground

* The ground immediately to the north of Colenso has been described in detail in Volume I., Chapter XXI.

is marked by Terrace Hill and Railway Hill, respectively 544 and 444 feet in height, which command the few hundred yards of comparatively level country between them and the Tugela. To the north-east of Railway Hill, and separated from it by a deep and narrow gorge along the western face of which runs the railway from Colenso to Ladysmith, is Pieters Hill.

The space between the Langewacht and the Onderbrook Spruits is filled by Horse-shoe and Wynne's Hills, which are about 400 feet lower than Grobelaar; while from the Onderbrook Spruit, a feature known as the Colenso Kopjes, and about 240 feet higher than the station, stretches southward to the railway bridge over the Tugela. Through this maze of hills there were two practicable roads. The western track lay through the defile between Vertnek and Grobelaar; the eastern ran between Wynne's Hill and the Tugela, then, circling round Terrace Hill, left Railway Hill to its right, and struck northward by Pieters Station to Nelthorpe. The road shown on the map between Grobelaar and Horse-shoe Hills was out of repair at the beginning of 1900, and virtually impassable.

Strength of the enemy;

The difficulty of determining the strength of the Boers during the fourteen days' struggle which ended with the relief of Ladysmith is more than usually great. By collating a large number of statements, made after the war by Boers who took part in this phase of the campaign, it appears probable that before any considerable reinforcements arrived from Ladysmith and from the Upper Tugela, nearly 7,000 burghers faced Sir Redvers Buller. The subsequent reinforcements, which included many outlying detachments, are estimated at between 1,500 and 2,000 men. To state with accuracy the number of

his artillery.

the enemy's guns is even more difficult than to give the strength of his commandos, not only because the Boers kept no official records, but because they continually changed the position of their artillery, thus causing it to appear more numerous than it really was. So frequently was it moved during each day's engagement from one cunningly prepared position to another, that in the maps illustrating these operations no attempt has been made to show the enemy's guns, though in the letterpress

RELIEF OF LADYSMITH. 433

the sites of the Boer cannon have been mentioned, as far as it has been possible to ascertain them. But, whatever may have been the exact number of guns which Botha was able to put into the field, it was quite insignificant compared to the British artillery.

In his message of February 7th* to General White, informing the defender of Ladysmith that the attempt to pierce the enemy's line at Vaal Krantz was abandoned, Sir Redvers Buller had foreshadowed the new scheme which was then forming in his mind for the relief of the garrison. He proposed first to seize Hlangwhane, Green Hill, Cingolo and Monte Cristo, and make himself master of the plateau they encircled. Next, if the track leading over Cingolo Nek proved practicable, he would cross the Tugela by a drift which had no name, and which lay a little to the south-east of the hill Intaba Ka Renga (map No. 30). Thence he would march to the Klip river, pass it to the north-east of Intaba Ka Renga, and sweep upon Umbulwana. But little was known of the Hlangwhane—Monte Cristo line of hills; even less of the track leading to the nameless drift; therefore, the whole of the project was necessarily tentative. Before deciding upon the details for the execution of the first part of his plan, the General desired to study closely the network of hills and valleys into which he must thrust his army. Hussar Hill presented suitable ground for his reconnaissance, and on the evening of February 11th, he gave Lord Dundonald orders to seize it with a mixed force of all arms; and next morning it was occupied, almost without resistance from the Boers. From the captured ground the General, through a telescope, made a long and careful examination of the terrain over which he was about to operate. When he had familiarised himself with its details, and noted the long and broken lines of trenches and sangars which ran from Hlangwhane to Monte Cristo, he withdrew the detachment. Though the rear-guard was hotly attacked as it fell back, the reconnaissance was successfullly effected with very small loss. In the afternoon Sir Redvers Buller verbally explained to his generals the outline of the plan, which his observations had

Details of Buller's plan.

Reconnaissance from Hussar Hill, Feb. 12th.

* See page 425.

enabled him to mature. The seizure of the hills stretching from Hlangwhane to Monte Cristo was to be the first step. Then the whole of the plateau between these hills and the Tugela was to be cleared of the enemy. Lastly, a pontoon bridge was to be thrown across the river, and the troops transferred from the right to the left bank, at some point which the operations of the next few days would enable him to select.

Buller's information about the Boer dispositions on right bank, Feb. 13th.

On the 13th, Lieut.-Colonel A. E. Sandbach, A.A.G. for intelligence, submitted a valuable report on the dispositions and entrenchments of the enemy south of the river:—

"INFORMATION OF ENEMY SOUTH OF TUGELA.

"13th February.

"1. Hussar Hill.—The enemy have been in the habit of occupying the dongas near this hill nightly. They also hold the bed of the Gomba Stream, where the natural formation of the ground affords good cover, and has been further improved by them.

"2. The enemy are reported to have five camps south of the Tugela, all within a three-mile radius of Hlangwhane:

On Hlangwhane itself.
Bloy's Farm.
Near the waterfall.
On N.W. spur of Cingolo Hill, north of the Nek.
On Gomba Stream.

"It is their custom, as far as has been ascertained, to have 'dummy' tents. Tents are often pitched to draw artillery fire. The Boers themselves, for the most part, sleep and live behind the hills, or in cover in the dongas.

"3. The bridge behind Hlangwhane is between the rapids and falls, and is made of rails laid on loose stone piers, with sleepers for a roadway. It is broad enough for two men or horses to cross abreast. There is also a square punt moved across the river by a wire, near the platelayer's cottage. It is capable of holding about twenty men.

"4. On Hlangwhane Hill there are certainly two guns, one a large gun, probably a long-range Creusot 3-in. gun, which fires shrapnel, and one Vickers-Maxim quick-firing 1-pr. Other guns may, however, have been brought across.

"5. North of the Gomba Stream there are some thirty schanzes built up; south of it, on Andries Pretorius' Farm, a long trench is reported to have been dug. The earth from this and other trenches has been carried about twenty yards in front of the trench itself, so as to conceal its real position. The force manning these defences is probably held concealed in the dongas, until after any preliminary artillery bombardment is completed. Shells in rear of the flanks of visible defences will probably delay their movements.

"6. The slopes of Cingolo Hill, facing the Gomba Stream, are reported to have been lately entrenched. No guns have yet been reported there, but may be expected.

"7. Six guns and two Maxims are reported to be mounted on the ridges between the railway and the Ladysmith main road, on left bank of the Tugela, *i.e.*, north and north-west of Fort Wylie. These guns can bring fire to bear on Hlangwhane Hill.

"One gun is reported on a kopje north-west of A. Pretorius' Farm."

After the enemy had been driven from the right bank of the Tugela, the entrenchments mentioned in this report were examined by Royal Engineer officers, who found that while a few on the extreme left of the Boer line were mere shallow trenches, the majority were formidable works, about four feet deep, with a parapet three feet in height, and several feet in thickness. Their occupants stood up to fire through small loopholes. In selecting sites for these entrenchments, the Boers had shown their usual skill, and to conceal them and blur their outline, bushes, rocks and boughs of trees had been scattered in front of them. Good use was made of dummy trenches, ostentatiously built in open ground to draw artillery fire. The only difference between the real and the dummy works was that the top of the parapets of the former were made of sacks of earth to stop bullets and splinters of stone, while the latter had no such protection. *Nature of works on right bank.*

In the account of the operations about to be described, it will be noticed that Sir Redvers Buller either gave verbal instructions to his generals, or, when orders in writing were issued by his Chief of the Staff, supplemented them by oral explanations. He adopted this course to minimise the chances of misunderstanding between his lieutenants and himself, for he realised the extreme difficulty of describing in writing the features of the mountainous country which his troops were about to enter. Like the district around Spion Kop and Vaal Krantz, it had indeed been surveyed, but solely with the view of settling the boundaries of the farms; and the map hurriedly compiled from these farm surveys on the outbreak of war often misrepresented or wholly ignored the military features of the ground. Great efforts had been made to correct these defects, but the only information obtainable was not that of soldiers trained to *Difficulty of issuing orders in writing, owing to nature of the country.*

study country from a professional standpoint, but of Natal colonists. Keen observers, from their own point of view, they were apt to leave out of their account details in the terrain which were really of vital military importance. Consequently the map, though far better than none at all, was frequently very misleading.

Absence of landmarks.

The difficulty in issuing formal written orders was increased by the absence of landmarks, such as would be found in most theatres of war. No hamlet clung to the sides of the mountains. No church steeple broke the sky-line. Hardly a farmhouse was to be seen. The shape of the kopjes had a different aspect when seen from various points of view. The perplexity due to these causes is to be traced, not only throughout the written orders for each day, but in the reports sent in by the generals describing the movements they had made, the ground they had gained, and their suggestions for the future employment of the troops under their command.

13th Feb., orders for the 14th.

Anxious though General Buller was to begin operations, various causes contributed to delay his movements, and it was not until the 13th that the following orders were issued for the advance of the IInd and Vth divisions upon Hussar Hill:—

" 1. It is intended to seize Hussar Hill to-morrow, and the spurs to the east of it, north of Moord Kraal, and to occupy this position with artillery.

" 2. Lieut.-Gen. Warren, with the Vth division, will move at 7 a.m. from Gun Hill, and will occupy Hussar Hill as far as the eastern slopes across the Weenen Road ; Maj.-Gen. Barton's brigade is placed under his orders.

" 3. Maj.-Gen. Lyttelton will move with his command (less Maj.-Gen. Hart's brigade) at the same hour by such route as he considers most suitable, and will occupy the eastern spurs of Hussar Hill, from Lieut.-Gen. Warren's right as far as the Blaauwkrantz, where that stream loops sharply to the north.

" 4. These positions will be entrenched under the orders of General Officers Commanding. The C.R.E. will make arrangements for an additional supply of entrenching tools.

" 5. As soon as Hussar Hill is occupied the two bde. divns. Field artillery, and the corps Field artillery battery, under Col. Parsons, will take up a position on it.

" The four Naval 12-prs., the two 5-in. guns, and the Howitzer battery will move with Gen. Warren's division, and take up a position with the Field batteries.

" The guns remaining on Gun Hill will endeavour to keep down the fire of the enemy's guns, should they open on Hussar Hill.

"6. Lord Dundonald's brigade will cover the movement. It will strike its camp, and bivouac on a site which will be pointed out to it.

"7. Maj.-Gen. Hart's brigade will move to Gun Hill, and remain in protection of the camp and railway station, watching the ground to his front and west. He will detail any working parties required to assist the movement of the Naval guns, on the requisition of the C.R.A.

"8. The troops will strike and pack their tents. They will carry on the man one day's rations, and in the wagons accompanying the troops, the men's great-coats. The remainder of the baggage will be parked; that of Maj.-Gen. Lyttelton's division, near Chieveley Station, and that of Lieutenant-General Warren's division, near Gun Hill.

"9. The General Commanding will be on Hussar Hill.
"By Order,
"H. S. G. MILES, Colonel,
"Chief of Staff."

Early in the morning of the 14th Sir Redvers Buller met the officers commanding his divisions, and issued verbal orders, which were thus summarised by his Chief of the Staff:— *14th Feb.; further orders issued verbally.*

"Vth division to advance at 7.30 a.m., and seize (the) Scrubby Hill immediately east of Hussar Hill. To use part of Barton's brigade for that purpose, keeping remainder on east end of Hussar Hill. Divisional batteries, Vth division, to remain with division.

"IInd division. As soon as Vth division has secured above hill, the IInd division will advance to reverse slope of it, and there orders will be issued as to further attack towards Cingolo by G.O.C. IInd division.

"The brigade division artillery and the Howitzer battery will act under orders of Colonel Parsons.

"The two 5-in. guns and the four 12-prs. will remain on Hussar Hill to keep down enemy's fire.

"Colonel Lord Dundonald will cover the right and left flanks and help the movement as far as he can."

The infantry divisions, preceded by the 2nd mounted brigade, marched from their bivouacs, and brushed away the Boer skirmishers, who were based on a deep wooded donga at the foot of Hlangwhane. Three guns opened upon the British. One, a 94-pr., posted at Fort Wylie, was speedily silenced by the heavy artillery at Gun Hill, near Chieveley. A second was concealed behind the reverse slope of Hlangwhane, while a third was placed some little distance to the north of Green Hill. About 9 a.m. Hussar Hill was reoccupied almost without loss, *Advance begins; Hussar Hill occupied.*

and at first it appeared that the Boers had completely retired from the south of the Gomba, but a skirmish on the right of the line between the 4th brigade and a party of the enemy at Moord Kraal Hill proved that this was not the case.

The artillery was brought up to Hussar Hill. Part of the Field batteries, and four Naval 12-prs. under Lieutenant F. C. A. Ogilvy and Mr. J. Wright (gunner), moved to its northern and north-eastern slopes, whence they shelled the centre of the enemy's line between Hlangwhane and Green Hill; the 61st Howitzer battery, from behind its south-western end, was in action against Green Hill.* Two 5-in. guns, in the course of the afternoon, were placed on the south side of Hussar Hill.

The three brigades of the Vth division bivouacked on the line extending from Hussar Hill on the east to the Colenso road on the west. The IInd division lay with the 2nd brigade on the south-eastern slopes of Hussar Hill, and the 4th brigade somewhat to the north-east. The Headquarters of the General Officer Commanding were established, early in the day, at Hussar Hill.

The troops were undisturbed during the night, save by a sudden cannonade from Gun Hill, where, by order of Major-General Hart, the Naval 4.7-in. guns fired in the direction of a laager reported to be concealed on the slopes of the far side of Hlangwhane.

Feb. 15th; artillery action.

On the 15th the artillery continued their bombardment of the trenches between Hlangwhane and Green Hill, searched with shrapnel the plateau behind these heights, and engaged the Boer ordnance. The Boer guns behind Hlangwhane and Green Hill were in the same places as on the 14th, and remained there till the 18th; the 94-pr. had disappeared from Fort Wylie, while a field gun and a 4.7-in. Howitzer came into action from the kopje south of the Onderbrook, which forms part of the hill frequently referred to in the following chapters as 244, from

* The daily expenditure of ammunition by each battery of the Royal Artillery and by the Naval brigade is given in Appendix 12.

It is impossible to state the total amount of small-arm ammunition used between the 12th February and the 3rd March, as a carefully prepared return on the subject was, unfortunately, lost in South Africa during the later stages of the war.

the figures on the map which denote its height. The artillery was on this day strengthened by the arrival of the remaining two 5-in. guns of the 16th company, Southern Division, R.G.A., from Port Elizabeth, but these two guns did not open fire till February 18th. While the gunners thus occupied the attention of the Boers, the eastward extension against the extreme eft of the enemy's line began slowly to develop. On the right the IInd division occupied Moord Kraal Hill and some rising ground to its north-west. Warren connected the right of his own division (the Vth) with Lyttelton (IInd division), by despatching the 6th brigade (Barton) to seize a wooded spur which lies about a mile east of Hussar Hill.

Movement against Boer left begins.

At 11.20 a.m. Major-General Lyttelton informed Sir Redvers Buller that the

"Boer position stretches much further back from Green Hill, just south of 'good camping ground,' towards Nek (*i.e.*, the Nek which divides Monte Cristo from Cingolo) than I thought.

"Report received on the Gomba Stream Valley, enclosed, shows position of Boer laagers. Ground on this side stream fairly easy—on far side difficult. I am going to send a skirmishing line towards the Gomba to try and disclose the Boer positions. This hill is suitable for artillery, but the Nek is beyond Field artillery range. The infantry on this hill should be entrenched. I will report further when skirmishers have advanced. The Boer position appears a very big one, and if adequately held would require more troops than are at my disposal."

To this message Buller replied at noon :—

"Reconnoitre carefully before you commit your troops further than the Gomba, and if you consider enterprise too difficult do not attempt it.

"We are holding a large number of Boers off Ladysmith, which is, after all, all we can expect to do.

"Let me know the conclusion you come to as soon as possible."

No further advance was made that day. It is a curious instance of the "fog of war" that, while the British generals hesitated to attack the Boer positions on account of their strength, Fourie, who commanded on the extreme left of the enemy's line, was thoroughly aware of his own weakness. Ever since the British force first moved into the valley of the Blaauwkrantz, he had frequently reported the danger of his situation, and on the 15th he urgently demanded reinforcements of men, artillery, and Kaffirs to dig emplacements for the guns.

Feb. 16th; artillery action; reconnaissance of Cingolo.

The artillery, on the 16th, kept up a very slow but steady fire upon the targets of the previous days, and the approaches to Cingolo were reconnoitred in force by the IInd division, while the Composite regiment, one of Dundonald's mounted infantry corps, lapped round the south-eastern base, and worked up the lower slopes. At 5.15 a.m., the Queen's (2nd brigade) and the Scottish Rifles (4th brigade) descended into the valley of the Gomba, with half of each battalion extended in first line, followed by the remaining half-battalions in reserve. In an hour they had crossed the river-bed, and gradually forced their way through the rugged and scrub-covered country to within a mile and a half of the foot of Cingolo, the south-eastern crest of which was now temporarily held by Captain R. N. Smyth, 21st Lancers, then doing duty with the 13th Hussars, who, with a patrol from the troop of regular cavalry attached to Lyttelton's division, had climbed the hill from the south-west. He came under fire from "snipers" hidden in the bush, but saw no sign of trenches or sangars. This patrol learnt much about the ground, and found the track, if track it can be called, by which Dundonald next day made his way upwards to the top of Cingolo. When the infantry was ordered to fall back, the Boer sharpshooters became active, but with little result. The rest of Lyttelton's troops did not cross the Gomba, and at 11 a.m. all were ordered to return to their bivouacs.

Dispositions on night of 16th.

At nightfall the disposition of the British force was as follows: On the extreme right the Composite regiment protected the outer flank of the IInd division, which bivouacked opposite Cingolo Mountain. In the centre were the 6th (Barton) and the 10th (Coke) brigades of the Vth division. On the left Warren's remaining brigade, the 11th (Wynne), held Hussar Hill, and connected with the 5th brigade at Chieveley and Gun Hill. The latter brigade (Hart) was charged with the double duty of protecting the valuable accumulation of stores at railhead, and of assuring the safety of such of the Naval pieces as were placed in battery upon Gun Hill. The South African Light

Horse were in reserve behind the centre of the line, while the left flank was watched by Thorneycroft's mounted infantry, who reported that the enemy was entrenching himself behind Colenso.

Throughout February 14th, 15th and 16th, Sir Redvers did not seriously push on, partly because he feared the effect on his men of the extreme and exhausting heat of the weather, partly because of the difficulty of supplying the troops with water in the arid region they were now occupying. So dry was the country between the Blaauwkrantz and the Gomba that water in tanks, each containing two hundred gallons, had to be conveyed to the troops on ox wagons, and a light railway was begun, but not completed, from Chieveley to Hussar Hill, to bring up the tanks, which were distributed by wagons. When Major-General Barton, in his camp at Chieveley, had heard that Sir Redvers Buller had stopped the transmission of supplies to the Upper Tugela, he had at once inferred that the army was returning from Vaal Krantz to Chieveley, and telegraphed to Maritzburg for every available water tank to be sent up country. These were filled at Frere, and thence forwarded to Chieveley. As soon as the troops occupied the banks of the Gomba, water was obtained by digging in the bed of the stream. But Sir Redvers Buller's slowness of movement was mainly due to another cause. The possibility that the enemy might attempt to turn his right flank by crossing the eastern drifts over the Tugela was ever present to his mind, and he would not launch his army into the hilly and wooded country north of the Gomba until he received news on February 14th, from Colonel Bethune, at Greytown, that his men had begun to guard these fords. His left flank also caused him some uneasiness. The enemy had skirmished with Burn-Murdoch, though with no great vigour, on the 12th, 13th and 14th, and it was not until the 15th that a considerable part of the commandos, left on the Upper Tugela to watch the 1st cavalry brigade (Burn-Murdoch), moved eastward to reinforce their comrades at Colenso.

Reasons for delay on 14th, 15th and 16th.

On the other hand, it cannot be ignored that the delays of these three days were very advantageous to the enemy, who had at first been little prepared for a vigorous attack ; nor is it clear that the heat would have prevented the force from advancing rapidly to the Gomba and thus solving the water difficulty.

<small>Orders for the 17th Feb.</small>

On the evening of the 16th orders were issued :—

"Moord Kraal Hill,
"16th February, 1900.

" 1. It is the intention of the G.O.C. to attack the Cingolo Ridge and the Green Hill to-morrow.

" 2. A brigade of General Warren's division will hold Hussar Hill, which will be entrenched. A battery R.F.A. will be attached to this brigade. The two 5-in. guns and the four Naval 12-prs. will remain in their present positions, to keep down the fire of the enemy's guns.

" 3. The 78th battery R.F.A. and the Howitzer battery will remain in their present position for the night, and the G.O.C. Vth division will provide for their safety. These batteries, with the remaining four batteries R.F.A., will act to-morrow under instructions from Colonel Parsons.

" 4. Two days' supply will be brought out under arrangements to be made by G.O.C. divisions.

"By Order,
"H. S. G. MILES, Colonel,
"Chief of Staff."

Lord Dundonald was instructed that :—

" 1. It is the intention of the General Commanding to try to turn the left flank of the enemy's position north of the Gomba Spruit to-morrow.

" 2. Two divisions will advance towards Cingolo Nek at daybreak for this purpose, one brigade holding Hussar Hill and securing the gun positions there.

" 3. You will divide your command : half will be on the right and, advancing in rear of the infantry, will endeavour as soon as opportunity offers to gain ground to the right and outflank any detachment of the enemy that may appear on the Nek.

" 4. The other half*, less one strong troop, will operate on our left up the Gomba Valley, taking such opportunities as may offer.

" The O.C. detached troop will report to General Wynne at Hussar Hill for orders.

" The General will be at the east end of Moord Kraal Hill."

<small>Feb. 17th ; supplementary orders issued.</small>

After a consultation at daybreak on the 17th, between General Sir Redvers Buller, Lieutenant-General Warren, and Major-General Lyttelton, supplementary orders were issued :—

" 1. It is the intention to attack Cingolo Ridge and Green Hill.

" 2. The right of General Lyttelton's division will be directed upon about

* Thorneycroft's mounted infantry.

RELIEF OF LADYSMITH.

the middle of the Cingolo Nek, the left brigade following in touch with it, the general advance being échelon from the right. The division will then swing to its left and move against the Green Hill, attacking it from the north-east.

"3. One brigade of General Warren's division will move on the left of General Lyttelton, conforming to the movements of that division; the other will be in support.

"4. The Field batteries and Howitzer battery under Colonel Parsons will support the attack.

"By Order,
"H. S. G. Miles, C. of S."

The troops were at once set in motion. The turning movement was to be strongly developed. Lyttelton was to cross the Gomba and, by an attack from the south, carry Cingolo, and the Nek which connects that mountain with Monte Cristo. This accomplished, the IInd division was to wheel to the left, and assail Green Hill from the north-east. Two brigades of the Vth division were to be in support of the IInd division, while the third held Hussar Hill. The formation was to be in échelon of brigades from the right. At this time Cingolo was but lightly held by the Boers. Green Hill was occupied by parts of the Bethel and Swaziland commandos. Hlangwhane was defended by the Standerton commando and by detachments of burghers from Heidelberg, Middelburg, Vryheid, and Krugersdorp. The remainder of the Heidelberg and Middelburg commandos, with that of Ermelo and some of the men of Boksburg, were on Monte Cristo. On the left bank of the Tugela another party of Krugersdorpers manned the works at Fort Wylie; among the Colenso kopjes were posted the remainder of Boksburg and Vryheid, while on the lower slopes of Grobelaar Mountain stood the laagers of Zoutpansberg, and of the remainder of the Bethel and Swaziland contingents.

At dawn the Naval 4.7-in. guns upon Gun Hill opened fire on the low kopjes west of Green Hill, and on a gun which had been emplaced on Hlangwhane during the night. The sailors made such excellent practice that after nine rounds the Boer artillerymen abandoned it till nightfall, when it was dragged down the hill, and transferred to the left bank. By 6 a.m., the remainder of the batteries, which extended from Hussar Hill to Moord

Artillery bombardment,

444   THE WAR IN SOUTH AFRICA.

covered by which IInd division advances on Cingolo. Kraal Hill, were in action against the enemy's works and guns between Hlangwhane and Monte Cristo. Half an hour later the IInd division was ordered to move upon Cingolo under cover of this bombardment. Major-General Hildyard's brigade (2nd) was in front; his leading battalion, the 2nd West Yorkshire, was followed by the 2nd Devon, 2nd Queen's, and the 2nd East Surrey. By 7.30 a.m., the West Yorkshire began to cross the Gomba, and Colonel F. W. Kitchener reported to the G.O.C., 2nd brigade, the points on which he was directing his attack, but the progress of the 2nd brigade was necessarily slow, for the hill-side was steep and rough with boulders of iron-stone, and the bush so thick that men had to be dropped every ten or fifteen paces to maintain connection between the various portions of the battalions. Until 9 a.m., the troops were unmolested by the enemy, when long-range fire was opened upon them by a detachment of Boers upon the northern slopes of Cingolo. Major-General Hildyard determined to manoeuvre these men out of their position, and at 9.50 a.m. ordered the Queen's to make a wide movement to the right, climb the south-western spur of the hill, and sweep along the crest on to the enemy's left flank. Though, during the morning, the troop of divisional cavalry which was on Hildyard's outer flank had for a short time been in touch with the 2nd mounted brigade (Dundonald), the rugged ground did not allow this contact to be long maintained, and Hildyard at this time was ignorant of the whereabouts of Lord Dundonald's men. It was not till 1 p.m. that the leading companies of the Queen's made their way to the top of the spur, where they found some of the South African Light Horse and the Composite regiment.

Mounted infantry scale eastern side of Cingolo. During the night of the 16-17th, it had been ascertained that the Boers had entrenched themselves on Cingolo. Lord Dundonald's sphere of operations was accordingly enlarged, and, construing his orders with a latitude fully justified by the result, he determined to attack the mountain from the rear. After a long sweep to the east, he circled round its eastern base, and in the face of very great physical difficulties forced his way up the hill, steep, strewn with boulders, and covered with dense undergrowth. He surprised a detachment of three hundred burghers, under Commandant Beyers, who, intent on observing the movements of the infantry to the westward, had neglected to watch their own outer flank. After a skirmish the Boers retired, abandoning their trenches on the top of the hill in succession as the approach of the mounted infantry threatened them in rear. Three hours after the Queen's had reached the south-western crest of Cingolo, the whole of the summit was occupied by the British troops, who were shelled by guns, one of which at least was on the south-western slope of Monte Cristo, near Bloy's Farm. Thanks to the large Naval telescopes with which they were equipped, the sailors discovered this gun and engaged it from Gun Hill, before its presence was signalled to them from the right of the line. Other Boer guns were posted on the northern slopes of Green Hill. *Cingolo captured by 4 p.m.*

At 4.10 p.m. Major-General Lyttelton summarised the situation on the right in a message to Colonel Miles, the Chief of the Staff, who received it ten minutes later: "Queen's have now reached north-west corner of Cingolo, and Devon are about to advance on Nek and Monte Cristo; it will take the whole division for this. I think C.-in.-C. should come here to see the position, so that he may direct General Warren to attack Green Hill simultaneously, if he thinks fit." On reading this, General Buller decided to halt, as, owing to the lateness of the hour and the fatigue of the men, he intended to postpone the assault on Cingolo Nek and Green Hill until the following day. Dundonald's mounted infantry and the IInd division bivouacked on the ground they had gained. Dundonald was on the north-east shoulder of Cingolo, looking down upon the Nek; the Queen's held Cingolo crest. Behind them, on its south-western slopes, lay the remainder of the 2nd brigade; in low-lying ground to the left rear was the 4th brigade. For part of the West Yorkshire and of the Devon night brought no repose. General Hildyard had reported that, when the fighting was broken off, the enemy had fallen back in strength on Monte Cristo. To pave the way for the attack upon this hill, the northern end of which was out of range of the field guns south of the Gomba, the 64th battery, *The situation.* *Buller decides to postpone further movements till next day.*

R.F.A. had been ordered to the western slopes of Cingolo. The hill was so steep that a road had to be made, but by working all night, detachments of the two battalions succeeded in dragging up four of the guns. The infantry so placed these that they were able to do good service in the engagement of the 18th.

The Vth division took no active part in the turning movement. Major-General Barton, whose front line was annoyed by musketry from a low knoll a few hundred yards north of the Gomba, occupied it with half a battalion of Royal Irish Fusiliers. At nightfall he was ordered to recall this detachment to the southern bank, where his brigade bivouacked.

CHAPTER XXV.

RELIEF OF LADYSMITH.

THE CAPTURE OF MONTE CRISTO ; THE RIGHT BANK SECURED.

THE plans for February 18th are fully set out in the orders issued by the General Officers Commanding the IInd and Vth divisions.

<small>Feb. 18th: orders.</small>

"ORDERS FOR IIND DIVISION.
"18th February, 1900.

" 1. The IInd division will advance this morning towards the Cingolo Nek, which is reported to be strongly held.

" 2. The 2nd brigade will move off at 5.30 a.m., and endeavour to take up a holding line from which long-range infantry fire can be brought to bear on the crest of Monte Cristo and its S.E. slopes, or to disclose the enemy's positions nearer the Cingolo Nek.

" The G.O.C. 2nd brigade will attack Monte Cristo when, in his opinion, the preparation has been sufficient.

" 3. The 4th brigade will move on the left of the 2nd brigade, its left pivoting on the kraal where the 3rd K.R.R. are now stationed. It will endeavour to bring infantry fire to bear on the Monte Cristo Hill and its southern slopes to assist in the preparation. It will keep two battalions in third line at the disposal of the G.O.C. IInd division.

" 4. The cavalry will move along the northern slopes towards Monte Cristo, will cover the right flank of the movement, and will join the attack on Monte Cristo.

" 5. The battery R.F.A.* will open fire directly the enemy's position is disclosed by the infantry advance. The heavy guns south of the Gomba Stream will assist in the preparation.

" Simultaneously with the attack the Vth division will threaten the Green Hill with one brigade.

" 6. G.O.C. will be in rear of the 4th brigade.
"By Order,
" B. HAMILTON, Col. A.A.G."

* The 64th battery R.F.A. It was reinforced at 8 a.m. by the 7th battery R.F.A.

"ORDERS FOR THE VTH DIVISION, 9.15 P.M., 17-2-1900.

" 1. General Lyttelton will attack to-morrow at daylight.

" 2. General Barton's brigade will form General Lyttelton's chief support. Its movements will be entirely regulated by those of General Lyttelton's division. A staff officer of General Barton's brigade will proceed as soon as the moon is sufficiently risen to see, to General Lyttelton's bivouac, to find out General Lyttelton's exact dispositions and the best means of the 6th brigade supporting him, and inform the G.O.C. 6th brigade.

" 3. General Coke's brigade will be in reserve, and will, in the first instance, occupy the same position as it did to-day in mobile formation.

" 4. Troops will move at daylight. Breakfasts to be arranged accordingly.

" 5. The G.O.C.-in-C. will be with General Lyttelton.

" By Order,
" T. CAPPER, for A.A.G."

2nd brigade attacks Cingolo Nek, at 6.40 a.m.,   At dawn the 5-in. guns on Hussar Hill began to shell Monte Cristo ; at 6.15, in accordance with a plan suggested by Major-General Lyttelton the night before, they ceased fire, but later, at that officer's request, re-opened upon the same target with great success. At 6.40, the 2nd brigade advanced, the Queen's on the right, the West Yorkshire on the left, followed in second line by the Devonshire and East Surrey. Half an hour later the 4th brigade (Norcott) moved off and, on the left rear of Hildyard's men, worked through the thick scrub in the valley between Cingolo and Green Hill. To the left of the 4th brigade was the 6th brigade (Barton). As the leading troops of the 2nd brigade approached the Nek they came under artillery fire from the north of Green Hill and of Hlangwhane, and from Pieters Hill, and under heavy cross musketry from the works which connected Green Hill with the base of Monte Cristo. Covered by the long-range volleys of the supporting battalions, and by machine guns, by the shells of the Naval 4.7-in. guns, of the 5-in. guns of the 16th company, R.G.A. at Hussar Hill, and of the four field guns, which, during the night, the brigade had helped to drag into position on the western slopes of Cingolo, the Queen's and West Yorkshire, moving with great rapidity, were able with
carries it, and comparatively small loss to cross the Nek, and to work up the lower slopes of the steep and bushy hill which they had to ascend. Here, thanks to ground, " dead " to the Boers on Monte Cristo, it was possible to bring up supports, and thus give

weight and driving power to the first line in the assault they were about to deliver. The last thirty or forty feet of the hill was covered with huge boulders, and so steep in places that men had to scramble up on hands and knees. By the time the troops had scaled this wall of rock, the Boers had fallen back to the further ridges of the Monte Cristo range, whence they opened a steady and annoying fire upon the 2nd brigade. Thus by 10.30, part of the Queen's and West Yorkshire, driving before them the occupants of the trenches which lay across their path, had made a lodgment on the southern knoll of the Monte Cristo range, marked 1,044 on the map. There they were quickly reinforced by the Devonshire and half the East Surrey, the remainder of which battalion was posted in reserve upon the Nek, while Dundonald's men, pressing onward to the right of the infantry, continued the turning movement across the eastern slopes of Monte Cristo. At about 1 p.m., Hildyard's first line began to push along the crest. It was still supported by the heavy guns on Hussar Hill, and by the two field batteries, which from the slopes of Cingolo played upon the laager and works of the Boers near Bloy's farm. In co-operation with Dundonald's mounted brigade, Hildyard drove the enemy from the southern end of Monte Cristo, and then re-formed his much-scattered battalions, while Lord Dundonald pursued the Boers northwards, until his progress was arrested by impassable precipices. As soon as Hildyard had assembled his brigade, which for some time had been considerably annoyed by a gun posted in the neighbourhood of Hlangwhane, he pushed forward the West Yorkshire to the knoll numbered 1,034, which marks the southern extremity of the main hill of Monte Cristo. From this point Colonel W. Kitchener poured a heavy fire at seven hundred yards range upon the trenches defending the Bloy's farm laager, which lay open at his feet. This laager was also assailed by the 4th brigade (Norcott), which on the left of the 2nd brigade (Hildyard) had worked through the scrub. Enfiladed by the West Yorkshire, attacked in front by the 1st Rifle Brigade (the leading battalion of the 4th brigade), to which they had hitherto offered a stout rear-guard opposition, and disconcerted by the capture

makes a lodgment on south of Monte Cristo by 10.30 a.m.

The IInd division carries the southern end of Monte Cristo and the laager at its western foot.

of Green Hill by Barton's brigade (6th), the Boers in the neighbourhood of Bloy's Farm retreated, abandoning their laagers and stores to the British troops.

<small>Buller orders the advance to cease.</small>

The East Surrey had advanced to the northern end of the main ridge of Monte Cristo, when orders were received from Headquarters to suspend operations for the day, although the works facing the right of the British line had been taken, and the hurried flight of numbers of wagons on the left bank of the Tugela showed that a panic had seized the rear of the Boer army. Sir Redvers Buller did not consider it advisable to continue the pursuit of the enemy into the dense bush which covers the plateau until he had reconnoitred the ground. He had, long before this, made up his mind to halt. From a message sent about noon to Major-General Hildyard, it appears that even thus early in the day Buller had no intention of actively following up the enemy till the morrow. After congratulating the 2nd brigade on its assault on Monte Cristo, he said: "Shall you be able to make yourself comfortable there for the night? Dundonald knows where water is. We see many mounted Boers running away from your front. If you can hold the hill-top, I propose to at once commence the construction of the road up the Nek, with a view to getting up big guns." These guns were to be mounted on Cingolo Nek, to cover the movements of the army north-east towards the drift near Intaba Ka Renga.

<small>Operations of the left wing of the army.</small>

The left wing of the army had this day again but little to do. The 5th brigade (Hart) was at Chieveley; the 11th brigade (Wynne) held Hussar Hill; from the 10th brigade Talbot Coke sent a battalion to the foot of Green Hill to assist the advance of the 6th brigade (Barton). It will be remembered that Barton had been recalled to the south bank of the Gomba at nightfall on the 17th; and was ordered to act as the chief support to Lyttelton's division in the operations of the next day. The directions he received were to follow in échelon with the IInd division, marching on Green Hill. He was not to attack it until the 2nd brigade had crowned Monte Cristo. On the morning of the 18th, after moving about a mile through thick bush towards Green Hill, Barton established contact with the left

<small>Barton's brigade, the 6th,</small>

battalion of the IInd division, and remained halted with it for several hours until he could see the 2nd brigade (Hildyard) fighting on Monte Cristo. At about 1.30 p.m., he ascertained that the progress of the 4th brigade was hindered by burghers in sangars on a low ridge running from Green Hill towards Cingolo Nek. Seeing that by occupying Green Hill he would be able to enfilade this ridge, and thus help on the advance of the 4th brigade, he wrote to General Warren to report his intention, and then sent the Royal Scots Fusiliers against its eastern, the Royal Irish Fusiliers against its western spur. The defenders, shaken by the bombardment of the 73rd Field battery from Hussar Hill, and by the Field batteries on Cingolo, shells from which began to fall among them about mid-day, and finding their line of retreat compromised by Hildyard's presence on Monte Cristo, retired after a very faint resistance. The infantry occupied the hill, on which the scrub was so thick that the Royal Scots Fusiliers, as they forced their way up the steep slope, fixed bayonets, in order that the glint of steel might show the artillery where they were. From the top of the kopje, the Royal Scots Fusiliers saw, about five hundred yards to their front, a line of works upon which men were employed. Beyond these trenches was a laager. The battalion rushed forward, driving the enemy before them, and captured both the works and the laager. This second laager was quite distinct from that previously captured by the IInd division, and to the north-west of it. Barton then began rapidly to organise his brigade (6th) for pursuit; but before he could lead it on he received explicit orders to stand fast. Late in the afternoon, Boer guns from the left bank near the Falls shelled Green Hill and the plateau to its front, but without result. *[marginal notes: carry Green Hill, and capture a laager.]*

The capture of Monte Cristo was the outcome of careful organisation. The 2nd brigade worked well together, and those of its battalions which were not actually engaged in the assault used with effect long-range volleys in support of the leading troops. The sweep of the 2nd mounted brigade (Dundonald) along the eastern slopes of Monte Cristo assured the safety of Hildyard's outer flank. The well-timed advance of the 4th brigade against the trenches and works which enfiladed Hildyard's left relieved the pressure upon his inner flank, while the movement of the 6th brigade against Green Hill enabled the 4th brigade to carry out its share in the day's work with small loss. The artillery co-operated admirably with the infantry, and by their excellent shooting and well-combined action largely contributed to the success of the turning movement. Thanks to signalling and to the use of the telephone, the fire of the artillery was easily directed and controlled, notwithstanding the long front occupied by the batteries. While the Field batteries, the 5-in. guns, and the Naval 12-prs. on Hussar Hill were employed, first in shelling Monte Cristo, and then in beating down the defenders of Green Hill and of the ravines and broken ground around it, the 6-in. and 4.7-in. Naval guns on Gun Hill dealt with the fire of the widely-scattered Boer artillery, especially that of a 94-pr. which came into action from the Colenso kopjes at about 2 p.m.; this they silenced after its seventh round. Before night fell, Colonel Parsons, who commanded the Field and Howitzer batteries, had brought five of them (63rd, 28th, 78th, 73rd and 61st Howitzer) from the valley of the Gomba up to the plateau and placed them in bivouac to the south of Bloy's Farm, where they were joined by the 7th and 64th batteries [see map No. 30 (a)].

The formation generally adopted by the battalions of the IInd division during the hill and bush fighting on the right bank of the Tugela was as follows :—

The first line consisted of groups of scouts under a specially selected officer. From 300 to 400 yards in rear followed two companies in line, extended to about six paces; about 300 yards behind them marched two more companies, similarly extended. The remaining four companies, under the battalion commander, brought up the rear, usually in column at 250 paces distance, each company extended to four or five paces.

The result of the operations of the 17th and 18th had been that the greater part of the eastern side of the girdle of hills encircling the plateau occupied by the Boers on the south of the Tugela, and part of the southern side, had been captured with small loss. The casualties during the fighting on these days amounted only to 20 killed, 218 wounded and 4 missing.

At 11.30 on the night of the 18th February Sir Charles Warren sent to General Buller the following proposal for the operations on the following day :— *Warren's suggestions for movements of 19th accepted in principle by Buller.*

"1. I have been in consultation with General Lyttelton, and unless I hear to the contrary, propose that the following should take place to-morrow, 19.2.00.

"At daybreak General Hildyard will advance and secure the remainder of the Monte Cristo hills, and such kopjes as lie on the right of our line of advance.

"Colonel Norcott's brigade will be available if necessary to support this advance.

"The two batteries (7th and 64th) under Major Paget, R.A., will take part in this advance.

"As soon as the right is secure, which it is expected General Hildyard's brigade can effect by itself, my left will advance. The 6th (General Barton's) brigade will then attack along the south-eastern slopes of Hlangwhane. General Hildyard will move at daybreak, at which hour I shall be glad if you will arrange that all available guns (Naval or other), at Hussar Hill and at Chieveley, open a heavy fire upon Hlangwhane. This fire to be sustained until I send word or signal that I intend to advance—that is, when my right is secure. General Lyttelton will then be able to assist my attack with his left brigade. I propose to keep on the S.E. slopes of Hlangwhane so far as possible to avoid shell fire from long-range guns, probably across the river.

"2. I propose sending General Coke with two battalions, leaving one for safety of supplies, etc., to support the two Naval batteries from Hussar Hill. This force will move west so that the guns may shell Hlangwhane along southern slopes, keeping a shrapnel fire well ahead of our advance.

"Please detail batteries (as many as possible) and instruct C.R.A."

Substantially, the plan so sketched was carried out on the 19th, but the infantry movements on the right of the line were fettered by the necessity of awaiting the arrival of heavy guns with which to beat down the fire of the Boer artillery on the far side of the Tugela, and especially from Grobelaar and Pieters Hill, where well placed guns caused much annoyance to the troops. The Field batteries early in the morning engaged the Pieters Hill guns, and also shelled the wooded ground on the northern and north-western edges of the plateau enclosed by Hlangwhane and Monte Cristo. *Feb. 19th. Causes of delay in execution of the plan.*

The 2nd mounted brigade (Dundonald) worked round the northern end of Monte Cristo down to the river, where their musketry dispersed a body of the enemy who were forming upon the left bank. They were supported by five companies of the East Surrey, who held the high ground from Clump Hill to the spurs two miles and a half to the eastward; the battalion reserve of three companies was at the north end of Monte Cristo, near the figures 1,024. The East Surrey remained as thus placed until dawn on the 22nd.

The Devon and the West Yorkshire were employed making roads towards Monte Cristo, to facilitate the supply of water and food, which hitherto could only be brought up by hand from the Gomba. Colonel Norcott, with the 4th brigade and the Queen's (2nd brigade), forced his way in a north-westerly direction towards the river, through a thick growth of trees which sheltered the enemy's skirmishers.

While the IInd division was establishing itself on the eastern side of the plateau, the G.O.C. Vth division received orders to attack Hlangwhane, supported on the right flank by three battalions of the 4th brigade. General Warren detailed the 6th brigade to capture the hill, and by 11 a.m. its summit and a deserted camp had passed into Major-General Barton's hands, without serious loss to him. The enemy's guns, however, from the Colenso kopjes, and from the heights on the left bank overlooking the Falls, brought an annoying fire on the infantry upon the hill, and his riflemen, clinging to the wooded knolls of the northern spur of Hlangwhane, attempted to entrench. Owing to a misunderstanding between the brigadiers of the 4th and 6th brigades, each thinking that the other was about to occupy these knolls, the enemy was allowed to remain on them all day. The 10th brigade (Coke) supported Barton, and by sending a battalion to Green Hill connected him with the IInd division. Wynne's brigade (the 11th) still held Hussar Hill.

Early in the forenoon, the heavy guns from Hussar Hill began to appear on the plateau. Major C. E. Callwell's four 5-in. guns of the 16th company, Southern Division R.G.A., came into action near Bloy's Farm. By 2 p.m., Lieut. Ogilvy's two Naval 12-prs. were posted on the north-western edge of the summit of Clump Hill, whence, after a breastwork had been thrown up, they also opened fire. Two Naval 4.7-in., under Commander A. Limpus, joined Callwell at 4.30 p.m. after an exhausting march from Gun Hill. The ox teams had given out, and the guns had to be dragged by hand for several miles by the sailors and men from the nearest infantry battalions. Limpus shelled the three guns which, from Pieters Hill, appeared to cover the movement of the enemy's wagons northward from the heights of the Tugela. In the small hours of the 20th the 4.7-in. were piloted to an underfeature on the north-western slope of Clump Hill by Mr. Schwickkard, a Natal scout, attached to the Field Intelligence Department, who, with Colonel L. W. Parsons, R.A., and Captain Jones, R.N., had already reconnoitred the hill to discover how heavy guns could best be dragged up its rugged slopes.

The British losses on the 19th were four killed, twenty-six wounded.

Effect of capture of Monte Cristo on Boers. — Though Commandant-General Joubert telegraphed to General Lukas Meyer that no movement, which would tend to make the British think that the Tugela was being evacuated, could be allowed, and though he also told Meyer that he was sending help from the besieging force round Ladysmith, yet all day long Boers could be seen trekking towards Umbulwana and Ladysmith, and there appeared to be a general retreat of Botha's army northwards. The flight caused consternation at Pretoria. On the 20th Kruger sent the following telegram to Lukas Meyer:—

Kruger's telegram to Meyer. — "Am I to understand from your telegram to Commandant-General that the great Boschkop (*i.e.*, Hlangwhane) on the other side of the Tugela, which we occupied during the battle of December 15th, has been evacuated by our men? If the British place their cannon on that kop, will they not be able to bombard our men out of their positions? This would really be a wretched situation, if this be correct. I thought that this was the key to our positions. Please reply at once about this, and *re* our new positions."

Boers recover from their partial panic, and take up new position. — But though the President's alarm was felt also in the laagers round Ladysmith, the flight was quite unauthorised, and very partial. Many burghers, indeed, fell back for a day or two, until shamed into returning to the fighting line. The best men remained with Botha, who, when he realised that the right bank was irretrievably lost, concentrated all his available troops behind the river, and took up a new position in rear of the former one. His right centre was entrenched among the dongas and bushy ridges of the lower slopes of Grobelaar Mountain, with strong detachments covering the guns posted on Vertnek and at the entrance to the defile below it. From Grobelaar his line ran north-east, across the flat-topped Horse-shoe and Wynne's Hills into the valley of the Langewacht, and onwards over Terrace Hill, Railway Hill, and the railway line till the left rested upon the heights of Pieters Hill. Never was the Boers' genius for hasty entrenchment displayed to greater advantage than in this phase of the campaign, when their unexpected defeat had compelled a sudden change of front and the adoption of a new scheme of defence. Before the battle of Colenso, and in the preparation of the works on the right bank of the river, practically unlimited time had been at their disposal, and on the Upper Tugela the long delays allowed them to erect fortifications at their leisure. But on the 19th and 20th February, though General Buller did not at once follow up his success of the 18th, Botha had rapidly to recast his plans, and, with men dispirited by defeat, to execute fresh works under artillery fire. In the neighbourhood of Colenso most of the hills are steep on the side facing the river. They have a well-defined crest line, which, seen from the foot, appears to mark their summit. In reality the tops of the kopjes are either flat, or else rise in gentle undulations from the apparent to the real crest, usually invisible from below. Botha, in his new line of defence, made full use of this characteristic. On the flat-topped hills his works were placed at the points furthest from the river, while on the kopjes with undulating summits, such as Terrace Hill, the sangars were drawn back to the real crest. In both cases he secured a fair field of fire, and minimised the effect of long-range supporting musketry, except where the infantry covering the attack were posted on heights commanding those he occupied. He was also able to keep the burghers, detailed to man his trenches, under shelter of the reverse slopes of the hills, safe from the British fire until the infantry assault was imminent. In some places, as, for instance, on Terrace and Railway Hills, works were thrown up on the lower slopes; but they appear to have been intended chiefly to detain the attackers under the flanking fire of inconspicuous sangars in the valleys between the hills, placed where they would escape the notice of the British gunners.

The distribution of the commandos, from the 20th until the night of the 27th, appears to have been as follows [see maps 30 (b) and (c)]. On the extreme right on the lower slopes of Vertnek was Zoutpansberg; Bethel was astride of the western road to Ladysmith; Swaziland, strengthened on the 23rd or 24th by the arrival from the Upper Tugela of Carolina, carried on the line to Horse-shoe Hill, which, with Wynne's Hill, was held by Heidelberg and Ermelo. On the Langewacht Spruit, Boksburg connected the defenders of Wynne's Hill with Krügersdorp, who manned the trenches on Terrace Hill. The Krugersdorpers were reinforced in the forenoon of the 23rd by a contingent of Johannesburgers. On Railway Hill was posted Vryheid, with Standerton drawn back on a kopje near the Twin Peaks from which it could rake the valley between Terrace and Railway Hill. A detachment of Pretoria joined Vryheid on the 23rd. The Standerton men were moved on the night of the 26th to Pieters Hill, and were reinforced by a further contingent of their own men from the Upper Tugela. Pieters Hill was guarded by Lydenburg and Heidelberg, with detachments of Piet Retief scattered along the heights above the river from Manxa Nest, past Intaba Ka Renga, to the junction of the Klip with the Tugela. General Louis Botha, whilst in supreme command of the whole force, himself directed the movements on the right, while General Lukas Meyer was in charge of the left wing. *Distribution of the enemy in the new position.*

At 4.15 a.m. on the 20th General Buller issued the following orders to the officers commanding the Vth and IInd divisions respectively :— *Orders for the 20th Feb.*

"To GENERAL WARREN,

"1. Arrange, by the formation of sufficient posts, for the security of our front, which, so far as your division is concerned, may be taken to be a line from Hussar Hill through any position you take up on Hlangwhane Mountain to Bowman's Farm, near which you will join the IInd division. The position you take up should be strong enough to prevent any attempt on the part of the enemy to advance, and to prevent sniping.

"2. I have ordered four more Naval 12-prs. from Chieveley to Hussar Hill. Select as good positions for them on your flank as you can find and prepare emplacements.

"3. Employ all available men of your division on :—

"(a) The improvement of your water supply.

"(b) The improvement of the road, if you can find a track from Hussar Hill to Bowman's Farm, or, preferably, to the position of your Headquarters the night before last."

"To GENERAL LYTTELTON,

"1. Order General Hildyard to come down to near your Headquarters with three battalions, leaving the one at the most northerly end of Monte Cristo.

"2. This battalion should, during the day, get two machine guns into position near the extreme north point of Monte Cristo and so entrench two small positions there that it will render it impossible for the enemy to keep any scouts on the 'Manxa Nest,' which is the prominent feature just across the Tugela. No attempt should be made to drive away the enemy's scouts now there until our men are securely entrenched.

"3. Positions in advance of our present piquet line will be taken up by two battalions at daylight, supported by such guns as you may think necessary to keep the camp clear of sniping shots and prevent any attempt on the part of the enemy to close on us.

"4. Parties will be sent round at daylight to collect any of the enemy's entrenching tools lying about, and throughout the day, under the direction of the C.R.E. IInd division, as strong a working party as can be furnished from the division will be employed making a good zigzag road up the gully by which the two Naval 12-prs. were taken yesterday, and northward along the western slope of the crest to Monte Cristo. The road should not be steep.

"5. General Hildyard before leaving his position is to instruct Lord Dundonald to arrange for the security of our right flank and to guard Cingolo Nek."

From these instructions it would appear that at the time they were issued it was the Commander-in-Chief's intention to retain possession of the heights of Monte Cristo.

Boers completely evacuate right bank.

At daylight it was found that the Boers still held the extreme north ridges of the Hlangwhane spur, but only with a rear-guard. They soon retired to the left bank, demolishing the ferry pont, and attempting, but with ill success, to destroy the bridge after they had crossed it. Very early in the morning reconnoitring parties found Colenso deserted; by 7 a.m., the reports from numerous patrols agreed that there were no Boers left south of the Tugela, and shortly afterwards the crests upon the right bank of the river were occupied by the IInd division, while on the left Sir Charles Warren moved part of the 6th brigade along the spur which, jutting out from the northern end of Hlangwhane, overlooks the course of the Tugela. The Royal Scots Fusiliers held this spur; the Royal Welsh Fusiliers held Hlangwhane, with the remainder of the brigade about three-quarters of a mile to the rear in support. In the early morning Warren had sent the 10th brigade (Coke) westward along the valley of the Gomba, to form a connecting link between the 11th brigade (Wynne) at Hussar Hill and the 6th brigade (Barton) at Hlangwhane; but later in the day Major-General Coke was desired to send one battalion to the latter mountain, the rest of his brigade falling back to Green Hill, in reserve, while Major-General Wynne swung his brigade round to the left and joined hands with the troops on Hlangwhane.

During the forenoon Sir Redvers Buller, from the top of Monte Cristo, carefully studied the country in all directions. To the eastward the ground seemed to promise no passage for an army over the river; and the Intelligence officer, Lieut.-Colonel Sandbach, on his return from a reconnaissance to the junction of the Klip with the Tugela, reported that the track, from Cingolo Nek to the river east of Pieters Hoek, was in a wretched condition. To make it fit for use would have needed time and labour that could not be spared if Buller was to save Ladysmith from starvation. To the north and north-west, the sides of the gorge in which the Tugela flows from Fuzzy Hill to Monte Cristo are so steep as to be impracticable. Buller considered that from Fuzzy Hill to the mouth of the Onderbrook, the river and its banks were commanded to such an extent by Wynne's and Horse-shoe Hills that the pontoon bridge, if thrown there, would have been blown out of the water. It must be noticed that Horse-shoe Hill and Wynne's Hill, seen from the summit of Monte Cristo, appear to be joined together, and not to be, as is the case, two distinct kopjes. This may account for some of the confusion in the orders of the 22nd. The conclusion to which his reconnaissance led Sir Redvers was that he must give up all idea of reaching Bulwana by the east of Monte Cristo, and, therefore, not thinking it worth while to

Buller reconnoitres from Monte Cristo,

abandons idea of crossing Tugela to east of Monte Cristo, and

<small>decides to bridge river near Hlangwhane.</small>

direct a search to be made for crossing places in the part of the river overhung by the heights he had captured, he decided to throw a pontoon bridge near Hlangwhane, to concentrate his troops for the passage of the river there, and to occupy Colenso. This done, he had—to quote his words to the Royal Commission[*]—" to take a hill on the north bank of the Tugela between the Onderbrook and Langewacht Spruits before any further advance in the direction of Bulwana was possible. It also appeared to me that certainly one-half, if not the whole of the enemy's main fortified position, was vulnerable only to attack from the south-west, or in other words from Colenso, for the nature of the ground forbade any attempt to force its passage from the south."

<small>Measures to carry out his plan.</small>

General Buller therefore sent instructions to the pontoon troop, Royal Engineers, to join him from Chieveley; repairs to the railway from Chieveley to Colenso were at once begun, and at 12.30 p.m., orders were issued to the General Officer Commanding the IInd division :—

> " Send the 2nd brigade and the 5-in. guns and baggage across by the main road through Bowman's Farm to Hlangwhane. Tell Lieut. Ogilvy, R.N., to get his guns down from the top of Monte Cristo and follow.
>
> " I intend to try and commence throwing a bridge across the Tugela to-night. The 4th brigade will bivouac in any positions that you may select adjacent to the south bank of the Tugela, on which they advanced this morning.
>
> " The regiment now on Monte Cristo will remain there to-night."

The 2nd brigade accordingly marched to the Divisional Headquarters, leaving the East Surrey and two machine guns to hold the northern end of Monte Cristo and to guard the Naval guns which still remained upon its underfeature, Clump Hill. When Major-General Hildyard arrived at the rendezvous, he was directed to keep the 2nd brigade as reserve to the 4th (Col. Norcott's) brigade, which then had two battalions, the Durham Light Infantry and the 1st Rifle Brigade, near the bank of the river. The rest of Norcott's troops were at Bloy's Farm. The 4th brigade continued to hold these positions throughout the night. At 1 p.m., the 2nd brigade was ordered to march to the eastern slopes of Hlangwhane and there bivouac. On the

[*] Royal Commission, Volume II., page 181.

RELIEF OF LADYSMITH.   461

extreme west of the British line Major-General Hart, with the 2nd Royal Dublin Fusiliers, pushed on from Chieveley into Colenso. A party of Thorneycroft's mounted infantry, who were scouting to the south of the Tugela, asked for orders from Hart, and were sent by him across the river by a ford, too deep for infantry, to ascertain if the kopjes overlooking the ruined bridges were clear of the enemy. In circling widely to the north-west, they came under heavy fire from the foot-hills of Grobelaar and fell back. At sunset, Hart, in obedience to an order from the Commander-in-Chief, returned to Chieveley with his detachment.

On the night of the 20th, Sir Redvers Buller was satisfied with the progress of the campaign. His turning movement had proved to be well conceived; the troops had executed it with spirit and intelligence and, looking as he did upon the ground as unfavourable to attack, with remarkably small loss. Since the 14th the casualties had been—Officers: killed 2, wounded 14; other ranks: killed 23, wounded 262, and 4 missing; total killed, wounded and missing of all ranks, 305. He was master of the right bank of the Tugela from Monte Cristo to Colenso. The Boer laagers had disappeared, but a trail of wagons was lumbering northwards. His infantry and artillery were so placed that, while covering the Royal Engineers as they threw the pontoon bridge over the river, they were ready to pour across it as soon as it was finished. There remained, indeed, the task of driving the enemy from the works which from Monte Cristo he had noted that morning, but, as he had reason to believe that the Boers were reduced in numbers and shaken in spirit, this did not appear to be very formidable. *Casualties between Feb. 14th and 20th, 1900.*

On the evening of the 20th the bivouacs ran roughly as follows from the left of Sir R. Buller's line :— *Position of troops on night of 20th.*

Vth division (Warren).

11*th brigade* (Wynne).—Stretching from Hussar Hill to Hlangwhane.

10*th brigade* (Coke).—One battalion on Hlangwhane, the remainder at Green Hill.

6th brigade (Barton).—On the spur which projects from the north of Hlangwhane, and overlooks the Tugela. (On the 20th this brigade was detached from the Vth division, becoming corps troops, and did not rejoin until the 28th.)

IInd division (Lyttelton).

2nd brigade (Hildyard).—On the eastern slopes of Hlangwhane, less one battalion at Monte Cristo.

4th brigade (Norcott).—Two battalions at Bloy's Farm and two overlooking the river Tugela.

5th brigade (Hart).—At Chieveley.

2nd mounted brigade (Dundonald) (less Thorneycroft's mounted infantry).—On the right rear of the infantry posted on Hlangwhane, with vedettes on Monte Cristo and along the Tugela to its junction with the Blaauwkrantz. (Thorneycroft's mounted infantry was on the left flank of the army.)

The disposition of the guns, which were then being concentrated round Hlangwhane, was approximately as follows :— The 7th, 63rd and 64th batteries were on the crest of Fuzzy Hill, with the 61st (Howitzer) to their right rear. The 19th battery was brought up to Hlangwhane from Hussar Hill, but returned at dusk; the 28th, 73rd, 78th batteries and No. 4 Mountain battery were near the track between Hlangwhane and Naval Hill; the 5-in. guns were moved to the east of Hlangwhane. The two Naval 12-prs. under Lieutenant Ogilvy, which had been ordered at 4 p.m. to march to Hlangwhane, by midnight reached its eastern slopes, where they were joined by two guns of similar calibre from Hussar Hill, under the command of Mr. J. Wright (gunner), and four from Gun Hill under Lieutenants F. W. Melvill and H. W. James. The two Naval 4.7-in. remained on Clump Hill, and in the afternoon engaged and silenced a Boer gun posted to the north of Terrace Hill.

During the night the enemy's guns fired occasionally, and there was much "sniping" from the left bank.

CHAPTER XXVI.

RELIEF OF LADYSMITH.

CROSSING OF THE RIVER ; ATTACK ON WYNNE'S HILL.*

SINCE February 14th, the IInd division, as it carried out the flanking movement which drove the Boers over the Tugela, had been in advance of the remainder of General Buller's army. On the 21st came the turn of the Vth division to lead. General Warren was to cross the Tugela as soon as the pontoon bridge was completed, while General Lyttelton remained on the right bank, to support the artillery, which, massed upon and around Hlangwhane, engaged the Boer guns across the river. On the spur of Hlangwhane were four 5-in. and eight Naval 12-pr. guns. At its northern extremity was posted the 64th Field battery, and at its foot, on the low ground close to the river, the 63rd, 7th and 19th Field batteries. Behind Fuzzy Hill was the 61st Howitzer battery, and on Clump Hill, the underfeature of Monte Cristo, was a detachment of sailors with two 4.7-in. guns. Very early in the morning of the 21st the Naval officers had observed five Boer guns and two pom-poms marching northwards along the road between Railway Hill and Pieters and had shelled them. They had afterwards dispersed a laager near Pieters station.

At 5.30 a.m. Major-General Barton was ordered to extend down the river to cover the Royal Engineers, engaged in the construction of the "heavy" pontoon bridge, 110 yards long, marked No. 1 on map 30 (b). Two of his battalions were employed on this duty : the Royal Fusiliers guarded the low ground near the river bank, the Royal Scots Fusiliers were posted

<small>Feb. 21st. Dispositions of Buller's artillery.</small>

* See map No. 30 (b).

on the high ground south of the Boer bridge. The remainder of the brigade bivouacked behind them in support.

Coke ordered to cross the pontoon bridge.

At 6.30 a.m. Major-General Coke received orders to concentrate his brigade (the 10th) behind Hlangwhane, in readiness to cross the bridge as soon as it was finished. At 12.45 p.m. the pontoon troop, aided by the two Field companies of Royal Engineers, had done their work unscathed, despite the shells of the Boer artillery. Just as the 10th brigade was about to pass the river, fresh orders for its movements on the left bank were received. General Buller had that morning heliographed to Sir George White :—

Buller heliographs his views to White,

" I am now engaged in pushing my way through by Pieters. I think there is only a rear-guard in front of me. The large Boer laager under Bulwana was removed last night. I hope to be with you to-morrow night. You might help by working north, and stopping some of the enemy getting away. A large camp has been moved to-day from the hill between the station and Cæsar's Camp."

He knew that many of the enemy had been withdrawn from Natal to resist Lord Roberts in the Orange Free State. Concluding that in consequence of this reduction in strength the Boer forces in his front could not seriously oppose him, Sir Redvers first intended that Lieut.-General Warren should push northward along the Tugela and, after making himself master of Horse-shoe Hill, should take up a position near the junction of the Onderbrook Spruit with the Tugela ; but later he learned from Thorneycroft's mounted infantry that parties of Boers were on the slopes of Grobelaar Mountain. As these parties threatened the left flank of his proposed advance, he changed his plans, and directed Warren* :—

and issues fresh orders to Warren.

" After crossing the pont (*the pontoon bridge*) to work across the low hills immediately to the west of it, on to the flat which is called the Tugela Drift on the blue map, ' D ' (*about half a mile south-west of kopje* 244), and then with your brigade division to shell heavily the valley of Onderbrook Spruit, and the back of kopjes that form the northern border of the flat on which you will be.

* In all the orders quoted in this and the following chapters describing the relief of Ladysmith, the words in italics (*e.g.*, *the pontoon bridge*) are explanatory and have been interpolated by the Editor.

RELIEF OF LADYSMITH.

"You should especially shell up the long kloof that runs in a north-westerly direction parallel to the Colenso-Ladysmith road.

"My idea is that what Boers there are are hiding in that kloof. If we leave them they will man the ridges and fire on us, but if we shell them heavily to-night, it is probable that by the morning they will have passed eastward.

"I do not propose to do more to-day than to endeavour to establish ourselves comfortably on what we may call the Colenso position. This order cancels our late conversation.

"P.S.—I shall not now send the Mountain battery, but you will take your whole brigade division."

Major-General Coke issued the following orders to his brigade :— *Coke's orders to his brigade.*

"Pontoon, 1.30 p.m., 21st Feb., 1900.

"1. The enemy are thought to be in the Onderbrook Spruit parallel to the westerly Ladysmith road, and lower down towards Tugela river.

"2. The 2nd Somerset Light Infantry will cross the bridge and advance in attack formation due west to the open ground marked 'Tugela Drift' on the blue map. The 2nd Dorset will form second line; the 2nd Middlesex, general reserve, at the disposal of the Major-General Commanding.

"3. On arrival at Tugela Drift the intention is to cover a position for our artillery to shell the enemy's position as supposed above.

"4. The G.O.C. will follow the Somerset Light Infantry."

Coke's troops crossed the river under a harmless fire from Grobelaar and from Pieters Hill, but when they left the shelter of the kopjes which fringe the left bank, and entered the plain known as the Tugela Drift, they were much annoyed by musketry. In order that they might avoid masking, and yet protect, Major Apsley Smith's brigade division of artillery (28th, 73rd and 78th), which had followed them over the bridge, the 10th brigade was pushed forward. Six companies of the Somerset Light Infantry, widely extended, preceded by their scouts, and followed by part of the Dorset regiment in second line, advanced to the north-west towards Grobelaar until they were completely checked by the riflemen who manned the rows of schanzes concealed in the bush on the lower slopes of the mountain. To the right rear an isolated combat was waged with equally unsuccessful results between the remainder of these battalions, and the parties of Boers who from Horse-shoe and Wynne's Hills enfiladed the main attack. The banks of the Onderbrook Spruit *10th brigade cross Tugela, and are checked.*

VOL. II.

had been cleverly cut away and scarped by the enemy, yet two companies of the Somerset, followed by four companies of the Dorset, succeeded in making their way over it to what was supposed to be the dead ground at the foot of these hills. Instead of finding themselves in safety at this point they were exposed, as were their comrades on the left, to so severe a fire from front and flanks that they were pinned to the earth, unable either to advance or retire until night fell. The Middlesex, held in reserve by Major-General Coke, fired a few rounds at Grobelaar, but otherwise took no active part in the engagement; and as Lieut.-General Warren did not deem it advisable to bring into action the 11th brigade, which, under Major-General Wynne, crossed the pontoon bridge about three o'clock, the Dorset and the Somerset Light Infantry were unsupported, except by Major Apsley Smith's guns posted a mile north-west of the pontoon bridge. Warren considered it unnecessary to assist Coke because his brigade was well able to protect the artillery and cover the bridge without further help. Though they were exposed for several hours to heavy musketry and shell fire the casualties of the Dorset and Somerset were not heavy; those of the former were insignificant; while the latter were fortunate in escaping with a loss among all ranks of ninety-one killed and wounded. The ammunition expended by the 10th brigade on February 21st, was: 2nd Somerset, 30,086; 2nd Dorset, 2,552; 2nd Middlesex, 352; total 32,990.

Warren does not support Coke; his reasons.

The Boers had few guns in action, but they had placed them so as to rake the Tugela Drift. One gun was concealed on Vertnek; another, with a pom-pom, was placed in the defile between that hill and Grobelaar; on the kopjes north of the Langewacht was a third Field gun, while hidden on the rocky summits of Onderbrook and Grobelaar Mountains were two more pieces of artillery. The energy with which the Boers resisted the 10th brigade, the volume of their fire, and the length of front which they occupied from Vertnek to Wynne's Hill, changed Sir Redvers' impression of the nature of the forces with which he had still to deal, while a heliograph message from Sir George White informed him that a considerable number

RELIEF OF LADYSMITH.

of the enemy had been brought by rail from northern Natal, and had detrained at Modder Spruit station.

Sir Charles Warren at 6.10 p.m. thus wrote to Sir Redvers Buller :—

"I will hold to-night the kopjes west of pontoon bridge and north of Colenso. There has been a good deal of opposition from the north, which will probably be repeated in the morning. Colonel Thorneycroft reports Boers in considerable numbers on each side of Ladysmith road and in the Onderbrook Spruit running north-west. Where do you propose I should attack in the morning ? I have been shelling heavily the points you mentioned. My line is enfiladed by long range guns from north-east which I cannot locate. The question arises whether the high ground north of Onderbrook Spruit will not have to be taken before any advance can be made. I know of about thirty casualties as yet." Warren's plan for the 22nd.

As soon as it was dark, Major-General Coke, believing that it would not be possible to retain throughout the night the ground gained during the afternoon, ordered his troops to fall back upon the Colenso kopjes, to the left of the 11th (Wynne's) brigade, now stretching from the pontoon bridge to the slopes of the northern of the two hills marked 244. When his battalions had been reassembled, he went to Lieut.-General Warren's bivouac, where he learned that the following orders had already been issued by that officer to the Vth division :— When Coke retires at nightfall to Colenso kopjes, he hears Warren has issued orders for the 22nd.

"1. It is the intention of the G.O.C. to occupy the line of kopjes overlooking Onderbrook Spruit to the front of the position to-morrow.

"2. General Coke will occupy the nearer kopjes occupied by him to-day before withdrawal, and he will also keep a detaining force in the plain. The force in the plain will not go so far as it did to-day. To move out at 4.30 a.m.

"3. General Wynne will, at the same time, occupy the forward position he held to-day, and after an artillery preparation he will turn the second line of kopjes by a movement by his right along the line of the river. General Coke will support this movement by an advance to second line of kopjes also.

"4. The Mountain battery on Hlangwhane will support this movement by fire.

"5. The C.R.A. will take his instructions from the G.O.C., reporting at 4.30 a.m. at his bivouac. His batteries will be ready to move at that hour.

"6. The O.C. Naval 12-prs. will also report at 4.30 a.m. for orders."

Coke, from his experience of the ground over which he had been fighting, urged that it would not be worth the loss which its reoccupation would entail. His brigade would be On Coke's representations,

468   THE WAR IN SOUTH AFRICA.

<small>Warren cancels his orders, and sends memorandum to Buller.</small>

under fire from Grobelaar Mountain and its underfeatures; and to extricate it, if once engaged, might bring on a general action. The orders were then cancelled, and Warren sent the following memorandum to the Chief of the Staff :—

> "I find from report made to me by General Coke at 10.30 p.m. that the right centre of his advanced line suffered very severely from a concentrated Boer fire from trenches on the hill in vicinity of Ladysmith road, in an established position of considerable strength, and any advance to-morrow across the plain where there is no cover must also meet with considerable loss until the enemy are shelled out of the trenches with lyddite. I consider, therefore, that further advance on hills on right which are commanded by the Onderbrook Hill should be prepared by some hours of shell fire from lyddite and long-range guns, as I consider the field guns by themselves are very inoperative against well-constructed trenches. There is no doubt that if the Boers come down in any force into the Onderbrook hills they entirely command the advanced kopjes held to-day, and the retaking of them will (depend ?) entirely on the number of Boers occupying the high ground to-morrow. I do not therefore consider it advisable early in the morning to occupy the hills to the right until it is ascertained to what extent the enemy occupy them, and would recommend that ground be selected to-morrow from which the Howitzer battery can shell these Boer trenches, and in the meantime I will direct the Naval guns in the morning upon some of the trenches, and will endeavour to place the Field artillery in positions where they may be useful without obliging the infantry to come so far forward as to come under fire from the Boer trenches until the enemy have been well shelled. Approximate casualties to-day were 3 officers killed, about 5 wounded and about 120 men killed and wounded."

<small>Hart near Colenso.</small>

While the 10th brigade was engaged on the left bank of the Tugela, Major-General Hart (5th brigade) had marched with two battalions and the 66th Field battery from Chieveley to Colenso. This battery had been destroyed at the battle of Colenso (December 15th), but had now been reformed. Colenso was deserted, but, as on the day before, Boers, concealed in the kopjes to the north of the river, kept up a steady fire, until they were dislodged by Thorneycroft's mounted infantry, who again forded the Tugela and threatened their line of retreat. Thanks to the energy of Lieutenant N. Chiazzari, Natal Naval Volunteers, who commanded a mixed detachment of bluejackets and men of his own corps, and had been left with Lieutenant T. Anderton, Natal Naval Volunteers, in charge of the 4.7-in. guns on fixed mountings at Chieveley,

RELIEF OF LADYSMITH. 469

a pont was brought up to Colenso, by which the Connaught Rangers were ferried across the river, while the 2nd Royal Dublin Fusiliers remained on the right bank. The 66th battery was ordered back to Chieveley for the night.

Among the Naval brigade some changes of position had taken place during the 21st. Lieutenant James, R.N., with two Naval 12-prs., was sent down from the Hlangwhane spur to the low ground on the left bank, which he reached at dusk. The two 4.7-in. were withdrawn from Clump Hill, and arrived at 11 p.m. at the pontoon bridge, where they were halted on the right bank. Thus, by the end of the operations of the 21st, Sir Redvers Buller had thrown the Vth division, three batteries of Field artillery, and two Naval 12-prs. across the river by the pontoon bridge; a battalion of the 5th brigade (Hart) had been ferried across the Tugela, while the remainder of the brigade stretched southward to Chieveley. The IInd division, the 6th brigade and nearly all the mobile artillery were concentrated near Hlangwhane. Buller expected to be reinforced on the 22nd and 23rd by Burn-Murdoch's troops, recently recalled from Springfield. *Positions of troops on evening of 21st.*

Throughout the night of the 21st-22nd the troops streamed without interruption across the pontoon bridge. During the morning of the 22nd February the whole of the 2nd brigade, the 2nd Scottish Rifles and the 3rd King's Royal Rifles (4th brigade), and the Inniskilling and Dublin Fusiliers (5th brigade), had joined the Vth division on the left bank, where it lay in the narrow strip of ground between the river and the Colenso kopjes. The remaining battalion of the 5th brigade, the 1st Border regiment, was left at Chieveley. The Vth division, posted among the Colenso kopjes, protected the bivouac of the rest of the army. Coke's brigade, the 10th, faced westward; the northern kopjes were held by Wynne's, the 11th brigade, whose leading battalion, the South Lancashire, occupied the hill (244 on the map) which overlooks the junction of the Onderbrook with the Tugela. Thus the greater part of the infantry was now concentrated on the left bank of the Tugela, on a space two and a half miles in length and in breadth varying from *Movements on Feb. 22nd.*

a mile and a quarter at the south to half a mile at the north. Behind them was the Tugela, passable only at the pontoon bridge, which was guarded by Major-General Barton, whose battalions extended along the heights overhanging the right bank as far as the Boer bridge. Three miles to the south-west of Hlangwhane Hill was the bivouac of the 1st cavalry brigade (Burn-Murdoch), which had now arrived from Springfield, where it had formed part of the small force of all arms left under Burn-Murdoch when the main army marched from Vaal Krantz to Chieveley. The moral effect of this detachment had been great, for its presence caused the Boers much anxiety about their right flank, and induced them to keep a considerable force on the Upper Tugela to watch its movements. On the 9th February, Commandant-General Joubert, in a long telegram to Botha, expressed his fear that the British might work up the river to its confluence with the Venter's Spruit, cross over the flats to the source of that stream, "where our men will not have the slightest cover. . . . They could thus easily reach Ladysmith." Though the flanking detachment was not intended for aggressive action, the alarm it excited is well shown by a telegram from De Villiers, captain of the despatch riders in Prinsloo's camp. It was not till February 23rd that he ventured to suggest that, as a "patrol on the 22nd had discovered that Springfield had been evacuated, there was now no occasion for keeping a strong force on the upper part of the river, and the brave burghers of Heilbron and Carolina can therefore be spared. . . . If no great movement is made by the enemy in the direction of the Upper Tugela, it would be advisable to send some of the Heilbron, Vrede and Carolina burghers from Spion Kop as reinforcements to Colenso." On the same day Botha informed Meyer that he had told General Schalk Burger, commanding on the Upper Tugela, to let Meyer have as many men as he could possibly spare. Among the reinforcements were to be the Lydenburg and Carolina commandos. There is reason to believe that several Free State commandos were retained at Spion Kop until the 27th to ward off a movement expected against the Boers' extreme right flank.

Effect of Burn-Murdoch's detachment at Springfield.

The enemy's guns were not moved during the night of the 21st, but during the 22nd two more pom-poms were brought into action on the slopes north of the Langewacht, about 1,000 yards west of Railway Hill. From the Colenso kopjes the British batteries opened fire upon the works stretching from Grobelaar to Wynne's Hill. The 73rd was on the extreme left, next came the 28th; then Lieut. James, with two Naval 12-prs., which were chiefly engaged against the pieces on Grobelaar Hill and the high ground to the west of Terrace Hill. Concealed among the kopjes, half a mile to the west of the pontoon bridge, was the 61st Howitzer battery, the target for which was Wynne's Hill, and on the extreme right, close to the river, were the 7th and 78th. From the Hlangwhane Range the four 5-in. guns of the Garrison artillery and the 64th Field battery shelled Wynne's and Terrace (Hart's) Hills, while two Naval 4.7-in., posted on the right bank of the river, about half a mile north of the pontoon bridge, and the 63rd Field battery and six Naval 12-prs. on the spur of Hlangwhane attacked the trenches on the crest of Terrace Hill, when no Boer guns were visible upon which to bear. The 6-in. Naval gun on Gun Hill at Chieveley assailed the enemy's gun emplacements on Grobelaar.

<small>Action of British artillery on 22nd.</small>

Thus, although in accordance with Sir Redvers Buller's wish to husband his ammunition, the guns fired slowly, many projectiles scourged the Boer positions. That the burghers manned their works and fought their guns on this and the succeeding days of the battle is a proof both of their courage and of the excellence of their trenches, schanzes and gun epaulments.

On the morning of the 22nd Lieut.-General Warren followed up his memorandum of the previous evening by sending that which here follows. With the new paper was a sketch. He now proposed again to issue the orders he had withdrawn on the 21st, but he required support from other troops, and for this he now asked.

<small>Warren's fresh proposals for Feb. 22nd.</small>

"I propose to take the Green Hill marked 'B' (*Wynne's Hill*) on the north side of Onderbrook Spruit with 11th brigade, 10th brigade to support (1 battalion), moving off at 1.15 p.m.

"I propose to leave 'D' (*Horse-shoe Hill*) alone, and it should be shelled until the advance is being made.

"The enemy's trenches at 'E' (*Terrace Hill*) should be shelled by the long-range guns during the operations and a machine gun or guns should be placed at 'A' (*the northern slopes of Naval Hill and Fuzzy Hill*) to fire up Langewacht Spruit. A fire up the Spruit between 'D' and 'B' would be useful during the morning before 1.15.

"The hill 'C' (*close to the junction of the Onderbrook and the Tugela, marked 244 on the map*) is held by 11th brigade, and all kopjes south, but 'F' (*rising ground to the south-west of the western end of the Hill 244*) is not occupied."

Buller directs Warren to attack with 11th brigade. This communication to Headquarters was crossed by a letter from Sir Redvers Buller directing General Warren to prepare the 11th brigade for attack. The part of the enemy's position to be assailed was not mentioned, but the letter stated that the IInd division was to support the 11th brigade. Receiving no further instructions, at 1 p.m. Warren went to the Commander-in-Chief and found that his proposals were in the main approved.

Buller's plan. Sir Redvers Buller intended that after the 11th brigade as a first step had carried Wynne's Hill, the troops should wheel to the right, follow the course of the river, and seize Terrace Hill, then described as "a high brown hill, which seemed strongly held, and appeared second in importance to Grobelaar." Since early morning the enemy from the works on Grobelaar had threatened the left flank of the projected advance. They had been kept back by the artillery, which also, by a steady bombardment, had paved the way for the movement on Wynne's Hill. The 10th brigade (Coke), posted among the kopjes running parallel to the river and west of the pontoon, guarded the *tête du pont*, and observed the Boers on Grobelaar, while the 5th (Hart's) brigade, to the north of the bridges at Colenso, guaranteed the safety of the extreme left of the line.

11th brigade ordered to attack Wynne's Hill. As soon as Lieut.-General Warren had received his instructions from Headquarters he gave Major-General Wynne orders to attack the ridge north of the position, i.e., Hill 244, then held by the South Lancashire regiment. Wynne pointed out to General Warren that to assault this ridge without having previously occupied Grobelaar Mountain would be like entering a pass without crowning its heights, and that the brigade, both during and after its attack, would be exposed to enfilade fire from the high ground on either side. Then, accompanied by the officers commanding the battalions of his brigade, he reconnoitred the hill which now bears his name from the outpost line of the South Lancashire, and pointed out to each unit the object it was to make for. The South Lancashire was to carry the right or eastern end of the ridge, the King's Own (Royal Lancaster) its centre, the Rifle Reserve battalion its left, or western, extremity. The operations of the Rifle battalion were to be bounded on the left by the donga running between Wynne's Hill and Horse-shoe Hill. The brigadier explained to his commanding officers that he had been promised protection on his left flank, and that he fully expected Horse-shoe Hill to be occupied by troops from another brigade immediately after he had seized Wynne's Hill.

While the commander of the 11th brigade was conferring with his colonels, Major-General Lyttelton was desired to support the 11th brigade, and at 1.10 p.m. Colonel Bruce Hamilton, his assistant adjutant-general, issued the following orders to Colonel Norcott, commanding the 4th brigade :— *IInd division to support 11th brigade. Lyttelton's orders to 4th brigade.*

"General Wynne's brigade is going to advance at 1.30 p.m. to attack a position occupied by the enemy north of Onderbrook Spruit. The 4th brigade will support this attack by sending one battalion écheloned in rear of the left flank of the 11th brigade (at about 100 yards) and a second battalion in rear of the first. The 2nd brigade will follow in reserve in rear of the left of the 11th brigade. The G.O.C. will be with the supporting battalion of 4th brigade."

At the time that Norcott was thus instructed to support the 11th brigade with two battalions, the only two units of his command on the left bank were engaged in holding the ground between the northern half of the Colenso kopjes and the Boers on Grobelaar Mountain. The Scottish Rifles were posted along the knolls about a mile to the west of the pontoon bridge; the 3rd King's Royal Rifles a little further to the north. It was found impossible to move them without imperilling the safety of the artillery in action on the hills behind them, and of Hildyard's (2nd) brigade, which, before it joined hands with the 11th brigade, had to march over the narrow strip of ground between these kopjes and the Tugela. *Position of Norcott's battalions.*

Wynne asks for long-range fire to support his attack.

Wynne, while making his final arrangements before setting his troops in motion, saw no sign of the promised battalions on the left rear, and thought it well to obtain, if possible, the aid of long-range supporting fire in his forward movement. At about 1.30 p.m. he accordingly sent this message to the G.O.C. IInd division :—

"Will you please send a battalion as soon as possible to occupy the ridge now held by the South Lancashire regiment, and to cover the advance of the 11th brigade."

The request duly reached the 4th brigade, but in consequence of the position of the battalions nothing was done. General Wynne's three battalions were therefore launched for the attack, with no troops nearer than the 2nd brigade at the southern end of the Colenso kopjes, immediately available to confirm their victory or to cover their retreat.

Advance of 11th brigade.

About 2 p.m. the 11th brigade advanced, the South Lancashire leading in widely extended order, followed by the Royal Lancaster and the Rifle Reserve battalion. The enemy opened upon them at very long range, but his shooting was rendered unsteady by the shells of the artillery and by the musketry volleys and machine gun fire from part of Major-General Barton's brigade (the 6th), which, from the western slopes of Naval Hill on the right bank of the river, covered the movement. Thanks to this support, the South Lancashire experienced little loss in effecting a lodgment upon that part of Wynne's Hill which overhangs the railway. Major-General Wynne was wounded at the beginning of the action and was succeeded by Colonel Crofton, Royal Lancaster, who next day was appointed to the lines of communication, Colonel F. W. Kitchener, West Yorkshire regiment, being selected to command the brigade in his stead. The Royal Lancaster, whose progress had been delayed in passing through a railway cutting, came up on the left of the South Lancashire, in a column of four extended lines of two companies, with 200 yards between each line. As the foremost companies approached a clump of trees, which had been chosen to mark the right of their attack, they found them-

RELIEF OF LADYSMITH. 475

selves under heavy fire, but pushed forward towards the rocks and boulders on the further crest of Wynne's Hill, along which the Boers had thrown up a line of well-placed stone breastworks. The whole brigade was now under severe cross fire from Grobelaar, from Terrace Hill, from the kopjes and broken ground in the valley of the Langewacht, and, above all, from Horse-shoe Hill, which had not been occupied by troops from another brigade, as Major-General Wynne had understood would be the case when he planned his assault on Wynne's Hill. To meet the musketry from the left rear, part of the Rifle Reserve battalion turned towards Horse-shoe Hill and made a lodgment upon it; but till this was done the rest of the brigade could not advance, and the delay thus caused did not allow of further progress before nightfall. Its progress delayed by non-occupation of Horse-shoe Hill.

At first Sir Charles Warren thought that all was going well. At 2.20 p.m. he wrote to the Chief of the Staff to say he "proposed to take the western end of high ridge to east of Green Hill (i.e., *Terrace Hill*), where Boers were entrenched this morning, and make an entrenchment there for the night, so that in the morning it may remain in our hands." In a further message to the Chief of the Staff, written at 3.35 p.m., he says that he "ought to have four Naval guns and the Howitzer battery on the position just taken (*Wynne's Hill*) or on the hill behind it (*Hill* 244), as the enemy are sure to put up guns on the surrounding hills to-night. I propose that these guns should come on to the hill south side of Tugela this afternoon, so that they may have no trouble in crossing and taking up positions during the night, and the officers should come and inspect the position to-day. I have brought up a Field battery to position on hill south of Tugela." But by 3 p.m. the increasing strength of the Boers, and the determination with which they were holding their ground, induced General Warren to apply for reinforcements to the G.O.C. IInd division. He asked Lyttelton "to send one battalion (half a battalion at a time) to the hill on the right occupied by our men now (*Wynne's Hill*). They had some difficulty in getting on owing to an enfilade fire." He also asked that a battalion should hold the "left hill (*Horse-* Warren, at first satisfied with his progress, asks for reinforcements at 3 p.m., and that Horse-shoe Hill should be

<small>occupied by IInd division.</small> shoe Hill), now lightly occupied by Major Stuart-Wortley's Rifle Reserve battalion."

<small>Movements of IInd division.</small> On receipt of this message Major-General Lyttelton ordered the 2nd brigade to move northwards along the left bank from the Colenso kopjes to the southern slopes of Hill 244. But it took time to send these orders to Major-General Hildyard, and then for his brigade to reach the spot, while from the north-west edge of Wynne's Hill the pressure on the King's Own (Royal Lancaster) increased every moment. Owing to the diversion of part of the Rifle Reserve battalion to Horse-shoe Hill, the Royal Lancaster had been obliged to extend widely to its left, <small>The situation on Wynne's Hill at sunset.</small> and by dusk a large part of its men were in the firing line. About sunset reinforcements began slowly to appear. The 3rd King's Royal Rifles (4th brigade) had just been relieved from outpost duty on the kopjes south of the Onderbrook facing the south- <small>3rd battalion K.R.R. ordered up,</small> eastern slopes of Grobelaar, when it was hurriedly sent off to help the Lancashire brigade. The commanding officer, Major R. C. A. B. Bewicke-Copley, directed his battalion upon Horse-shoe Hill and the west end of Wynne's Hill.

As night fell the British guns ceased fire. Emboldened by their silence, and especially by that of the two 4.7-in. guns, which were then being dragged down to the pontoon bridge from the spot on the right bank where they had been in action, the Boers attacked Wynne's Hill with such vigour that further aid was urgently required. The 2nd brigade had now reached the southern slopes of Hill 244; and Major-General Hildyard had desired Lt.-Colonel R. H. W. H. Harris, commanding the East Surrey, to take up an outpost line in relief of the 11th brigade as soon as it became dark, when an A.D.C. from Major-General Lyttelton brought an order for the East Surrey to go forward immediately, as the 11th brigade had been driven in. General Hildyard at once sent on this battalion, soon followed by the <small>and the East Surrey and Devonshire.</small> Devon, but before these troops had crossed the Onderbrook valley the attack on the western portion of Wynne's Hill became so severe that part of two companies of the Royal Lancaster was forced across the plateau to the southern crest. On their right was the South Lancashire, who held the eastern portion of the hill, with posts along the railway up to the bridge over the Langewacht. When Lieut.-Colonel W. McCarthy-O'Leary saw that part of the battalion on his left had been driven in, he instantly brought up his supporting companies from the cover they had occupied below the southern crest. But this reinforcement was not needed. One company of the 3rd King's Royal Rifles, under Captain the Hon. R. Cathcart, and portions of three other companies of the same corps, were then moving forward separately to take up their places in the outpost line. To stem the retreat, and to give time for the broken troops to rally behind the supporting companies of the Royal Lancaster, which, under Major E. W. Yeatherd, were then hastening to the front, the officer commanding one of these small parties of the King's Royal Rifles, of his own initiative, fixed bayonets* and charged the pursuing Boers who, with a considerable loss in killed and wounded, fell back before him upon their works. Not satisfied with this success, the ardent Riflemen dashed onwards, through a gap in the line still held by the King's Own (Royal Lancaster) until they found themselves within seventy to one hundred yards of the entrenchments, whence so venomous a fire was poured upon them that they flung themselves into a stone cattle kraal. While placing the men for the defence of this post Cathcart was mortally wounded and the command passed to Lieutenant D. H. Blundell-Hollinshead-Blundell. This officer was unable in the darkness to see that not only in front but on both flanks he was faced by the enemy's works. He believed, on the strength of a message, brought to him by a non-commissioned officer, that he would be reinforced at dawn, and he hoped that then the whole of the summit of Wynne's Hill could be regained. He therefore decided not to send his men back to the valley under cover of the darkness, but to hold the kraal throughout the night as an advanced post for a fresh attack. It was a wise and gallant decision, for his company to some extent filled the break in

<small>K.R.R. reach Wynne's Hill at critical moment, relieve the strain,</small>

<small>but advance too far across the plateau,</small>

<small>and occupy a kraal close to enemy's works.</small>

---

* Rifle regiments always give the order to fix *swords*, but the word bayonet is adopted throughout this history, as less liable to confuse.

the line caused by the partial retirement of the battalion on his flank. The presence of his men in the kraal checked the occupants of the enemy's sangars throughout the night, and thus prevented a counter-stroke against the East Surrey and Devonshire, who lay upon the southern part of Wynne's Hill, unconscious for many hours of the danger to which the party of Riflemen was exposed.

<small>East Surrey come up to Wynne's Hill and Horse-shoe Hill.</small>

It was nearly dark when the East Surrey, marching in column of half companies extended to six paces between the men, reached the Nek which connects Horse-shoe and Wynne's Hills. Here they were informed by a private soldier that help was required on both sides of the defile, that the firing line was hard pressed, and that it was running short of ammunition. Lieut.-Colonel Harris, who commanded the battalion, left Major H. W. Pearse with four companies to hold the Nek and reinforce such part of Horse-shoe Hill as was in our possession, while he himself, with the rest of the battalion, passed up the western end of Wynne's Hill. To his front Pearse found a detachment of the Rifle Reserve battalion, and spent the night in throwing up sangars with strong traverses to guard against the enfilading fire that he had been warned to expect from two kopjes on the south side of the Onderbrook, from which the Boers had not yet been dislodged. During the hours of darkness occasional bursts of hostile musketry were directed upon this western end of Horse-shoe Hill, but they were never very serious.

<small>Situation on Horse-shoe Hill,</small>

<small>and Wynne's Hill.</small>

As the half battalion under Lieut.-Colonel Harris was scrambling over the boulder-strewn slopes of Wynne's Hill, their commanding officer met Colonel Crofton, who told him that the firing line was about a hundred and fifty yards further on; but when Harris reached the southern crest no firing line was to be found, except about 150 men of the 11th brigade, who, having lost their officers and non-commissioned officers, before his return had rallied on his companies of the East Surrey. Placing a company of his own battalion upon each flank of these men, he fronted towards the position which he imagined the enemy to occupy, and, like the other corps then on Wynne's Hill, threw up stone breastworks. The lessons of

Vaal Krantz had not been forgotten by those who had fought there, and all ranks now thoroughly knew the need for working by night in order to obtain shelter from the enemy's fire by day. Leaving his men thus employed, Lieut.-Colonel Harris, with a small party, searched for the firing line of which Colonel Crofton had spoken, but without success, as it lay further to the eastward than he was able to patrol. He then returned to his sangars, and as it was possible some of the 11th brigade might be in front, ordered that there was to be no firing; any attack by the enemy was to be repelled with the bayonet. Throughout the night the Boers maintained a fairly heavy fire, but made no attempt to close upon his works.

To Harris' front was the kraal occupied by Blundell's Riflemen; some distance to their right the Devon, on the southern slopes of the hill, supported the Royal Lancaster, which was now commanded by Major F. B. Matthews, Major E. W. Yeatherd having been mortally wounded; to the westward the crest line was held by part of the Rifle Reserve battalion.

In the evening, before the true nature of the struggle for the possession of these kopjes had been realised, General Buller issued orders. They were intended to collect the scattered brigades and were in the nature of "instructions" rather than "marching orders." They were cancelled soon after they had been given out, and have therefore no bearing on events.

The reports sent in after nightfall show how hard it is to know what has really happened during an action fought in the dark over broken and hilly ground. Major-General Lyttelton wrote to the Chief of the Staff at 9.50 p.m. that as far as he could judge :— *Knowledge possessed by the Generals of the situation on these hills.*

"The position, the Green Hills (*Wynne's and Horse-shoe Hills*), have never been really carried, though portions of them were, and the Boers still hold their positions both in front and on each flank. Just before dark a sharp attack was made on them and it appeared that part of the line gave way; however, Sir C. Warren informs me that our men kept their position. I reinforced with two battalions and have two more ready to support, if required. The left flank is none too strong and along the whole line the units are mixed up. I hear there are a good many casualties."

At 11 p.m. General Warren wrote to the Chief of the Staff :—

"There are altogether, I believe, seven battalions in position on the east and west of Green Hills (*Wynne's and Horse-shoe Hills*), three of 11th brigade and four of the IInd division, and there are two of the IInd division on hill to south of the Onderbrook Spruit in reserve, and yet constant requests for reinforcements keep coming in. It is useless to send reinforcements in the darkness, as it will only result in the troops firing into each other, and yet I am quite satisfied that daylight will show that there are quite sufficient troops to hold the ground if properly placed. When daylight arrives, with the assistance of General Lyttelton and General Hildyard, I will endeavour to reinforce any points where there is weakness.

"But before I can place the 11th brigade in an efficient condition I must replace General Wynne (wounded), and I ask permission to place Colonel Kitchener (West Yorkshire regiment) in command of the brigade (11th). General Lyttelton and General Hildyard will, I believe, both concur. Unless we are all very much mistaken to-morrow's affair will be a big thing and will require all our guns in good positions to keep the fire of the enemy down sufficiently to enable us to hold the positions we have taken without considerable loss, if the enemy appear in the same strength and spirit they have shown at sunset this evening.

Warren's suggestions for the 23rd.

"To the following points I would call particular attention :—

"(a) On the right the Boers possess a very high hill entrenched (*Terrace Hill*), which I had hoped to have taken to-night, and also some brown kopjes (*the lower slopes or foot-hills of Terrace Hill, north of the Boers' bridge*) between that hill and the river which I thought had been cleared of Boers by the recent shelling. These latter kopjes ought to have their fire kept down from the Hlangwhane-Monte Cristo line.

"That is to say, that General Barton's brigade and the guns with him should be pushed forward to the high ground overlooking the Tugela and keep down the fire from the kopjes which enfilade the right flank of our position.

"(b) The guns brought up here to-morrow morning should also keep down the fire on these kopjes and the entrenched hill on our right (*Terrace Hill*), and also on the high plateau on our left.

"If both these are carried out I think we can hold the position we have taken to-day satisfactorily.

"I have just received your orders for to-morrow's march, but they seem a little advanced for the position we are in at present unless the enemy retire during the night. I have, for the convenience of the situation, made my camp for the night on the south side of the hill overlooking Onderbrook Spruit near General Lyttelton's bivouac, and I am in direct signalling communication with the officer commanding 2nd brigade.

"CHARLES WARREN, Lieut.-Gen.
"Commanding Vth division."

CHAPTER XXVII.

RELIEF OF LADYSMITH.

HART'S HILL.*

DURING the night, 22nd-23rd, after the arrival of the Devon and the East Surrey (2nd brigade) at the Onderbrook kopjes, little change occurred. There was much intermingling of units, due to the conditions under which the advance of the reinforcing battalions was made. Companies and even sections were thrust forward singly to fill gaps in the front line. The firing was intermittent, with occasional heavy bursts of musketry during which parties of adventurous Boers came so close to the troops on Wynne's Hill that in two or three cases they had to be driven back with the bayonet. No attempt was made to turn the right of our line. Patrols of the East Surrey, pushing some distance along the railway, which runs at the eastern foot of Wynne's Hill, found no trace of activity in that direction. Situation on Wynne's Hill night of 22nd-23rd.

Until break of day on the 23rd neither side gained ground. At dawn the detachment of the King's Royal Rifles was withdrawn from the kraal into which Lieut. Blundell had thrown himself with them. During the night Lieut. H. Wake, King's Royal Rifles, volunteered to go back across the plateau in search of help and orders. After many difficulties in the black darkness, he succeeded in finding Colonel Crofton and Capt. W. P. Braithwaite, brigade major, of the 11th brigade. He told them of the desperate plight of the Riflemen, with ammunition almost ex- Feb. 23rd. At break of day part of the King's Royal Rifles are withdrawn,

* See map No. 30 (b).

hausted, surrounded on front and flanks by the enemy's works. Two companies of the East Surrey at once lined the southern crest, with orders to await the first glimmer of dawn before trying to bring away the Riflemen. It was still dark when, guided by Wake, the East Surrey moved forward to a spot on the plateau from which they could bring their rifles to bear upon the sangars round the kraal. There they halted while Wake crept on to tell Lieut. Blundell that help was at hand, and that he was to work his men back in driblets to the East Surrey. One by one the Riflemen began to steal away from the kraal which had, though inadequately, hitherto sheltered them. They were not noticed until an unlucky sound attracted the Boers' attention, and brought a hail of bullets. Then, as the retreat could no longer be concealed, the men rushed towards the troops who had come to rescue them, passed through their extended ranks, and, covered by the steady volleys which the East Surrey poured upon the works around the kraal, re-formed in rear. This detachment of the King's Royal Rifles had lost nearly half its men killed and wounded. One of the companies of the East Surrey, that commanded by Major H. L. Smith, was able to retire to the southern crest, under the protection of the Riflemen whom they had rescued and who had now rallied. But on the other hand, the company of his battalion to which Lieut.-Colonel Harris had attached himself, had a harder fate. It was commanded at this time by Lieutenant C. H. Hinton. In supporting Major Smith's company, Lieut.-Colonel Harris and Lieut. Hinton pressed on too far; Harris fell, pierced with several bullets;* Hinton was killed, and the command devolved upon Sergeant F. C. Leavens, who greatly distinguished himself by the coolness and skill with which he handled his men. The enemy's musketry was so sustained that it was impossible to withdraw from the dangerous ground for fourteen hours. At dusk Sergeant Leavens fell back, with a loss of thirteen killed and twenty-one wounded. Not only did he bring away such of the wounded within reach as were fit to be moved, but also some of the rifles of the dead and

covered by two companies of the East Surrey.

---

* For gallantry in succouring Lieutenant-Colonel Harris under very heavy fire, Private A. E. Curtis, the East Surrey, received the Victoria Cross.

wounded. The following letter was sent afterwards to Major Pearse, 2nd East Surrey regiment :—

"The Major-General desires me to inform you how highly he appreciates the conduct of all ranks of the 2nd East Surrey regiment in the operations of the 22nd-23rd instant, when the battalion was employed in most trying conditions. The Lieutenant-General commanding has asked him to intimate the high appreciation of the 3rd King's Royal Rifles of the service rendered them on the morning of the 23rd, and to add his own cordial thanks.

"By Order,
"CHRISTIAN VICTOR,
"Bde. Major, 2nd Brigade."

Reinforcements sent to Wynne's Hill.

Seeing Lieut. Blundell's company running back in order to form up again, as ordered, behind the East Surrey, some of the King's Own followed their example, and from the plateau sought shelter on the southern slope of the hill. They were replaced by a company and a half of the Devon. Along the rest of the western crest line of Wynne's Hill the Devon relieved the two Lancashire battalions, and about 5.30 a.m. the Queen's furnished half a battalion, under Major W. S. Burrell, to hold the southern part of the western face of Wynne's Hill, till then only defended by two companies of the Rifle Reserve battalion. Two Maxims were sent to Burrell, one from the East Surrey, the other from the Royal Lancaster. With the help of volunteers from the Riflemen, they were placed in position, and did excellent work throughout the day in keeping down the heavy enfilading musketry which the Boers poured upon them. The other half battalion of the Queen's, on the south bank of the Onderbrook, held the kopjes which lie near the great bend in the spruit. Facing westward it checked the attempts of Boer sharpshooters to work down the bed of the stream. It gradually became necessary to throw all the companies into the trenches and sangars of the firing line, which were within a few hundred yards of the enemy's works. Thus, in the course of the forenoon of the 23rd, most of the units which had been engaged throughout the afternoon of the 22nd and the night of the 22nd-23rd in the attack on the Onderbrook kopjes, were relieved by fresh troops, and lay behind such shelter as they could improvise at the foot of Wynne's and Horse-shoe Hills. The freshly arrived infantry held parts of these hills, though heavily and continuously shelled, and assailed with musketry by a large number of the enemy concealed among the kopjes and broken ground which faced and flanked the British line.

The fighting on the west end of Wynne's Hill during the early morning of the 23rd has been described in considerable detail because it illustrates the difficulties encountered by subordinate officers when an attack has been launched, and the conduct of the actual fire fight has passed into the hands of the battalion and company commanders. It also emphasises the absolute necessity that in the fire fight every intended movement, however local, should be communicated to the troops in the immediate neighbourhood.

Movement of the artillery to the left bank.

The heavy guns at Chieveley and four Naval 12-prs. on Hlangwhane ridge were still left on the right bank. An attempt was made to bring the 5-in. and the Naval 4.7-in. guns over the bridge on the evening of the 22nd, but the 4.7-in., each of which in its improvised carriage weighed in all six tons and a half, proved too heavy. By taking the guns out of their "cradles," the sailors reduced the weight to four tons and a half, and the heavy ordnance passed over in safety. As such part of the artillery as had not hitherto crossed arrived on the left bank,

Its disposition.

Colonel L. W. Parsons, C.R.A., placed his guns in two lines, one behind the other. The 61st Howitzer battery was concealed among the kopjes near the railway, a little to the south of the bridge over the Onderbrook. On its left was the 28th Field battery, which had run considerable risk of being captured or destroyed by the Boers in the grey of the morning. On the evening of the 22nd, Lieut.-General Warren had ordered Major Apsley Smith to post at earliest dawn a battery on a site which he pointed out. Apsley Smith, while it was still dark on the 23rd, had led the 28th battery forward, and was nearing the spot when he was ordered back by General Warren, as owing to the outpost line having been drawn in during the night, the guns would have been dangerously exposed. The burghers, less than one thousand yards off, opened fire upon the battery as it retired, and, though protected by the volleys of the nearest

RELIEF OF LADYSMITH.

outposts, it was forced to take shelter in a rocky gorge, so narrow that a road had to be cut to extricate the guns and wagons. Fortunately, only five men and three horses were wounded in this adventure. To the right front and right rear of the 61st and 28th, the 64th and 78th batteries were placed close to the river. Behind these guns on the crest of the ridge stood the second line of artillery. The 73rd Field battery was on the left; in the centre came two Naval 4.7-in. and four Naval 12-pr. 12-cwt.; to the right were three 5-in. guns of the Royal Garrison artillery with the fourth detached to the left flank. The fire was directed on the same targets as on the 22nd, which included "Terrace Hill," the kopje to the north-east of Wynne's Hill. The General-in-Chief had intended to carry Terrace Hill after the seizure of Wynne's Hill. In the morning this height was known to the gunners as "Terrace Hill," but by the evening it had received the name of "Hart's Hill" to commemorate the gallant effort made during this day by the 5th brigade to capture it. It was not possible to use all the guns to prepare for the attack on Terrace Hill. The second line of artillery was occupied in keeping down the fire of the Boer guns, which, when they could be seen at all, appeared to be in the same positions as on the 22nd, and in searching the ground to the south of Grobelaar Mountain, to prevent any movement against the left and left rear of the army; while from Gun Hill, near Chieveley, the sailors fought a 6-in. gun and a 4.7-in. mounted on a platform against Boer artillery concealed on Grobelaar Mountain. From the northern slopes of Hlangwhane four Naval 12-prs. bombarded the trenches on Terrace (Hart's) Hill; and in the course of the day they were joined by Field batteries from the left bank, where the area in which artillery could be employed with safety to itself was so limited that the 7th, 19th and 63rd batteries were sent back over the bridge to come into action, two from Hlangwhane, and one from Fuzzy Hill against Terrace (Hart's) Hill.

When Sir Redvers Buller had realised that the 11th brigade was not strong enough to carry out the task assigned to it, viz., the capture not only of Wynne's Hill, but also of Terrace (Hart's) Hill, he decided to employ the 5th brigade to storm

Movement of Hart's brigade.

the latter on the 23rd. Instructions were accordingly issued to Major-General Hart to leave his bivouac on the left bank of the Tugela, opposite Colenso, and to join the Vth division at the Onderbrook Spruit. At 5 a.m. Hart, who had just been reinforced by half a battalion of the Imperial Light Infantry from Chieveley, set his brigade in motion, and, although steadily shelled by guns on Grobelaar, sustained few casualties on his march to Hill 244, where he halted about 7 a.m. There he received verbal orders from General Buller to attack as soon as the artillery bombardment had sufficiently shaken the occupants of the trenches. The Royal Inniskilling Fusiliers having joined him, his brigade was now complete with the exception of the Border regiment left to hold Chieveley and Gun Hill. In addition his command included half a battalion of the Imperial Light Infantry (11th brigade), and also the 1st battalion Rifle Brigade and 1st battalion Durham Light Infantry, which two battalions, under Colonel Norcott, were sent to him from the 4th brigade. After studying the terrain as far as it was possible for him to do so, Major-General Hart pointed out to the officers commanding his battalions the general line of advance by which the hill was to be reached, and allotted to each his duties in the assault. A march of a mile and a half would bring the brigade to a long kopje, the lower half of which ran back from the river in a series of terrace-like slopes from which it took its name of Terrace Hill. The slopes varied in degree, but were uniformly rocky, with many mimosa trees scattered over their surface. On the highest and broadest terrace lay the railway, while above it frowned the upper part of the hill, steep, rugged and strewn with boulders. The Royal Inniskilling Fusiliers were to lead, followed in succession by the Connaught Rangers and the half battalion Imperial Light Infantry. The second line was to be formed by the Royal Dublin Fusiliers, while the 1st battalion Rifle Brigade and the Durham Light Infantry were to follow in third line as close to the Dublin Fusiliers as cover permitted, but in no event far behind them. When the Inniskilling Fusiliers arrived at the foot of the terrace, they were to leave the ravine, form for attack, and wait until the Connaught

RELIEF OF LADYSMITH. 487

Rangers had assumed the same formation on their right. The Imperial Light Infantry were to work their way still further to the right, lapping well round to the east of the base of the hill, and, when the frontal attack was started, attempt to turn the enemy's left flank. To support the assaulting column General Warren called up four Naval 12-prs. under Lieutenants Melvill and James, from the Colenso kopjes to the Hill 244, while the 11th brigade was to help the attack by long-range musketry. Lieut.-General Warren at noon sent to Col. Kitchener this message :— Supporting artillery and long-range musketry.

"General Hart will move out to the attack at 12.30 p.m. His first objective will be the brown kopjes (*the foot-hills or lower terraces of Hart's Hill*) to east of your position. Having taken these, he will work on to the higher Green Hill (*Hart's Hill*) to the north of them, attacking its eastern end and working westward along the crest so as to outflank the long trench on the western slope of the hill. Two batteries follow him when clear of infantry fire. Support his advance as far as practicable from your position by Maxim and musketry fire."

A little after midday, Major-General Hart was ordered to advance; the artillery shelled the hill with redoubled vigour, while the troops on the right of Wynne's Hill, and two battalions of the 6th brigade (the Royal Fusiliers and Royal Scots Fusiliers), from Naval Hill on the right bank of the Tugela poured long-range volleys upon the trenches and works which concealed the defenders of Terrace Hill. Throughout its course over the battlefield of the 14th-27th February, the Tugela flows in a deep bed, the sides of which, varying in height from forty feet at Colenso to several hundred feet below Pieters Hill and Manxa Nest, are sometimes steep enough to be described as cliffs. In places the river almost laps the base of its enclosing walls; elsewhere there is a space of a few feet between the water and the sides of the ravine. Thus men marching along this space between the river and the cliffs would be entirely sheltered from fire from the hills above them, and might be brought untouched to a point fairly close to the enemy's position, and could be launched against it without having their order disturbed by distant fire. Moreover, during the time that, unseen by the enemy though not unknown to him, they were making the greater part of Hart advances; the terrain.

their advance, the artillery could continue to play upon the entrenchments they were about to attack, so that the infantry assault would follow closely on the bombardment. It was of this opportunity that General Hart meant to take advantage. Unfortunately the path on which he moved was so narrow that much of the march had to be made in single file, so that numbers could only be delivered very slowly at the front, and it took a long time to form the men up into their proper units when they had reached the required point. Hart first made his way along the bottom of the gorge, and when that was not wide enough to afford foothold to his troops, scrambled along the side of its left bank. The difficulties of the ground did not allow the men to press forward quickly in single file. The column wound in a string which seemed interminable, moving behind the railway embankment or floundering knee-deep in the mud and reeds of the bank of the river. Upon the narrow railway bridge at the junction of the Langewacht Spruit with the Tugela the Boers concentrated such a storm of rifle bullets and pom-pom shells that the soldiers could only attempt to cross one at a time. Each man rushed singly through the twenty yards of this defile, leaping over the gaps in the roadway through which could be seen the water in the spruit many feet below. Once over the bridge he flung himself down the eastern side of the embankment to gain momentary shelter, and then followed his comrades in their dash for the river bank, the next stage in their onward march. Not a few dropped dead or wounded on the bridge. The delay due to this running the gauntlet at "Pom-pom Bridge," as the soldiers named it, was increased by the impossibility of inducing the ammunition mules of the Inniskilling Fusiliers and Connaught Rangers to face the fire. It was found necessary to unload the boxes of reserve ammunition and carry them across by hand. From these various causes the march was so slow that it was late in the afternoon before the men could form up at the spot selected.

Difficulty of crossing "Pom-pom Bridge."

Major-General Hart, fearing the approach of darkness, therefore decided at about 5 p.m. to deliver the assault without waiting for his third line. He formed the Inniskilling Fusiliers

5 p.m. Hart decides to attack without waiting for

RELIEF OF LADYSMITH. 489

for attack on a front of four companies, with their left opposite to the western end of the hill. The remainder of the battalion was drawn up behind them in successive lines of double companies. The Connaught Rangers were ordered to prolong to the right with one company, with the rest of the battalion ranged behind it in column. The Imperial Light Infantry were to guard the right flank. When the leading company of the Rangers was level with the Inniskillings, all moved forward, rushing from hillock to hillock, and firing volleys at the crest line above them. It was impossible for the infantry as they climbed the sides of the mountain to discover that this crest line did not mark the true summit, which was at that time wholly invisible to them. The top of Hart's Hill is a lozenge-shaped plateau, which rises in gentle undulations for several hundred yards, and then rapidly falls into the valley which separates it from Railway Hill. The Boers had thrown up strong breastworks, connected by a deep trench, about two hundred yards back from the southern, or false crest, and until they were driven from these defences Hart's Hill could not be won. Owing to the great extension of the firing line the Connaught Rangers were crowded on the right, and some of their companies were therefore sent by their Colonel (L. G. Brooke) to work up the donga which runs into the Tugela along the eastern side of Hart's Hill. These companies directed their fire upon the trench at the head of this donga and the crest of Railway Hill, the kopje to their right front. Passing through a deserted laager, from which the enemy had retreated when the Inniskillings emerged from the river bed, the troops rapidly worked up to the railway which alternately ran through cuttings and over embankments. Its double fence of barbed wire proved a formidable obstacle, and this delay, under effective fire, cost many lives. During this stage of the combat General Hart caused the regimental call of the Inniskilling Fusiliers and the Connaught Rangers to be frequently sounded, followed by the "Advance," the "Double," and the "Charge." The men needed no encouragement, and the bugle sounds induced such haste as to imperil, if not destroy, cohesion among the units.

his third line to come up. His dispositions.

At first all went well; the artillery beat down the fire of the enemy's guns and bombarded his works with ever-increasing vigour; the enemy's advanced parties fell back from the railway, and by hard fighting were gradually driven up the slopes and over the false crest. A sudden check in front decided the Major-General to throw part of his reserve into the fight. Half a battalion of the Royal Dublin Fusiliers, under Bt. Lieut.-Colonel C. G. H. Sitwell, was sent to reinforce the Inniskilling Fusiliers. The Dublin Fusiliers dashed forward, climbed the hill, and, as their leading company,* under Captain C. F. Romer, was nearing the left of the Inniskillings, the latter fixed bayonets and charged with their commanding officer, Lieut.-Colonel T. M. G. Thackeray, at their head. They reached the false crest of the hill, only to find themselves confronted by the stone works on the plateau, which were held by the Krugersdorp commando. Unfortunately at this moment the artillery had to cease fire, lest in the fast waning light they should drop their projectiles among the Irish brigade. The Boers, relieved from the bombardment, and with nerves unshaken by a cannonade which in their deep trenches they had been able to avoid, plied their rifles so fiercely that the attackers were mown down as soon as they became visible over the crest line. Among those who fell was Lieut.-Colonel Thackeray, mortally wounded. Nor was this withering musketry from their front the only fire that General Hart's troops had to face, for marksmen, in the valleys to the right and left of the hill upon which they stood, smote them heavily on both flanks.

<small>Hart throws part of his reserves into firing line.</small>

<small>A check at the false crest.</small>

Romer established his men among the boulders which marked the south-western corner of the false crest line, and waited to attack the Boer works until the remainder of the half battalion of the Dublin Fusiliers came up. On the right the leading companies of the Connaught Rangers had sustained considerable losses in crossing the railway and in scaling the upper slopes of the hill. They had taken shelter behind a low stone wall which

---

* This company, about 90 strong, was ordered to advance in a line extended to ten paces interval, a formation which, on a rocky hill, made the exercise of control very difficult.

RELIEF OF LADYSMITH.

ran for a hundred yards a little below the false crest. Here they halted until reinforced by some of the companies of their own battalion and two of the Dublin. It was now almost dark; the stars were beginning to appear. The remainder of the half battalion of Dublin Fusiliers had reached the false crest, and Romer had begun to creep with his company along the summit of the hill towards the enemy's sangars when suddenly the Inniskillings rose to their feet, and, led by Major F. A. Sanders, on whom the command had now devolved, rushed upon the enemy with a terrific yell. The Dublins at once joined the Inniskillings and both went headlong at the entrenchments. The Connaught Rangers, seeing the Inniskilling and Dublin charge, leaped over the wall and joined in the assault. Instantly from the trenches and sangars on the far side of the crest burst a deadly fire. Now that the guns were no longer playing upon them, the Boers stood up in their trenches the better to use their rifles. The line staggered; then recovered itself and rushed fiercely on. Though the soldiers fell fast, and many of the officers were shot as they led their men, not a few of the gallant Irishmen dashed forward until struck down when within a few yards of the enemy. So much were the Boers impressed by their courage that in some cases they refrained from firing upon men who had specially attracted their notice. These they allowed to leap into the works, where they were pulled down and disarmed before they could use their bayonets. *[A charge by the whole line is beaten back.]*

The Irish brigade was not strong enough to force the Boer trenches, and there were no fresh troops behind it to lend weight and driving power to the assault. Half the Dublin Fusiliers, the only battalion which Hart had in reserve, had been thrown into the fight, and the third line, under Colonel Norcott, did not arrive until 9 p.m., when the murky darkness made it impossible to employ them. *[The third line arrive at night, when darkness makes it impossible to use them.]*

The greater part of the troops sullenly fell back about two hundred yards below the false crest, and then collected behind the stone wall. Here they halted, and prepared to hold the slopes which they still retained, while above them small parties of officers and men covered their retreat with musketry, and then *[The assaulting troops cling to the false crest, and await reinforcements.]*

themselves retired, a few at a time, crawling backwards on their stomachs under heavy fire. Gradually the ranks were re-formed, and the soldiers did their best to improve the shelter afforded by the wall, behind which the men were dangerously crowded. Here they anxiously awaited water, orders, and reinforcements, but for many hours no messages of any kind reached them. While reorganising his shattered troops, Colonel Brooke, Connaught Rangers, the senior officer present, took measures to guard his flanks. Recalling the two companies which had worked up the donga to the east of the hill, he placed them on the railway cutting as outposts on his right rear, while he ordered part of the Imperial Light Infantry to move further down the line, i.e., towards Pom-pom Bridge, as a protection for his left rear. The Boers made no counter-attack; but during the night there was much intermittent firing, in the intervals of which could be heard the groans and cries of the wounded, who, with the dead, lay between our troops and the works of the enemy. To some of the wounded help could be given; others, until the armistice of the 25th, had to remain untended, exposed for forty-four hours alike to the elements and to the shot and shell of the combatants. The fighting on the 23rd and 24th was so continuous, and so much of it took place during the night, that it is impossible to discriminate accurately between the losses on each day. The casualties for the two days will be found on page 500. They included Lieut.-Colonel C. C. H. Thorold, Royal Welsh Fusiliers.

Brooke's measures for security.

During the progress of Hart's attack, the enemy's musketry against the left of our line, which earlier in the day had been heavy, decreased greatly, and in the course of the evening the 11th brigade, after having been under continuous fire for twenty-eight hours, was marched back to the shelter of Hill 244. During the 22nd and 23rd this brigade expended nearly 125,000 rounds of small-arm ammunition :—

South Lancashire	46,991
King's Own (Royal Lancaster)	45,000
Rifle Reserve Battalion	32,930
	124,921

RELIEF OF LADYSMITH. 493

Major-General Hildyard, whose brigade (the 2nd) was now strengthened by the arrival of the Royal Fusiliers and the Royal Welsh Fusiliers, attached to him from the 6th brigade, occupied the southern part of the plateau of Wynne's Hill with the Queen's, Royal Fusiliers, Devon, West Yorkshire, and Royal Welsh Fusiliers. In second line on the slopes lay the East Surrey. Two battalions of the 4th brigade, the Scottish Rifles, and part of the King's Royal Rifles were in the positions they had taken up on the 22nd, facing Grobelaar Mountain on the left rear of the line of hills held by Major-General Hildyard's troops. During the night the men laboured continuously, improving and enlarging the existing sangars, and there was much firing. *Feb. 23rd. Positions of the remainder of troops near Wynne's Hill.*

In the course of the day Sir George White signalled to General Buller that bodies of the enemy were in movement towards Umbulwana, Onderbrook, and Potgieter's, besides a detachment of 1,500 men who had been despatched to strengthen the garrison of Helpmakaar, now threatened by Bethune's column. *Reported movements of Boers.*

On the night of the 23rd the position of Sir Redvers Buller's troops was approximately as follows :* *Situations of Buller's army on night of 23rd.*

Hart, with two battalions of the 4th brigade in support of his brigade (the 5th), was clinging to the slopes of the hill he had partially captured. To Hart's left rear was Lyttelton's division (the IInd). It was composed of Hildyard's brigade (the 2nd), the Royal Fusiliers and Royal Welsh Fusiliers (both of 6th brigade), with the Scottish Rifles and King's Royal Rifles (both of the 4th brigade). These last two battalions were on the left rear of the division. Behind the Hill 244 lay the 11th brigade (Kitchener). The 10th brigade (Coke) continued to protect the line of advance from the Colenso kopjes. Thorneycroft's mounted infantry guarded the left of the 10th brigade (Coke), while the remainder of the 2nd mounted brigade (Dundonald) connected Coke's right with the left flank of the 11th brigade. The 1st cavalry brigade (Burn-Murdoch) bivouacked near the pontoon bridge, and on the right bank the rest of Barton's brigade acted as escort to the artillery on the heights of Hlangwhane.

* See map No. 30 (c).

494   THE WAR IN SOUTH AFRICA.

Communications over the Tugela.

The Boer bridge under the northern end of the Hlangwhane spur, partially destroyed by the burghers when they fell back to the left bank, was repaired by the Royal Engineers; but it proved of comparatively little value, as it was unfit for wheeled traffic, difficult of approach, and exposed to fire. Since neither the railway bridge nor the road bridge at Colenso had as yet been restored, and the drift across the river near them was unfit for the passage of heavily-laden wagons, the only available means of communication between the right and left banks was by the pontoon bridge (No. 1). To relieve the pressure of traffic across it, the Royal Engineers threw an aerial tram, capable of bearing half a ton weight of stores at a time, across the Tugela at Colenso, whence the supplies were carried to the troops at the front in railway trollies, which had been left on the line by the Boers. But this aerial tram, though very useful, was, like another thrown by the Royal Engineers over the river near the Boer bridge, only a temporary expedient. For the future supply of the army north of the river it was essential that one of the Colenso bridges should be made fit for heavy traffic. To rebuild the railway bridge would obviously be the work of months; but the gap in the road bridge could be made good in a few days.

Natal Pioneer Corps begin work on the road bridge at Colenso, Feb. 23rd.

This important duty was entrusted to Lieut.-Colonel H. E. Rawson, C.R.E., on the lines of communication. He directed the operations of the Natal Pioneer Corps, a body of civilians composed of the staff and white artisans of the Natal Public Works Department, with native labour supplied by loyal chiefs. The Natal Pioneer Corps, which had already done good service in fortifying Pietermaritzburg during Joubert's raid into southern Natal, volunteered for the repair of the bridge. They began work at sunrise on the 23rd, when parties of the enemy were still within rifle shot, and under an annoying shell fire, which on the 26th and 27th so frightened the natives that they refused to go on. By dint of strenuous exertions by night and day a trestle bridge was thrown over the gap on the 2nd March. The wagons, laden with the supplies collected by various committees for the defenders of Ladysmith, were at once sent on by the bridge thus restored, across which all traffic from bank to bank of the Tugela was carried until the railway bridge was made good.

No change in the relative positions of the British and Boer forces took place during the night of the 23rd–24th, but at dawn on the 24th Major-General Hildyard was ordered to support Major-General Hart with two battalions. The East Surrey and the West Yorkshire were sent forward to the right of the 5th brigade, neither of them in full strength, as some of their companies were then so hotly engaged on Wynne's Hill that they could not be withdrawn from the fire fight. Therefore, half a battalion of the Scottish Rifles was summoned from Hildyard's left, and followed the West Yorkshire towards Hart's Hill. In consequence of this drain on Hildyard's strength, the South Lancashire was lent to him from the 11th brigade, still in reserve among the Colenso kopjes. At midnight on the 23rd General Hart had received detailed accounts of that evening's failure, and at 5 a.m. he sent Major C. R. R. McGrigor, his brigade major, to judge of the situation and report to him. Major McGrigor, on reaching the front, at once saw how serious was the case, and hastened to General Hart for orders. Hart decided to reinforce, but it was too late to do so. The foremost troops could not maintain their hold upon the upper slopes of the hill. Not long after Major McGrigor had left the Connaught Rangers, a brisk musketry fire opened upon the rear of the Irish brigade from the loop of the railway to the south-west of Hart's Hill, where a number of Boers had seized a cutting, which should have been held by a company of the Imperial Light Infantry. A company of the reserve half battalion of Dublin Fusiliers under Captain W. J. Venour, dislodged these Boers and drove them into the donga which skirts the western foot of Hart's Hill. A number of men of the Imperial Light Infantry, attaching themselves to this company of Dublin Fusiliers, did excellent service, as another party of the same corps had done the night before with the companies of the Connaught Rangers in the fighting round the donga on the right flank. Meantime other burghers, who had crept into the broken ground on either side, turned their fire upon the men who had clung throughout the

Feb. 24th.
Movements at dawn.
Hildyard supports Hart with two battalions.

Hart decides to reinforce the Irish brigade, but is too late.

night to the shelter of the wall below the false crest. The little additional stone works which the troops had thrown up did not protect them from this new attack. Men fell fast; there was no sign of reinforcements; the Boer fire redoubled in intensity. Finally Colonel Brooke reluctantly ordered the men to retire down the hill and re-form behind the railway; and by 8 a.m. the ground between the false crest and the line was occupied only by the dead and wounded who had so gallantly helped to capture it. On the right, part of the Connaught Rangers continued to act as a flank defence, and prevented the Boers from working down the donga between Hart's and Railway Hills, while on the left, Captain Venour's company was reinforced and guarded the railway throughout the day.

Irish brigade retires from the false crest and re-forms behind the railway, 8 a.m., Feb. 24th.

When Hart saw that the Irish brigade had been compelled to evacuate the upper part of the hill, he promptly sent the Durham Light Infantry, supported by the 1st Rifle Brigade to retake the ground. This was done with very small loss, owing to the covering fire of the Maxims of the 5th brigade, which had been collected on a small kopje south of the railway line. The local situation, as regards the 5th brigade, and the Boers facing it on the true crest of Hart's Hill, was peculiar. Owing to the shape of the false crest, neither the Boers on the real summit of Hart's Hill nor the British on its lower slopes could see each other. Between them lay the false crest, upon which, from their trenches on the true crest, the burghers could bring so devastating a fire as to stop for the moment any further British effort to seize it. Half-way up the kopje Hart's main body held the hillocks on the southern edge of the terrace along which the railway runs, and, by firing over the heads of the advanced detachment, could sweep the false crest with musketry, while the rifles of the advanced detachment could also be brought to bear upon it from the slopes on which they were posted. Thus the false crest was untenable by either Briton or Boer. General Hart would not recall the advanced detachment, because if he did so the volume of British fire directed upon the false crest would be diminished, the Boers might occupy it, and by fire from thence might drive his main body back to the banks of the Tugela.

Hart sends D. L. I. and 1st Rifle Brigade to re-occupy the ground given up by Irish brigade.

RELIEF OF LADYSMITH.

During the forenoon the enemy's musketry chiefly fell upon Hart from his front and left, but at midday an annoying fusilade was opened from the lower slopes of Railway Hill. Throughout the day the British heavy guns were turned upon the Boer trenches on Hart's Hill, and an officer, lying wounded on the slope between the false and the true crest, noticed that many lyddite shells made good direct hits on the enemy's works.

For a time Sir Redvers Buller proposed to make a further attack on Hart's Hill, intending to launch at the same time two battalions against Railway Hill. The capture of Hart's Hill was to be undertaken, and by the storming of Railway Hill the enemy's left flank was to be turned and driven in. But before the arrangements for these assaults were completed, a welcome discovery caused the General-in-Chief entirely to recast his plans. Lieut.-Colonel Sandbach, his Intelligence officer, had suggested to him that a crossing, lower down the stream than the site of the existing pontoon bridge (No. 1), would be of very great help to the operations. Buller agreed, and ordered him to seek for such a crossing place. While studying the lie of the land from the ground held by Hart's brigade, Sandbach noticed on the heights on the right bank signs of a horse-track, leading from the east of Naval Hill down to the Tugela. Hastening there, he reconnoitred the descent to the river, and found that the track could be made practicable; that it was completely screened from the fire and view of the enemy, and that there the conditions of the river were favourable to pontooning. On receiving this information, Sir Redvers directed Sandbach to take Major J. L. Irvine, the officer commanding the pontoon troop, to see the place. Major Irvine also considered that a bridge could be thrown at the spot selected, which was about half a mile further down stream than the Boer bridge, and on the joint report of these two officers, the General decided to withdraw a great portion of his army from the left to the right bank, bridge the Tugela to the south of the ground then occupied by General Hart, and, using the bed of the river as a covered way, make a heavy attack on the centre and left of the Boer line, so as to drive them off the approach to Ladysmith.

Discovery of a track from Naval Hill to the Tugela enables Buller to recast his plans.

His fresh scheme.

Its difficulties. The difficulty of the manœuvre was greatly increased by the fact that the material of the pontoon train was only sufficient to supply one bridge long enough to span the Tugela below Colenso. Therefore, the whole of the troops selected to recross the river, with their baggage, supplies, and other impedimenta, had to be transferred to the right bank before the existing pontoon bridge could be dismantled, and a fresh one thrown at the point now chosen [see map No. 30 (d)].

Movements on the 24th. The 1st cavalry brigade (Burn-Murdoch), during the 24th, was moved to the right bank, south of Colenso, while A. battery R.H.A., which had hitherto been attached to it, was sent to the neighbourhood of Hlangwhane. The exposed flank on the left bank was still protected by the 2nd mounted brigade (Dundonald), less the South African Light Horse detached to Gourton, west of Frere, to intercept a party of four hundred Boers reported to be in that neighbourhood. In the morning four Naval 12-prs. moved from the Colenso kopjes to Monte Cristo, whence in the afternoon they opened upon the heights of Pieters Hill. They were followed after dark by two 4.7-in., which reached the pontoon bridge at 11 p.m., and crossed it early on the 25th, as also did the 5-in. guns. These preliminaries do not appear to have given the Boers any idea that a change of plans had taken place. The necessary road making, which was at once vigorously taken in hand by the Royal Engineers, did not rouse their suspicions, if, indeed, they noticed it. The artillery duel and the exchange of incessant musketry fire continued throughout the day, and two guns mounted on Grobelaar caused the 2nd brigade much annoyance by enfilading their sangars. The Boer gun at Vertnek seems to have been transferred to Grobelaar. The pom-pom in the defile to the north of Vertnek was not seen during the 24th, but it reappeared on the 25th on the western side of Pieters Hill. At 6 p.m. the enemy made a half-hearted attack on Major-General Hildyard, but were easily beaten off; and at dusk a demonstration in the upper valley of the Onderbrook was dispersed by the shells of the 61st Howitzer battery.

In the night of 24th, Boers On the left of their line the Boers attempted to create a panic among the troops of the British right wing. With the exception of the Durham Light Infantry, who, by the recall at dusk of the 1st Rifle Brigade, had been left alone below the false crest of Hart's Hill, the whole of the heterogeneous mass of battalions, then under Major-General Hart's command [Inniskilling and Dublin Fusiliers and Connaught Rangers (5th brigade); half the Imperial Light Infantry (10th brigade); the West Yorkshire and East Surrey (2nd brigade); 1st Rifle Brigade, Durham Light Infantry, and half the Scottish Rifles (4th brigade)], were closely packed in hastily constructed sangars on the lower slopes of the hill. It was not till the evening of the 25th that the Durham Light Infantry were recalled from their advanced position. General Hart, considering that the Durham Light Infantry adequately guaranteed his force against surprise, did not place other outposts, and contented himself with posting sentries on a ridge of rocks which ran along the left of his bivouac. Some of the battalions took measures for their own protection, but their precautions were purely local and lacked the cohesion of a chain of properly organised piquets and supports. At about 9 p.m. a party of Boers, creeping down the donga to the west of Hart's Hill, opened a heavy fire into the densely packed bivouac. In some units this sudden fusilade caused confusion; but on the first alarm the officers commanding the 1st Rifle Brigade, the West Yorkshire, and the East Surrey, formed their battalions into quarter column, fixed bayonets and lay down to await orders. Thus, when two staff officers, Captain H. H. Wilson, brigade major, 4th brigade, and Major A. W. L. Bayly, Indian Army, called upon them to drive away the enemy, they were able to do so with ease. The hillocks to the right and left were cleared of the Boers; part of the East Surrey were posted on the extreme right, in the donga which runs from the east of Hart's Hill into the Tugela, while the West Yorkshire took charge of the river bank as far as "Pom-pom" bridge.

disturb Hart's brigade with musketry.

During the whole of the 24th the 11th brigade remained in reserve among the kopjes about a mile north of the pontoon bridge; it was shelled for several hours, fortunately without great effect. Of the 6th brigade, three of the battalions were fighting on the left bank of the river. The Royal Fusiliers and

Royal Welsh Fusiliers held Horse-shoe Hill with the 2nd brigade; the Royal Irish Fusiliers escorted the heavy guns; only the Royal Scots Fusiliers were employed on the right bank, where they held the Hlangwhane spur, with piquets watching the Boer bridge.

<small>Casualties on Feb. 23rd-24th.</small>

The casualties on the 23rd and 24th were heavy. Sixty officers fell, of whom 11 were killed, 48 wounded and one missing. Among the other ranks 163 were killed, 872 wounded and 74 missing. Most of the latter were probably killed or wounded and their fate unknown when the returns were made up. The total was 1,169. Among the greatest sufferers were the battalions which attempted to storm the works on the top of Hart's Hill. The Inniskilling Fusiliers lost three officers (including their lieut.-colonel), killed or mortally wounded, eight wounded, one disabled from a fall and one missing. The command changed hands four times and ultimately devolved upon a captain, who brought the battalion out of action. Of the other ranks 56 were killed, 159 wounded and 23 missing. In the Connaught Rangers seven officers were wounded; of the non-commissioned officers and men 19 were killed, 105 wounded, and eight missing. Among the officers of the Royal Dublin Fusiliers, one was killed and four wounded; in the other ranks there were eight killed, 62 wounded and 18 missing. In the 11th brigade, the largest casualty return was that of the King's Own (Royal Lancaster). Fourteen officers and 660 non-commissioned officers and men went into action on the 22nd at Wynne's Hill; by the night of the 24th three officers had been killed and three wounded; and in the other ranks 21 were killed, 106 wounded and 15 missing (see Appendix 2).

For gallantry on the 24th February, Lieut. E. T. Inkson, R.A.M.C., was awarded the Victoria Cross.

CHAPTER XXVIII.

RELIEF OF LADYSMITH.*

PIETERS HILL.

IN pursuance of Sir Redvers Buller's new plan a stream of artillery and of supply wagons was directed to the pontoon bridge (No. 1) throughout the night of the 24th–25th. There had been heavy rain during the afternoon; and so much mud had been brought on to the bridge by the oxen that it became dangerously slippery, and Major Irvine, R.E., had to suspend all traffic till the morning. Thus the accumulation of vehicles on the slopes above the river was great. Happily the Boer artillery did not seize this opportunity, for a few shells, well placed in the early morning, might have done much damage. By 10 a.m. on the 25th all the guns, with the exception of the 73rd Field battery left with the 10th brigade, were once more upon the right bank.

_{Night of Feb. 24th-25th, 1900.}

Though many of those who had been wounded in the attacks on Hart's and Wynne's Hills had been carried into safety, not a few still lay between the works of the two armies. Their condition was pitiable in the extreme. Not only were they suffering the pangs of thirst and the agony of untended wounds, but they were exposed to imminent and unceasing danger from the projectiles, which swept over the ground upon which they had fallen. In the interests of humanity, Sir Redvers Buller arranged with the Boer leaders for a local truce, during which no fire was to be directed by either side upon these kopjes, so that the surgeons might superintend in safety the removal of

_{Feb. 25th. Local truce to collect wounded.}

* See maps No. 30 (c) and (d).

the sufferers from the bullet and shell-swept slopes on which they had lain for nearly forty-four hours. When this news had run round the Boer line, numbers of burghers, cramped with long crouching in their sangars and trenches, stood up to stretch their weary limbs, and thus disclosed the exact spot from which their fire had been directed. In many parts of the field the British works were within two hundred yards of those of the enemy ; in some cases, indeed, not more than seventy yards lay between the piles of stones from the cover of which Britons and Boers had fired upon one another without cessation for nearly three days and nights. Thanks to this local truce, which did not preclude the movement of troops, the artillery were able to transfer their guns to the positions, described below, without being shelled by the enemy, and much work was done on the right bank in making roads to the site of the proposed pontoon bridge, marked upon the map [No. 30 (d)] as No. 2 pontoon bridge. Nearly all of the roads shown on the right bank were made by the army during the relief of Ladysmith.

Boers disclose their positions during truce.

Among the measures taken during the 25th was the division of the British front into two sections. Lieut.-General Warren was placed in command of the troops to the east of the Langewacht Spruit, while Major-General Lyttelton was in charge of the line to the westward of that stream. The 10th brigade (Coke), on the Colenso kopjes, continued, however, to be under General Warren's immediate orders. By a curious coincidence, the Boers also adopted the Langewacht Spruit as the line of demarcation between their right wing, under Botha, and their left, under Lukas Meyer.

By nightfall nearly all the guns had reached their new positions. Four Naval 12-prs., which on the 24th had been sent back from the left bank, were on Clump Hill. At each end of Fuzzy Hill were posted two 5-in. guns, with the 63rd battery R.F.A. between them. On the reverse slopes of the kopje which lies to the north-east of Fuzzy Hill was the 61st Howitzer battery ; while to the south of the Howitzers was the 19th battery. The northern end of Naval Hill was ringed with three tiers of fire. From its summit frowned the Naval guns, under Captain E, P,

New positions of guns on right bank.

RELIEF OF LADYSMITH.

Jones, R.N. Highest of all were two 4.7-in. guns on travelling carriages, under Commander Limpus, R.N. A little lower and to the left were stationed four 12-prs., under Lieut. Ogilvy, R.N., and Mr. Wright, R.N. Two more 4.7-in., on fixed mountings were on their way from Chieveley, under Lieut. Anderton, Natal Naval Vounteers, and Midshipman W. R. Ledgard, R.N., to be placed on a knoll a little to the south of the Howitzer battery. Further down the slope, below the 12-prs., the guns of the 64th Field battery were perched on a series of rocky steps. To the left front of the 64th, and on a somewhat lower level, four guns of No. 4 Mountain battery were concealed among the rocks and bushes which overhang the river. To the right of the 64th was A. battery R.H.A. Below the Naval 12-prs. three Field batteries, the 7th, 78th and 28th, stretched from east to west along the western spur of Naval Hill.

Shortly after 8 p.m., when the truce expired, the enemy poured heavy musketry upon Hart's brigade and upon the left and centre of our line at Onderbrook Spruit, and advanced, probably hoping to find out whether the troops had begun to fall back. This frontal attack was repulsed with small loss to the British, but the fire from Grobelaar for some time continued to be severe upon Hildyard's left rear; and about an hour later a demonstration in some force was made against Coke's brigade. *8 p.m., Feb. 25th. Hostilities resumed.*

Among the infantry there were no movements of importance; but, to meet a threatened attack from the direction of Weenen, nearly all the mounted troops were moved to the right bank, the protection of which was entrusted to Major-General Barton. The 2nd mounted brigade, leaving part of Thorneycroft's mounted infantry near Colenso, moved rapidly to Cingolo Nek; they occupied it, and threw out a chain of posts to watch the Tugela from Monte Cristo to its junction with the Blaauwkrantz river. The 1st cavalry brigade arrived at Hussar Hill at 8.30 a.m., and detached a squadron of the 13th Hussars to feel for the enemy. These were a force of six hundred to seven hundred Boers, who had been despatched from Ladysmith to attack the lines of communication. Erasmus, who was in command, reached the confluence of the Tugela and the Blaauw- *Threatened attack from Weenen.*

krantz, about fifteen miles to the west of the line of drifts which were watched by Colonel Bethune's flanking detachment. There he halted, contenting himself with sending towards Weenen a few scouts, whose presence was detected and at once reported to Sir Redvers Buller by the Civil Magistrate, Mr. Jackson. Then, without an effort to harass the lines of communication, to attack the rear, or to draw the cavalry away from the main advance on Ladysmith, Erasmus retired northwards. Joubert's plan was sound, but he had entrusted it to a feeble hand. Sir Redvers was served in very different fashion by Bethune, who, boldly crossing the Tugela, led a reconnaissance in force towards Helpmakaar on the 24th. His movements were reported, and created such alarm that 1,500 men, who might otherwise have been used to reinforce Botha's commandos, were detached from the siege of Ladysmith to strengthen the garrison of Helpmakaar. Bethune found the Boers well posted, with four guns, four pom-poms, and Maxims, and in numbers far superior to his own. He fell back a few miles, and on the 27th again strongly demonstrated against Helpmakaar, in order to detain as many Boers as possible there, and thus relieve the pressure upon Ladysmith and upon the main army. At the same time he sent on a party of fifty men, who volunteered to blow up the Waschbank bridge on the Sundays river. The attempt, though it failed because a spruit became impassable from a sudden flood, was well conceived, and helped to shake the *moral* of the burghers, and to hasten their retreat.

<small>Bethune's reconnaissance.</small>

On the morning of the 26th Sir Redvers Buller, accompanied by Sir Charles Warren and several Staff officers, examined the enemy's position from various points on the heights on the right bank, to settle the details of the projected movement from both sides of the Tugela. Among other questions, the exact site for the new pontoon bridge was then discussed. General Warren urged that it should be thrown further down the stream than the spot selected by the Royal Engineer officers. Sir Redvers Buller reminded him that on the 20th Lieut.-Colonel Sandbach had reconnoitred along the heights of the right bank from Monte Cristo to the junction of the Klip and the Tugela

<small>Feb. 26th, 1900. Discussions as to exact spot where pontoon bridge should be thrown.</small>

rivers, and had reported that it would require much time and labour to make practicable the track leading from Cingolo Nek to the low ground east of Pieters Hoek; but invited General Warren to satisfy himself by a personal inspection. Sir Charles Warren did so, and on his return agreed that the country was impassable; but he then suggested the possibility of throwing the bridge across the Tugela where it washes the foot of Pieters Hill. Lieut.-Colonel Sandbach and Brevet-Major T. Capper (acting A.A.G., Vth division) were accordingly sent to see if the river could be bridged at this point. They reported to Sir Redvers Buller that rocks and broken water made bridging impossible, and added that from the spot already selected for the pontoon bridge, i.e., to the south of Hart's brigade, troops could move unseen to the foot of Pieters Hill along the left side of the river bed.

At 5 p.m., General Buller assembled his Generals and Staff officers, and issued verbal orders, which were afterwards reduced to writing and distributed by the Chief of the Staff.

Orders for the 27th.

After the bombardment of the Boer positions by every available gun had shaken the defenders of the hills which were to be successively attacked, Major-General Barton (6th brigade) was to descend from the Hlangwhane plateau to the Tugela, cross it by the new pontoon bridge (No. 2), then work down stream under cover of the left bank, and carry Pieters Hill, upon which it was now definitely ascertained that the left of the enemy's line rested. (The brigades had become so intermingled in the course of the last five days' fighting, that it is necessary to name the units of which they were to be composed on the 27th.) Major-General Barton was to lead the 2nd Royal Scots Fusiliers, and the 2nd Royal Irish Fusiliers of his own brigade, and the 2nd Royal Dublin Fusiliers of the 5th brigade, who were to join him at the pontoon bridge. Colonel Kitchener, who had been brought over from the left bank, had under his orders the King's Own (Royal Lancaster), South Lancashire, and York and Lancaster of his brigade (11th), with the West Yorkshire from the 2nd brigade. He was to follow Barton, picking up the King's Own and the West Yorkshire at the pontoon bridge (No. 2), and, as soon as Barton's pressure began to make itself felt, to assail the centre of the Boer line at the hill then known as Railway, and now as Kitchener's, Hill. As soon as Colonel Kitchener's attack had developed, Colonel Norcott's brigade (the 4th), from its bivouac on the terraces of Hart's Hill, was to carry the summit. The 4th brigade now consisted of the 1st Durham Light Infantry, 1st Rifle Brigade, and half the 2nd Scottish Rifles of the 4th brigade, and the 2nd East Surrey of the 2nd brigade. Colonel Norcott's remaining troops (the other half-battalion of the Scottish Rifles, and the King's Royal Rifles), were on the extreme left flank of the IInd division. The 5th brigade was in reserve guarding the bridge-head. This brigade was now formed of the 1st Royal Inniskilling Fusiliers, 1st Connaught Rangers, and half of the Imperial Light Infantry from the 10th brigade. The 1st Border, from Chieveley, was on the right bank. The movements were to be covered by the musketry of the 2nd mounted brigade, the 1st Border and the Rifle Reserve battalion, which were to line the right bank of the Tugela. The 6th brigade acted directly under the orders of the Commander-in-Chief. The other two brigades (4th and 11th), as will be seen from the map, were working on the east of the Langewacht and, therefore, in accordance with the distribution of the army made on the 25th, under Sir Charles Warren's command. West of the spruit, Major-General Lyttelton, with part of Hildyard's brigade (2nd), and the various battalions temporarily attached to it, was to hold in check the Boer right, and to support Warren's column with long-range fire. Hildyard's command in all now consisted of the 2nd Queen's and 2nd Devon of the 2nd brigade ; the 2nd Royal Fusiliers and 1st Royal Welsh Fusiliers of the 6th brigade, and half of the 2nd Scottish Rifles and the 3rd battalion, King's Royal Rifles of the 4th brigade. The 10th brigade (Coke) still remained as before : 2nd Somerset Light Infantry, 2nd Dorset, 2nd Middlesex. It was in its old position, and was to guard Colenso, and maintain touch with the left of Lyttelton's division.

Feb. 26th.
Artillery duel.
Beyond a slow artillery duel between the Boer guns and the artillery massed on the right bank of the Tugela, there was no serious fighting on the 26th, for the British gunners were

RELIEF OF LADYSMITH.

chiefly occupied in thoroughly testing the ranges of the various hills, sangars, and other works which in the coming battle might become their targets. The enemy posted a new gun on the north shoulder of Manxa Nest, but otherwise made no change in the position of his artillery. The Royal Engineers established, on the site of the proposed pontoon bridge (No. 2), a raft by which the 37th company, R.E., crossed the Tugela, and worked upon a road leading up the river bank, until heavy fire compelled them to cease their operations. Among the cavalry and infantry the only movements were those of concentration upon the Hlangwhane plateau. Two battalions of infantry, the 1st Border (5th brigade) and the 1st York and Lancaster (11th brigade) were ordered up from Chieveley, where they were replaced by the 2nd battalion, Lancashire Fusiliers from Frere. The Border reached the plateau during the night of the 26th-27th and the York and Lancaster on the morning of the 27th. The main body of the 2nd mounted brigade was brought down from Cingolo Nek, leaving outposts along the course of the Tugela as far as the Blaauwkrantz, and the South African Light Horse rejoined Dundonald's Headquarters from their patrol to the west of Frere. The South Lancashire and the Rifle Reserve battalion crossed from the left to the right bank. *Movements of troops.*

Major Irvine, "A." pontoon troop, R.E., received instructions to dismantle the bridge at 6 p.m., and relay it below the Tugela Falls; but owing to later orders it was not until 8.30 p.m. that the work was begun. The pontoons, of which there were forty-four sections in the water, were water-logged, and many had one or two inches of mud in them; they had to be hauled, a section at a time, up the bank by the Sappers. The task of dismantling and packing up the bridge was finished by 2.30 a.m. on the 27th, and the pontoon troop then marched to the Nek, north-east of Hlangwhane Hill. The Nek was so closely covered with bivouacs that Major Irvine found it impossible to guide his wagons through them, and was forced to halt till daylight. By 9 a.m. a "heavy" bridge of a total length of ninety-five yards, made of sixteen pontoons and Weldon trestles, had been thrown over the Tugela below the Falls. Owing to the happy selection of the site, which *Pontoon bridge dismantled, and re-laid by 9 a.m., Feb. 27th.*

was protected from the enemy's projectiles, the work was carried out without loss of life. There were only two casualties, caused by stray bullets which fell among the men as, their task being at an end, they were resting on the left bank.

Warren's orders, Feb. 27th.

At 6 a.m., on the 27th, General Warren issued the following orders to the troops holding his section of the front :—

1. Under instructions from General Officer Commanding-in-Chief an attack will be made to-day on the enemy's positions on the hill previously attacked by 5th brigade, on the Green Hill north-east of that (*Kitchener's or Railway Hill*), and on Pieters Hill.

2. The forces operating under Sir C. Warren will be as follows :—

Inniskilling Fusiliers
Connaught Rangers } under General Hart.
Half Imperial Light Infantry

Durham Light Infantry
Rifle Brigade
Half battalion Scottish Rifles } under Col. Norcott.
East Surrey Regiment

South Lancashire Regiment
Royal Lancaster Regiment
York and Lancaster Regiment } under Col. Kitchener.
West Yorkshire Regiment

3. The Dublin Fusiliers will operate under General Barton. Orders for moving will be issued. Battalions to be ready to move at 8 a.m.

4. The plan of attack is as follows :—

General Barton, with three battalions, will attack Pieters Hill.

Colonel Kitchener will attack Green Hill (*Kitchener's or Railway Hill*), starting from the railway corner.

Colonel Norcott will make a frontal attack on the hill previously attacked by 5th brigade.

(a) General Barton's attack will be started first; Colonel Kitchener's attack will follow, and will be delivered as soon as General Barton's attack begins to be felt.

Colonel Norcott's attack will not be seriously developed until the attack under Colonel Kitchener has gained the slopes of the Green Hill (*Kitchener's or Railway Hill*).

(b) Troops under Sir C. Warren to be ready to move at 10 a.m.

5. The artillery on **Hlangwhane and Monte Cristo** is going to support these attacks.

6. Two battalions of infantry **are** also going to be placed down the northern slopes of Hlangwhane and Monte Cristo line to keep down enemy's fire from opposite side.

7. Ammunition Column is at top of Hlangwhane plateau.

RELIEF OF LADYSMITH.

8. The P.M.O. will arrange field hospitals and dressing stations. Ambulances remain on Hlangwhane plateau; stretcher bearers accompany brigades.

9. Infantry will work well extended so as to be able to turn small positions held by the enemy, and offer a bad target to enemy's fire.

10. The G.O.C. will be near the signal station here at the beginning of the action.

11. The force under General Hart will guard the present position, relieving Colonel Norcott's troops before the latter move off.

12. The following telegram has been received from the Secretary of State for War:—" The whole country is watching with admiration your steady advance in the face of tremendous difficulties, the magnitude of which are fully understood here. The conduct of your troops is beyond all praise."

By Order,
T. CAPPER,
for A.A.G., Vth division.

Special Instructions for Artillery of Vth division.

1. Attention is specially directed to the trench at head of donga in which the railway causeway arch is situated. Please shell this well.

2. Follow the infantry attacks up closely. When no longer safe to shoot at enemy's position, do not cease fire, but shoot over the enemy's trenches, "pitching them well up," * so as to make the enemy think he is still being shelled, and also catch him as he runs down the other side.

By Order,
T. CAPPER,
for A.A.G., Vth division.

27th February.

Before the action began, Colonel Parsons, C.R.A., summoned the commanders of batteries to meet him upon Naval Hill, where the greater part of the guns had been massed since the evening of the 25th. After explaining the orders, and allotting targets for brigades and individual batteries, he pointed out that it was essential that officers should keep their eyes fixed upon the infantry whose attack they were to support, as, if once lost to view, it would be almost impossible to pick up the lines of skirmishers among the rocky scrub-covered hills they had to scale. Fire was to be maintained up to the very last moment; then, when it became impossible further to shell the works occupied by the Boers without running too great risk of hitting our own men, elevation and fuses were to be increased by

Instructions to the artillery by the C.R.A.

---

* Intended and understood as a cricket-field phrase.

at least five hundred yards, so as to bring grazing fire upon the reverse slopes of the hills, and thus harass the Boers as they fled before the bayonets of the stormers. The guns remained throughout the day in the positions taken up on the 25th and 26th, with one alteration made by the direct order of the Commander-in-Chief, who despatched two guns of No. 4 Mountain battery to Clump Hill—a selection of ground which proved to be of the greatest assistance to Barton's brigade during its attack on Pieters Hill. On the Clump Hill and Hlangwhane heights were posted four Naval 4.7-in. and eight Naval 12-prs., forty-two field guns, six Howitzers, six guns of the Mountain battery, and four 5-in. guns. On the left bank, with Coke's brigade, were six field guns, while between Colenso and Chieveley were six guns and the following Naval ordnance: one 6-in., two 4.7-in., and six 12-prs. In all the total strength of Sir Redvers Buller's artillery on the 27th was ninety-one guns.

Barton's plan. Some hours before the bridge was finished, Major-General Barton met on Clump Hill Colonel J. Reeves and Lieutenant-Colonel E. E. Carr, who commanded respectively the 1st Royal Irish Fusiliers and the 2nd Royal Scots Fusiliers. Barton explained his plan for the taking of Pieters Hill to the two commanding officers. From the right bank Pieters Hill appeared to be a smooth down, sloping north-west from the gorge of the Tugela up to a line of small kopjes, which lie north and south and overhang the valley through which the railway runs past Pieters Station to Ladysmith. After crossing the pontoon bridge, the brigade was to make its way down the bed of the river, hugging the left bank, until the head of the leading battalion, the Royal Scots Fusiliers, reached the mouth of a donga a few hundred yards below the point where the Tugela, after bending for a short distance to the south-east, again turns sharply to the north-east. Then the column was to halt, form for attack, and scale the steep side of the gorge with the Royal Scots Fusiliers on the right, the Royal Irish Fusiliers on the left, in rough échelon from the right, followed in second line by the Royal Dublin Fusiliers, who were to join the brigade at the bridge. He pointed out that when the brigade reached the down, they might be exposed to fire from the donga which runs into the river opposite Clump Hill, and from a detachment of the enemy which had been seen the day before near Manxa Nest. To guard against this danger, he directed that, as soon as the leading battalion had scaled the slope of the down, part of it should turn eastward and hold suitable ground to protect the right of the brigade, while the remainder of the troops in first line swept in a wide enveloping line westward over Pieters Hill. He impressed upon his subordinates that the movement must be rapid in order that it might be effective as a surprise.

The artillery opened fire at 8 a.m., and began a general bombardment of the Boer position. During the battle the Boer guns on Grobelaar and Onderbrook mountains and one of the pom-poms on the northern side of the Langewacht disappeared. The other guns were in their old places. The works on Pieters Hill, visible from Naval Hill, were continuously shelled by two platform 4.7-in. Naval guns, three batteries of Field, and one of Horse artillery. The Naval 12-prs. and the two Mountain guns on Clump Hill played upon such works on Pieters Hill as they were able to see. The remainder of the artillery fired upon those of the sangars on Railway Hill which bore upon Pieters. The 61st Howitzer battery, by shelling the deep, wooded kloof between these kopjes, dispersed a large reserve which had been placed there in readiness to reinforce either hill as occasion needed. The wheeled 4.7-in. Naval guns on Naval Hill first engaged the enemy's guns, and, when these had been temporarily silenced, turned their attention to the Boer trenches. The moment that the pontoon bridge was reported ready for traffic, Barton set his brigade in motion. Covered both by the shells of the artillery and by the long-range fire from the Maxims and rifles of Dundonald's brigade, the 1st battalion Border regiment and the Rifle Reserve battalion, which lined the heights overhanging the right bank, he assembled his command on the left bank by 10.30 a.m. Then his men, elated by the news of Cronje's surrender at Paardeberg, which had just been announced to the army, began to thread their way along the river bed, among huge boulders and slippery ledges of rock that made progress

Bombardment begins, 8 a.m., Feb. 27th.

Barton crosses river by 10.30 a.m.

difficult and slow. So narrow was the path that the soldiers could keep no formation, but had to scramble as best they could along the bottom of the gorge. A gun, posted to the north of Manxa Nest, shelled them fitfully and without result, but, with this exception, their march down the natural covered-way formed by the ravine was unmolested. It is not clear how far the Boers had expected an attack on Pieters Hill. It certainly was not strongly held at first, a fact which lends weight to the statements made later by various Boer Generals, that they thought such an attack might be attempted, but could not succeed.

Terrain of Pieters Hill.

When General Barton, after emerging from the river bed, reached Pieters Hill, he found that the terrain which, from the high ground on the right bank looked comparatively easy, was, in fact, difficult for an attacking force. It proved to be a down, bare and treeless indeed, but with a surface more rugged than could be seen from a distance. On the south it is skirted by the Tugela; on the north and east it is encircled by a large wooded donga, which rises about a mile north-west of Railway Hill and falls into the Tugela, under the pinnacle of rock known as Manxa Nest. Its western boundary is the valley, traversed by the railway, and overhung by a line of kopjes, which form the highest part of Pieters Hill. These run from south to north, and end in a low isolated hill, crowned by a well-defined clump of rocks, which marks their northern limit. The down is seamed by several subsidiary watercourses; and overlooking the main wooded donga, where it bends southward towards the Tugela, are two or three hillocks and ridges, which lie like low outworks covering the approach to it from the west. The tactical value of these dongas was great, for they afforded a covered line of communication by which reinforcements could be brought unseen to the hill from other parts of the Boer line of battle; and even more important was the isolated hill with the clump of rocks. Not only did it enfilade the western kopjes, but it commanded the down in every direction. General Barton realised that he must dislodge the enemy from the western line of kopjes, and at the same time protect his right and rear against musketry from the eastern ridges and dongas. He therefore sent the Irish

Fusiliers against the southern knolls of the western line of kopjes. Barton's movements. These they carried. He ordered three companies of the Royal Scots Fusiliers to front to the east and north-east, and the main body of the battalion to swing round, so as to mask the northern rock-crowned hill, and turn it by the east. Notwithstanding the efforts of the detachment ordered to keep down the fire from the east and north-east, the Boer bullets fell so heavily upon the right flank and right rear of the main body of the Scots Fusiliers that they somewhat lost direction, and veered westward, to the left of their intended line of advance. This attack was made in the usual way, in rushes by sections. One company ("E"), however, moved across the plain in ordinary "quick time," without halting or lying down, and did not suffer as much as the others. Although reinforcements were sent to the main body from the companies facing eastwards, yet at 2 p.m. when the main body of the Scots Fusiliers had carried the centre of the western line of kopjes, their right was considerably to the south of the rock-crowned kopje which they were intended to turn. Barton, with his small force of three battalions, had no troops in hand to rectify this mistake. The kopje remained unmasked. Its fire completely enfiladed the western hillocks. Two guns, and two pom-poms repeatedly swept the down with their shells. Riflemen, posted in the trenches near Railway Hill and the rugged ground beyond it, harassed the brigade from the southwest, and the musketry from the east and north-east became so annoying that to meet it Barton sent four companies from his reserve to take post on suitable ground in the centre of the down. Against the burghers in the trenches near Railway Hill he could do little; but he knew that Colonel Kitchener's attack upon that part of the line could not be long deferred. The enemy on the east and north-east, if not subdued, was at least kept in check; but the fire from the northern kopje grew intolerable, and he decided to carry it with two companies of the Dublin and one of the Scots Fusiliers. Captain J. A. E. MacBean, Barton's brigade major, organised the assault, and, under cover of the musketry of the company of the Scots Fusiliers, the detachment of the Dublin Fusiliers, led by Captain W. J. Venour, succeeded in getting within three hundred yards of the kopje they were assaulting, but there the enemy's riflemen forbade further progress, and Venour settled his men among the rocks, in readiness for a fresh attempt.

About this time the enemy began a series of efforts to reinforce his extreme left with burghers hitherto stationed near Grobelaar Mountain, and with men who arrived from the laagers round Ladysmith. In varying numbers and at irregular intervals, parties of Boers galloped round the back of Pieters Hill; some succeeded in reaching the kopje which the Dublin Fusiliers were facing; others attempted to descend the eastern donga, but were driven back by the shells of the two mountain guns posted on Clump Hill and by the long-range volleys of their escort, a half-company of the Border regiment. Late in the afternoon Barton, feeling that it was essential to carry the northern hill, directed Major F. F. Hill, Irish Fusiliers, to renew the attack with three companies of his battalion, supported by the fire of Venour's detachment of Dublin Fusiliers and Scots Fusiliers. The assault, in which the covering parties also joined, was partially successful. The hill was captured and held; but the ground beyond was so piled with sharp-edged boulders that the troops could not charge across it. Men could only move over it at a walking pace, and in attempting to do so the casualties became so heavy that the advance was checked. It was impossible to drive the Boers from the neighbouring dongas, into which they had thrown themselves. All the officers of the detachment of Royal Irish Fusiliers were killed or wounded; the companies remained under the command of non-commissioned officers until next day, and Captain Venour was left the senior and almost only surviving officer on this part of the field. While this combat was taking place, the capture of Kitchener's Hill made Barton's left flank secure, but not before every man of his reserves had been thrown into the firing line, and his supply of ammunition reduced dangerously low. By 7 p.m. the enemy's fire began to die down; and in the night an officer's patrol discovered that the Boers had stealthily retired, carrying with them most of their dead and wounded.

CHAPTER XXIX.

RELIEF OF LADYSMITH.

PIETERS HILL (*continued*).*

IMMEDIATELY after Barton's troops had crossed the Tugela Colonel Kitchener followed with his two battalions, from the Hlangwhane plateau. At the pontoon bridge (No. 2) he was joined by the Royal Lancaster and the West Yorkshire, and his whole brigade (the 11th) began to move along the bed of the river. The West Yorkshire, commanded by Major W. Fry, who were to be on the right of the front line, led the column. On the summit of the left bank of the gorge moved their scouts, watching the comparatively level ground which lay between the Tugela and the railway. Then came the King's Own (Royal Lancaster), as left of the front line, next the South Lancashire, in second line, with the York and Lancaster behind them, in reserve. For an hour the 11th brigade closely followed, and, indeed, occasionally overlapped, the rear of Barton's column; then, on reaching the mouth of the donga which runs into the Tugela from the valley between Pieters and Kitchener's Hills, Colonel Kitchener halted and formed for attack. At about 1.30 p.m. he ordered the West Yorkshire forward to secure ground from which they could effectually cover with musketry the movements of the remainder of the brigade. Major Fry, with two companies, first occupied the railway cutting due east of Kitchener's Hill, and then sent two other companies to seize a ridge of rocks above it, from which they poured heavy fire upon

Kitchener follows Barton across the bridge and down the river bed.

His order of march.

1.30 p.m. He begins to attack.

* See maps Nos. 30 (c) and (d).

large parties of Boers, who were seen hastening to reinforce the works upon the northern and eastern slopes of Hart's Hill. Two companies prolonged the line to the right along the railway, and made their way towards the eastern shoulder of Kitchener's Hill. After dislodging at the point of the bayonet a party of the enemy concealed in the neighbouring donga and capturing many of them, the West Yorkshire attempted to scale the hill assigned to them. But the British artillery were shelling the trenches of its defenders so assiduously that it was impossible to advance until Fry, to attract the attention of the gunners, moved two of his companies up the most open part of the kopje. The artillerymen understood the signal, and turned their shells in another direction; the West Yorkshire rushed on and established themselves upon the eastern crest line, with their left thrown back, firing heavy volleys to meet the storm of bullets which burst upon them from the Hart's Hill sangars, the riflemen in which, disdaining concealment, boldly stood up and fired over the parapets of their works.

So far the operations of the 11th brigade on the right had been thoroughly successful, but on the left matters were not equally satisfactory. In order to prevent overlapping between Kitchener's and Norcott's troops in their respective attacks, the donga, which runs into the Tugela from the Nek connecting Kitchener's and Hart's Hills, had been agreed upon as the boundary between the 11th and 4th brigades. Kitchener had ordered the King's Own (Royal Lancaster) to treat this donga as the southern limit of their sphere of action; but in their advance more than half the battalion became confused as to the kopje they were to assault, and, attracted by the fire from Hart's Hill, which smote them on their flank, crossed the donga and attacked that kopje. The want of trained company leaders accounts for this mistake. The Royal Lancaster had lost so many officers at Spion Kop and Wynne's Hill that when it went into action on the 27th three of the companies were commanded by sergeants, and with the battalion there were but seven officers, all told, more than one of whom had less than a year's service. At the end of the day only four officers and one colour-sergeant

A mistake in the leading of a battalion

RELIEF OF LADYSMITH.

remained fit for duty. Though the ultimate result of this loss of direction was to help the 4th brigade to capture Hart's Hill, its immediate effect was to leave a dangerous gap, several hundred yards in width, between the right and left of Kitchener's front. In this gap a small kopje on a spur running southward from Kitchener's Hill, was the centre of a series of cunningly-devised trenches stretching backwards in échelon from its flanks. Further to the south were three more trenches, also in échelon, about four hundred yards north-east of Hart's Hill. Many of these works could not be seen by the West Yorkshire and Royal Lancaster.* To make headway against the burghers who manned them, Kitchener thrust part of the South Lancashire into the centre of his line, sent another part to the right, and half the battalion of York and Lancaster to support the left companies of the South Lancashire. *[leaves a dangerous gap in Kitchener's line. He fills it from his second line and reserve.]*

The leading companies of the latter battalion with difficulty forced their way through the wire fences of the railway, and then found themselves under heavy fire. Gradually working forward over undulating ground, they arrived within seventy or eighty yards of the southern group of trenches, undiscovered by the enemy, upon whom the Maxims of the 5th brigade were vigorously playing. Then they fixed bayonets and charged. The Boers in two of the trenches fled before them, panic stricken; but in one were many men of truer metal, who fought stoutly to the end. The South Lancashire were excited by the loss of their colonel, McCarthy-O'Leary, whom they had seen fall mortally wounded at their head; their nerves were strung to the highest pitch by the incessant fighting of the last few days; it was not till the last moment that the enemy surrendered. Under these circumstances onlookers were greatly impressed by the discipline shown in the fact that when the surrender took place the officers were able at once to stay the bayonets. The arms were sloped and the ranks reformed. Forty prisoners were taken. As soon as the gunners on the right bank of the Tugela saw the flight of the Boers from the trenches, they covered the ground over which the fugitives had to pass with a hail of shells, which was kept *[The charge of part of the South Lancashire.]*

---
* For characteristics of these works, see freehand sketches.

up so long that, while hurrying on the enemy, it effectually prevented the British infantry from following in pursuit.

A detachment of the South Lancashire now worked up the eastern shoulder of Hart's Hill, the top of which was being heavily shelled. To warn the artillery of their presence, the infantry fixed bayonets and held their rifles high over their heads. Dislodging a party of Boers from a sangar, they brought a flanking fire upon the western end of Kitchener's Hill in support of the attack of the West Yorkshire, while the central companies poured bullets over the broken ground between that hill and Hart's.

At 2.45 p.m. the 4th brigade (Norcott) begins to move.

To Colonel Norcott had been allotted the task of capturing Hart's Hill. At about 2.45 p.m., his brigade (the 4th) began to move from its sangars; the East Surrey was on the right, the 1st Rifle Brigade on the left of the first line, the half battalion Scottish Rifles and the Durham Light Infantry in second line. When the leading companies neared the railway they halted, in accordance with Lieut.-General Warren's instructions not to cross the railway until they received a written order from him to do so. When Warren considered that the 11th brigade had made sufficient progress in their attack on Kitchener's Hill, he allowed the 4th brigade to advance. Crossing the railway with little loss, the East Surrey and the 1st battalion Rifle Brigade were pressing up the slopes of Hart's Hill, and had just passed the Boer prisoners captured by the South Lancashire, when a verbal order arrived that half a battalion of the East Surrey, which had been kept in local reserve to the first line, and the half battalion of Scottish Rifles should report at once to Colonel Kitchener, who was said to require immediate reinforcements. These troops hastened to the 11th brigade, only to find on their arrival that their help had not been asked for and was not required. The remainder of the East Surrey, and the 1st battalion Rifle Brigade, aided by the fire which the artillery was now directing upon the works on the real crest of Hart's Hill, gradually won their way up the southern side of that kopje, and reached the false crest, to see the Boers retiring over the opposite side of the summit, their retreat admirably covered by the sharpshooters in the broken ground near the Langewacht Spruit. Portions of the South Lancashire and other battalions of the 11th brigade pressed towards the northern system of trenches, upon which was now concentrated a terrific fire of shells from the 5-in., the Naval 4.7-in., and Naval 12-prs., the Howitzers and the Field artillery. Many of the defenders sought safety in flight; but in the trenches there remained not a few gallant men who could clearly be seen standing up to fire at the British infantry as they gradually lapped round the works. At 5.30 p.m. the glitter of bayonets gave notice that the troops were now within charging distance of their object. The guns ceased fire, and the infantry rushed on, and at the point of the bayonet carried the trenches which had been so splendidly defended. Part of the Royal Lancaster, under non-commissioned officers, captured the eastern end of Hart's Hill, where they were joined by the detachment of South Lancashire, who had already occupied its eastern shoulder. About this time the West Yorkshire completely carried Kitchener's Hill after sharp fighting, in which Captain C. Mansel-Jones, West Yorkshire regiment, so greatly distinguished himself that he was awarded the Victoria Cross. Then, from the right bank of the Tugela, loud cheering burst from the covering troops, who, on the heights they occupied, could see much of the field of battle. The answering shouts from Barton's brigade on Pieters, from the 11th brigade on Kitchener's Hill, and from Norcott's brigade on Hart's Hill, announced to the battalions on the left of the British line that victory was won at last, that the Boer left and centre had been turned and captured, and that the way to Ladysmith at length lay open. *5.30 p.m. Hart's Hill carried. Kitchener's Hill carried.*

The attacks of the 11th and 4th brigades were magnificently supported by the artillery, who hotly shelled the enemy's sangars up to the last possible moment. When Kitchener's men were approaching the enemy's works, the Field batteries were compelled to cease fire, lest their shrapnel should injure the infantry; but the Howitzer battery, owing to the steep angle of descent of its projectiles, and the 5-in. and Naval guns, thanks to the fact that they were firing common shell, were able to continue *Action of the artillery.*

a terrific bombardment almost to the moment of the actual bayonet charge. The powerful telescopes which formed part of the equipment of the Naval officers, proved of very great value on this, as on many other occasions. In the Field batteries the want of such glasses was severely felt. As soon as Kitchener carried his hill, the guns turned on the works on Hart's, then being attacked by the 4th brigade; they fired upon the trenches until the Boers broke, and then shelled the fugitives. Yet the Boers never fought better than in the rear-guard action. After they had lost Pieters, Kitchener's and Hart's Hills, they clung most stubbornly to the broken ground behind these kopjes, and so fierce were the exchanges of musketry across the valley of the Langewacht that Sir Redvers Buller abandoned his intention of launching his cavalry and Horse artillery in pursuit. His preparations were already made; his mounted troops were concentrated on the Hlangwhane plateau, and A. battery R.H.A., and the 73rd Field battery stood limbered up, ready to follow, when, on his return from the railway, to which he had gone as soon as Kitchener's Hill was carried, he countermanded their advance. Not until darkness set in did the firing cease; then the enemy began to ebb away so slowly and silently that it was not for several hours that the outposts discovered that the burghers were retiring.

Buller decides not to launch his cavalry in pursuit.

The duty of the troops under Major-General Lyttelton had been to hold in check the enemy's right during Major-General Barton's and Lieutenant-General Warren's attacks on the left and centre of the Boer position. In the morning the musketry on this part of the field was intermittent, but at 2 p.m., when it became necessary to support the 6th and 11th brigades in every way, a very heavy fusilade was opened all along Lyttelton's line; it raged for two hours, and prevented a large number of the enemy from leaving their trenches and reinforcing the hills on their left, where the actual assault was delivered. During the afternoon the battalions under Lyttelton expected to be called upon to attack the works on their immediate front, and Sir Redvers Buller sent an order to "advance the moment the assault was successful," but by some mischance the message

The work of the left wing.

Lyttelton with musketry prevents large number of enemy from moving to support Boer left.

An order which miscarried.

RELIEF OF LADYSMITH.

was not received. Therefore, General Lyttelton's part in the battle was necessarily limited; he pinned the Boers opposite to him to their works; he co-operated when occasion offered with Major-General Hart in supporting the attacking troops with long-range volleys, and he poured a tremendous fire upon the burghers when they retired from the sangars on Hart's and Kitchener's Hills. At 6 p.m. the 2nd brigade (Hildyard) was directed to march to Hlangwhane plateau and cross the Tugela by the pont which the Natal Naval Volunteers had established at Colenso, but as this ferry-boat proved to have broken down, it was impossible to obey the order, and thus enable Sir Redvers Buller to reinforce Barton and extend his right further towards the valley of the Klip.

The guns on Grobelaar fired occasionally upon Hildyard's brigade, at the 10th brigade (Coke), posted among the Colenso kopjes, and at the Natal Pioneer Corps, employed in rebuilding the road bridge across the Tugela. But they were quelled by the 4.7-in. guns on fixed mountings on Naval Hill, by the Naval 6-in. on Gun Hill, and by a 4.7-in. mounted on a railway truck at Chieveley.

During the day half of the Middlesex battalion had been sent to join the IInd division; the remainder of Coke's brigade did not move; the extreme left of the British line was watched by Thorneycroft's mounted infantry.

The casualties on the 27th amounted to 503, of which the three battalions under Barton's command contributed more than 200. Among the officers eight were killed, 28 wounded. In the other ranks 59 were killed, 399 wounded, and nine missing. Between February 14th and 27th the total British loss was 27 officers killed, 100 wounded, and one missing; in the other ranks 280 were killed, 1,762 wounded, and 89 missing (see Appendix 2). For the same period the Boers reported their casualties at 420 killed and wounded; and 60 burghers and European adventurers were made prisoners. *Casualties on Feb 27th.* *Casualties between 14th and 27th.*

The fighting on the 27th differed entirely from that of the last few days in several important points. For the first time, since the passage of the Tugela on the 21st, the army had elbowroom; and the whole of the infantry and artillery were brought effectively into action. The co-operation between the infantry and the artillery was excellent; the gunners supported the attacking infantry to the very last moment, and the infantry had so thoroughly realised the importance that the ground over which they had to advance should be swept by the artillery, that they were known to grumble if our shells were not constantly bursting in front of them, as they moved forward to the attack. Thanks to the good arrangements made by Colonel Parsons the direction and control of the Royal artillery was admirable, and fire was shifted rapidly from target to target as occasion required. The Naval gunners, grasping the situation, co-operated with great success. The rifles of those of the troops not engaged in the actual attack on the three hills, Pieters, Kitchener's, and Hart's, were brought into use for long-range covering and supporting fire. Above all, the plan of operations was intelligible, properly explained, and understood by all concerned.

Great fatigue of troops. During the last ten days the labours of the men had been very great, for though there were no movements which entailed long marching, the necessity of constantly throwing up entrenchments caused ceaseless work. Directly each hill was carried, every man who had been engaged in winning it, as soon as he could be spared from the actual fire-fight was employed in building up stone breastworks, as a protection from the musketry from the neighbouring kopjes still in the hands of the enemy. By day, and under aimed fire, such defences could only be hastily made; but under cover of darkness they were improved, and while part of a battalion was on outpost, another detachment of the corps was erecting sangars, while the remainder brought food, water, and ammunition for their comrades. For several nights running the men did not get more than two or three hours sleep, for there were guns to be "man-handled" up steep and rocky hills, wagons to be dragged out of bad places, roads to be made, gun emplacements to be built. For the officers there *Want of officers.* was even less rest. Bullets and disease had reduced the numbers of the commissioned ranks so much that it was no uncommon thing to find but one officer in each company left fit for duty.

Owing to the absence of any reserve of trained subalterns to fill the gaps so caused, companies in some cases were commanded by lads with only a few months' service in the Army. The troops had fought by day as hard as they had worked by night. With the exception of the few hours' truce on the 25th, firing was continuous between dawn on the 17th and dark on the 27th. By day the roar of guns and the crackle of musketry never ceased. By night Boer skirmishers "sniped" at the British works, while not infrequent bursts of well-sustained musketry threatened an attack in force, and kept the soldiers alert behind their sangars. Owing to the confined space in which, for a great part of the time, the army was herded together, the building of stone shelters for protection of the bivouacs—even of the second and third lines—against long-range fire, involved constant work.

In the course of the evening of the 27th Dundonald and Burn-Murdoch received instructions for the morrow. Dundonald was to work north and north-west towards Ladysmith, followed over the pontoon bridge by Burn-Murdoch, who was to move eastward, cross the Klip, and reconnoitre Umbulwana. Lord Dundonald, as a Colonel, was senior to Burn-Murdoch, who was a Lieutenant-Colonel; but the regular cavalry and the mounted infantry had not been formed into a cavalry division, and had been treated as independent units throughout the campaign on the Upper Tugela. Orders to Burn-Murdoch had always been issued, not through Dundonald, but direct from the Headquarters Staff, to whom on all occasions he had reported. On the evening of the 27th, each brigadier, as usual, received his orders from the Headquarters Staff. Orders to Dundonald and Burn-Murdoch for the 28th.

During the night of the 27th-28th, Major-General Barton, who, though wounded at Pieters Hill, still remained in command of his brigade upon the heights which he had carried, thus wrote to Sir Redvers Buller :— Night of Feb. 27th-28th. Barton urges immediate advance.

"I am only about three miles from Umbulwana Mountain—cavalry, infantry, and light guns are quite sufficient to push on with, give battle and defeat the enemy. Bringing heavy guns will delay, and give the Boers every advantage. They and baggage can follow later. The opportunity now is not one to be missed. I have been strongly opposed and heavily attacked since I occupied this ground. There is only one thing to do now, viz., to push on and press back the Boers and seize their communications on this side. I ought to be reinforced at dawn. Can you not send me my regiments from Colenso?

"G. BARTON, Major-General.

"P.S.—If you complete me to a division I can take Umbulwana Mountain, cavalry watching on my right."

Major-General Barton in this message much under-estimated his own distance from Umbulwana, which was nearer five miles than three.

<small>6.30 a.m., Feb. 28th. Barton reports Boer movements to the north.</small>
At 6.30 a.m. on the 28th, Barton further heliographed to the Commander-in-Chief that there was a considerable movement of men and wagons northwards from the camp east of Umbulwana, and strongly recommended a rapid reconnaissance with mounted troops and machine guns. This information, which, like the letter just quoted, was received by General Buller a long time after it was despatched, confirmed the reports from the other brigades that the enemy had retired, and was supplemented by signals from Ladysmith to announce that a panic had set in and that the Boers were everywhere in flight.

<small>Troops begin to cross the bridge,</small>
At earliest dawn the 63rd Field, and four guns of No. 4 Mountain batteries, crossed the pontoon bridge, and were posted, the former in the saddle between Hart's and Kitchener's Hills, the latter on the kopjes which formed the bridge-head. Three officers' patrols of the 2nd mounted brigade had followed; but an interruption to the traffic across the bridge then occurred, causing a serious check to the cavalry, which was well mounted <small>which breaks down temporarily.</small> on fresh horses, and eager to pursue the enemy. One of the legs of a trestle which connected the pontoons with the bank sank into the ground, and in setting it right much valuable time was lost. Dundonald's brigade was unable to pass over the <small>Dundonald crosses, followed by Burn-Murdoch. Dundonald's movements.</small> Tugela until 7.30 or 8 a.m.; an hour later Burn-Murdoch's troops, some of whom used the Boer bridge, began to follow, with orders simply to cross the bridge. Advancing through the positions held by the infantry, Dundonald threw out patrols —the South African Light Horse to the right, Thorneycroft's

mounted infantry to the front and left. The former scouted towards the Klip river, then in flood and passable only at a wooden bridge lately built by the Boers south of Umbulwana for military purposes; the latter were met by the fire of a rear-guard of the Standerton commando, concealed in the kopjes which lie near the railway line north of Pieters Station. After driving back the Standerton men, Dundonald had just occupied the kopjes south of Davels Spruit, when he was brought to a complete standstill by the enemy's musketry, and sent an officer, Major A. Weldon, Leinster regiment, to find, and bring up, infantry and artillery reinforcements. During this time the cavalry brigade (Burn-Murdoch) was halted in the gorge between Pieters Hill and the railway, while Sir Redvers Buller, from the top of a kopje near the station, was studying the ground to the north and east. At 1 p.m. Burn-Murdoch, in answer to his repeated requests to be allowed to go on, was told to advance towards the right front. Before he had reached the railway line south of Pieters Station, Weldon met him, and informed him that Dundonald was asking for help in his engagement at Davels Spruit. Burn-Murdoch accordingly turned westward, and after remaining some time in support of the 2nd mounted brigade (Dundonald), until the Boers were driven away, largely by machine gun fire, and their laager captured, he turned eastward towards the Klip river. On nearing the high ground about Nelthorpe, the cavalry brigade (Burn-Murdoch) found itself in presence of another portion of the enemy's rear-guard, which covered the operations of burghers busily passing their guns and wagons down the eastern side of Umbulwana. Reports had been sent by General Barton and Colonel Sandbach describing the retreat and movements of the Boers and indicating the spots from which guns could usefully be employed against them. Hardly any use was made of such of the artillery as had been brought across the river; and the Naval 12-prs. on Clump Hill, opening fire of their own initiative against the burghers who covered the dismantling of the works on Umbulwana, were silenced by a Staff officer. The Boer rear-guard opened heavy musketry fire upon the leading squadrons of the 13th and 14th

1 p.m. Burn-Murdoch allowed to advance.

After helping Dundonald, Burn-Murdoch turns eastward

Hussars from both sides of the river, and guns played upon them from the south-eastern end of Umbulwana. Though checked, Burn-Murdoch held his ground, and occupied a farm which overlooked the bridge thrown over the Klip by the Boers. At nightfall, after he had off-saddled and watered his horses, he sent to report to Sir Redvers that he proposed to stay the night on the farm, and to pursue the enemy at dawn.

<small>and occupies a farm commanding a bridge over the Klip.</small>

Throughout the 28th the Commander-in-Chief had been considering the question whether he should launch his mounted troops in pursuit of the burghers who had retired before him during the night of the 27th-28th, or should devote his whole energies to passing into Ladysmith the long column of supply wagons which stood on the right bank laden with food for White's starving soldiery. He decided in favour of the food.* After the capture by the infantry of Hart's, Kitchener's, and Pieters Hills, he had deemed it impossible to send forward his mounted troops. Thus the Boers gained a long start in their retreat. This start had been greatly increased by the temporary breakdown of the pontoon bridge. He had had large personal experience of Boer skill in rear-guard fighting when he had burghers with him in the war against the Zulus. To pursue them now without artillery seemed to him hopeless. If he was to get food into Ladysmith at once he could not use adequate artillery in the pursuit, for nearly all his guns were on the right bank of the Tugela massed around the plateau of Naval Hill. These would have to be lowered down the steep side of the right bank of the river, passed over the pontoon bridge, and hauled up the even steeper slopes on the left bank, an operation which, as he estimated, must take the driver and teams of each gun or wagon three-quarters of an hour to accomplish. But when the guns had reached the left bank the difficulties would not be over, for the Klip river, as well as the Tugela, was in flood, and therefore impassable except by the Boer bridge south of Umbulwana. As he did not know whether the Boers had not destroyed this means of passage, he had to take into his calculations the possibility of being himself obliged to bridge the Klip,

<small>Buller's dilemma—to pursue or not to pursue.</small>

* See Appendix 13.

in order to attack Umbulwana, the occupation of which he considered necessary to protect the right of his advance. Now he had but one pontoon bridge, which was at present employed on the Tugela below Naval Hill. If he dismantled this to use it at the Klip River, he cut off the only means by which the supply wagons could cross the stream, for he knew that Colonel Rawson's restoration of the Colenso road-bridge could not be finished for two or three days. Therefore he replied to Burn-Murdoch's message with an order to fall back behind the line occupied by the infantry since the end of the battle of the 27th. Burn-Murdoch accordingly left a detached post to hold the bridge, and fell back behind the infantry outposts south-west of Pieters Station. He decides not to pursue and recalls Burn-Murdoch.

Under cover of Burn-Murdoch's movement to the eastward Dundonald had resumed his advance towards Ladysmith; the Composite regiment led by Captain H. Gough, 16th Lancers, scouted in front, followed by the remainder of the brigade. In search of ground suitable for mounted men, Dundonald at first moved to the east, but coming under fire from Umbulwana, turned north again, waiting at each ridge until Gough reported that the country beyond it was clear of the enemy. At a flat-topped hill south of Intombi, Dundonald halted. The afternoon was far spent. The kopje in front of him was so steep and rocky that horses could only be led up it in single file. The country was so rough that he considered it impossible to scout widely enough to the right and left to ascertain whether the enemy was not hanging on his flanks. He did not wish to compromise the safety of the whole of his brigade, the only mounted infantry with the Natal army, and he therefore sent the greater portion of it, under Colonel Thorneycroft, back to a position which he had previously selected, and galloped himself into Ladysmith with part of the Imperial Light Horse and Natal Carbineers. On his arrival at Sir George White's outposts he wrote to Headquarters, asking that the remainder of his brigade might be sent after him, but the report was not handed to General Buller until next morning (March 1st), and on the night of the 28th, the troops under Thorneycroft remained in bivouac near Nelthorpe.

After writing this message Dundonald, by lamp signal, repeated his request that his two regiments might be sent to him, and added such information about the movements of the Boers as White's Intelligence officers had been able to collect.

As soon as Dundonald reached Ladysmith, General White's Staff organised a patrol to Umbulwana, composed of men from the main body of the Imperial Light Horse, which formed part of the garrison. Starting at dawn on March 1st, they found the mountain clear of the enemy, and sending to Ladysmith for wagons, carried back to the starving troops a certain amount of food, which the Boers had left behind them.

March 1st. Bulwana found evacuated.

While the mounted troops were thus employed at the front, General Warren and General Lyttelton firmly established themselves on the positions which had been carried on the 27th. Both divisions were reorganised, and the battalions restored to the brigades from which they had been borrowed in the stress of combat. Major-General Hart was placed in command of the troops near the pontoon bridge, viz.: the pontoon troop, the 5th brigade, four 5-in. R.G.A., two Naval 4.7-in. platform guns, and the Naval 12-prs. The two wheeled 4.7-in. were posted between Hart's and Kitchener's Hills.

Reorganisation of divisions and brigades in Buller's army, Feb. 28th.

The army, with the exception of the 5th and 10th brigades, marched next day towards Ladysmith, and bivouacked at Nelthorpe. The 5th brigade was employed in making roads from the pontoon bridge to the Colenso—Pieters—Nelthorpe road, and in helping the wagons, which contained the stores for Ladysmith and for the relieving force, up the steep slopes of the chain of hills which rise between the Tugela and the valley of the Klip. The 10th brigade remained among the Colenso kopjes to guard the rear and protect the Pioneer Corps in their work on the road-bridge.

March 1st. Buller advances.

The advance was covered by the mounted troops. Dundonald, who had rejoined his brigade early in the morning from Ladysmith, protected the left front and left flank, while Burn-Murdoch guarded the right front, flank and rear. Sending out two squadrons which were intended to act as contact squadrons, one to the front and the other to the right front,

RELIEF OF LADYSMITH.

Burn-Murdoch crossed the Klip by the Boer bridge, which he had reached the night before and, arriving at the shoulder of Umbulwana at 11.30 a.m., looked down into Intombi Hospital. He then sent to ask to be liberated from his clearly detailed employment of guarding the right flank, right front and right rear of the infantry and to be allowed to go on, but Sir Redvers refused, and ordered the cavalry back to Nelthorpe. The squadron (one of the 13th Hussars, under Major C. Williams), which had been sent scouting to the front, was, however, beyond recall; for it had reached Ladysmith at 7 a.m. On his arrival there, Major Williams was taken to Sir George White, who enquired whether, in Williams' opinion, Sir Redvers Buller would object to the employment of the squadron with the column under Colonel W. G. Knox, then sallying out to attempt to harass the retreat of the enemy. Williams reassured Sir George White on the point, adding that no doubt all the cavalry were following in pursuit. After feeding his horses, Williams started to catch up Knox's column, but when he had advanced about a mile he received an order from Sir Redvers Buller, who then had ridden into Ladysmith, to halt his men, and return to Ladysmith himself.* There General Buller, according to Major Williams' recollection, informed him that he did not wish for any pursuit of the enemy; but gave him leave, while resting his horses before going back to Nelthorpe, to ride on to the front where Knox's troops were in action. Williams did so, accompanied by one or two other officers; from the neighbourhood of Pepworth Hill they watched the Boers as, retiring across Modder Spruit, they placed a gun upon a train which they set in motion, and then blew up the culvert over which it had just passed. Colonel Knox's troops were so weak from the sickness and starvation of the four months' siege that they were virtually unable to march, and their sortie was fruitless.

Burn-Murdoch ordered back from Intombi to Nelthorpe.

Knox's sortie from Ladysmith.

The 1st cavalry brigade (Burn-Murdoch) remained on March 2nd in the neighbourhood of Nelthorpe, watching the country

March 2nd.

---

* It will be noticed that Sir Redvers Buller's remembrance of the order he gave to Major Williams is much at variance with this account. General Buller's statement to the Royal Commission will be found in Appendix 13.

on the north and east, while a long convoy of seventy-three wagons laden with food and medical comforts slowly made its way into Ladysmith. Dundonald's brigade, now officially described as the 3rd mounted brigade, patrolled in the direction of the Weenen road, and along the Dundee road as far as Modder Spruit. The infantry and guns took up positions for the triumphal march into the town they had relieved. With this procession, on March 3rd, the campaign on the Tugela ended.

March 3rd.

The final chapters of this volume describe the course of the siege, which had thus been brought to an end.

CHAPTER XXX.

THE DEFENCE OF LADYSMITH. *

FROM THE ACTION OF LOMBARDS KOP TO THE ATTACK OF JANUARY 6TH, 1900.

THE action of Lombards Kop† practically decided both the British and Boer Generals, the latter to besiege, the former to be besieged. To Sir G. White, indeed, a siege, so far from appearing a calamity, seemed now to be the best, if not the only, means by which to "cover the vitals of Natal" from invasion.‡ The events of October 30th had opened his eyes to the determination and the peculiarly intangible strength of the Boers. Granted that a siege of Ladysmith would paralyse his power of offence, would lock up a force originally designed to be mobile, and colour irrevocably the whole strategy of the campaign, it would nevertheless detain north of the Tugela the bulk of the Boer invading forces, and thus, and thus only, save Pietermaritzburg, and perhaps Durban itself, from falling into the hands of the enemy. Retreat across the Tugela was still possible; but, considering the intricate character of the intervening country, the enveloping nature of the enemy's advance, and his now undoubted confidence, to attempt a march southward would be to risk the army upon the integrity of which the fate of Natal at this moment depended, and of course to sacrifice, with incalculable loss of prestige, the town of Ladysmith and the vast accumulation of stores therein. Finally, there did not appear to exist, within reasonable distance, any defensible positions better than those

<small>Result of action of Lombards Kop, Oct. 30th, 1899.</small>

---

* See map No. 31.   † Volume I., Chapter X.
‡ Royal Commission on the War in South Africa, Volume II., page 144.

in which the Field Force was now disposed. At Ladysmith White had found troops sufficiently strong, sufficiently concentrated, and sufficiently supplied, to make a stand until southern Natal was strong enough to protect itself. The one serious disability had been removed by the opportune arrival of the long-range Naval guns. At Ladysmith, therefore, he would remain, accepting rather than submitting to an investment.

Joubert decides to lay siege to Ladysmith,

Commandant General Joubert, on the other hand, who had previously been so despondent as to compare himself with Napoleon at Moscow,* was made aware of his strength by his unexpected success. He now regarded the capture of the town and garrison as not only an easy matter, but one which might quickly decide in his favour a campaign which he was anxious to bring to an end as speedily as possible. The fall of Ladysmith would draw every Boer sympathiser in South Africa —and he knew there were many thousands—to his side in arms. It would thus lay not Natal alone, but Cape Colony also at his mercy, by calling suddenly into existence a strong body of rebels in the very midst of that largely sympathetic territory. Sharing not at all, moreover, the loudly expressed opinion of many of his subordinates, that he was already strong enough both to besiege Ladysmith and to overrun the rest of Natal, he refused to leave Sir G. White's force in his rear, and would consent to

and to raid southern Natal.

nothing more than a foray towards the south, whilst his main body closed in around the town. At a council of war held at his Headquarters at Modder Spruit on November 1st, it was decided that, whilst the Free State forces under General A. P. Cronje drew a line of investment through the north, west and south, the Transvaalers should occupy the ground east of the town, the two contingents joining hands across the Klip river on the north, and at Nelthorpe on the south.

With the exception of the raid southward, which was postponed for the present, these movements were set on foot at once.

His operations begin, Nov. 1st, 1899.

Before the evening of November 1st, the Free Staters had pushed

* Letter from General Joubert to State Secretary, Pretoria, October 27th, 1899: "Our case is serious. We are now even as Napoleon in the time in Moscow."

THE DEFENCE OF LADYSMITH. 533

advanced posts as far southward as Grobelaar Kloof, whence, as described in Volume I., Chapter XVI., next day they shelled the garrison of Colenso, forcing it to retire by a night march to Estcourt. Early on November 2nd a cavalry reconnaissance from Ladysmith drew fire from a strong Boer force beyond Middle Hill, and on the afternoon of the next day Transvaalers and Free Staters had linked forces, as arranged, at Nelthorpe. A train conveying Major-General French and his staff, who were travelling southward in response to instructions from Sir R. Buller, narrowly evaded capture as it passed between the Boer horsemen converging on the railway. The train escaped under fire, and the destruction of the line at this point a few moments later may be said to mark the completion of the investment of the British force in Ladysmith. *French, ordered to join Buller at Cape Town, nearly captured, Nov. 3rd, 1899.*

Ladysmith, a town consisting of two main streets of villas and tin-roofed shops containing some 4,500 inhabitants, lay in a deep bend on the left bank of the river Klip, at 3,268 feet above sea level, and about 30 miles distant from the Drakensberg Mountains. Of strategic importance, since it formed the junction of the Transvaal and Orange Free State railways, which had replaced the old main roads, the town itself, from the configuration of the ground about it, was tactically ill adapted to defence unless held by a garrison with sufficient strength and time to man and fortify the outermost of two roughly concentric circles of heights which commanded it. Upon the circumference of this outer circle, which was distant from 6,000 to 10,000 yards from the centre of the town, lay the following heights (see map No. 31) :— *Description of Ladysmith;*

On the North.—Thornhill's Kopjes, Surprise Hill, Bell's Kop and Pepworth Hill, all within 7,500 yards of the centre of the town, commanding both the Harrismith and the Elandslaagte railways, and covering the routes to the Drakensberg passes. *the hills around the town; the outer ring.*

On the East.—Lombards Kop, a pointed hill, and Umbulwana Mountain, a flat-topped mass, the former at 8,000, the latter 7,500 yards range from the centre of Ladysmith, flanking the road to Helpmakaar, and the railway and road to Colenso.

Gun Hill and Umbrella Hill, two large under-features of Lombards Kop, projected from its western side. A range of lower kopjes, running northward parallel to the Modder Spruit, connect these eminences across the Elandslaagte railway line, with Pepworth Hill to the northward.

On the South.—Middle Hill, with its continuation, End Hill, and the northern spurs of that series of tumbled heights which, in Grobelaar Kloof and the Pieters Hills, dominate the river Tugela about Colenso. These average some 9,000 yards from the centre of Ladysmith.

On the West.—Lancer's Hill, 11,000 yards range, and Rifleman's Ridge, 8,000 yards measured from the same point, commanded the main Colenso road, and the roads from Acton Homes and Van Reenen's Pass; Telegraph Ridge, 7,500 yards range from Ladysmith, commanded the railway and road to Harrismith.

Such was the outer perimeter which, covering roughly some 36 miles of circumference, had to be yielded to the enemy, since the British force was inadequate in strength, in means of supply, and in mobility to retain lines of defence so distant from its base. Only by a chain of forts, provisioned and munitioned, might such a line possibly have been held. The incessant work in the field of the staff and troops from the beginning of the concentration at Ladysmith had allowed neither the time nor the labour to construct such forts, even had the standing of a siege been designed from the outset. Within this circumference, and separated from it on the west and north by valleys intersected by dongas, on the east by undulating scrub, and on the south-east by the level grass-land fringing the river Klip, a horse-shoe of rough kopjes were grouped about the town. They somewhat resembled the parapet of a field-work, having its " salient " pointing north-west, and its " gorge " to the eastward. This, but for the natural protection of the bends of the river and the beds of the tributary spruits, was open. These kopjes, on the northern and eastern side, were rocky outcrops of low elevation, the western arm alone rising to considerable eminence where, at its lower termination,

<small>The inner ring of hills.</small>

it turned to face squarely southward. Facing Surprise Hill, the heights about Bell Spruit and Pepworth Hill, and some 3,000 yards from the first-named, a range of rocky knolls joined the river Klip to the Elandslaagte railway. Across the line, interrupted only by a deep cutting, the range continued in an easterly direction along the left bank of the Klip, until it broke off abruptly under 4,000 yards from Gun Hill, at which it pointed straight from the direction of the town. Three miles of flat grass-land, intersected by the river and railway, divided this point from the southern termination of the western arm of the defences. There rose the commanding plateau known to the Boers as the Platrand, but re-named by the British "Cæsar's Camp," from its resemblance to a hill of this name at Aldershot. It was a feature prolonged, after a shallow depression at its western end, by the slightly higher and more broken Wagon Hill, so called from a clump of trees upon it (subsequently felled), which was supposed to resemble a wagon with its span of oxen. Both faced southerly, Cæsar's Camp confronting End Hill at about 4,000 yards from crest to crest, Wagon Hill looking upon Middle Hill at 2,800 yards, with a knoll called "Mounted Infantry Hill" about midway between. Separating the Cæsar's Camp and Middle Hill ridges ran the Bester's Valley, watered by the Fourie's Spruit, and cut by many dongas.

<small>Cæsar's Camp and Wagon Hill.</small>

North of Cæsar's Camp Ridge, the kopjes of the western arm subsided somewhat, as they led irregularly, but without interruption, up to the salient. Rifleman's Ridge of the outer perimeter inclined inwards towards them, varying from 6,000 yards opposite Maiden Castle, to under 3,000 yards at Rifleman's Post, where, at the junction of the Klip river and Flagstone Spruit, the northern defences began. This inner line measured over 14 miles in circumference, and presented, in addition to its extent, the disadvantages that it was unprepared for prolonged defence, was for the most part commanded in enfilade, that it was open on one side, and that, except from the north, it provided no good second line of resistance at any point. Especially detrimental was the proximity of Lombards Kop and

Umbulwana on the eastern side. Certain to be occupied by the enemy, if not held by the British, these mountains not only looked into the rear or flank of the town and every defence about it, but commanded the whole of the only grazing ground at the disposal of the garrison, namely, the flats fringing the river Klip; commanding also the railway and other approaches from the southward. These heights indeed, to pursue the analogy, formed the proper topographical "gorge" to the field-work of the Ladysmith kopjes; and since there were no eminences outside them of similar command, it is plain that there could have been no complete artillery investment of the town and camps themselves, had it been possible to include them in the defensive circuit. For that purpose there existed no objections on the score of lack of water, fuel, material for entrenching, or good communication with Headquarters. The appearance of heavy hostile artillery on such heights was not, it is true, foreseen; yet a gun of position had already fired from Mount Impati. Nevertheless, for the reasons given, the inner line was all that seemed to the General possible, and, having already surveyed and, to some extent, allocated troops to its various parts, he now issued orders for a full occupation. The enceinte was divided into four sections, as follows:—

The defences; Section A.

Section A, under Colonel W. G. Knox. Boundaries, from the kopjes at the end of the ridge pointing to Gun Hill (now called Helpmakaar Ridge) to Junction Hill, close to the Orange Free State railway junction at the north-east angle of the town, including the kopjes henceforward known as Devon Post, Cemetery Hill, and Tunnel Hill (or Liverpool Castle). This section, the aforementioned eastern arm, was exposed to flanking artillery fire from Gun Hill and Lombards Kop, to fire partially in reverse from Umbulwana, and to fire at various angles from Pepworth and Long Hills, and even from Surprise Hill. The garrison was primarily (3rd November) as follows:—1st Devon, 1st (King's) Liverpool, 2 companies 1st Gloucester regiment, half company 2nd Royal Dublin Fusiliers, 2 guns No. 10 Mountain battery, 2 Howitzer (6.3-in.) detachments, four other gun detachments.

THE DEFENCE OF LADYSMITH. 537

Section B, under Colonel (local Major-General) F. Howard. Section B. Boundaries, from Gordon Hill across the northern salient to the junction of the Klip river with the Flagstone Spruit, including Observation Hill, Cove Redoubt, Leicester Post, King's Post,* Ration Post, and Rifleman's Post. This section, which formed the northern defences, was in the first instance garrisoned as under :—

Six companies, 1st Leicestershire regiment, 2nd King's Royal Rifles, 2nd Rifle Brigade, and, until November 9th, the 1st King's Royal Rifles. Whilst this section lay open to a wide range of frontal fire from Pepworth Hill to Thornhill's Kopje, Telegraph Ridge enfiladed the left flank, and Rifleman's Ridge, Middle Hill, and even Umbulwana took the positions in reverse from varying angles.

Section C, under Colonel I. S. M. Hamilton. This formed Section C. the western arm. Boundaries, from Flagstone Spruit to Cæsar's Camp, including Range Post, Signpost Ridge, Maiden Castle, Wagon Hill. First garrison: 1st Manchester regiment, 4 companies, 2nd Gordon Highlanders, 2 companies, 1st Royal Irish Fusiliers. This section was much exposed, its southern end especially, being within artillery range from Rifleman's Ridge and Umbulwana on right and left flanks respectively, the latter height also searching it in reverse, as did Pepworth Hill also, at extreme range. Middle and End Hills faced the Cæsar's Camp portion frontally, as previously described.

Section D, under Colonel W. Royston. From Cæsar's Camp, Section D. across the valley of the Klip river to where the eastern arm ended at Helpmakaar Ridge, consisting of three miles of flat, here and there grown with thorn scrub, and cut at all angles by dongas. To the Town Guard was allotted a line of observation stretching from Maiden Castle to the foot of Cemetery Hill, whilst the levels in front were piqueted by the mounted troops of the Volunteer brigade, consisting of detachments of the Natal Carbineers, Natal Mounted Rifles, and Border Mounted Rifles.

The troops not assigned as above were at first formed into a general reserve.

* See freehand sketch in the map case.

538   THE WAR IN SOUTH AFRICA.

Artillery dispositions.

The first dispositions of the artillery were as follows:—The Naval artillery under Captain the Hon. H. Lambton, R.N., who exercised an independent command, to the northern defences; one 4.7-in. on Junction Hill, another on Cove Redoubt. These heavy pieces had arrived unmounted, their cradles, carriages, shields, and holding-down appliances being unassembled. Nevertheless, by dint of the exertions of their crews, and infantry and Royal Engineer fatigue parties, they were in position, the Junction Hill gun on November 2nd, that on Cove Redoubt the day after. The four Naval 12-prs. being on field mountings which had been improvised at Simon's Town by Captain P. Scott, R.N. (Volume I., pp. 117–119), had gone into action at the moment of their arrival,* and were now placed on Gordon Hill. The six Field batteries were primarily treated as units of the movable Reserve, and were not assigned frontal positions. Of the remaining artillery in Ladysmith, two 6.3-in. Howitzers were first mounted on the Helpmakaar Ridge, the two remaining guns of No. 10 Mountain battery being placed in rear of the Liverpool regiment on Tunnel Hill. Two 3-pr. Hotchkiss (Natal Naval Volunteers) were stationed at Devon Post, and the two Vickers quick-firing pieces, the trophies of Elandslaagte, in a re-entrant behind the left centre of the Helpmakaar Ridge. This then was the preliminary arrangement of Sir G. White's force.

Numbers of the garrison and of civil population.

Supply of food,

On November 2nd the effective garrison numbered 13,496 officers and men, with 51 guns,† the civilian population at that date numbering some 5,400. There were also about 2,400 Kaffirs and natives of India in the town, bringing the total approximately to 21,300 souls. The reserves of military supplies in hand were as follows—estimated at full rates of ration:—

Breadstuff	65 days' supply.
Meat	50 ,, ,,
Groceries	46 ,, ,,
Forage	32 ,, ,,

This supply, Brevet-Colonel E. W. D. Ward, the A.A.G. (B), who had early investigated with care the resources of the

* See Volume I., page 185.   † For fuller state see Appendix 2.

THE DEFENCE OF LADYSMITH.

town, took measures to augment, as soon as the prospect of investment became a certainty, by requisition from the shops, hotels, etc., securing by these means an addition of about 14 days' breadstuffs, 18 days' groceries, and 26 days' grain; two mealie mills were also taken over to be worked under military supervision.

Of ammunition the following was in store:— *ammunition.*

S. A. A.	$5\frac{1}{2}$ million rounds, over and above 150 rounds carried by each soldier.
15-pr. B. L.	250 rounds per gun.
4.7-in. Naval	300 ,, ,,
12-pr. Naval	290 ,, ,,
6.3-in. Howitzer	430 ,, ,,

Throughout November 2nd and 3rd, the enemy's commandos were circling about the town, finally taking up the following positions: north of the town, from the Harrismith railway to Pepworth Hill, the Pretoria commando (2,300 strong), with a detachment of the State artillery (here and elsewhere 400) and the Johannesburg Police (600), all on Pepworth Hill; the Irish Brigade (200) lying upon the Elandslaagte railway line. To the eastward, the Lydenburg commando (1,100) possessed the kopjes running parallel to and west of the Modder Spruit, covering General Joubert's Headquarters; the Heidelberg (1,700) and Wakkerstroom (800), with artillery detachments, took post on Gun Hill, Lombards Kop and Umbulwana. To the southward the Krugersdorpers (800) camped above Nelthorpe, the commandos of Utrecht (900) and Vryheid (944), supported by a small German Corps, prolonging and completing the Transvaal line westward across the heights closing the valley of the Klip. On the left of Vryheid a portion of the Winburg (here and elsewhere, 2,114) and the Harrismith commando (915) of the Orange Free State forces, in this order from east to west, occupied End and Middle Hills; the Heilbron commando (1,670) seized Lancer's Hill, whilst on the west of the town the Kroonstad commando (2,500) made for Rifleman's Ridge, Star Hill, and high ground running northward to the Sand Spruit.

The positions taken up by Boers, Nov. 2nd-3rd, 1899.

Numbers of the investing commandos,	The rest of the Winburgers here joined the Kroonstad men with the Pretoria commando across the Klip, thus completing the first circle of investment with about 17,000 men.
and of reinforcements immediately at hand.	Besides the above, there were at hand at this date the following commandos: Bethel (700), Germiston and Boksburg (620), Standerton (1,100), Ermelo (800), Piet Retief (250), Vrede (1,006), Bethlehem (1,605). When these came up within a few days they swelled the total around Ladysmith to over 23,000 men, an army which, well equipped and well mounted, had enveloped the town with a celerity which seemed to augur an instant effort to reduce it. Before the end of December these were joined by the following reinforcements:—Middelburg (1,317), Zoutpansberg (1,200), Johannesburg commando (1,000), Swazi Police (200), Carolina (310), in all about 4,000 men. At the same time a body of Free Staters of about the same strength quitted Natal to oppose Lieut.-General Lord Methuen on the western border, leaving the total Boer forces in Natal much the
Boer guns open fire, Nov. 2nd, 1899.	same as before. The hostile artillery was not slow in development. On November 3rd, the fire of the 94-pr. gun upon Pepworth, which had bombarded intermittently throughout the 2nd, killing an officer and wounding two men, was joined by that of long-range field guns from Umbulwana, from the kopjes about Aller Park, and from other widely separated points of the outer peri-
Cavalry reconnaissance, Nov. 3rd.	meter. On the morning of the 3rd a reconnaissance was sent out towards Lancer's Hill under Major-General J. F. Brockle-hurst, who had succeeded Major-General French in command of the cavalry. It consisted of: 5th Dragoon Guards; 18th and 19th Hussars, four squadrons; Imperial Light Horse; mounted infantry company, 1st Manchester regiment; 21st battery, Royal Field artillery. It met with strong opposition from the Heilbron burghers, who fired so sharply with two Field guns and many rifles that, even with a reinforcement of two batteries (42nd and 53rd) and the Natal Volunteers, the Imperial Light Horse, who had ventured too far forward in pursuit of a supposed retirement, were only extricated with considerable difficulty. (Casualties, November 3rd: Killed, 2 officers, 2 men; died of wounds, 1 officer; wounded, 3 officers, 25 men;

THE DEFENCE OF LADYSMITH.

missing, 1 man.) A demonstration by the enemy against Devon Post on the opposite side of the defences followed the withdrawal of Brocklehurst's force, and a bombardment so severe that the Town Council, at a meeting convened in the evening, drew up an address to Sir G. White on the subject of the removal of non-combatants into a place of safety. Their representations, joined to those of the Principal Medical Officer, whose hospitals, especially the prominent Town Hall, were greatly exposed, and finally the arrival of 89 wounded sent down from Dundee, induced Sir G. White to despatch a letter to General Joubert, asking that the sick and wounded, and the non-combatant inhabitants of Ladysmith might be allowed to depart southward by train. In reply Joubert, whilst declining to allow any exodus from the zone of operations, chivalrously sanctioned the formation of a neutral camp on the Intombi Spruit below Umbulwana, and agreed to a cessation of hostilities until midnight, November 5th, to enable the arrangements to be carried out. Next day, therefore, Colonel Ward took the matter in hand, and before the expiration of the armistice, a vast camp sheltered, beside sick and wounded soldiers, a number of families who dared not remain in their homes. *Joubert agrees to formation of a camp on Intombi Spruit for wounded and non-combatants.*

For three days both sides now did little but consolidate their respective positions. The enemy was seen to be entrenching assiduously, especially upon Umbulwana. His only movement of importance was the seizure on the 4th of Limit Hill, hitherto piqueted by a squadron, 5th Dragoon Guards. In the British lines the chief occurrences were the emplacing of the 13th battery in position east of Junction Hill, of two 6.3-in. Howitzers on the Helpmakaar Ridge, and of two guns, 69th battery on Leicester Post. On November 7th a general bombardment, opening at dawn, continued all day, and at midday a force of about 1,000 Boers gathered below Middle Hill, and attacked Wagon Hill by long-range fire. The latter height was promptly occupied by 1 company, 1st Manchester regiment and 2 squadrons, Imperial Light Horse, with the machine gun of the 5th Dragoon Guards, and the attack came to nothing. (Casualties, November 7th: Killed, 1 man; wounded, 2 officers, 5 men.) *Boers seize Limit Hill, Nov. 4th, and bombard and threaten Wagon Hill, Nov. 7th.*

In the evening four guns of the 42nd battery were strongly posted on Cæsar's Camp. During the day the enemy sent into the town 200 natives of India from the abandoned Dundee mines. On the morning of November 8th another heavy gun (94-pr.) opened fire from the flat summit of Umbulwana. Wagon Hill was this day permanently garrisoned by 3 companies, 1st King's Royal Rifles; and the two remaining guns of the 42nd battery, for which pits had already been dug, were entrenched upon Cæsar's Camp, somewhat to the east of the rest of the battery. (Casualties, November 8th: Killed, 1 man; wounded, 1 officer, 4 men.)

<small>Nov. 8th. Boers open from Umbulwana; White permanently occupies Wagon Hill.</small>

This occupation proved timely. The importance of the position had been early recognised by the Boers, who at a Krijgsraad held in the afternoon had decided upon a night attack. The project was, however, abandoned in favour of a general daylight assault next day. At 5 a.m. on the 9th, a heavy bombardment, directed chiefly at the northern and eastern defences, began from Surprise Hill, Pepworth Hill, and Lombards Kop, to which the Naval guns and the 69th battery replied, the latter from positions at Rifleman's and King's Posts. The Boer fire gradually concentrated upon Observation Hill, which was held only by piquets of the 5th Lancers, and when, about 7 a.m., sharp musketry was directed upon the same ridge and grew momentarily more severe, it seemed as if Observation Hill were to be attacked forthwith. Two companies of the 2nd Rifle Brigade were therefore sent forward to reinforce the cavalry piquets from Leicester Post, and these, advancing under heavy fire, reached the position at 9 a.m., and were exposed all day to 3 guns and many rifles, losing only an officer and 5 men. Simultaneously, a feeble demonstration against the Helpmakaar Ridge by the Utrecht and Wakkerstroom commandos, supported by artillery, kept the garrison of that part alert in their defences, the enemy appearing in some force in front of Lombards Kop. They were speedily dispersed by the shells of the Howitzers, and the attack not being pressed, the assistance of the 1st King's Royal Rifles, who were sent from General Howard's section to support, was not required.

<small>Nov. 9th. Boers bombard from north and east, demonstrate elsewhere, and</small>

THE DEFENCE OF LADYSMITH.

Meanwhile, a raking shell fire from east to west, and south to north, had opened at 5 a.m. upon the Cæsar's Camp plateau, and continued without intermission until, about 10.30 a.m., the Free Staters advanced across the Bester's Valley to attempt to carry out what was the real purpose of the day's operations. Gradually developing an encircling rifle attack against the British left, they pushed forward boldly to within 500 yards of the defences. At one point a formed body of men on foot, led by a standard bearer, advanced in close order, and only retired after suffering considerable losses from a hot fire directed upon it by the Manchester regiment. The steady musketry of the infantry, and the accurate practice of the 42nd battery, soon checked the attack, and though the Manchester was incessantly engaged until nightfall, by midday the heaviest pressure was over there, as at the other threatened points of the defences. A royal salute of 21 shotted guns, fired by the Naval guns at noon in honour of H.R.H. the Prince of Wales' birthday, celebrated also the discomfiture of the enemy's plans, though firing continued intermittently until 7 p.m. (Casualties, November 9th: Killed, 4 men; wounded, 3 officers, 20 men; died of wounds, 1 officer, 3 men.) *attack Cæsar's Camp without success.*

As a result of the day's experience, both Observation and Wagon Hills were more permanently occupied, the former by 4 companies, 1st King's Royal Rifles, and 1 company, 2nd Rifle Brigade, the latter by 2 squadrons, Imperial Light Horse, in reinforcement of the 3 companies, 1st King's Royal Rifles already there. The remainder of the 2nd Rifle Brigade held King's and Leicester Posts, exchanging duties with the 4 companies, 1st King's Royal Rifles on Observation Hill on alternate days. Orders were also issued for the following movements of Field artillery, which it will be seen was thus gradually being transformed into artillery of position: 2 guns, 69th battery to Observation Hill; 4 guns, 69th to Leicester Post; 4 guns, 67th to Ration Post. *Changes in position caused by the fighting of Nov. 9th.*

After his repulse on the 9th, the enemy was quiet for four days, sending only a desultory bombardment into the town. (Casualties, November 10–13th: Wounded, 1 officer, 1 man;

missing, 2 men.) All in Ladysmith daily became more secure, the troops by the strengthening of walls and traverses of stone, the inhabitants by the excavation of bomb-proofs in their gardens, and of large caves in the sandy soil of the deep banks of the Klip, to which the civilian population henceforward resorted during bombardments. Many, indeed, took up permanent residences in these dark shelters, which they provisioned and furnished from their homes. A reconnaissance, consisting of the 5th Lancers, 19th Hussars, 21st and 67th batteries, parties of the Imperial Light Horse, Natal Mounted Rifles, and mounted infantry, supported by the 42nd and 53rd batteries, was sent out on the 14th to ascertain the enemy's strength behind Rifleman's Ridge. It proved abortive, the Ridge being too strongly held for investigation, and again a Boer demonstration against the Helpmakaar Ridge on the east of the town followed the retirement of the British force on the west. (Casualties, November 14th: Killed, 1 man; wounded, 1 officer, 2 men.)

During the next three weeks the siege became purely monotonous and uneventful. The enemy, distrusting his own half-heartedness, as evinced by the futile demonstrations of the 9th, watching anxiously, moreover, the concentration of British troops now in process south of the Tugela, dared nothing against the garrison which might be decisive. Schemes there were broached and discussed, notably a plan for another attack on Cæsar's Camp plateau towards the end of November, but the Krijgsraads which sanctioned these designs had more than once to experience the extraordinary humiliation of hearing their decisions promptly discussed and vetoed by councils composed of the very officers to whom the execution of their orders had been allotted.* The Boer Army, therefore, lay inert in its laagers from November 15th to December 6th, entrusting the reduction of Ladysmith to the artillery, which bombarded daily, and often by night, with so little unanimity of purpose, and with so little loss to the besieged, as not to further the fall of the town, whose capture the Boers had made the vital item of

* See Appendix 14.

THE DEFENCE OF LADYSMITH. 545

their campaign. (Casualties, November 15th—December 6th: Killed, 5 men; wounded, 1 officer, 52 men. On November 30th there were in hospital from all causes, 432 officers and men.)

Not less passive was the defence, but with more reason. Sir G. White, in his *rôle* of holding back the invading armies, between which and the heart of the Colony he deemed himself alone to stand, did not consider that sorties would serve any useful purpose. If the Boer forces were too timid to assault him, they were yet strong enough at all points to offer formidable resistance to any attack on his part; and, even presuming a successful rupture of their investing line, no further result could follow until General Sir F. Clery's command should be concentrated and ready to co-operate. Sir George White was in constant communication with that General, and as early as the 7th November, and again on the 28th and 30th, had signalled his intention of joining hands, and named the best route for that purpose; receiving in reply General Sir R. Buller's repeated assurances of an early attempt at co-operation. Meanwhile, therefore, he did no more than organise (November 28th) a mobile column of all arms, which by constant assemblies and nightly exercise of route marching, he kept ready to move out at half-an-hour's notice. It consisted of 4 regiments of cavalry, 4 batteries of Royal Field artillery, 4 battalions of infantry, 15 mixed companies of infantry, and 2 detachments of Colonial Forces, with ammunition and supply columns, carrying 3 days' rations. Nevertheless there seemed no immediate prospect of relief. The enemy brought new guns into position daily, notably a 94-pr. on Gun Hill on the 24th, a 4.7-in. Howitzer north of Range Post on the 26th, and a 94-pr. on Middle Hill on the 28th. The British artillery ammunition was scarce, and orders were issued for the most scrupulous husbanding of it. On November 25th, Sir G. White considered it prudent to reduce the rations for the troops, and declined to receive another party of 250 natives whom the enemy attempted to introduce into the town. The chief internal movement during this period was the removal on November 28th of the two Howitzers from the Helpmakaar Ridge to a depression near the extremity of Wagon Hill,

Reason why White's defence was passive.

Mobile column organised, and kept exercised by night marches.

Boers bring more guns into action.

whence they engaged, and after a duel of two days silenced, the heavy Boer gun upon Middle Hill.

On November 29th Sir G. White issued orders for an attack on Rifleman's Ridge. But when that position appeared to be strongly reinforced at sunset, it was feared that the British plans had been disclosed to the enemy, and the project was abandoned. The British General constantly and bitterly complained of leakage of information by channels impossible to discover. As another of many examples may be taken an occurrence on the night of December 5th, when two companies of the Rifle Brigade, stealing out at 1.30 a.m. to attempt a surprise on a Boer post at Thornhill's Farm, found the farm, which up to then had been consistently occupied, empty.

<small>Boer spies in Ladysmith.</small>

<small>Night of Dec. 7th-8th. Hunter's sortie against artillery on Gun Hill.</small>

Better fortune attended a sally on the night of December 7th. The practice of the 94-pr. gun and a 4.7-in. Howitzer on Gun Hill had for some time been so harassing that Brevet-Major D. Henderson, Argyll and Sutherland Highlanders, D.A.A.G. for Intelligence on Sir G. White's Staff, asked leave to make an attempt with 50 men to destroy them at night. Permission was at first refused; subsequently, however, it was decided to carry through the enterprise with a stronger body. A force of 650 men was therefore placed under the command of Major-General Sir A. Hunter, the Chief of the Staff. It consisted of 500 Natal Carbineers, under Colonel Royston; 100 Imperial Light Horse, under Lieut.-Colonel A. H. M. Edwards, 5th Dragoon Guards; 18 of the Corps of Guides, under Brevet-Major D. Henderson; a detachment Royal Engineers, under Captain G. H. Fowke, R.E.; and a detachment No. 10 Mountain battery. The venture was perfectly successful. As a preliminary, the 1st Devon regiment, moving out after dark, entrenched in a covering position north of the Helpmakaar Ridge. Skilfully led by Major Henderson and his guides, the column, marching in sections, then covered the two miles of rough scrub-grown country between the Helpmakaar Ridge and Gun Hill without incident or confusion, despite the black darkness, and by 2 a.m. reached the base of the flat-topped underfeature whereon stood the Boer guns. Shortly before this the force had divided. The

THE DEFENCE OF LADYSMITH. 547

main body of the Natal Carbineers branched out to right and left to cover the flanks, and now, between these wings, 200 men, taken equally from the Imperial Light Horse and the rest of the Natal Carbineers, lined up for assault. The surprise was complete. Sweeping aside the piquet, which confronted them with a hurried fire, the troopers of the Imperial Light Horse broke into the work containing the 94-pr., the Natal Carbineers soon afterwards discovering that of the 4.7-in. Howitzer. Charges of gun-cotton were fixed in the breeches and muzzles of both guns and successfully fired with fuses ignited by burning cigars. Sir A. Hunter then called for three cheers for H.M. the Queen, and collecting his force, of which Major Henderson and 7 men were wounded, withdrew in safety, taking with him a Maxim captured on the hill. By 7 a.m. all were back in Ladysmith. *Its success.*

Simultaneously with this brilliant adventure, two companies of the 1st Liverpool regiment, accompanied by a squadron 19th Hussars, had attacked and captured Limit Hill; and the Hussars, riding four miles beyond, destroyed the telegraph line and burnt many shelters occupied by the enemy. An attempt of the 1st Leicester regiment to surprise the piquets at Hyde's and a neighbouring farm was less productive, the buildings being found to be evacuated. (Casualties, December 7th: Wounded, 1 officer, 10 men.) *Other sorties the same night.*

During the day preceding these occurrences, heliographic communication had been successfully established with Sir R. Buller, who had previously made partially successful attempts to communicate with Ladysmith by means of searchlight signals flashed upon the clouds at night. After December 7th heliographic communication was never interrupted. The first of these messages which Sir G. White received from Frere ran as follows :— *Dec. 7th. Heliographic communication permanently established with Buller. Buller announces his plans to White.*

No. 65. 7th December.
"I have definitely decided to advance by Potgieter's Drift. Expect to start 12th December, and take 5 days,"

qualified later by the following:

"The date given above is 6 days earlier than I find possible."

Encouraged by this news, and surmising from the success of the sallies of the previous night that the Boer line of investment had been considerably weakened by the detachment of a force to watch Buller, on the morning of December 8th, Sir George White sent out the 5th Lancers and 18th Hussars, supported by the 5th Dragoon Guards and 53rd battery, Royal Field artillery to reconnoitre along the Newcastle road. But the enemy, chagrined by the events of the night, was keenly on the alert, and meeting the reconnaissance with a heavy fire of guns and rifles from all directions, forced a hasty retreat at 6.20 a.m. (Casualties, December 8th : Killed, 3 men ; wounded, 3 officers and 18 men.) As a result of this activity of the garrison, 2,000 Boers who had gone south to face Sir R. Buller on the Tugela returned to Ladysmith next day, when a false order to attack Umbulwana at night, which was signalled openly to Colonel Hamilton on Cæsar's Camp, added to the uneasiness of the enemy, which further increased when a party of guides under Major A. J. Murray went out after dark and fired sharply near that mountain.

Dec. 8th. Reconnaissance.

The next night (December 10th) another enterprise was undertaken, this time against the 4.7-in. Howitzer on an eminence to the north of Ladysmith, henceforward to be known as Surprise Hill. Lieut.-Colonel C. T. E. Metcalfe, commanding the 2nd Rifle Brigade, who had previously reconnoitred the approaches to the position occupied by this gun, volunteered, and received permission, to make an attempt to destroy it. Moving out from Observation Hill at 10 p.m. with five companies (12 officers and 488 men) of his battalion and a detachment, Royal Engineers under Lieutenant R. J. T. Digby Jones, Metcalfe concealed his men in a donga until the setting of the moon, which was due at midnight. The force then emerged and, though the advance lay directly between Thornhill's and Bell's Kops—both occupied by the enemy—succeeded in reaching the foot of Surprise Hill by 2 a.m. undetected. On the way one half of " E." company was dropped at the railway, and the other half in a donga under Surprise Hill. Two companies (" A." and " H.") were then told off for first line, and two (" B." and " G.") for second, and the

Night of Dec. 10th-11th. Metcalfe's sortie against guns on Surprise Hill.

THE DEFENCE OF LADYSMITH. 549

ascent up the hill began, the supporting companies forming outwards to the flanks as they climbed, in order to leave a gap through which the two assaulting companies might retire when necessary. "A." and half "H." companies then extended to single rank, the remaining half of "H." company, together with the demolition party, following in rear of the centre. The summit was all but gained when a Boer sentry challenged and fired, the report of his rifle being immediately followed by that of a gun from Bell's Kop. Thereupon the Riflemen swarmed over the crest, and running past the emplacement, formed up beyond it into a semi-circular firing-line, and opened with volleys at the enemy, who replied from a short distance back. The emplacement itself was found to be empty. Some little time elapsed before the piece was discovered concealed beneath a tarpaulin outside the work. The charges were then quickly lit in muzzle and breech, the storming party still firing volleys as it awaited the explosion. The charges failed to ignite, and another half-hour passed before the desired detonation from a second fuse gave the signal for retreat. Although the muzzle of the gun was thereby destroyed, Jones fired a third to render the work complete. By this time the enemy was thoroughly alarmed. The half-company, which had been detached at the foot of the hill, became hotly engaged before the main body left the summit, and by the time the latter had come back to it, the enemy was everywhere in force and firing furiously at close quarters. Then the column, hemmed in on both flanks, fixed bayonets, and closed. After a spirited mêlée, in which the enemy emptied magazines point-blank and the soldiers freely used the steel, the battalion fought its way clear, followed by a heavy cross fire. Reforming his units at the railway crossing, Metcalfe marched back to Ladysmith in triumph. (Casualties: Killed 1 officer, 16 men; died of wounds, 3 men; wounded, 4 officers, 34 men; missing, 6 men.) *Its success.*

Next day (December 11th) the Boer 94-pr. gun, which had been silent since its discomfiture by the Howitzers on Middle Hill, re-opened from Telegraph Ridge. The Howitzers were therefore moved from Wagon Hill to Ration Post, whence on the 12th they again proved too much for their adversary. Beyond this, there was for some days little action by either besiegers or besieged, both of whom now turned to watch anxiously the development of events on the Tugela. A battle there was imminent; and whilst the enemy detached largely from the lines of investment to strengthen his field army, Sir G. White, eagerly looking forward to co-operation, revised the strength of his mobile column, and placed the artillery in positions likely to be useful in view of the expected attempt at his relief.

<small>White, anxious to co-operate with Buller, re-organises his mobile column; its composition.</small>

The column, as now formed, was made up of 4 regiments cavalry; 5 batteries, Royal Field artillery; 7th brigade infantry (2 battalions and 2 companies), 8th brigade (1 battalion and 11 companies); 2 regiments Colonial troops, with 1 company, Royal Engineers, Ammunition and Supply columns.

Sir George had received repeated messages from Sir R. Buller, in which, though the intended date of the latter's advance had been varied with the fluctuation in the arrivals of his artillery and transport, the direction of Potgieter's Drift had always been unchanged. A message of December 11th (Telegram No. 72. See Volume I., Chapter XXI.) gave the programme more in detail.

On the 13th Sir G. White received Sir R. Buller's signal informing him of his change of plans (Heliogram No. 78. See Volume I., Chapter XXI.). Sir G. White thereupon asked for a probable date on which to expect the advance, receiving the following in reply:—

" (Extract) No. 83 Cipher, 13th December.
" Actual date of attack depends on difficulties met with; probably 17th."

Two days later heavy firing, sounding at dawn from the direction of Colenso, warned the garrison of Ladysmith that the battle for its relief had unexpectedly begun.

The anxiety of the hours which followed was deepened at noon by the arrival of the news of the disastrous action at Magersfontein. Nor did any message more cheering come from the battlefield immediately to the southward, the echoes of which

THE DEFENCE OF LADYSMITH.

died away in the early afternoon. Instead, there was received from Sir R. Buller next day the following disquieting communication, dated from Frere :—

Buller heliographs to White to announce his failure at Colenso.

"No. 88 Cipher, 16th December.

"I tried Colenso yesterday, but failed. The enemy is too strong for my force, except with siege operations, which will take one full month to prepare. Can you last so long ? If not, how many days can you give me in which to take up defensive positions ? After which I suggest your firing away as much ammunition as you can, and making best terms you can. I can remain here if you have alternative suggestion, but unaided I cannot break in. I find my infantry cannot fight more than 10 miles from camp, and then only if water can be got, and it is scarce here."

A correction and an addition to this message were subsequently received (but were not specifically acknowledged). These ran as follows :—

"No. 92 Cipher, 16th December.

"My message, No. 88 Cipher. Groups 31 to 43 were correctly sent, but in place of them, and of first number of 44 Group, read as follows : ' How many days can you hold out ? ' Also add to end of message, ' whatever happens, recollect to burn your Cipher and Decipher and Code Books and any deciphered messages.' "

The effect of these alterations was to amend the original heliogram (No. 88) to the following reading in full :—

"I tried Colenso yesterday, but failed. The enemy is too strong for my force except with siege operations, which will take one full month to prepare. Can you last so long ? How many days can you hold out ? I suggest your firing away as much ammunition as you can, and making best terms you can. I can remain here if you have alternative suggestion, but unaided I cannot break in. I find my infantry cannot fight more than 10 miles from camp, and then only if water can be got, and it is scarce here. Whatever happens, recollect to burn your Cipher, Decipher and Code Books, and any deciphered messages."

To this Sir G. White replied as follows :—

White's reply.

"Your No. 88 of to-day received and understood. My suggestion is that you take up strongest available position that will enable you to keep touch with the enemy, and harass him constantly with artillery fire, and in other ways as much as possible. I can make food last for much longer than a month, and will not think of making terms unless I am forced to. You may have hit enemy harder than you think. All our native spies report that your artillery fire made considerable impression on enemy. Have your casualties been very heavy? If you lose touch of enemy, it will immensely increase his opportunities of crushing me, and have worse effect elsewhere. While you are in touch with him and in communication with me, he has both of our forces to reckon with. Make every effort to get reinforcements as early as possible, including Indian, and enlist every man* in both Colonies who will serve and can ride. Things ought to be looking brighter. The losing of 12,000 men here would be a heavy blow to England. We must not yet think of it. I fear I could not cut my way to you. Enteric fever is increasing to an alarming extent here. There are 180 cases all within the last month. Answer fully. I am keeping everything secret at present until I know your plans."

Further messages between Buller and White.

Sir R. Buller replied with the following message :—

" No. 93, 17th December.

" I find I cannot take Colenso, and I cannot stay in force near it, as there is no water, but I am leaving there as large a force as I can supply with water. I will do anything I can to help you, but recollect that in this weather my infantry cannot be depended on to march more than 10 miles a day. Can you suggest anything for me to do? I think in about three weeks from now I could take Colenso, but I can never get to Onderbrook."

Sir G. White answered the above as follows :—

" No. 33P, 18th December.

" Your No. 93, 17th December, received and understood. It is difficult for me to make suggestions, as I do not know situation outside, or whether you have made serious attempt to take Colenso, and with what casualties. Your messages were previously confident, and I had made preparations to fight towards Onderbrook, and could still do so if you had Colenso. I cannot advise leaving small force in advance of main body. It would probably be invested and be no real threat to enemy. (Your front line should be held in full strength. Abandonment of this garrison seems to me most disastrous alternative on public grounds. Enemy will be doubly strong on Tugela if Ladysmith falls.)† I can only suggest getting every available reinforcement in men and guns, and attacking in full strength as quickly as possible. Meanwhile I will do all I can to maintain an active defence, and will co-operate with you to the extent of my power if you advance again. How are you getting on in Orange Free State? We know nothing. Detailed news desirable to contradict mischievous rumours here."

* This was in the first instance received as " jungle men."

† The passage enclosed in brackets was read with considerable differences by Sir R. Buller's signallers, as follows :—

"Your front line should be held in full strength on Tugela river if Lady smith falls."

THE DEFENCE OF LADYSMITH.

The next message received by Sir George White gave hope of an intention to persevere. It ran thus :—

" No. 97, December 17th.
" Fifth division just arriving at the Cape. Have telegraphed for it to come on at once. It will make me strong enough to try Potgieter's. How long can you hang on ? "

Reply by Sir G. White :—

" No. 34P, December 18th.
" Your 97 Cipher of yesterday received and understood. Delighted to get it. I have provisions for men for 6 weeks, and I have confidence in holding this place for that time, but bombardment becomes more trying. I had 22 casualties this morning from one shell. Enteric and dysentery increasing very rapidly. I can get on well for 3 weeks, keeping even horses moderately fit. If you wish to wait for siege guns, it is worth waiting a little to dominate and overwhelm the enemy's guns. Bring every heavy gun, Naval and others, you can get. Water will be difficulty as regards occupying a position near Tugela river from which you can maintain continued attack. Could you arrange pipes, pumping station, or reservoir ? "

As a result of the set back of Colenso, Sir George White, informing his garrison that they " must not expect relief as early as had been anticipated,"* disbanded his mobile column, and on December 17th made a fresh allocation to the defences of the troops thus rendered disposable. Dec. 17th. White breaks up his mobile column.

From this date until the close of the year no events of importance occurred at Ladysmith. (Casualties, December 12th–31st : Killed, 1 officer, 16 men ; died of wounds, 1 officer ; wounded, 12 officers, 40 men.) The enemy, whose artillery now numbered from 20 to 25 pieces of all calibres, continued to bombard daily, and with increasing effect. On December 18th there were 18 casualties from shell fire, a single projectile from Umbulwana killing 4 men and wounding 7 men and 12 horses. On the 22nd another shell from Umbulwana killed 9 and wounded 3 men of the 1st Gloucestershire regiment near Tunnel Hill ; another shell on the 27th killed 1, mortally wounded 1, and wounded no less than 8 officers and 1 man who were in the dug-out mess shelter of the 1st Devon regiment by the railway cutting at Tunnel Hill ; whilst Sir G. White's Headquarters,

* Special Field Force Order, December 17th.

Sickness among the garrison of Ladysmith.

the position of which was well known to the Boer gunners, had become so favourite a target, that on the 22nd it was considered advisable to remove to another building. During this period, moreover, enteric fever and dysentery, the most formidable assailants of besieged armies, began to make their presence felt severely. At the end of November, the number of patients in the hospitals from these causes had been but 87 (15 enteric, 72 dysentery), with a weekly death-rate of 5. The last week of December, during which between 50 to 60 men went to hospital daily, saw the figures increased to 802 (441 enteric, 361 dysentery), whilst the death-rate had risen to 23 weekly.* On the last day of the year there were in hospital from all causes over 1,650 officers and men.

Dec. 30th, 1899. Buller advises White that he is about to make fresh attempt to reach him.

On December 30th Sir G. White heard from Sir R. Buller,† that the latter intended to begin another attempt at relief on January 6th, by way of Lancer's Hill, which, it was hoped, would be reached, *vîâ* Potgieter's Drift, about the 12th. Sir George White replied‡ on January 2nd, with a promise of co-operation in an attack on Lancer's Hill, reiterating his confidence in his power to hold his own at Ladysmith.

Jan. 1900. The first five days of the month.

That power was soon to be severely tested. The first days of 1900 passed uneventfully. Only the usual shelling occupied the attention of the garrison, resulting in a few more casualties,§ and in the wrecking of the house occupied by the Staff of the 7th brigade, whereupon, on January 3rd, Colonel Ian Hamilton moved his Headquarters up to Cæsar's Camp. To that hill were ordered on the 4th a Hotchkiss gun from Devon Post, and to Wagon Hill a 4.7-in. Naval gun from Junction Hill. The movement of these weapons was, however, postponed on account of heavy rain until the night of the 5th. On that very night, and upon that very position, the enemy suddenly delivered an attack so fierce and sustained, that for seventeen hours the fate of Ladysmith trembled in the balance.

---

* For fuller Hospital Statistics, see Appendix 15.

† Heliograms 131, of 30th December, 1899, and 133, of 2nd January, 1900.

‡ Heliogram 39 P., 2nd January, 1900.

§ Casualties, January 1st–5th: Killed, 2 men; wounded, 11 men.

CHAPTER XXXI.

THE DEFENCE OF LADYSMITH.

WAGON HILL.*

FROM the earliest days of the investment, the Boers, with that unerring tactical eye which distinguished them, had marked the Cæsar's Camp—Wagon Hill plateau as the key of the British defences. Such it was indeed. Situated no more than 3,000 yards from the centre of Ladysmith, with a command of 600 feet, it not only dominates the town itself within extreme rifle range, but if lost, would have rendered impossible the occupation of every other position without exception, for there is none which it does not overlook from flank to rear within field artillery range. The general position of this ridge has already been described, and the accompanying maps show plainly its relation to the other eminences about it. The feature itself must be considered more in detail. Running almost due west and east, about two and a quarter miles from end to end, it includes, as aforesaid, two separate heights of unequal length, joined by a Nek. The eastern and larger of these, called Cæsar's Camp, is a long, flat-topped hill, divided into two bold salients by a re-entrant which indents its southern face about its centre. The summit, which heightens gradually from the eastern crest, is about two miles long, and from 800 to 1,000 yards in breadth, the rear, or northern crest being slightly higher than the southern. Below the latter the hillside falls steeply to the Bester's Valley, covered with boulders and scrub, and broken by small but rough salients and re-entrants, rounding into more even gradients

^{marginal note:} Importance of Cæsar's Camp and Wagon Hill

* See maps Nos. 31, 32 and 32 (a).

across the face of the eastern spur, which points towards Umbulwana (see map No. 32).

A shallow Nek, the parting between the two re-entrants, which cleaves on opposite sides the faces of the hill, connects the extremity of Cæsar's Camp with Wagon Hill to the westward. This is of much smaller dimensions than Cæsar's Camp, its crest measuring no more than 900 yards from flank to flank and less than 300 from front to rear. Two knolls with a dividing depression break up the summit. The easternmost of these, on which stood two small works, is higher than the western, or Wagon Point, commanding indeed so much of the southern crest of Cæsar's Camp itself, that it may be called the key of both positions. A salient, protruding towards the Bester's Valley, renders the hillside for the most part dead to the view of the occupants of the crest, and a donga, trifurcating near the summit, runs like a covered way up the spur. Wagon Point forms the western end of the whole feature, and is separated from Mounted Infantry Hill by a valley 800 yards wide, the outlet from the Bester's Valley into the broad plain where stands Rifleman's Ridge. The summit, on which stood the clump of trees from which the hill took its name, here narrows considerably, and the sides towards the enemy are precipitous, though from the many boulders and irregularities they are by no means insurmountable.

At no point in the defences of Ladysmith were the dangers of their undue extent more apparent than on Cæsar's Camp and Wagon Hill. The plateau itself had a perimeter of over five miles. Of this a front of no less than three miles was liable to assault, whilst there was scarcely any part of the summit immune from artillery fire from either Umbulwana on the one flank, Rifleman's Ridge on the other, or Middle Hill on the front. It was therefore only properly defensible by closed works, or by the more expensive method of strong entrenchments. To fill the latter men were not available. Without troops to hold them, indeed, extensive trenches would only have added to the insecurity of the positions by forming shelters and *points d'appui* for an assaulting enemy.

THE DEFENCE OF LADYSMITH.

The defences crowning the heights on January 6th, though somewhat slight on Wagon Hill, were on Cæsar's Camp by no means insignificant. On both positions they were proportionate to the available garrisons, and on both, the northern crests had been constituted the lines of resistance, the southern the lines of observation. Pits and emplacements sheltered the guns, and stone sangars the piquets, which, disposed on the cordon system, lined the outer crests of the two kopjes. On Cæsar's Camp the 1st Manchester regiment had two enclosed, and two semi-enclosed works, built up of stones. The latter contained the supports to the piquets, the former, of which the western called Manchester Fort, was of considerable strength, stood upon the line of resistance. The other troops on this hill were the 42nd battery, Royal Field artillery, a detachment, Royal Navy with a 12-pr. gun, and a detachment, Natal Naval Volunteers with a Hotchkiss. On Wagon Hill, the eastern of the two small works, a redoubt called the "Crow's Nest"—a name, though it was not universally used at the time, which will be adhered to for the sake of clearness in the description which follows— formed the Headquarters of three companies of the 2nd King's Royal Rifles, under Major H. Gore-Browne, which found six posts of double sentries. Next to these, in the work to the west (marked I.L.H. on map) commanding the depression which separated Wagon Hill proper from Wagon Point, was a squadron (38 men) of the Imperial Light Horse; another squadron (41 men) occupied Wagon Point itself. Three piquets watched the front of these, one holding the Nek.

Defences on Cæsar's Camp and Wagon Hill.

On the afternoon of January 5th, Joubert held a Krijgsraad, at which, for the fourth time since the siege began, it was decided to assault the Platrand, or the Cæsar's Camp plateau. The force detailed was 4,000 men, 2,000 from the armies of each Republic, a reinforcement of 600 burghers being called up from the commandos lying on the Tugela. The Transvaalers were to attack Cæsar's Camp, the Free Staters Wagon Hill, the whole under the direction of General Schalk Burger. Both contingents would leave their laagers at midnight. To divert attention from the assault, feints were arranged against other portions of the British lines.

Jan. 5th, 1900. Boers decide to attack them.

About 7.15 p.m. on January 5th, a party of 33 Sappers of the 23rd company, Royal Engineers, under Lieutenant R. J. T. Digby Jones, arrived at Wagon Hill. Their mission was threefold, to finish an emplacement for a 12-pr. Naval gun near the centre of the summit of Wagon Point, to erect a platform in a similar emplacement, partially completed just below the extreme western point, and to mount the 4.7-in. Naval gun, which was on its way from Junction Hill, in a work which had already been prepared for it about midway between the two 12-pr. emplacements, i.e., near the western crest of Wagon Point. A fatigue party of 50 men of " C." company, 1st Manchester regiment met the Royal Engineers on their arrival, and the work commenced. The 4.7-in. gun arriving soon after, escorted by 13 bluejackets and two officers of H.M.S. *Powerful*, and 170 men of the Gordon Highlanders, was left at the foot of the hill, in the wagon in which it had travelled, until the emplacement should be ready for its reception. For hours all was quiet. An officer of the Imperial Light Horse, who had patrolled to within a short distance of Middle Hill, returned about 2 a.m., reporting nothing stirring in the enemy's lines. At 2.30 a.m., the tasks being nearly completed, the fatigue party of the Manchester left for their own bivouacs.

Assault on Cæsar's Camp begins, 2.40 a.m., Jan. 6th.
Ten minutes later the piquet of the Imperial Light Horse on the Nek, between the western work and Wagon Point, heard sounds of movement in the donga below their sangar; a sentry challenged, and receiving no reply, fired. A crash of musketry replied from the darkness; the Light Horse supports ran up, four men falling shot at once. Lieutenant J. J. Richardson, commanding the squadron, thereupon made his way towards the spot, and descending a little below the summit of the Nek, found himself in the midst of a press of men climbing the hill. Thinking they were soldiers of his regiment, he called to them, was immediately fired upon, and fell wounded. A moment later the Royal Engineer party of 25 men, who with Jones were still working on the upper 12-pr. emplacement (the remaining 8 Sappers being engaged on the lower), came under heavy fire from no more than 150 yards from their left front. The enemy

was already on the hill. Jones immediately extinguished the lanterns, extended his small command, and returned the fire, some men of the Gordon Highlanders, who had come up from the 4.7-in. gun, lining up with the Sappers. After a few moments of shooting, Jones, ordering bayonets to be fixed, led his men about 40 yards forward to the outer crest of the hill. The Imperial Light Horse on either hand conformed to the movement, and attempted to find a position commanding the re-entrant from whence the Mauser fire apparently came. But those on Wagon Point found the enemy already above them on the glacis of the I.L.H. work to their left, and in a few moments their casualties numbered 17 out of 22 officers and men present. The Bluejackets now joined the Royal Engineers in the western gun emplacement, and the 2nd King's Royal Rifles, who had two half-companies on piquet, reinforced with two more half-companies, and these lined the crest irregularly in whatever cover they could find. The third company, commanded by Bt.-Major D. Mackworth, the Queen's (Royal West Surrey) regiment (attached), remained in the Crow's Nest. Shortly after, Gore-Browne received an urgent appeal for support from the Imperial Light Horse, and in response ordered part of this reserve company to their assistance. Mackworth thereupon quitted the Crow's Nest, and taking 20 of his men, led a charge in the darkness against the band of Boers who were doing such mischief from the outer contour of the knoll, on which stood the I.L.H. work. He was met with a fierce fire, and fell shot through the head, most of his party falling dead or wounded around him.

Meanwhile, on Cæsar's Camp, the Manchester regiment had stood to arms. This battalion had furnished five piquets, that on the right joining hands with the King's Royal Rifles, the left—which found three groups upon the eastern edge of the plateau—looking towards Umbulwana, and connecting with the line of outposts of Royston's Natal Volunteers, which crossed the valley of the Klip back towards the town. For about 15 minutes after the outburst on Wagon Hill nothing happened in this quarter, and the Manchester were able to reinforce their outposts. Suddenly, at 3.45 a.m., the left-hand piquet was swept

560   THE WAR IN SOUTH AFRICA.

The enemy, passing between outposts, make lodgment on crest of Cæsar's Camp.

by a volley at short range from its unprotected left rear, and in a few moments was practically annihilated. The enemy, having penetrated between the left of the Manchester and the right of the Natal Volunteers, were upon the crest of the plateau, from whence the whole summit would be exposed to their fire when daylight came. But though the musketry here, as across on Wagon Hill, grew momentarily more fierce, the Boers on Cæsar's Camp, either from uncertainty as to their position, or from lack of support, fortunately pushed on no farther.

The attack on Wagon Hill, on which Boers also make a lodgment.

Very different was the nature of the attack in progress against Wagon Hill. The Free Staters climbed uninterruptedly, stealing up in scattered bands, firing incessantly from every hollow and boulder, and pressing with such determination that the squadron of the Imperial Light Horse, which filled the low-lying gap between the I.L.H. work and Wagon Post, was speedily outflanked, outnumbered, and forced to give back to higher ground. Day was now dawning, and as the men showed against the skyline, many fell to a storm of fire which was scarcely diminished by the shooting of the Natal Volunteers' Hotchkiss, which endeavoured to cover the retirement. So close was the enemy, indeed, that the gun itself barely escaped capture, and Lieutenant Mathias, retiring last of his squadron, found himself amongst the Boers, escaping, however, unnoticed. At this moment another party of the enemy, moving completely around the western extremity of Wagon Hill, fell upon the 4.7-in. gun, still lying in its wagon at the foot of the slope. But the guard beat them back, and dismantled the wheels of the wagon to render it immovable should the enemy after all succeed in capturing it. Thus at 3.45 a.m. the whole position was enveloped in a confusion of musketry; the defenders, who were in many parts intermingled with, or actually in advance of the enemy, finding themselves attacked from so many directions at once, that no man knew whether to meet with the bayonet the Boers close upon him, or to reply to the rifles of those more distant.

White at once reinforces.

In Ladysmith the seriousness of the attack had been instantly recognised by Sir G. White. In less than an hour from the first firing the following units received his orders to reinforce: the rest

THE DEFENCE OF LADYSMITH.

of the Imperial Light Horse to go to Wagon Hill, the 2nd Gordon Highlanders to Cæsar's Camp. A wing of the latter regiment had always been at a camping ground under Maiden Castle, and Colonel Hamilton who, since the destruction by shell-fire of his quarters in Ladysmith, had passed the nights near this spot, had already collected three companies, two of which, under Major C. C. Miller-Wallnutt, he took with him to Wagon Hill. The third, under Captain the Hon. R. F. Carnegie, he sent to reinforce the Manchester on Cæsar's Camp. The Imperial Light Horse galloped out of the town at 4.30 a.m., followed shortly by the rest of the Gordon Highlanders. Scarcely had the latter crossed the iron bridge which spanned the Klip at the south-west corner of the town, when they came under a thin rain of bullets which, after clearing the crest of the Cæsar's Camp plateau, were dropping all but spent. One of these struck Lieut.-Colonel W. H. Dick-Cunyngham, V.C., as he rode at the head of his battalion, and he fell mortally wounded.

At 4.20 a.m., Sir G. White sent orders also to the Headquarters, 1st and 2nd King's Royal Rifles, who were in bivouac near Observation Hill, to move out. In about half an hour four companies of each battalion, under Major W. P. Campbell, were on the march to Wagon Hill. Of all these reinforcements, the Imperial Light Horse, who had ridden fast from Ladysmith, and the three companies Gordon Highlanders, previously mustered by Colonel Hamilton, arrived first, and almost simultaneously, at about 5 a.m. The Light Horse at once went forward into the fighting line of their comrades on Wagon Hill. For a time Miller-Wallnutt's two companies of Gordon Highlanders were held back under Wagon Hill, whilst Carnegie, pursuing his way to Cæsar's Camp, led his company straight to the assistance of No. 5 (the left) Manchester piquet, which, as before described, was at this time outflanked, at such close quarters, that Lieut. R. Hunt-Grubbe, of the Manchester, who went forward slightly in advance of Carnegie, fell into the hands of the Boers on the very spot where a group of the piquet had recently been. But the Gordons, dropping amongst the stones, opened so hot a fire that the Boers lying in this part began to melt away to their left. They thus relinquished their dangerous enveloping position for one more in front of the Manchester, whose fire, assisted by that of the Highlanders on the left, and of 45 men of the mounted infantry company, 1st (King's) Liverpool regiment, who now came into line on the right, held the enemy without difficulty, though it could not dislodge him.

Action of Boer artillery.

Meanwhile day had broken, and every Boer gun about the town had opened on the various sections of the defences, most severely at first upon Observation Hill. There the first of the pre-arranged feints began with a skirmishing attack by the Pretoria commando upon the Leicester regiment, which, assisted by the shells of the 69th battery, repulsed this feint without loss. The Cæsar's Camp plateau itself came under fire of heavy guns upon Umbulwana, Middle Hill, and Rifleman's Ridge, and these raked the defences at all angles. Nor could the Naval 12-pr. on the summit, which in reply opened at Middle Hill, or the 42nd battery succeed in silencing the enemy's artillery, though the shrapnel had a noticeable effect on the musketry of his supports on Mounted Infantry Hill. But additional artillery was soon at hand. At 5.30 a.m. the 53rd battery (Major A. J. Abdy), and ten minutes later the 21st battery (Major W. E. Blewitt) trotted out of Ladysmith, the former towards the eastern, the latter towards the western end of the plateau. Marching unobserved by the Boer gunners past Range Post, the 21st battery, escorted by the 5th Dragoon Guards, came into action at a point upon Sign Post Ridge, whence it was possible to shell the whole of the ground below the western extremity of Wagon Hill, which was thus, during a critical time, secured from being turned from this direction. The 53rd battery unlimbered in the scrub in the flats behind Maiden Castle, and opened both at the shoulder of Cæsar's Camp and into the bushy slopes and dongas which sheltered the Boer supports, which were massed in the wake of the attackers of the crest. The 94-pr. and a 15-pr. on Umbulwana assailed the battery at once, inflicting considerable losses. But the enemy's practice was much hampered by the accurate shooting of the 4.7-in. gun at Cove Redoubt, and Abdy's gunners, disregarding all

21st and 53rd battery R.F.A. do good work.

THE DEFENCE OF LADYSMITH.

dangers but that menacing Cæsar's Camp, soon scattered the Boers lurking in front of them in all directions. The battery fired 138 rounds of shrapnel from this point.

The bold action of the 53rd battery produced immediate and valuable effect upon the situation on the summit. Though the Boers on the left rear of the Manchester had, on the arrival of the Gordons, shifted ground somewhat, they had yielded none, and were still in force on the eastern crest of Cæsar's Camp, their fire being at least equal to, if not master of, that of the British. When, however, they felt Abdy's shrapnel and saw their supports dispersing behind them from the same cause, they began to waver, and Carnegie, seizing the opportunity, instantly ordered his company to advance with fixed bayonets. The Boers did not await the charge. Chasing them from the crest, the Gordons reoccupied the advanced sangars recently tenanted by the left of the Manchester piquets and released Lieut. Hunt-Grubbe. *Boers lose eastern crest of Cæsar's Camp,*

The left rear and left flank were thus (about 6 a.m.) clear; but the Boers on the front, that is on the southern crest, remained in undiminished numbers, and once more the contest here settled down to a fire fight of great intensity and uncertain issue. Sir G. White, who was in close touch by telephone with every phase of the action, had already, at 5.30 a.m., ordered the 2nd Rifle Brigade in Ladysmith to reinforce Cæsar's Camp. At 7 a.m. eight companies of the 1st and 2nd King's Royal Rifles, under Campbell, arrived at Wagon Hill, where a vehement rifle combat was in progress at such close quarters, that it was hard to say whether the hill was in British or Boer hands. The Imperial Light Horse had been absorbed into the firing line two hours, the Gordon Highlanders under Miller-Wallnutt, one hour previously, and both now lay within a few yards of the enemy, the former along the southern crest of Wagon Point, the latter below the south-western extremity. Miller-Wallnutt had at first attempted to creep around this western point, hoping to take the assailants of the hill in flank, but the tremendous fire which broke out against him from all sides, from Middle Hill in front, and from the hidden dongas which seamed the valley below his right *but hold the southern crest.* *The struggle on Wagon Hill.*

and right rear, rendered the attempt impossible, and the Gordons were pinned to the crest on the right of the Naval and Royal Engineer detachments. The most damaging fire directed upon the Imperial Light Horse came from the small band of Boer marksmen, who lay just above the donga by which they had climbed, on the outer crest of the I.L.H. work. These took the troops on either side of them directly in enfilade, and the effect was galling.

On his arrival, Campbell halted his command under the reverse slope of the Crow's Nest, and, having ascertained the situation, pushed forward four companies King's Royal Rifles into the firing line between the Crow's Nest and the I.L.H. work, above the re-entrant, keeping the other four companies under cover close behind. *Fruitless efforts to drive the Boers from its summit.* He at once decided upon another effort to dislodge the Boers from in front of the I.L.H. work. In response to his request, Major R. S. Bowen, selecting eight men of his company, volunteered to make the attempt. But Bowen, charging gallantly, was killed, as Mackworth had been, within ten yards of the outcrop which sheltered the enemy, and the whole of his little party were destroyed upon the narrow belt of open ground behind him. The shooting from this quarter continued to be so intolerable, that about 8.45 a.m., Colonel Hamilton ordered Lieut. N. M. Tod, of the Cameronians, attached to the King's Royal Rifles, to lead a third attack on the outcrop. But Tod, too, was instantly killed, his party of twelve men annihilated, and Colonel Hamilton, relinquishing for the present all hope of turning out the enemy by these means, forbade any further attempts. After these events, the firing on Wagon Hill slackened somewhat, and by 11 a.m. had so nearly ceased, that some of the men and officers were able to procure food. Meanwhile Sir G. White had received urgent demands for further reinforcements, *White, having no more infantry available, sends cavalry as reinforcements.* and his reserve of infantry being exhausted, had despatched three squadrons of the 5th Lancers, and two squadrons of the 19th Hussars to Cæsar's Camp, and the 18th Hussars to Wagon Hill. The 18th Hussars arrived about 9 a.m., and, as the firing above them had diminished, dismounted until further orders under Wagon Hill, near to the 4.7-inch gun, still in its wagon.

THE DEFENCE OF LADYSMITH.

Turning again to Cæsar's Camp, the situation here continued to improve, and by 10 a.m. there were ample troops on the hill for all contingencies. About 8 a.m. six companies of the 2nd Rifle Brigade and a little later two squadrons of the 19th Hussars reached the position. Lieut.-Colonel Metcalfe at once pushed the Riflemen forward into the firing line, sending one company to Carnegie's right to fill a gap between the Gordons and Manchester. Other four companies made a wide sweep around Carnegie's left, and, clearing the last stragglers of the enemy from the eastern crest, reoccupied it completely, and linked up with Carnegie on their right, retaining a company in support. The 19th Hussars remained in reserve. An hour later the four Headquarter companies of the Gordon Highlanders and three squadrons of the 5th Lancers arrived simultaneously from Ladysmith, having been shelled by the Umbulwana gun on the way out. As there was no immediate need of further troops on the hill, the 5th Lancers remained with the 19th Hussars in reserve below Manchester Fort, whilst the Gordons, closely supporting the front, were very gradually absorbed into the firing line. Here, too, as on Wagon Hill, the volume of fire abated somewhat about 11 a.m., and it seemed as though the Boers were wearying of the struggle. They were, in fact, already morally defeated. The weakly held positions which they had failed to snatch in the dark, they knew well the impossibility of forcing in the broad light of day, when the defences had been reinforced. They were conscious, too, of being betrayed by their comrades. Their supports, cowed on the right by Abdy's shrapnel, on the left fearful of the fierce fighting in progress on the crest line, lurked under cover on the other side of the Bester's Valley, and but few had ventured to come down even to the Fourie's Spruit.

<small>Situation at Cæsar's Camp.</small>

Nevertheless, certain bold spirits determined to risk all on a supreme effort. At 12.30 p.m., a band of Free Staters, led by Commandant de Villiers, formerly chief of the Free State army, and Field-Cornet de Jagers, of Harrismith, suddenly charged in loose order over the crest-line of Wagon Point, and made for the 4.7-in. gun emplacement. The troops in front, whose watchfulness had relaxed after an hour of comparative quiet,

<small>12.30 p.m. A fresh Boer effort on Wagon Hill for the moment succeeds, but is beaten back.</small>

gave back in surprise before the rush, and in a moment the Boer leaders, followed fortunately by but a few of their men, were at the emplacement, wherein lay a small party of Royal Engineers and Imperial Light Horse. Miller-Wallnutt and Digby Jones were just outside the emplacement, beneath a tarpaulin shelter. Here, at the moment of these occurrences, they were joined by Colonel Hamilton. From their covered position these officers had not noticed the retirement, and the first hint of the presence of the enemy was given by a Sapper falling dead to a shot fired by one of the Boers over the very parapet of the work itself. Jones, seizing a rifle, immediately dashed out into the open, and encountering de Villiers shot him dead, de Jagers falling simultaneously to a bullet sent from inside the emplacement. The rest of the Boers on the crest had now opened a withering fusilade on the retiring infantry, who fell back further, and once more the position seemed lost. But Jones, accompanied by 2nd Lieut. G. B. B. Denniss, R.E., by Sergt. G. Howard and Trooper H. Albrecht, of the Imperial Light Horse, by the Bluejackets, under Mr. W. Sims (gunner), R.N., and a few more of whom only the gallantry and not the names are known, led his Sappers forward at a run towards the crest with fixed bayonets, reoccupied the abandoned front line, and replied so fiercely to the burghers' musketry that they dared not follow de Villiers ; and the hill-top was for the moment rescued.

18th Hussars, dismounted, come into action on Wagon Hill,

Meanwhile, some of the infantry repulsed from the crest-line, were recoiling down the reverse slope. At the bottom lay the 18th Hussars, under Major E. C. Knox, who promptly ordered two squadrons to advance. They did so with great dash, breasting the spurs on either side of the re-entrant, and carrying upward with them the retiring soldiers, were soon on the summit by the side of Jones' men. But the infantry, though re-encouraged, were still in disorder, and Jones, seeing the urgent need of an officer to direct them, himself rose and went along the line, adjusting it to the best advantage. Whilst thus engaged, a bullet struck him in the throat, and he was instantly killed. Denniss, going to his assistance, fell by his side, whilst about the same time, Miller-Wallnutt, who had returned to the fire-swept

THE DEFENCE OF LADYSMITH.

point of the hill, which his men had so long maintained, was also killed.

The situation on Wagon Hill was now (1.30 p.m.) once more critical. The enemy was again in force on the crest-line and around the I.L.H. work; and his fire was searching, as was also that of the Boer artillery, which maintained a rapid practice from the surrounding heights. The defenders, who had suffered heavy losses, were worn out, and despite the assistance of the fresh men of the 18th Hussars, were in no condition to withstand a determined assault. At 1.45 p.m., therefore, the three squadrons 5th Lancers and the two of the 19th Hussars, which had lain behind Cæsar's Camp, were sent across to Wagon Hill. Thither two squadrons of the 5th Dragoon Guards were at the same moment hurrying from another direction. The latter, together with a third squadron, had been lately the escort to the 21st battery, in which duty they had been replaced by the last squadron of the 19th Hussars, which came out from Ladysmith for the purpose. Dismounting at 2.30 p.m. below the Crow's Nest, the Lancer and Hussar squadrons climbed the hill. On arriving at the summit, their commanding officer was informed that the front line of defence was all but denuded. He thereupon ordered his men to extend and advance dismounted. They instantly doubled under heavy fire straight across the flat, past the left of the Crow's Nest, until they reached the sangars originally occupied by the piquets of the King's Royal Rifles, in front of the Crow's Nest. On their right lay a belt of flat ground, swept by the fire of the party of the enemy, who were still immovably established on the outer contours of the I.L.H. work, hidden in the rib of rock, in attempting to dislodge them from whence Mackworth, Bowen and Tod had lost their lives in turn. As the troopers ran forward, a heavy rainstorm broke over the field. They then dropped into the shelters, and, supported on the left by the Maxim gun sent forward from the 5th Dragoon Guards, replied to the enemy's fire for the next hour in drenching rain. During that time Campbell contrived to distribute three of his reserve companies of the King's Royal Rifles in a supporting fire position along the northern crest, which was

supported by the 5th Lancers and 19th Hussars.

soon after strengthened by the inclusion of the two squadrons of the 5th Dragoon Guards. Once more a musketry duel raged across the few yards separating the combatants, and neither side seemed to obtain even a momentary mastery.

<small>White sends part of the Devonshire regiment to Wagon Hill.</small>

To Sir G. White it appeared of supreme importance to turn the enemy off the hill before nightfall. His reserves, and more than his reserves, were now deep in the fight; but to attain his object he decided to draw further upon the actual defenders of his perimeter for a last effort. At 4 p.m., the Headquarters of the 1st Devon regiment, which had already moved down from Tunnel Hill near to the iron bridge in readiness for emergencies,* received orders to march at once for Wagon Hill with every available man. Within a quarter of an hour three companies (5 officers and 184 men), under Major C. W. Park, were marching rapidly out of the town, and at 5 p.m. were under the hill. Park reported his arrival to Colonel Hamilton, who requested him to attempt to turn out with a bayonet charge the party of sharpshooters occupying the front of the I.L.H. work. Park at once formed up his detachment in a depression upon the reverse slope, a shelf so shallow and narrow, that there was no room for any formation but quarter column. Bayonets were fixed, and magazines charged, and Park described the point to be cleared to the company officers.

<small>Their bayonet charge;</small>

He then ordered the charge, and followed by his men, emerged over the crest, on to the flat intervening between the I.L.H. work and the right of the 5th Lancers on the left, his units forming line as they entered the open. Arrived abreast of the Lancers, Park saw that he was leading too much to the left. He therefore signalled a change of direction, and the companies behind him, responding as if at exercise, swung the left shoulder up, the pivot company dropping to the ground and instantly opening magazine fire. They then rushed on, cheering, straight for the outcrop which sheltered the enemy. At this moment, by a curious coincidence, the storm which had raged without cessation, culminated in a stupendous burst of thunder and hail, which drowned even the loud shouts of the charging soldiers and

* Three companies of this battalion were on Observation Hill.

THE DEFENCE OF LADYSMITH. 569

the uproar of the tempest of fire which broke out from the enemy. So destructive a blast had not been delivered at any time during the action. In the brief time required to traverse the 130 yards of naked flat, an officer and some forty men fell. But the onset neither wavered nor deflected. The soldiers, close on the heels of their commander, bore down upon the rocks, and the enemy, shunning the bayonet attack, fled down into the valley. Thus the position was finally cleared. But the Devon, dropping into a fire position in the captured outcrop, now came under severe long-range musketry from the enemy's covering troops, and their losses were still further augmented. Two more officers were killed as they lay, and another, Lieut. J. E. I. Masterson, was severely wounded as, leaving cover, he ran back under a heavy fire across the open, to direct the attention of the Imperial Light Horse to the Boers who were causing the losses.* Of the officers, therefore, Park alone survived; and until dusk he kept his men steady in their exposed situation, where they showed a fortitude scarcely less than that which had inspired their brilliant assault.

The Boers, who now fled from all parts of the position, suffered severely in their retirement. As they rushed down the slopes, the whole British line opened upon them with independent musketry, and many fell, more especially at the drifts, for these had become the only means of crossing the dongas which were now in high flood after the torrential downpour. Many of these passages were in full view of the crest, especially of that of Cæsar's Camp. There the troops had been continuously and hotly engaged since the recrudescence of the attack at 12.30 p.m., and now, with every rifle in line, they dealt destruction to the Boers as they gathered in confused crowds at the drift heads. Many Boers, it is said, were drowned as they attempted to cross, and it is certain that some of the wounded, who had sheltered in these natural trenches, were swept away by the sudden freshets. Soon darkness, falling at 6.30 p.m., put an end to fighting, of which the closeness, the peril, the anxiety, and the magnitude of the issues at stake are not to be measured by

its success. Flight of the Boers from Wagon Hill.

---

* For Victoria Crosses awarded for this day, see next page.

the mere numbers engaged, or the length of the casualty list. Had the plateau remained in the enemy's possession, the fall of Ladysmith would have been possible at any moment. The enemy, greatly encouraged, would not have guarded feebly their acquisition. The British strength which had been unable to retain the plateau, had then almost certainly been unequal to the task of reconquering it, and Ladysmith lay defenceless beneath its close and commanding crest-line.

<small>Operations of the enemy against other parts of the perimeter.</small>
The demonstrations against other parts of the works, though accompanied by heavy firing, came to nothing, as they were probably designed to do. Only against Observation Hill was there anything like a serious attack. Here the enemy advanced boldly under cover of a sustained bombardment, pressing on to within a few yards of the trenches, only to be beaten back with considerable* loss by the detachment of the 1st Devon regiment, supported by three companies 1st Leicester regiment, and the guns of the 69th battery. Nevertheless, a heavy shell fire fell into nearly every British position about the town, and all the troops were kept in their sangars throughout <small>Jan. 6th. Casualties.</small> the day. (Casualties, January 6th: Killed, 14 officers, 135 N.C.O.'s and men; died of wounds, 3 officers, 23 N.C.O.'s and men; wounded, 28 officers, 221 N.C.O.'s and men; total 424.)

* The bodies of twenty Boers were collected here.

VICTORIA CROSSES AWARDED FOR GALLANTRY ON JANUARY 6TH, 1900.
Lieut. R. J. T. Digby Jones, R.E. (posthumous).
Lieut. J. E. I. Masterson, 1st battalion Devonshire regiment.
Private J. Pitts, 1st battalion Manchester regiment.
Private R. Scott, 1st battalion Manchester regiment.
Trooper H. Albrecht, Imperial Light Horse (posthumous).

CHAPTER XXXII.

THE DEFENCE OF LADYSMITH.

LAST PHASE OF SIEGE, 7TH JANUARY TO 3RD MARCH, 1900.

THE action of January 6th profoundly discouraged the enemy. His losses were heavy. During an armistice on the following day, seventy-nine bodies, found within the British position alone, were handed over for burial to the Boer authorities, and very many corpses lay undiscovered amongst the shrubbery and winding dongas of the Bester's Valley. On January 11th, a letter was received from Commandant-General Joubert complaining that all the dead in the British lines had not been handed over. A well-informed Transvaaler records the Boer losses on January 6th as 184 killed, 380 wounded. Though no official casualty list was ever compiled, it is certain that from 500–700 Boers fell on this day, a total heavy indeed for the numbers engaged of an army averse to, and unequipped for, close combat. Those who died, moreover, were the finest of the fighting material, and the spirit which vanished with them left a gap more irreparable than the want of their rifles. Even more than the losses did the conduct of the whole attack dishearten, by its lack of cohesion, both the burghers themselves and the Republican Generals who witnessed the fighting from the lofty platform of Umbulwana. Of the men told off to the assaulting columns, many had not left their laagers at all; and of the remainder, not one quarter ventured beyond the limit of the long-range zone, not one eighth dared to follow their intrepid leaders to the attack on the crest.* From this date the Boers abandoned all idea

Marginalia: Effect on Boers of repulse, Jan. 6th, 1900. Their casualties.

* For the fundamental causes of this and other failures on the part of the Boers, see Volume I., page 73; and, in the present instance, Appendix 14.

of taking the town by assault, and resolved to rely upon the potent allies of besiegers—starvation, exhaustion, and disease. These they knew must be coming to their assistance within the lines, which they themselves could not force.

Their inaction during remainder of January.

The remainder of January therefore passed in stagnation more exhausting than battles for the imprisoned garrison. There was the usual daily shelling, the usual sharp-shooting of piquets; but the former never rose to the volume of a bombardment, nor the latter to an intensity sufficient to cause a general manning of the trenches. Much and arduous work was accomplished during the month. Cæsar's Camp plateau, its former garrison increased by a dismounted squadron of the 18th Hussars in Manchester Fort, and by five companies of the 2nd Rifle Brigade (from Section B) on Wagon Hill, was more strongly fortified. Elsewhere, the perimeter of the town was further safeguarded by constant improvement of the defences, and by utilising the Field artillery as guns of position. (Casualties, January 7th–31st: Killed, 3 N.C.O.'s and men; wounded, 2 officers, 19 N.C.O.'s and men.)

White reorganises his mobile forces.

On January 8th, Sir G. White, who had been in constant communication with Sir R. Buller, heard that the army on the Tugela was about to start upon its second attempt at relief. Once more, therefore, he prepared the flying column, which had been temporarily disbanded, though he had previously informed Sir R. Buller that not much in the way of co-operation was to be expected from his men in their exhausted condition.* The Ladysmith sick list was, indeed, approaching a formidable total. There were on January 13th no less than 2,150 men in hospital, of whom 671 were cases of enteric fever.† Four days later the total non-effectives had risen to 2,400,‡ leaving only 9,500 men fit for duty.

At 3.30 p.m. on January 12th, Lord Dundonald's heliograph was seen flashing from above Potgieter's Drift on the Upper Tugela. The days which followed were full of anxiety for the

* Heliogram No. 44 P, of January 7th.
† See Appendix 15.
‡ Heliogram No. 48 P, January 17th.

THE DEFENCE OF LADYSMITH.

garrison. On the 14th Sir R. Buller signalled* that since the enemy's position at Potgieter's Drift was too strong to assault, it would have to be turned, and that this would entail a delay of four or five days. On the 16th, the enemy, obviously uneasy at Buller's progress, kept up fire on the town all day, a mortar at the foot of Surprise Hill joining for the first time in the bombardment. Next day heavy firing was heard from the direction of Springfield, and Buller, signalling in the evening, conveyed the welcome news that he had crossed the Tugela, and hoped "to be knocking at Lancer's Hill in six days . . ." †

<small>Jan. 17th. Buller announces he has crossed the Tugela.</small>

Throughout the next two days the distant firing encouraged whilst it tormented the garrison, and the guns of the defence replied vigorously to the Boer artillery, which was further (on the 18th) reinforced by a 15-pr. gun on Rifleman's Ridge. On the 19th intelligence came of Lord Dundonald's successful affair near Acton Homes. On the 21st Buller signalled that he was "slowly fighting his way up-hill,"‡ and a considerable number of the enemy were observed to leave their laagers round Ladysmith and ride towards the Upper Tugela. Sir G. White thereupon ordered an active fire by his artillery, both to induce them to return, and to detain as many more as possible from reinforcing the commandos on Buller's front. On the 23rd, full rations were restored to the garrison, and the delighted troops were informed that "the relief of Ladysmith may now be held to be within measurable distance."§ That evening Buller signalled that he was about to attack Spion Kop, and when next day the summit of that lofty hill was seen to be wreathed with the smoke of bursting shells, the tension in Ladysmith was extreme. At 10 p.m. a lamp signal announced the capture of the mountain, and Sir G. White replied ‖ with the thanks of himself and the garrison for the efforts of Buller's force.

<small>Jan. 19th. News of the Acton Homes skirmish received by White.

White, seeing some of enemy leaving their laagers round Ladysmith, tries to detain them.

Jan. 23rd. Relief of Ladysmith appears imminent; full rations issued to garrison, but very soon reduced.

Jan. 24th., 10 p.m. Buller announces capture of Spion Kop.</small>

* Heliogram No. 156, of January 16th.
† Heliogram No. 159, January 17th.
‡ Heliogram No. 166, January 21st.
§ Field Force Orders, January 23rd.
‖ Heliogram No. 54 P, January 24th.

The morning of the 25th opened with a brisk cannonade by the Boer artillery on Telegraph Ridge. No further messages came from Buller; but figures were discernible at work upon Spion Kop, many of the Boer laagers behind the kop were seen to be in retreat, and the situation seemed to be assured. Next day was cloudy, and though no heliograms could therefore be expected, doubt began to creep in upon the garrison, which was not allayed when the rations were once more reduced to the half scale. On the 27th the sun, shining again, brought darkness into the lines with a message which it had refused to transmit for two days.

Jan. 27th. Buller's signal of 25th, reporting his withdrawal to Potgieter's, received.

Sir R. Buller heliographed as follows :—

No. 170, January 25th.

"Warren took Spion Kop the 24th, and held it all day, but suffered very heavily. General Woodgate dangerously wounded, 200 killed and 300 badly wounded, and his garrison abandoned it in the night. I am withdrawing to Potgieter's, and mean to have one fair, square try to get into you, but my force is not strong enough, I fear."

White's reply.

Sir G. White replied with the following :—

No. 55 P, January 27th.

"Your No. 170 of 25th only received to-day. We must expect to lose heavily in this campaign, and be prepared to face it. If you try again and fail, Ladysmith is doomed. Is not 7th division available to reinforce you? I could feed the men another month, but not all the horses, and without guns my force could do nothing outside. My medical supplies are nearly out, and the mortality is 8 to 10 daily already. I put it to you and the Government whether I ought not to abandon Ladysmith and try to join you. I could, I think, throw 7,000 men and 36 guns into the fight. If you would commence preparing an attack and draw off the enemy, say, in the afternoon of a day to be settled between us, I would attack that night, and do my best to join you. The attack from here ought to have great effect, but I fear my men are weak, and in some instances morally played out. The fall of Ladysmith would have a terrible effect, especially in India. I am deeply impressed with the gravity of the situation, and trust you will repeat this to the highest authorities. Deserters report Boers lost severely on 24th, and were quite disheartened by your artillery fire. If we stick to them we may effect a junction, but my proposal is a desperate one, and involves abandoning my sick and wounded, Naval guns, and railway rolling-stock. I could not keep the field more than two or three days. I would hold on to the last here if political considerations demand it, or if there is a prospect of sufficient reinforcement to relieve us."

THE DEFENCE OF LADYSMITH.

On January 28th the following messages passed between the Generals, which, as giving the situation as it stood in Natal, and Field-Marshal Lord Roberts' broad and encouraging forecasts of his future movements, are inserted here in full.

Messages between Buller and White.

From General Sir R. Buller to General Sir G. White :—

"No. 173, 28th January.

"We had awful luck on the 25th : I had got two Naval guns and a mountain battery half way up Spion Kop when the troops came down. If we had had the luck out of all the Colonels up there to have found a really good fighting man, we should have been in Ladysmith in four days. As it is, we are no better off, and some regiments have had a severe shake. On the other hand the Boers themselves admit very heavy casualties, and that they are tired out. We have held them in their trenches at a distance of from 1,000 to 1,400 yards for a week, and our artillery fire has been very good. We have lost, say, 1,400. I cannot think their casualties less than 1,000. The question is, can I get within a day's fight of you ? At the present time they have the position at Potgieter's. I think I can certainly take that, but it will leave them on my left in the Acton Homes-Spion Kop position. They may not remain there, but if they do, I doubt if I can get forward to the Roodepoort position, which is, I hear, heavily entrenched. I propose about Wednesday to attack at Potgieter's. If I get through I shall be able to arrange with you for a simultaneous attack, you on Lancer's Hill, and me on Roodepoort, and that I think offers the best chance of success. Believe me, I will leave nothing untried.

"Your No. 55 P. received since above was written. I agree with you that breaking out is only a final desperate resort. I shall try to force this position, and then we shall see. Some old Boers, who were very civil to our doctors on Spion Kop, told them that there were 16,000 of them in front of us, and not more than 4,000 left at Ladysmith. I have no means of knowing how true this is, but deserters say that most of the men are here. Lord Roberts says he cannot reinforce me, but that if you will wait till the end of February, he will by then be in Bloemfontein, and will have relieved Kimberley, which will, he says, reduce the pressure on Ladysmith. I doubt Roberts' forecast coming off, and think I had better play my hand alone, and as soon as I can. What do you think ? "

From General Sir R. Buller to General Sir G. White :—

"No. 174, 28th January.

"Following telegram just received for you from Lord Roberts : ' Please communicate following to White : I beg you will yourself accept and offer all those serving under your command my warmest congratulations on heroic, splendid defence you have made. It is a matter of the deepest regret to me that the relief of Ladysmith should be delayed, but I trust you will be able to hold out later than the date named in your recent message to Buller. I fear your sick and wounded must suffer, but you will realise how important it is that Ladysmith should not fall into the enemy's hands. I am doing all that is possible to hurry on my movements, and shall be greatly disappointed if, by the end of February, I have not been able to carry out such operations as will compel the enemy to materially reduce his strength in Natal.' "

From General Sir G. White to General Sir R. Buller :—

" No. 56 P., 28th January.

" Thanks for your No. 173 of to-day. It is most provoking about losing Spion Kop. I think it would be better if you stick to bombardment, and slow progress by something like sap rather than commit yourself to another definite attack. Information, which I believe correct, says Boers are discouraged by superiority of your armament, and say they cannot stand it. Keep them, therefore, in their trenches and bombard them as heavily as you can. I don't think they will stand it long. I trust to your preventing them from throwing their strength on me. I will hold on six weeks more by sacrificing many of my horses, and that period of bombardment, coupled with Roberts' advance, will make Orange Free State men at all events clear off. I believe your estimate of enemy's numbers here and before you may be correct, but his guns here are protected by wire entanglements and mines. Boers can, however, come here from Potgieter's in 90 minutes. In this lies their great strength; you must not let them leave you and throw their strength on me."

From General Sir G. White to General Sir R. Buller :—

" No. 57 P., 28th January.
"Your No. 174 of to-day. Please communicate following reply to Lord Roberts : 'Many thanks from self and force for message and congratulations. By sacrificing rest of my horses I can hold out for six weeks, keeping my guns efficiently horsed and 1,000 men mounted on moderately efficient horses. I should like to publish your intention to advance via Orange Free State as early as you can permit me to do so. It will encourage my garrison and will be certain to reach and discourage Orange Free State men.' " *

Condition of garrison of Ladysmith.

Once more, therefore, Sir G. White resigned himself to maintaining a passive defence—passive, because his mobility, the only means of offence, was rapidly disappearing. The physical strength of his infantry was dwindling daily. Even the short marches entailed by the relief of posts were already as much as many of the soldiers could manage, and that often only with

* Many of these messages are necessarily quoted or referred to in other chapters in this volume.

THE DEFENCE OF LADYSMITH.

many halts for rest by the way. His sick and wounded had already exceeded to an alarming extent the medical resources at his command. The Intombi Camp, composed of portions of two field hospitals and a stationary hospital, possessed a proper capacity of only 300 beds, with a proportionate staff and supply of drugs and appliances. By the end of January no less than 1,900 sick and wounded, of which 842 were cases of enteric fever, and 472 of dysentery, lay crowded within its tents, inadequately sheltered, hastily tended, and ill fed. The death-rate had risen to eight per diem. Food for the healthy was becoming as scarce as comforts for the sick. There was no more bread, and not much biscuit. Horse meat had for some time replaced beef; the issues of such accessories as tea or coffee had fallen to $\frac{1}{6}$ oz., salt to $\frac{1}{4}$ oz., sugar to $1\frac{1}{2}$ oz., whilst tobacco, almost as necessary to British soldiers as any of these, was not to be had except by payment of from eight shillings to sixteen shillings per ounce. Even the drinking water supply, which had never been good, began to give grave cause for anxiety for reasons somewhat curious. Since the destruction of the main by the enemy at the beginning of the siege, the garrison had been dependent on the dirty water of the Klip river. This had been rendered comparatively innocuous by boiling and the use of Berkefeld filters; but the alum necessary for precipitating impurities in the water before it passed through these filters was early exhausted, the mud clogged the machines, and they became unserviceable. Three improvised condensers, and a system of filtration through sheets sprinkled with wood ashes, were then installed, and until January 25th succeeded in delivering 12,000 gallons of clean water per diem. On that date, however, the coal supply gave out, and these devices became inoperative.

The sick.

Food supplies.

Water supply.

Turning now to the animals, forage was so scarce that on January 30th it became necessary to order the cavalry to turn adrift all their horses, except seventy-five per regiment, to shift for themselves on the withered veld. Over 1,100 horses were therefore driven out to prearranged grazing grounds. But they quickly herded together, and at feeding time was witnessed the distressing spectacle of the mob of starving animals, stampeding

Owing to want of forage, 75 per cent. of cavalry horses turned adrift.

back to their lines, bleeding from the cuts of rocks and barbed wire, and whinnying for their accustomed food. The troopers, thus dismounted, handing in their lances, swords, and carbines, drew rifles and bayonets from the Ordnance Stores, and took post in the defences as infantry, at the rate of some 175 men per regiment. From this time onward, the cavalry soldiers received at intervals the unwelcome order to drive batches of their valued horses to the commissariat to be killed and converted into " chevril," a species of soup. Now, indeed, must be described the most striking feature of the whole defence, and that on which its ultimate success essentially depended. To the officers of the Army Service Corps and Indian Commissariat Department under Colonel E. W. D. Ward, was alone due the extension of time during which the provisions within the enclosed area would keep the troops alive. It was, in fact, entirely by their skill in utilising the meagre resources at their disposal that Sir George White was able to advance the date up to which he calculated he would be able to hold out from the middle of January to 1st April.

<small>Troopers, armed with rifles, are used as infantry.</small>

<small>Horse-flesh as food.</small>

<small>Methods of using horse-flesh and Indian corn.</small>

The methods adopted are, therefore, of extreme interest. Had it not been for their success Ladysmith must have fallen, and it is hardly possible to estimate the influence which the release of the Boers retained around it for active service elsewhere must have had on all points of the theatre of war, and the effect which its fall would have had, not only on Boers and natives, but on the population of India, and even, perhaps, in the Councils of the States of Europe.

Mealie flour, mealie bran and crushed mealies were obtained from two mills worked by employés of the Natal Government Railway under the superintendence of Lieut.-Colonel J. Stoneman, A.S.C., D.A.A.G., aided by Major D. M. Thompson, Assistant Commissary-General of the Indian Commissariat. This made it possible to use as food the Indian corn, otherwise nearly valueless for the purpose. The supply of this had been obtained where wheat grain could not have been secured. From the horses which could no longer be fed (1) chevril, a strong meat soup, issued nightly to the troops; (2) a condensed form of the

THE DEFENCE OF LADYSMITH.

same, used in the hospitals to replace the exhausted meat extracts; (3) a jelly similar to calf's-foot, for the sick and wounded; (4) chevril paste, very like potted meat, and (5) "neat's-foot oil," needed for lubricating the heavy Naval ordnance, were worked up in a factory organised for the purpose. This factory was under Lieut. C. E. I. McNalty, A.S.C., while Captain J. R. Young, R.E., improvised a factory for food in a locomotive shed. A sausage factory was worked by Mr. R. Beresford Turner, a Natal colonist. Whilst the "slaughter" cattle were still sound, many of them were converted into "biltong," as a reserve against a time when disease might break out and make them unfit for food. This was managed by Captain A. Long, A.S.C. All dairy cows were requisitioned, and a system for the supply of milk to the sick and wounded was set up. The feeding of the whole of the civil population was arranged under Lieut.-Colonel Stoneman and Major Thompson. The various methods of filtering the water by Berkefeld filters, condensers, improvised by Mr. Binnie of the Natal Government Railway service, under the direction of Engineer C. C. Sheen, R.N., H.M.S. *Powerful*, and finally the barrack sheeting holding wood ashes, have already been referred to. Only 300 men now remained horsed of all the mounted force in Ladysmith, the batteries alone, and portions of two ammunition columns being kept mobile with 850 horses, i.e., 120 per battery. Thus January closed in scarcity, with hope of relief growing fainter, and means of defence apparently failing, except the unabated courage of the garrison. *Milk for sick and wounded.*

On February 2nd, the enemy began to put into execution a fantastic plan which had been suggested by Krantz, the commander of the German Corps, namely, to dam with bags of earth the Klip river, at a defile beneath the southern foot of Umbulwana. By this they hoped to "put a great part of the Ladysmith plain under water," thereby (*a*) safeguarding the guns on Umbulwana and Lombards Kop from any repetition of the sorties of December 7th and 10th, (*b*) cutting off the defenders of Cæsar's Camp from the remainder of the garrison, (*c*) flooding the British magazines, (*d*) in case of their having to raise the siege, rendering the Klip unfordable by blowing up the dam and *Feb. 2nd. Boers begin to dam the Klip.*

creating an artificial flood.* Hundreds of thousands of mealie bags and much other material had been collected since January 13th. A tramway extension of the railway had been completed to the river bank, and a large number of Kaffirs enlisted for the work. But though from this day the dam rose steadily above the river, to the chagrin of its projectors and the expectant burghers, the river itself rose not an inch behind it, nor caused to the defenders of the town even the most transitory annoyance.

At this time Sir R. Buller was engaged in the operations described elsewhere,† before Vaal Krantz, and the enemy removed the 94-pr. from Telegraph Ridge to oppose him from Doorn Kop.‡ The 6.3-in. Howitzers were, therefore, on February 8th, removed from Ration Post, and replaced behind Wagon Hill Nek. News of Sir R. Buller's intended retirement was conveyed to Sir G. White in the following heliogram :—

Buller informs White he is falling back from Vaal Krantz. His new plan.

"No. 190, February 7th.

"Enemy too strong for me here, and though I could force position, it would be at great loss. .... My plan is to slip back to Chieveley, take Hlangwhane .... and next night try and take Bulwana from the south. Can you think of anything better? I find I cannot take my guns and trains through these mountains. I hope to be at Hlangwhane on Saturday ...." §

To this Sir G. White replied ‖ that though he could offer no suggestions, he could assist Sir R. Buller at Umbulwana. On the 9th the Boers celebrated their success at Vaal Krantz by a searchlight bombardment of the town, from 2 a.m. onward. For the third time the hopes of the straitened garrison were deferred. The prospects were gloomy in the extreme. The condition of the town has already been described, and it grew worse daily. On the 9th the biscuit ration was reduced by one half, and the grain ration discontinued, even for the seventy-five horses per regiment which had been retained. Of the horses out at grass, no less than seventy per diem were being killed for

Rations in Ladysmith greatly cut down.

---

* Report of the surveyors rendered by order of Commandant-General Joubert on January 13th.
† See Chapter XXIII.
‡ See map No. 21 (b).
§ Amended (No. 190 C, February 8th) to Monday.
‖ Message No. 64 P, February 8th.

THE DEFENCE OF LADYSMITH. 581

food. Most alarming of all was the increasing feebleness of the soldiers still in the ranks. Practically unable to march, or even to use their weapons in a long day's fighting, they seemed alike at the mercy of an assault, and unequal to any co-operative movement with the army of the Tugela. Only their spirit continued to burn brightly in their wasting frames, and this, communicating its fervour to the civilians, drew no less than 900 men from the ranks of the railway employés, transport riders, and artisans in the town to answer a call for volunteers made at this time. They were enrolled as a battalion, which took its place in the defences. *[Physical weakness of troops from short commons.]*

On February 13th, the enemy on the Tugela showed signs of uneasiness, breaking up some of his laagers, whose occupants marched east and southwards towards Potgieters and the country about Pieters. One of the actually investing laagers, that at Lancer's Hill, was not to be seen on the morning of this date. It was evident that Buller's march to Chieveley was being closely followed, and in strength, and Sir G. White signalled to Buller his anxiety for news.* That which came in reply on the 14th was welcome indeed, and it came not from Sir Redvers Buller, but from Lord Roberts:— *[Effect of Buller's re-appearance before Colenso on the laagers round Ladysmith.]*

"I have entered the Orange Free State with a large force specially strong in cavalry, artillery, and mounted infantry. Inform your troops of this, and tell them from me I hope result of next few days may lead to pressure on Ladysmith being materially lessened."†

From this day, the clamour of Buller's progress, the thunder of his guns, and even the low murmur of his musketry sounded clearly to the ears of the soldiers in Ladysmith, in whom confidence and apprehension alternated hourly as the firing seemed now to be drawing nearer, now receding, now, most ominously of all, to be lulled altogether. The enemy was in constant movement. On February 15th, a commando with all its transport came north, and laagered at Surprise Hill,‡ another of *[Constant movements of the enemy near Ladysmith.]*

* Heliogram No. 66 P, February 13th.
† Telegram No. 1,780, transmitted through Sir R. Buller.
‡ Heliogram No. 68 P, February 15th.

much the same strength (400–600 with 50 wagons) apparently relieving the first in a position about Onderbrook. Next day there were some signs of retreat, a strong body of the enemy, estimated at 2,000, moving northwards towards the Cundycleugh Pass, firing several farms belonging to Natalians as they passed up the Dewdrop Valley.* Then a message from Buller† announced that he was fighting under Cingolo and Monte Cristo. Throughout the 17th shells were watched bursting along these mountains, and on the 18th, to the delight of the garrison, Buller's attacking lines were seen to roll up the heights and crown the summits amid a great hum of firing. Sir G. White thereupon signalled his congratulations, and again offered to co-operate if Sir R. Buller would inform him of his line of advance,‡ receiving, on the 21st, a reply to the effect that Buller was coming through by Pieters, that he hoped to be in Ladysmith next day, and that the Ladysmith troops could best assist by sallying not south, but north to intercept the retreating enemy.§ But the Boers now seemed to rally, and for a time no further signs of flight were noticeable. The bombardment of Ladysmith, indeed, which had never ceased, actually increased in severity, especially from the batteries on Surprise Hill, which caused numerous casualties to the troops on Observation Hill. As a counterblast, however, the Naval 12-pr., mounted on Cæsar's Camp, opened fire on the crowd of men working at the great dam on the 21st, and scattered them in all directions, thereby drawing upon itself the fire of the 6-in. gun on Umbulwana.

White, on seeing result of Buller's action at Monte Cristo, offers to co-operate. Buller's reply.

Boers bombard Ladysmith with increased activity.

On the 22nd Buller signalled that, though he was making progress, he was meeting with more opposition than he had expected, and would therefore not be able to enter Ladysmith by the date he had anticipated; ‖ and later, that his occupation of Monte Cristo could only be temporary.¶ Throughout the

Buller's heliogram of 22nd.

---

* Heliogram No. 70 P, February 16th.
† Heliogram No. 202, February 16th.
‡ Heliogram No. 72 P, February 19th.
§ Heliogram No. 207, February 21st.
‖ Heliogram No. 208, February 22nd.
¶ Heliogram not dated or numbered.

THE DEFENCE OF LADYSMITH. 583

23rd and 24th, the sound of battle continued to the southward, and Sir G. White for the fourth time moved one of the 4.7-in. Naval guns, which, owing to the scarcity of ammunition,* had not fired for a month, up to Cæsar's Camp, from whence Grobelaar Kloof could be bombarded, sending at the same time one of the Howitzers to Observation Hill, to deal with the Surprise Hill artillery, whose activity continued. On the 26th no news came from Buller, the day being cloudy and unfit for signalling. On the previous day the firing on the Tugela had died away, and the garrison of Ladysmith, ignorant of the cause, which was the observance of an armistice between the belligerents on the Langewacht, regarded the silence with foreboding as an omen of yet another failure. The reduction of rations to a quarter of the scale seemed confirmation of disaster on the Tugela. But on the 26th the distant sound of the firing rose again, continued all day, swelled on the morning of the 27th to an incessant and tremendous uproar, and subsided to silence once more at nightfall. In the evening lamp communication was successfully established with Cingolo Mountain. Buller, however, uncertain as to the extent of his victory at Pieters Hill, and unwilling to arouse hopes which might prove to be too great, signalled no more than that he was " doing well," replying at the same time to White's previous offer, with the information that he was not yet close enough for active co-operation.† The news of Lord Roberts' triumph at Paardeberg, which he transmitted to Ladysmith, was received by a burst of cheering from every camp and sangar around the town. That night a panic, partly started by an attempt by a detachment of the Gloucester regiment to destroy the entanglements around Gun Hill, fell upon the Boers, and a furious discharge of rifles, beginning at midnight, ran completely around the investing lines, and continued for half an hour. It was the farewell from the besieging forces. When dawn broke on the 28th, every road leading northward was rising in dust over retreating artillery, transport, cattle, and

Rations further reduced.

On night of 27th, after Pieters Hill, White again offers co-operation.

At dawn of Feb. 28th the Boers seen to be in general retreat.

* Only 80 rounds remained for these pieces. For ammunition expenditure throughout the siege, see Appendix 15.
† Heliogram No. 211, February 27th.

horsemen, and the soldiers, gazing from their trenches, lamented that their enfeebled limbs condemned them only to watch instead of falling upon the fugitives and destroying them. But the wasted garrison was now almost completely immobile. At noon the following message was heliographed by Sir R. Buller :—*

"Have thoroughly beaten enemy, believe them to be in full retreat. Have sent cavalry to ascertain which way they have gone."

Up on Umbulwana the Boer gunners, having fired one last round from the 94-pr., were now hurriedly removing the weapon by means of a large tripod crane, and though the 4.7-in. guns dropped shell after shell around the emplacement, the enemy succeeded in saving the great piece just before the crane itself was shattered.

<small>6 p.m., Feb. 28th. Dundonald enters the town.</small>

At 5 p.m. the head of Buller's cavalry was descried near Intombi, and an hour later 300 men of Lord Dundonald's Imperial Light Horse, Border Mounted Rifles, and Natal Carbineers pressed through the drift over the Klip, and made their way into the town through a throng of cheering soldiers and civilians, and the siege which had lasted 120 days was raised.†

<small>March 1st. Food and medical stores brought in.</small>

Next morning (March 1st), Sir Redvers Buller entered Ladysmith, and after an interview with Sir G. White, returned temporarily to his army at Nelthorpe. A large convoy of food and medical appliances was driven in during the day, and distributed at once. Sir G. White had at 9 a.m. detailed a flying column to move out and make an effort to intercept the routed enemy. At 11 a.m. Colonel W. G. Knox led out the column to hasten the enemy's retreat.‡ His force was as weak in numbers as it was in physical strength ; for but few soldiers remained in Ladysmith who could march at all, and of those who paraded, none were capable of any but the briefest of operations. Knox moved

<small>Knox's attempt to pursue breaks down from weakness of men.</small>

---

* Not numbered or dated.

† Casualties, February 1st–28th : Killed, 1 man ; wounded, 1 officer, 17 men. For various statistics relating to the siege, see Appendices 2 and 15.

‡ Flying Column Orders, 1st March, 1900. The force consisted of portions of the Liverpool and Devon regiments, and Gordon Highlanders, with two guns 10th Mountain battery, parts of the 53rd and 69th batteries R.F.A., and two squadrons 5th Dragoon Guards.

THE DEFENCE OF LADYSMITH. 585

by Limit and Flag Hills to Pepworth Hill, where he became slightly engaged, the artillery shelling effectively the enemy still lingering by the Modder Spruit. On the 2nd, Sir R. Buller established his Headquarters at the Convent, and the next day he led the army of the relief through the streets between the ranks of the garrison, whose emaciated forms contrasted strangely with the bronzed and healthy soldiers whom they loudly cheered. Completely traversing the town, Buller distributed his corps into various bivouacs about the abandoned Boer positions close to the northward, where they awaited their camp equipment and supplies.

<small>March 3rd, 1900. Buller's army marches into Ladysmith.</small>

END OF VOLUME II.

APPENDICES

APPENDIX I.

CHAPTER VII.

"Bothaville Drift,
"4 p.m., 17th February.

"DEAR LORD ROBERTS,

"I telegraphed to you to-day how we are getting on. Nothing can exceed the marching and spirit of our people. Marching day and night; we made an eleven-mile march this morning. After a rest we start again at 5 o'clock, and again, as your plan has suggested, we march at 3 a.m. to-morrow; we will bivouac at Paardeberg, I hope, this afternoon. So far to-day there was little opposition. The wounded yesterday I under-estimated about a hundred. We are doing all we can to send them to Klip Drift camp. The Boers lost heavily yesterday. Reported 100 killed and 300 wounded. We are doing what we can to help them. You will get the Jacobsdal Hospital people to take them there. I am marching very soon, only awaiting report from the mounted infantry. With regard to my position and Lord Kitchener's, your description of it I perfectly understand. This is not a time to enter into personal matters. Till this phase of the operation is completed I will submit to even humiliation rather than raise any question connected with my command. We are doing well in regard to fresh meat, and this must be replenished soon. I believe a column is coming in. Artillery horses are very soft. I have one Navy gun, a 12-pounder.

"Yours truly,

"T. KELLY-KENNY."

APPENDIX 2.

SHOWING THE CASUALTIES, ETC., IN THE PRINCIPAL ENGAGEMENTS DESCRIBED IN VOLUME II.

THE BATTLE OF PAARDEBERG.
February 18th, 1900.

The total casualties on February 18th, 1900, were approximately 85 officers and 1,185 other ranks, killed, wounded and missing. In the following units the losses were as follows:—

Units.	Officers.			Other ranks.			Total all ranks.
	Killed.	Wounded.	Missing.	Killed.	Wounded.	Missing.	
1st battn. Yorkshire	1	3	—	38	84	3	129
2nd battn. Duke of Cornwall's Light Infantry	3	4	—	25	48	—	80
1st battn. West Riding	1	2	—	22	104	—	129
1st battn. Welsh	1	5	1	18	63	—	88
2nd battn. The Black Watch	1	5	—	16	69	—	91
1st battn. Oxfordshire Light Infantry	3	4	—	6	26	—	39
1st battn. Essex	—	3	1	15	47	3	69
2nd battn. King's Shropshire Light Infantry	—	4	—	8	32	—	44
2nd battn. Seaforth Highlanders	2	5	—	49	95	1	152
1st battn. Argyll and Sutherland Highlanders	1	6	—	19	66	—	92
Royal Canadian Regiment	—	2	—	18	61	—	81

CHAPTERS I. TO XIV.

SUMMARY OF CASUALTIES IN LORD ROBERTS' MAIN ARMY DURING THE MARCH FROM THE MODDER TO BLOEMFONTEIN.

Action.	Killed.		Wounded.		Missing.		Prisoners.		Total.	
	Officers.	Men.	Officers.	Men.	Officers.	Men.	Officers.	Men.	Officers.	Men.
Hannay's Action, 11th February	—	3	—	20	—	21	1	10	1	54
De Kiel's Drift, 13th February	—	—	1	2	—	1	—	—	1	3
Waterval Drift, 15th February	1	1	—	21	1	29	1	3	4	54
Jacobsdal, 14th to 15th February	—	2	2	25	—	3	—	—	2	30
Cavalry division, 13th to 17th February	2	9	13	82	4	85	—	—	19	176
Klip Kraal, 16th to 17th February	—	11	6	99	—	7	—	—	6	117
Paardeberg, 18th to 27th February	14	225	72	1,023	7	60	1	—	94	1,308
Paardeberg, 28th February	—	—	—	1	—	—	—	—	—	1
Osfontein, 1st to 6th March	—	1	1	7	—	1	—	—	1	9
Poplar Grove, 7th March	2	2	3	41	—	1	—	—	5	44
Driefontein, 10th March	4	58	20	342	—	14	—	—	24	414
Total	23	312	119	1,663	12	222	3	13	157	2,210

N.B.—Of these casualties nearly half, viz., 1,020, fell on the 6th division, whose marching-in strength to Bloemfontein was thus reduced to 130 officers and 5,115 men. The Welsh and Buffs had each only 10 officers left for duty; the Yorkshire and Essex but 11. 2,167 horses of the Cavalry division died or otherwise became non-effective during the 30 days, 11th February to 13th March; the chief cause of these heavy casualties in horse-flesh was reported by the Veterinary-surgeon in charge of the division to have been "exhaustion, the result of hard and continuous work on short rations."

MAJOR-GENERAL CLEMENTS' FORCE.

CHAPTER XV.

CASUALTIES FROM 7TH FEBRUARY TO 15TH MARCH, 1900.

Date.	Units.	Officers.				Other ranks.			
		Killed.	Wounded.	Missing.	Total.	Killed.	Wounded.	Missing.	Total.
Various ...	6th (Inniskilling) Dragoons	—	1	—	1	4	5	1	10
12th Feb	Royal Artillery	—	—	—	—	—	1	—	1
12th Feb.	1st battn. Royal Irish regiment	—	—	—	—	—	—	1	1
12th to 15th Feb.	2nd battn. Worcestershire regiment.	2	3	—	5	17	28	18	63
12th to 15th Feb.	2nd battn. Wiltshire regiment	—	3	2	5	15	9	132	156
12th Feb.	South Australian Mounted Rifles	1	—	—	1	1	—	—	1
10th to 12th Feb.	Victorian Mounted Rifles...	1	2	1	4	5	12	11	28
9th to 12th Feb.	West Australian Mounted Infantry	—	—	—	—	1	7	—	8
19th to 25th Feb.	French's Scouts	—	—	—	—	—	2	1	3
24th Feb.	Various	1	2	—	3	1	11	10	22
20th to 26th Feb	New South Wales Mounted Infantry	—	1	—	1	2	1	—	3
22nd Feb.	Prince Alfred's Volunteer Guard	—	—	—	—	—	—	11	11
	Totals... ...	5	12	3	20	46	76	185	307

APPENDIX 2.

Major-General Clements' Column near Rensburg.

CHAPTER XV.

Approximate strength of the force on 6th February, 1900.

Units.	Officers.	Other ranks.	Horses.	Guns. 5-in.	Guns. Howitzers.	Guns. 15-prs.	Guns. 12-prs.	Machine.
Brigade Staff	3	21	3	—	—	—	—	—
6th (Inniskilling) Dragoons (2 squadrons only)	12	160	180	—	—	—	—	—
J. battery R.H.A.	5	179	196	—	—	—	6	—
4th battery R.F.A.	5	174	139	—	—	6	—	—
37th Howitzer battery R.F.A. (one section)	2	64	52	—	2	—	—	—
Ammunition column	3	107	93	—	—	—	—	—
Australian regiment (6 coys.)	20	490	520	—	—	—	—	—
2nd battn. Bedfordshire regiment	22	880	2	—	—	—	—	1
1st battn. Royal Irish regiment	14	700	2	—	—	—	—	1
2nd battn. Worcestershire regiment	23	900	3	—	—	—	—	1
2nd battn. Royal Berkshire regiment (4 coys. only)	12	500	2	—	—	—	—	—
2nd battn. Wiltshire regiment	18	800	3	—	—	—	—	1
Detachment A.S.C.	5	60	20	—	—	—	—	—
Detachment R.A.M.C.	8	100	80	—	—	—	—	—
Total—6th February	152	5,135	1,295	—	2	6	6	4
Reinforcements about 21st Feb.								
2nd battery R.F.A.	5	170	135	—	—	6	—	—
39th battery R.F.A.	5	170	137	—	—	6	—	—
36th company R.G.A. (1 section)	2	75	4	2	—	—	—	—
Mounted Infantry (2 companies)	5	180	190	—	—	—	—	—
2nd contingent Victorian Mounted Rifles	6	175	180	—	—	—	—	—
Uitenhage Rifles (2 coys.) Eastern Province Horse (1 coy.) Prince Alfred's Guard (2 coys.) 1st City Mounted Infantry (1 coy.)	15	500	520	—	—	—	—	—
Total—21st February	190	6,405	2,461	2	2	18	6	4
On Lines of Communication.								
4th battn. Derbyshire regiment	30	630	4	—	—	—	—	—

VOL. II.

GENERALS GATACRE'S AND BRABANT'S FORCES.

CHAPTER XV.

CASUALTIES FROM 7TH FEBRUARY TO 15TH MARCH, 1900.

Date.	Units.	Officers.				Other Ranks.			
		Killed.	Wounded.	Missing.	Total.	Killed.	Wounded.	Missing.	Total.
23rd February	De Montmorency's Scouts	2	—	1	3	4	4	3	11
12th March	1st battn. Royal Scots	—	—	—	—	—	1	—	1
12th March	1st battn. Derbyshire regiment	—	—	—	—	—	2	—	2
GENERAL BRABANT'S COLONIAL DIVISION.									
5th to 11th March	Kaffrarian Rifles	—	1	—	1	2	8	—	10
5th February	The Border Horse	—	—	—	—	2	—	—	2
4th to 5th March	Frontier Mounted Rifles	—	—	—	—	3	7	—	10
7th Feb. to 11th March	Cape Mounted Rifles	—	1	—	1	10	23	1	34
7th Feb. to 11th March	1st regt. Brabant's Horse	—	—	—	—	3	2	5	10
7th Feb. to 11th March	2nd regt. Brabant's Horse	2	—	—	2	6	10	1	17
	Totals...	4	2	1	7	30	57	10	97

APPENDIX 2.

LIEUT.-GENERAL GATACRE'S AND BRIGADIER-GENERAL BRABANT'S FORCES.

LIEUT.-GEN. GATACRE—APPROXIMATE STRENGTH 11TH FEBRUARY, 1900.

Units.	Officers.	Other Ranks.	Horses.	Naval 12-prs.	15-prs.	2.5-in.	Machine.
IIIrd division Staff	11	14	14	—	—	—	—
Brigade division Staff R.A.	4	13	13	—	—	—	—
74th battery R.F.A.	5	162	137	—	6	—	—
77th battery R.F.A.	5	168	135	—	6	—	—
79th battery R.F.A.	5	162	139	—	6	—	—
Ammunition Column	5	128	93	—	—	—	—
Det. Royal Garrison Artillery	1	30	2	2	—	—	—
12th coy. R.E.	8	190	33	—	—	—	—
De Montmorency's Scouts	2	58	75	—	—	—	—
Mounted Infantry	22	639	636	—	—	—	—
1st battn. Royal Scots	24	895	4	—	—	—	1
2nd battn. Northumberland Fusiliers	20	550	4	—	—	—	1
1st battn. Derbyshire regiment	25	889	5	—	—	—	1
2nd battn. Royal Berkshire regiment (4 coys. only)	12	500	2	—	—	—	—
2nd battn. Royal Irish Rifles	12	683	3	—	—	—	1
Det. A.S.C.	5	60	20	—	—	—	—
Det. R.A.M.C.	8	100	80	—	—	—	—
Totals	174	5,246	1,395	2	18	—	4
ON LINES OF COMMUNICATION.							
3rd battn. Durham Light Infantry	28	680	4	—	—	—	—
Brigadier-General Brabant's Colonial Division— Approximate strength 11th February, 1900	—	1,600	—	—	2	4	—

SANNAH'S POST, MARCH 31st, 1900.

CHAPTER XVII.

SUMMARY OF BRITISH CASUALTIES.

	Killed or died of wounds.	Wounded.	Missing or prisoners.
Officers	6	14	17
Other ranks	24	99	411
	30	113	428

The principal losses in individual corps were as follows :—

		Killed or died of wounds.	Wounded.	Missing or prisoners.
10th Hussars	officers	—	—	2
	other ranks.	3	3	22
Royal Horse artillery	officers	1	4	5
	other ranks.	4	29	128
Mounted infantry	officers	3	4	4
	other ranks.	7	39	126
Roberts' Horse	officers	1	4	3
	other ranks.	7	15	49
New Zealand Mounted infantry	officers	—	—	—
	other ranks.	—	—	17
Army Service Corps	officers	—	—	2
	other ranks.	—	—	23

APPENDIX 2. 597

SPION KOP (17TH-24TH JANUARY, 1900).

CHAPTERS XX., XXI., XXII.

DETAILED LIST OF THE PRINCIPAL BRITISH CASUALTIES.

Units.	Officers.			Other ranks.			Remarks.
	Killed.	Wounded.	Missing.	Killed.	Wounded.	Missing.	
2nd battn. Royal West Surrey regiment	2*	3	—	7*	30	—	* 2 officers and 3 men died of wounds.
2nd battn. Royal Lancaster regiment	3	4	1	69*	98	31	* 18 men died of wounds. 21.17 % of strength.
2nd battn. West Yorkshire regiment	1	1	—	5	38	—	
2nd battn. Lancashire Fusiliers	5	13	1	83*	169	137	*19 men died of wounds. 40.72% of strength.
2nd battn. Scottish Rifles	4	6	—	35*	45	1	*10 men died of wounds.
1st. battn. Border regiment (20-26th Jan.)	1	4	—	14*	120	—	* 3 men died of wounds. 16.72% of strength.
1st battn. South Lancashire regiment	2	—	—	6*	33	13	* 3 men died of wounds.
2nd battn. Middlesex regiment	4	4	—	38*	49	7	*2 men died of wounds.
3rd battn. King's Royal Rifles (20-27th Jan.)	3	5	—	21	73	—	
1st battn. York & Lancaster regiment (20-27th Jan.)	—	4	—	13*	92	—	* 6 men died of wounds.
2nd battn. Royal Dublin Fusiliers	—	—	—	3	47	2	
Imperial Light Infantry	2	3	—	30*	28	64	* 2 men died of wounds. 14.6% of strength.
Thorneycroft's mounted infantry	7	5	—	21*	43	10	* 1 man died of wounds. 17.2% of strength.
Other Corps (various)	8	13	—	25	104	20	
Total	42	65	2	370	969	285	
	109			1,624			
			1,733				

VAAL KRANTZ OPERATIONS.

CHAPTER XXIII.

APPROXIMATE STRENGTH OF THE FORCE ENGAGED, 5TH-7TH FEBY., 1900.

Arms.	Officers.	Other Ranks.	Horses: Riding and Draught.	Guns.							Remarks.
				Naval.		Field.			2.5-in. Mtn.	Machine.	
				4.7-in.	12-prs.	5-in.	Howr.	15-prs.			
The Naval Bde.....	25	208	6	2	8	—	—	—	—	—	Includes A. Battery R.H.A.
Natal Army Staff..	34	132	123	—	—	—	—	—	—	—	
Mtd. Troops (2 Bdes.)...........	87	2,666	2,798	—	—	—	—	6	—	3	
Royal Artillery ...	64	1,815	1,535	—	—	2	6	42	6	—	
Royal Engineers...	23	711	376	—	—	—	—	—	—	—	
Infantry (4 Bdes.)*.........	407	14,614	908	—	—	—	—	—	—	16	
Army Service Corps	14	188	436	—	—	—	—	—	—	—	
Royal Army Med. Corps ...	29	385	336	—	—	—	—	—	—	—	
Total... ...	683	20,719	6,518	2	8	2	6	48	6	19	

* NOTE.—(1) The 10th Bde., left to guard Spearman's Camp, not included above. (2) The 6th Bde. (not included above) demonstrated from Chieveley towards Colenso.

SUMMARY OF CASUALTIES AT VAAL KRANTZ, 5TH-7TH FEBY., 1900.

Ranks.	Killed	Wounded.	Missing.	Total.
Officers	2	18	—	20
Other Ranks	25	282	6	313
				333

APPENDIX 2.

RELIEF OF LADYSMITH.

CHAPTERS XXIV. TO XXIX.

SUMMARY OF BRITISH CASUALTIES, 14TH TO 27TH FEBRUARY, 1900.

Dates.	Officers.			Other ranks.		
	Killed.	Wounded.	Missing.	Killed.	Wounded.	Missing.
14th February, 1900	—	1	—	1	19	—
15th ,, ,,	—	1	—	—	—	—
16th ,, ,,	—	—	—	—	—	—
17th ,, ,,	—	1	—	4	31	—
18th ,, ,,	1	7	—	15	179	4
19th ,, ,,	1	2	—	3	24	—
20th ,, ,,	—	2	—	—	9	—
21st ,, ,,	4	5	—	12	97	2
22nd ,, ,,	2	5	—	20	87	—
23rd ,, ,,	4	13	—	55	225	16
24th ,, ,,	7	35	1	108	647	58
25th ,, ,,	—	—	—	2	11	—
26th ,, ,,	—	—	—	1	34	—
27th ,, ,,	8	28	—	59	399	9
Totals	27	100	1	280	1,762	89

THE WAR IN SOUTH AFRICA.

RELIEF OF LADYSMITH.
CHAPTERS XXIV. TO XXIX.

Statement showing the principal Casualties among the Infantry Battalions engaged, 14th to 27th February, 1900.

Unit.	Officers. Strength.	Officers. Casualties.	Officers. Percentage.	Other Ranks. Strength.	Other Ranks. Casualties.	Other Ranks. Percentage.
2nd battalion Royal West Surrey regiment	21	6	28·57	861	124	14·41
2nd ,, ,, Lancaster regiment	14	9	64·28	843	180	21·35
2nd ,, ,, Fusiliers	28	4	14·29	980	80	8·16
2nd ,, Devonshire regiment	24	2	8·33	941	84	8·93
2nd ,, Somersetshire Light Infantry	28	5	17·86	981	87	8·87
2nd ,, West Yorkshire regiment	26	8	30·77	855	107	12·51
2nd ,, Royal Scots Fusiliers	28	9	32·14	980	95	9·69
1st ,, ,, Welsh Fusiliers	28	4	14·29	980	63	6·43
1st ,, ,, Inniskilling Fusiliers	18	13	72·22	877	238	27·14
2nd ,, East Surrey regiment	25	7	28·00	840	141	16·79
1st ,, South Lancashire regiment	19	6	31·58	942	100	10·62
3rd ,, King's Royal Rifle Corps	24	5	20·83	830	84	10·12
1st ,, Durham Light Infantry	17	0	0	770	70	9·09
2nd ,, Royal Irish Fusiliers	28	9	32·14	980	95	9·69
1st ,, Connaught Rangers	26	7	26·92	833	132	15·85
2nd ,, Royal Dublin Fusiliers	19	7	36·84	911	130	14·27
1st ,, Rifle Brigade	19	7	36·84	768	96	12·5

Note.—In many instances the *numbers of strength are approximate only*, consequently, the percentages are also approximate.

DEFENCE OF LADYSMITH.
CHAPTERS XXX. TO XXXII.

Summary of British Casualties from 2nd November, 1899, to 28th February, 1900 (inclusive).

Ranks.	Killed.	Wounded.	Missing (Prisoners).	Died of Wounds.	Died of Disease.	Total Casualties.
Officers	18	70	—	8*	12	100
Other ranks	193	559	10	51*	529	1,291
Total	211	629	10	59*	541	1,391

* Omitted from totals.

DEFENCE OF LADYSMITH.

CHAPTERS XXX. TO XXXII.

Strength of Troops on 2nd November, 1899.

Arms.	Effective Officers	Effective Other Ranks	Sick & Wounded Officers	Sick & Wounded Other Ranks	Horses	Mules	Oxen	Attendants (Natives, &c.)	Guns 4.7-in.	12-pr. Naval	Howitzers	15-pounders	9-pounders	2.5-in.	Maxim-Nordenfeldt	Machine	Remarks
The Naval Brigade	19	261	1	—	2	30	—	4	2	4	—	—	—	—	—	4	
Staff & Miscellaneous	70	200	—	1	150	41	—	13	—	—	—	—	—	—	—	3	
Cavalry	121	2,314	6	21	2,226	764	—	230	—	—	—	—	—	—	—	—	Includes Imperial Light Horse.
Royal Artillery	36	1,308	1	21	1,161	512	202	197	—	—	2	36	—	2	2	7	
Royal Engineers	13	271	10	2	47	101	48	33	—	—	—	—	—	—	—	—	
Infantry	197	7,207	—	103	456	1,876	—	454	—	—	—	—	—	—	—	—	
Army Service Corps	5	96	—	—	6	497	1,429	335	—	—	—	—	—	—	—	—	Includes Supply Park.
Royal Army Medical Corps	33	175	—	—	17	462	22	976	—	—	—	—	—	—	—	—	Includes Indian Field Hospitals.
Army Ordnance Corps	8	62	—	—	6	—	—	119	—	—	—	—	—	—	—	—	Includes Indian Ordnance.
Natal Volrs. & Town Guard	70	1,030	2	81	1,238	256	—	51	—	—	—	—	3	—	—	4	
Total	572	12,924	20	229	5,309	4,539	1,701	2,412	2	4	2	36	3	2	2	18	

NOTE.—In Stores—4 guns.

APPENDIX 3.

CHAPTER X (MAP No. 24).

DETAIL OF ENTRENCHING CARRIED OUT BY THE ROYAL ENGINEERS AND 14TH BRIGADE DURING THE INVESTMENT OF CRONJE'S LAAGER.

Date.	Work done.	Remarks.
21st-22nd.	*Left Bank.* Trench A constructed, and bush cleared to front.	Executed by 9th Co. R.E. in anticipation of arrival of 14th brigade.
22nd-23rd.	*Right Bank.* Trench, 50 yards long, dug at L, with a horn work at top of the river bank; 100 yards of trench dug at M in rear.	Executed by infantry working parties.
	Left Bank. 65 yards trench dug at B (250 yards in advance of A), and B's flank prolonged another 40 yards to river bed.	do.
23rd-24th.	*Right Bank.* Trench M completed and prolonged 35 yards. Trench, 150 yards long, with a return of 25 yards, dug at N.	do.
	Left Bank. Trench B extended 90 yards further.	do.
24th-25th.	*Right Bank.* Flanking work, covering the right of existing trenches, excavated at O. A new trench dug at P. Trench N extended 70 yards.	do.
	Left Bank. Trench 90 yards long constructed at C.	do.
25th-26th.	*Right Bank.* A new trench made at Q; trench P extended; trench N completed.	do.
	Left Bank. An attempt to construct flanking work at D was frustrated by enemy's heavy fire; a new trench was, however, made at E, on a level with Q.	do.
26th-27th.	The C.R.E. had proposed to direct an approach trench from the end of P to knoll R, and there to have constructed a work commanding all the Boer trenches north of the river, but owing to a misunderstanding this task was not attempted. Trenches N and P on the right were improved.	do.

APPENDIX 4.

CHAPTER X.

Prisoners taken at Paardeberg 27.2.00.

O.F.S. Artillery under Major R. Albrecht :—
    Officers—Lieut. E. von Dewitz.
              Lieut. K. von Heister.
              Lieut. O. Augenstein.
        45 men.

Orange Free State.

District.	Commandant.	Field-Cornet.	Men.	
Kroonstad	S. W. Meintjes	F. P. Nel	154	
Ladybrand	R. J. Snyman	T. N. van der Walt	160	
Ficksburg	I. J. de Villiers	N. J. P. Kriek	49	
Winburg	J. P. Jordaan / J. W. Kok	G. H. Prinsloo / J. A. Cronje / C. J. Oosthuizen	163	
Hoopstad	J. J. C. Greyling	T. Nieuwoudt / S. J. A. van Zyl / A. H. Theron	333	
Bloemfontein	J. J. Boshoff	—	148	
Dewetsdorp	N. P. Fourie	—	37	1,327
Jacobsdal	A. Smidt	—	20	
Boshof	—	J. W. Groenewald	99	
Petrusburg	—	—	19	
Fauresmith	—	—	51	
Brandfort	—	—	32	
Senekal	—	—	21	
Ventersburg	—	—	23	
Various	—	—	18	

Guns taken were—3 7.5 c/m. Krupps.
                    1 old pattern Q.F. about 12-pr.
                    1 3.7 c/m. Vickers-Maxim.

PRISONERS TAKEN AT PAARDEBERG 27.2.00—continued.

TRANSVAAL.

District.	Commandant.	Field-Cornet.		Men.	Brought forward, 1,327.
Potchefstroom	F. Roos	W. Lemmer D. Hattingh	300 315	615	
,,	M. J. Wolmarans	Du Plessis P. De Villiers	100 61	161	
Schoenspruit	,,	J. Venter		275	
,,	,,	J. J. Naude		210	2,592
Gatsrand	J. Maartens	A. J. G. Oosthuizen H. W. Alberts Naude	349 37 60	446	
Scandinavians	—	J. De Friis		49	
Bowyk	—	D. J. Terblanche		318	
Bloemhof	J. Woeste	Badenhorst P. Snyman J. Bosman	107 171 240	518	
Grand Total (besides about 150 wounded, etc.)					3,919

The Boer casualties at Paardeberg between the 17th and 27th February, 1900, were (about) 117 killed, 297 wounded. The British losses between the 19th and the 27th February—*i.e.*, exclusive of those sustained at the battle of Paardeberg—were 9 officers and 123 other ranks.

APPENDIX 5.

CHAPTER XI.

Redistribution of the mounted infantry into four brigades on the 6th March. 1900 :—

      1st Brigade.
Lt.-Col. E. A. H. Alderson.
  1st regiment M. I.
  3rd regiment M. I.
  Roberts' Horse.
  New Zealand M. I.
  Rimington's Guides.
  Tasmanian M. I.
  New South Wales Lancers.

      2nd Brigade.
Lt.-Col. P. W. J. Le Gallais.
  6th regiment M. I.
  8th regiment M. I.
  C. I. V. Mounted Infantry.
  Kitchener's Horse.
  Nesbitt's Horse.
  New South Wales M. I.

      3rd Brigade.
Lt.-Col. C. G. Martyr.
  2nd regiment M. I.
  4th regiment M. I.
  Burma M. I.
  Queensland M. I.
  South Australian M. I.
  West Australian M. I.

      4th Brigade.
Col. C. P. Ridley.
  5th regiment M. I.
  7th regiment M. I.
  1st 'City of Grahamstown Volunteers.
  Ceylon M. I.
  1st Canadian M. I.
  2nd Canadian M. I.

This organisation of the mounted infantry was not adhered to in the action of 7th March. The New South Wales Lancers and West Australian mounted infantry did not join till after Poplar Grove.

APPENDIX 6.
CHAPTER XIV.

Return of Troops Marching into Bloemfontein on its Surrender, 13th March, 1900.

Units	Officers.	Other Ranks.	Horses (Riding and Draught).	Guns.							Remarks.
				6 in. Howitzers.	5 in. Howitzers.	4·7 in. Naval.	12 pr. Naval.	15 pr.	12 pr.	Machine.	
Army Headquarter staff	50	65	73	—	—	—	—	—	—	—	
CAVALRY DIVISION.											
Divisional staff	13	40	66	—	—	—	—	—	—	—	
1st Cav. brigade staff	6	14	22	—	—	—	—	—	—	—	
6th Dragoon Guards	20	333	300	—	—	—	—	—	—	—	
2nd Dragoons	19	311	321	—	—	—	—	—	—	—	
6th Dragoons (det.)	4	46	49	—	—	—	—	—	—	—	
14th Hussars (det.)	7	108	74	—	—	—	—	—	—	1	
Q. battery R.H.A.	5	147	154	—	—	—	—	—	6	—	
T. battery R.H.A.	5	148	139	—	—	—	—	—	6	—	
U. battery R.H.A.	5	142	154	—	—	—	—	—	6	—	
Ammunition column	4	72	32	—	—	—	—	—	—	—	
Field hospital	2	20	30	—	—	—	—	—	—	—	
Bearer company	2	15	23	—	—	—	—	—	—	—	
Brigade division staff R.H.A.	4	16	18	—	—	—	—	—	—	—	
1st Australian Horse	5	112	101	—	—	—	—	—	—	—	
New South Wales Lancers	6	89	90	—	—	—	—	—	—	—	
2nd Cav. brigade staff	4	13	20	—	—	—	—	—	—	—	
Household Cavalry	22	291	292	—	—	—	—	—	—	—	
10th Hussars	26	386	414	—	—	—	—	—	—	1	
12th Lancers	20	288	265	—	—	—	—	—	—	—	
Brigade division staff R.H.A.	4	15	21	—	—	—	—	—	—	—	
G. battery R.H.A.	5	147	139	—	—	—	—	—	6	—	
P. battery R.H.A.	5	145	130	—	—	—	—	—	6	—	
Carried forward	243	2,963	2,927	—	—	—	—	—	30	3	

APPENDIX 6.

Units.	Officers.	Other Ranks.	Horses (Riding and Draught).	6 in. Howitzers.	5 in. Howitzers.	4.7 in. Naval.	12 pr. Naval.	15 pr.	12 pr.	Machine.	Remarks.
Brought forward	243	2,963	2,927	—	—	—	—	—	30	3	
Ammunition column	2	43	36	—	—	—	—	—	—	—	
Field hospital	3	16	25	—	—	—	—	—	—	—	
Bearer company	3	46	—	—	—	—	—	—	—	—	
Field hospital (attached)	2	15	19	—	—	—	—	—	—	—	
3rd Cav. brigade staff	4	10	15	—	—	—	—	—	—	—	
9th Lancers	21	397	316	—	—	—	—	—	—	1	
16th Lancers	24	373	368	—	—	—	—	—	—	2	
Brigade divn. staff R.H.A.	4	10	15	—	—	—	—	—	—	—	
O. battery R.H.A.	5	154	142	—	—	—	—	—	—	6	
R. battery R.H.A	7	163	153	—	—	—	—	—	—	6	
Ammunition column	2	94	40	—	—	—	—	—	—	—	
Left ½ No. 11 Field hospital	2	16	2	—	—	—	—	—	—	—	
No. 9 Bearer company	3	42	6	—	—	—	—	—	—	—	
C. coy. Army Service Corps	2	28	13	—	—	—	—	—	—	—	
Field Troop R.E.	7	117	104	—	—	—	—	—	—	—	
B. coy. Transport	3	21	12	—	—	—	—	—	—	—	
C. coy. Transport	2	11	13	—	—	—	—	—	—	—	
D. coy. Transport	1	12	8	—	—	—	—	—	—	—	
L. coy. Transport	3	9	6	—	—	—	—	—	—	—	
S. coy. Transport	2	33	20	—	—	—	—	—	—	—	
Alderson's M. I.											
1st M. I. regiment	21	404	423	—	—	—	—	—	—	3	
3rd M. I. regiment	12	195	228	—	—	—	—	—	—	—	
Carried forward	378	5,172	4,891	—	—	—	—	—	42	9	

RETURN OF TROOPS MARCHING INTO BLOEMFONTEIN ON ITS SURRENDER, 13TH MARCH, 1900—*continued*.

Units	Officers	Other Ranks.	Horses (Riding and Draught).	Guns.							Remarks.
				6 in. Howitzers.	5 in. Howitzers.	4.7 in. Naval.	12 pr. Naval.	15 pr.	12 pr.	Machine.	
Brought forward	378	5,172	4,891	—	—	—	—	—	42	9	
ALDERSON'S M. I.—*continued*.											
Roberts' Horse	35	353	387	—	—	—	—	—	—	—	
New Zealand Mtd. Rifles	5	60	72	—	—	—	—	—	—	—	
Rimington's Guides	7	102	110	—	—	—	—	—	—	—	
LE GALLAIS' M. I.											
Staff	3	10	13	—	—	—	—	—	—	—	
6th M. I. regiment	13	391	330	—	—	—	—	—	—	—	
8th M. I. regiment	15	311	254	—	—	—	—	—	—	—	
City Imperial Volunteers	11	185	145	—	—	—	—	—	—	—	
Kitchener's Horse	26	402	270	—	—	—	—	—	—	2	
Nesbitt's Horse	8	119	136	—	—	—	—	—	—	—	
New South Wales M. I.	22	408	345	—	—	—	—	—	—	—	
H. Coy. Transport A.S.C.	2	23	317	—	—	—	—	—	—	—	
Supply det. A.S.C.	1	2	1	—	—	—	—	—	—	—	
MARTYR'S M.I.											
Staff	3	—	6	—	—	—	—	—	—	—	
2nd M. I. regiment	18	483	489	—	—	—	—	—	—	—	
4th M. I. regiment	15	327	251	—	—	—	—	—	—	—	
Burma M. I.	17	292	332	—	—	—	—	—	—	—	
1st Queensland M. I.	8	184	211	—	—	—	—	—	—	—	
2nd Queensland M. I.	8	128	158	—	—	—	—	—	—	—	
Carried forward	595	8,952	8,718	—	—	—	—	—	42	11	

APPENDIX 6.

Units	Officers	Other Ranks	Horses (Riding and Draught)	Guns 6 in. Howitzers	5 in. Howitzers	4.7 in. Naval	12 pr. Naval	15 pr.	12 pr.	Machine	Remarks
Brought forward	595	8,952	8,718	—	—	—	—	—	42	11	
RIDLEY'S M. I.											
Staff	3	1	9	—	—	—	—	—	—	—	
5th M. I. regiment	12	287	276	—	—	—	—	—	—	—	
7th M. I. regiment	17	337	262	—	—	—	—	—	—	—	
1st City Grahamstown Vols.	12	245	231	—	—	—	—	—	—	—	
Ceylon M. I.	6	86	109	—	—	—	—	—	—	—	
F. Coy. Transport A.S.C.	2	31	20	—	—	—	—	—	—	—	
Supply det. A.S.C.	1	8	—	—	—	—	—	—	—	—	
Royal Naval Brigade	33	393	10	—	—	4	3	—	—	—	
Comdr.-in-Chief's Body-Guard	1	43	53	—	—	—	—	—	—	—	
Staff, Howitzers	6	15	14	—	—	—	—	—	—	—	
15 coy. S.D. R.G.A.	5	138	7	4	—	—	—	—	—	—	
Ox Ammunition Reserve	1	2	2	—	—	—	—	—	—	—	
9th Field coy. R.E.	7	161	14	—	—	—	—	—	—	—	
1st Telegraph division R.E.	4	112	34	—	—	—	—	—	—	—	
GUARDS BRIGADE.											
Brigade staff	4	26	11	—	—	—	—	—	—	—	
3rd bn. Grenadier Guards	26	899	8	—	—	—	—	—	—	1	
1st bn. Coldstream Guards	25	927	8	—	—	—	—	—	—	1	
2nd bn. Coldstream Guards	20	858	8	—	—	—	—	—	—	1	
1st bn. Scots Guards	15	516	6	—	—	—	—	—	—	1	
Carried forward	795	14,037	9,800	4	—	4	3	—	42	15	

VOL. II.

RETURN OF TROOPS MARCHING INTO BLOEMFONTEIN ON ITS SURRENDER, 13TH MARCH, 1900—continued.

Units.	Officers.	Other Ranks.	Horses (Riding and Draught).	Guns. 6 in. Howitzers.	5 in. Howitzers.	4.7 in. Naval.	12 pr. Naval.	15 pr.	12 pr.	Machine.	Remarks.
Brought forward	795	14,037	9,800	4	—	4	3	—	42	15	
GUARDS BRIGADE—continued.											
Field hospital	4	33	7	—	—	—	—	—	—	—	
Bearer company	2	52	4	—	—	—	—	—	—	—	
Supply det. A.S.C.	1	16	2	—	—	—	—	—	—	—	
11th coy. A.S.C.	2	19	19	—	—	—	—	—	—	—	
VITH DIVISION.											
Divisional staff	15	53	54	—	—	—	—	—	—	—	
Brigade divn. Staff R.F.A.	3	2	5	—	—	—	—	—	—	—	
76th battery R.F.A.	5	46	88	—	—	—	—	6	—	—	
81st battery R.F.A.	4	79	73	—	—	—	—	6	—	—	
82nd battery R.F.A.	5	99	94	—	—	—	—	6	—	—	
65th Howitzer battery	5	169	162	—	6	—	—	—	—	—	
R.E. staff	2	5	4	—	—	—	—	—	—	—	
38th coy. R.E.	6	131	19	—	—	—	—	—	—	—	
13th Brigade staff	3	19	7	—	—	—	—	—	—	—	
2nd bn. East Kent regt.	10	560	8	—	—	—	—	—	—	—	
2nd bn. Gloucester regt.	22	563	8	—	—	—	—	—	—	—	
1st bn. West Riding regt.	18	593	5	—	—	—	—	—	—	—	
1st bn. Oxfordshire L.I.	15	424	7	—	—	—	—	—	—	—	
13th Bearer company	2	39	4	—	—	—	—	—	—	—	
Supply det. A.S.C.	1	15	2	—	—	—	—	—	—	—	
18th Brigade staff	4	37	7	—	—	—	—	—	—	1	
2nd bn. R. Warwickshire regt.	20	834	7	—	—	—	—	—	—	—	
1st hn. Yorkshire regt.	12	705	4	—	—	—	—	—	—	—	
1st bn. Welsh regt.	11	654	7	—	—	—	—	—	—	—	
Carried forward	967	19,184	10,397	4	6	4	3	18	42	19	Arrived on 17th.

APPENDIX 6.

Units.	Officers.	Other Ranks.	Horses (Riding and Draught).	Guns. 6 in. Howitzers.	5 in. Howitzers.	4.7 in. Naval.	12 pr. Naval.	15 pr.	12 pr.	Machine.	Remarks.
Brought forward	967	19,184	10,397	4	6	4	3	18	42	19	
1st bn. Essex regiment	12	738	4							1	
18th Field hospital	4	32	1								
18th Bearer company	2	24	—								
VIITH DIVISION.											
Divisional staff	11	77	43								
Brigade divn. staff R.F.A.	4	8	18								
18th battery R.F.A.	5	134	113					6			
62nd battery R.F.A.	5	128	113					6			
75th battery R.F.A.	5	141	122					6			
No. 1 Ammn. column	3	102	78								
A Sec. 1-pr. Maxims	2	27	29							3	
26th coy. R.E.	7	126	18								
Divnl. Supply det. A.S.C.	1	30	21								
14th Brigade staff	3	15	7							1	
2nd bn. Norfolk regiment	16	763	5							1	
2nd bn. Lincoln regiment	19	752	6							1	
1st bn. K.O.S. Borderers	22	803	5							1	
2nd bn. Hampshire regiment	18	578	5								
Field hospital	5	31	33								
Bearer company	3	54	4								
Supply det. A.S.C.	1	7	1								
Transport coy. A.S.C.	2	25	14								
15th Brigade staff	4	19	8								
Carried forward	1,121	23,798	11,045	4	6	4	3	36	42	27	

RETURN OF TROOPS MARCHING INTO BLOEMFONTEIN ON ITS SURRENDER, 13TH MARCH, 1900—continued.

Units.	Officers.	Other Ranks.	Horses (Riding and Draught).	Guns.							Remarks.
				6 in. Howitzers.	5 in. Howitzers.	4.7 in. Naval.	12 pr. Naval.	15 pr.	12 pr.	Machine.	
Brought forward	1,121	23,798	11,045	4	6	4	3	36	42	27	
VIIth Division—continued.											
2nd bn. Cheshire regiment	22	688	6							1	
2nd bn. S. Wales Borderers	22	795	5							1	
1st bn. E. Lancashire regiment	19	695	6							1	
2nd bn. N. Staffordshire regiment	19	737	8							1	
Bearer company	3	48	4								
Field hospital	4	31	5								
Supply det. A.S.C.	1	9	11								
Transport coy. A.S.C.	2	9	8								
IXth Division.											
Divisional staff	10	50	32								
Brigade divn. staff R.F.A.	3	13	13								
83rd battery R.F.A.	5	156	127					6			
84th battery R.F.A.	5	158	131					6			
85th battery R.F.A.	5	167	131					6			
Ammn. column	6	120	88								
7th Field coy. R.E.	6	163	35								
Highland brigade staff	4	43	10								
2nd bn. Royal Highlanders	13	513	7							1	
2nd bn. Seaforth Highlanders	12	538	7							1	
1st bn. A. and S. Highlanders	14	637	7								
Field hospital	4	27	5								
Bearer company	2	45	3								
19th Brigade staff	3	26	8								
Carried forward	1,305	29,466	11,702	4	6	4	3	54	42	34	

APPENDIX 6.

Units.	Officers.	Other Ranks.	Horses (Riding and Draught).	Guns.							Remarks.
				6 in. Howitzers.	5 in. Howitzers.	4.7 in. Naval.	12 pr. Naval.	15 pr.	12 pr.	Machine.	
Brought forward	1,305	29,466	11,702	4	6	4	3	54	42	34	
2nd bn. Duke of Cornwall's L.I.	15	654	5							1	
2nd bn. Shropshire Light Infantry	19	739	7							1	
1st bn. Gordon Highlanders	19	738	9							2	
Royal Canadian regiment	30	745	18								
Y Transport coy. A.S.C.	1	33	1								
Supply det. A.S.C.		16									
Bearer company	4	65	6								
Field hospital	4	33	5								
Supply Park A.S.C.											
No. 1 section	1	5	1								
No. 22 unit	2	6	2								
No. 25 ,,	2	8	2								
No. 29 ,,		3									
No. 5 company		2									
No. 21 ,,		3									
No. 29 ,,		1									
No. 34 ,,											
1st Balloon section R.E.	2	27	10								
Grand Total	1,405	32,549	11,773	4	6	4	3	54	42	39	

Government House,
Bloemfontein.

W. F. Kelly, Major-General,
D. A. G. South African Field Force.

APPENDIX 7.

CHAPTER XIX.

REASONS FOR THE REMOVAL OF LIEUT.-GENERAL GATACRE.

S. A. Desp. In a memorandum to the Secretary of State for War, dated 16th April, 1900, Lord Roberts set forth his reasons for the step he had taken in removing Lieut.-General Sir William Gatacre from the command of the IIIrd division.

With reference to the defeat at Stormberg, Lord Roberts explained the view he had taken as follows :

" In my opinion, Lieut.-General Gatacre on this occasion showed a want of care, judgment, and even of ordinary military precautions, which rendered it impossible for me, in justice to those who might be called on to serve under him, to employ him in any position where serious fighting might be looked for. I was, however, most anxious to avoid, if it were possible, the infliction on him of the slur which necessarily attaches itself to a General who is removed from his command while on active service. I, therefore, refused to supersede him at the time when I assumed the chief command in South Africa, believing that I might safely employ him on the lines of communication or in any position not actually in the front.

" On 28th March I telegraphed to Lieut.-General Gatacre as follows :—

" 'No. C. 696. If you have enough troops at your disposal I should like you to occupy Dewetsdorp. It would make the road to Maseru safe, and prevent the enemy from using the telegraph line to the south. *Let me know what you can do to this end.*'

" To the question italicised above, Lieut.-General Gatacre gave me no reply. In answer to my telegram he sent a list of movements then in progress in the southern part of the Orange Free State, east of the railway, which included a movement of two companies Royal Irish Rifles towards Dewetsdorp, where they were due to arrive on Sunday (1st April).

APPENDIX 7. 615

"On 30th March he wired that two companies mounted infantry and three companies Royal Irish Rifles were moving on Dewetsdorp.

"On 31st March I wired to Lieut.-General Gatacre that I considered Dewetsdorp too far advanced for security, and on the 1st April he informed me that he had sent a despatch rider to Dewetsdorp with orders for the troops there to fall back on Reddersburg.

"The result of these movements was that in falling back these companies were surrounded east of Reddersburg and, being without food or water, were eventually compelled to surrender. For this result I must hold Lieut.-General Gatacre responsible. Dewetsdorp is some forty-five miles by road east of the railway on which the mass of the troops were stationed, and is therefore a position in which a small force is much isolated and might be in great danger if attacked. It appears, however, that Lieut.-General Gatacre ordered two companies mounted infantry and three companies Royal Irish Rifles to Dewetsdorp on his own responsibility, and failed to give me the information I asked for as to what he could do with the troops at his disposal as regards holding the place, which, if supplied, would have enabled me to judge of its adequacy or otherwise, and therefore whether Dewetsdorp should or should not be occupied. The small force he actually sent was entirely incapable of holding its own so far from sufficient support, and being partly composed of infantry was unable to move rapidly when a retirement became necessary. I consider that in thus isolating a small detachment, Lieut.-General Gatacre has shown a grave want of judgment which must necessarily shake the confidence of those under his orders and have a bad effect on the *moral* of his troops. I am therefore unable to retain him in command of his division and have given orders for his relief and return to England.

"ROBERTS, Field-Marshal."

"Bloemfontein,
"April 16th, 1900."

APPENDIX 8.

CHAPTER XX.

THE SPION KOP CAMPAIGN.

APPENDIX 8 (A).

GENERAL SIR. R. BULLER'S ORDERS OF THE 8TH JANUARY, 1900.

FIELD ORDERS.

Frere Camp,
8th January, 1900.

1. A memorandum giving the organization of the Field Army is issued herewith.

2. The following moves will take place under the orders of Lieut.-General Sir C. F. Clery, K.C.B., on the night of the 9th-10th January, 1900 :—

IIND DIVISION AND ATTACHED TROOPS.

(a) Major-General Hildyard's Column :—
    Mounted Brigade : 400 of all ranks (including one squadron 13th Hussars).
    2nd Infantry Brigade.
    Divisional Troops : a battery, Royal Field Artillery.
    Corps Troops : two Naval 12-pr. guns.

To move from Chieveley by the south of Doorn Kop to the camp already selected in the vicinity of Pretorius Farm.

(b) Major-General Hart's Column :—
    Mounted Brigade : 400 of all ranks.
    5th Infantry Brigade.
    73rd Battery, Royal Field Artillery.
    17th Field Company, Royal Engineers.
    Corps Troops : six Naval 12-pr. guns.

To move from Frere by the Frere-Springfield road to the camp selected south of Pretorius Farm.

APPENDIX 8.

(c) Headquarters and Divisional Troops, IInd Division :—

Mounted Brigade : headquarters and main body supply column (from Frere), Medical unit.

Divisional Troops : a battery, Royal Field Artillery, ammunition column, supply column (from Frere), field hospital (from Frere).

Corps Troops : two squadrons 13th Hussars, two guns 66th Battery, Royal Field Artillery, two Naval 4.7-in. guns, supply column (from Frere).

To move from Chieveley (except where otherwise mentioned) by the Frere-Springfield road to the camp selected south of Pretorius Farm, except that one squadron 13th Hussars for the Vth Division, and two guns 66th Battery, Royal Field Artillery, will be left at Frere.

3. Vth Division and attached troops.

The following troops will move on the evening of the 10th January, 1900, from Frere to Springfield, under the orders of Lieut.-General Sir C. Warren, G.C.M.G., K.C.B. :—

Vth Division.

4th Infantry Brigade.
11th Infantry Brigade.
Divisional Troops.

Corps Troops :—
   10th Brigade.

Artillery :—
   61st Battery, Royal Field Artillery (Howitzer).
   78th Battery, Royal Field Artillery.
   Ammunition Column.

Engineers :—
   Pontoon Troop.
   Balloon Section.
   Section Telegraph Division.

Supply Park.

4. Ammunition.

(a) Ammunition will be taken as follows :—

15-pr. :—
   With batteries .... 150 rounds per gun
   With ammunition column ..... 150 ,, ,,
   Total 300

5-in. Howitzer :—
   With batteries .... 88 rounds per gun
   With ammunition column ..... 130 ,, ,,
   Total 218

4.7-in. Naval gun :—
   With gun .... 150 rounds per gun
   With ammunition column ...... 100 ,, ,,
   Total 250

12-pr. Naval gun :—
　　With gun.................... 250 rounds per gun
　　With ammunition column...... 50　　,,　　,,
　　　　　　　　　　　　　　　　　───
　　　　Total.................... 300

Small arm ammunition, according to war establishment.

(b) A small ammunition park will be held in readiness at Frere, with 1,260 rounds of 15-pr. ammunition, 300 rounds of 5-in. Howitzer, and 125,000 rounds of small-arm ammunition.

The park will be organized under an officer and 20 non-commissioned officers and men, Royal Artillery, to be detailed from the general depôt by the General of Communications.

5. Medical arrangements.

(a) The Corps Troops will avail themselves of the nearest Divisional field hospital.

(b) No. 4 Stationary Hospital will accompany the force to receive such sick and wounded from field hospitals as may be directed by the Principal Medical Officer of the force.

(c) The Volunteer Ambulance Corps (European), divided into four companies, will be attached to Brigade field hospitals of the IInd and Vth Divisions.

The Officer Commanding the corps will accompany and take his instructions from the Principal Medical Officer.

(d) 100 men of the Ambulance Corps (native) will accompany No. 4 Stationary Hospital, the remainder will stay at Estcourt until further orders.

6. Supplies.—The arrangements for supplies will be in accordance with a memorandum, which is issued herewith to General Officers Commanding Divisions and Corps Troops.

7. Transport Equipment.—The following will be carried in regimental transport wagons :—

Tents, one blanket for every two men, one waterproof sheet per man, 50 rounds of ammunition per infantry soldier, 3 days' rations less 1 day's meat, 750 lbs. wood to make up 3 days' supply, 3 days' grain ration, officers' baggage, and such regimental stores as may be considered necessary, not to exceed 3,000 lbs.

　　　　　　　　　　　By order,
　　　　　　　　　　　　A. WYNNE, Colonel,
　　　　　　　　　　　　　　　　Chief of Staff.

───

ARRANGEMENTS FOR SUPPLIES.

The supply columns will carry 4 days' and the supply park 4 days'. Springfield will be filled up with reserve rations and forage as follows :—

1st day.—Supply park to Pretorius Farm, off-loads, and returns to Frere. The force at Pretorius Farm will be rationed by regimental wagons drawing daily from Frere.

2nd day.—All supply columns to Springfield and off-load. Supply park to Pretorius Farm, off-loads, and returns to Frere.

APPENDIX 8.

3rd day.—All supply columns from Springfield to Pretorius load and return to Springfield. Supply park from Frere to Pretorius and remain loaded ready to march next day.

4th day.—Supply columns from Springfield to Pretorius load and return to Springfield. The supply park from Pretorius to Springfield.

The troops at Springfield will draw on their regimental wagons, replenishing from the depot there.

The force at Pretorius will join at Springfield with full regimental wagons.

By order,

A. WYNNE, Colonel,
Chief of Staff.

APPENDIX 8 (B).

GENERAL SIR R. BULLER'S ORDERS OF THE 9TH JANUARY, 1900.

Frere Camp,
9th January, 1900.

1. The General proposes to effect the passage of the River Tugela in the neighbourhood of Potgieters Drift, with a view to the relief of Ladysmith.

2. Forces (already detailed) will be left at Chieveley and Frere to hold these points, while the remainder of the Army is operating on the enemy's right flank.

3. Springfield will be seized and occupied, and the march of the main body and supplies to that point will be covered by a force encamped about Pretorius Farm.

4. With reference to Field Orders, dated 8th instant, paragraph 2 (a), the primary duty of Major-General Hildyard's column is to protect the march of the troops from Frere to Springfield during the formation of a supply depôt at Springfield but he will also operate so as to induce the enemy to believe that our intention is to cross the River Tugela at Porrit's Drift.

5. As stated in paragraph 2 (b) and (c) of the Field Order above quoted, the remainder of Lieut.-General Clery's force will encamp south of Pretorius Farm. Major-General Hart will, under General Clery's orders, assist in every way the supply columns as they pass his camp, and he will also be prepared to support Major-General Hildyard, if necessary.

6. On the afternoon of the 10th instant, General Clery will send a sufficient force from the mounted brigade with artillery, to reconnoitre, and, if possible, occupy Springfield.

7. The force under General Warren's command (Field Order, dated 8th instant, paragraph 3) will reach Springfield on the morning of the 11th instant, in support of the mounted troops referred to in paragraph 6 of this order.

8. It is anticipated that the supplies intended to be put into Springfield will be completed on the 13th instant, when General Clery's force will march to Springfield.

9. The Commanding Royal Engineer will arrange for a field telegraph between Frere and Springfield, with an office in General Clery's Camp, south of Pretorius Farm.

10. The General Officer Commanding, 10th brigade, will provide a party of signallers under the Brigade Signalling Officer, with Field Army Headquarters.

11. The General Commanding-in-Chief will proceed to Springfield on the 11th instant.

By order,

A. WYNNE, Colonel,
Chief of Staff.

APPENDIX 8 (c).

NATAL ARMY ORGANIZATION, 8TH JANUARY, 1900.

MOUNTED BRIGADE—COMMANDING, COLONEL THE EARL OF DUNDONALD.

1st Royal Dragoons.
Mounted Infantry: 2nd K. R. Rifles, 1 company.
      "   "   2nd R. Dublin Fusiliers, 1 section.
Natal Police, 1 squadron.
Natal Carbineers, 1 squadron.
Imperial Light Horse, 1 squadron.
Bethune's Mounted Infantry.
Thorneycroft's Mounted Infantry.
South African Light Horse.
Supply Column (No. 6 company, A.S.C.).
Medical Unit.

IIND DIVISION.—COMMANDING, LT.-GENERAL SIR C. F. CLERY.

2nd Brigade, Maj.-Gen. H. J. T. Hildyard.

2nd R. West Surrey Regiment.
2nd Devonshire Regiment.
2nd West Yorkshire Regiment.
2nd East Surrey Regiment.
Supply Column (No. 16 Co. A.S.C.).
Bearer Co. (No. 2 Co. R.A.M.C.).
Field Hosp. (Depot Cos. R.A.M.C.).

5th Brigade, Maj.-Gen. A. F. Hart.

1st R. Inniskilling Fusiliers.
1st Border Regiment.
1st Connaught Rangers.
2nd R. Dublin Fusiliers.
Supply Column (No. 4 Co. A.S.C.).
Bearer Company (No. 16 Co. R.A.M.C.).
Field Hosp. (No. 10 Co. R.A.M.C.).

Divisional Troops.

Squadron, 13th Hussars.
Brigade Division Staff, R.F.A.
7th Battery, R.F.A.
64th Battery, R.F.A.
73rd Battery, R.F.A.
Ammunition Column.
Regimental Staff and 17th Co. R.E.
Supply Column (1 Auxiliary Co. A.S.C.).
Field Hosp. (No. 5 Co. R.A.M.C.).

APPENDIX 8. 621

VTH DIVISION.—COMMANDING, LT.-GEN. SIR CHARLES WARREN.

4th Brigade, Maj.-Gen. Hon. N. G. Lyttelton.

2nd Scottish Rifles.
3rd K. R. Rifle Corps.
1st Durham Light Infantry.
1st Rifle Brigade.
Supply Column (No. 14 Co. A.S.C.).
Bearer Co. (No. 14 Co. R.A.M.C.).
Field Hosp. (No. 14 Co. R.A.M.C.).

11th Brigade, Maj.-Gen. E. R. P. Woodgate.

2nd R. Lancaster Regt.
2nd Lancashire Fusiliers.
1st South Lancashire Regt.
1st York and Lancaster Regt.
Supply Column (No. 25 Co. A.S.C.).
Bearer Co. (No. 6 Co. R.A.M.C.).
Field Hosp. (Depôt Cos. R.A.M.C.).

Divisional Troops.

Squadron, 13th Hussars.
Brigade Division Staff, R.F.A.
19th Battery, R.F.A.
28th Battery, R.F.A.
63rd Battery, R.F.A.
Ammunition Column.
Regimental Staff and 37th Co. R.E.
Supply Column (No. 27 Co. A.S.C.).
Field Hosp. (No. 16 Co. R.A.M.C.).

CORPS TROOPS.

Cavalry.

Headquarters and squadron, 13th Hussars.

Artillery.

61st Howitzer Battery, R.F.A.
78th Battery, R.F.A.
Two Naval 4.7-in. Guns.
Eight Naval 12-pr. Guns.
Ammunition Column.

Engineers.

Pontoon Troop, R.E.
Balloon Section, R.E.
Section Telegraph Div. R.E.

Army Service Corps.

Supply Col. (No. 2. Aux. Co. A.S.C.).
Supply Park.

10th Brigade, Maj.-Gen. J. T. Coke.

2nd Somerset Lt. Infy.
2nd Dorsetshire Regt.
2nd Middlesex Regt.
Supply Column (No. 32 Co. A.S.C.).
Bearer Co. (No. 10 Co. R.A.M.C.).
Field Hosp. (No. 11 Co. R.A.M.C.).
[Imperial Lt. Infantry joined later.]

Garrison at Chieveley, Maj.-Gen. G. Barton.

Mounted Brigade, 200 all ranks.
Four Naval 12-pr. Guns.
6th Brigade :—2nd Royal Fusiliers.
    2nd R. Scots Fusiliers (less half battalion).
    1st R. Welsh Fusiliers.
    2nd R. Irish Fusiliers.
    Supply Column (No. 24 Co. A.S.C.).
    Bearer Co. (No. 17 Co. R.A.M.C.).
    Field Hosp. (No. 11 Co. R.A.M.C.).

Garrison at Frere, Lt.-Col. Blagrove, 13th Hussars.
Mounted Brigade, 400 all ranks (including M. I. Cos. 4th and 5th Brigades).
Two Guns, 66th Battery, R.F.A.
Two Naval 12-pr. Guns.
Half Battalion, R. Scots Fusiliers.
Detachment, K. R. Rifle Corps.
Detachment, Rifle Brigade.

APPENDIX 8 (D).

ORDERS ISSUED TO COLONEL THE EARL OF DUNDONALD ON THE 10TH JANUARY, 1900.

O. C. Mounted Brigade.

You will move forward this afternoon with the force under your command, accompanied by one battery of artillery.

You will leave General Clery's camp (Pretorius) at about 2.30 p.m. to reconnoitre, and, if possible, occupy Springfield.

If you can occupy Springfield, you will hold it until the arrival of General Warren's column to-morrow morning.

You will keep up communication with General Clery and report your movements and dispositions.

By order,

B. HAMILTON, Colonel.

Chieveley, 10th January, 1900, 8.30 a.m.

APPENDIX 8 (E).

THE CONCENTRATION OF SUPPLIES AT SPRINGFIELD, JANUARY, 1900.

19th January, 1900.

ASSISTANT ADJUTANT-GENERAL,

The transport used to convey the 16 days' supply from Frere to Springfield Bridge was as follows :—

Supply park	164	wagons
Supply column	160	,,
Total	324	,,

Each did two treks—648 wagons, and carried :—
464,000 rations for men.
64,000 rations for horses.
56,000 rations for mules.
55,000 lbs. of hay.

APPENDIX 8.

NOTE ON THE FIRST TRIP.

Twenty supply park wagons were used to take on supplies to Cavalry Brigade at Spearman's, and were replaced on second trip by a similar number of regimental transport wagons from IInd Division. A further 17 regimental wagons brought as far as Pretorius Camp, from Frere, 11,700 lbs. hay, 28,000 rations of biscuit and groceries, and eight Frere local transport wagons brought out additional rum, lime juice, disinfectants, bran and hay; total weight, 44,000 lbs.

SUMMARY.

FRERE TO SPRINGFIELD BRIDGE.

No. of wagons.	Rations, men.	Rations, horses and mules.	Rations, hay, at 5 lb.	Weight in lb.
648 (a)	464,000	120,000	11,000	3,575,000 (b)

(a.) Average weight, 5,517 lb. gross.
(b.) Men's rations calculated at 5 lb., including cases, and ¼ lb. wood per man carried in addition.

FRERE TO PRETORIUS.

17 (c)	28,000 (d)	—	340	99,700 (e)

(c.) Average weight, 5,865 lb.
(d.) Less meat.
(e.) Men's rations, less meat, calculated at 3½ lb.

FRERE TO SPEARMAN'S.

8 (f.)		Lime juice, rum, disinfectants, bran, hay,		44,000
673	492,000	120,000	11,340	3,718,700

(f.) Average weight 5,500 lb.

The weight loaded on the wagons was adjusted in accordance with the distance to be covered.

H. G. MORGAN, Major,
Director of Stores.

APPENDIX 8 (F).

GENERAL SIR REDVERS BULLER'S SPECIAL ORDER TO THE TROOPS.

FIELD ORDER.

Springfield,
12th January, 1900.

The Field Force is now advancing to the relief of Ladysmith, where surrounded by superior forces our comrades have gallantly defended themselves for the last ten weeks.

The General Commanding knows that everyone in the Force feels as he does, we must be successful.

We shall be shortly opposed by a clever, unscrupulous enemy; let no man allow himself to be deceived by them. If a white flag is displayed, it means nothing unless the Force displaying it halt, throw down their arms, and throw up their hands at the same time.

If they get a chance the enemy will try and mislead us by false words of command and false bugle sounds; everyone must guard against being deceived by such conduct.

Above all, if any are ever surprised by a sudden volley at close quarters, let there be no hesitation; do not turn from it, but rush at it. That is the road to victory and safety. A retreat is fatal; the one thing the enemy cannot stand is our being at close quarters with them.

We are fighting for the health and safety of our comrades; we are fighting in defence of our flag against an enemy, who has forced war upon us for the worst and lowest motives by treachery, conspiracy and deceit. Let us bear ourselves as our cause deserves.

By order,

A. WYNNE, Colonel,
Chief of Staff.

APPENDIX 8 (G).

TELEGRAM FROM GENERAL SIR R. BULLER TO THE SECRETARY OF STATE FOR WAR, 13TH JANUARY, 1900.

Spearman's Camp,
13th January, 1900.
1.55 p.m.

The following is the situation here :—The river looked at from the south forms deep doubles. At the apex of one re-entering bend is Potgieters Drift. The Boer position lies 6,000 yards off across the two salients, having command of from 200 to 500 feet; the intervening plain is without cover and flat; the enemy's flanks are unassailable; their defences are in two and three lines, the second line being out of sight of the plain with 8 guns. This position I do not think we can force. On the 14th we shall be concentrated here with 16 days' supplies, which I am unable to increase. My force consists of 5 brigades, less 1 battalion; 42 guns, Field artillery; 1 Howitzer battery; 6 Naval 12-pr. and 2 guns 4.7-in. I propose that Warren—taking 36 guns, Field artillery, 3 brigades, and 1,500 mounted men—shall cross 5 miles to the west at Trickhardt's Drift; the mountain which forms right flank of enemy's defence will be turned by his advance, while we do the best we can here with 1 brigade and 3 battalions, Howitzer battery and Naval guns. He agrees to this, but as he can only take supplies for 3 days, and will have to march not less than 15 miles from the river, and as he will have difficulty in obtaining water, the operation is undoubtedly risky. But this is the only possible chance for Ladysmith, where supplies are running short, and the sick list is already over 2,000.

APPENDIX 8 (H).

SECRET ORDERS ISSUED BY GENERAL SIR R. BULLER TO GENERAL SIR C. WARREN, 15TH JANUARY, 1900.

From General SIR REDVERS BULLER.
To Lieut.-General SIR CHARLES WARREN.

Mount Alice.
15th January, 1900.

1. The enemy's position in front of Potgieters Drift seems to me to be too strong to be taken by direct attack.

2. I intend to try and turn it by sending a force across the Tugela from near Trickhardt's Drift and up to the west of Spion Kop.

3. You will have command of that force, which will consist of the 11th brigade of your division, your brigade division, Royal Field artillery, and General Clery's division complete, and all the mounted troops, except 400.

4. You will of course act as circumstances require, but my idea is that you should continue throughout refusing your right, and throwing your left forward till you gain the open plain north of Spion Kop. Once there you will command the rear of the position facing Potgieters Drift, and, I think, render it untenable.

5. At Potgieters there will be the 4th brigade, part of the 10th brigade, one battery Royal Field artillery, one Howitzer battery, two 4.7-in. Naval guns. With them I shall threaten both the positions in front of us, and also attempt a crossing at Skiet's Drift, so as to hold the enemy off you as much as possible.

6. It is very difficult to ascertain the numbers of the enemy with any sort of exactness. I do not think there can be more than 400 on your left, and I estimate the total force that will be opposed to us about 7,000. I think they have only one or, at most, two big guns.

7. You will take $2\frac{1}{2}$ days' supply in your regimental transport, and a supply column holding one day more. This will give you four days' supply, which should be enough. Every extra wagon is a great impediment.

8. I gathered that you did not want an ammunition column. I think myself that I should be inclined to take one column for the two brigade divisions. You may find a position on which it is expedient to expend a great deal of ammunition.

9. You will issue such orders to the Pontoon Troop as you think expedient. If possible, I should like it to come here after you have crossed. I do not think you will find it possible to let oxen draw the wagons over the pontoons. It will be better to draw them over by horses or mules, swimming the oxen; the risk of breaking the pontoons, if oxen cross them, is too great.

10. The man whom I am sending you as a guide is a Devonshire man; he was employed as a boy on one of my own farms; he is English to the backbone, and can be thoroughly trusted. He thinks that if you cross Springfield flat at night he can take you the rest of the way to the Tugela by a road that cannot be overlooked by the enemy, but you will doubtless have the road reconnoitred.

11. I shall endeavour to keep up heliographic communication with you from a post on the hill directly in your rear.

12. I wish you to start as soon as you can. Supply is all in, and General Clery's division will, I hope, concentrate at Springfield to-day. Directly you start I shall commence to cross the river.

13. Please send me the 10th brigade, except that portion which you detail for the garrison at Springfield, as soon as possible; also the eight 12-pr. Naval guns, and any details, such as ammunition column, etc., that you do not wish to take.

REDVERS BULLER,
General.

APPENDIX 8 (1).

FORCE UNDER THE COMMAND OF SIR CHARLES WARREN ON LEAVING SPRINGFIELD FOR TRICKHARDT'S DRIFT, 16TH JANUARY, 1900.

G. O. C.—Lieut.-General Sir C. Warren.

TROOPS.

Mounted Brigade :—Commanding, Colonel the Earl of Dundonald.
    Royal Dragoons.
    13th Hussars (2 squadrons).
    Thorneycroft's M.I. (less 100 men).
    South African Light Horse.
    Imperial Light Horse (1 squadron).
    Natal Carbineers (1 squadron).
    Natal Police (1 squadron).
    M.I. 2nd K. R. Rifles (1 company).
    M.I. 2nd R. Dublin Fusiliers (1 section).

Artillery :—
    7th, 73rd, 78th, and 19th, 28th, 63rd Batteries R.F.A.

Engineers :—
    "A" Troop, Bridging Battalion, R.E.
    17th Company, R.E.

Infantry :—Commanding, Lieut.-Gen. Sir C. F. Clery :—
    2nd Brigade, Major-General Hildyard.
        2nd The Queen's, R. West Surrey Regiment.
        2nd Devonshire Regiment.
        2nd West Yorkshire Regiment.
        2nd East Surrey Regiment.

    5th Brigade, Major-General A. F. Hart.
        1st R. Inniskilling Fusiliers.
        1st Border Regiment.
        1st Connaught Rangers.
        2nd R. Dublin Fusiliers.

Attached :—
    11th Brigade, Major-General Woodgate.
        2nd The King's Own (R. Lancaster) Regiment.
        2nd Lancashire Fusiliers.
        1st South Lancashire Regiment.
        1st York and Lancaster Regiment.

Details :—
    Ammunition Column, Supply Column, Bearer Companies, Field Hospitals, &c.

APPENDIX 8.

SPION KOP OPERATIONS.

Approximate Strength of the Force under Lieut.-General Sir C. Warren, 17th January, 1900.

Arms.	Officers.	Other Ranks.	Horses (Riding and Draught.)	Guns.	
				15-pr.	Machine.
Vth Division Staff	12	55	46	—	—
Mounted Troops	110	2,160	2,300	—	2
Royal Artillery	54	1,262	1,048	36	—
Royal Engineers	21	606	318	—	—
Infantry (3 brigades)	298	10,336	565	—	12
Army Service Corps	11	144	327	—	—
Royal Army Medical Corps	23	290	252	—	—
Total	529	14,853	4,856	36	14

APPENDIX 8 (J).

FORCE UNDER THE COMMAND OF MAJOR-GENERAL THE HON. N. G. LYTTELTON AT POTGIETERS DRIFT AND SPRINGFIELD.

G. O. C.—Major-General the Hon. N. G. Lyttelton.

TROOPS.

The Naval Brigade :—Commanding, Captain E. T. Jones, R.N.

Mounted Troops :—13th Hussars (1 squadron).
Bethune's M.I.

Artillery :—61st (Howitzer) and 64th batteries R.F.A.

Engineers :—37th company, R.E.

Infantry :—4th Brigade, Major-General the Hon. N. G. Lyttelton.
        2nd Scottish Rifles.
        3nd King's Royal Rifle Corps.
        1st Durham Light Infantry.
        1st Rifle Brigade.

    10th Brigade, *Major-General Talbot Coke.*
        2nd Somerset Light Infantry.
        2nd Dorset Regiment.
        2nd Middlesex Regiment.

AT POTGIETERS DRIFT AND SPRINGFIELD.

Approximate Strength of the Force under Major-General the Hon. N. G. Lyttelton, 17th January, 1900.

Arms.	Officers.	Other Ranks.	Horses (Riding and Draught).	Guns. Naval.		Guns. Field.		Machine.
				4·7-in.	12-pr.	Howitzers.	15-pr.	
The Naval Brigade	25	225	6	2	8	—	—	—
Natal Army Staff	34	137	123	—	—	—	—	—
Mounted Troops	16	400	420	—	—	—	—	—
Royal Artillery	16	473	421	—	—	6	6	—
Royal Engineers	4	111	84	—	—	—	—	—
Infantry (2 brigades)	201	7,060	198	—	—	—	—	7
Army Service Corps	6	88	218	—	—	—	—	—
Royal Army Medical Corps	14	164	168	—	—	—	—	—
Total	316	8,658	1,638	2	8	6	6	7

APPENDIX 9.

CHAPTER XXI.

APPENDIX 9 (A).

GENERAL SIR CHARLES WARREN'S ORDERS FOR THE MARCH TO TRICKHARDT'S DRIFT, 16TH JANUARY, 1900.

FORCE ORDERS BY LIEUT.-GENERAL SIR C. WARREN.

Camp, Springfield,
16th January, 1900.
1 p.m.

Confidential.

The following is the order of march for the force acting under General Sir C. Warren this day :—

1. All tents will be left standing on their present ground.

2. The only baggage that will be taken with the column are the great-coats of the men, camp kettles, a certain proportion of regimental tools, and 20 lbs. per officer, including their canteens.

3. All other baggage, blankets, waterproofs, and other gear will be packed in separate wagons, and will proceed to Spearman's Hill with specially told off men at the rate of 1 per wagon, who will be responsible for the custody of the baggage. A N.C.O. from each Bn. will be in charge of his regimental section of wagons. Other units will conform to this arrangement. The G.O.C. IInd Division will detail an Officer to take charge of this Baggage Column and conduct it to Spearman's Hill Camp. To march from here to-night after the troops have marched. To be ready to start at 7 p.m.

Thus the only wagons which will go with the Column operating against the enemy are those carrying regimental supplies and great-coats and authorised allowance of officers' baggage.

4. In addition to above wagons will be told off by Brigades and units to take the whole of the tents of the force when struck to-morrow to Spearman's Hill. In cases where units of Corps Troops occupy less than a wagon a combination must be made with other units of Corps Troops. This Column will march under the command of the Officer left in command of the camp here.

5. The 50 extra rounds of ammunition per man will be carried for the first march on the wagons, after that by the men.

6. The wagons with the great-coats, as far as is practicable, will be kept up close to the Brigades so that they will be available for the troops when night falls.

7. Each man will carry ½ a day's rations for to-morrow in his haversack in addition to his emergency ration and the unexpired portion of to-day's rations, in accordance with instructions issued to-day.

8. The emergency ration will consist of two biscuits in addition to the tinned ration.

9. Care will be taken that water carts and men's water-bottles are filled before starting, and that men get tea before leaving Camp.

10. One company per Brigade will stay behind in camp; this party will carry on the usual routine of Camp, simulating the usual fires, outposts, bugle calls, etc., and will guard the encampment. A Field Officer to be detailed by G.O.C. 11th Brigade will command and will report to the A.A.G. at 4 p.m. to-day for orders. A squadron of Bethune's Mounted Infantry has been detailed to report to this officer at this camp.

11. Camp here will be struck not earlier than sunset to-morrow. On arrival at Spearman's Hill tents will be packed with remainder of baggage.

12. Regimental supply and great-coat wagons referred to in order 2 accompanying the force, will be ready to move at 3 p.m. to-day under the order of the Divisional Baggage master. Guide, Lieut. Schwickkard. To move in following order :—

V. Div. H.Q. XI. Bde.—Vth Div. Troops—Mounted Troops, II. Division.

13. The Ammunition Column of all troops will march at 1.30 p.m., and will park alongside the Pontoon wagons to the W. of Spearman's road and wait for orders.

<small>A. G. Comd.
G. O. C. 2 Bde.
*1st R.Dragoons
Thorneycroft's
M. I.
1 By. 5 Bde.
2nd Bde. Div.
(less F. H.)</small>

14. Troops will march as follows, advanced guard as in margin, clearing a point on the road to Spearman's Hill, just opposite the H.Q. Camp of Sir C. Warren at 5 p.m. Commanders of units to report on receipt of these orders to General Hildyard, 2 Bde. Camp.

15. Main body will march as follows, under command of the G.O.C. IInd Division :—

Vth Div. Squadron Cavalry to clear the same point as in 14, at 5.10 p.m.
1 Bn. 11th Bde.
Remainder Bde. Div. Vth Div.
Bde. Div. R.F.A. IInd Div.
Remainder 11th Bde.
F.H. 2nd Brigade.
Remainder of IInd Div.

16. On arrival at the rendezvous about 3 miles from this Camp the G.O.C. the force will meet the Column and make further dispositions.

17. All units in rear must be careful to maintain touch with the unit in front of them.

By order,

A. W. MORRIS, Colonel, A.A.G.

Sir C. Warren's Force.

Circulated to Officers.

* Unless already disposed of under the orders of Lord Dundonald.

APPENDIX 9 (B).

FROM SIR R. BULLER (JAN. 17TH, 1900. RECEIVED JAN. 18TH).

My dear Warren,—

    I am carrying coals to Newcastle, probably, but on the chance I write to say I wish you would, if you have not already done so, point out to Woodgate that his advance from Smith's Farm to-day was all wrong. The one thing if we mean to succeed is to keep our left clear. He was at Smith's Farm; the Yorkshires had occupied a kopje to the east, and he had advanced north-east; this was wrong. I give a small diagram. (*Here follow two diagrams, with explanations. See Royal Commission on the War in S. Africa. Vol II., p. 655.*) If your direct road is blocked, we must go forward by moving off to the left, and this will have the further advantage that it will keep you near the water at Venter's Spruit—consequently the left flank must always be thrown outward. If you can make a direct advance, it will be in line, but if you are checked, the next advance must be by moving half left; I mean that to get on, your left will creep outward and forward, and your right follow. I don't know if I have made myself clear. Wynne will explain, but until you have so far encircled the enemy that you can wheel to the east, pray always try to overlap their right with your left.

REDVERS BULLER.

APPENDIX 9 (C).

MESSAGES EXCHANGED BETWEEN SIR C. WARREN AND LORD DUNDONALD, 18TH JANUARY, 1900.

From Sir C. Warren to Lord Dundonald, 18th January, 1900 :—

    "The G.O.C., as far as he can see, finds that there are no cavalry stationed near the camp, and nothing to prevent the oxen being swept away; you are to send 500 mounted men at once to be stationed round the camp."

From Sir C. Warren to Lord Dundonald, 18th January, 1900, 11.45 a.m :—

    "In case I may not have been explicit this morning in my instructions, I send the following :—500 mounted men to be employed on our rear and flanks to protect the oxen, cover our infantry, and feel for the enemy. The remainder to be employed in scouting to the front, with instructions to cut off any Boers. Parties to patrol about 10 miles to the west and north-west."

From Lord Dundonald to Sir C. Warren, 18th January, 1900, 2 p.m. :—

    "I had already arranged to protect your advance by piqueting kopjes. The Royal Dragoons will do this and look after your rear and flanks. I am having sketches made of the Rangeworthy Hills, which will be sent you; the Boers occupy them. To advance with your infantry to attack Rangeworthy (Venter's Spruit) in flank, you will have to cross to the left over the Venter's Spruit, about a mile above its junction with the Tugela, coming along the back of the kopjes which line the south-west bank of the Venter's Spruit; you can then re-cross the Venter's Spruit farther on to make your flank attack; there is plenty of water here and all along the Venter's Spruit, and also camping ground. If you wish to keep on the north-east side of the Venter's Spruit, you will have to advance on the Rangeworthy Hills, without making your *detour* flank attack, as there is broken ground close under the hills, and it would also be within rifle-fire. I should recommend your crossing yourself to where I address this letter from, and you will see enough. An officer who knows the road will take this note, and will inform you. I find that the Royals are weaker than I thought they were, being only some 412 instead of 500. As it is a unit, I have detailed them alone, and if you wish more I can send you more men to make up the 500; without the Royals I have about 1,100 men only. I have sent patrols to west and north-west."

From Lord Dundonald to Sir C. Warren, 18th January, 1900 (evening) :—

" My advanced squadrons are engaged with the enemy. I am supporting them. Can you let me have the Royals ? "

From Sir C. Warren to Lord Dundonald, 18th January, 1900, 7.30 p.m. :—

" I did not intend you should force on an action until I had arranged to proceed from here and take the initiative ; unless you are sure of success you should retire upon the camp. I am sending you 3 squadrons of the Royals to support you."

From Lord Dundonald to Sir C. Warren, 18th January, 1900 (despatched 6.50 p.m., received 9 p.m.) :—

" The position about two miles west of Acton Homes occupied after a fight ; about 20 Boers killed and wounded, 15 prisoners ; am holding position and kopjes commanding the west of your line ; details further."

From Lord Dundonald to Sir C. Warren, 18th January, 1900 (later) :—

" I remain here for the night with 880 men ; the two squadrons 13th Hussars have to connect with occupying a kopje *en route*."

From Sir C. Warren to Lord Dundonald, 18th January, 1900 (in reply to the above) :—

" The position you have occupied seems to be too far to the north-west, but of this I cannot be certain. I am marching towards Venter's Spruit to-morrow morning, and expect advanced guard to arrive there about 7 a.m. What number of mounted men can you send me, as I have practically none ? "

Sir C. Warren to Lord Dundonald, 7 a.m. :—

" Yours of 4 a.m. Our objective is not Ladysmith. Our objective is to effect a junction with Sir Redvers Buller's force and then to receive orders from him. By detaching your cavalry from me you are hampering all my movements, and forcing me to alter my plans. I am moving up towards you and desire you will not move forward unless you are actually forced to do so. I require your mounted men to act as part of my force. I am shelling a hill close to this in order to draw attention off you."

Lord Dundonald to Sir C. Warren, 9 a.m. :—

" Please understand that I have taken up my position here to protect your left flank and assist your plans. I am in close touch with you. If I am to operate on your left flank, the road across which I came is the only one available for my wheeled first-line transport. I quite understand your general plan, and that it is to unite with Sir R. Buller. I am quite able to protect myself where I am, and shall there await your instructions."

APPENDIX 9 (D).

Sir C. Warren to Sir C. F. Clery, 19th January, 1900, 6 a.m. :—

"You command the whole of the troops in rear of General Hildyard, including the rear-guard. The object is to push all the baggage and supply wagons to the front as quickly as possible, as until they are away from the vicinity of the camp (Trickhardt's Drift) General Woodgate's Brigade cannot be moved. My objective is to render assistance to Lord Dundonald, who has been in action. I am now shelling the Boer position in order to distract attention from him, but until the whole of our wagons are well to the front I cannot render him assistance."

APPENDIX 9 (E).

From Sir C. Warren to Lord Dundonald, 20th January, 1900, 5.20 a.m. :—

"General White states that a force of 1,500 to 2,000 Boers marched from Clydesdale to Acton Homes yesterday at 5 p.m., 19th January. You must take care that you are not cut off, and must keep touch with the main force."

APPENDIX 9 (F).

From Sir C. Warren to Sir R. Buller, 19th January, 1900 (sent 7.45 p.m., received 8.15 p.m.) :—

"To CHIEF OF STAFF.

"Left Flank, 19th January.

"I find there are only two roads by which we could possibly get from Trickhardt's Drift to Potgieters on the north of the Tugela, one by Acton Homes, the other by Fairview and Rosalie. The first I reject as too long : the second is a very difficult road for a large number of wagons, unless the enemy is thoroughly cleared out. I am, therefore, going to adopt some special arrangements which will involve my stay at Venter's Laager for two or three days. I will send in for further supplies and report progress.

"C. WARREN."

APPENDIX 9 (G).

ORDERS ISSUED BY SIR C. WARREN TO SIR C. F. CLERY, 19TH JANUARY, 1900 (EVENING).

"General Officer Commanding IInd Division,

"I shall be glad if you will arrange to clear the Boers out of the ground above that at present occupied by the 11th brigade, by a series of outflanking movements. In the early morning an advance should be made as far as the Hussars reconnoitred to-day,* and a shelter trench there made across the slope

* Three Tree Hill.

of the hill. A portion of the slopes of the adjoining hill to the west can then be occupied, the artillery assisting, if necessary, in clearing the western side and upper slopes. When this is done I think that a battery can be placed on the slopes of the western hill in such a position that it could shell the schanzes of the Boers on Spion Kop and the upper portion of the eastern hill. When this is done a further advance can be made on the eastern hill, and artillery can be brought to bear upon the upper slopes of the western hill. It appears to me that this might be done with comparatively little loss of life, as the Boers can in each turn be outflanked. The following cavalry are at your disposal: two squadrons Royal Dragoons and Vth divisional squadron.

"C. WARREN,
"Lieut.-General."

APPENDIX 9 (H).

From Sir C. Warren to Sir C. F. Clery, 20th January, 1900 (evening) :—

"I quite concur that a frontal attack is undesirable, and that a flank attack is more suitable. I intended to convey that we should hold what we get by means of entrenchments when necessary, and not retire, continuing the advance to-morrow if it cannot be done to-night; frontal attack, with heavy losses, is simply playing the Boer game."

APPENDIX 9 (I).

From Sir C. Warren to Chief of Staff, 21st January, 1900, 6.30 p.m. :—

"I am under the impression, from various indications, that the Free State Boers are preparing a great trek to the west, and that the present fighting is to secure their line of retreat. If you can push on three battalions to reinforce me as quickly as possible I think I can manage to close the road to the west and secure some of the wagons."

APPENDIX 9 (J).

From Sir C. Warren to Sir R. Buller, 21st January, 1900 (evening) :—

"I find that there is a position now being fortified behind the one we are now engaged on, so that it is impossible to say when decisive attack will take place, but I am under the impression that with continuous fighting we shall clear the range of hills we are now attacking up to the Acton Homes-Ladysmith road in two or three days. I fancy the Boers are fighting as much to retain possession over their communications as to prevent our getting to Ladysmith, and I have great hopes that the Howitzers will add greatly to our progress to-morrow. I find that there are some guns placed concealed in a donga, together with a large number of Boers, overlooking the road between here and Acton Homes, and as soon as the extra battalions arrive I shall endeavour to surround both."

APPENDIX 9 (K).

From Sir R. Buller to Sir C. Warren, 22nd January, 1900, 5.6 a.m. :—

"I think it possible the enemy may try a counter-attack. They are concentrated. Your troops are widely extended and do not support each other. I should be cautious how I attempted any enterprise further to the left at present. I thought Woodgate's troops very badly placed on your right yesterday, the bulk of them were much too far back to have been of any use in the event of a sudden attack upon the guns. I think before you do anything else, at least one battalion should be strongly entrenched close to the guns. I am riding over this morning and should like to see you. Will you leave an orderly on the hill where I met you out yesterday to tell me where to find you?"

APPENDIX 9 (L).

FORCE ORDERS BY SIR C. WARREN, 22ND JANUARY, 1900.

Venter's Laager, 22.1.00, 1.20 p.m.

1. As a temporary measure the following arrangements for staff duties are being made :—

    A.A.G.—Major Capper,
    Provost Marshal—Major Williams.
    Signalling Officer—Capt. McHardy.

2. The following tactical distribution of troops is made :—

    Right Attack and Right Flank. Troops east of a line dividing Three Tree Hill from Fair View Farm spur and the 10th brigade. These are under General Talbot Coke.

    Left Attack and Left Flank. Troops to the west of above line. These are under General Sir F. Clery.

3. General Talbot Coke will arrange for immediate security of camp and baggage.

4. The Lancashire Fusiliers will rejoin 11th brigade.

5. The G.O.C. the force will be stationed near the artillery on Three Tree Hill.

6. Two mounted orderlies from each division and one from each brigade division R.A. will be permanently stationed with the Headquarters of the force. To report as soon as possible.

T. CAPPER, Maj. for A.A.G.

APPENDIX 9 (M).

ORDERS BY SIR C. WARREN FOR THE OCCUPATION OF SPION KOP, 23RD JANUARY, 1900.

To G.O.C. Right attack.

1. The G.O.C. the force has decided to seize Spion Kop to-night.

2. You will detail from the troops under your orders 2 battalions and Thorneycroft's Mounted Infantry and ½ company R.E. to carry out this operation.

3. Major-General Woodgate is to command this force.

4. The Column will parade at the place appointed by you, and you will issue all necessary orders. The Column should move off not later than 12 midnight.

5. Extra ammunition must be carried on ammunition mules drawn from the Regiments of your own force.

6. One day's complete rations are to be carried on the man, and wagons with supplies and great-coats brought up as far as possible at present without exposure.

7. All natives in the vicinity of the commencement of your line of advance should be confined to their kraals by cavalry piquets, which should act after dark to-night. WRIGHT'S FARM should also be piqueted and inhabitants confined to the building.

8. The Imperial Light Infantry now at the Pontoon Bridge will be ordered to occupy the heights E. and W. of the gully above WRIGHT'S FARM after dark to-night, ready to support you and keep open your communications.

9. A mountain battery has been ordered to come up, and will be sent up the SPION KOP as soon as they arrive, after you have made your lodgment on the hill.

10. The artillery and infantry of your right attack must be prepared to support the Column occupying SPION KOP by their fire as soon as it is light.

11. Entrenchments must be made on the top of SPION KOP as soon as it is taken; the half company R.E. will bring their extra tools for this purpose.

12. The G.O.C. desires that the regiments you may detail for the SPION KOP Column should be relieved from further duty to-day.

13. Endeavour will be made to collect any puckall mules* there may be in camp to carry water. Failing this, water can be carried on mules in waterproof sheets.

14. Signalling communication must be established as soon as secrecy is no longer possible.

15. A special party from the R.A. to observe and report by signal the effect of Howitzer fire must also accompany the Column.

By order,

T. CAPPER,

for A.A.G.

* Mules provided with the Indian equipment for carrying water in skins.

APPENDIX 9 (N).

ATTACK ORDERS ISSUED BY MAJOR-GENERAL COKE, COMMANDING RIGHT ATTACK, JANUARY 23RD, 1900.

1. The General Officer Commanding has decided to seize Spion Kop.

2. The operations will be conducted by Major-General Woodgate, who will detail two battalions of his own brigade, to which will be attached about 100 men of Thorneycroft's Mounted Infantry and half company Royal Engineers.

3. Rendezvous just east of the encampment Royal Engineers, at 7 p.m. Men must be kept concealed from the front.

4. One hundred and fifty rounds of ammunition will be carried by the men. The General Officer Commanding 11th brigade will attach three mules to each battalion, and the Officer Commanding 10th brigade three mules, this afternoon. Ammunition for these mules will be furnished by the battalions concerned. One day's complete ration to be carried by the men. All horses to be left at the Royal Engineer bivouac. The mules will follow in rear of the Column. Men will carry entrenching tools in stretchers.

5. The Officer Commanding the Royal Dragoons will arrange to piquet all native kraals on the line of advance, and also Wright's Farm. All inhabitants should be confined to the buildings.

6. Men will of course carry filled water-bottles, and should be cautioned that a re-fill may be difficult. Battalions will endeavour to make some arrangement, by fastening biscuit boxes on to mules, or in some other manner, to carry extra water.

7. The General Officer Commanding 11th brigade will arrange that the Volunteer ambulance and the bearer company of the brigade send detachments. No ambulance to be nearer than the Royal Engineer bivouac till daylight.

J. TALBOT COKE, Major-General.

APPENDIX 9 (O).

BRIGADE ORDERS BY MAJOR-GENERAL WOODGATE, 23RD JANUARY, 1900.

1. The General Officer Commanding has decided to seize Spion Kop this night.

2. The following troops will compose the force :—
   Royal Lancaster regiment (6 companies).
   2nd Lancashire Fusiliers.
   Thorneycroft's Mounted Infantry (180 men).
   Half company 17th company Royal Engineers.

3. The above troops will rendezvous at White's Farm* about half mile north-west of Pontoon Bridge at 7 p.m.

* On the map called Wright's Farm.

4. Extra ammunition will be carried on the mules supplied by the 10th brigade.

5. One day's complete rations will be carried. Wagons with supplies and great-coats will be brought up as soon as possible without exposure; also water carts and machine guns.

6. The South Lancashire regiment will hand over six mules, three to each battalion, for water-carrying purposes.

7. Pack mules will be utilized for carrying water in waterproof sheets.

8. Twenty picks and twenty shovels to be carried in regulation stretchers.

9. Password, " Waterloo."

APPENDIX 9 (P).

FORCE ORDERS BY SIR CHARLES WARREN, RELATIVE TO THE OCCUPATION OF SPION KOP.

Three Tree Hill,
23rd January, 1900.
7 p.m.

I. An attack on Spion Kop will be made to-night by a force of about $3\frac{1}{2}$ battns. under General Woodgate, the march commencing about midnight.

II. This attack will be supported from Three Tree Hill by the troops under the orders of the G.O.C. Right attack.

If firing takes place from Spion Kop during the night, the artillery from Three Tree Hill will fire Star Shell and will open fire at the rear of the enemy's position to prevent reinforcements being brought up. Infantry from Three Tree Hill will fire at daylight with the same object.

III. The G.O.C. Left attack will use his discretion about opening fire against the enemy to his front, if firing breaks out on Spion Kop with a view to creating a diversion.

IV. A Staff Officer from Right and Left attacks will report to the G.O.C. the force at midnight at Three Tree Hill.

V. All troops are to be warned of the operations which will be carried out. No firing must take place without the orders of Battalion Commanders.

VI. Countersign is *Waterloo*.

VII. If firing commences frequent reports are to be sent to the G.O.C. the force at Three Tree Hill by signal or messenger.

By Order,
T. Capper, A.A.G.

VIII. The division of the Force into Right and Left attack is to be considered purely tactical. For administrative purposes, the troops will be organised as before into IInd and Vth divisions and Corps Troops. This arrangement will apply to casualty returns.

IX. General Talbot Coke will temporarily command the Vth division and will nominate his own Staff.

X. The Imperial Light Infantry joined the force to-day and comes under the orders of the G.O.C. Right attack.

By Order,
T. Capper, A.A.G.

APPENDIX 10.

CHAPTER XXII.

COLONEL CROFTON'S MESSAGE.

APPENDIX 10 (A).

Colonel Crofton subsequently stated that the message delivered verbally by him to the signalling officer of his battalion, and by the latter to the signaller, also verbally, ran thus :—

"General Woodgate dead. Reinforcements urgently required."

The signalling officer on the other hand stated that the message he handed in was as follows :—

"General Woodgate is killed, send reinforcements at once."

APPENDIX 10 (B).

From General Warren to General Lyttelton. Sent from Left Flank Attack Office, 9.53 a.m., received 9.55 a.m., 24.1.00 :—

"Give every assistance you can on your side ; this side is clear, but the enemy are too strong on your side, and Crofton telegraphs that if assistance is not given at once all is lost. I am sending up two battalions, but they will take some time to get up."

APPENDIX 10 (C).

Heliogram from someone unknown on Spion Kop to General Lyttelton. Received 10.15 a.m., 24.1.00 :—

"We occupy all the crest on top of hill, being heavily attacked from your side. Help us.—Spion Kop."

APPENDIX 10 (D).

General Talbot Coke to General Warren. Sent (by hand) from "Top of Spion Kop," 5.50 p.m., and delivered by Colonel Morris to General Warren at 7.50 p.m., 24.1.00 :—

"The situation is as follows : The original troops are still in position, have suffered severely, and many dead and wounded are still in the trenches. The shell-fire is and has been very severe. If I hold on to the position all night, is there any guarantee that our artillery can silence the enemy's guns ? Otherwise to-day's experience will be repeated, and the men will not stand another complete day's shelling. I have in hand Bethune's Mounted Infantry and the Dorset regiment intact to cover a withdrawal. If I remain I will endeavour to utilise these units to carry food and water up to the firing line. The situation is extremely critical. If I charge and take the kopje in front, the advance is several hundred yards in the face of the entrenched enemy in strength, and my position as regards the quick-firing guns is much worse. Please give orders, and should you wish me to withdraw, cover retirement from Connaught's Hill."

APPENDIX 10 (E).

From Colonel Thorneycroft to Chief Staff Officer to Sir C. Warren. Sent by hand, from the summit of Spion Kop, at 6.30 p.m., 24.1.00 :—

"The troops which marched up here last night are quite done up, Lancashire Fusiliers, Royal Lancaster regiment, and Thorneycroft's Mounted Infantry. They have had no water, and ammunition is running short. I consider that, even with reinforcements which have arrived, it is impossible to permanently hold this place, so long as the enemy's guns can play on this hill. They have one long-range gun, three of shorter range, and one Maxim-Nordenfeldt, which have swept the whole of the plateau since 8 a.m. I have not been able to ascertain the casualties, but they have been very heavy, especially in the regiments which came up last night. I request instructions as to what course I am to adopt. The enemy at 6.30 p.m. are firing heavily from both flanks, with rifles, shell, and Nordenfeldt, while a heavy rifle-fire is kept up in front. It is all I can do to hold my own. If casualties go on occurring at present rate, I shall barely hold out the night. A large number of stretcher bearers should be sent up, and also all water possible. The situation is critical.

"ALEX. THORNEYCROFT,

"Lt.-Colonel."

APPENDIX 10 (F).

From Colonel Thorneycroft to Sir C. Warren. Sent from Spion Kop, by Lieut. Winston Churchill, 24.1.1900. Delivered 2 a.m., 25.1.00.

"Spion Kop, 24th January, 1900.

"Regret to report that I have been obliged to abandon Spion Kop, as the position became untenable. I have withdrawn the troops in regular order, and will come to report as soon as possible.

"ALEX. THORNEYCROFT,

"Lt.-Colonel."

APPENDIX 10 (G).

General Lyttelton to General Warren. Received 8.35 p.m., 24th January, 1900 :—

" My position to-night is this : The Scottish Rifles and 2 squadrons Bethune's have joined your extreme right and remain there. The K.R.R. scaled Sugar Loaf Hill, and reached the top, but as they were 2 miles in advance of your extreme right, and as I had no troops to support them, I have ordered them to withdraw again to the foot of my position here. Let me know how you stand, and what you propose to do in the morning."

APPENDIX 10 (H).

General Warren to General Lyttelton. Sent from Left Flank 6.45 p.m., received 6.48 p.m., 24.1.00 :—

" The assistance you are giving most valuable. We shall try to remain *in statu quo* during to-morrow ; balloon would be of incalculable value to me."

APPENDIX 10 (I).

FORCE ORDERS, ISSUED BY GENERAL WARREN ON THE EVENING OF THE 24TH JANUARY, 1900.

24.1.1900.

1. The action of to-day commenced with the surprise of Spion Kop by General Woodgate's force, which consisted of :—

    The Lancashire Fusiliers.
    The Royal Lancaster regiment.
    Thorneycroft's Mounted Infantry.
    ½ Co. R.E., and detachment R.A.

About 8.30 a.m. the enemy made a determined attempt to retake the hill, which was gallantly held by our men all day, in spite of a damaging shell-fire.

At the close of the day the following regiments were occupying Spion Kop, in addition to the original force :—

    The Dorsetshire regiment.
    The Middlesex regiment.
    Part of the Connaught Rangers.
    2 companies Bethune's M.I.
    The Scottish Rifles.

The two last operating from Potgieters.

The remainder of General Lyttelton's brigade also operated on our right.

The G.O.C. is confident that the spirit of gallantry and endurance which has marked the conduct of the troops will be continued to-morrow.

2. An issue of rum is sanctioned for all troops.

3. Captain C. B. Levita, R.A., is appointed D.A.A.G. (a), to the force as a temporary measure, from 23.: .00.

4. The East Surrey and Devonshire regiments have been temporarily transferred to the right attack.

By Order,
T. CAPPER,
for A.A.G.

The countersign to-night is " Victoria."—T.C.

APPENDIX 10 (J).

Letter from General Warren to Colonel Thorneycroft. Sent at 8.20 p.m. by Lieut. Winston Churchill, and delivered at 10.30 p.m., 24th January, 1900 :—

" The General Officer Commanding Force would be glad to have your views of the situation and measures to be adopted, by Lieut. Winston Churchill, who takes this note.

" By Order,
" T. CAPPER, A.A.G."

APPENDIX 11.

CHAPTER XXIII.

APPENDIX 11 (A).

ORDERS FOR THE OPERATIONS AT VAAL KRANTZ.

SPEARMAN'S.

3rd February, 1900.

1. It is the intention of the General Commanding to attack the extreme left of the enemy's positions and to endeavour to take the hill Vaal Krantz.

2. The attempt will commence by a demonstration against the Brakfontein position. This will be carried out by the two brigade divisions Royal Field artillery and the 61st Howitzer battery, covered by the 11th (Wynne's) brigade, Vth division, now across at Kopje.

3. During this demonstration the 4th brigade (Lyttelton), supported by the IInd (Clery, Hildyard, Hart) division, the whole under the command of General Clery, will be formed in a suitable position east of No. 2 Pontoon Bridge, the general idea being to cause the enemy to think that these troops are about to move from east to west across the bridge. The 4 guns 64th battery are placed under General Clery's orders.

4. After a certain bombardment, sufficient to cause the enemy to enter their trenches, the left battery of the Field artillery will limber up, and retire by No. 2 Pontoon Bridge to its new position, covering the throwing of the Pontoon Bridge No. 3 at Munger's Drift.
Simultaneously with this movement, the 4th brigade will move out to cover the movement and the battery of 14 guns on Zwart Kop and the two 5-inch guns under it will open on Vaal Krantz and bombard the few trenches there. (Underneath Zwart Kop there are two 5-inch guns.)

5. As soon as the Pontoon No. 3 is completed, the rest of the six batteries will follow each other, passing from left to right, at 10 minutes' interval, the whole taking up positions to support the attack on Vaal Krantz under the orders of Colonel Parsons, R.A., who will report to General Clery.

6. After a sufficient bombardment, the 4th (Lyttelton) brigade, supported by the IInd (Clery, Hildyard, Hart) division, will, under General Clery's orders, attack Vaal Krantz.

7. As soon as the hill is occupied the artillery will ascend it and shell the trenches at Brakfontein, doing all they can to enfilade any that admit of it. Colonel Parsons will arrange that two batteries always watch the hills on the right.

8. The 1st brigade cavalry (Burn-Murdoch's) will, when feasible, pass Vaal Krantz, and getting into the plain, bring the battery Royal Horse artillery into action on any convenient target.

9. The 2nd brigade (Dundonald's) cavalry will watch the right and rear throughout the operations.

10. The Officer (Colonel Nutt) Commanding Royal artillery will command the 14 guns on Zwart Kop and the two 5-inch below. Their duties will be to prevent the enemy receiving any reinforcements from our right rear; to shell any points whence rifle-fire is brought to bear on our advancing infantry; to keep any guns the enemy may bring to bear out of action. The Royal Scots Fusiliers will be under the orders of the Officer Commanding Royal artillery for the day—this battalion practically at Zwart Kop.

11. The Naval guns on Signal Hill and plateau below will contribute, their mission being to keep the enemy's guns out of action; to stop the enemy passing from his right to his left; to shell any trenches whence fire is directed on our attack.

12. The Officer Commanding Pontoon Troop will arrange to throw No. 3 Bridge at the earliest hour possible. Its formation will be covered by the 4th (Lyttelton) brigade, the 4 guns of the 64th battery, and the battery mentioned in paragraph 4.

13. The General Officer Commanding 10th (Talbot-Coke) brigade will be responsible for the camp at Spearman's Hill and the kopjes at Potgieters.

14. The 61st Howitzer battery will come into action in front of The Kopjes, and, under the orders of its Commanding Officer, will follow the Field artillery to the right, taking up a position, to be selected by its Commanding Officer, whence it can shell Krantz Kloof, Doorn Kloof, and the Brakfontein trenches.

15. The Signalling Officer, Natal, will arrange, in communication with Officer Commanding Telegraphs, for communication being kept up between Signal Hill, Zwart Kop, The Kopjes, and General Clery's Headquarters, and, if possible, between Signal Hill and the plateau where the two 12-pounders are, and between Zwart Kop and the two 5-inch guns.

16. The balloon will ascend and will send messages to all batteries whose fire can be observed.

17. The General Officer Commanding Vth (Warren) division will superintend the duties specified in paragraphs 2 and 13, and will, as soon as he thinks it safe, move all or a portion of the 11th brigade to the right in support of the IInd division.

18. The General Commanding will, at the commencement of the action, be on the hill, where the two 5-inch guns are placed.

By Order,

H. S. G. MILES, Colonel,

Chief of Staff.

APPENDIX 11 (B).

2nd Brigade Orders,
VAAL KRANTZ.
7.12 p.m.   7.2.1900

1. The force will withdraw from the Vaal Krantz ridge to-night.

2. The withdrawal will be carried out as follows :—

By 9 p.m. each battalion will be ready concentrated below its present position on the W. slope of the hill, except that the present firing line will be thinly occupied by about one section per company. At 9 p.m. battalions will move off to the new pontoon bridge, and will cross in the following order :—

    Half battalion 2nd Devon.
    2nd Queen's.
    2nd East Surrey.
    2nd West Yorkshire.
    Half battalion 2nd Devon.

3. Half battalion of the 2nd Devon regiment will take up a covering position on the left bank of the river by 8.45 p.m. The other half battalion which crosses first will, as soon as it has crossed, take up a position on the right bank to cover the retirement and the breaking up of the bridge.

4. At 9.15 p.m. the men left to occupy the firing line will be withdrawn simultaneously, and will cross the bridge in the same order as their battalions. After they are all through, the half battalion 2nd Devon regiment on the left bank will follow the brigade over the bridge.

5. The O.C. 2nd Devon regiment will have an officer at each end of the bridge to regulate the traffic, to be there by 8 p.m.

6. The utmost silence will be preserved during the retirement. No lights of any kind will be allowed, and care should be taken to break step and make no noise crossing the bridge.

7. All vehicles, animals, and bulky articles will be sent on at once.

By Order,
H. E. GOGARTY, Captain.
Brigade Major, 2nd Brigade.

APPENDIX 11 (C).

ORDERS FOR THE RETIREMENT FROM VAAL KRANTZ.

Orders by General Sir R. Buller to Lieut.-General Sir C. Warren for the evacuation of Spearman's Camp.

1. G.O.C. to superintend evacuation of Spearman's Camp.

2. Get everything away as quickly as possible to Springfield Bridge, where I propose to leave 1st cavalry brigade, A. battery R.H.A., two Naval guns and two battalions infantry.

3. I wish the Howitzer battery and the 4.7-in. Naval guns, and four of the 12-prs. sent forward first thing to Chieveley. Everything else may come in the same order as you may select. I have already given orders for the Naval guns to be got off Zwart Kop, and until they and the mountain battery and all the troops now in Zwart Kop Valley are withdrawn, you should keep a good garrison there.

4. The O.C. 1st cavalry brigade will be directed to report himself to you for orders.

5. My address till further notice will be Springfield Bridge.

6. I have not yet seen the P.M.O., but I intend to leave all bad cases in hospital there. It will want no protection.

7. I should like you to relieve the R. Scots Fusiliers in Zwart Kop Valley, and send them to Springfield Post this evening or early to-morrow.

APPENDIX 12.

CHAPTERS XXIV. TO XXIX.

EXPENDITURE OF AMMUNITION BY THE ROYAL ARTILLERY DURING THE RELIEF OF LADYSMITH.

14TH—28TH FEBRUARY, 1900.

Battery.	Brigade Divn.	14th	15th	16th	17th	18th	19th	20th	21st	22nd	23rd	24th	25th	26th	27th	Total.	Remarks.
7th R.F.A.		—	11	30	31	307	107	10	82	—	464	137	—	88	272	1,539	
63rd R.F.A.		—	29	21	157	266	160	234	83	—	536	174	—	—	203	1,863	
64th R.F.A.		110	24	52	104	98	220	206	220	—	368	161	—	104	413	2,080	
28th R.F.A. ⎫	5th	146	—	—	249	625	376	62	964	359	—	—	—	98	450	3,329	⎫ No returns showing expenditure of each battery.
73rd R.F.A. ⎬																	⎬
74th R.F.A. ⎭																	⎭
19th R.F.A.		—	—	—	—	78	—	—	343	548	424	—	—	95	284	1,772	
61st (How.) R.F.A.		110	—	—	151	140	68	43	67	261	374	268	—	66	145	1,693	
A. R.H.A.		—	—	—	—	—	—	—	—	—	326	—	—	—	239	565	
16th Co. Southern Divn., R.G.A.		—	20	79	131	236	100	7	62	130	286	220	—	76	179	1,526	
No. 4 Mountain R.G.A.		—	—	—	—	—	—	—	—	—	907	—	—	5	170	1,082	
66th R.F.A.		—	—	—	—	—	—	—	—	—	58	—	—	—	—	58	
Total		366	84	182	823	1,750	1,031	562	1,821	1,298	3,743	960	—	532	2,355	15,507	

APPENDIX 12 (*continued*).

DAILY EXPENDITURE OF AMMUNITION BY THE NAVAL GUNS WITH SIR REDVERS BULLER FROM THE 14TH TO THE 28TH FEBRUARY, 1900, INCLUSIVE.

Date.	6-in. gun.	Two 4.7-in. on wheels.	Four 4.7-in. on Platforms and Railway Trucks.	12-prs.	Remarks.
February 14th	—	77	—	31*	* At Springfield.
,, 15th	—	48	—	50	
,, 16th	—	30	—	43	
,, 17th	25	43	—	65	
,, 18th	30	78	22	110	
,, 19th	15	19	—	82	
,, 20th	17	47	—	65	
,, 21st	—	40	—	237	
,, 22nd	12	131	—	318	
,, 23rd	48	244	19	375	
,, 24th	26	180	15	226	
,, 25th	—	—	—	—	Armistice.
,, 26th	6	111	6	337	
,, 27th	28	146	125	1,133	
,, 28th	—	—	—	—	
Total	207	1,194	187	3,072	

APPENDIX 12 (continued).

NAVAL GUNS WITH GENERAL SIR REDVERS BULLER'S FORCE IN NATAL, SHOWING AMMUNITION EXPENDED DURING THE PRINCIPAL ACTIONS.

Description of Guns.	Name of Commander of Gun Sections.	Ammunition expended in Rounds.			Remarks.
		6-in.	4.7-in.	12-prs.	
COLENSO, 15TH DECEMBER, 1899.					
4.7-in. wheeled gun No. 1 4.7-in. ,, ,, No. 2	Comndr. Limpus	—	160	—	
12-pr. gun No. 1 12-pr. ,, No. 2 12-pr. ,, No. 3 12-pr. ,, No. 4 12-pr. ,, No. 17 12-pr. ,, No. 18	Lieut. Deas Mr. Wright Lieut. Ogilvy Lieut. James	—	—	300	
12-pr. ,, No. 7 12-pr. ,, No. 8 12-pr. ,, No. 9 12-pr. ,, No. 10	Lieut. Wilde Lieut. Richards	—	—	600	
Total rounds ...		—	160	900	
SPION KOP, JANUARY 17TH–24TH, 1900.					
4.7-in. wheeled gun No. 1 4.7-in. ,, ,, No. 2	Comndr. Limpus	—	598	—	
12-pr. gun No. 1 12-pr. ,, No. 2 12-pr. ,, No. 3 12-pr. ,, No. 4 12-pr. ,, No. 11 12-pr. ,, No. 12 12-pr. ,, No. 17 12-pr. ,, No. 18	Lieut. Deas Mr. Wright Lieut. Ogilvy Burne Lieut. James	—	—	946	
Total rounds ...		—	598	946	
Total rounds carried forward			758	1,846	

APPENDIX 12 (continued).

Description of Guns.	Name of Commander of Gun Sections.	Ammunition expended in Rounds.			Remarks.
		6-in.	4.7-in.	12-pr.	
	Total rounds brought forward	—	758	1,846	
	VAAL KRANTZ, FEBRUARY 5TH–9TH, 1900.				
4.7-in. wheeled gun No. 1 4.7-in. ,, ,, 2	Comndr. Limpus Lieut. Hunt	—	785	—	
12-pr. gun 1 12-pr. ,, 2 12-pr. ,, 3 12-pr. ,, 4 12-pr. ,, 17 12-pr. ,, 18 12-pr. ,, 11 12-pr. ,, 12	Lieut. Deas Mr. Wright } Lieut. Ogilvy Lieut. James Lieut. Burne	—	—	1,808	
	Total rounds ...	—	785	1,808	
	RELIEF OF LADYSMITH, FEBRUARY 14TH–28TH, 1900.				
6-in. gun...............	Lieut. Drummond	207	—	—	
4.7-in. guns, Nos. 1 & 2 (wheeled).........	Comndr. Limpus	—	1,194	—	
4.7-in. guns (four) on railway & platforms	Lieut. Anderton, N.N.V. & others	—	187	—	
12-prs., Nos. 1, 2, 3 & 4	Lieut. Deas Mr. Wright } Lieut. Ogilvy	—	—	2,069	
12-prs., Nos. 17 & 18	Lieut. James	—	—	526	
12-prs., Nos. 13 & 14	Lieut. Melvill ...	—	—	446	
*12-prs., Nos. 11 & 12	Lieut. Burne	—	—	31	* At Springfield.
	Total rounds ...	207	1,381	3,072	
	Grand total ...	207	2,924	6,726	

NOTE.—12-pr. guns Nos. 5 & 6 { Lieut. Steel } were south of Frere and not in
12-pr. guns Nos. 15 & 16 { Lieut. Halsey } action until after 27th Feb., 1900

APPENDIX 13.

CHAPTER XXIX.

SIR REDVERS BULLER's reasons for not pursuing the Boers on the 28th February, 1900.

Extract from Royal Commission, Minutes of Evidence, Vol. II., pages 182-3.

" I had no doubt from what I saw, and from General White's information, that the enemy were in full retreat, and retreating Boers are very difficult to catch, especially when they have twenty-four hours' start of you. I divided my mounted men into two bodies, the Irregulars to go north and west, the Regulars to go north and east ; and with the Regulars I sent the only Horse artillery guns that I had. I thought it was possible they might come up about Modder River with such of the enemy's guns as had been left in action to the last, and seeing that all the laagers had been moved clear away on the 20th, I considered that if they failed to catch the enemy at Acton Homes, on the Cundycleugh Road, or at Modder River, pursuit would be useless. Parthian tactics are those which long experience in native wars has made almost a second nature to the Boers. All that I know worth knowing about rearguards I learned from the Boers whom I commanded in 1879 ; and I was, and am still, deeply impressed with the belief that unless there is some paramount object to be gained, an attempt to force a Boer rearguard is merely a waste of men. Moreover, in the face of White's telegram, the reprovisioning of Ladysmith became a matter of supreme importance. The river was high. The drifts were impassable. I had only one bridge, a pontoon bridge, leaky, crazy, and worn out. The roads were execrable. Every gun and every vehicle other than a provision wagon brought over that bridge meant nearly three-quarters of an hour's delay in the reprovisioning of Ladysmith. The left division of the cavalry reached Ladysmith during the night, and reported that the whole of my left front was clear of the enemy. The right division crossed the Klip river, and were checked under the south-east corner of Bulwana by a very strongly-posted rearguard of the enemy, who disclosed three guns and considerable rifle power. The country was covered with bush, and much intersected with dongas. This rearguard stopped Burn-Murdoch, who commanded the cavalry on the right; but, watching the action, I felt certain that the Boers would retire at dark. I was satisfied, too, that if I supported him with infantry I should lose many men and gain nothing, because any pursuit to be effective ought to have been by the west and not by the east side of Bulwana.

* * * * * * * *

"On the 1st March I intended to advance to attack Bulwana; but some of Burn-Murdoch's scouts, who had got up the mountain in the night, reported at daybreak that it was evacuated, and that no enemy was visible on our right. Heavy rain had fallen in the night. I ordered an advance on Nelthorpe, where was the drift over the Klip river, though at the time it was impassable. Colonel Rawlinson and a correspondent had ridden into our camp from Ladysmith during the night, and I at once rode back with them into that town. On meeting General White I learnt that he had sent a force out to the Newcastle Road, where he said there was a large Boer laager and Boers in force. Calling up Major Williams, 13th Hussars, whose squadron formed the left of the right pursuing brigade, I told him to proceed at once with it to the place where General White's troops were said to be in action, to get round and beyond them if possible, and to send to me in Ladysmith as soon as possible a report as to whether any enemy worth pursuing were within reach or in sight. Before I left Ladysmith that afternoon I received a report from Lord Dundonald that he was pressing forward to Van Reenen's Pass with no enemy in front of him. He sent in two ambulances which he had taken beyond Dewdrop. I received reports also from Major Williams that there was no one but a very small rearguard among the hills on the Cundycleugh Road in front, and from General Burn-Murdoch that all was clear to Modder River. I then returned to Nelthorpe.

"Passing through Ladysmith, on my way I met Colonel Stoneman, and asked him for how much longer he could really have kept

APPENDIX 13.

the garrison. He replied, 'The garrison, sir, could have lived for three weeks longer, but the natives and sick in hospital would have been starved to death a fortnight earlier.' On my return to my camp I was glad to be able to telegraph to England that seventy-three wagons, the first nine of which contained hospital supplies, were then entering Ladysmith.

"Early on the 2nd March I ascended Bulwana Hill. It was an extraordinarily good day for seeing. Van Reenen's Pass was perfectly clear, with the exception of some wagons at the extreme top, and there was not a soul to be seen in the direction of Sunday River on the enemy's line of retreat to Dundee and Newcastle. I moved my camp that evening to Ladysmith, and on the morning of the 3rd sent the following telegram (No. 214) to Lord Roberts :—' I find that the defeat of the Boers is more complete than I dared to anticipate. This whole district is completely clear of them, and except at the top of Van Reenen's Pass, where several wagons are visible, I can find no trace of them. Their last train left Modder Spruit about one o'clock yesterday [Note—This telegram was written on the 2nd], and they then blew up the bridge. They packed their wagons six days ago, and moved them north of Ladysmith, so I had no chance of intercepting them, but they have left vast quantities of ammunition of all sorts, entrenching tools, camp and individual necessaries. They got away all their guns but two."

APPENDIX 14.

DEFENCE OF LADYSMITH.

CHAPTERS XXX. TO XXXII.

Decision of Boer Council of War vetoed by Subordinates.

(1) A telegram dated 1st December, 1899, from "*State Attorney, Ladysmith*," to "*Government, Pretoria*," is extant which begins by declaring that "so far all the Boer losses may be ascribed to the incompetence of their officers." The truth of this accusation is then proved: "At the Krijgsraad held on the 30th November, it was decided that an assault upon the Platrand should be made early on 1st December. Reinforcements were held in readiness, and if only the assault had been carried out, Ladysmith would have now been in the hands of the Boers. The Krijgsraad had felt no doubts whatever as to the practicability of the attempt, but after they had arrived at their decision, the junior officers convened themselves to another meeting, at which they took it upon themselves to resolve that the plan was too dangerous to attempt—a resolution which only became known to their superiors on 1st December. Much anger is felt by the latter, who will, however, not venture to punish their juniors for this insubordinate act."

(2) A telegram from General Erasmus to the Government at Pretoria under the same date, states that "the officers (fifteen in number) who had been detailed to lead the assault on the position this morning had in the meantime" (*i.e.*, between the time when the Krijgsraad rose and the hour prescribed for the assault) "resolved amongst themselves to disobey the resolution of the Krijgsraad."

"When dawn broke the covering parties of Boers fired heavily upon the Platrand with the object of assisting the assaulting column"—whose leaders, however, had in the meantime determined not to assault at all.

APPENDIX 15.

DEFENCE OF LADYSMITH.

EXPENDITURE OF AMMUNITION DURING THE SIEGE.

4.7-in.	12-prs. Naval.	Howitzers.	15-prs.	9-prs.	2.5-in.	Maxim Nordenfeldt.	Hotchkiss.	Lee-Metford.
514	784	776	3,768	25	101	48	80	213,400
EXPENDITURE ON 6TH JANUARY, 1900 (INCLUDED IN ABOVE).								
29	39	23	744	—	—	20	—	127,210

DEFENCE OF LADYSMITH.

HOSPITAL STATISTICS.

(1) TOTAL ADMISSIONS TO HOSPITAL DURING THE SIEGE.

Total Admissions from all Causes.	Total Deaths from all Causes.	Enteric Fever.		Dysentery.		Wounds.		Other Causes.	
		Admissions.	Deaths.	Admissions.	Deaths.	Admissions.	Deaths.	Admissions.	Deaths.
10,688	600	1,766	393	1,857	117	524	59	6,541	31

APPENDIX 15 (continued).

(2) FIGURES SHOWING THE NUMBER OF TROOPS IN HOSPITAL EACH WEEK SUFFERING FROM ENTERIC FEVER OR DYSENTERY.

Dates.	Enteric Cases in Hospital.	Dysentery Cases in Hospital.
4th November	—	12
11th November	2	21
18th November	7	56
25th November	15	72
2nd December	37	92
9th December	89	126
16th December	190	194
23rd December	254	234
30th December	441	361
6th January	594	433
13th January	671	458
20th January	820	489
27th January	842	472
3rd February	847	447
10th February	875	388
17th February	826	330
24th February	744	311
3rd March	708	341

INDEX

INDEX TO VOLUME II.

Aasvogel Kop and Farm, 214, 231, 233-4.
Abandonment of convoy at Waterval Drift, 77-9.
Abdy, Major A. J., 562-3, 565.
Abon's Dam and Farm, 33, 36-7, 64, 73, 80.
Abraham's Kraal, 186, 189, 208, 213-19, 227, 231; *see also* Driefontein, Battle of; Boers concentrate at, 210.
Abraham's Kraal Drift (Modder river), 147, 213.
à Court, Lieut.-Colonel C., 379, 382.
Acton Homes, 339, 347, 350-1, 360, 362, 364-5, 372-3, 573, 575.
Acton Homes road, 368, 534.
Adye, Colonel J., 182, 212.
Aerial tramway, over the Tugela, 494.
Africander families, in Kimberley, 57.
Ainsworth, Lieut. W. J., 289.
Airlie, Lieut.-Colonel D. S. W., The Earl of, 26.
Albrecht, Major R., 101.
Albrecht, Trooper H., 566, (awarded the Victoria Cross) 570.
Aldershot, 535.
Alderson, Lieut.-Colonel E. A. H., 24, 27, 33, 93-4, 158, 181, 190, 194, 201-2, 212, 215, 217-18, 232-5, 275, 280, 284-5, 289-91, 321-2.
Alderson's Mounted Infantry. *See* Infantry, Mounted.
Aldworth, Lieut.-Col. W., 129, 138-40.
Alexander, Lieut.-Colonel The Hon. W. P., 24, 222.

Alexandersfontein, 37, 54, 58, 64, 66, 68, 92.
Alexandra Berg, 224-5.
Aliwal North, 157, 213, 231, 246, 301, 304, 312-14, 318; bridge at, 246, 258.
Alleman's Drift (Orange river), 255.
Allen, Major E., 312-13.
Allen, Major-General R. E., 320.
Allenby, Major E. H. H., 18, 234-5.
Aller Park, 540.
Altham, Major E. A., 39-40.
Ambuscades: at Acton Homes, 361; at Korn Spruit, 281-2, 288, 294.
Ammunition, 154, 163, 166, 168, 178, 224, 257, 375-6; expended at Kimberley, 43, 49-50, 59; at Spion Kop, 371; at the Tugela Heights, 438, 466, 492; at Vaal Krantz, 418; at Wepener, 318; in Ladysmith, 539, 583.
Ammunition columns. *See* Regular Units.
Amphlett, Major C. G., 259-60, 275-9, 285, 287.
Anderton, Lieut. T., 468, 503.
Argyll and Sutherland Highlanders. *See* Regular Units.
Armistice, at Hart's Hill, 492, 501-2, 583; at Kimberley, 57; at Ladysmith, 541, 571; at Spion Kop, 401; Cronje asks for, 148.
Armoured trains, 47, 55-6, 58, 60; captured at Kraaipan, 47.
Arms, Boers', how obtained, 206; collection of, 257, 260-1, 301.
Army. *See* British Army.

Army Corps, 1st, arrival of, 239.
Army Headquarters, 12–13, 21, 28–30, 75–6, 80, 87, 115, 189, 190–1, 211, 214, 220, 227–8, 234; composition of the forces at, March 13th, 241.
Army Medical Corps, Royal. See REGULAR UNITS.
Army organisation, objects of, 111–12.
Army Service Corps. See REGULAR UNITS.
Artillery, Royal. See REGULAR UNITS.
Artillery in action, concealment and dispersion, use of, inefficiency of such methods, 418.
Arundel, 89, 152, 250, 252–4.
Ashburner, Lieut. L. F., 289.
Ashmore, Lieut. E. B., 288.
Asiatics in Kimberley, 65; in Ladysmith, 538.
Assembly of troops for relief of Kimberley, February 8th, 4.
Atkinson, Sergeant A. (awarded the Victoria Cross), 124.
Australian contingents: Horse, New South Wales, Queensland, South Australia, Victoria, West Australia. See COLONIAL UNITS.

BABERSPAN, 214–18, 223.
Baden-Powell, Colonel R. S. S., 44.
Bainbridge, Major E. G. T., 329, 331.
Bainbridge, Captain N., 277–9, 281.
Bainbridge's Mounted Infantry. See INFANTRY, MOUNTED.
Bain's Vlei, 209–10, 213, 230.
Balance of power in South Africa, changed February 11th–March 15th, 1900, 240.
Balloon at Paardeberg, 168, 173.
Banfield, Lieut.-Col. R. J. F., 130, 134.
Bank's Drift (Modder river), 109, 116, 122, 129, 161.
Bank's Drift Farm, 158, 168–9.
Bannatine-Allason, Major R., 26.
Barbed wire fences, 41, 51, 94, 160, 223, 235, 489, 578.
Barker, Colonel J. C., 120.

Barkly West, 90, 332.
Barton, Major-General G., C.B., 403, 423–4, 429, 436–7, 439–41, 446, 448, 450–1, 453–4, 459, 462–3, 470, 474, 480, 493, 503, 505–6, 508, 510–15, 519–21, 523–5.
Bastard's Nek, 251.
Bastion Hill, 346–51, 357, 366–73, 377.
Basutoland, 157, 213, 259, 261, 263, 304, 318.
Bates, Major A., 45.
Batson, Major H., 427.
Bayly, Major A. W. L., 499.
Beaconsfield, 41, 51–2, 60.
Beaconsfield Town Guard. See COLONIAL UNITS.
Bearcroft, Captain J. E., R.N., 90, 92, 147, 198.
Bechuanaland, 44–5.
Beit, Mr. A., 315.
Bell Spruit, 535.
Bell's Kop, 533, 548–9.
Belmont, 11, 59, 135.
Benaudheidsfontein, 54.
Berkefeld filters, 577, 579.
Berkshire regiment, Royal. See REGULAR UNITS.
Besters Kraal, 312–13.
Bester's Valley, 535, 543, 555–6, 565, 571.
Bethanie, 256, 303, 308–9, 311–12, 320.
Bethel commando. See COMMANDOS.
Bethlehem commando. See COMMANDOS.
Bethulie, 213, 231, 236, 249, 254, 256–8, 263–4, 300–1, 312, 327.
Bethulie bridge, 165, 180, 248–9, 258.
Bethulie commando. See COMMANDOS.
Bethune, Lieut.-Colonel E. C., 341–2, 354, 385, 406, 426, 429, 441, 493, 504.
Bethune's Mounted Infantry. See COLONIAL UNITS.
Bewicke-Copley, Major R. C. A. B., 428, 476.

INDEX.

Beyers, Commandant, 445.
Bezuidenhout Pass, 184.
Biggarsberg, 184–5, 188, 238, 242, 338.
Biltong, 579.
Binnie, Mr., 579.
Bird river, action at, 245.
Birkbeck, Major V. M., 245.
Blaauwbank (Natal), 338.
Blaauwbank Drift, 20–1.
Blaauwboschpan Farm, 25, 28, 79.
Blaauwkrantz river, 421, 431, 436, 439, 441, 462, 503, 507.
Black Watch, The. *See* REGULAR UNITS.
Blankenburg's Vlei, 37.
Blewitt, Major W. E., 562.
Bloemfontein, 4, 7, 10, 16, 29, 38, 59, 68, 81, 93, 95–6, 99, 106–7, 135, 146, 154–5, 157, 161, 164, 166, 171, 173, 180, 185–6, 188–92, 203, 208–10, 212, 215, 218, 222–4, 228, 247, 254–7, 308, 311–12, 314, 318, 319–21, 325–7, 332, 575; advance on, from Paardeberg, 213–14, 231; British halt at, 243, 274–313; capture of railway plant at, 237; cavalry action outside, 235–6; conference at, 42; Cronje supposed to be aiming for, 79, 83, 88, 97, 110; preparations for defence of, by Boers, 210, 213; proclamation to inhabitants of, 234; railway re-opened to Cape Town, 258; scheme for French to move on, 164, 171; surrender of, 238; the occupation of, 230–40; water supply at, 241, 259, 281.
Bloemfontein commando. *See* COMMANDOS.
Bloemhof commando. *See* COMMANDOS.
Bloemspruit Farm, 236, 295, 303.
Bloy's Farm, 434, 445, 449–50, 452, 454, 460, 462.
Blundell-Hollinshead-Blundell, Lieut. D. H., 477, 479, 481–3.

Boat, ferry, on Tugela, 343, 354, 458.
Boats, James' collapsible, 120, 126, 163.
Boers : activity of, renewal of, after fall of Bloemfontein, 265–6 ; assault the Platrand at Ladysmith, 557–70 ; begin movement on Kimberley, 47 ; casualties of, 56, 59, 95, 160, 170, 178, 203, 229, 251, 333, 361, 411, 477, 521, 570–1 ; condition of, in Cronje's laager, 170–1 ; counter-attack by, at Klip Kraal Drift, 86 ; at Thaba Mountain, 330 ; demoralisation of, 208, 241–2, 304 ; depression of, 5, 207, 265 ; deserters from, 79, 109, 152, 164, 187, 189, 210 ; discipline among, want of, 166, 168 ; effect of Sannah's Post on, 298–9 ; entrenchments of, at Paardeberg, 102 ; at Poplar Grove, 187 ; at Tugela Heights, 435 ; furloughs granted to, by De Wet, 241–2 ; horses of, 1, 36, 98 ; inactivity of, at Ladysmith, 544, 572 ; after success at Stormberg, 244 ; Intelligence Department of, *see* INTELLIGENCE ; investment of Kimberley by, 54, 57, 66 ; of Ladysmith by, 531–85 ; *moral* of, at Poplar Grove, 187 ; passes to, Lord Roberts offers, 260 ; plan of campaign of, included early attack on Kimberley, 42, 44 ; position of, at Paardeberg, 109–10 ; at Poplar Grove, 185–7 ; around Kimberley, 54 ; around Ladysmith, 539–40 ; at Karee Siding, 270 ; at Sannah's Post, 281–99 ; at Spion Kop, 344–402 ; at Vaal Krantz, 403–22 ; on the Tugela, 424, 530 ; proclamations by, 188, 266–7 ; raids of, in Natal, 184, 532 ; rearguard, actions of, 82, 90, 103, 201–2, 228, 520, 526 ; reasons of, for not holding Spion Kop, 383–4 ; retreat of, from Bloemfontein, 237, 241 ; from Driefontein, 230 ; from Ladysmith, 583–4 ; from Magers-

Boers: retreat of—*continued*.
fontein, 81, 96; from Pieters Hill, 514; from South-east Cape Colony, 213, 245, 246–8, 259, 263–4; from South-east Orange Free State, 324; responsibility for supply to, 266; Steyn and Kruger attempt to revive, 188; strength and dispositions of, 14, 59, 89, 94, 146, 165, 187–90, 211, 230–1, 249, 259, 265, 316, 414, 539–40; surprise of (Acton Homes), 361; tactics of, at Spion Kop, 384; telegrams from, 10–11, 17, 167, 170–1, 185, 210–11, 218, 314, 317, 425, 455, 470; transport of, property of burghers, 108; War Councils of, *see* KRIJGSRAAD; women and children of, in laagers, 1, 98, 107, 162, 171; wounded, 162.

Boesman's Kop, 259, 261, 276–81, 283–93, 295–8.

Boileau, Captain F. R. F., 174.

Bokpoort, 264.

Boksburg commando. *See* COMMANDOS.

Bombardment at Colenso, 335; at Kimberley, 55, 57, 68–9; at Ladysmith, 531–85; at Paardeberg, 110–11, 114–15, 150, 155, 168, 174, 176; at Spion Kop, 334–402; at Vaal Krantz, 403–22; at Wepener, 316–17; of the Tugela Heights, 438–530.

Border Horse. *See* COLONIAL UNITS.

Border Mounted Rifles. *See* COLONIAL UNITS.

Border regiment, The. *See* REGULAR UNITS.

Borderers, King's Own Scottish. *See* REGULAR UNITS.

Borderers, South Wales. *See* REGULAR UNITS.

Bosch Kop, 202–3.

Boschkop (Natal). *See* HLANGWHANE.

Boschrand, 209, 218–24, 227.

Boschvarkfontein, 88, 99.

Boshof, 46, 56, 81, 93, 166, 183, 187, 189, 231, 314, 332–3.

Boshof commando. *See* COMMANDOS.

Boshof road, 92–3, 208.

Bosjespan Farm, 32, 79, 87, 108, 181.

Botha, General Louis, 188, 238, 242, 265, 348, 399, 413, 424–5, 433, 455–7, 470, 502, 504.

Botha, Petrus, 56.

Botha, Commandant Philip, 136, 168–71, 189.

Bothashoek Farm, 99, 140.

Bowen, Major R. S., 564, 567.

Bowles, Colonel H., 124.

Bowman's Farm, 457–8, 460.

Boyes, Major-General J. E., 320.

Brabant, Brig.-General E. Y., C.M.G., 165, 241, 244–6, 301–4, 312–13, 318–20, 324, 327, 332.

Brabant's Horse. *See* COLONIAL UNITS.

Brabazon, Major-General J. P., C.B., 321, 324.

Braithwaite, Captain W. P., 481.

Brakfontein, 345–8, 352, 365, 377, 385, 405–10, 412, 414.

Brandfort, 79, 241, 268–9, 273, 281, 298, 317.

Brand Kop, 233–8.

Brandvallei, or Brand Vlei, 98, 103, 190.

Bredenbach, Commandant, 110, 189.

Bridges: Boer, over Tugela, 425, 434, 464, 494, 497, 524, 526; construction of, 355–6, 425, 460, 463, 527; destruction of, 248, 255, 458, 504; guarding of, 257, 267–9, 303; over Tugela, 344, 494; railway, repair of, 258–9, 274, 332–3.

Brigades. *See* CAVALRY *and* INFANTRY.

Bright, Private, 289.

British Army: casualties in, *see* CASUALTIES; composition of, at Bloemfontein, March 13th, 241; in Natal, February 12th, 425–9; condition of, at Bloemfontein, 242; before Ladysmith, 522; conditions met by, in South Africa, 204–5; congratulations to, 183, 238–9;

INDEX. 663

dispositions of, out of Natal, April 29th, 327–8; organisation of, in Natal, 340, 528; redistribution of, 320, 327; after Paardeberg. 180; after Sannah's Post, 305; cavalry into two brigades, 164; mounted infantry into four brigades, 181; Natal army after relief of Ladysmith, 528; Natal army before Pieters Hill. 505; Natal army before Spion Kop, 340; Natal army before relief of Ladysmith, 429; Staff system in, prior to 1888, 181; strength of, on March 6th, before Poplar Grove, 190; Brabant's division, February 16th, 245, 318; Broadwood's force, March 30th, 275; Clements' force, February 22nd, 254; Dundonald's brigade, January 10th, 341; Dundonald's brigade, January 18th, 360; Gatacre's division, February 11th, 246; Hart's command, April 14th, 318; Lyttelton's force, at Potgieters Drift, January 16th, 354; Natal Field Force, February 12th, 425–9; Tucker's division, March 28th, 270; Warren's force at Spion Kop, 352–3; Wepener garrison, 315; temporary immobility of, December, 1899, 335.

British, proclamations of, 234, 260; shooting of, compared with that of Boers, 388.

Britstown, 266.

Broadwood, Brig.-General R. G., 4, 18–19, 24, 26, 33–5, 92, 96–7, 99–102, 140, 149–52, 158–9, 164, 171, 195, 201–3, 217, 219, 222–3, 227–8, 234, 236–7, 269, 275–99, 300, 303, 308, 327–8, 331–2.

Brocklehurst, Major-General J. F., M.V.O., 540–1.

Brooke, Colonel L. G., 429, 489, 492, 496.

Brown, Major F. J., 134.

Brown's Drift (Modder river), 32, 90–1.

Buchan, Lieut.-Colonel L., 174.

Buckley, Lieut. B. T., 283.

Buffalo river, 338–9.

Buffs, The (East Kent regiment). *See* REGULAR UNITS.

Buller, The Right Hon. General Sir Redvers H., G.C.B., K.C.M.G., 5, 7, 10, 16, 62, 71, 89, 155, 161, 173, 544, 548, 580–5; advice of, to Warren for Spion Kop operations, 348; asks for reinforcements, 9; difficulties of, after Vaal Krantz, 424–5; entry of, into Ladysmith, 178; messages from, to General White, 337, 358–9, 404, 419, 425, 433, 464, 550–4, 572–6; to Lord Roberts, 5–11, 89, 155, 183–4, 405, 419; new plan of, after Spion Kop, 403, 407; after Vaal Krantz, 419; orders issued by, 340, 343, 347, 407, 419–20, 436–7, 442–3, 457–60, 464–5; plans of, for relief of Ladysmith, 7, 183, 425, 433–4, 472, 547; proposals of, after relief of Ladysmith, 184; scheme of, for Spion Kop campaign, 337, 339, 357, 359.

Bultfontein (Orange Free State), 322.

Bultfontein mine, 41.

Bulwana. *See* UMBULWANA.

Burger, General Schalk, 384, 470, 557.

Burghers. *See* BOERS.

Burghersdorp, 167, 213, 247.

Burma Mounted Infantry. *See* INFANTRY, MOUNTED.

Burn-Murdoch, Brig.-General J. F., 406, 421, 426, 429, 441, 469–70, 493, 498, 523–9.

Burne, Lieut. C. R. N., R.N., 426.

Burnham, Mr. F. R., 188, 195.

Burrell, Major W. S., 483.

Bushman's Kop, 302.

Bushman's river (Natal), 335.

Butler, Lieut.-General Sir W., K.C.B., 42.

Byng, Lieut.-Colonel The Hon. J. H. G., 427.

CABLE. See TELEGRAPHS.
Cactus Knolls, 186, 200.
Cæsar's Camp, 464, 535, 537, 548, 554, 572, 579, 582–3; attacks on, 336, 542–4, 555–70.
Caledon river, 260, 264, 312, 315.
Callwell, Major C. E., 454–5.
Cameron Highlanders. See REGULAR UNITS.
Cameronians (Scottish Rifles). See REGULAR AND MILITIA UNITS.
Campaign, whole aspect of, changed, after capture of Cronje and entry into Ladysmith, 178–9, 206.
Campbell, Major-General B. B. D., M.V.O., 320.
Campbell, Major W. P., 561, 563–4, 567.
Canadian regiments. See COLONIAL UNITS.
Canadians, Royal (Leinster regiment). See REGULAR UNITS.
Cape Colony, 425; Boer, raid in, proposed, 166; retreat from, 213, 247–8, 257; Botha believes Natal army moving to, February 10th, 425; British in, inadequacy of, 239; disaffected Dutch in, 335–6; effect in, of Labuschagne's Nek fight, 246; frontier defence of, 44; Gatacre and Clements, operations of, in, 241–58; Government of, 43, 46; local forces in, see COLONIAL UNITS; military situation in, 184, 238, 336; Ministry of, 42; north-west of, Lord Kitchener to command, 212; ports of, 155, 243; Prieska district of, 182, 212; railways in, 155, 243; republic in, proposed, 167.
Cape Garrison (Volunteer) Artillery. See COLONIAL UNITS.
Cape Mounted Rifles. See COLONIAL UNITS.
Cape Mounted Rifles Artillery. See COLONIAL UNITS.
Cape Police. See COLONIAL UNITS.

Cape Town, 2, 20, 39, 42–5, 47, 62, 153, 178, 240, 243, 359; railway re-opened to, from Bloemfontein, 258.
Capper, Major T., 448, 505, 509.
Captures: by Boers, 47, 76, 79, 136, 253, 282, 291, 298–9, 310; by British, 37, 79, 82, 87, 99, 160, 169–70, 178, 229, 237, 246, 256–7, 333, 361, 451, 517.
Carabiniers. See REGULAR UNITS.
Carnegie, Captain the Hon. R. F., 561, 563, 565.
Carolina Commando. See COMMANDOS.
Carr, Lieut.-Colonel E. E., 429, 510.
Carter, Lieut.-Colonel H. M., 250–2.
Carter's Farm, 60–1.
Carter's ridge, 41, 54, 57–61.
Casualties: Boer, see BOERS; British, at Acton Homes, 361; at Driefontein, 228–9; at Glen, 268–9; at Jacobsdal, 79; at Karee Siding, 272–3; at Leeuwkop, 321; at Osfontein, 136–7; at Paardeberg, 143, 169–70, 176; at Poplar Grove, 203; at Reddersburg, 309–10; at relief of Ladysmith, 453, 455, 461, 466, 468, 482, 500, 508, 514, 521; at Sannah's Post, 288, 299; at Spion Kop, 369–72, 378, 398, 402; at Vaal Krantz, 410, 421; at Wagon Hill, 570; at Wepener, 319; at Wolvekraal, 14; in Brabant's force, 246; in cavalry division, 27, 34–6, 95, 101, 160, 323, 327; in Chermside's brigade, 159; in Clements' force, 251–3, 255; in Duke of Cornwall's Light Infantry, 140; in Gatacre's force, 247; in Kelly-Kenny's division, 86; in Kimberley, 56, 61–2, 69, 72; in Ladysmith, 570; in Pilcher's force, 263. See also APPENDIX 2.
Cathcart, Captain the Hon. R., 477.
Cavalry, 2, 37–8, 92–3; advance of, after Pieters Hill, 525–30.
Cavalry Brigades:—
   1st (Porter), 12, 18–20, 24–6, 33–7,

INDEX. 665

93–5, 97, 152, 158, 194, 201, 203, 212, 214–15, 219–23, 227–8, 232–5, 237, 241, 269–70, 295–6, 298, 303, 328, 332.
2nd (Broadwood), 18–19, 24–6, 33–7, 96–7, 99–102, 140–1, 149–52, 158–9, 191, 201–3, 214–15, 219, 222–3, 227–8, 233–4, 236–7, 241, 269–70, 275–99, 300, 303, 327–8, 331–2.
3rd (Gordon), 18–20, 24–6, 33–7, 93–5, 97, 140–1, 150, 152, 191, 201, 214, 234, 237–8, 241, 268–70, 295–6, 298, 303, 320–6, 332.
4th (Dickson), 320–3, 332.
1st (Natal) (Burn-Murdoch), 406, 408, 426, 469–70, 493, 498, 503, 523–9.
2nd Mounted (Natal) (Lord Dundonald), 334, 341–3, 353, 356–7, 360–5, 368–9, 406, 421, 427, 437, 442, 444–5, 449, 451, 453, 462, 493, 498, 503, 506–7, 511, 523–30.
Cavalry division, 3–4, 11–29, 32–7, 66, 68, 72–3, 79–80, 93–5, 110, 116, 122, 140–1, 150, 152, 154, 158–61, 172, 180, 190–7, 201–3, 212–15, 219, 222, 227–8, 233–8, 269–73, 294–8, 300, 321–3, 326, 328 ; charge of, before relief of Kimberley, 35 ; march of, to Koodoos Drift, 103 ; strength of, February 24th, 172 ; March 6th, 190 ; to advance on Bloemfontein, 164, 171 ; to relief of Kimberley, 11 ; weight carried by horses of, 36.
Cemetery Hill, 536–7.
Chamier, Lieut.-Colonel G. D., 58, 60–1, 66.
Charles, Lieut. E. M. S., 236–7.
Chermside, Major-General Sir H. C., G.C.M.G., C.B., 123, 142, 147, 157, 159, 161–2, 167, 270–1, 320, 326–7.
Chesham, Colonel Lord C. C. W., 183.
Cheshire regiment. See REGULAR UNITS.

Chester-Master, Captain R., 87–8, 91, 96.
Chevril, paste, soup, etc., 578–9.
Chiazzari, Lieut. N., 468.
Chief of the Staff. See KITCHENER and MILES.
Chieveley, 334–7, 340–1, 344–5, 402–3, 419–23, 425–9, 431, 437, 440–1, 450, 453, 458, 460–2, 468–71, 484–6, 503, 506–7, 510, 521, 580.
Cholmondeley, Lieut.-Colonel H. C., 79.
Christiana, 97, 166.
Christmas greetings from H. M. the Queen, 65.
Cingolo, 404 ; the capture of, 423–46.
Cingolo Nek, 433, 447–51, 459, 503, 505, 507, 582–3.
City of London Imperial Volunteers Mounted Infantry, 28, 79, 147, 270.
City Mounted Volunteers. See COLONIAL UNITS.
Civilian employés (railway), 155.
Civilians enrolled as Volunteers, in Kimberley, 48 ; in Ladysmith, 581.
Clements, Major-General R. A. P., D.S.O., 3, 89, 152, 154–5, 164, 172, 182, 213, 231, 250–3, 259, 267, 300–1, 303, 320.
Clery, Lieut.-General Sir C. F., K.C.B., 334, 336–7, 341–2, 366, 368–9, 373–4, 376, 388, 402, 407, 420, 545.
Clocolan, 262, 264, 281, 302, 332.
Clowes, Lieut.-Colonel P. L., 331–2.
Clump Hill, 430, 454–5, 460, 462–3, 469, 502, 510–11, 514, 525.
Coke, Major-General J. Talbot, 371–6, 378, 385, 387, 389, 391, 394–7, 399–401, 428, 450, 453–4, 459, 461, 463–4, 466–9, 472, 493, 502–3, 506, 510, 521.
Coldstream Guards, The. See REGULAR UNITS.
Colenso, 8–9, 70, 211, 334, 336, 338–40, 345, 347–8, 350, 367, 399, 404, 423–5, 430–2, 438, 441, 443, 456, 458, 460–1, 467–9, 472, 486–7, 494,

Colenso—*continued*.
498, 503, 506, 510, 521, 524, 528, 533–4, 550–3, 581.
Colenso heights and kopjes, 421, 432, 452, 454, 465, 467, 469, 471, 473–4, 476, 487, 493, 495, 502, 528.
Colesberg, 13, 15–17, 29, 79, 89, 106, 110, 135, 146, 152, 154–5, 157, 161, 165–6, 186, 189–90, 209–10, 213, 242, 250, 253–4, 259, 261, 263–4, 335, 383.
Coleskop, 252.
Colonial Contingents, South African and oversea, 240. *See also* COLONIAL UNITS.
Colonial division. *See* COLONIAL UNITS.
Colonial Government, 40, 62.
Colonial Scouts. *See* COLONIAL UNITS.
Colonial staff officers, 40.
Colonial troops, command of, 45.
Colonial Units :—
 Australian Horse (1st), 222, 228, 269.
 Australian Mounted Infantry, 301.
 Beaconsfield Town Guard, 60.
 Bethune's Mounted Infantry, 341–2, 354, 385, 406, 493.
 Border Horse, 312–13, 318.
 Border Mounted Rifles, 537, 584.
 Brabant's Horse (1st and 2nd), 244, 246, 302–4, 315–16, 318.
 Canadian Artillery, 145.
 Cape Garrison (Volunteer) Artillery, 318.
 Cape Mounted Rifles, 244–5, 247, 303-4, 315-16.
 Cape Mounted Rifles Artillery, 315–16.
 Cape Police, 43, 45, 47–9, 52, 55, 58–61, 92, 248–9, 256.
 City Mounted Volunteers (1st), 254.
 Colonial division, 241, 244–7, 301, 304, 312, 315–33.
 Colonial Scouts, 428–9.
 Composite regiment of Mounted Infantry, 341–2, 360, 368, 427, 440, 444–5, 527.
 Corps of Guides, 546, 548.
 De Montmorency's Scouts, 247–9, 256, 310–11.
 Diamond Fields Artillery, 40, 42, 44, 46, 52, 55–6, 58, 60–1, 68, 92–3.
 Diamond Fields Horse, 40, 42, 44, 46, 55, 60, 92.
 Driscoll's Scouts, 315–16.
 Durban Light Infantry, 429.
 East London Volunteers, 244.
 Eastern Province Horse, 254.
 French's Scouts, 236.
 Grahamstown Volunteers Mounted Infantry, 28.
 Imperial Light Horse, 355, 361, 406, 499, 527–8, 540–1, 543–4, 546–7, 557–61, 563–4, 566, 569, 584.
 Imperial Light Infantry, 375, 385, 387, 400, 426, 486–7, 489, 492, 495, 506, 508.
 Kaffrarian Mounted Rifles, 244, 304, 312–13, 315–16, 318.
 Kimberley Light Horse, 47–50, 55, 58–61, 94.
 Kimberley Mounted Corps, 333.
 Kimberley regiment, 46, 56, 58, 92.
 Kimberley Rifles, 40, 42.
 Kimberley Town Guard, 46, 48–9, 58, 69.
 Kitchener's Horse, 12–13, 18, 25, 28, 75, 121–2, 130, 133, 136, 329–30.
 Ladysmith Town Guard, 537.
 Mashonaland Mounted Police, 47.
 Natal Carbineers, 357, 361, 406–7, 527, 537, 546–7, 584.
 Natal Field Artillery, 426, 429.
 Natal Mounted Police, 407, 426.
 Natal Mounted Rifles, 537, 544.
 Natal Naval Volunteers, 468, 521, 538, 557, 560.
 Natal Pioneer Corps, 494, 521, 528.
 Natal Royal Rifles, 429.
 Natal Volunteers, 540, 559–60.
 Nesbitt's Horse, 191.
 New South Wales Artillery, 145.
 New South Wales Lancers, 222, 228.

INDEX. 667

New South Wales Mounted Infantry, 81, 117, 191, 254.
New South Wales Mounted Rifles, 13.
New Zealand Mounted Infantry, 13, 95, 291, 299, 329.
New Zealand Mounted Rifles, 12, 275.
New Zealand Rough Riders, 318.
Prince Alfred's Volunteer Guard, 254, 332.
Queensland Mounted Infantry, 95, 191, 287, 292, 296.
Queenstown Rifle Volunteers, 244, 312, 318.
Railway Pioneer regiment, 155.
Rimington's Guides, 12, 18, 81–2, 87, 96, 235, 275.
Roberts' Horse, 20, 140, 152, 156–7, 194, 275, 280, 282–4, 289, 299.
Royal Canadian regiment, 75–6, 126–7, 139–42, 148–9, 157–8, 174–5, 200–1, 325, 329, 331.
Royal Victorian Navy, 156.
South African Light Horse, 341, 343, 360–1, 368, 406, 423, 427, 440, 444, 498, 507, 524.
South Australian Infantry, 254.
Tasmanian Infantry, 254.
Thorneycroft's Mounted Infantry, 341, 343, 360, 368, 375–6, 379, 384, 386, 406, 427, 441–2, 461–2, 464, 468, 493, 503, 521, 524, 527.
Uitenhage Rifles, 254.
Umvoti Mounted Rifles, 426.
Victorian Infantry, 254.
Victorian Mounted Infantry, 251–2, 331.
Victorian Mounted Rifles, 254.
West Australian Infantry, 254.
West Australian Mounted Infantry, 251, 332.
Colquhoun, Lieut.-Commander W. J. (Royal Victorian Navy), 156.
Columns, flying, for Prieska district, 182.
Colvile, Lieut.-General Sir H. E., K.C.M.G., C.B., 4, 15, 22, 74, 80, 90–1, 103–5, 114–16, 118, 121, 123, 126, 128, 131–2, 138, 142, 173, 178, 180–1, 199–200, 213, 227, 277, 285, 287, 292–300, 325, 327.
Commandant-General. *See* JOUBERT.
Commander-in-Chief. *See* WOLSELEY and ROBERTS.
Commandos :—
  Bethel, 443, 457, 540.
  Bethlehem, 89, 129–30, 187, 290, 540.
  Bloemfontein, 187.
  Bloemhof, 20, 54.
  Boksburg, 443, 457, 540.
  Boshof (Kolbe's), 54, 166, 187, 199.
  Carolina, 344, 393, 398, 457, 470, 540.
  Cronje's (Andries), 78, 89, 99, 168, 211.
  De Beer's, 122, 209.
  De la Rey's, 54, 166–7, 250.
  De Wet's, 17, 19, 99, 130, 135, 157, 165, 168, 211, 237, 286.
  Despatch Riders, 17, 106.
  Edenburg, 187.
  Edwardes' Scouts, 393.
  Ermelo, 344, 349, 443, 457, 540.
  Fauresmith, 135, 256.
  Ferreira's, 37, 99, 166.
  Ficksburg, 187.
  Free State Artillery, 101.
  Free Staters, 10, 23, 29, 54, 93, 152, 165, 233, 344, 349, 384, 408, 470, 532–3, 540, 543, 557, 560, 565.
  French corps, 211.
  Froneman's, 30–1, 33, 168–9, 308, 312.
  German corps, 539, 579.
  Germiston, 540.
  Griqualand West (rebels), 93–5.
  Harrismith, 539, 565.
  Heidelberg, 187, 201, 443, 457, 539.
  Heilbron, 89, 470, 539–40.
  Irish brigade, 539.

668 THE WAR IN SOUTH AFRICA.

Commandos—*continued*.
   Jacobsdal, 54.
   Johannesburg, 344, 411, 457, 540.
   Johannesburg Police (Zarps), 210, 218, 225–7, 539.
   Kroonstad, 54, 539–40.
   Krugersdorp, 349, 443, 457, 490, 539.
   Ladybrand, 187, 210.
   Lichtenburg, 54.
   Lubbe's, 25–7, 33, 135.
   Lydenburg, 344, 457, 470, 539.
   Middelburg, 443, 540.
   Mounted Police (Kruger's escort), 203.
   Philippolis, 135, 187.
   Piet Retief, 457, 540.
   Potchefstroom, 20, 187.
   Pretoria, 349, 457, 539–40.
   Senekal, 89, 165, 187, 211, 408.
   Standerton, 443, 457, 525, 540.
   Swaziland, 443, 457.
   Swaziland Police, 540.
   Transvaal Artillery, 539.
   Transvaal Police, 209–10.
   Transvaalers, 28, 54, 165–6, 532–3, 557.
   Utrecht, 539, 542.
   Van der Post's, 14.
   Vrede, 408, 470, 540.
   Vryheid, 344, 443, 457, 539.
   Wakkerstroom, 539, 542.
   Wepener, 160.
   Winburg, 165, 169, 187, 192, 211, 290, 539–40.
   Wolmaranstad, 54.
   Zoutpansberg, 443, 457, 540.
Commissariat. *See* SUPPLIES.
Commissie bridge, 312.
Commissie Drift, 263–4.
Commissie Poort, 262, 264–5.
Commission Royal, on the War in South Africa, 181, 193, 404, 460, 529, 531.
Communications, over the Tugela at Colenso, 494; with Kimberley, 63.
Composite regiment. *See* COLONIAL UNITS.
Composition of columns marching on Bloemfontein, 214.
Congratulations, on defence of Ladysmith, 575; on entry into Bloemfontein, 238–9; on relief of Ladysmith, 575; to 2nd East Surrey regiment, 483.
Conical Hill, 352, 377, 382, 387.
Coningham, Lieut.-Colonel C., 251.
Connaught Rangers, The. *See* REGULAR UNITS.
Constantia, 322.
Convoys: Boer—march from Cape Colony, 263–4; British—captured near De Kiel's drift, 76; captured at Waterval drift, 75–9; from Honey Nest Kloof, 78, 90; from Osfontein, 241; of wounded from Paardeberg, 182; through Poplar Grove, 232, 238; to army after Paardeberg, 181; system of, 12. *See also* VOLUME I., CHAPTER XXV.
Cooke, Lieut.-Colonel E., 428.
Cooper, Colonel C. D., 429.
Cornwall's, Duke of, Light Infantry. *See* REGULAR UNITS.
Corps of Guides. *See* COLONIAL UNITS.
Cove Redoubt, 537–8, 562.
Cramer-Roberts, Captain W. E., 133.
Creusot guns, 4, 66, 94, 414–16, 418, 434–5.
Crofton, Colonel M. E., 384–5, 389–90, 420, 428, 474, 478–9, 481.
Cronje, Commando of. *See* COMMANDOS.
Cronje, General Andries, 20–1, 23, 25, 78, 89, 99, 168, 189, 210, 532.
Cronje, General P., 1–3, 5, 16–17, 20, 22–3, 28, 30, 32–3, 37, 54, 72, 90, 93, 96–7, 104–5, 159, 191, 193, 203–4, 238, 242–3, 511; assault on laager of, by British, 173–5; bombardment of, 150, 154–6; clings to Magersfontein, 1, 80; convoys of, 85, 88, 98, 100–2, 123; correspondence of, with Lord Roberts, 148, 163, 177; De Wet urges him to cut his way

INDEX.

out, 170; fails to out-march his pursuers, 98; laager of, 85, 108, 117-18, 134; laager, investment of, 145-61; lines of communication of, 29, 38; pursuit of, 73-105; realises his danger, 80; rearguard actions of, 83-7, 100, 102; rejects De Wet's advice to break out, 151; reports of deserters from Paardeberg, 164; retreat, choice of lines of, 81; cut off by French, 100-3; on Bloemfontein, 79, 83; strength of, 89; the surrender of, 162-79; transport of, belongs to burghers, 107; surrender of, mistake as to, 148; wagons of, set on fire, 156; white flag raised by, 175.
Crow's Nest, 557, 559, 564, 567.
Cruickshank, Major D. T., 275, 289-90.
Cundycleugh Pass, 582.
Curtis, Private A. E. (awarded the Victoria Cross), 482.
Cyclists, Boer, as orderlies, 263.

DALGETY, LIEUT.-COLONEL E. H., 315-19, 326-7.
Dalzell, Lieut.-Colonel the Hon. A. E., 83-5, 150-1.
Dam, Klip river, 579-80.
Damfontein, 195-6, 203.
Damfontein Farm, 322.
Damvallei, 209, 211, 216-21, 224-7.
Davels Spruit, 525.
Davidson, Lieut.-Colonel W. L., 35, 99-102, 222.
Dawson, Lieut.-Colonel H. L., 275, 283.
De Aar, 166, 182, 212, 243.
Dean, Lieut. F. W., R.N., 28, 34, 82, 87, 98, 150, 156, 200.
De Beer, Commandant T., 30, 81-2, 100-1, 107, 122, 141; commando of, see COMMANDOS.
De Beers Mining Company, 39, 41, 49-51, 53, 66, 69, 140, 181.

Débris heaps, aids to defence of Kimberley, 41-2, 68.
Deel Drift, 343.
Defences, Kimberley, scheme of, discussed in 1896, 40; Kimberley, plan of, worked out, 51; Ladysmith, 536-38.
De Jagers, Field-Cornet, 565-6.
De Kiel's Drift, 3, 18-25, 28, 74, 76.
Delagoa Bay, 324.
De la Rey, General H. J., 166-7, 189, 209-11, 218-19, 227, 230, 233, 250, 265; commandos of, see COMMANDOS; grants furloughs to the burghers, 242.
De Lisle, Lieut.-Colonel H. de B., D.S.O., 13-14, 131-2, 191, 329-30.
De Lisle's Mounted Infantry. See INFANTRY, MOUNTED.
De Montmorency, Captain the Hon. R. H. L. J., V.C., 247-8.
De Montmorency's Scouts. See COLONIAL UNITS.
Denniss, 2nd Lieut. G. B. B., 566.
Derbyshire regiment. See REGULAR and MILITIA UNITS.
Despatch riders, Boer. See COMMANDOS.
De Villebois Mareuil, Colonel, 1, 66, 187, 211, 333.
De Villiers, Commandant, 565-6.
De Villiers, Commandant, 281, 294, 308.
De Villiers, Captain, 470.
Devon Post, 536, 538, 541, 554.
Devonshire regiment. See REGULAR UNITS.
Dewdrop, 340, 364-5, 582.
De Wet, Commandant Christian, 19-25, 29, 72, 74, 78-9, 89, 99, 106-7, 115, 130, 165, 167, 170, 176, 181, 185-9, 192-3, 202-4, 207-10, 218-19, 222, 237, 265-6, 275, 278, 281, 285-6, 290-1, 296, 298-9; appointed to command of Orange Free State burghers, 165; at Reddersburg, 300-13; at Wepener, 314-33; com-

De Wet, Commandant Christian—*con.* mando of, *see* COMMANDOS; counter-attack by, at Paardeberg, 135–8, 143–4, 149–52, 154, 157–62, 164–5, 168–9; grant of furloughs to the burghers by, 242; retirement of, from Driefontein, 227; "Three Years' War," by, 17, 159, 230.

De Wet, Commandant Piet, 172, 209–11, 281, 322, 324.

Dewetsdorp, 259–61, 264, 302–8, 314, 317, 320–2, 324, 326–7.

Diamond Fields Advertiser, 63.

Diamond Fields Artillery. *See* COLONIAL UNITS.

Diamond Fields Horse. *See* COLONIAL UNITS.

Diamond mines, 39, 41.

Dick-Cunyngham, Lieut.-Colonel W. H., V.C., 561.

Dickson, Major-General J. B. B., C.B., 320, 322–3.

Dingwall, Captain K., 76.

Director of Railways. *See* GIROUARD.

Director of Supplies. *See* RICHARDSON.

Director of Telegraphs. *See* HIPPISLEY.

Disease, contracted at Paardeberg, 164.

Divisions. *See* CAVALRY and INFANTRY.

Dobell, Major C. M., 287, 291.

Donald, Lieut.-Colonel C. G., 429.

Donker Poort, 256, 301.

Doornboom, 214, 231–2.

Doorn Kop or Doorn Kloof, 345–6, 348, 352, 372, 414–16, 418, 420, 580.

Dordrecht, 89, 146, 152, 244–5.

Dorsetshire regiment. *See* REGULAR UNITS.

Douglas, Colonel C. W. H., A.D.C., 145, 166.

Draaibosch Pan, 219–20.

Drafts, of troops, 153, 244, 405, 423.

Dragoon Guards. *See* REGULAR UNITS.

Dragoons. *See* REGULAR UNITS.

Drakensberg Mountains and Passes, 184, 242, 338–9, 533.

Driefontein, 230–1, 237, 241, 255; battle of, 208–29.

Drie Kopjes, 196–7, 201.

Driekop, 214, 231–2, 234, 238.

Drieputs Drift (Modder river), 25, 33, 97.

Drieputs Kopjes, engagement at, 82–3, 90, 98.

Driscoll's Scouts. *See* COLONIAL UNITS.

Dronfield ridge, 41, 54–6, 92–5.

Dronfield Station, 55, 93.

Droogfontein, 94–5, 97.

Dublin Fusiliers, The Royal. *See* REGULAR UNITS.

Dundee, 184, 188, 541–2.

Dundee road, 530.

Dundonald, Major-General D. M. B. H., The Earl of, C.B., M.V.O., 183, 341–3, 347, 353, 356, 360–5, 368–9, 373, 406, 427, 433, 437, 440, 442, 444–5, 449–51, 453, 458, 462, 493, 498, 507, 511, 523–30, 572–3, 584.

Durban, 184, 430, 531.

Durban Light Infantry. *See* COLONIAL UNITS.

Durham Light Infantry. *See* REGULAR UNITS.

Du Toit, Commandant, 54, 93–4, 166, 189, 242, 266.

Du Toit's Pan, 41.

Dysentery, 553–4, 577.

EAST LANCASHIRE REGIMENT. *See* REGULAR UNITS.

East London, 173, 183–4, 243–4.

East London Volunteers. *See* COLONIAL UNITS.

East Surrey regiment. *See* REGULAR UNITS.

East Yorkshire regiment. *See* REGULAR UNITS.

Eastern Province Horse. *See* COLONIAL UNITS.

INDEX. 671

Eddy, Major G. E., 251–2.
Edenburg, 135, 256–7, 303, 310–11 ; VIIIth division concentrates at, 320.
Edenburg commando. *See* COMMANDOS.
Edwardes' Scouts. *See* COMMANDOS.
Edwards, Lieut.-Colonel A. H. M., 546.
Elandslaagte, 538.
Elandslaagte railway, 533–5.
Electric searchlights, 41, 50.
End Hill, 534–5, 537, 539.
Endangwe Hill, 347.
Engineers, Royal. *See* REGULAR UNITS.
Engines, railway, capture of, 237, 256.
Englebrecht, Commandant, 189.
Engleheart, Sergeant H. (awarded the Victoria Cross), 237.
Enslin, 4, 11, 15, 22, 64, 95 ; capture of convoy from, 76.
Enteric fever, 164, 552–4, 572, 577.
Entrenchments : Boer—at Karee Siding, 270 ; at Ladysmith, 541 ; at Paardeberg, 102, 109, 168, 173, 175, 186–7 ; at Pieters Hill, 517 ; at Poplar Grove, 201 ; at Spion Kop, 358, 369 ; at Vaal Krantz, 406 ; near Colenso, 434–5, 456 ; British—at Paardeberg, 109, 134, 167, 173, 175 ; at Spion Kop, 381–2.
Entrenching tools, at Spion Kop, 376 ; Boers leave, at Magersfontein, 109.
Erasmus, Commandant, 503–4.
Erste Geluk, 322.
Ermelo commando. *See* COMMANDOS.
Erthcote, 360, 368.
Escort to convoys, at Waterval Drift, 75 ; reinforced, 76–7 ; at Sannah's Post, 276.
Essex regiment. *See* REGULAR UNITS.
Estcourt, 335, 533.
European adventurers with the Boers, 329–30, 521.
Eustace, Lieut.-Colonel F. J. W., 34.
Ewart, Colonel J. S., 119.

FAIRVIEW FARM, 351, 304–6.
Fairview road, 372.
Families of burghers in camp, 1, 98, 107.
Farms in Natal, fired by Boers, 582.
Fauresmith, 15, 29, 135, 301.
Fauresmith commando. *See* COMMANDOS.
Fearon, Major J. A., 169.
Ferdinand's Kraal, 194.
Ferreira, General J. S., 4–5, 29, 37–8, 54, 79, 81, 89, 93, 99, 106–7, 140–1, 166, 189.
Ferreira, commando of. *See* COMMANDOS.
Ferreira Farm, 235, 237–8.
Ferreira Siding, 234, 236–7, 303.
Ferreira Spruit, 234.
Ferries over the Tugela, 343, 354, 434, 458.
Fever, enteric, 164, 552–4, 572, 577.
Ficksburg commando. *See* COMMANDOS.
Field artillery, Royal. *See* REGULAR UNITS.
Field Cornets, duties of, 266.
Field Intelligence Department, 89. *See also* INTELLIGENCE, BRITISH.
Field telegraphs, 36, 96, 196, 213.
Filters, Berkefeld, 577, 579.
Firth, Sergeant J. (awarded the Victoria Cross), 254.
Fischer, Mr. A., 166.
Fisher, Lieut.-Colonel R. B. W., 101, 286–7.
Flag Hill, 585.
Flags of truce, 148, 162, 177, 315.
Flagstone Spruit, 535, 537.
Flint, Lieut.-Colonel E. M., 145, 181, 191.
Flying columns, Prieska district, 182.
Food, convoy with, arrives in Ladysmith, 530 ; scarcity of, in cavalry division, February 17th, 102 ; in army at Paardeberg, 163 ; supply of, in Kimberley, 53, 65–6 ; in Ladysmith, 538, 577.

Forage. *See* SUPPLIES.
Forestier-Walker, Lieut.-General Sir F. W. E. F., K.C.B., C.M.G., 44, 80.
Fort Wylie, 435, 437–8, 443.
Fourie, Commandant P., 210–11, 281, 308, 324.
Fourie, General, 425, 439.
Fourie's Spruit, 535, 565.
Fourteen Streams, 45, 94, 152, 166, 187, 231, 242, 266, 332.
Fowke, Captain G. H., 546.
Franco-German campaign, comparisons with, 113, 204–5.
Fraser, Major J. R., 60, 68.
Free State, Orange, 41, 106, 188, 215, 238, 257.
Free Staters' commandos. *See* COMMANDOS.
Free Staters, demoralisation of, 231; from Natal, 3, 165.
French Corps. *See* COMMANDOS.
French, Lieut.-General J. D. P., C.B., 1–32, 68, 73–82, 90, 92–106, 108, 110, 116, 118, 121, 123, 131, 139–41, 145, 149–61, 164, 169, 172, 178, 191–204, 207, 212, 216–25, 232–8, 249–50, 300, 321–6, 328–35, 540; at Karee Siding, 269–73; commands left column at Driefontein, 214; intercepts Cronje, 88, 96; learns Cronje's situation, 99; leaves Ladysmith, 533; marches to Koodoos Drift, 99–100; to rescue Broadwood, 294–8; to Thabanchu, 259–68; orders issued by, 97, 195, 215, 261–2, 322–3; reports from, 122, 196–7, 213, 217.
French's Scouts. *See* COLONIAL UNITS.
Frere, 334, 337, 341–2, 402, 429, 431, 441, 498, 507, 547, 551.
Frere's Store, 361.
Frewen, Major S., 35, 160.
Froneman, Commandant C. C., 30–1, 33, 73, 82, 149, 168–9, 308, 312, 324.
Froneman, commando of. *See* COMMANDOS.
Fry, Major W., 515–16.

Funchal (Madeira), Lord Roberts at, 336.
Fusilier regiments. *See* REGULAR UNITS.
Fuzzy Hill, 430, 459, 462–3, 472, 485, 502.

GALLWEY, LIEUT.-COLONEL E. J., 428.
Garrison artillery, Royal. *See* REGULAR UNITS.
Garrisons of: Kimberley, 48–9, 52; Ladysmith, 538; South Africa, August, 1899, 42; Wepener, 315.
Gatacre, Lieut.-General Sir W. F., K.C.B., D.S.O., 164–5, 184, 213, 241–59, 267, 320, 335; division, strength of, February 11th, 246; marches to Reddersburg, 300–13; succeeded by Chermside, 320.
German Corps. *See* COMMANDOS.
Germiston commando. *See* COMMANDOS.
Girouard, Lieut.-Colonel E. P. C., D.S.O., 155, 165.
Glasock, Driver H. H. (awarded the Victoria Cross), 290.
Glen Siding, 321, 327; bridge at, 256, 267–9, 274; concentration of troops at, 268–70.
Gloucestershire regiment. *See* REGULAR UNITS.
Godfrey-Faussett, Captain O. G., 133.
Goemansberg, 89, 146.
Gomba Stream and Valley, 424, 430–1, 434–5, 438–47, 450, 452, 454, 459.
Goodenough, Lieut.-General Sir W., 39–40, 42.
Goold-Adams, Major H. J., 44.
Gordon, Brig.-General J. R. P., 4, 18–20, 24, 26, 33–6, 93–4, 97, 140–1, 150, 152, 156, 164, 201, 203, 238, 269, 320.
Gordon Highlanders, The. *See* REGULAR UNITS.
Gordon Hill, 537–8.
Gore-Browne, Major H., 557, 559.
Gorle, Captain H. V., 53.

INDEX. 673

Gough, Captain H. De la P., 347, 427, 527.
Gourton, 498.
Government of Orange Free State to Kroonstad, 230, 241.
Graham, Major H. W. G., 360–1.
Grahamstown Volunteers Mounted Infantry. *See* COLONIAL UNITS.
Grant, Captain P. G., 249.
Grant, Commander W. L., R.N., 28, 80, 90, 155.
Grant, General (U.S.A.), 207.
Graspan, 4, 11, 15, 22, 59 ; starting point of Army, 3.
Great-coats, 392.
Green Hill (Spion Kop), 350–2, 357, 365–7, 377, 382, 395 ; (Vaal Krantz), 412–13 ; (Relief of Ladysmith), 424, 430–1, 433, 437–9, 442–3, 445, 447–8, 450–2, 454, 459, 461, 471, 475, 487, 508.
Grenadier Guards. *See* REGULAR UNITS.
Grenfell, Lieut.-Colonel H. M., 245.
Greytown, 426, 441.
Grierson, Lieut.-Colonel J. M., M.V.O., 181, 192, 233.
Griqualand West, 45.
Griqualand West commando. *See* COMMANDOS.
Griqualand West rebels, 93–5, 152.
Griquas, 335.
Griquatown, 189.
Grobelaar, Commandant, 189, 260, 262, 308.
Grobelaar, commando of. *See* COMMANDOS.
Grobelaar, Mr., 166.
Grobelaar Kloof, 533–4, 583.
Grobelaar Mountain, 431–2, 443, 453, 456, 461, 464–6, 468, 471–3, 475–6, 485–6, 493, 503, 511, 514, 521.
Grover, Lieut. P. C., 289–90.
Grubb, Lieut. A. H. W., 168.
Guards' Brigade. *See* INFANTRY BRIGADES.
Gun-cotton, 236, 547.

Gun Hill (Chieveley), 426, 436–8, 440, 443–4, 452, 455, 462, 471, 485–6, 521 ; (Ladysmith), 534–6, 539, 545–6, 583 ; (Paardeberg), 101, 109, 117, 126, 128–9, 138, 142, 150, 152, 156.
Guns : Boer—19, 34, 36, 47, 54, 57, 61, 66, 77, 79, 85–6, 88–9, 101, 129–30, 146, 158–9, 166, 187, 189–91, 196, 200, 211, 216, 218, 220–6, 230–1, 235, 246, 249–50, 271, 273, 279, 281, 291–2, 295, 308–9, 316, 328, 364, 366, 369, 371, 382, 388, 392, 404, 406, 409, 411, 413–14, 418, 432–3, 435, 437, 445, 451, 462–3, 466, 498, 504, 511, 513, 541, 545, 548–9, 553, 562, 565, 567, 573, 580, 582, 584 ; British— *see* REGULAR *and* COLONIAL UNITS ; captured by Boers, 47, 291 ; by British, 45, 178, 547 ; at Wepener, 315 ; in Kimberley, 40, 49–50, 52, 58 ; in Ladysmith, 538 ; with the Natal Field Force, 429, 510 ; *see also* CREUSOT, HOWITZERS, KRUPP, MAXIM, NAVAL, etc.

HAIG, LIEUT.-COLONEL D., 18, 24, 195, 215, 232, 262, 323.
Hall, Lieut.-Colonel F. H., 147, 150, 156–7.
Hallowell, Major H. L., 312.
Hamilton, Colonel Bruce M., 327–8, 331–2, 447, 473.
Hamilton, Lieut.-Colonel E. O. F., 427.
Hamilton, Colonel I. S. M., C.B., D.S.O., 10, 320, 324–32, 537, 548, 554, 561, 564, 566, 568.
Hamilton's Mounted Infantry. *See* INFANTRY, MOUNTED.
Hampshire regiment. *See* REGULAR UNITS.
Hankey, Captain H. M. A., 132–3.
Hannay, Colonel O. C., 4, 11–14, 18, 22, 28–30, 32, 73, 80–1, 83, 86, 91, 98, 100, 103, 114–19, 121–2, 129–33, 138.

VOL. II. 43

Hannay's Mounted Infantry. *See* IN-
FANTRY, MOUNTED.
Harding's Farm (Natal), 410, 420.
Harding's Farm (Orange Free State), 64.
Harris, Lieut.-Colonel R. H. W. H., 427, 476, 478–9, 482.
Harrismith commando. *See* COM-
MANDOS.
Harrismith railway, 533–4, 539.
Harrison, Major R. A. G., 85.
Hart, Major-General A. FitzR., C.B., 318–19, 324, 327, 341–2, 357, 364, 366–70, 388, 407, 429, 436–8, 440, 450, 461–2, 468–9, 485–99, 505, 508–9, 521, 528.
Hart's Hill, attack on, 481–501, 506, 516–22, 524, 526, 528.
Hatting's Farm, 402, 405.
Headquarters. *See* ARMY HEAD-
QUARTERS.
Heidelberg commando. *See* COM-
MANDOS.
Heilbron commando. *See* COM-
MANDOS.
Helvetia, 302, 304, 306, 312–13.
Henderson, Major D., 546–7.
Henderson, Colonel G. F. R., 20, 89, 146.
Henderson, Major J. A., 246.
Henderson, Mr. R. H. (Mayor of Kimberley), 50.
Hennessey, Captain G. P., 256.
Henry, Lieut.-Colonel St. G. C., 30, 191, 194, 199, 200–1, 287, 291–2, 294–6.
Henry's Mounted Infantry. *See* IN-
FANTRY, MOUNTED.
Helpmakaar, 493, 504, 533.
Helpmakaar Ridge, 536–8, 541–2, 544–6.
Hertzog, Commandant, 135.
Hertzog, Judge, 167, 210.
Hesketh, Lieut. A. E., 35.
Hickson, Colonel R. A., 149, 169, 218, 225.
High Commissioner, South Africa, 44, 63, 153. *See also* ROSMEAD *and* MILNER.
Highland brigade. *See* INFANTRY BRIGADES.
Highland Light Infantry. *See* REGU-
LAR UNITS.
Hildyard, Major-General H. J. T., C.B., 341, 343, 345, 355, 362–4, 366, 369, 373, 388, 407, 411–12, 416–17, 419, 427, 444–5, 448–53, 458, 460, 462, 473, 476, 480, 493, 495, 498, 503, 506, 521.
Hill, Lieut.-Colonel A. W., 397, 428.
Hill, Major F. F., 514.
Hill " 244 " on Map, 469, 472, 475–6, 486–7, 492–3.
Hinton, Lieut. C. H., 482.
Hippisley, Lieut.-Colonel R. L., 214.
Hlangwhane, 339, 404, 419, 424–5, 430–8, 443–4, 448–9, 453–5, 457–64, 467, 469–71, 480, 484–5, 493–4, 498, 500, 505, 507–10, 515, 520–1, 580.
Hobkirk's Farm, 251–2.
Hogg, Mr., 236.
Hollams' Farm, 249.
Hondenbeck Hill, 270–2.
Honey Nest Kloof, 75, 78, 90.
Hoopstad, 332.
" Hooters " in Kimberley, 47.
Hopetown, 146.
Hore, Lieut.-Colonel C. O., 44.
Horse Artillery, Royal. *See* REGULAR UNITS.
Horse-Shoe Hill, 432, 456–7, 459, 464–5, 472–3, 475–6, 478–80, 483, 500.
Horses, 3, 27, 50, 119, 144, 180, 319, 576–9; Boers', condition of, 1, 167, 171, 204; want of, 81, 164; cavalry, led, 12, 23, 262; cavalry short of, 269, 275; exhausted condition of, 32, 37–8, 85, 92, 94–6, 102, 122, 141, 160, 171–2, 180, 182, 202–4, 220, 228, 242, 270, 273, 296, 307, 327; Horse artillery short of, 269–70; stampede

INDEX. 675

of, at Sannah's Post, 283; supplied by De Beers Company, 30; used as food, in Kimberley, 65; in Ladysmith, 7, 577-81; weight carried by British and Boer, 30.

Horton, Private, 289.

Hoskier, Lieut.-Colonel F. H., 247.

Hospitals, 153, 162-3, 182, 231, 307, 577, 579; statistics, 554; stores in Ladysmith run out, 8. *See also* ROYAL ARMY MEDICAL CORPS.

Hostilities, continuance of, decided upon by Krijgsraad, March 17th, 265.

Hotchkiss, 14-pr. Q.F. guns, 315, 318; 3-pr. guns, 538, 554, 557, 560.

Household Cavalry. *See* REGULAR UNITS.

Hout Nek, 327-8.

Howard, Major-General F., C.B., C.M.G., 537, 542.

Howard, Sergeant G., 566.

Howitzers, batteries of, *see* REGULAR UNITS; 4.7-in. (Boer), 545-8; 6-in. (British), 174-6, 371-2, 414, 429; 6.3-in. (British), 536, 538-9, 541-2, 545, 549, 580, 583.

Hughes-Hallett, Lieut.-Colonel J. W., 126, 200.

Humphreys, Captain C., 288-9.

Hunter, Lieut.-General Sir A., K.C.B., 4, 10, 327, 546-7.

Hunter-Weston, Major A. G., 236-7.

Hunt-Grubbe, Lieut. R., 561, 563.

Hussar Hill, 431, 433-4, 436-43, 448-54, 457-9, 461-2.

Hussars. *See* REGULAR UNITS.

Hutton, Major-General E. T. H., C.B., 327.

Hutton's Mounted Infantry. *See* INFANTRY, MOUNTED.

Hyde's Farm, 547.

"I. L. H." Work, on Wagon Hill, 557, 559-60, 564, 567-8.

Imperial Light Horse. *See* COLONIAL UNITS.

Imperial Light Infantry. *See* COLONIAL UNITS.

Imperial Yeomanry, 145, 153, 183, 321, 324, 326, 333.

India, effect in, if Ladysmith fell, 578; Horse artillery from, 7; Steyn reports imaginary Russian action against, 265.

Indian Commissariat Department, 578.

Indian corn as food, 578.

Infantry Brigades :—

1st (Guards) (Pole-Carew, later Jones), 12, 123, 142, 145, 147, 180-1, 191-2, 194, 199, 211, 214-15, 227-8, 233, 237-8, 241, 257, 300, 303, 320, 332.

2nd (Hildyard), 334, 337, 355, 362-3, 369-70, 388, 407, 410, 416-17, 419, 427, 438, 440, 444-5, 447-51, 453-4, 460, 462, 468, 473-4, 476, 480-1, 483, 493, 495, 498-9, 505-6, 521.

3rd (Highland) (MacDonald), 4, 11, 15, 75, 80, 91, 103, 114-15, 119-21, 125-6, 128, 142, 157, 162, 177, 199-200, 293-8, 325, 328.

4th (Lyttelton, later Norcott, then Cooper), 334, 340, 342-3, 354, 407-8, 410, 412-13, 416, 428, 438, 440, 445, 447-9, 451-4, 460, 462, 469, 473-4, 476, 486, 493, 499, 506, 516-20.

5th (Irish) (Hart), 318, 327, 334, 340-2, 357-8, 364, 366-70, 388, 407, 410, 420, 429, 437, 440, 450, 462, 468-9, 472, 485-93, 495-7, 499, 503, 505-9, 517, 528.

6th (Barton), 327, 334, 337, 340, 423, 429, 436-7, 439-40, 443, 446, 448, 450-4, 459, 462-3, 469, 474, 480, 487, 493, 499, 503, 505-6, 508, 510-15, 519-21.

7th (Ian Hamilton), 550.

8th (Howard), 550.

9th (Douglas), 12, 145.

10th (Coke), 340, 342, 371-6, 401, 428, 440, 443, 448, 450, 454,

VOL. II. 43*

Infantry Brigades (10th)—*continued.*
459, 461, 464, 466–7, 469, 471–2, 493, 499, 501–3, 506, 521, 528.
11th (Woodgate, later Wynne, then Kitchener), 342–3, 357–8, 364, 366, 375, 406–10, 428, 440, 450, 454, 459, 461, 466–7, 469, 471–6, 478–9, 480–1, 485–6, 492–3, 495, 499, 505, 507–8, 515–21.
12th (Clements), 152, 241–58, 301, 303, 320, 343.
13th (C. E. Knox), 80–4, 87, 91, 98, 114, 117, 119, 123–5, 132, 149–50, 157, 161–2, 198, 218, 220, 296, 298, 303.
14th (Chermside, later Maxwell), 77, 80, 123, 147, 157, 159, 161–2, 167, 191–2, 194, 199, 270–3, 327.
15th (Wavell), 70, 147, 180–1, 190, 213, 270–3, 327.
16th (Campbell), 320.
17th (Boyes), 320.
18th (Stephenson), 80, 87, 98, 114–15, 117–18, 122, 130, 131–4, 137, 149–50, 161–2, 167, 198, 218, 220–1, 223–7, 320, 332.
19th (Smith-Dorrien), 4, 11, 15, 75, 80, 91, 103, 114–15, 121, 126, 128, 138, 140, 162, 173–7, 200, 293–8, 325, 328–9, 331.
21st (B. M. Hamilton), 327–8, 331–2.
22nd (Allen), 320–1, 326.
23rd (W. G. Knox), 320.
Infantry Divisions :—
Ist (Methuen), 12, 63, 79, 91, 240–1, 332–3.
IInd (Clery, later Lyttelton), 340–1, 344, 366–70, 420, 427, 436–40, 443–5, 447–8, 450–2, 454, 457–8, 460, 462–3, 469, 472–6, 480, 493, 506, 521, 528.
IIIrd (Gatacre, later Chermside), 241–9, 257, 300–13, 320–1, 327.
Vth (Warren, later Hildyard), 184, 337–43, 355, 358, 362, 364–71, 420, 428–9, 436–40, 442–3, 446–8, 454, 457, 461–7, 469, 471, 480, 486, 505, 508–9, 528, 553.
VIth (Kelly-Kenny), 4, 11, 15, 21–2, 29–34, 36, 73–4, 80–4, 87, 91, 98, 100, 102–5, 110, 113–15, 118, 120, 123–4, 132, 136–7, 161, 191–2, 194–5, 197, 199, 211–12, 214–20, 223–8, 232, 237–9, 241, 303, 320, 327, 335.
VIIth (Tucker), 4, 11, 15, 19, 21–2, 25, 28–9, 32, 74, 79–80, 91, 147, 167, 181, 191, 194, 199, 211, 213–14, 228, 238–9, 241, 269–73, 303, 327, 332, 574.
VIIIth (Rundle), 153, 240, 320–3, 326, 328, 333.
IXth (Colvile), 4, 11, 15, 21–2, 28–30, 74–5, 80, 91, 103, 110, 114–15, 119–20, 123, 128–9, 132, 137–8, 145, 180–1, 191–2, 199–200, 212–15, 227–8, 233, 237–8, 240–1, 277, 285, 287, 291–8, 325, 327.
Xth (Hunter), 327.
XIth (Pole-Carew), 320–3, 326–7, 332.
Infantry, marches of :—
VIth and IXth divisions to Paardeberg, 31, 103.
VIIth division to Paardeberg, 147.
Guards' brigade into Bloemfontein, 238.
Royal Irish Rifles and Queenstown Volunteers to Aliwal North, 313.
Infantry, Mounted, 12, 20, 77, 98, 102–3, 105, 120, 126, 130, 134, 136–7, 153, 169, 181, 190, 198, 200, 247–9, 257, 262, 270, 277, 285, 287, 301–11, 315–16, 320, 324–6, 330, 361, 407 ; inefficiency of, 13 ; companies, method of formation of, 128 ; reorganisation of, into four brigades, 181.
Alderson's, 18, 24–5, 32–3, 35–6, 93–5, 158, 190, 194–5, 201–2, 212, 214–15, 218, 232–5, 241, 275–99, 321.
Bainbridge's, 329.

INDEX.

Burma, 219, 275, 284–5, 289.
De Lisle's, 191, 329.
Hamilton's (Ian), 327.
Hannay's, 4, 11–14, 18, 21, 28–30, 32, 73, 76, 80–5, 91, 98, 100, 103, 114–19, 121–2, 129–33.
Henry's, 191, 199, 287, 291–2, 294–6.
Hutton's, 327.
Le Gallais', 191, 214–15, 219, 228, 233, 241, 269–70.
Legge's, 329.
Martyr's, 83, 119, 191, 194–5, 199, 213–14, 219, 222, 228, 233, 241, 277, 285–7, 291–2.
Pilcher's, 262–7, 275–6, 291.
Ridley's, 30, 32, 91, 190, 194, 214, 241, 269, 328.
Sitwell's, 321.
Inkson, Lieut. E. T. (awarded the Victoria Cross) 500.
Inniskilling Dragoons. See REGULAR UNITS.
Inniskilling Fusiliers, The Royal. See REGULAR UNITS.
Intaba Ka Renga, 433, 450, 457.
Intelligence: Boer, 10–11, 30, 324; compared with British, 17; fails, 16; British, 16–17, 23, 29, 43, 59, 79–80, 89, 100, 146, 152, 157, 161, 188–9, 211, 213, 230–1, 264, 278, 302, 304, 306, 309, 347, 355, 434–5.
Intintanyoni, 338.
Intombi Camp and Hospital, 529, 541, 577.
Intombi Spruit, 527, 584.
Investment of, Cronje's laager, 145–61; Kimberley, 54–72; Ladysmith, 531–85.
Irish Brigade (Boer), see COMMANDOS; (British) see INFANTRY, 5TH BRIGADE.
Irish Fusiliers, The Royal. See REGULAR UNITS.
Irish Rifles, The Royal. See REGULAR UNITS.
Ironstone Kopje, 59–60.

Irvine, Lieut. F. S., 288.
Irvine, Major J. L., 355, 410, 497, 501, 507.
Isabellafontein, 332.
Israel's Poort, 261, 276, 324–5.

JACKSON, MR., 504.
Jacobsdal, 4, 11–12, 15, 17, 20–1, 25, 29–30, 74, 78, 80, 87–8, 90–2, 95, 103, 110, 120, 123, 142, 146–8, 163; occupation of, by British, 30, 79.
Jacobsdal commando. See COMMANDOS.
Jacobs, General, 135.
Jacobsrust Farm, 328, 332.
Jagersfontein, 257, 303.
Jagersfontein commando. See COMMANDOS.
James, Lieut. H. W., R.N., 462, 469, 471, 487.
James' collapsible boat. See BOATS.
Jamestown, 244–6.
Jammersberg bridge, 264, 315, 317, 319.
Johannesburg, 59, 243, 305.
Johannesburg commando. See COMMANDOS.
Johannesburg Police. See COMMANDOS.
Johnson, Colonel F. F., 75–7.
Jones, Captain E. P., R.N., 426, 455, 503.
Jones, Major-General I. R., 320.
Jones, Lieut. R. J. T. D., 548–9, 558–9, 566, (awarded the Victoria Cross) 570.
Jonono's Kop, 338.
Joubert, Commandant-General, 178, 188–9, 211, 265–6, 455, 470, 494, 504, 539, 541, 571, 580; decides to assault Cæsar's Camp, 557; to invest Ladysmith, 532.
Junction Hill, 536, 538, 541, 554, 558.

KAAL SPRUIT, 147, 209, 214, 231, 234.
Kaffir Drift, 385, 3 1–2.

Kaffir drivers, etc., 119, 580; stampede of, at Sannah's Post, 280, 282.
Kaffirs in Ladysmith, 538; sent out of Kimberley, 51.
Kaffir River bridge, 257, 303.
Kaffir spies, inaccuracy of, 341.
Kaffrarian Rifles. See COLONIAL UNITS.
Kalkfontein Farm (near Paardeberg), 110; (near Poplar Grove) 196-7, 201; (near Karee Siding) 270.
Kameelfontein Farm, 99-102, 108, 122, 149, 152, 156.
Kamfer's Dam, 42, 58-9, 66, 92-3.
Karee Siding, 274, 295, 303-4, 320, 327-8, 332; action at, 269-73.
Katdoorn Farm, 213, 219.
Kekewich, Colonel R. G., 4-5, 43-65, 67-8, 70, 92; to command Colonial troops in Griqualand West, 45.
Kelly, Major-General W. F., C.B., 214.
Kelly-Kenny, Lieut.-General T., C.B., 4, 21-2, 30-1, 34, 74, 80-5, 88, 90, 100, 103, 105, 113-14, 116-18, 120-4, 128, 130, 132, 134, 136-8, 168-9, 177-8, 191-2, 195-9, 212, 218, 220, 223-5, 227, 230, 320; position of, with regard to Lord Kitchener, 103, 116, 143.
Kenhardt, 189.
Kenilworth, 41, 51-2, 57.
Kimberley, 1-5, 73, 79-82, 88-100, 104, 106, 110, 140, 145-6, 152, 154, 156, 158, 166, 180-3, 206, 208-9, 212, 238, 240-1, 243, 320, 327, 332-3, 336, 575; ammunition and rifles sent to, 43; bombardment, effect of, 68-9; Chamber of Commerce remonstrates on removal of inhabitants, 63; deaths in, 69; defence works, begun 18th September, 1899, 46; scheme of, 51-2; evacuation of, by civil population, 62-3; garrison of, 44-5, 48, 52; inhabitants, number of, 51; local forces of, see COLONIAL UNITS; mines at, 39, 62; rations reduced in, 65; relief fund, for poor of, 66; scheme of defence for, 40-4, 54; scurvy in, 69; sorties from, 58, 60, 66, 68, 92; strategic value of, 39; summoned to surrender, 56; supplies in, 53, 64-6, 70; telephones in, 52; water supply of, 44, 53.
Kimberley Volunteers, strength of, etc., 40, 44, 46-8.
Kincaid, Lieut.-Colonel W. F. H. S., 173-5.
King's Royal Rifle Corps, The. See REGULAR UNITS.
King's Post, 537, 542-3.
Kitchener, Colonel F. W., 369-70, 427, 444, 449, 474, 480, 487, 493, 505-6, 508, 513-20.
Kitchener, Major-General H. H., Lord, G.C.B., K.C.M.G., 11, 21, 25, 27-31, 36-7, 67, 79, 84, 88, 90-1, 95-6, 98, 103, 110-11, 120, 122, 126, 128-9, 131-3, 135-8, 145-8, 151, 165, 172, 182, 196, 244, 254, 276, 296-7; dispositions of, at Paardeberg, 113-18; inadequacy of staff of, 105, 111-12, 116; messages from, and to Lord Roberts, 88, 90, 123, 142; position of, as to other Generals, 104, 116, 143; to North-West Cape Colony, 212.
Kitchener's Hill, 506, 514-22, 524, 526, 528. See also RAILWAY HILL.
Kitchener's Horse. See COLONIAL UNITS.
Kitchener's Kopje, 121-2, 130, 135-8, 141, 149-50, 152, 154, 157-61, 164-5, 168-9, 171, 185.
Kits, weight of officers', 353.
Klein Klipkraal, 287.
Klerksdorp, 29, 266.
Klerksdorp commando. See COMMANDOS.
Klip Drift, 25-6, 28, 30-1, 33, 36-7, 73-4, 84-5, 87-91, 95-6, 98, 103, 147, 180.
Klip Kraal Drift (near Paardeberg), 25-6, 75, 79-81, 83-5, 91, 98, 103,

120, 123, 143, 147, 155, 177, 180, 194.
Klip Kraal Drift (Waterworks), 298, 308, 325.
Klip river (Natal), 433, 457, 459, 504, 521, 523, 525–9, 533–7, 539–40, 544, 559, 577, 579.
Klokfontein Farm, 59.
Kloof Camp, 252.
Knox, Major-General C. E., 81–7, 90–1, 97–8, 114, 117, 119, 123–5, 161–2, 218, 220, 296–8.
Knox, Major E. C., 566.
Knox, Colonel W. G., C.B., 320, 529, 536, 584.
Koffyfontein, 14, 20, 22–3, 75, 79, 106–7, 135, 146.
Kolbe, Commandant, 166, 187, 199–200, 209, 211.
Koodoos Drift, 91, 96–7, 99–103, 108, 116, 121–2, 140–1, 156–8, 180.
Koodoosrand, 100–2, 107–9, 122, 141, 171, 186, 194.
Korn Spruit and Drift, 277, 280–2, 284–94.
Kraaipan, 45, 47.
Krantz, Commander of German Corps, 579.
Krantz Kloof, 406, 412, 415.
Krantz Kraal Drift, 296, 298, 327, 332.
Krijgsraad, 66, 81, 168, 176, 209–10, 265, 274, 281, 399, 542, 544, 557.
Kroonstad, 230, 241, 265, 267, 274, 300, 305, 308, 333; burghers to re-assemble at, after fall of Bloemfontein, 242.
Kroonstad commando. *See* COMMANDOS.
Kruger, H. E. President S. P. J., 46, 166–7, 170, 176, 179, 187–8, 203, 233, 265–6, 305, 314, 455.
Krugersdorp commando. *See* COMMANDOS.
Kruger's Siding, 303.
Krupp guns, 95, 187, 200, 211, 413, 541.
Kuilfontein, 254.
Kuruman, 45.

LAAGER, 191, 464; capture of (Monte Cristo), 449, 451; Cronje's, at Paardeberg, 145–61.
Labram, Mr. G., 50.
Labuschagne's Nek, action at, 245–6.
Ladybrand, 242–3, 256–7, 261–3, 267, 274–5, 302, 304–5, 315; commando, *see* COMMANDOS.
Ladysmith, 4–5, 9, 52, 66, 110, 172, 178, 206, 238, 240, 327, 334–6, 346, 348–51, 353–5, 368, 370–1, 373, 377, 401, 405, 414, 416, 419; abandonment of, discussed, 6–9, 574; ammunition in, 539, 583; artillery in, disposition of, 538, 541–3; Boers believed *en route* from, 146, 189, 230; Boers, strength of, at, 89; bombardment of, 540–4, 580, 582; bomb-proof shelters in, 544; Buller enters, 585; congratulations on defence of, 7, 575; death-rate in, 8, 554, 574; defences of, 536–8, 544; description of, 533–8; Dundonald enters, 527; food supply of, 538–9, 577–9; inhabitants, numbers of, 533, 538; leakage of information from, 546; messages from, 337, 358, 550–4; messages received in, 547, 550–4; mobile columns in, 545, 550, 553, 572; non-combatants in, removal of, 541; rations in, reduction of, 574, 577, 580, 583; roads to, 364–5; sickness in, etc., 358, 553–4, 572, 577, 581; spies in, 546; supplies for the defenders of, 494, 526, 584; terrain of, 338–40, 531–42, 555–7; Town Guard of, *see* COLONIAL UNITS; water supply of, 577.
Ladysmith Garrison, condition of, 576–9; inadequacy of, 534; offers to co-operate with Buller, 582–3; strength of, 538, 572, 574; unable to co-operate with Buller, 358.

Ladysmith, Relief of, attack on Cingolo, 443–5; on Cingolo Nek, 448; on Hart's Hill, 481–500; on Monte Cristo and Green Hill, 449–51; on Pieters Hill, 501–30; on Wynne's Hill, 463–80; Boers evacuate Colenso, 458; bombardment of enemy's positions during, 438, 443–5, 505–7, 509–11, 519–20; bridging the Tugela, 460, 504, 507–8; Buller decides not to pursue, 520, 527; Buller's scheme for, 433; cavalry brigades, advance of, at, 525–30; delay in, 441; disposition of Buller's force during, 440–1, 461–2, 468–71, 493, 505–9; of enemy during, 457; enemy attacks Wynne's Hill, 476–7; enemy's positions on the Tugela during, 433–5, 439, 443, 455–7, 465–6, 490–1, 502; fire, long-range, during, 474, 478, 511, 521; fronts, British and Boer, divided into same two sections at, 502; guns, disposition of, during, 438–9, 452–5, 462–5, 471, 475, 484–5, 502–3, 510; Hart's advance against Terrace Hill, 487–92, 495–7; Hlangwhane occupied by British, 454; infantry, difficulties of advance, 488–9; messages from G.O.C.'s during, 439, 445, 467–8, 471, 474–5, 479–80, 523–4; must be carried out, 416; new plans for, 403, 425, 433–4, 472, 497–8; night alarm during, 499; orders for, attack on Cingolo ridge, 442–3, 447–8, 464–5, 467, 472–3, 486, 505, 508–9, 520; difficulty of issuing, 436; proposals by General Warren for, 453, 467–8, 471–2; reconnaissances during, 433–4, 440, 459; retreat of Boers northwards, 461, 514, 524, 526; river (Tugela), crossing of, during, 463–80; signalling during, 452; situation, at Cingolo, 445; on Horse Shoe Hill, 478–80; on Wynne's Hill, 476–81; terrain on the Tugela, 430–2, 486–7, 512.

Langewacht Spruit, 431–2, 456–7, 460, 466, 471–2, 475, 477, 488, 502, 506, 511, 519–20.
Laing's Nek, 184.
Lamb, Major C. A., 428.
Lambton, Captain the Hon. H., R.N., 538.
Lancashire Fusiliers, The. See REGULAR UNITS.
Lancaster regiment, The King's Own Royal. See REGULAR UNITS.
Lancer's Hill, 339, 359, 364, 405, 534, 539–40, 554, 573, 575, 581.
Lancers. See REGULAR UNITS.
Landrosts, 256, 261–2, 301.
Lansdowne, The Most Hon. H. C. K., Marquis of, K.G., G.C.S.I., G.C.M.G., G.C.I.E., 6.
Lanshoek Farm, 19.
Law, Lieut.-Colonel C. H., 428.
Lawrence, Major the Hon. H. A., 188, 195.
Lean, Major K. E., 331.
Leavens, Sergeant F. C., 482.
Ledgard, Midshipman W. R., R.N., 503.
Leeuwberg, 214, 232–3.
Leeuwberg Kopje, 303.
Leeuwkop, 185–7, 200–1, 264, 304, 321.
Leeuw river mills, 262, 276, 327.
Le Gallais, Lieut.-Colonel P. W. J., 181, 191, 214–15, 219, 228, 233, 269–70, 273.
Le Gallais' Mounted Infantry. See INFANTRY, MOUNTED.
Le Gallais' Kopje, 194, 197–8.
Legge, Lieut.-Colonel N., D.S.O., 329.
Legge's Mounted Infantry. See INFANTRY, MOUNTED.
Leicester Post, 537, 541–3.
Leicestershire regiment. See REGULAR UNITS.
Lemmer, General, 260, 281, 294, 308.
Lennox, Captain A. M. A., 136.
Leper Hospital (Bloemfontein), 235.
Lichtenburg commando. See COMMANDOS.

INDEX. 681

Liebenberg, General, 266.
Likhatlong, 298.
Limit Hill, 541, 547, 585.
Limpus, Commander A., R.N., 455, 503.
Lincolnshire regiment. *See* REGULAR UNITS.
Lindsell, Lieut.-Colonel R. F., 151.
Lines of Communication : Boer—29, 38, 81, 190, 245, 371 ; British—12, 78, 80, 155, 164–5, 180, 182, 242–4, 250, 254, 257–8, 266, 274, 308, 333, 335, 339 ; General Officer Commanding, *see* FORESTIER-WALKER.
Little, Major M. O., 26, 35.
Little Tugela river, 340, 342, 344.
Liverpool Castle, 536. *See* TUNNEL HILL.
Liverpool regiment, The King's. *See* REGULAR UNITS.
Llander, Trooper, 357.
Lloyd, Lieut.-Colonel G. E., 124.
Local forces, South Africa, *see* COLONIAL UNITS ; organisation of, in Kimberley, 43.
Lodge, Gunner I. (awarded the Victoria Cross), 290.
Logageng, 322.
Lombards Kop, 533–6, 539, 542, 579 ; action of, 531.
Long, Captain A., 579.
"Long Cecil," 50, 66.
Long Hill, 536.
Long Kopje, 351, 366, 370.
Long-range supporting fire, 474, 487, 511, 521, 523.
"Long Tom," 5, 92.
"Look-out Hill." *See* SPION KOP.
Lothian regiment, The Royal Scots. *See* REGULAR UNITS.
Loyal North Lancashire regiment. *See* REGULAR UNITS.
Lubbe, Commandant, 23, 25–7, 33, 75, 83, 89, 135.
Lubbe's commando. *See* COMMANDOS.
Lukin, Captain H. T., 315.
Lund, Captain F. T., 168–9, 202.

Lyddite, 156, 383, 418, 468, 497.
Lydenburg commando. *See* COMMANDOS.
Lyttelton, Major General the Hon. N. G., C.B., 354, 358, 364–5, 374, 377, 385–6, 391–2, 398, 407, 411–15, 417, 420, 427–8, 436–7, 439–40, 442–3, 448, 450, 453, 458, 462, 473–6, 479–80, 493, 502, 506, 520–1, 528.

MACBEAN, CAPTAIN J. A. E., 513.
McCarthy-O'Leary, Lieut.-Colonel W., 428, 477, 517.
McCracken's Hill, 252.
MacDonald, Major-General H. A., C.B., 15, 103, 114–15, 120, 125–6, 162, 293, 295–6.
Macdonell, Lieut. A. H., 175.
Macfarlane's Farm, 55.
Macfarlane's Knoll, 56, 94.
Macfarlane's Siding, 55, 94–5.
McGrigor, Major C. R. R., 495.
Machine guns, 13, 352, 376, 429, 448, 458, 460, 472, 474, 511, 541.
MacInnes, Lieut. D. S., 43, 51.
McKenzie, Major D., 361.
Mackenzie, Lieut.-Colonel C. J., 146.
Mackworth, Major D., 559, 564, 567.
MacMullen, Major F. R., 253.
McNalty, Lieut. C. E. I., 579.
McNeill, Captain A. J., 248.
Maconochie's Kopjes. *See* "THE KOPJES."
McWhinnie, Captain W. J., 306–11.
Mafeking, 39, 44–5, 47, 54, 59, 97, 183, 189, 242, 332.
Mafeteng, 318.
Magersfontein, 17, 20–1, 48, 54, 63–4, 70, 79, 87, 102, 106, 146, 205, 314, 339, 550 ; Cronje's position at, 1, 3, 32, 73, 243 ; entrenching tools left at, 109 ; evacuation of, by Boers, 81, 88, 90–1, 96 ; still occupied, February 15th, 80.
Maiden Castle, 535, 537, 561–2.
Majuba, 176, 198.

Makauw's Drift, 141, 152, 156, 158, 160–1, 194–5, 199.
Malta, mounted infantry from, 318.
Manchester Fort, 557, 565, 572.
Manchester regiment. See REGULAR UNITS.
Mansel-Jones, Captain C. (awarded the Victoria Cross), 519.
Manxa Nest, 457–8, 487, 507, 511–12.
Maps, incompleteness of, affects British, 339, 435–6 ; superiority of British, over Boer, 20.
Marches, of VIth and IXth divisions, 31, 103 ; of VIIth division, 147 ; of detachment Irish Rifles and Queenstown Volunteers, 313 ; of Guards' Brigade into Bloemfontein, 238.
Maritzburg. See PIETERMARITZBURG.
Maritz Ferry, 346.
Martial law, Kimberley, 48, 70.
Martin, Sergeant-Major J., 282–3.
Martini-Henry rifles issued to Kimberley Town Guard, 49.
Martins, Commandant, 79.
Martyr, Lieut.-Colonel C. G., D.S.O., 83, 119, 181, 191, 194–5, 199, 213–14, 219, 222, 228, 233, 277, 285–8, 291–2.
Martyr's Kopje, 222–3.
Martyr's Mounted Infantry. See INFANTRY, MOUNTED.
Maseru, 264, 302.
Mashonaland Mounted Police. See COLONIAL UNITS.
Masterson, Lieut. J. E. I., 569; (awarded the Victoria Cross) 570.
Mathias, Lieut., 560.
Matthews, Major F. B., 479.
Mauser rifles, 87, 381, 383, 413, 559.
Maxims (see also MACHINE GUNS), 50, 55, 58, 92, 149, 160, 172, 262–3, 281, 371, 410, 412, 435, 483, 487, 496, 504, 511, 517, 547, 567.
Maxim-Nordenfeldt guns, 20.
Maxwell, Major Cedric, 245, 315, 319.
Maxwell, Lieut. F. A., 289 ; (awarded the Victoria Cross), 290.

Maxwell, Major-General J. G., D.S.O., 327.
Maxwell, Lieut.-Colonel R. C., 167.
May, Major S., 56.
Mayor, of Bloemfontein, 234, 238.
Mayor, of Kimberley, 63, 66.
Mealie flour, etc., 578.
Mealie Spruit, 277, 287, 291.
Meat. See FOOD.
Medical arrangements, 191.
Medical Service, 153. See also ROYAL ARMY MEDICAL CORPS.
Medicines, offer of, to Boers, 164.
Melvill, Lieut. F. W., R.N., 462, 487.
Merton Siding, 91.
Messages, miscarriage of, after relief of Kimberley, 88 ; after relief of Wepener, 326.
Metcalfe, Lieut.-Colonel C. T. E., 548–9, 565.
Methuen, Lieut.-General Lord P. S., K.C.V.O., C.B., C.M.G., 4, 12, 29, 37, 54, 58–60, 62–4, 71, 74, 79, 81, 89–91, 108, 145, 166, 182–3, 241, 314, 332–3, 325–6, 540.
Meyer, General Lukas, 424–5, 455, 457, 470, 502.
Middelburg (Transvaal) commando. See COMMANDOS.
Middelpunt Farm, 197, 201–2.
Middelpunt ridge, 201.
Middlebosh Farm, 26.
Middlebosh Hill, 28.
Middleburg (Cape Colony), 243.
Middle Hill, 533–5, 537, 539, 541, 545–6, 549, 556, 558, 562–3.
Middlesex regiment. See REGULAR UNITS.
Miles, Colonel H. S. G., M.V.O., 406, 437, 442–3, 445.
Militia Units, 80, 145, 153 ; The Cameronians (Scottish Rifles) (4th), 333 ; The Sherwood Foresters (Derbyshire) (4th), 254.
Miller-Wallnutt, Major C. C., 561, 563, 566.
Milne, Captain G. F., 161, 188.

INDEX.

Milner, The Right Hon. Sir A., K.C.M.G., (High Commissioner), 43-7, 49, 62-3, 152, 335-6; sends Kekewich to Kimberley, 44.
Mines, Diamond, at Kimberley, 39.
Mobile column in Ladysmith, 545, 550, 553, 572.
Mobilisation, Boer, begins, 44.
Modder Poort, 262, 302.
Modder river, 3, 9, 11-12, 16-17, 22, 24-9, 31-3, 53, 58-9, 62, 64, 73-4, 79-80, 90, 93, 97, 100, 103-4, 106, 108, 118-19, 124, 141, 172, 178, 191-3, 199, 205, 209, 212, 243, 261, 268, 276-99, 322-3, 325, 328, 335; battle of, 2, 62; Boers retreat along, 211; camp, line of supply from, 4, 15, 80, 180-2; Cronje's position on, 83, 123, 125; crossing of, at Paardeberg, 120-1; Glen Siding, bridge over, 256, 259, 267-9, 274.
Modder Spruit and Station (Natal), 467, 529-30, 532, 534, 539, 585.
Modder-rivier-poort. See POPLAR GROVE DRIFT.
Montagu-Stuart-Wortley, Major the Hon. E. J., 429, 476.
Monte Cristo, 339, 424-5, 430-1, 433-4, 439, 443-5, 463, 480, 498, 503-4, 508, 582; the capture of, 447-62.
Moor, Captain H. G., 251.
Moord Kraal Hill, 431, 436, 438-9, 442-4.
Moral, causes affecting, at Reddersburg, 304-6.
Mostershoek Farm, 140.
Mostert's Farm, 55.
Mount Alice, 339-40, 342, 345-6, 358, 377-8, 383, 387-8, 398, 404, 406-8, 410, 420.
Mount Impati, 526.
Mountain battery. See REGULAR UNITS.
Mountain guns, 429.
Mounted Infantry. See INFANTRY, MOUNTED.
Mounted Infantry Hill, 535, 556, 562.

Mounted Police. See COMMANDOS.
Mules, 50, 182, 376; brigade transport, 12, 32; difficulty of crossing rivers with, 74, 356.
Munger's Farm, 406, 410-13, 417, 420.
Munger's Farm Drift, 407, 410.
Murch, Lieut. D. J., 288.
Murray, Major A. J., 548.
Murray, Lieut.-Colonel W. H. F., 55-6, 68, 92-3, 95.

NAAUWPOORT, 80, 165, 172, 182, 243, 247, 250, 252, 254.
Napoleon at Moscow, Joubert's comparison, 532.
Natal, army in, composition and dispositions of, 425-9; estimate of number of Boers in, March 11th, 231; Boers from, 3, 6-7, 79, 89, 106, 129, 146, 152, 157, 161, 165, 190; defensive position in, Buller to take up, 6; Government Railway, work done by officials of, 578-9; local forces in, see COLONIAL UNITS; Public Works Department employés repair Colenso road bridge, 494; reinforcements asked for by Buller, February 9th, 9; troops to hold, if Ladysmith abandoned, 8.
Natal Pioneer Corps, 494.
Natives, 375-6, 426; in Kimberley, 51, 62, 65, 69-70; in Ladysmith, 538, 542.
Naval Brigade, The Royal, 63, 75, 147, 190, 214-15, 228, 233, 237, 241, 354, 426, 430, 564, 566.
Naval Brigade, guns of: **12-Prs.**, 22, 28, 31, 33-4, 62, 73, 82, 87, 90, 98, 117, 147, 150, 155-7, 191, 194, 200, 212, 332, 334-5, 354, 377-8, 385-6, 393, 396, 399, 401, 406-7, 413, 415, 418, 421, 423-4, 426, 429, 436-8, 440, 442, 452, 454, 458, 460, 462-3, 467, 469, 471, 484-5, 487, 498, 502-3, 510-11, 519, 525, 528, 538-9, 542-3, 557-8, 562, 582; **4·7-In.**, 28, 74, 80, 90, 143, 147, 155-7,

Naval Brigade, guns of, 4·7-In.—*contd.*
  176, 191, 194, 198, 332, 335, 343, 377–8, 383, 385, 393, 406–7, 415, 418, 420–9, 438, 440, 443, 448, 452, 455, 460, 462–3, 468–9, 471, 476, 484–5, 498, 502–3, 510–11, 519, 521, 528, 538–9, 542–4, 558–60, 562, 564–5, 583–4; **6-In.,** 426, 452, 471, 485, 510, 521.
Naval Gun (Signal) Hill. *See* SIGNAL HILL, NATAL.
Naval Hill, 425, 430, 462, 472, 474, 487, 497, 502–3, 509, 511, 521, 526–7.
Naval telescopes, 445, 520.
Nek, near Kimberley, through which French charged, 33–6, 82.
Nel, Commandant, 281.
Nelthorpe, 432, 525, 527–9, 532–3, 539, 584.
Nesbit, Captain R. C., V.C., 47.
Nesbitt's Horse. *See* COLONIAL UNITS.
Netherlands Railway, repair of Boer guns by, 5.
Newberry's Flour Mills, 262–3, 265.
Newcastle road, 548.
New South Wales, corps from. *See* COLONIAL UNITS.
New Year's greetings from H.M. the Queen, 65.
New Zealand, contingents from. *See* COLONIAL UNITS.
Neylan, Major J. N., 249.
Nicholson, Lieut.-General Sir W. G., K.C.B., 181.
Nicholson's Nek, 338, 383–4.
Nieuwenholdt, Field Cornet, 101.
Nieuwjaarsfontier, 322.
Nooitgedacht Farm, 185, 196, 201.
Norcott, Colonel C. H. B., 428, 448–9, 453–4, 460, 462, 473, 486, 491, 506, 508, 516, 518–19.
Norfolk regiment. *See* REGULAR UNITS.
North Staffordshire regiment. *See* REGULAR UNITS.
Northumberland Fusiliers. *See* REGULAR UNITS.

Norval's Pont, 164–5, 172, 180, 189, 213, 231, 243, 254–8, 263–4, 300–1; Clements crosses Orange river at, March 15th, 255; railway communication completed at, March 30th, 258
" Notes for Guidance in South African Warfare," 113, and Vol. I., pages 448–50.

OBSERVATION HILL, 537, 542–3, 548, 561–2, 568, 570, 582–3.
Oertel's Drift, 208.
Officers, casualties amongst, *see* CASUALTIES *and* APPENDIX 2; special service, 43; paucity of, 153, 522–3; loss of, effect on troops, 309.
Ogilvy, Lieut. F. C. A., R.N., 438, 454, 460, 462, 503.
Oliphantsfontein, 37, 54, 99.
Oliphantsfontein Kop, 58.
Oliver, Mr. H. A. (Mayor of Kimberley), 50.
Olivier, General J. H., 172, 231, 260, 308.
O'Meara, Captain W. A. J., 43–4, 46, 58.
Onderbrook Mountain and Kopjes, 431, 438, 466, 468, 481, 483, 486, 493, 498, 511, 582.
Onderbrook Spruit, 431–2, 459, 464–5, 467, 469, 471–3, 476, 478, 480, 483–4, 503.
Oorlog's Poort, 321.
Orange Free State, arms in, collection of, 257, 260–1; commandos, position of, around Ladysmith, 539–40; frontier, defence of, given by Boers as reason for withdrawal from Ladysmith, 185; Government of, to Kroonstad, 230, 241; invasion of, 5, 11–17, 155, 244, 246, 576, 581; operations in, during halt at Bloemfontein, 274–333; railway systems in, 243, 533, 536; south-east portion of, De Wet's incursion into, 300–33.

INDEX. 685

Orange river, 3–5, 12, 44–5, 58, 155, 165, 172–3, 213, 242–8, 250, 254–9, 263, 274, 300–1, 320, 327, 336 ; situation on, March 15th, 257.
Orange River bridge, 12–13, 75, 145.
Orange River station, 4, 11, 44, 89.
Orders, absence of, for French, after entry into Kimberley, 95 ; congratulatory to Army, on occupation of Bloemfontein, 238–9 ; difficulty of issuing, in Natal, 435 ; from Kruger to De la Rey to assist Free Staters, 233 ; for attack at Poplar Grove, 190–2 ; for march on Bloemfontein, 213–14, 232–3 ; issued by French, 23, 96–7, 195, 215 ; issued by Kitchener, 104 ; lack of, at Paardeberg, 143 ; miscarriage of, 326 ; mode of conveyance of, in British Army system, interference with, etc., 112 ; to Buller, from Lord Roberts, 155, 184 ; to Clements, from Lord Roberts, 155, 172, 182, 254–5 ; to Coke, from Warren, 375–6 ; to Colvile, 80, 91, 120, 227, 294, 297 ; to Dundonald, 356, 360, 442 ; to French, 88, 91 ; to Gatacre, 247, 301–3, 311 ; to Girouard, 165 ; to Guards' Brigade, 227 ; to Hamilton (Ian), 324–6 ; to Hannay, 116, 132 ; to Kelly-Kenny, 80, 88, 91, 104–5, 197, 225 ; to Methuen, 12, 183 ; to Natal Field Force, 436–7, 442–3, 447–8, 457–60, 464–5, 473, 486, 505, 508–9, 520, 523 ; to Pole-Carew, 322–3 ; to Porter, 216–17 ; to Rundle, 322–3 ; to Stephenson, 122, 225 ; to Tucker, 15–16, 78, 80, 91, 269 ; to Warren, 347, 357.
Ordnance Stores, 578.
Organisation of brigades and divisions (out of Natal), April 18th, 320 ; of mounted infantry, 181 ; of Natal army, January 9th, 340 ; of Natal army, February 1st, 406. See also BRITISH ARMY, REDISTRIBUTION OF.

Osfontein (Cape Colony), 248.
Osfontein homestead, 121, 136–7, 169, 180–1, 183, 189–90, 194–5, 212, 241.
Otter, Lieut.-Colonel W. D., 127, 139, 174.
Otto's Kopje Mine, 52, 59.
Oversea Colonials, 240. *See also* COLONIAL UNITS.
Oxen, 3, 74–6, 78, 108, 111, 118, 144, 147, 257, 356, 360, 362, 455.
Oxfordshire Light Infantry. *See* REGULAR UNITS.

PAARDEBERG, 90–1, 101–3, 146, 151, 154–5, 158, 165, 172, 183, 193–4, 203–6, 240, 242, 294, 511, 583 ; attack at, February 18th, want of combination in, 127–8 ; " Big Donga " at, 128, 138–42, 148 ; Boers entrench at, 109 ; British sapping at, 154, 163, 167 ; communication of orders at, difficulty of, 129 ; communication opened with French at, 122 ; counter-attack at, by De Wet, 135, 143–4 ; effect on British of, 138 ; Cronje decides to give battle at, 107–8 ; Cronje's laager at, 2, 100 ; position of, 108–9 ; wagons in, set on fire, 117 ; De Wet arrives near, 135 ; drift at (Modder river), 88, 98, 102–5, 109, 114–21, 132–7, 142–7, 150, 156, 158, 164, 171 ; effects in South Africa of surrender at, 178–9 ; failure at, causes of, 143 ; fording the river at, 120, 126, 133 ; Hannay's charge at, 132–3 ; Mounted Infantry at, gain touch with cavalry, 121 ; insanitary conditions at, 164, 171 ; Lord Kitchener's, plan of action at, 113–16 ; reasons for attacking at, 110–11 ; Lord Roberts, arrives at, 148 ; reasons for not assaulting laager at, 153–5 ; sick and wounded at, removal of, 182 ; situation at

686   THE WAR IN SOUTH AFRICA.

Paardeberg—*continued*.
  February 18th, 8 a.m., Kitchener's views of, 123; February 18th, 7 p.m., Kitchener's views of, 142.
Paardeberg Hill, 128.
Paardekraal, 321.
Paget, Major W. L. H., 427, 453.
Pain, Lieut.-Colonel G. W. Hackett, 250.
Panfontein, 185, 214, 238, 241.
Panfontein Kopjes and Ridges, 186–7, 199.
Park, Major C. W., 568–9.
Parker, Sergeant C. (awarded the Victoria Cross), 290.
Parry, Private, 289.
Parsons, Colonel Sir C. S. B., K.C.M.G., 182, 212.
Parsons, Lieut. F. N. (awarded the Victoria Cross), 137.
Parsons, Lieut.-Colonel L. W., 408–10, 436–7, 442–3, 452, 455, 484, 509, 522.
Passages of Riet and Modder rivers, 15, 74, 120, 126, 194; Tugela, 460, 463–80.
Passes, granted to burghers under proclamation, 260.
Patrols, inefficiency of, at Sannah's Post, 278–9.
Peakman, Lieut.-Colonel T. C., 60–1, 66.
Pearse, Major H. W., 478, 483.
Peck, Lieut. H. R., 288.
Pelletier, Lieut.-Colonel O. C. C., 174, 176.
Pelly, Major J. S., 429.
Penhoek, 245.
Penny, Private, 236.
Pepworth Hill, 529, 533–7, 539–40, 542, 585.
Perrott, Lieut.-Colonel T., 233.
Petrusburg, 107, 135, 159, 166, 170, 189, 202, 214–16, 228, 232.
Philippolis, 135, 301; commando, *see* COMMANDOS.
Phillips, Captain H. G. C., 400.

Phipps-Hornby, Major E. J., 283, 288–9, 292; (awarded the Victoria Cross), 290.
Pickford, Private, 289.
Pienaar's Farm, 247.
Piet Retief commando. *See* COMMANDOS.
Pietermaritzburg, 423, 429, 441, 494, 531.
Pieters Hill, 183, 430, 432, 448, 453, 455–7, 463–5, 487, 498, 534, 581–3. *See also* LADYSMITH, RELIEF OF.
Pieters Hoek, 459, 505.
Pieters Station, 430–2, 463, 510, 525, 527.
Pilcher, Lieut.-Colonel T. D., 262–7, 275–6, 291.
Pilcher's Mounted Infantry. *See* INFANTRY, MOUNTED.
Piquet Hill, 351, 357, 385.
Pitts, Private J. (awarded the Victoria Cross), 570.
Platrand, 535, 537. *See also* CÆSAR'S CAMP.
Pohlmann, Commandant, 384.
Pole Carew, Major-General R., C.B., 145, 257–8, 261, 300, 320–4, 326–7.
Pom-Pom bridge, 488, 492, 499.
Pom-poms (Vickers-Maxims), 76–7, 83, 101, 136–7, 174, 178, 221–6, 235, 250, 273, 281, 292, 326, 328, 371, 382, 388, 392, 409, 411, 413, 419, 434, 463, 466, 471, 488, 498, 504, 511, 513, 538.
Pondos, 335.
Pontoons, 120, 194, 255, 342, 348, 353–6, 402, 407, 409–10, 412, 420–1, 434, 459–65, 469, 493–4, 497–8, 501–5, 507, 510–11, 515, 523–4, 527–8.
Poore, Major R. M., 233.
Popham, Second Lieut. R. S., 249.
Poplar Grove, 164–5, 168, 172, 180–1, 188–9, 208, 212, 232, 238; Boers' panic and flight from, 201, 203; Colvile's advance at, 199–201; De Wet's escape from, 203–4;

INDEX. 687

drift at, 185-7, 190, 192, 213; enemy's retreat from Seven Kopjes at, 196-7; French's advance at, 196-7; homestead at, 187, 191; hour of starting, effect of misunderstanding as to, 192; Kelly-Kenny's advance at, 198-9; Lord Roberts' scheme for attack at, 190-3, 207; medical arrangements at, 191; reasons for failure at, 197, 204-7.
Porrit's Drift, 343.
Porter, Colonel T. C., 4, 18-19, 22, 24, 27, 33, 35, 92-4, 97, 152, 158, 169, 201, 203, 212, 215, 217-23, 228, 232, 234-5, 237, 269, 328.
Port Elizabeth, 243, 439.
Potchefstroom commando. *See* COMMANDOS.
Potgieter, Commandant F. J., 149.
Potgieters Drift, 5, 339-48, 353-4, 358, 364, 377-8, 385, 391-2, 402, 413, 420, 493, 547, 550, 553-4, 572-6, 581.
Poundisford, 241.
Powder, made in Kimberley, 50.
Powerful, H.M.S., 558, 579.
Premier Mine (Kimberley), 41-2, 52-3, 56-7.
Presidents of the Boer Republics. *See* KRUGER *and* STEYN.
Pretoria, 4-5, 16, 66, 166, 211, 233, 236, 243, 305, 314, 319, 327, 413, 455.
Pretoria commando. *See* COMMANDOS.
Pretorius Farm, 341-5, 421.
Pretorius, Andries, Farm, 434-5.
Pretyman, Major-General G. T., C.B., 177-8.
Prieska, 152, 182, 189, 238, 266.
Prince Alfred's Volunteer Guard. *See* COLONIAL UNITS.
Prinsloo, General, 242, 409, 413, 470.
Prisoners of War: Boer—27, 36, 59, 79, 93, 160, 169-70, 178, 229, 238, 256, 260, 262, 333, 361, 517, 521; British—47, 76, 79, 133, 136, 253, 281, 298-9, 310, 390, exchange of, 163.

Proclamations: Boer—188, 266-7; British—234, 260.
Public opinion, effect on the Army, 205-6.
Public Works Department, Natal, 494.

QUEEN, THE, HER MAJESTY, 239, 547; message from, 65.
Queensland Mounted Infantry. *See* COLONIAL UNITS.
Queenstown Rifle Volunteers. *See* COLONIAL UNITS.

RADCLIFFE, CAPTAIN N. R., 285, 292, 295.
Rafts, 344.
Raids, into Cape Colony, proposed, 166; into Southern Natal, 532-3.
Railway Hill, 430, 432, 456-7, 463, 471, 489, 496-7, 506, 508, 511-13.
Railways, 44, 47-8, 63-4, 145, 155, 165, 184, 247, 252, 254-5, 257-9, 268, 275, 300, 305, 308, 319, 327, 332-3, 533; best supply route, 243; bridge over Orange river, 12-13; capture of rolling stock of, 227; cut by Boers, at Bethulie, 248, at Norval's Pont, 255, north of Ladysmith, 529; cut by British south and north of Bloemfontein, 234, 236; materials for, 165; Norval's Pont line of, 164, 258; raid on, by Boers, proposed, 166; re-opened to Cape Town, 258; south of Bloemfontein, 232-6.
Railway Pioneer regiment. *See* COLONIAL UNITS.
Ramah Spring, 12-13.
Ramdam, 16, 19, 21, 25, 30, 107, 172; concentration at, 11, 13-18, 22, 28; water at, 3.
Range Post, 537, 545, 562.
Rangeworthy Heights, 350, 359-60, 364-6, 368, 373, 381, 388, 402-3.
Ration Post, 537, 543, 549, 580.
Rations. *See* SUPPLIES.

Rawson, Lieut.-Colonel H. E., 494, 527.
Reade, Major R. N. R., 58.
Rebels, Cape Colony, 532; Griqualand West, 93–5, 146, 182.
Reconnaissances, from Kimberley, 55–6; in Natal, 335, 433–4, 440, 459, 504, 533, 540–1, 544, 548.
Reddersburg, 236–314; attack on McWhinnie's force near, 307–10; Gatacre to the rescue of, 311; loss of officers at, effect of, 309; retreat on, 306–7; surrender of British at, 310; water at, scarcity of, 310.
Reddersburg commando. *See* COMMANDOS.
Reeves, Colonel J., 429, 510.
Refugees, from Thabanchu, 276.

REGULAR UNITS.

Cavalry :—
Household Cavalry, 26, 99, 101–2, 131, 150, 158–9, 275, 285–7.
5th (Princess Charlotte of Wales's) Dragoon Guards, 540–1, 546, 548, 562, 567–8, 584.
6th Dragoon Guards (Carabiniers), 12, 18, 22, 37, 96–7, 99–100, 102, 122, 149, 158, 169, 217, 219, 221–2, 227–8, 269.
1st (Royal) Dragoons, 334, 341, 360, 362, 376, 401, 406, 426, 428.
2nd Dragoons (Royal Scots Greys), 18, 20, 24, 169, 216–17, 222, 235, 269.
5th (Royal Irish) Lancers, 542, 544, 548, 564–8.
6th (Inniskilling) Dragoons, 18, 221–2, 228, 251.
8th (King's Royal Irish) Hussars, 246, 331.
9th (Queen's Royal) Lancers, 19, 26, 33, 35–6, 140–1, 158, 168, 202, 268–9.
10th (Prince of Wales's Own Royal) Hussars, 20–1, 99, 101–2, 149, 158, 196, 222, 228, 237, 275, 285–7, 299, 427.
12th (Prince of Wales's Royal) Lancers, 26, 99, 101–2, 121–2, 149, 158, 196, 222, 269, 295.
13th Hussars, 356–7, 360, 406, 426–7, 440, 503, 525–6.
14th (King's) Hussars, 12, 22, 221–2, 405, 426, 525–6.
16th (Queen's) Lancers, 19, 24–5, 34–6, 140–1, 152, 156, 158, 160, 268–9, 426–7.
18th Hussars, 540, 548, 564, 566–7, 572.
19th (Princess of Wales's Own) Hussars, 540, 544, 547, 564–5, 567.

Artillery :—
Royal Horse, 18, 20, 25, 94–5, 122, 131, 139, 169, 190, 195–6, 201, 235, 261, 269, 299, 328, 331–2, 511, 520.
A. battery, 7, 405–6, 426, 498, 503, 520.
G. battery, 26, 34, 99–102, 149–50, 158, 222.
J. battery, 251, 253.
O. battery, 19, 34, 140–1, 158, 268, 273.
P. battery, 34, 99–102, 158, 222, 325.
Q. battery, 34, 217, 219, 275, 280, 283–4, 288–91, 293.
R. battery, 19, 34, 140–1, 152, 156, 158, 160, 268, 273.
T. battery, 34, 217, 219–21, 223.
U. battery, 34, 218–21, 223, 275, 280, 282–3, 295.
Royal Field, 30, 80, 157, 190, 270, 301, 311, 321, 328, 331, 335, 343, 366, 381, 412, 436, 438, 442–3, 446, 466, 469, 510–11, 519, 550.
2nd battery, 253, 325.
4th battery, 333.
5th battery, 303.

INDEX.

7th battery, 352, 366, 408-9, 427, 447, 452-3, 462-3, 471, 485, 503.
8th battery, 318.
13th battery, 541.
18th battery, 76-7, 147, 159.
19th battery, 352, 366, 370, 377, 408-9, 426, 462-3, 485, 502.
20th battery, 145.
21st battery, 540, 544, 562, 567.
28th battery, 352, 366, 370, 408-9, 411, 428, 452, 462, 465, 471, 484-5, 503.
38th battery, 145.
39th battery, 253.
42nd battery, 540, 542-4, 557, 562.
53rd battery, 540, 544, 548, 562-3, 584.
61st (Howitzer) battery, 354, 407-9, 426, 452, 462-3, 471, 484-5, 498, 502, 511.
62nd battery, 77, 147, 159, 168-9.
63rd battery, 352, 366, 408-11, 427, 452, 462-3, 471, 485, 502, 524.
64th battery, 342, 354, 406-7, 410-11, 427, 445, 447, 452-3, 462-3, 471, 485, 503.
65th (Howitzer) battery, 91, 120-1, 137, 142, 150, 156, 214-15, 233.
66th battery, 468-9.
67th battery, 543-4.
69th battery, 541-3, 562, 570, 584.
73rd battery, 352, 366, 408-9, 428, 451-2, 462, 465, 471, 485, 501, 520.
74th battery, 247-9, 320.
75th battery, 79, 147, 158, 169.
76th battery, 34, 84-6, 114, 117, 121, 130, 136-7, 150-1, 155-6, 218, 220, 223, 226, 229.
77th battery, 247, 320.
78th battery, 352, 366, 408-9, 428, 442, 452, 462, 465, 471, 485, 503.
79th battery, 244-5, 320.
81st battery, 34, 81, 83-5, 114, 117, 129-30, 133, 135-7, 150, 152, 156, 218, 220-1, 223, 226, 229.

82nd battery, 91, 114, 120-1, 126-8, 142, 150, 156, 218-19.
83rd battery, 145.
84th battery, 145, 257.
85th battery, 145.
Ammunition columns, 18, 24-5, 27, 30, 32, 91, 195, 214-15, 233, 354, 427-8, 508, 550, 579.
Royal Garrison, 45, 52, 58, 61, 174, 176, 214-15, 233, 251, 253, 315, 328, 332, 405-7, 410, 413, 415, 418, 427, 436, 438-9, 442, 448, 454, 460, 462-3, 471, 484-5, 498, 502, 510, 519, 528.
4th Mountain battery, 375, 396, 399, 401, 406, 418, 423, 427, 462, 465, 503, 510-11, 524.
10th Mountain battery, 536, 538, 546, 584.
Engineers :—
Royal Engineers, 13, 18, 24, 45, 58, 60-1, 91, 98-9, 109, 120, 126, 134, 147, 155, 157, 159, 163, 167, 173-5, 190, 194, 196, 214-15, 233-4, 236, 255, 257, 268, 275, 315, 317, 344, 348, 353-5, 375-6, 379, 381-2, 395-6, 401, 407, 410, 420, 427-8, 460-1, 463-4, 494, 498, 507, 546, 548-50, 558-9, 564, 566.
Foot Guards :—
Grenadier Guards (2nd), 320.
Grenadier Guards (3rd), 177, 257, 268.
Coldstream Guards (1st), 268.
Coldstream Guards (2nd), 177, 268.
Scots Guards (1st), 257.
Scots Guards (2nd), 320.
Infantry :—
The Royal Scots (Lothian) (1st) [formerly 1st Foot], 39, 245, 249, 301-4, 315-16.
The Queen's (Royal West Surrey) (2nd) [formerly 2nd Foot], 355, 369-70, 416, 427, 444, 448-9, 454, 483, 493, 506.

Regular Units (Infantry)—*continued*.
The Buffs (East Kent) (2nd) [formerly 3rd Foot], 83–4, 119, 137, 149, 169, 176, 218, 223, 225–8.
The King's Own (Royal Lancaster) (2nd) [formerly 4th Foot], 366, 376, 379, 383–4, 401, 408, 421, 428, 473–4, 476–7, 479, 483, 492, 500, 505, 508, 515–17, 519.
The Northumberland Fusiliers (2nd) [formerly 5th Foot], 244, 301–3.
The Royal Warwickshire (2nd) [formerly 6th Foot], 132.
The Royal Fusiliers (City of London) (2nd) [formerly 7th Foot], 423, 429, 463, 487, 493, 499, 506.
The King's (Liverpool) (1st) [formerly 8th Foot], 536, 538, 547, 562, 584.
The Norfolk (2nd) [formerly 9th Foot], 77, 133, 147, 157, 161, 271.
The Lincolnshire (2nd) [formerly 10th Foot], 77, 147, 157, 159, 160–1, 271.
The Devonshire (1st) [formerly 11th Foot], 536, 546, 553, 568–70, 584.
The Devonshire (2nd) [formerly 11th Foot], 343, 355, 369, 377, 402, 411–12, 417, 419, 427, 444–5, 448–9, 454, 476, 478–9, 481, 483, 493, 506.
The Prince Albert's (Somersetshire Light Infantry) (2nd) [formerly 13th Foot], 318, 327, 371, 385, 399, 420, 428, 465–6, 506.
The Prince of Wales's Own (West Yorkshire) (2nd) [formerly 14th Foot], 343, 355, 369–70, 416, 427, 444–5, 448–9, 454, 493, 495, 499, 505, 508, 515–19.
The East Yorkshire (2nd) [formerly 15th Foot], 320, 331.
The Leicestershire (1st) [formerly 17th Foot], 537, 547, 562, 570.

The Princess of Wales's Own (Yorkshire) (1st) [formerly 19th Foot], 30, 98, 114, 117–19, 123–4, 142, 149, 150–1, 161, 169, 218, 220–1, 224, 226.
The Lancashire Fusiliers (2nd) [formerly 20th Foot], 366–7, 370, 376, 379–80, 383–4, 387, 408, 428–9, 507.
The Royal Scots Fusiliers (2nd) [formerly 21st Foot], 421, 423, 427, 429, 451, 459, 463, 487, 500, 505, 510, 513–14.
The Cheshire (2nd) [formerly 22nd Foot], 271–2.
The Royal Welsh Fusiliers (1st) [formerly 23rd Foot], 423, 429, 459, 492–3, 500, 506.
The South Wales Borderers (2nd) [formerly 24th Foot], 271–2.
The King's Own Scottish Borderers (1st) [formerly 25th Foot], 76–7, 147, 157, 159–61, 168–9, 271, 273.
The Cameronians (Scottish Rifles) (2nd) [formerly 90th Foot], 354, 385, 391–2, 394, 398, 400, 410–12, 428, 469, 473, 493, 495, 499, 506, 508, 518, 564.
The Royal Inniskilling Fusiliers (1st) [formerly 27th Foot], 327, 370, 429, 486, 488–91, 499–500, 506, 508.
The Gloucestershire (1st) [formerly 28th Foot], 536, 553, 583.
The Gloucestershire (2nd) [formerly 61st Foot], 83–5, 119, 137, 150–1, 177, 218, 223–7.
The Worcestershire (1st) [formerly 29th Foot], 320.
The Worcestershire (2nd) [formerly 36th Foot], 250–2.
The East Lancashire (1st) [formerly 30th Foot], 271–3.
The East Surrey (2nd) [formerly 70th Foot], 355, 369–70, 416, 427, 444, 448–9, 454, 460, 476, 478, 481–3, 493, 495, 499, 506, 508, 518.

INDEX.

The Duke of Cornwall's Light Infantry (2nd) [formerly 46th Foot], 120, 128, 132, 138–42. 174, 201, 325, 329.

The Duke of Wellington's (West Riding) (1st) [formerly 33rd Foot], 83–5, 119, 124, 149, 218, 254, 289.

The Border (1st) [formerly 34th Foot], 318, 367, 370, 429, 469, 486, 506–7, 511, 514.

The Hampshire (2nd) [formerly 67th Foot], 77, 147, 157, 161, 271.

The South Staffordshire (1st) [formerly 38th Foot], 320.

The Dorsetshire (2nd) [formerly 54th Foot], 354, 371, 385, 394, 398, 402, 420, 428, 465–6, 506.

The Prince of Wales's Volunteers (South Lancashire) (1st) [formerly 40th Foot], 366, 376, 379, 383, 408, 428, 469, 472–4, 476–7, 483, 492, 495, 505, 507–8, 515, 517–19.

The Welsh (1st) [formerly 41st Foot], 82, 87, 114–15, 117, 122, 130, 133–4, 137, 149, 157, 218, 220–8.

The Black Watch (Royal Highlanders) (2nd) [formerly 73rd Foot], 43, 121, 125–6, 174, 177.

The Oxfordshire Light Infantry (1st) [formerly 43rd Foot], 83–6, 119, 124, 142, 150–1, 218.

The Essex (1st) [formerly 44th Foot], 30, 114–15, 117, 122, 130, 133–4, 136–7, 149, 157, 169, 218, 220–8, 289.

The Sherwood Foresters (Derbyshire) (1st) [formerly 45th Foot], 301, 303, 311.

The Loyal North Lancashire (1st) [formerly 47th Foot], 43, 45, 49, 55, 58, 60–2, 68, 92.

Princess Charlotte of Wales's (Royal Berkshire) (2nd) [formerly 66th Foot], 244, 246, 249.

The Queen's Own (Royal West Kent) (2nd) [formerly 97th Foot], 320.

The King's (Shropshire Light Infantry) (2nd) [formerly 85th Foot], 126–8, 138–9, 142, 148–9, 152, 157, 162–3, 173–5, 201, 289, 325, 329, 331.

The Duke of Cambridge's Own (Middlesex) (2nd) [formerly 77th Foot], 371, 383, 387, 390, 392, 394, 428, 465–6, 506, 521.

The King's Royal Rifle Corps (1st) [formerly 60th Foot], 537, 542–3, 561, 563–4, 567.

The King's Royal Rifle Corps (2nd) [formerly 60th Foot], 537, 557, 559, 561, 563–4, 567.

The King's Royal Rifle Corps (3rd) [formerly 60th Foot], 377–8, 392–4, 398–9, 411–12, 416, 428, 447, 469, 473, 476–9, 481–3, 493, 506.

The Duke of Edinburgh's (Wiltshire) (2nd) [formerly 99th Foot], 250–3.

The Manchester (1st) [formerly 63rd Foot], 537, 540–1, 543, 557–63.

The Manchester (2nd) [formerly 96th Foot], 320.

The Prince of Wales's (North Staffordshire) (2nd) [formerly 98th Foot], 213, 271.

The York and Lancaster (1st) [formerly 65th Foot], 366–7, 370, 408, 426, 428, 505, 507–8, 515, 517.

The Durham Light Infantry (1st) [formerly 68th Foot], 284, 289, 377, 385, 391, 411, 416, 428, 460, 486, 496, 499, 506, 508.

The Highland Light Infantry (1st) [formerly 71st Foot], 103, 120, 177.

Seaforth Highlanders (Ross-shire Buffs, The Duke of Albany's) (2nd) [formerly 78th Foot], 121, 125–6, 139, 177, 248.

The Gordon Highlanders (1st) [formerly 75th Foot], 75–6, 126–8, 131, 139, 142, 148–9, 157, 163, 173–4, 177, 201, 325, 329–31.

Regular Units (Infantry)—*continued.*
  The Gordon Highlanders (2nd) [formerly 92nd Foot], 537, 558–9, 561–5, 584.
  The Queen's Own Cameron Highlanders (1st) [formerly 79th Foot], 311.
  The Royal Irish Rifles (2nd) [formerly 86th Foot], 249, 301–2, 306–10, 312–13, 318.
  Princess Victoria's (Royal Irish Fusiliers) (1st) [formerly 87th Foot], 537.
  Princess Victoria's (Royal Irish Fusiliers) (2nd) [formerly 89th Foot], 423, 429, 446, 451, 500, 505, 510–12, 514.
  The Connaught Rangers (1st) [formerly 88th Foot], 364, 367, 417, 420, 429, 469, 486–92, 495–6, 499–500, 506, 508.
  Princess Louise's (Argyll and Sutherland Highlanders) (1st) [formerly 91st Foot], 120, 125, 174, 177, 546.
  The Prince of Wales's Leinster (Royal Canadians) (1st) [formerly 100th Foot], 320.
  The Royal Dublin Fusiliers (1st) [formerly 102nd Foot], 429.
  The Royal Dublin Fusiliers (2nd) [formerly 103rd Foot], 367, 370, 429, 461, 469, 486–91, 495, 499–500, 505, 508, 510, 513–14, 536.
  The Rifle Brigade (The Prince Consort's Own) (1st), 354, 385, 391, 411, 417, 428, 449, 460, 486, 496, 499, 506, 508, 518.
  The Rifle Brigade (The Prince Consort's Own) (2nd), 537, 542–3, 546, 548–9, 563, 565, 572.
  Rifle Reserve Battalion, 423, 429, 473–4, 476, 478–9, 492, 506–7, 511, 513.

Army Service Corps (includes Supply parks and columns):—18, 45, 48, 53, 76, 190, 214, 257, 275, 299, 428–9, 550, 578–9.
Royal Army Medical Corps (includes Bearer companies, Field hospitals, etc.):—18, 24, 45, 48, 182, 190, 195, 214, 257, 275, 315, 428–9.

Reichman, Captain, United States Attaché, 202.
Reinforcements: Boer—29, 59, 77, 99, 107, 110, 135, 154, 166, 172, 250, 384, 467, 540; from Colesberg, Natal, etc., 79, 89, 106, 129, 146, 155, 157, 161, 165, 186, 189, 209, 230; from the Transvaal, 233; British—at Bloemfontein, 319; at Paardeberg, 102, 122, 147; at Thaba Mountain, 331; for Clements, 254; for Gatacre, 244; for Natal, 9; from Cape Town, 80; from England, 12, 153, 320.
Remounts, 140, 172, 242, 269.
Rensburg, 152, 250, 252–4.
Republics, Boer, 39, 155, 179, 265, 305.
Republic in Cape Colony, proposed, 167.
Reserve, men of, 423; officers of, 153.
Rhodes, The Right Hon. C. J., 39, 41, 50–1, 53, 57, 62–3, 65–8, 70–1.
Rhodes, Lieut.-Colonel E., D.S.O., 191.
Rhodesia, Southern, 43.
Richards, Lieut. S. R. S., R.N., 423.
Richardson, Lieut. J. J., 558.
Richardson, Colonel W. D., 78, 91.
Ridley, Colonel C. P., 75–7, 181, 190, 194, 201, 214, 269, 328.
Ridley's Mounted Infantry. *See* INFANTRY, MOUNTED.
Rietfontein, 322.
Riet river, 3–4, 12, 15, 17–24, 27, 29–30, 32, 74–5, 79, 113, 154.
Riet river bridge, 256–7, 303.
Rifle Brigade, The. *See* REGULAR UNITS.
Rifle Reserve battalion. *See* REGULAR UNITS.

INDEX. 693

Rifleman's Post, 535, 537, 542.
Rifleman's Ridge, 534-5, 537, 539, 544, 546, 556, 562, 573.
Rifles, Boer, for Cape Colony, 167.
Rimington, Major M. F., 275.
Rimington's Guides. *See* COLONIAL UNITS.
Riverton, 41; waterworks at, 55.
Roberts, Field-Marshal, The Right Hon. F. S., Lord, K.P., G.C.B., V.C., etc., etc., 1-22, 25, 28-31, 36-8, 95-6, 100, 113, 116, 135, 170, 172-4, 177-84, 188, 192-4, 199-200, 207-8, 211-18, 225, 227, 237-47, 250, 254-61, 264-8, 274-5, 285, 308, 321, 325-8, 335-6, 359, 404-5, 419, 426, 464, 575-6, 581, 583; Buller and Clements, action urged on by, 155; Buller, a strict defensive ordered to, by, 184; ordered by him, to relieve Ladysmith at any cost, 416; Bloemfontein, march on, after Poplar Grove, arranged by, 213-14; final march on, ordered by, 232-3; enters and issues congratulatory orders at, 238-9; at, causes of delay of, 242; cavalry march on Bloemfontein, designed by, 154-5; choice of route by, misleads Boers, 16, 22-3, 107; Chermside's and Guards' brigades, sent on by, 123; Clements, orders to, modified by, 172; ordered a strict defensive by, 182; Colvile sent to Waterval Drift by, 277; correspondence with, 297-8; convoy to replace loss at Waterval arranged by, 80; Cronje's, correspondence with, 162; immobility modifies plans of, 73; move, February 16th, reported to, 87-8; unconditional surrender, demanded by, 148; surrender received by, 177; decision, after Spion Kop, 7-8; after Vaal Krantz, 8-9, 11, 416; to abandon convoy, 77-8; to besiege not assault Cronje, 153; distributes detachments to pacify Free State, 301-2, 304-5; De Wet, driven from Kitchener's Kopje by, 157-60; causes of failure to capture, by, 326; flying column recalled to Springfield by, 298; French, congratulated by, 38; ordered to avoid Boers at Driefontein by, 217; plan for seizing Karee Siding, explained to, by, 269; sent to Bloemfontein with proclamation by, 233-4; to Thabanchu, March 18th, by, 261; to Waterval Drift by, 294; from Le Gallais Kopje sees French and Kelly-Kenny halted, 197; Gatacre's return to Bethanie ordered by, 312; halt after Cronje's surrender forced on, 180; Kekewich reports to, 5, 67; Kimberley, rides to, March 1st, 182; Kitchener, given control in name of, 104-5; warned by, of outside help for Cronje, 110; reports on Paardeberg battle to, 123, 142; sent by, to organise southern forces and new line, 164-5; sent to west by, 212; Kelly-Kenny ordered to push on at Driefontein by, 225; orders back to Waterval, support for convoy, 76-7; orders forward further reinforcements to Paardeberg, 147; Paardeberg, double line formed at, by, 161; Pieters Hill, on news of, telegrams from, 183; Pole-Carew, to meet Gatacre and Clements, sent by, 256; report from, March 17th, received by, 257; Poplar Grove, scheme for, read to general officers by, 190; disappointment at, 203; promises Kimberley relief, 5; reasons, for choice of route in Orange Free State, 3, 16, 71; for date of starting, 5, 67; Reddersburg, reinforcements for, ordered by, 311; Rhodes appeals to, 67; influence on action of, 71; sends on Colvile's division to Paardeberg, 91; Sannah's Post, orders after, by, 302-3,

Roberts, Field Marshal, Lord—*contd.*
305; starts for Klip Drift, 143, 148; telegraphs Cronje's move to Kitchener, French and Kelly-Kenny, 88; White in Cape Colony, scheme for using, proposed by, 184; Wepener relief columns to trap De Wet, ordered by, 318-19.
Roberts' Horse. *See* COLONIAL UNITS.
Robin, Major A. W., 275.
Robinson, Commissioner M. B., 43.
Rochfort, Colonel A. N., 34, 280, 288.
Rodger, Captain T. H., 61.
Romer, Captain C. F., 490-1.
Rondeval Drift, 24-6, 30-2, 87.
Roodekop Ridge, 322-3.
Roodepan, 14-15.
Roodepoort (Natal), 365, 405, 575.
Roodepoort Hill, 322.
Rooidam, 25.
"Rooineks" (British), 305.
Rooipoort, 212.
Roos, Commandant, 82, 86, 209.
Rosalie, 351, 364-5, 372.
Rosendal, 321.
Rosmead, Lord, H. E., Governor and High Commissioner, 40.
Ross, Lieut.-Colonel W., 75.
Rouxville, 301-2, 304, 312-13, 318.
Royal Army Medical Corps. *See* REGULAR UNITS.
Royal Artillery. *See* REGULAR UNITS.
Royal Canadian regiment. *See* COLONIAL UNITS.
Royal Cavalry regiments. *See* REGULAR UNITS.
Royal Commission on the War in South Africa. *See* "COMMISSION."
Royal Engineers. *See* REGULAR UNITS.
Royal Infantry battalions. *See* REGULAR UNITS.
Royal Navy. *See* NAVAL BRIGADE.
Royal Victorian Navy. *See* COLONIAL UNITS.
Royston, Colonel W., 537, 546, 559.

Rundle, Lieut.-General Sir H. M. L., K.C.B., C.M.G., D.S.O., 320-4, 328, 333.
Russell-Brown, Lieut. C., 256.
Rustfontein, 303.

SALVOES, fired at Paardeberg, 164.
Sanatorium (Kimberley), 57.
Sand Drift, 344.
Sand Spruit, 539.
Sandars, Major F. A., 491.
Sandbach, Lieut.-Colonel A. E., 434, 459, 497, 504-5, 525.
Sannah's Post, 300, 302-3, 305, 314; Broadwood's dispositions at, 284-6, withdrawal from, 290-1; capture of U. battery at, 283-4; cavalry division arrives at, 296; Colvile's division arrives at (Boesman's Kop), 292; De Wet arrives at, 281; effect of De Wet's success at, 305; escape of Q. battery from, 283; information of Boers' presence at, 278; Martyr's dispositions at, 287; messages to and from, 294, 296-8; moral effect of De Wet's success at, 298-9; situation at, difficulty of, 284, 288; terrain at, 276-7, 284.
Sap, at Paardeberg, 154, 163, 167.
Scheepers, G. J., 23.
Scheme, for defence, Kimberley, 40, 42.
Schleswig-Holstein, Major H. H. Prince Christian V. A. L. E. A. of, G.C.B., G.C.V.O., 483.
Schmidt's Drift road, 60.
Schoeman, General, 253, 335.
Scholtz Nek, 5, 64.
Schreiner, The Hon. W. P., C.M.G., M.L.A., 42-3.
Schuinshoek, 202.
Schwickkard, Mr., 455.
Scobell, Major H. J., 215-17, 235.
Scobell's Knoll, 216.
Scots Fusiliers, The Royal. *See* REGULAR UNITS.
Scots Greys, Royal. *See* REGULAR UNITS.

INDEX. 695

Scots Guards. *See* REGULAR UNITS.
Scott, Captain P., R.N., 538.
Scott, Major R. G., 94.
Scott, Private R. (awarded the Victoria Cross), 570.
Scouse, Colour-Sergeant, 331.
Scrubby Hill, 437.
Scurvy, in Kimberley, 69.
Seaforth Highlanders. *See* REGULAR UNITS.
Searchlight, Kimberley, 41, 50; signals, 58–9, 67, 547.
Secretary of State for War, 6, 335, 346, 419, 509.
Senekal commando. *See* COMMANDOS.
Settle, Brig.-General H. H., 182, 212.
Seven Kopjes, 187, 191–2, 196, 198–9, 201.
Sheen, Engineer C. C., R.N., 579.
Shells, made in Kimberley, 50.
Shooting of British soldiers compared with that of Boers, 388.
"Shop, The" (Driefontein), 222–3, 228.
Shropshire Light Infantry. *See* REGULAR UNITS.
Sick and wounded, at Ladysmith, 572, 577–9; from Paardeberg, 182.
Siege, of Kimberley, 54–72; of Ladysmith, 531–85.
Signal Hill (Natal), 406, 410, 415; (Paardeberg) 108, 117, 128, 142, 147, 156–7, 161.
Signalling, arrangements for, 191, 375, 391, 400; unsatisfactory, between balloon and guns, 167.
Signpost Ridge, 537, 562.
Simon's Town, 156, 538.
Sims, Gunner W., R.N., 566.
Situation, in Cape Colony, North-West, 212, 335–6; in Natal, after Colenso, 335; after Spion Kop, 6; on the Modder river, February 16th, 90–1; on the Orange river, March 16th, 257; in Western theatre of War, 88, 238; Sannah's Post action, changes, 305; throughout South Africa, March 13th, 238.

Sitwell, Lieut.-Colonel C. G. H., D.S.O., 490.
Sitwell, Lieut.-Colonel W. H., 248, 321.
Sitwell's Mounted Infantry. *See* INFANTRY, MOUNTED.
Skiet's Drift, 345–7, 354, 406, 410, 414.
Slaag Kraal Hill, 187, 202–3, 212.
Slaagslaagte, 201.
Slingersfontein, 250–1.
Smartt, The Hon. T. W., M.L.A., 66.
Smith, Major H. L., 482.
Smith, Major W. Apsley, 428, 465–6, 484.
Smith-Dorrien, Major-General H. L., D.S.O., 15, 91, 103, 114–15, 126, 128–9, 138, 142, 148, 162–3, 173–6, 200–1, 207, 293, 296, 325, 327–31.
Smithfield, 259, 263–4, 301–4, 306, 312–14.
Smithfield commando. *See* COMMANDOS.
Smut, Commandant, 30.
Smyth, Captain R. N., 440.
Snyman, Commandant, 189, 242.
Sol. de Jager's Farm, 350.
Soldiers. *See* TROOPS.
Somersetshire Light Infantry. *See* REGULAR UNITS.
South Africa, 2, 7, 40, 50, 71, 265; British forces in, adequate after four months, 239; situation throughout, March 13th, 238.
South African Colonial troops. *See* COLONIAL UNITS.
South African Light Horse. *See* COLONIAL UNITS.
South Australian Infantry. *See* COLONIAL UNITS.
South Lancashire regiment. *See* REGULAR UNITS.
South Staffordshire regiment. *See* REGULAR UNITS.
Sorties, from Kimberley, 58, 60, 68, 92; from Ladysmith, 66, 529, 546–9.
Spearman's Hill, 342–4, 354, 371–2, 420–1.

Spearman's Hollow, 405.
Special Service officers, 43.
Spens, Lieut.-Colonel J., 127–8, 138, 140, 201.
Spies, Boer, in Ladysmith, 546; Native, unreliable, 341.
Spiller, Field-Cornet T., 160.
Spion Kop, 403, 405, 409, 412–13, 423, 429, 435, 470, 516, 573–6; Acton Homes, surprise of Boers at, 360–3; advance on, 367–9; armistice at, 401; Boer movements at, 344–5, 368; Boers re-occupy, 401; Buller acquiesces in scheme for attack on, 375; Buller and Warren confer at, 372; Buller's fresh plans for, 345, 357; Clery's dispositions at, January 20th and 21st, 366–71; concentration of troops at, 341–8; Council of War at (Warren's), 365, 373; difficulties of ascent of, 380; entrenchments on, Boer, why none, 383–4; *see also* 358 and 368–9; British, 381–2; exhaustion of troops at, 389, 396; failure at, effects of, 5–6; food and water at, want of, 389, 391, 394–6; Lyttelton's dispositions at, 377; measures taken by Warren to hold, 396–7; messages from, Coke at, 391, 394–7, Crofton at, 385, Thorneycroft at, 394, 397; night march to, 353–4; orders for attack on, 375–6; reinforcements at, 384–5, 387, 390, 396; re-organisation of forces at, 374; situation on, critical, 386, 389, 391, 394–6; signalling difficulties at, 391, 400; Springfield as base for, 343–4; terrain of, 338–40, 345–7, 350–2, 373–4; Thorneycroft to command on, 388–9; "Twin Peaks" adjoining, attack on, 392–4; Warren's plans at, 363, 365, retirement from, 397, 400–2; Woodgate, in charge of the assault on, 375, dispositions of, at, 382.
Spitz Kop, 61, 213–14, 230.

Sprigg, The Right Hon. Sir J. Gordon, M.L.A., 40, 42.
Springfield (Natal), 340–5, 353, 405, 420–1, 424–6, 469–70, 573.
Springfield bridge (Natal), 343–4, 421.
Springfield Farm (Orange Free State), 277–9, 292–3, 295, 298, 303, 321, 325, 328, 332.
Springfontein, 242–3, 256–8, 300–3, 306–7, 311.
Sprot, Major A., 219, 221–3, 227–8.
Spytfontein, 48, 64, 68.
Staff, 153, 181; Lord Kitchener's, inadequacy of, 105, 111–12, 116.
Stairs, Captain H. B., 175.
Standerton commando. *See* COMMANDOS.
Star Hill, 539.
Star shells, 369, 376, 381.
Stateberg, 302.
Steam-Sappers, 344.
Steele, Corporal, 289.
Steenkamp, General, 266.
Stephenson, Major-General T. E., 87, 98, 114–18, 122, 129–34, 139, 149, 161–2, 167, 218, 221–6, 320, 332.
Sterkfontein, 234.
Sterkstroom, 244, 335.
Sternberg, Count, 1, 23.
Steyn, H. E. President M. T., 106–7, 154, 161, 165–7, 171, 179, 187–8, 210–11, 214, 236, 241, 264–7, 305, 308, 314, 317, 324.
Steyn, Commandant, 115, 129–30, 135–6, 143–4.
Stinkfontein Farm, 121–2, 129–30, 159–61.
Stirling, Lieut. G. M. H., 289.
Stockenstroom Drift, 255.
Stoneman, Lieut.-Colonel J., 578–9.
Stores, in Ladysmith, 531; protection of, 440; hospital, in Ladysmith, run out, 8.
Stormberg, 70, 89, 146, 165, 172, 189–90, 230, 242–7, 259–64, 306.

INDEX. 697

Strength of: Boers—89, 146, 165, 187–90, 211, 230–1, 249, 259, 265, 414, 432, 539–40; British—*see* BRITISH ARMY.
Strydomspan Farm, 227.
Stubbs, Major A. K., 251.
Sugar Loaf Hill. *See* TWIN PEAKS.
Sundays river, 338, 504.
Supplies: Boer—29, 110, 191, 210, 268, 375–6; captured, at Bosjespan, 87; at Oliphantsfontein, 37; British—90, 105, 154, 180–2, 258, 261, 287, 340–2, 494; arrival of, at Bloemfontein, 241, 319; at Osfontein, 181–2, 195; at Paardeberg, 102, 164; biscuit ration reduced, at Paardeberg, 78, 168, in Ladysmith, 580; Cape Town, main depôt of, 243; cavalry, 11, 21, 23–5, 27–8, 33, 74, 96; columns, days carried by, 11–12; committee on, Kimberley, 53, 65; convoys of, 30, 78, 172, 212, 241, lost at Waterval Drift, 78; difficulties of, 242; for Ladysmith, 526, 528, 530; inadequacy of, at Paardeberg, 163; in Ladysmith, 538–9, 577, 580, 583; line of, from Modder camp, 4, 80, 147, 172, from Norval's Pont, 164; Natal Field force, base for, 343–4; parks of, 74, 214–15; rations of, reduced, 242; statistics of, 344; scarcity of, 102–3.
Surgeons, offer of, to Boers, 162.
Surprise Hill, 533, 535–6, 542, 548–9, 573, 581–3.
Surrenders, of Boers, 160, 170, 257, 361, 517; of British, 47, 76, 282–3, 310, 390.
Surrey Farm, 222, 228.
Susanna Farm, 99.
Swaziland commando. *See* COMMANDOS.
Swaziland Police. *See* COMMANDOS.
Systems, of railways, 243.

TAAIBOSCHLAAGTE HEIGHTS, 252, 254.
Tabanyama plateau, 350–2, 360, 373.
Table Mountain (Poplar Grove), 160–1, 185–7, 191–2, 195–7, 199–201.
Talana, 393; result of loss of documents at, 16.
Tasmanian Infantry. *See* COLONIAL UNITS.
Taungs, 45.
Taylor, Major W. H. F., 44.
Telegrams: from Boers—10–11, 17, 167, 170–1, 185, 210–11, 218, 314, 317, 425, 455, 470; from British—between Buller, White, and others, 359, 404, 419, 425, 464, 547, 550–4, 572–6, Roberts and Buller, 5–10, 155, 183–4, 405, 416, 419, Roberts and Kelly-Kenny, 88; Roberts and Kitchener, 88, 90, 123, 142, Roberts and White, 575–6, 581; *re* Driefontein battle, 217; to the War Office, 6, 8.
Telegraph lines broken, cut, etc., 20, 27, 48, 90, 96, 234, 236.
Telegraph Ridge, 414, 534, 537, 549, 574, 580.
Telephones, in Kimberley, 52; in Ladysmith, 563.
Telescopes, Naval, 445, 520.
Temporary rank, 104.
Tents left standing, at Modder, 11; at Springfield (Natal), 353.
Terrace Hill, 430, 432, 456–7, 462, 471–2, 475, 480, 485–7. *See also* HART'S HILL.
Terrible, H.M.S., 426.
Thaba Mountain, fight at, 328–32.
Thabanchu, 242, 257, 259, 273–81, 286, 292, 294, 298, 304, 310–11, 314, 322–32.
Thabanchu road, 236, 323.
Thackeray, Lieut.-Colonel T. M. G., 429, 490.
"The Kopjes," 354, 378, 391, 396, 398, 405, 407–10, 420.
Theron, Commandant G., 281.

Theron, Daniel, 170, 176; reports from Cronje's laager, 170–1.
"The Shop" (Driefontein), 222–3, 228.
Theunissen, Commandant H., 169–70.
Thompson, Major D. M., 578–9.
Thorneycroft, Lieut.-Colonel A. W., 341, 343, 368, 375–6, 379, 382, 384, 386, 388–92, 394–5, 397–9, 401, 406, 427, 441–2, 461–2, 493, 502.
Thorneycroft's Mounted Infantry. *See* COLONIAL UNITS.
Thornhill's Farm, 546.
Thornhill's kopjes, 533, 537, 548.
Thorold, Lieut.-Colonel C. C. H., 429, 492.
Three Stone Hill, 186, 200.
Three Tree Hill, 351, 366–7, 372–80, 387, 402.
Tintwa Pass, 184, 338.
Tod, Lieut. N. M., 564, 567.
Tools, entrenching. *See* ENTRENCHING.
Town Guards. *See* COLONIAL UNITS.
Towse, Captain E. B. (awarded the Victoria Cross), 330.
Tramway, aerial, over the Tugela, 494.
Transport, 74, 154, 243, 282–3, 341, 344, 348, 353–4, 356, 358–9, 363–5; Boer, 107–8, 191, 209–10, 402; brigade, mule, 12; difficulties of, 181–2, 242; divisional, 75, 147, 321; from Osfontein, 212; insufficiency of, 231; reorganisation of, 2, 5. *See also* VOLUME I., CHAPTER XXV.
Transvaal, 28, 155, 166, 233, 533; Cronje's communications with, cut, 38.
Transvaal Artillery and Police. *See* COMMANDOS.
Transvaalers, 54, 93, 165–6, 532–3, 557; lines of investment of, at Ladysmith, 539–40.
Transvaalers commando. *See* COMMANDOS.

Tremayne, Captain J. H., 357.
Trestle-bridge, 344.
Trestles, sinking of, causes delay to Buller's cavalry, 524.
Trickhardt's Drift, 346–9, 396, 399, 401–2.
Troops, British, disposition of, April 29th, 327–32, after relief of Ladysmith, 183–4; exhaustion of, at Paardeberg, 141, 153, in Ladysmith, 581, in Natal, 522; position of, February 8th, near Modder river, 4; scattered, motives for, 304; weight carried by, 353.
Trotter, Lieut.-Colonel J. K., 40, 42–3, 71.
Tucker, Lieut.-General C., C.B., 4, 15, 19, 21–2, 25, 28, 73, 77–8, 80, 90–1, 147, 194, 199, 201, 214, 228, 231, 234, 238, 269–70, 303, 327.
Tugela river, 6–7, 9, 179, 339, 345–7, 350–9, 360, 364–5, 391, 398, 401, 403, 407, 411, 420, 531, 534, 544, 548, 550, 552–3, 557, 581, 583; communication over, at Colenso, 494; defensive position on, suggestion to take up, 6; in flood, 526; right bank secured, 447–62.
Tugela River Drift, 464–5.
Tugela river, Little, 340, 342, 344.
Tugela river, Upper, 338, 441, 456–7, 470, 523, 572–3.
Tunnel Hill, 536, 538, 553, 568.
Turner, Captain H. G., 256.
Turner, Major H. S., 43–4, 46, 55–6, 58–61.
Turner, Mr. R. Beresford, 579.
Tweede Geluk, 322.
Tweefontein, 333.
Twin Peaks, 345–6, 352, 383, 387, 392–4, 397–9, 401, 406, 457.
Tyson, Captain T. G., 66.

UITENHAGE RIFLES. *See* COLONIAL UNITS.
Ultimatum, Boer, 47.
Umbrella Hill, 534.

INDEX. 699

Umbulwana, 419, 425, 433, 455, 459–60, 464, 493, 523–9, 533, 536–7, 539–42, 548, 553, 556, 559, 562, 565, 571, 579–80, 582, 584.
Umvoti Mounted Rifles. *See* COLONIAL UNITS.
Union Jack, hoisting of, at Bloemfontein, 238.
Untrained condition of Mounted Infantry, 13, 32, 81.
Untrained staff, 112.
Urmston, Major E. B., 125–6, 128.
Utrecht commando. *See* COMMANDOS.

VAAL (river), 37, 41, 53, 81, 93–4, 96–7, 106, 166, 183, 266, 332.
Vaalbank Farm, 222.
Vaalbank Hill, 222–3.
Vaal Krantz, 9, 344–5, 352, 423–4, 426, 433, 435, 441, 470, 479, 580; abandonment of, 418; ammunition expended at, 418; Boers attempt to recapture, 416; Buller wishes to use, as a pivot of attack, 414; concentration of troops at, 406–7; conference of Generals at, 407, 418; evacuation of, 419–22; feint at Brakfontein, 408; guns, British, number of, at, 418; on Zwart Kop, 406; Hill " 360," 412–18; impossible to mount guns on, 415; plan for attack of, 407; preparations for the battle of, 405–6, 410–11; relief of Ladysmith *viâ*, 8, 404–5; retirement from, 419–20; sangars and shelters at, 417; terrain of, 404–6.
Van Aswegen, Commandant, 93.
Vanderberg Drift, 109, 116, 121, 129–30, 133, 137, 139, 149, 157, 159, 161, 180.
Van der Merwe, Commandant M. G., 281.
Van der Post, Commandant, 14.
Van der Post, commando of. *See* COMMANDOS.
Van Druyten's Farm, 52.
Van Goosen's Farm, 247.

Van Reenen's Pass, 184, 189, 534.
Van Wyk's Vlei, 182, 212.
Vendutie Drift, 97–109, 116, 118, 121–2, 130, 178.
Venour, Captain W. J., 495–6, 513–14.
Venter's, laager, 365, 369; Spruit, 338, 346, 350–1, 360–4, 369–70, 372, 470; Spruit Drift, 366.
Venter's Vallei, 214, 232–4, 237.
Vertnek Mountain, 430, 432, 456–7, 466, 498.
Vice, Mr. 247.
Vickers-Maxims. *See* POM-POMS.
Victoria, corps from. *See* COLONIAL UNITS.
Victoria Crosses, 123, 137, 237, 254, 290, 330, 482, 500, 519, 570.
Victoria West, 266.
Vieh Kraal Hill, 219–25.
Viljoen, Commandant B., 344, 411.
Vilonel, Commandant, 211.
Vlakfontein, 322.
Vlaklaagte, 223.
Volunteer corps: British, *see* CITY OF LONDON IMPERIAL VOLUNTEERS; Colonial, 40, 42–6, 62; Kimberley in 1896, 40; in Ladysmith, 581. *See also* COLONIAL UNITS.
Voortrekkers, 352.
Vrede commando. *See* COMMANDOS.
Vryburg, 44–5, 47, 53.
Vryheid commando. *See* COMMANDOS.
Vryheid district, 184.

WAAIHOEK, 181, 212, 215–16.
Wagon Hill, 535, 537, 541, 545, 549, 554, 572, 580; attack on, November 9th, 542–3; January 6th, 336, 383, 555–70.
Wagon Point, 556–9, 563, 565.
Wagon Post, 560.
Wagons, 263, 342–4, 356, 362–3, 371, 421, 494; capture of Cronje's, 82, 87; destruction of, at Waterval drift, 78; recapture of, by Pole-Carew at Edenburg, 257; set on fire, 156.

Wake, Lieut. H., 481–2.
Wakkerstroom (Orange Free State),321.
Wakkerstroom commando (Transvaal). See COMMANDOS.
Wakkerstroom district (Transvaal),184.
Wallace entrenching tools, 102.
War Commission. See "COMMISSION."
"War Notes," by Colonel de Villebois Mareuil, 1, 187.
War Office, 42, 346, 405; telegrams, from and to, 6, 8, 509.
Ward, Colonel E. W. D., C.B., 538, 541, 578.
Warren, Lieut.-General Sir C., G.C.M.G., K.C.B., 334, 338, 341–3, 347–53, 355–65, 368, 371–7, 382, 384–6, 388–91, 394–401, 418, 420–1, 428, 436–7, 439–40, 442–3, 445, 451, 453–4, 457, 459, 461, 463–4, 466–8, 475, 479–80, 484, 486, 502, 504–6, 520, 528 ; orders by, 366, 467, 508–9, 518 ; plans of, 467, 471–2.
Warrenton, 81, 93, 189, 332.
Warwickshire regiment, The Royal. See REGULAR UNITS.
Waschbank bridge, 504.
Water, 36–7, 147, 192, 281, 335, 376, 389, 391, 395, 454, 458, 553, 577 ; pollution of, at Paardeberg, 164; scarcity of, 2–3, 20–2, 25, 27, 31, 38, 81, 94, 99, 118, 148, 208, 242, 310, 334, 441 ; supply of, at Bloemfontein, 241 ; tanks for, 441.
Waterworks, 308, 320, 325, 327. See also SANNAH'S POST.
Waterworks Drift, 276–7, 279–80, 285–7, 290–1, 293, 324–5.
Waterval Drift (Modder river), 276, 291–8, 325–8 ; (Riet river), 17–22, 24, 28–33, 72, 74, 87, 89, 135 ; (Riet river) capture of convoy at, 75–8, 181, 257.
Waterval Hill, 19, 21.
Wavell, Major-General A. G., 79, 147, 270–3, 327.
Way, Lieut A. S., 289.

Webb, Sapper, 237.
Webster, 2nd Lieut. A. McC., 55, 60.
Weenen, 503–4.
Weenen road, 436, 530.
Wegdraai Drift, 29–30, 32, 73–8, 80, 87, 90–1.
Weight, carried by soldiers, 353 ; carried by British and Boer horses, 36.
Weldon, Major A., 525.
Weldon trestles, 507.
Welsh Fusiliers, The Royal. See REGULAR UNITS.
Welsh regiment. See REGULAR UNITS.
Wepener, 160, 236, 261–4, 304, 324–7 ; ammunition at, expenditure of, 318 ; limited supply of, 317 ; bombardment at, 316–17 ; De Wet moves on, 312 ; entrenchments at, 316–17, 319 ; garrison at, composition of, 315 ; position at, 315 ; relief columns for, 318 ; troops sent to, 301–3 ; troops at, summoned to surrender, 315.
Wepener commando. See COMMANDOS.
Wessels, Commandant C. J., 54, 56–7, 166, 308.
Wesselton, 41.
West Australia, corps from. See COLONIAL UNITS.
West Kent regiment, The Royal. See REGULAR UNITS.
West Riding regiment. See REGULAR UNITS.
West Surrey regiment, The Royal. See REGULAR UNITS.
West Yorkshire regiment. See REGULAR UNITS.
White flag, 263, 310.
White, Lieut.-General Sir G. S., G.C.B., G.C.S.I., etc., 5–10, 155, 183–5, 327, 336–9, 346, 359, 364–5, 404–5, 419, 425, 433, 464, 466, 493, 526–9, 531–85 ; messages from, 337, 358–9, 550–3, 574–6, 581.
Williams, Major C., 529.
Wilson, Captain H. H., 499.

Wiltshire regiment. *See* REGULAR UNITS.
Wimbledon, 41, 61.
Wimbledon ridge, 54, 57–8, 61.
Winburg, 281, 310, 314, 327–8, 332; commando, *see* COMMANDOS.
Windmill camp, 252.
Winterhoek, 23, 78–9.
Wire fences, 35, 41, 51, 94, 160, 223, 235, 489, 517.
Wolmarans, Commandant, 82.
Wolmaranstad, 149; commando, *see* COMMANDOS.
Wolseley, Field-Marshal, The Right Hon. G. J., Viscount, K.P., G.C.B., G.C.M.G., etc., 6.
Wolseley, Lieut. E. J., 272.
Wolvekraal, action at, 29, 146; homestead, 98.
Wood, Major-General Elliot, 173.
Woodgate, Major-General E. R. P., C.B., C.M.G., 357, 364, 366–7, 373, 375–9, 381–5, 389, 395, 406, 574.
Woodland, Lieut.-Colonel A. L., 428.
Worcestershire regiment. *See* REGULAR UNITS.
Wounded: Boer—Lord Roberts offers help to, 162; British—at Driefontein, 228, 231; at Hart's Hill, 492, 501; at Spion Kop, 396, 398, 400. *See also* CASUALTIES.
Wright, Colonel A. J. A., 272.
Wright, Gunner J., R.N., 438, 462, 503.
Wright's Farm (Kimberley), 60.
Wright's Farm (Natal), 351, 355, 362, 375–7, 385.
Wynne, Major-General A. S., C.B., 406–10, 428, 440, 442, 450, 454, 459, 461, 466–7, 469, 472–5, 480.
Wynne's Hill, 432, 456–7, 459, 463–81, 483–5, 487, 493, 495, 500–1, 516.

YEATHERD, MAJOR E. W., 477, 479.
Yeomanry. *See* IMPERIAL YEOMANRY.
York and Lancaster regiment. *See* REGULAR UNITS.
Yorkshire Kopje, 219–25, 228.
Yorkshire regiment. *See* REGULAR UNITS.
Young, Captain J. R., 579.

ZARPS. *See* COMMANDOS—JOHANNESBURG POLICE.
Zastron, 301–2, 304.
Zoutpans Drift, 12.
Zoutpansberg commando. *See* COMMANDOS.
Zululand, borders of, 339, 426; expected Boer concentration on, 335.
Zulus, 335, 526.
Zwart Kop, 339, 346, 354, 404–8, 410, 412–13, 415–16, 418, 420–1.
Zwart Kopje Fontein, 333.

Printed at The Chapel River Press, Kingston, Surrey.

www.ingramcontent.com/pod-product-compliance
Lightning Source LLC
Chambersburg PA
CBHW052008290426
44112CB00014B/2158